America's New Racial Battle Lines

Chicago Studies in American Politics

A series edited by Susan Herbst, Lawrence R. Jacobs, Adam J. Berinsky, and Frances Lee; Benjamin I. Page, editor emeritus

Also in the series:

RESPECT AND LOATHING IN AMERICAN DEMOCRACY: POLARIZATION, MORALIZATION, AND THE UNDERMINING OF EQUALITY *by Jeff Spinner-Halev and Elizabeth Theiss-Morse*

COUNTERMOBILIZATION: POLICY FEEDBACK AND BACKLASH IN A POLARIZED AGE *by Eric M. Patashnik*

RACE, RIGHTS, AND RIFLES: THE ORIGINS OF THE NRA AND CONTEMPORARY GUN CULTURE *by Alexandra Filindra*

ACCOUNTABILITY IN STATE LEGISLATURES *by Steven Rogers*

OUR COMMON BONDS: USING WHAT AMERICANS SHARE TO HELP BRIDGE THE PARTISAN DIVIDE *by Matthew Levendusky*

PERSUASION IN PARALLEL: HOW INFORMATION CHANGES MINDS ABOUT POLITICS *by Alexander Coppock*

DYNAMIC DEMOCRACY: PUBLIC OPINION, ELECTIONS, AND POLICYMAKING IN THE AMERICAN STATES *by Devin Caughey and Christopher Warshaw*

RADICAL AMERICAN PARTISANSHIP: MAPPING VIOLENT HOSTILITY, ITS CAUSES, AND THE CONSEQUENCES FOR DEMOCRACY *by Nathan P. Kalmoe and Lilliana Mason*

THE OBLIGATION MOSAIC: RACE AND SOCIAL NORMS IN US POLITICAL PARTICIPATION *by Allison P. Anoll*

A TROUBLED BIRTH: THE 1930S AND AMERICAN PUBLIC OPINION *by Susan Herbst*

POWER SHIFTS: CONGRESS AND PRESIDENTIAL REPRESENTATION *by John A. Dearborn*

PRISMS OF THE PEOPLE: POWER AND ORGANIZING IN TWENTY-FIRST-CENTURY AMERICA *by Hahrie Han, Elizabeth McKenna, and Michelle Oyakawa*

RACE TO THE BOTTOM: HOW RACIAL APPEALS WORK IN AMERICAN POLITICS *by LaFleur Stephens-Dougan*

DEMOCRACY DECLINED: THE FAILED POLITICS OF CONSUMER FINANCIAL PROTECTION *by Mallory E. SoRelle*

THE LIMITS OF PARTY: CONGRESS AND LAWMAKING IN A POLARIZED ERA *by James M. Curry and Frances E. Lee*

AMERICA'S INEQUALITY TRAP *by Nathan J. Kelly*

GOOD ENOUGH FOR GOVERNMENT WORK: THE PUBLIC REPUTATION CRISIS IN AMERICA (AND WHAT WE CAN DO TO FIX IT) *by Amy E. Lerman*

WHO WANTS TO RUN? HOW THE DEVALUING OF POLITICAL OFFICE DRIVES POLARIZATION *by Andrew B. Hall*

FROM POLITICS TO THE PEWS: HOW PARTISANSHIP AND THE POLITICAL ENVIRONMENT SHAPE RELIGIOUS IDENTITY *by Michele F. Margolis*

THE INCREASINGLY UNITED STATES: HOW AND WHY AMERICAN POLITICAL BEHAVIOR NATIONALIZED *by Daniel J. Hopkins*

LEGISLATIVE STYLE *by William Bernhard and Tracy Sulkin*

LEGACIES OF LOSING IN AMERICAN POLITICS *by Jeffrey K. Tulis and Nicole Mellow*

Additional series titles follow index.

America's New Racial Battle Lines

Protect versus Repair

ROGERS M. SMITH
AND DESMOND KING

THE UNIVERSITY OF CHICAGO PRESS   CHICAGO AND LONDON

The University of Chicago Press, Chicago 60637
The University of Chicago Press, Ltd., London
© 2024 by The University of Chicago
All rights reserved. No part of this book may be used or reproduced in any manner whatsoever without written permission, except in the case of brief quotations in critical articles and reviews. For more information, contact the University of Chicago Press, 1427 E. 60th St., Chicago, IL 60637.
Published 2024
Printed in the United States of America

33 32 31 30 29 28 27 26 25 24   1 2 3 4 5

ISBN-13: 978-0-226-83402-3 (cloth)
ISBN-13: 978-0-226-83404-7 (paper)
ISBN-13: 978-0-226-83403-0 (e-book)
DOI: https://doi.org/10.7208/chicago/9780226834030.001.0001

Library of Congress Cataloging-in-Publication Data

Names: Smith, Rogers M., 1953– author. | King, Desmond, author.
Title: America's new racial battle lines : protect versus repair / Rogers M. Smith and Desmond King.
Other titles: Protect versus repair | Chicago studies in American politics.
Description: Chicago : The University of Chicago Press, 2024. | Series: Chicago studies in American politics | Includes bibliographical references and index.
Identifiers: LCCN 2023044861 | ISBN 9780226834023 (cloth) | ISBN 9780226834047 (paperback) | ISBN 9780226834030 (ebook)
Subjects: LCSH: United States—Race relations.
Classification: LCC E184.A1 S6625 2024 | DDC 305.800973—dc23/eng/20231002
LC record available at https://lccn.loc.gov/2023044861

♾ This paper meets the requirements of ANSI/NISO Z39.48-1992 (Permanence of Paper).

To the memory of Charles W. Mills, friend, scholar, and inspiration

Contents

List of Figures and Tables   ix

PART 1.   **America's Racial Battles: An Overview**

CHAPTER 1.   America's New Racial Battle Lines   3

CHAPTER 2.   Racial Orders as Institutional Orders: Race, Class, and Intersectionality   33

PART 2.   **The Protect Alliance**

CHAPTER 3.   The Rise of the Protect Policy Alliance: New Actors, New Money, Resurgent Causes   69

CHAPTER 4.   The Conservatives' Story: Who and What to Protect   97

CHAPTER 5.   The Protect Alliance at Work: Policies and Reforms   124

PART 3.   **The Repair Alliance**

CHAPTER 6.   The Rise of the New Repair Groups   153

CHAPTER 7.   The Repair Story and Transformative Visions   198

CHAPTER 8.   Today's Repair Alliance: Current Initiatives across Policy Regimes   221

PART 4.   **The Rough Roads Ahead**

CHAPTER 9. Lessons for and from Theories of Racial Politics   253

CHAPTER 10. Views from the Battleground: Paths and Prospects for America's New Racial Politics   269

Acknowledgments   305

APPENDIX A. Research Strategies and Methodologies   307

APPENDIX B. Organizations in the Protect Alliance   317

APPENDIX C. Organizations in the Repair Alliance   327

Notes   347

References   353

Index   429

Figures and Tables

Figures

2.1 The Political Spiral of Racial Institutional Orders   43

2.2 Core Members of Today's Protect and Repair Racial Policy Alliances   47

2.3 Repair Racial Policy Groups   48

2.4 Protect Racial Policy Groups   49

Tables

1.1 Varieties of Racial Policy Alliances   20

5.1 Trump Administration Protect Policies   129

6.1 Organizations Signing In Support of HR 40, 2020–2022   171

A.1 Organizations in Social Network Analyses   312

A.2 Organizations Interviewed   314

B.1 A Sampling of Protect Alliance Members   317

C.1 A Sampling of Repair Alliance Members/HR 40 Supporters   327

PART I
America's Racial Battles
An Overview

CHAPTER ONE

America's New Racial Battle Lines

Racism is alive in our country, our state, in Queen Anne's County, and our schools. —Dr. Andrea Kane, Queen Anne's County School District Superintendent, in her letter to 7,700 district households on June 5, 2020

We do not have a racist county. We do not have a racist board. —Mr. Richard A. Smith, School District Board President, responding to Superintendent Kane's letter (Green 2021)

What is happening in the politics of race in America? We have been scholars of American racial politics, individually and collaboratively, for more than a quarter of a century, largely focused on national developments. But in the last decade, a rising number of local clashes like this one between two Maryland school officials—one a female African American educational administrator, the other a white male businessman and recurrent local Republican candidate—showed us it was time for some fundamental rethinking. This book is the result.

Because of the furor her June 2020 letter generated, Superintendent Kane gave up her long administrative career and became an Ivy League academic, escaping what she experienced as a poisonous race-charged political climate. Her critic, Richard Smith, originally an appointee to the board, remains in office, scheduled to serve as board president through 2024 (Queen Anne's County Public Schools n.d.).

In our previous work, we (like many others) depicted modern American racial politics as centered on a debate as to whether the nation should have strictly color-blind policies, conferring neither benefits nor burdens on the basis of race, or race-conscious policies like affirmative action, designed to fully integrate African Americans and others long denied opportunities into major American institutions. In 2011, we devoted a book to delineating how these two rival racial policy stances shaped developments across a remarkably wide range of American institutional systems and policy arenas, including employment, education, voting rights, immigration, housing, census categories, and many more (King and Smith 2011).

Superintendent Kane and Board President Smith were, however, not arguing over affirmative action policies. Smith, moreover, was not suggesting that the school district's curriculum should be fully "color-blind," with no discussion of race at all. Their dispute was different, and deeper. It was about what Americans should think and say to each other about the place of race in their nation's past and especially in its present—and therefore about how they should understand the core identities of America and themselves.

Superintendent Kane, like most progressives today, clearly thought racism had been prominent throughout American history and remained so in the twenty-first century, despite affirmative action programs and despite the gains in the civil rights era of the 1950s and 1960s. Board President Smith, like most conservatives today, dismissed any idea that America had always been fundamentally a racist country, and that many of its officials, perhaps including himself, remained racist. Superintendent Kane wrote her letter because she believed strongly that all the reforms pursued since the 1960s had not been nearly enough to overcome American racial injustices, and that much more was still needed. Board President Smith made his reply because he believed just as strongly that accusations like Kane's were wrong and harmful.

Reflecting on this controversy—and a vast and expanding array of similar disputes we had been witnessing in previous years—and on the shocking rise of Donald Trump to domination of the Republican Party and to the US presidency, we came to conclude that racial disputes in America were moving or indeed had moved beyond the color-blind/race-conscious debates we had examined. We believed we were witnessing the rise of a new and still more polarized American racial politics. On one side of this new divide are Americans who believe that racial injustices are still so pervasive in American life that sweeping institutional transformations, not just integration, must be achieved to end many forms of "systemic racism." Consequently, they call not simply for race-conscious policies, but for initiatives to *repair* what they see as the nation's fundamental flaws.

They are opposed by Americans who view their country as in its essence great and exceptional, not flawed and with no significant historical debts. These other Americans consequently regard liberal (let alone radical) efforts to achieve sweeping transformations as dangerous, and borne of what they regard as the only really potent form of racism in the nation today: "anti-white bigotry," in the words of Stephen Miller, former adviser to President Trump (Reinhard and Dawsey 2022). Because this side believes America and most Americans need to be defended against their opponents, its members focus not on "color-blind" policies but on measures to *protect*, and also restore, those characteristics of America and Americans that they regard as traditional sources of its greatness. For many, those characteristics include having always been a predominantly white, Christian, male-led capitalist nation.

This emerging racial policy divide presents Americans with a profound choice about whether they should seek most to "protect" or to "repair" their nation and themselves. We undertook the research for this book to explore whether we are right about this new politics of race in America, and if so, what these developments may mean for America's present and future.

The Racial Orders Framework

To do so, we employed but also felt compelled to revise the analytical framework for understanding racial conflicts in America that we developed at an earlier stage of our careers. We have both long been concerned about issues of inequality, including racial justice and civil rights. But truth be told, when we embarked on our academic careers—both white men from comfortably middle-class families—American racial politics were not at the center of our studies of politics. In the fall of 1980, Dublin-born Desmond King was new to America, beginning his doctoral program at Northwestern University and chiefly studying labor market inequalities and political economy. Rogers Smith had just completed his doctorate focused on civil liberties in American constitutional law and was starting university teaching at Yale. Both of us worried about the languid pace of change following landmark civil and voting rights laws in the 1960s. But we each had real confidence as we began our careers that the years ahead would bring continuing improvements in economic and social justice, with a continuing erosion of racist discourse and of violent racial conflicts in the US. Moreover, in July 1980, as Smith prepared his first lecture course on American constitutionalism, a Supreme Court with seven justices appointed by Republican presidents decided *Fullilove v. Klutznick* by a 6–3 vote, upholding congressional power to target federal spending toward companies owned by racial minorities—a major explicitly race-conscious economic measure. The racial reform initiatives of the 1960s and 1970s appeared constitutionally and politically secure, and the violence of the 1960s appeared to have faded.

If all this sounds like we exhibited what James Baldwin excoriated as the "incredible, abysmal, and really cowardly obtuseness" of white liberals, that was probably far more the case than it should have been, given our admiration for Baldwin's analytic acuteness and eloquence (Baldwin 1963, 58). Then, like many other liberal academics, we were stunned by the massive victory to which the conservative Ronald Reagan led Republicans on November 4, 1980. Living in the Chicago area, King soon was bolstered by the election of Harold Washington in 1983 as the city's first Black mayor. But he was dismayed by the narrowness of Washington's victory; by the decisions of many leading white Democrats, including the chair of the Cook County Democratic Party, Edward Vrdolyak, to support Washington's Republican opponent; and by the upsurge of racial vitriol the campaign stirred. That year Smith began a project on American citizenship laws, seeking to assess how "liberal individualist" or "communitarian republican" those laws had been historically—only to make two disillusioning discoveries. The first was that through much of the nation's history, many more legislators and judges than he was aware of had explicitly endorsed the view that America was and should be a white man's nation. The second was that their reasons for doing so invoked vicious mischaracterizations of African Americans that appeared to be on the rise again in Reagan-era public and even intellectual discourse.

Consequently, by the 1990s both of us were working extensively on different aspects of American racial politics, with mounting alarm. Increasingly, economic and racial conservatives joined in repudiating government aid targeted to disadvantaged racial minorities—the former because they opposed all government aid programs, the latter because they argued that racial minorities did not deserve such aid and would not benefit from it. In 1994, the Harvard psychologist Richard Herrnstein and the MIT-trained political scientist Charles Murray published *The Bell Curve*, intentionally seeking to revive the respectability of the intellectual school of scientific racism, including its insistence that, due to the ineradicably lower IQs of Blacks and Latinos, an increase in their share of the population would place "downward pressure on the distribution of intelligence" (Herrnstein and Murray 1994, 360–61, 549). In 1995, a Supreme Court increasingly hostile to affirmative action overturned *Fullilove v. Klutznick* in *Adarand Construc-*

tors v. Peña, putting an end to many state as well as national initiatives to aid minority-owned enterprises. That same year, King published *Separate and Unequal: African Americans and the US Federal Government*, and in 1997 Smith published *Civic Ideals: Conflicting Visions of Citizenship in US History*. Both works documented how pervasive policies of white supremacy had been in different aspects of American governance historically, with legacies that appeared all too alive in the late twentieth century.

After our books made us aware of our common interests, we also found we shared a belief that our earlier neglect of racial issues was all too common in the political science literature on American politics, even in the emerging subfield of American political development with which we were aligned. We began working out how we thought American racial politics could be studied better, resulting in our first article, "Racial Orders in American Political Development" (King and Smith 2005). The "racial orders" framework we formulated then proved useful for many years in discerning the character and impacts of the nation's racial politics, including in our book-length overview, *Still a House Divided: Race and Politics in the Obama Era* (King and Smith 2011). The framework has more recently helped us organize the evidence that the politics we portrayed then has been significantly changing with the rise of Trump and Black Lives Matter (Smith and King 2020, 2021).

Agreeing with most contemporary political scientists, though not Charles Murray, that systems of racial identities and racial inequalities are to a substantial degree products of politics and not nature, we have sought to discern patterns in those political processes. We have maintained that American racial politics can best be understood as having an enduring "deep structure" comprised of competing networks of political actors, civil society organizations, and government institutions that take opposing positions on the major racial issues of their eras—networks we have called "racial institutional orders" and "racial policy alliances." Up through roughly 2010, the predominant, era-defining racial policy dichotomies were: enslavement versus emancipation (up until 1865); *de jure* segregation versus integration (from the 1890s through the 1960s); and the permissibility of race-targeted policies, as opposed to color-blind policies (from the late 1970s through the early twenty-first century). Though the racial policies in dispute changed, the conservative stances on them consistently operated to preserve or extend many economic, political, and social advantages for those persons deemed "white" and those who aligned with them. The opposing alliances consistently sought to achieve greater racial equality in some or all of these dimensions of American life. Their clashes made conflicts over racial statuses and inequalities a central and enduring driver of American political development.

We called these networks not simply "racial policy alliances" but "racial institutional orders" because we were struck by the fact that, far more than is the case for many other concerns, all through US history some political advocates on each side of these major issues have always been in control of some governing institutions, authoritatively ordering citizens' conduct in their preferred directions. States and cities enforced either free or enslaved labor prior to the Thirteenth Amendment; some moved to *de jure* segregation or more open public institutions prior to the judicial decisions and congressional civil rights laws of the 1950s and 1960s; and many either adopted or banned race-conscious policies in the late twentieth century, with different federal agencies aligning one way or the other on all these issues from era to era.

We have therefore long argued that while for some purposes it makes sense to speak of the aggregate patterns of state and national racial policies in different eras as constituting "the" American racial order of their times, it is imperative to recognize that in fact the nation has always had not just clashing racial policy advocates, but two main and evolving *rival* "racial institutional orders," with different governing institutions as well as their supporters championing one side or the other of the major racial issue of their day. This deep structure of American politics generated the clashes that constituted the prevailing national racial patterns in each period, and their outcomes then ushered in subsequent eras. Rather than a unified and unchallenged white hegemony, then, unresolved conflicts over racial issues have characterized America and its governance.

We have also emphasized that historically, the changes in racial policies have swung back and forth, in pendulum-like fashion, with progress toward greater racial equality invariably encountering partly successful resistance and reversals, leaving many inequalities entrenched. Consequently, the nation's deep structure of race-related conflicts has endured. The changes have meant, however, that the pendulum swings have not gone back and forth on the same horizontal plane. Color-blind racial conservatism accompanied by mass incarceration was not the same as Jim Crow racial segregation, which was not the same as enslavement. The swings have rather been part of a spiral of politics visible in political development—but a spiral that can spin off in many directions, down as well as up (Smith 2015). History therefore has provided no guarantees that major changes in America's racial policy coalitions will not continue, or that modern politics will not produce a still more deeply inegalitarian nation. But history also does not justify concluding that progress in racial equality never has been and never will be possible.

Like many millions of others, we hoped for a time that the election of Barack Obama to the White House in 2008 signaled that American racial politics were changing for the better, if still not as rapidly as many, including ourselves, would have liked. But as we suggested in 2011, although Obama's election was authentically historic, he largely sought to finesse rather than transcend the color-blind versus race-conscious policy dichotomy, using a rhetoric that leaned toward the first while quietly pursuing policies that often embodied the second. As Obama embarked on his embattled second term, we saw no major shift in the substance of the nation's racial policy debates at the national level, despite how stale they had become in many eyes (leading them to be pursued far more in legislative and administrative hearings and in courtrooms than in electoral contests and broader public debates).

Yet even as we published *Still a House Divided*, changes were stirring, in part because of that very staleness, that would soon erupt in ways few analysts, including ourselves, foresaw (King and Smith 2011). Over the years, a number of thoughtful academic critics have taken issue in various ways with our framework for studying American racial politics. These unexpected developments underlined for us the force of their concerns.

Many of our critics have judged our portrait of an evolving dichotomous structure of America's racial politics, focused on national policies and meant to be theoretically parsimonious, to be unduly simplistic and likely to lead scholars to look for change in the wrong places. These colleagues have generally interpreted "racial institutional orders" as focused primarily on elite-driven, top-down components of national politics. Some see the framework as reflecting and reinforcing beliefs in the existence of fixed and homogeneous racial identities, interests, and preferred policies on each side of the divides we have depicted. They have argued that racial politics are far more complex, involving a great variety of actors in local, state, and national politics and in social life. They have stressed that conceptions of racial identities, interests, and policies often alter as part of processes of contestation and political, economic, and social change. Our critics contend that issues and outcomes in any period often differ prodigiously by geographical region and level of government. Most have also stressed that major developments are often driven from the bottom up, by social movements, by organized and spontaneous protests, by shifting tides in public opinion and social practices, and by the collective consequences of individual choices.[1]

We do not agree with all these criticisms. We have not denied that the nation's racial politics, like the politics of other issues, have always exhibited a great range of goals and strategies on the part of diverse groups in different locales and at different levels of government. We have also recognized that who governmental and social institutions and practices have categorized as "white" or as one of many types of "non-white" persons has varied considerably, often as a result of political struggles in which opposing forces have sought to add allies or taint opponents through inclusive or divisive classifications. We have noted, moreover, that through processes of "critical ideational development," discourses including advocacy of color-blindness have at times shifted from one racial policy alliance to an opposing one (King and Smith 2014).

Yet we have thought and continue to think that when it comes to racial policies in America, far more than on many other matters, the exigencies of coalition-building and the construction of popular appeals to American voters still tend to compel otherwise distinctive actors to position themselves, at least loosely, on one side or the other of what emerges as the major racial policy issue of their time. Those issues are contested at all levels of government and in other arenas of social life. Left-leaning scholars often long for and sometimes predict the emergence of a similarly dichotomous class politics pitting the poorer majority against the affluent few. But the multiple cleavages among small and large businesses; agricultural, manufacturing, distribution, service, and financial sectors; and labor and consumer interests have frustrated those hopes throughout US history. Until very recently, unions in particular have often divided rather than united workers across race. Moreover, in some economic sectors both workers and employers are helped by economic protectionist policies; other workers and employers are harmed by them. Consequently, class alliances often prove hard to sustain.

In contrast, we believe the historical record shows plainly that on racial issues, overarching policy dichotomies have been far more dominant, even as the policies in question have changed over time. We do not regard this pattern as inevitable or desirable, particularly in the present era when polarization has again become so profound that it often makes progress impossible and threatens frequent violence. We note in our conclusion that one lesson that might be drawn from our analysis is the need for Americans to seek to imagine their politics, including how politics engages racial divisions, in very different ways than they have done in the past. We maintain, however, that our focus on rival racial policy alliances accurately captures much of the reality of American politics in the past and present.

Still, our critics have been right on many points. While both national and state policymakers must act for major changes to occur, historically they have done so to a large extent as the result of mounting pressures from grassroots forces: the escapes and insurrections by enslaved people as well as the abolitionist movement during the antebellum years; and the boycotts, sit-ins, and protest marches of the civil rights era. Americans' actions have also been keenly shaped by international factors, especially the rise and fall of racially justified European empires. Our past discussions insufficiently stressed the roles of both domestic and international social movements and other global economic and political forces. Consequently, in recent years we have monitored both formal and informal American racial politics at all levels, as well as international politics, looking for signs that significant shifts might be underway. As discussed in chapter 2, we have also further developed our framework in an effort to do more justice to these complexities.

While we did this work, it became increasingly clear that, after more than three decades, major changes were happening. A fourth era within America's enduring structure of racial policy conflicts was underway, a clash between new Protect and Repair racial policy alliances, with the first far more powerful, especially in the Trump years, but with each in control of enough governmental entities to be called "racial institutional orders."

The Intensifying Divides

We will see in later chapters that leaders of today's opposed racial policy alliances have distinct (though overlapping) narratives regarding why they have come to adopt postures they acknowledge to be more militant than those of their predecessors in the late twentieth century. To a considerable degree, each side blames the other for becoming more extreme, compelling heightened opposition on their own part. We do not seek to assess the evidence for and against these accusations here. Our aim is to describe each of today's racial policy alliances, and what their rise may mean for the nation's politics and its enduring racial inequalities, as accurately as we can. We should clarify, however, that our research suggests these rival alliances have been emerging more or less simultaneously since roughly 2010, with the increasing prominence of each relentlessly fueling the other.

Why did they arise? We doubt that there was any single reason, and we also believe that political developments rest ultimately on the contingent choices people make, though always within constraints. Still, we think it likely that a number of factors contributed to the emergence of the new policy alliances, even if we cannot assign those factors precise weights.

By the dawn of the twenty-first century, the contestation between the color-blind and race-conscious institutional orders had achieved what some scholars perceptively characterize as "racial stasis" and "stagnation" (Desante and Smith 2020). The color-blind alliance had, to be sure, achieved growing success over the race-conscious alliance in the two decades following Ronald Reagan's 1980 victory. The Supreme Court had chipped away at affirmative action programs not only in public contracting but also in employment, college admissions, and other venues; permitted and eventually required school districts to abandon school desegregation programs; and weakened voting rights protections. Striking Republican success in winning control of state legislatures also facilitated legislative terminations of affirmative action, public set-asides, and desegregation initiatives, sometimes supported by popular referenda. After the Democrats passed the National Voter Registration Act in 1993 to increase voter participation, Republican legislatures fought back by narrowing voting eligibility and access in many states—a trend that would accelerate after the Court voided important parts of the 1965 Voting Rights Act through its 2013 decision in *Shelby County v. Holder* (King and Smith 2016). And even as they sought to expand their voter base, centrist Democrats led by Bill Clinton increasingly joined Republicans in rejecting "big government" in favor of neoliberal deregulation and increased reliance on the private sector, thereby diminishing public aid programs as well as some antidiscrimination initiatives aimed at reducing racial inequalities (Gerstle 2022).

Throughout, however, this determined color-blind policy alliance faced a resolute race-conscious policy alliance, whose members advocated obverse measures. They managed to sustain more limited affirmative action programs; and in governmental agencies, in educational institutions, in nonprofit and many for-profit corporations, as well as through the work of racial, ethnic, and immigrant advocacy groups, they won adoption of "diversity, equity, and inclusion" initiatives that created institutionalized bases for sustaining many race-conscious policies. Many of the advocacy groups supported new federal voting laws to insure a diverse, inclusive electorate, and some of their proposals were enacted by Democratic Party officeholders. Not coincidentally, national discussions and support for color-blind or race-conscious policies became more firmly aligned with partisanship over time, even if Democrats never supported race-conscious measures as unequivocally as Republicans urged their demise (King and Smith 2011).

With support for color-blind approaches to racial issues and neoliberal economic policies in the ascendancy, the nation's patterns of substantial racial inequalities in most spheres of American life, including wealth, income, employment, homeownership, educational attainment, health outcomes, life expectancy, and incarceration rates all persisted. Consequently, many who identified with the concerns of communities of color grew more and more dissatisfied with the nation's status quo and persisting inequities (Sharkey, Taylor, and Serkez 2020). At the same time, as the nation's economic and social policies increasingly favored those with high "human" as well as financial capital, many less educated, working-class whites were experiencing diminished economic opportunities, stagnant or declining living standards, and mounting uncertainties that would only grow in the ensuing two decades. Many observers believe their anxieties "fed resentments about race" (Abramowitz and Teixeira 2009, 400, 417). Public opinion surveys show a steady decline from World War II onward in the willingness of whites to proclaim open support for white supremacy. But many scholars argue that the generations born in the latter part of the twentieth century, shaped by the predominant public ideology of color-blindness, ceased to be more liberal on racial policies, or more resistant to negative racial stereotypes, than their predecessors (DeSante and Smith 2020, 30–36).

By the year 2000, even though racial issues had moved far from the foreground of American politics, many advocates and analysts were insisting that major changes were needed. That year saw revitalized interest in reparations, aroused in part by Randall Robinson's book *The Debt: What America Owes to Black*s and by the formation of a Reparations Assessment Group by the late Harvard law professor Charles Ogletree, among other efforts (Robinson 2000; Shepard 2000). Those discussions dwindled, however, once the 9/11 attacks on the World Trade Center and the Pentagon shifted national attention to the "war on terrorism."

The economic and national security failures of the George W. Bush administration then facilitated the extraordinary rise to the presidency of Barack Obama. The Obama administration stirred many diverse reactions. Some conservatives saw it as egregiously "race-conscious," and new right-wing armed groups formed in opposition to it, including the Oath

Keepers and the Three Percenters (Caldwell 2020, 188; ADL 2009). In contrast, many progressives, particularly those supporting reparations, were dismayed that Obama did not do more to address the nation's widespread racial inequalities (Darity 2016). And while conservatives frequently accused Obama of unjustly favoring people of color, especially African Americans, the burst housing bubble that brought on the Great Recession as Obama entered office proved particularly devastating for Black homeowners. Many never recovered in the ensuing years. By 2022, Black homeownership stood at 43.4 percent, nearly 30 points lower than white homeownership, and lower than it had been at the start of Obama's second term (Bahney 2022). Real estate industry studies suggest that often Black homes are severely undervalued as well (Alcorn 2021). Since home-owning has long been a major source of wealth for most Americans, many Black Americans hardly felt they had received especially beneficial treatment from the Obama administration or from American institutions in general during his time in office. Few saw their situations as aided by either party in the ensuing Trump years.

Nonetheless, Black voters remained loyal to Obama and the Democrats throughout. Observers agree, moreover, that it was the passage of the Affordable Care Act, not racial issues per se, that sparked the mobilization of the predominantly white Tea Party movement and contributed to a "shellacking" of the Democrats in the 2010 midterm elections. Those losses put militantly conservative Republicans in control of the House of Representatives, and expanded their presence in the Senate, state governorships, and state legislatures (Aldrich et al. 2014, 472). Yet while the various Tea Party groups often stressed regulatory and tax issues, analysts have also documented significant opposition among Tea Party supporters to governmental initiatives to promote racial equality (Parker and Barreto 2013). Ever since the Census Bureau issued a report in 2008 indicating that the US would likely have a majority non-white population by the mid-twenty-first century, formed in part by an influx of immigrants that included a large unauthorized population from Latin America, researchers have found evidence that many whites become more conservative on race-related issues whenever they hear that these demographic changes are underway (Resnick 2017).

After Obama won reelection by a narrower margin in 2012, already weakened hopes that genuine progress against racial inequality might occur under his leadership were blown apart by a series of horrifying racial incidents that continued through the ensuing decade, including the killings of Trayvon Martin in Sanford, Florida in February 2012, of Michael Brown in Ferguson, Missouri in August 2014, of Breonna Taylor in Louisville, Kentucky in March 2020, and of George Floyd in Minneapolis, Minnesota in May 2020. Those deaths—three at the hands of police officers—punctuated countless other murders of Black people by white people, official and unofficial, before and since.

Unlike in much of America's past, however, in the twenty-first century phone videos of killings spread by social media regularly transformed those local tragedies into drivers of national and international politics. The story is now familiar of how a Twitter hashtag created in 2013 by Patrice Cullors, Alicia Garza, and Opal Tometi, outraged by the acquittal of George Zimmerman for his shooting of Trayvon Martin, soon burgeoned with the aid of the internet into a national and international social movement, fostering many new organizations including the Black Lives Matter Global Network (Rickford 2015; Cullors 2020; Ray 2022). In 2015, Black Lives Matter also partnered with roughly fifty other groups to orchestrate an umbrella organization, the Movement for Black Lives (M4BL), which has since continued to grow. In 2016 M4BL adopted a broad-ranging platform called a "Vision for Black Lives" that featured reparations, along with demands for an end to what it described as wars on Black people; protection of voting rights for Black political power; enhancement of Black community control over many policies and programs; a restructuring of the economy to serve people and not corporations; divestment from military expenditures, militant policing, and fossil fuels and investment in health care, housing, sustainable environment, and education in Black communities; and more (Movement for Black Lives 2023).

The growth of BLM was aided by mounting disillusionment across the political spectrum with the ways American criminal justice policies and practices fostered a costly and destructive system of mass incarceration (Garland 2022; Sharkey 2022). That disillusionment built broad support for protests against police abuses and for racial justice issues more generally. Mass demonstrations grew in the Trump years to the highest levels in US history, culminating in the huge and geographically widespread protests in 2020 following the killing of George Floyd (Buchanan, Bui, and Patel 2020; Chenoweth et al. 2021).

The campaign and election of Donald Trump in 2016 proved an even greater catalyst for the emergence of new polarized racial policy alliances than Obama's presidency. The ensuing chapters document in detail how Trump's rhetoric and subsequent policies on immigration, crime, housing integration, cultural issues like public monuments and Critical Race Theory in education, and much more featured all the central themes of the Protect alliance and fostered the formation of numerous supportive groups.[2] However, Trump's administration simultaneously persuaded many more liberal-minded Americans to embrace beliefs that moderate efforts to promote integration into what was becoming "MAGA America" were insufficient. Millions joined in both protests and new organizations and initiatives aimed at repairing a nation seen as pervasively marred by systemic racism.

Though the appalled reactions of many to Trump's rise and to the multiplying videos of the killing of Black people probably did most to mobilize the new Repair policy alliance, it is likely that the emergence of modern "big data" documentation of racial disparities also contributed to broadening the sense of urgent need for change, since researchers have found that data reports often do more than stories to give people accurate estimations of how significant and persistent racial gaps really are (Kraus 2022). In any case, as the twenty-first century unfolded, racial controversies began to return to the forefront of public concern. Since 1935, the Gallup organization has polled Americans on the issues they regard as most important. In the mid-1960s, "civil rights and race relations" were often #1 or #2, but those issues faded in salience through the 1970s and vanished almost entirely with the coming of the Reagan era. They began regaining prominence early in the twenty-first century, and surged in importance in the public's mind when evidence of what many saw as racial injustices, and all saw as racial disputes, multiplied (Aisch and Parlapiano 2017). Then the murders of Taylor and Floyd triggered the 2020 summer of historically massive protests and an upsurge in support for racial justice initiatives, though white receptivity soon declined when critics portrayed the protests as fomenting violence and destruction of property (Brimelow 2021).

As racial issues moved back to center stage for American voters, the publicized killings of Black people and the ensuing protests and counter-protests did not prompt people to renew disputes over color-blind versus race-conscious policies. Nor were those the main themes when Americans confronted the mounting evidence that many forms of suffering, eventually including the burdens of the COVID pandemic, were falling disproportionately on America's communities of color (Hooijer and King 2022). Instead, as American politics were realigning more generally in the polarized twenty-first-century American political climate partly stirred up by racial divisions, conservatives and liberals drew acutely different lessons from the burgeoning racial controversies (Skocpol and Tervo 2020; Kalmoe and

Mason 2022). Many began shifting away, to the right and to the left, from the racial policy positions prevailing in America from, roughly, the Reagan Revolution through Obama's reelection in 2012.

The Emerging Racial Policy Alliances: A Preview of What Is to Come

The chapters that follow lay out the results of our research into what these developments have produced. Chapter 2 prepares the way by presenting our revised racial orders framework and comparing it with other theoretical approaches to understanding racial politics. Parts 2 and 3 focus on the Protect and Repair racial policy alliances respectively. Chapter 3 elaborates the rise and composition of the Protect alliance; chapter 4 outlines its members' stories of how and why they have mobilized; and chapter 5 details their preferred policies. Chapters 6, 7, and 8 do the same for the Repair alliance. In part 4, we discuss the implications of our findings for theories of racial politics (chapter 9), and offer alternative scenarios of where the clash of the Protect and Repair racial policy alliances may take the nation in the short- to mid-term future (chapter 10).

Before diving deep into different theories of racial politics and the specifics of our claims about America's new racial politics, however, we should help readers to be clear on just what we see as novel in these new racial policy alliances, what sorts of evidence has led us to our conclusions, and why we see this fourth phase in America's historical racial conflicts as likely to endure whatever the results of the 2024 elections.

There are inevitably significant continuities as well as breaks with the past, and so it is reasonable to wonder at the outset: is there anything really new here—and in any case, doesn't it all turn on what happens to Donald Trump? We think the answers are yes and no.

The New Substance of Opposed Racial Policies

Though there are some disagreements over what led to the rise of the modern racial policy alliances, today racial conservatives almost uniformly view the past few decades as years in which liberal elites, and a pernicious new diversity, equity, and inclusion (DEI) industry of human resource staffs and consultants in educational institutions, corporations, foundations and the media, have together imposed a racially discriminatory "woke" ideology on almost all the major arenas of American life. Racial liberals, in contrast, perceive the same period as an era in which national political discourse and national policies have moved further and further away from substantial, targeted efforts to ameliorate the nation's entrenched and pervasive patterns of racial inequality, along with economic inequality more generally. Both sides therefore feel that they and the nation urgently need to pursue a new course.

For conservative leaders and for many voters who feel both ignored and actively oppressed by liberal policies, late twentieth-century color-blind policies, often allied with beliefs that governmental aid of all sorts should be limited so that individual striving can drive change and determine the distribution of goods, now seem inadequate (Hochschild 2015; Jardina 2019; Tesler 2012, 2016a). Most conservatives now believe the government needs to do much more to defend what they see as the traditional virtues and interests of America and of more traditionalist Americans. Most define those virtues and interests in ways that reflect long-disputed but very understandable beliefs that the core of American identity lies in its European and Christian heritage and its commitments to private property and market systems, along with republican systems of popular self-governance that include limits on majoritarian democracy. Those beliefs are understandable because the United States *did* originate in a revolution led by a coalition of propertied, European-descended Christian men who favored such republicanism. Those traits went on to characterize most of the nation's leadership and predominant groups throughout American history, including every US president, with the partial exception of the Afro-European-descended Barack Obama.

For millions who see the nation's history as showing that America has been the world's greatest nation—American traditionalists like themselves, and especially white Christian men, now appear to be the greatest victims of public and private racial and religious injustices, as well as rising economic radicalism, potential majoritarian tyranny, and outright violence. This perspective is shared not only by large numbers of white Americans but also by conservative Americans of color. Consequently, in policy arenas including not just civil rights but also immigration, crime, voting rights, religious liberties, abortion, gender and sexuality, education, housing, public commemorations, and economic and social regulation in general, conservatives are stirred not by bland calls for neutral, color-blind policies, but by fierce promises to protect people like themselves against all threats to what they value most. Their ambitions to defend traditionalist America and Americans compose the substance of the Protect racial policy alliance. That alliance, like all coalitions, is nonetheless made up of diverse members, ranging from a minority who are overt white supremacists to some who still feel color-blind policies are sufficient to defend their core interests. All advocates and supporters of the alliance agree, however, that the focus throughout American policy-making today must be on protection against the dangers posed by the American Left to the cluster of qualities and constituencies they believe once made America great.

On the left, many liberals and progressives, convinced that America's history displays huge injustices despite achievements, and embittered by the undeniable racial disparities, growing overall economic inequalities, police violence, and increasingly militant Right so visible in the nation today, now regard older civil rights demands for integration into existing institutions as at best naïve. Progressives seek an agenda that pursues pervasive egalitarian transformations to end what they view as systemic racism in America's main political, economic, social, and cultural institutions. Because progressives and liberals commonly understand racial discrimination to be bound up with class injustices and also cultural norms and practices privileging men, traditional forms of Western religiosity, heterosexuals, the able-bodied, and the native-born, those transformations now often extend to all the long list of areas that agitate conservatives.

Some more moderate liberals continue to refer to the policies they desire as "racial equity" initiatives. But the most radical activists and intellectuals instead speak forthrightly of a new "abolitionism" that aims at ending mass incarceration, conventional policing, immigration enforcement, and much more. Our research indicates, however, that many and perhaps most racial justice advocates today are increasingly embracing the term "reparations" as the label for the transformations they seek—while giving it new meaning. Instead of defining reparations as financial compensation for past proven specific harms alone, usually in the form of one-time checks to affected individuals, most modern reparationists employ the term as a synonym for changing institutional systems to achieve greater diversity, equity, and inclusion in a wide range of areas, including employment, business, land and resource ownership, political rights, education, housing, health care, immigration, and more. Even more conservative Black thinkers who have been skeptical of one-time cash reparations, like the columnist and academic John McWhorter, have written favorably of "this new conception of reparations" (McWhorter 2023). But because this ex-

TABLE 1.1 **Varieties of Racial Policy Alliances**

Conservative Racial Policy Spectrum

White Supremacist	White Protectionist	Multicultural Protectionist	Color-Blind/Self-Help

Liberal Racial Policy Spectrum

Self-Help/Color-Blind	Race-Conscious Integration	Systemic Initiatives/ Reparations	Abolitionism

pansive, umbrella-like conception of reparations is novel, it is still far from universally understood, much less universally embraced. Consequently, we refer to the modern liberal racial coalition as the Repair policy alliance, acknowledging that for the most moderate this term means integrative racial equity initiatives, while for abolitionists the goal of Repair signifies "Radical Reconstruction."

These positions represent not a total rupture, but an indisputable shift within the range of positions both on the right and on the left that American politics has long displayed. To put our argument graphically, the spectrum of America's historical conservative and liberal racial policy stances can be conceptualized as in table 1.1.

Conservative positions range from (1) overt white supremacy, the predominant position up through the mid-twentieth century and resurgent on the far right today; to (2) demands to protect whites, especially, from all the losses for themselves and the nation that they feel will result from efforts to undo systemic racial inequalities; to (3) milder forms of "multicultural protectionism," a position that accepts greater racial, ethnic, and religious diversity in America so long as all groups embrace conservative economic and social policies that preserve many of the advantages that traditionalist Americans, especially propertied white Christian men, have long possessed; to (4) rigid adherence to color-blind public policies, whether or not this promotes greater inclusion and racial equality over time, often in the belief that if those things are to be achieved, it will be through the self-help of individuals.

Liberal positions range from (1) a counterpart to this last conservative view, an emphasis on achieving racial progress chiefly through Black self-help, rather than governmental aid, but with an end to racial segregation and the adoption of color-blind policies—positions long advanced (sometimes covertly) by Booker T. Washington and later openly by the

Urban League; to (2) the race-conscious measures to achieve integration that became core to many civil rights advocates in the 1970s; to (3) the calls to repair systemic racism that some refer to as racial equity initiatives, and that many now call reparations; to (4) abolitionism, which at its most radical calls for ending all enforcement of the policies in the US and around the globe that have generated a profoundly unequal world system, with predominantly white nation-states still economically and politically hegemonic.

Our central arguments in the pages that follow are first that America's conservative racial policy alliance has shifted rightward, from colorblindness toward white protectionism, though with the possibility that it may rest on multicultural protectionism. Second, America's liberal racial policy alliance has moved leftward, toward systemic racial equity initiatives commonly called "reparations," which some see as a step toward "abolition." It should be clear that these shifts do not mean that all on the right are now "white protectionists," or that all on the left are now "reparationists." The alliances today continue to include some representatives of all the right and left positions just identified, as well as other more minor variations. Again, coalitions are by definition made up of people with distinct but overlapping views and we do not impute an artificial cohesiveness to either alliance.

We nonetheless contend that virtually all on the conservative spectrum now agree that it is most vital to protect against what they see as a radically militant Left, while virtually all on the liberal spectrum now agree that American institutions need systemic if not radical repair.

The two alliances are not similarly situated, however, in many vital regards. The Protect policy alliance has the considerable advantage that it is seeking to mobilize groups—traditionalist whites, Christians, conservatives on issues of gender and sexuality, believers in property rights and less regulated markets, and more—who have tensions among them but who have often worked in coalition with each other ever since the nation's inception. They also have great advantages in how the deliberately fragmented structures of power in the American political system, and the biases of its representative institutions in favor of less populous areas which are now more often conservative, make it far easier to protect traditional features of American life than to transform them (Johnson and Miller 2023). Though many Left constituencies support transformations because they believe they have been subjected to unjust disadvantages, their particular experiences of status discrimination and economic exploitation have varied sharply, in ways that make reaching agreement on policies and strategies for change challenging.

As many conservatives recognize, however, the groups that are current or potential members of today's Repair alliance are dominant in many cities and some states, where by controlling governing institutions they constitute a racial "institutional order." Liberal and progressive groups also undeniably have a strong presence in the nation's educational, cultural, and media institutions, and attract corporate supporters in increasing numbers. And though their structural disadvantages in the American political system make it hard for them to translate their numbers into nationwide political power they are likely to comprise a majority of the US population in the years ahead. Consequently, surveys show that many Americans who are alarmed by what they see as a militant Left empowered by increasing numbers of Black and Hispanic Americans and immigrants are now willing to reject compliance with the results of majoritarian democratic processes (Bartels 2020).

These circumstances mean that while the clash between color-blind and race-conscious policy alliances appeared to leave the nation stuck with a relatively unchanging racial status quo, the new, more intensely polarized Protect and Repair racial policy alliances have the potential to be far more destructive. Many in each camp now see their commitments as central not simply to their partisan preferences, but to their core identities (Mason 2018). All too many regard their opposites as so demonic that political cooperation with them is impossible, social mixing with them is repellent, and the possibility of resorting to illegality and violence to defeat them appears acceptable, perhaps inescapable (Kalmoe and Mason 2022).

So, let us note at the outset that, perhaps surprisingly, the evidence in this book suggests that it is still possible to discern ways Americans might find some shared ground on racial issues. There remains a potential for many to unite around principles of color-blindness, despite the obstacles arising from the fact that conservatives associate these principles with policies promoting individual self-help while liberals link them with universalistic regulatory and redistributive public programs. Moreover, at least some whites seeking greater protection, notably those in the multicultural protectionist camp, are willing to view some limited "repair" measures for African Americans, such as race-targeted educational and job training programs, as likely to enable whites and all Americans to feel safer and more secure. Others who continue to champion color-blindness are willing to see some reparations as justified due to proven specific violations of those principles. And some liberals and progressives are willing to accept not only universalistic color-blind policies but even some protectionist remedies, such as enhanced funding for criminal justice and immigration enforcement, if they believe they are structured to reduce racial inequalities, injustices, and tensions.

Nonetheless, the seriousness of this newest stage in the evolution of America's racial orders should not be underestimated. The emergence of these new racial policy alliances threatens to deepen the divides that already profoundly trouble the United States. Their clash may produce significant hurdles to any further progress toward racial justice, however defined, and toward reducing persistent racial inequalities. The passions they reflect and inspire have alarming potential to foster frequent violence in the years ahead in many regions of the country, and all too often in the nation's capital—violence appearing to many observers as a new kind of guerrilla civil war.

The Evidence of Change

Previously, we have documented racial institutional orders and alliances by investigating the public positions taken by different actors, organizations, and government agencies in publications and speeches, legislative and administrative testimony, and judicial briefs. We do so in this book too, but because we discuss very recent developments, we have supplemented those sources with interviews and surveys of contemporary racial policy advocates across the political spectrum and at national, state, and local levels, as well as with illustrative network mappings of the contemporary alliances.[3] We detail these methods in appendix A.

The roughly thirty interviews we did (via Zoom or email, due to pandemic constraints) with conservative and progressive racial policy advocates proved valuable, and we are grateful to all who took time to speak with us. On both sides of today's racial policy divide, we encountered intelligent, conscientious people whose positions express genuine convictions that they are opposing evils that must be confronted.

That is *not* to suggest that we view the two sides as morally equivalent. We acknowledge throughout that we regard the conservative protectionist racial policy alliance as seeking to protect many features of American life that are unworthy of preservation and that indeed should never have existed in the first place. We accept the judgments of many progressives that egalitarian transformations are needed in many American institutional systems.

Yet we know that our own judgments and those of the advocates with whom we agree are fallible, and we recognize that many of the criticisms of Left positions that conservatives advance have force. We seek in this book to depict the realities of contemporary American racial politics, including the views of those on each side, as accurately as possible, not to compile a scorecard of who is right or wrong, and not to offer a brief for one side or the other. We know that, given our own views, we may not have succeeded. Readers may observe that we identify the progressive activists and analysts with whom we spoke more often than we do those on the conservative side. That is in large part because we have not wished to make people who generously aided us appear at all responsible for the contents of a book with which they may disagree. Only when conservative interviewees explicitly stressed that they were comfortable with being identified as the source of the views we attribute to them have we done so. We have not reported anyone's views in either camp without their consent.

Though this evidence has given us confidence in our findings and arguments, we recognize that there are reasons to doubt whether its core claims will endure beyond the period in which they were formulated, during the Trump presidency and in the extraordinary protest-filled summer of 2020. At this writing, despite robust GOP voter support, Trump's political prospects are in doubt, while public support for Black Lives Matter and racial justice causes more generally, which peaked in June 2020 following George Floyd's death, has since receded (though it stabilized in late 2021 — Pew Research Center 2021). Nonetheless, in the period since Donald Trump's presidential defeat, the evidence for the emergence of the two new racial policy alliances has in fact continued to accrue.

The Protect Alliance since 2020

We will see in the chapters to come that no American leader has proclaimed Protect alliance themes as passionately and effectively as Donald J. Trump. He did so at the very start of his presidential campaign, he did so throughout his presidency, and he did so vociferously in the summer of 2020, as he was running for reelection amid health and economic crises he could not stem, and as he faced turbulent protests demanding racial justice. To give readers a vivid sense of the Protect alliance's themes, we can do no better than to quote Trump's Independence Weekend speech in 2020, a howling battle cry against all those calling for systemic change:

> Seventeen seventy-six represented the culmination of thousands of years of Western civilization and the triumph of not only spirit, but of wisdom, philosophy, and reason. And yet, as we meet here tonight, there is a growing danger that threatens every blessing our ancestors fought so hard for, struggled, they bled to secure. Our nation is witnessing a merciless campaign to wipe out our history, defame our heroes, erase our values, and indoctrinate our children. Angry mobs are trying to tear down statues of our founders, deface our most sacred memorials, and unleash a wave of violent crime in our cities. Many of these people have no idea why they're doing this, but some know exactly what they are doing. They think the American people are weak and soft and submissive. But no, the American people are strong and proud and they will not allow our country and all of its values, history, and culture to be taken from them. (Trump 2020)

But even though Trump catalyzed and has since kept a high profile in the emergent Protect alliance, it began to form before his 2016 candidacy and it is now sustained by many other figures, including conservative media voices and the numerous new Trump-like Republican candidates. Strikingly, many members of the immense network of think tanks, academic centers, policy advocacy organizations, litigation groups, and funding agencies wealthy conservatives like the Koch brothers established and enriched from the early 1970s on, largely to advance a conservative economic agenda, have shifted in recent years to emphasizing protectionist cultural themes. New organizations focused on those messages have also proliferated, especially since Trump's defeat, like the America First Policy Institute, populated by many Trump administration alumni and other leading conservatives, and Stephen Miller's America First Legal organization.

After the 2020 elections, these actors pressed hard on new and continuing themes presenting all whites and conservatives more generally as in dire need of protection in America today. They accused all Democrats of wanting to "defund" the police, leaving law-abiding citizens defenseless against criminal predators and protesters. They denounced the undeniable failures of the Biden administration to stifle the influx of largely non-white immigrants and refugees. Along with others, then-Fox commentator Tucker Carlson ratcheted up anxieties about this influx by endorsing "replacement theory," the idea that Democrats are recruiting non-white people so that they may become the nation's dominant voting bloc, and one hostile to whites (McCarthy 2022). For some those anxieties have resonated malevolently: Payton Gendron, the eighteen-year-old accused of killing ten people in a Buffalo, New York, supermarket on May 14, 2022, invoked the threat of a "great replacement" to justify his violence (Jones 2022a).

Conservatives across the country also launched intense new campaigns against the heretofore recondite academic school of Critical Race Theory (CRT) and the alleged indoctrination of children into anti-white and anti-American beliefs in public schools. By March 2023, eighteen states had through legislation, executive order, or administrative action banned or restricted the teaching of "divisive concepts" that explicitly or implicitly included Critical Race Theory, and Republicans in forty-four states were advancing proposals with similar aims (Schwartz 2023). A number were derived from the "Teaching Racial and Universal Equality" or TRUE Act proposed by the Alliance for Free Citizens, one of many new right-wing advocacy groups (Flaherty 2021; Smith 2021; World Population Review 2022). Increasingly, conservatives' proposals also aimed at banning the teaching of "divisive concepts" in public higher education institutions, not just K-12 schools (Reilly 2022). Two of the GOP's most successful candidates, Florida's Governor Ron DeSantis and Virginia's Governor Glenn Youngkin, especially highlighted their opposition to CRT and their championing of parental rights. As DeSantis geared up for his 2022 reelection campaign, he signed into law a "K-12 Education" bill enhancing parental power to compel withdrawal of books from school libraries and from reading lists to which parents objected (Papaycik 2022). After his massive victory, as he prepared for what most observers expected to be a 2024 presidential run, DeSantis undertook a range of further measures, successfully pressing his department of education to ban a new Advanced Placement course on African Americans, appointing a majority of conservative educational advocates to the board of trustees of the famously progressive New College of Florida, and signing bills to defund diversity, equity, and inclusion programs, while mandating Western civilization courses, at all Florida public universities (Hartocollis and Fawcett 2023; Atterbury 2023). The College Board, the creator of the proposed AP course, then revised it to give less attention to CRT and Black queer scholarship and to the Black Lives Matter movement—while denying that the changes were due to political pressure (Anderson and Rozsa 2023). Though educators pushed back against the standards for teaching African American history that Florida adopted under DeSantis's leadership, and his "culture war" initiatives failed to ignite his presidential campaign, conservatives in many states advanced similar policies (Mervosh 2023).

Conservatives have also raised alarms about threats to the free speech of those on the right, arising from what they see as a "woke" leftist "cancel culture" reigning in American universities, media outlets, and even many corporate boardrooms (Mishan 2020; Pew Research Center 2021). After finally (in 2023) succeeding in getting the Supreme Court to overturn most forms of affirmative action in higher education, conservative activists quickly turned to legal challenges to corporate diversity, equity, and inclusion policies (Mark and Tan 2023). So, although Trump was out of office and off Twitter after January 2021 (despite a Twitter reinstatement by Elon Musk), the message that whites in America need protection continued to be advanced on more fronts and in more ways than ever before.

The Repair Alliance since 2020

The race-conscious policy alliance has continued to give way to its successor as well. As we have noted, this reconfiguration was partly in response to Trump's belligerence, but also because of pre-2016 discontents about the inadequate pace of federal civil rights reforms; meager efforts to reduce racial gaps in income, wealth, housing, health, and education; the enactment of voter suppression laws in many states; failures in combating racialized criminal justice; and the apparent ease with which civil rights could be pushed back (Hackett and King 2019; K. Johnson 2016; R. Johnson 2020; King 2014; Miller 2015). Racial justice advocacy in the 2020 campaign included heightened emphasis by many candidates on what they saw as the need to address systemic racism in America. In the election's wake, efforts to advance racial equity and reparations initiatives gained notable new successes.

A significant example was the fresh attention given in Congress to HR 40, the bill to create a commission to study and develop reparations proposals that US Representative John Conyers of Michigan began repeatedly introducing in 1989 (Biondi 2003, 11; Henry 2007, 97, 118). Now sponsored by Rep. Sheila Jackson Lee of Texas, the bill has always had the official support of mainstream civil rights groups like the NAACP, the Leadership Conference on Civil and Human Rights, and the Southern Christian Leadership Conference. Nonetheless, calls for reparations long remained at the margins of

American racial politics. When reparations are defined in the traditional fashion, moreover, as cash payments to the descendants of persons subjected to enslavement, over two-thirds of Americans oppose them, with only 18 percent of whites in favor, compared with 77 percent of Black Americans (Blazina and Cox 2022).

Yet it is not misleading to say that talk of reparations has moved ever closer to the center of the political stage. Most Democratic presidential candidates endorsed HR 40 in the 2020 campaign, including, after a history of skepticism, the eventual nominee, Joe Biden (Lillis and Wong 2019; Gambino 2020). In 2021, with now-President Biden's support, the House Judiciary Committee approved the bill for the first time and sent it to the House for floor action (Freking 2021a, 2021b). Since it had no chance of passing the Republican-led Senate, the House leadership opted not to pursue it until and unless Democrats regained full control of Congress; but the Judiciary Committee's favorable vote helped place the reparations commission higher on the party's future legislative agenda.

On some issues, the Democrats' agenda (like those of many racial justice organizations) also bears the imprint of BLM movement advocacy, especially as elaborated in the 2020 M4BL Vision for Black Lives. Though the Vision lists "reparations" as just one of its six sections, its authors, like many of their contemporaries, define reparations sufficiently capaciously that their reparations demands overlap with those in each of the other sections. Again, the demands do not focus on individual payments to those directly harmed by enslavement or segregation in ways increasingly measured by scholars (Aneja and Xu 2022). Instead, the platform calls for free access to higher education and forgiveness of student loans; a guaranteed minimum income for all Black people; corporate and government payments to Black communities to support health care, housing, food, and land; and revisions in public school curricula and cultural and historical sites to recognize enslavement, segregation, and discrimination and to honor struggles against such oppressive institutions. The platform echoes many of the Black Panther Party demands from the 1960s.

Receptivity to reparations, frequently defined with similar breadth, has since increased in many locations, some unexpected. On July 14, 2020, the city council of Asheville, North Carolina, a southern city that is 83 percent white, voted unanimously to apologize for the city's past complicity in slavery. The council created a Community Reparations Commission tasked to recommend funding to increase minority homeownership and to aid minority businesses, and it has since added other personnel for reparations work. Their mandate neither includes nor rules out payments to individuals. Asheville followed the prominent lead of Evanston, Illinois, which resolved in November 2019 to adopt a new tax to fund housing and employment opportunities for its African American residents. Providence, Rhode Island; Burlington, Vermont; Amherst, Massachusetts; Boston, Massachusetts; Iowa City, Iowa; Detroit, Michigan; Richmond, Virginia; Kansas City, Missouri; and San Francisco, California, among other cities, have similar measures in progress (Fies 2020; Pereira 2021a; Har 2023; Koch 2023).

Beyond the city level, in 2020 the California State Assembly created a state Task Force to Study and Develop Reparations Proposals for African Americans. Related efforts are underway in Maryland, New Jersey, New York, Vermont, and Oregon (Bonta 2022). In June 2023, the final report of the California Task Force called for a comprehensive reparations program to be administered by a new California African American Freedmen Affairs Agency (California Task Force to Study and Develop Reparation Proposals for African Americans 2023, 687). In December 2022, New York Mayor Eric Adams, a moderate to conservative African American Democrat, stated that he supported the efforts in New York's state legislature to create a reparations commission similar to that in California (Gartland and Slattery 2022). These governmental initiatives demonstrate why the current push for policies to achieve systemic racial repairs deserves to be called not just a movement but an emerging Repair "racial institutional order," just as much as the Protect order that conservatives have begun crafting at all levels of American governance, even if the Repair order remains much less extensive and powerful.

In addition to these cities and states, moreover, many civil society institutions and groups are pursuing active reparations agendas. We will see in part 2 that higher education institutions including Georgetown University, the Princeton Theological Seminary, and Harvard University have acknowledged their past complicity in enslavement, including income gained from enslavement via direct ownership or gifts, and they have sought to aid those victimized by their institutions—in Georgetown's case by paying direct descendants of people it owned and sold. Nuns living in Louisiana have developed a similar response to past injustices (Jones 2020). The Jesuit Conference of Canada and the United States, with which Georgetown is affiliated, has pledged $100 million toward a goal of providing $1 billion in reparations to descendants of enslaved persons, an effort it is pursuing through the Descendants Truth & Reconciliation Foundation (Andrew 2021). Universities' historical mistreatment of Native Americans through the usurpation of or underpayment for lands looms over many of these institutions as well, leading Cornell University, among others, to set up a research project assessing land it took from Indigenous communities (Hatzipanagos 2023).

A network of activist groups fostered by the Institute of the Black World 21st Century and including the National African American Reparations Commission (NAARC) and the National Coalition of Blacks for Reparations in America (N'COBRA) is undertaking wide-ranging private reparations initiatives they see as complementing their advocacy for public measures. Many are working in solidarity with white groups like Showing Up for Racial Justice (SURJ) and the Fund for Reparations NOW! (FFRN). Some whites are using Venmo and PayPal to make small-level transfers to African American individuals, groups, and organizations as a form of reparations.

One of the most important findings of this book is not only that these new initiatives are occurring in both public and private venues in many different places, local, state, and national, but that they have recently become startlingly well funded. Especially in the wake of the murder of George Floyd, foundations, corporations, churches, and wealthy individuals, including some of the new tech billionaires, began donating in not just the tens but the hundreds of millions to a wide variety of social justice groups, including many that are now pursuing aspects of the Repair agenda. The Black Lives Matter Foundation raised $90 million in 2020 alone (Jones 2021). Aided by new progressive donor-assisting organizations such as Bridgespan, older groups like Community Change received generous endowment gifts from wealthy progressives like Mackenzie Scott as they embarked on initiatives jointly with Black community groups. We will encounter many other examples in the chapters ahead.

Furthermore, the possibility that governmental support for reparations as well as other initiatives aimed at ending systemic racism may increase over time, even at the federal level, cannot be ruled out. Many of the progressive Democratic candidates who fared well against establishment figures in 2020, like New York's Jamaal Bowman and Missouri's Cori Bush, have affirmed the justice of reparations and won reelection in 2022 (Gabriel et al. 2023). In 2023, Bush introduced a House resolution calling for $14 trillion in reparations to be paid to Black Americans, based in part on research by the Duke University economist and reparations advocate William Darity Jr. (Felton 2023b). Advocates of reparations such as the late author and activist Randall Robinson have argued that past race-conscious policies such as affirmative action "will never close the economic gap" because sweeping "structural" changes are needed. Although the sources of racial gaps and disparities remain much disputed, along with appropriate policy responses to them, scholars continue to find fresh evidence of shocking racial inequalities in innumerable arenas of American life, such as the manner in which IRS computer algorithms make Black Americans three times more likely than others to be audited by the Internal Revenue Service (Tankersley 2023). Examples of such unintended racial disadvantages, reinforced by evidence that even Black police officers can adopt abusive practices toward Black men, exemplified in the killing of Tyre Nichols in 2023, have persuaded many more Americans that "systemic racism" is indeed pervasive in American life and requires fundamental repair and restructuring (Jervis and Guynn 2023).

Darity has called the resulting surge in political receptivity to reparations a "sea change," even if America remains far from taking the concerted and massive federal actions he judges to be necessary and obligatory (Goldberg 2020; Darity and Mullen 2020). There is no doubt that, given the unpopularity of reparations with virtually every American demographic except Blacks, many Democrats will remain wary of endorsing massive reparations payments. But as Marc Morial, the president of the National Urban League, has argued, "talk of reparations for Black Americans is not going away," and it is likely to drive support for a broad range of racial equity initiatives that may or may not be labeled reparations (Gabriel et al. 2023). We conclude that in the 2020s, most political actors seeking to present themselves as liberals or progressives will feel both empowered and compelled to advance a demanding Repair racial agenda, though some activists and many mainstream Democrats will resist calling it "reparations."

We believe the ensuing chapters provide abundant further evidence that rival Protect and Repair institutional orders are indeed coming to the fore, with their clash doing much to shape American political development. We do not profess to know with any certainty where this emerging Protect or Repair dichotomy in American racial politics and policy disputes will lead, or what are the best political and policy responses to its emergence. Again, this book is not written to defend the particular claims or the general stances of either racial policy alliance, or some third course, though the desire to aid the discovery of practical ways to reduce racial injustices that has driven all our work remains central to it. Our closing chapter does sketch the possible directions the nation appears to face, and we regretfully judge some sort of conservative multicultural protect agenda that we do not favor to be most probable. Yet politics sometimes shows that people are capable of imagining alternatives beyond those that observers identify, especially when many come to be profoundly dissatisfied with their society's current course.

Our primary aim, however, is not prediction. It is rather to answer the question with which we began: what is happening now in American racial politics? Developing a rigorous response requires deploying a theoretical framework that can help identify and organize the huge array of pertinent evidence, enabling judgments about how to distinguish signals from noise. Building on what we regard as the most promising general approaches in the contemporary social sciences, chapter 2 elaborates one such framework.

CHAPTER TWO

Racial Orders as Institutional Orders

Race, Class, and Intersectionality

Institutions are supra-organizational patterns of human activity by which individuals and organizations produce and reproduce their material subsistence and organize space and time. They are also symbolic systems, ways of ordering reality and thereby rendering experience of time and space meaningful. —Friedland and Alford (1991)

Institutional Orders and Alternative Theoretical Frameworks

The recent transformations in American civil rights policy debates have spurred us along with many others to renewed exploration of different theoretical approaches to racial politics. Those inquiries have led us to develop further our long-standing "institutional orders" framework, seeking to incorporate insights both from other conceptualizations of racial issues, and from other schools of institutionalist analysis in the social sciences. This chapter elaborates the results, which may legitimately be placed in the perhaps off-putting category of "inside the academic beltway" discourse. We offer them nonetheless, for two related reasons.

First, we believe the form of institutionalist analysis we elaborate here lays out a promising path forward for social science research not only on racial politics, which many institutionalists long neglected, but on many other kinds of social and political phenomena as well.[1]

Second, the other scholarly perspectives on racial politics we discuss are each associated with distinctive strategies of political advocacy and policy design that leading activist groups debate. Our institutional orders framework provides a means of assessing the strengths and limitations of these alternative accounts, and it can therefore aid reflections on effective advocacy and policy-making.

To vindicate these two claims, *America's New Racial Battle Lines* analyzes the searing American racial politics of the current moment.

Policy Alliances and Institutional Orders

Our approach emerged from the school of historical institutionalism in political science, particularly those historical institutionalists who assign a significant role to ideas in political development.[2] Here we connect it with parallel theorizing in sociology and management studies about institutions and especially "institutional orders," because those disciplines have advanced institutionalist theories that are more ambitious than most of those to be found in political science, accounts that deserve to be foundational in all the social sciences.[3]

Though leading scholars of politics often speak of societies as having an institutionalized "racial order" and "capitalist order," among other "orders," often these terms are used without much detailed specification. We have from the outset of our work defined "institutional orders" as "coalitions of state institutions and other political actors and organizations that seek to secure and exercise governing power in demographically, economically, and ideologically structured contexts," contexts which "define the range of opportunities open to political actors" (King and Smith 2005, 75). Without, admittedly, much elaboration, we have conceived of political societies as made up of innumerable institutional orders—congeries of governing institutions and other groups and organizations that shape governance in particular policy arenas, such as labor policies, corporate policies, religious policies, racial policies, gender policies, environmental policies, infrastructure policies, and on down a lengthy list. Because we have understood these coalitions of governmental and nongovernmental actors as formed around their shared support for various regulatory policies, we have sometimes referred to them as "policy alliances" as well as "institutional orders."

We continue to believe that when it comes to racial institutional orders, for most purposes it is appropriate to use these terms interchangeably: again, the major racial policy alliances in America have always been in control of at least some governing institutions, and all governing institutions are always supported by at least some allied civil society groups and other political actors, as well as many prevailing social norms and practices. However, such close linkages between leading policy advocates, governing institutions, and dominant cultural and social traditions have not always existed in many other major policy arenas. As examples, for long stretches of American history, women, disabled persons, and LGBTQ+ individuals and groups did not control any governing institutions authoritatively structuring gender roles and statuses, accommodations for different forms of disability, or the status of non-heterosexual identities and practices, respectively; nor were their concerns socially recognized or validated. Indeed, even in the case of class politics, although movements with clashing economic agendas have controlled different governing institutions in different times and places, rarely if ever in America have the poor captured key governing institutions from the predominant influence of the rich. And apart from some liberal versions of Christianity and other religions, the most prominent American cultural traditions and practices have valorized the wealthy few far more than the many struggling to survive.

Consequently, on many topics we now think it appropriate to recognize that historically there have been American "policy alliances" too disempowered to be called "institutional orders," even though some have succeeded in gaining control of governing institutions over time. Even in the area of racial policies, where major rival policy alliances have always formed parts of governing institutional orders, it often makes sense to attend to smaller, usually more radical policy alliances that have not fully captured any governing institutions, but that nonetheless affect the agenda and the outcomes of local, state, and national contests over racial issues.

We have always contended that racial institutional orders include social movement activists and other civil society groups, and through researching this book, we have concluded that they are playing an increased role today.[4] As scholars like Megan Ming Francis and Fredrick Harris have stressed, it is impossible to analyze contemporary American racial politics without recognizing that in recent years the landscape has been fundamentally reshaped on the left by social movement organizations, especially Black Lives Matter (Francis 2014, 7, 14; Harris 2015; and see Lieberman 2023). Many groups are primarily active locally, though they are also often in communication with national and transnational counterparts and allies. It is also necessary to recognize that contemporary conservative racial politics, though centered after 2016 on the persona of Donald J. Trump, cannot be understood without attention to the prior Tea Party movement, which wealthy conservatives sponsored but which generated genuine grassroots enthusiasm; to extremist white supremacist organizations, generally active locally, that previously seemed politically marginal; and to related ideologies of white victimization that formerly seemed less prominent than proclamations of a merit-focused "color-blindness."

Beyond social movements, it is also true that, as Stuart Hall influentially argued after the racially motivated killing of a Black teenager, Stephen Lawrence, by whites in South London in 1993, a variety of racialized "sociological processes," "practices," and "institutional cultures" often do more than formal policies to shape social behavior and experiences, in ways that may ultimately drive racial politics (Hall 1999, 188–89).[5] The dilatory police response to Lawrence's murder led an official inquiry to apply the label of "institutional racism" to the culture of the London police force (MacPherson 1999). Many perceive the 2023 killing of twenty-nine-year-old Tyre Nichols in Memphis and eleven-year-old Aderrien Murry in Mississippi by Black police officers as indelible evidence that such racialized institutional cultures remain potent in America (Jervis and Guynn 2023; Oxenden and Jaglois 2023). Recent research confirms that it is still customary for police of all backgrounds to stop Blacks and Hispanics at much higher rates than whites when they are seen as "out of place" in the neighborhoods where they are met (Schenker et al. 2023).

Moreover, the diffusion through many social and economic institutions of ideas urging the importance of "diversity, equity, and inclusion" and "intersectionality" has contributed to the more transformative Repair policy proposals and political strategies of contemporary Left advocacy groups and candidates. The spread of conservative critiques of "political correctness" and now "wokeness" has in recent years similarly fostered new Protect policy initiatives in the areas of education, corporate regulation, employment, and much more. While such social practices, discourses, processes, and institutional cultures have always been vital parts of the ideational contexts that both shape and are shaped by institutional orders, their importance is especially apparent today.

Some scholars suggest that greater attention to the broad range of grassroots actors and organizations, as well as to social practices, discourses, and processes, makes it difficult to claim that American racial politics has tended to center on overarching issues that define different eras, with groups acting in loose concert on those issues. In our view, the evidence does not show that to be the case. Today as in the past, the politics of building coalitions and constructing resonant popular appeals are still fostering alliances on each side of the nation's fundamentally dichotomous racial policy divides. Supporters of extreme positions like overtly white supremacist policies on the right, or allegiance to the African diaspora rather than to any modern state on the left, still act in American politics on most issues in support of one or the other of today's major racial institutional orders. We agree with our critics, however, that it is often useful to analyze such groups as "racial policy alliances" that are not integral parts of any governing "institutional order," and we do so at appropriate points in this book. We also agree that many of these extremist groups' resources and influence are found in the realms of social practices, processes, and cultures.

By specifying that it is sometimes appropriate to speak of "policy alliances" as distinguished from governing "institutional orders," even in reference to racial politics, while also highlighting the roles of sociological features of American life, we enable our framework to find more common ground with two largely distinct groups of scholars. The first consists of researchers focused on severely marginalized groups, who often stress social practices, social movements, and radical racial policy alliances rather than mainstream political processes, policies, and governing institutions. The second is the many political scientists who prefer to reserve the term "institutional orders" for the formal governmental institutions of the state on which they focus, such as the Congress, the executive branch, and the judiciary in the United States. By highlighting how social movements form policy alliances that may or may not become governing institutional orders, our framework encompasses both these camps.

Doing so also places our approach midway between the many political scientists who study governing institutions and the even greater number of social scientists in other disciplines who refuse to confine the term "institutional orders" to the formal institutions of governments. Many sociologists, anthropologists, and students of management and organizational behavior maintain that there are major social "institutional orders" that do not include governing "state" institutions at all. While we have learned much from them, we do not go so far.

Social Institutional Orders and Political Institutional Orders

Most prominently, in 1991, the sociologists Roger Friedland and Robert R. Alford pushed back against political scientists' and political sociologists' then-recent efforts to "bring the state back in"—engagements to which they had previously made major contributions. They published a seminal article, "Bringing Society Back In: Symbols, Practices, and Institutional Contradictions," in the landmark volume *The New Institutionalism in Or-*

ganizational Analysis, edited by Walter W. Powell and Paul J. DiMaggio. There they argued for conceiving of every modern society as "an interinstitutional system," much as we do. They defined "institutions" and "institutional orders," terms they often used interchangeably, as fundamental units of analysis that were broader than specific organizations (Friedland and Alford 1991, 232). They were "supraorganizational patterns of human activity by which individuals and organizations produce and reproduce their material subsistence and organize space and time. They are also symbolic systems, ways of ordering reality and thereby rendering experience of time and space meaningful" (243).

Like us, Friedland and Alford thought of societies as containing innumerable institutional orders; but they refrained from undertaking the daunting task of considering how all those many orders might be studied. Instead they argued for analyzing "contemporary Western societies" as comprised of a small set of "important institutional orders," each with its own "central logic—a set of material practices and symbolic constructions" (248). Without providing any elaborate arguments for their typology, they delineated the "central institutions" of such Western societies as the "capitalist market, bureaucratic state, democracy, nuclear family, and Christian religion" (232). They argued that these "major institutions" or "institutional orders" were "interdependent and yet also contradictory," with the result that "institutional contradictions are the bases of the most important political conflicts in our society," as many political scientists also contend (256).

Scholars from several disciplines, notably Patricia Thornton, William Ocasio, and Michael Lounsbury, then built on Friedland and Alford and similar conceptions of societies as "interinstitutional systems" with "subsystems, termed 'institutional orders,'" that contain those societies' "key cornerstone institutions" (Thornton, Ocasio, and Lounsbury 2012, 53). In *The Institutional Logics Perspective* (2012), Thornton, Ocasio, and Lounsbury argued that, in addition to a central "cornerstone institution," each institutional order has related organizations and actors with pertinent material practices and symbolic constructions—a definition similar to the way we have defined racial institutional orders. As their title suggested, these scholars also stressed even more than Friedland and Alford that all the institutional orders have their own distinctive "institutional logics" (53). In addition, Thornton, Ocasio, and Lounsbury argued for a somewhat different list of basic institutional orders, or "central institutions," than their predecessors had used. They proposed family, community, religion, state, market, profession, and corporation as the cornerstone institutions of the main institutional orders in modern Western societies. They saw democracy and democratic participation as a source of state legitimacy, not a separate institutional order (74).

Though these different forms of "institutionalist" scholarship have made many contributions, the quest to study societies as complex systems of interacting institutional orders remains more ambitious aspiration than achievement. One reason is that, in seeking to keep scholarly tasks reasonably manageable by focusing on a handful of "important" or "central" institutions, these leading theorists have neglected a number of institutional orders that are also undeniably significant.

We believe institutionalist research can better realize its tremendous promise if scholars do not presume in advance that certain institutional orders are "central." It is wiser to pursue exploration of all the institutions and their intersections that we can discern, in order to develop more comprehensive and convincing typologies of institutional orders; to investigate their interactions and contradictions; and to see what descriptive and explanatory insights emerge. Doing so is admittedly a massive task. Here, for example, we can only note a few of the intersections of racial orders with America's capitalist economic order, its institutional orders of gender and sexuality identities and statuses, its church-state order, and many others. Yet if researchers in many disciplines adopt institutional orders as their basic units of analysis, over time the social sciences collectively should be able to make progress on many difficult and enduring theoretical and empirical issues, including but going well beyond the racial topics examined here.

There are, to be sure, reasonable objections to this expansive "institutional orders" research agenda. It may well seem too open-ended and ill-defined. We think scholars will discover, however, that it is not really any more amorphous than traditional social science inquiries focused on "groups" or "economic interests" or "individual rational action" or "attitudes and beliefs." When employed as units of analysis, all of those conceptions logically imply terrains of research too vast to be mapped exhaustively, and all prompt similar debates concerning how their core concepts should be defined and how they can be operationalized. Over time, moreover, many scholars adopting these other units of analysis have felt compelled to take "institutionalist" turns, attending to how institutional structures shape the rational or not-so-rational choices of individuals, groups, and classes; their competitive options and prospects; and their beliefs, values, and very senses of identity. In the last generation the social sciences have also made progress in developing concepts and tools for mapping social networks, in ways that aid empirical identification of the members of institutional orders, as we discuss below.[6]

The fundamental reason for pursuing a wide-ranging institutionalist social science agenda, however, is that it ensures including all significant social and political phenomena, even if not all rise to the level of "central" institutions. Most pertinently, such a broad-gauge institutionalism could and should have a prominent place for analyzing racial issues and identities—topics on which these seminal works of institutionalist theory were largely silent. Friedland and Alford's pioneering article does not mention race at all. *The Institutional Logics Perspective* does so only twice, listing "race" as just one of the many social identities people possess (Thornton, Ocasio, and Lounsbury 2012, 85, 87). As a result, these accounts of societies as "interinstitutional systems" may not seem like the most promising points of departure for analyzing racial politics, in comparison with the many views that foreground racial identities, statuses, and concerns.

We believe instead that if properly elaborated, these accounts of societies as systems of intersecting institutional orders provide especially fruitful approaches for studying racial politics, as well as most of the other major concerns of social science research. We depart from the frameworks advanced by scholars outside political science, however, first by insisting on bringing *politics* back into all such analyses. Unlike many sociologists and economists, we do not think it correct to treat "the state" or "the bureaucratic state" as simply one institutional order among others with which it intersects. Governance, exercised both through claims to legitimate authority and through coercive power, and almost always politically contested, has more pervasive impacts than these theories acknowledge. In our view, every institutional order, including capitalist markets, professions, corporations, families, religions, and all others, necessarily includes at least some state governing institutions, rules, and policies that help to authorize and structure the order, often against resistance. In some cases, such as religious or professional institutional orders, those state structures may not be the "cornerstone institution" of the order, and the degree of their importance for different institutional orders varies. The power and authority governing institutions can assert means, however, that they play vital roles within every institutional order.

Consequently, while we agree that all institutional orders should be seen as containing "cornerstone institutions," which may or may not be institutions of state governance, as well as other associated organizations, individuals, symbolic systems, and practices, we continue to restrict the term "institutional order" to those associations or coalitions that *do* include governing institutions, and we refer to those that do not as simply "policy alliances." That label is, to be sure, not always the most felicitous for conveying the main purposes and practices of many associations, such as churches and entertainment organizations. It is, however, appropriate for institutional analyses in political science. Even though the members and activities of many associations may not give much attention to government policies much of the time, that remains true only while those policies do not hinder their preferred pursuits. Once governmental measures impinge on them, some members of every form of human association—including families, professions, corporations, labor unions, professional groups, religious congregations, and entertainment and social media companies—soon become at least part-time participants in a contesting "policy alliance."

In addition to confining "institutional orders" to those orders that include state institutions, while adding attention to less empowered "policy alliances," our framework departs from these predecessors in another crucial respect. As noted, while we concede that it is sometimes appropriate to speak of "the state" as a single institutional order, because at any one time the aggregate of all governing institutions' pertinent policies and practices have empirically identifiable impacts, we also maintain that treatments of "the state" as a unitary actor should be deployed far more carefully and sparingly than is often the case. As historical institutionalists in political science have stressed, the many governing institutions and actors that make up "the state" are often in tension with or outright opposition to each other, so that the "institutional contradictions" Friedland and Alford stress arise *within* the "bureaucratic state," as well as with external institutions.

As we have previously emphasized, in the making of racial policies as on many other issues, clashing political coalitions have often been in control of different governing institutions, making their policy disputes also institutional disputes. For example, when Radical Republicans controlled Congress in the late 1860s and early 1870s, their legislative Reconstruction program faced opposition first from the chief executive, then from a majority of the Supreme Court. Later, racial segregationists continued to rule many southern state governments into the 1960s, a time when national governing institutions, buffeted by civil rights protests and international pressures, came to embrace anti-segregation initiatives. In these and in many other instances, major political developments arose from battles between governing institutions under the influence of rival racial policy alliances (Orren and Skowronek 2004, 71–74, 133–35; King and Smith 2005, 81).

Our modified institutional orders framework, then, embraces more fully than ever the conception of human societies as interinstitutional systems with subsystems of institutional orders, while insisting that all institutional orders contain at least some state institutions; that those state institutions most often should not be conceived as unitary actors comprising a single, distinct institutional order; and that those policy alliances that do not control any state institutions are nonetheless often important subjects of institutionalist analyses.

The last point prompts a further refinement of our institutional orders framework that will be evident in the chapters that follow: the addition of attention to particular "policy regimes," issue arenas affected by the contestation of the dominant orders in particular periods.[7] All the candidates for "important" institutional orders, such as families, religions, professions, corporations, and more, shape a wide range of policies and practices, such as the gender division of labor, public educational practices, privacy rights, benefits packages, and much more. Similarly, we have always defined racial institutional orders as coalitions of governmental institutions and nongovernmental actions with shared ideas on how the major racial policy issues of their time should be decided. But those major policy issues—slavery, Jim Crow, color-blind policies, Protect or Repair policies—are "major" precisely because they have roles, sometimes highly visible, sometimes largely unseen, in a wide range of more particular policy disputes, such as the right to distribute abolitionist tracts, state powers to regulate interstate commerce, the placing of waste sites, the forms and locations of housing aid, and many more.

We therefore conceive of competing racial institutional orders, like all major institutional orders, as seeking to structure governance not only on the main issue around which they are formed but also a number of other "policy regimes"—in the case of racial orders, examples including voting rights, employment, education, housing, transportation, health care, religious rights, environmental measures, and others. Members of radical minority "racial policy alliances" that do not really agree with the dominant policies of the two leading racial institutional orders nonetheless frequently act as part of one or the other in battles over some specific policy regimes, even as groups that are steadfast members of a dominant racial institutional order on most issues sometimes defect on a few.

Figure 2.1 depicts the resulting political relationships of racial policy alliances to racial institutional orders to racial policy regimes in the spiral of politics that our framework envisions. As we have suggested, the

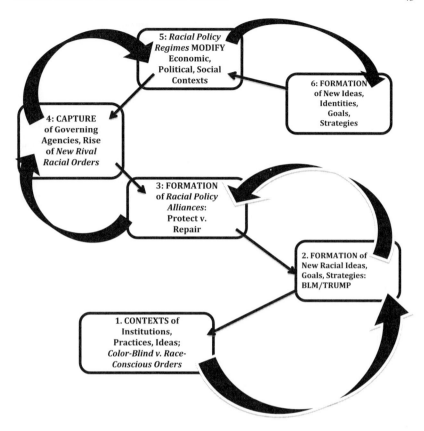

FIGURE 2.1. The Political Spiral of Racial Institutional Orders

late twentieth-century era when racial policies were dominated by disputes over color-blind and race-conscious policies produced little racial progress in many eyes. It instead contributed to economic, political, social, demographic, and ideological contexts that gave rise to new racial policy ideas and goals, including the Repair goals of Black Lives Matter and the Protect goals of Donald Trump, and so to new racial policy alliances. Each of these alliances has since gained control of some governing institutions, transforming into racial institutional orders and enacting new racial policy regimes. These regimes are in turn changing American contexts in ways that may eventually give rise to further developments, though it is too soon to tell what those will be.

Moreover, while political developments primarily follow the sort of path just sketched, it is also true that impacts run the other way. The formation of new ideas already alters ideological contexts; the processes of forming racial alliances can change conceptions of racial identities; contestations to gain power and establish institutional orders can foment shifts in the makeup of racial policy alliances; and so forth. The arrows pointing back in figure 2.1 signal these realities.

A perennial question in the social sciences is whether changes are "top-down" or "bottom-up," arising from the initiatives of elites or from grassroots movements and other social developments. The racial politics we describe have always had elements of both: widely shared mass dissatisfactions, demands, and aspirations are often the ultimate sources of change, but the particular policies that are considered and adopted by governing agencies are often formulated and implemented by more elite political actors. The roles of those elites, however, should not obscure recognition that both Protect and Repair alliances have emerged from deep popular discontents in the early twenty-first century, expressed in racial justice protests after police killings and the rise of the Black Lives Matter movement on the left, and in the Tea Party movement and the unexpectedly passionate popular support for Trump's Make America Great Again campaign on the right. To be sure, wealthy elites funded and sometimes sought to shape both sides, especially the Right; but the breadth and intensity of popular support for these rival movements have not been manufactured.

Even so, it is important to underline that racial policy alliances, like all coalitions, are made up of individuals, groups, and organizations with partly overlapping but partly distinctive agendas, so while participants in each racial order join with their racial policy allies on most issues, few do so on all. Consequently, racial institutional orders—again, like all significant institutional orders—have partly fluctuating memberships, with the variations generally tied to differences over specific policy regimes, despite other agreements. These fluctuations explain why, even when one racial institutional order is more powerful than its rival for long stretches of US history, policy outcomes still vary in different policy arenas, as well as in different regions and at different levels of government.[8]

Racial Institutional Orders as Social Networks

These additional complexities make empirical mappings of racial institutional orders challenging. In this book we can provide only illustrative, not comprehensive inventories of the memberships of the emerging Protect and Repair racial policy alliances, as well as the allied governing institutions that make them racial institutional orders. It is therefore reasonable to wonder how real what we are terming "racial policy alliances" and "institutional orders" are—whether alleged participants perceive them as existing, and whether those participants' actions can plausibly be interpreted as manifestations of their putative memberships.

Although those doubts are reasonable, they are not well-founded. In our interviews, in our reviews of organization publications and websites, and in the accounts provided by journalistic and scholarly secondary sources, we found massive evidence that most participants are vividly aware of the ideas and activities of at least some of the other advocacy groups, politicians, and governing agencies in the policy alliance to which we assign them. Both conservatives and progressives speak readily about the general movements of which they see themselves as parts, and about a variety of kindred particular groups. They also characterize those opposing them on racial policies as united and frequently cooperating with each other on the most contentious issues. Indeed, anxious partisans on each side often see their opponents as much more unified and purposeful than they are themselves.

In part to make vivid the concept of racial policy alliances, and in part to show the potential of new tools of social network analyses to provide rich empirical depictions of policy alliances and institutional orders of many types over time, we have undertaken some illustrative mapping of the networking among a small number of groups that we and others identify as conservative or liberal on racial policies. If these groups are indeed acting as members of racial policy alliances, it is reasonable to hypothesize that their websites will have many hyperlinks to each other's websites, resources, blogs, and other materials.

As detailed in appendix A, we used website crawling software (uncharmingly named "Screaming Frog") to compile and graph how frequently the different groups' websites have had hyperlinks to each other since the sites were created.[9] Because control of many government agencies can shift with each election, and because groups and individuals may link with government bodies for a wide variety of purposes, these figures are confined to nongovernmental groups. Links to the Obama Department of Justice would, for example, have a different significance than links to the Trump Department of Justice. Consequently, these figures depict *racial policy alliances*, not racial institutional orders. The ensuing chapters then add extensive documentation of the government bodies controlled by each of the rival modern racial policy alliances at the time of this writing.

The three figures below illustrate the networks of fifty American political groups, selected to represent both older conservative and liberal organizations, like the American Enterprise Institute and the American Civil Liberties Union, and newer ones, like the National Conservativism Conference and Black Lives Matter. Because we found a greater variety among liberal groups, they are slightly overrepresented, with twenty-eight organizations as opposed to twenty-two conservative ones.

Figure 2.2 depicts both of the two contemporary racial policy alliances, with liberal groups clustered, suitably enough, on the left, and conservative groups on the right. Figure 2.3 depicts the liberal racial policy alliance in isolation, while figure 2.4 does the same for the conservative alliance.

The circles or "nodes" on the figures represent the websites of those groups. The size of each group's node indicates its degree of connectedness — that is, to how many other groups' websites any given website is connected via hyperlinks. A small node represents no or only very few connections, as in the case of Conservative Headlines (CHead) in the conservative cluster. A large node means a group's website has many hyperlinks to many other groups, as is true of the National Association of Scholars (NAS) in the same figure.

The lines or "edges" between the nodes represent the frequency of the hyperlinks connecting one group's website to the websites of the other groups in the figure on a logarithmic scale. The thinnest edges, such as the one connecting Institute of the Black World 21st Century (IBW21) to the journalist Peter Brimelow's anti-immigration nationalist conservative group VDare, show a single hyperlink, while the thickest represents the most frequent interaction: there are almost eighty-five thousand hyperlinks from the Institute of the Black World 21st Century (IBW21) website to that of the National African American Reparations Commission (NAARC) that IBW21 helped to create.

As the nodes and edges demonstrate, within each cluster there are some extensively connected and presumably influential organizations, such as the American Enterprise Institute and VDare among conservatives, and the ACLU and the Institute for the Black World 21st Century among progressives. Other groups have more limited linkages, and we have included groups whose websites show no connections to any of the other groups in either network. Their presence shows that internet hyperlinks are not so ubiquitous that all groups appear to have some connection to all other groups, which would make the results less informative.[10]

In figure 2.2, the conservative and liberal clusters do interact with each

RACIAL ORDERS AS INSTITUTIONAL ORDERS 47

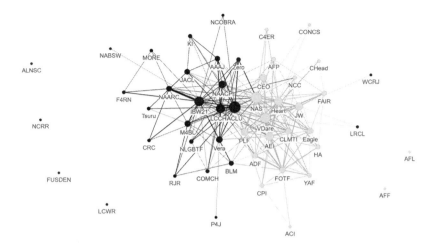

FIGURE 2.2. Core Members of Today's Protect and Repair Racial Policy Alliances

AAAJ: Asian Americans Advancing Justice; ACLU: American Civil Liberties Union; ALNSC: Alabama New South Coalition; BLM: Black Lives Matter; COMCH: Community Change; CRC: CARICOM Reparations Commission; F4RN: Fund for Reparations NOW!; FUD: First Unitarian Denver; IBW21: Institute of the Black World 21st Century; JACL: Japanese American Citizens League; KI: Korematsu Institute; LCCHR: Leadership Conference on Civil and Human Rights; LCWR: Leadership Conference of Women Religious; LRCL: La Raza Centro Legal; M4BL: Movement for Black Lives; MORE: Mayors Organized for Reparations and Equity; NAACP: National Association for the Advancement of Colored People; NAARC: National African American Reparations Commission; NABSW: National Association of Black Social Workers; NCOBRA: National Coalition of Blacks for Reparations in America; NCRR: Nikkei for Civil Rights and Redress; NLGBTF: National LGBTQ Task Force; P4J: Partners for Justice; RJR: Racial Justice Rising; Tsuru: Tsuru for Solidarity; Vera: Vera; WCRJ: Workers Center for Racial Justice; Zero: Campaign Zero; ACI: American Cornerstone Institute; ADF: Alliance Defending Freedom; AEI: American Enterprise Institute; AFF: America First Foundation; AFL: America First Legal; AFP: America First Policy Institute; C4ER: Californians for Equal Rights; CEO: CEO USA; CHead: Conservative Headlines; CLMTI: Claremont Institute; CONCS: The Conservative Caucus; CPI: Conservative Partnership Institute; Eagle: Eagle Forum; FAIR: Federation for American Immigration Reform; FOTF: Focus on the Family; HA: Heritage Action; Heart: Heartland Institute; JW: Judicial Watch; NAS: National Association of Scholars; NCC: National Conservatism Conference; PLF: Pacific Legal Foundation; VDare: VDare; YAF: Young America's Foundation

other to a limited degree, but they network far more extensively with their allies on racial policies. This software social network mapping of the interconnections of racial policy organizations illustrates vividly the existence of distinct racial policy alliances, on the internet at least. Our subsequent discussions of these organizations and others working with them will show why, based on other evidence, we believe these alliances merit the labels Protect and Repair, and how they are impacting policies in many governing venues today.

Prominent among the liberal racial justice organizations depicted in figure 2.3 are not only older civil rights groups such as the NAACP, but newer groups such as the National African American Reparations Commission (NAARC) that clearly advance the Repair policy agenda we delineate in the ensuing chapters. The figure also suggests that the Institute for the Black World 21st Century, which takes as its mission the increase in communications and coordination among racial justice groups, is indeed promoting extensive interconnections and networking.

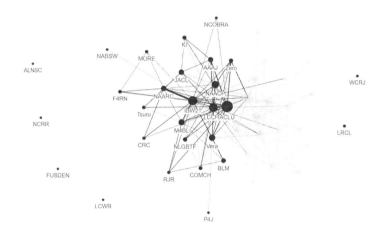

FIGURE 2.3. Repair Racial Policy Groups

AAAJ: Asian Americans Advancing Justice; ACLU: American Civil Liberties Union; ALNSC: Alabama New South Coalition; BLM: Black Lives Matter; COMCH: Community Change; CRC: CARICOM Reparations Commission; F4RN: Fund for Reparations NOW!; FUD: First Unitarian Denver; IBW21: Institute of the Black World 21st Century; JACL: Japanese American Citizens League; KI: Korematsu Institute; LCCHR: Leadership Conference on Civil and Human Rights; LCWR: Leadership Conference of Women Religious; LRCL: La Raza Centro Legal; M4BL: Movement for Black Lives; MORE: Mayors Organized for Reparations and Equity; NAACP: National Association for the Advancement of Colored People; NAARC: National African American Reparations Commission; NABSW: National Association of Black Social Workers; NCOBRA: National Coalition of Blacks for Reparations in America; NCRR: Nikkei for Civil Rights and Redress; NLGBTF: National LGBTQ Task Force; P4J: Partners for Justice; RJR: Racial Justice Rising; Tsuru: Tsuru for Solidarity; Vera: Vera; WCRJ: Workers Center for Racial Justice; Zero: Campaign Zero

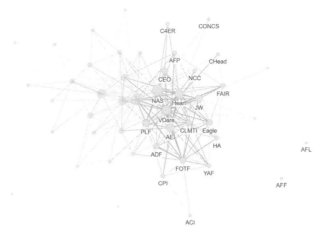

FIGURE 2.4. Protect Racial Policy Groups

ACI: American Cornerstone Institute; ADF: Alliance Defending Freedom; AEI: American Enterprise Institute; AFF: America First Foundation; AFL: America First Legal; AFP: America First Policy Institute; C4ER: Californians for Equal Rights; CEO: CEO USA; CHead: Conservative Headlines; CLMTI: Claremont Institute; CONCS: The Conservative Caucus; CPI: Conservative Partnership Institute; Eagle: Eagle Forum; FAIR: Federation for American Immigration Reform; FOTF: Focus on the Family; HA: Heritage Action; Heart: Heartland Institute; JW: Judicial Watch; NAS: National Association of Scholars; NCC: National Conservatism Conference; PLF: Pacific Legal Foundation; VDare: VDare; YAF: Young America's Foundation

Figure 2.4 shows that some of the oldest and most established conservative groups, such as the American Enterprise Institute and the National Association of Scholars, are still more interlinked with a variety of conservative racial policy organizations than most newer groups. For example, the Conservative Partnership Institute, founded in 2017, seeks to connect and assist conservative groups much as the Institute for the Black World 21st Century does among left-leaning racial justice organizations, but it is at this point not so thickly interconnected as the IBW21 or as older conservative entities. We will see, however, that many of the older conservative groups have shifted toward the Protect policy agenda advanced by the newer entities, so there is good reason to believe that the conservative racial policy alliance is as strongly mutually supportive on key issues as its progressive counterpart, even though differences inevitably persist within each alliance.

This internet mapping makes us confident that racial policy alliances are empirically tangible and politically significant, even if they are difficult to inventory comprehensively. We expect that as institutionalist research proceeds, scholars will make great progress in such mapping, often extending it to governing agencies, helping institutionalist social science to realize its great potential.

Turning to Alternative Theoretical Frameworks

Precisely because many institutionalist analyses have not focused on racial politics, we believe it is vital to explore how our framework of competing racial alliances and institutional orders can both inform and be informed by other theoretical approaches concerned specifically with racial conflicts and political processes. Our thinking has been especially influenced by scholars with three overlapping but distinguishable perspectives, which we call here the *capitalism-focused* camp, the *white hegemony* camp, and the *intersectional* camp. There is a long history of some advocates and scholars in each of these camps firing on the others, with the first accused of "class-reductionism," the second of "race-reductionism," and the third dismissed as hopelessly complex, even as its proponents criticize both of the other camps for neglecting, especially, gender and sexual aspects of intersectional systems of inequality.

Yet all three approaches share with ours the premise that American systems of racial inequality do not arise from natural differences, but instead are political and social constructions, the products of political forces. That premise has never been shared by many influential conservative understandings of race in America, some of which are gaining renewed visibility through the advocacy of the far-right wing of today's Protect alliance. Though it would take us too far afield from this book's main tasks to examine these understandings in detail, they are too significant to go unacknowledged.

Deterministic Conservative Theories of Racial Differences and Inequalities

Few readers will be surprised to learn that many older and some contemporary conservative accounts portray racial inequalities as primarily the natural outgrowths of biological differences among the races, or as the products of cultural differences so deeply rooted that they have effectively become an almost immutable second nature. A number of scholars have documented how the United States has a long history of intellectual contributions to "scientific racism," going back at least to Thomas Jefferson's speculations on inherent Black inferiority in *Notes on the State of Virginia* (Smedley and Smedley 2012). Not all will be aware of how such accounts continue to be advanced by prominent scholars, including conservative political scientists. The leading example probably remains Charles Murray, the W. H. Brady Scholar at the American Enterprise Institute. Murray opened his 2020 book *Human Diversity: The Biology of Gender, Race, and Class* by observing that if readers are "convinced that gender, race and class are all social constructs . . . [t]his book isn't for you" (Murray 2020, 1).[11] As his title promised, Murray went on to stress biological sources of racial inequality, as he and Richard Herrnstein did earlier in *The Bell Curve*.

In contrast, Lawrence Mead, a professor of politics and public policy at New York University, contends that America's racial gaps have cultural roots. Summarizing the message of his 2019 book, *Burdens of Freedom: Cultural Difference and American Power*, Mead has written: "Today, the seriously poor are mostly blacks and Hispanics, and the main reason is cultural difference. . . . Fifty years after civil rights, their main problem is no longer racial discrimination by white people, but rather that they face an individualist culture they are unprepared for. Their native stance toward life is much more passive than the American norm. . . . They now must strive to get ahead . . . while avoiding crime and personal problems. . . . They are thus at a disadvantage in competing with the European groups—even if they face no mistreatment on racial grounds" (Mead 2019, 2021). Mead insists that his view, unlike Murray's, is not about race. Yet since most Black Americans and many Hispanic Americans are not descendants of recent immigrants but rather come from families that have lived in the United States for generations, Mead's argument assumes that the traits of non-European cultures have been sustained for centuries by the Black and Hispanic communities within the United States. Thus, in his account these alleged cultural attributes appear to be as deeply ingrained as biological characteristics.

Though our work has long been motivated in part by concerns about the resurgence of views like those of Murray and Mead, our racial orders framework, focused on political coalitions, is not a useful lens for examining claims of biological and cultural differences, and we have not done so in this book. We acknowledge that we believe these claims recurrently garner attention because of their value as tools of conservative political movements, rather than because of their merits as objective assessments of the realities of race, however earnest their authors may be in advancing them. In this respect, our approach sides with progressive perspectives on racial identities and inequalities, including the three camps we engage with here. In chapter 4, we will give attention to some considered conservative accounts of race that emphasize political factors, rather than biological or cultural determinants of racial identities, characteristics, and statuses. In seeking to strengthen our racial orders framework, however, we have primarily considered the accounts of racial politics that share our basic premise and strike us as most intellectually powerful.

The Ambiguities of Racial Capitalism

While the three camps of racial analysis that have most influenced us all share our focus on how politics structure racial identities and statuses, they have important differences in their accounts of what political factors should be stressed. However, those differences can be unclear, particularly because, though some capitalism-focused scholars resist, all three camps can be interpreted as embracing a term now commonly deployed in both academic and political discourse: "racial capitalism." And because the phrase has become so ubiquitous, especially among groups in today's Repair alliance, it might seem a suitable label for that alliance's central target.

We are reluctant, however, to place great reliance on the "racial capitalism" phrase, in characterizing either the different theoretical approaches to understanding racial politics or the concerns of the Repair alliance. The term's renewed popularity arises in part because it provides an inspiring rallying cry for those opposed to both racial and capitalist injustices, while remaining sufficiently ambiguous on the character and mechanisms of the linkages between them to permit it to be interpreted in a number of different ways. Though the concept of "racial capitalism" has much deeper roots, particularly in 1970s Marxist debates in apartheid South Africa, many now trace the phase to a political scientist, the late Cedric Robinson. He maintained in his 1983 book, *Black Marxism: The Making of the Black Radical Tradition*, that even European feudal systems of labor exploitation racialized their workers to justify their lowly statuses (Robinson 2020 [1983], 3; cf. Levenson and Paret 2022, 2–3, 6–10).[12] Consequently, Robinson saw capitalism as having emerged within already racialized nations, and as an inherently racially exploitative system. As Robinson put it in *Black Marxism*, rather than arising from inequities originating with capitalism, "the social, psychological, and cultural origins of racism and nationalism both anticipated capitalism in time and formed a piece with those events that contributed directly to its organization of production and exchange" (9).

There are nonetheless passages in Robinson's book that some read as suggesting that distinctive modern conceptions of race arose later, out of capitalism's efforts to justify its specific systems of economic inequality (Levenson and Paret 2022, 11). In any case, other analysts of racial capitalism do not follow Robinson's chronology or his account of racial and capitalist linkages. They instead portray modern racial ideologies as developing after feudalism in order to justify the violent expropriation of labor, land, and resources from populations subjected to European systems of capitalist imperial expansion. Some racial capitalism analysts advance these views in amendment to or in explicit disagreement with Robinson. Some do not refer to his work at all.[13] The legal scholar Nancy Leong, for example, has analyzed how contemporary capitalist systems use "nonwhite people" as valuable economic commodities by citing Critical Race Theory, but not Robinson (Leong 2013). The political scientist Michael Javen Fortner has drawn on but revised Robinson's conception of racial capitalism by stressing how the "co-constitutive dynamics of racial capitalism" can foment "intra-racial fissures and cross-racial" class alliances, such as those between Black and white urban landlords, in ways that generally work to bolster capitalism while perpetuating or exacerbating the hardships of the urban Black poor (Fortner 2023). Similarly, the historian Jennifer L. Morgan argues that racism and capitalist profitability have been "co-constituted"—though she, like Fortner, does not specify the mechanisms of their linked emergence and persistence (Morgan 2021, 10). As Zachary Levenson and Marcel Paret note, in both contemporary scholarship and political advocacy most invocations of "racial capitalism" do not in fact seek to resolve whether there is "a preexisting racism that helps constitute capitalism, or whether racial differentiation is an effect of capitalism itself," or whether some other relationship is at work (Levenson and Paret 2022, 13). Nor do many clarify whether racism can survive without capitalism, or capitalism without racism.

It might seem that for the many activists and scholars who see both racism and capitalism as ineradicably unjust, no resolution is needed. Both are to be opposed, along with many other systems of injustice. Yet bitter conflicts have long arisen over how that opposition is to be pursued. The three camps we consider here differ significantly over which issues should be foregrounded, both in political organizing and in policy prescriptions.

The first, capitalism-focused camp favors mobilization around interracially shared economic interests, emphasizing class rather than racial identities. It stresses "universal," or at least pro-working-class, economic policies, believing that these will reduce racial inequalities along with unjust economic inequalities.

The second, white hegemony camp calls for sweeping efforts to end all forms of systemic racism, in tandem with or often prior to addressing systemic economic transformations. Believing that a class-focused agenda will leave too many racial injustices intact, it views a wide range of sometimes radical race-targeted policies as necessary parts of such transformations.

The third, intersectionality camp calls for broad intersectional coalition-building and for policies that innovatively blend race and class concerns with measures addressing many other kinds of inequities, especially those of gender and sexuality. It seeks simultaneously to publicize and to transform multiple forms of discrimination and disadvantage that are often mutually reinforcing.

The Contributions of the Racial Orders Framework

We believe these three perspectives collectively pose the most significant questions for analyses of racial politics today. Our institutional orders framework is, however, neither committed to nor confined to any of them. It is in important respects humbler in its premises. It does not assume that all racial inequalities are or are not rooted in capitalism; or that the US is or is not an ineradicably white supremacist regime; or that multiple intersecting systems of inequality must or must not be understood to be equally mutually constitutive, so that none, or at least very few, should be given priority in analytic understandings or political action. It also does not assume that capitalism can or cannot be disentangled from the racialization of labor, from unjust economic inequalities, and from many forms of global imperialism. It offers no certain estimate of how inclusively intersectional and transformative racial policy alliances can hope to be, and no full theoretical portrait of what the intersectional relationships are among race, class, gender, sexuality, disability, and many other aspects of identities and inequalities. Though it does contend that racial institutional orders are real and important, it is not even committed to any typology of the "central" or "most important" institutional orders in the US or any other society. We are pleased for others to develop such accounts, but we regard them as, at this point, still speculative in important respects.

The fundamental contribution of our framework is to highlight the need to explore these important rival claims about racial politics empirically, and to guide how empirical inquiries can be productively structured to generate evidence pertinent to evaluating them. It calls for identifying the memberships, ideas, and internal dynamics of racial institutional orders and for mapping their historical and current interactions with other institutional orders and policy alliances, including those structuring economic entities, families, genders and sexualities, religious bodies, and many more. Such investigations appear to us the most promising path available for assessing the strengths and limitations of these alternative theoretical perspectives, and for developing richer accounts of racial politics past, present, and future. To see why, let us more fully consider each of these alternative camps.

Most theorists in the first, *capitalism-focused* camp reject Cedric Robinson's claim that the racism visible in the last several centuries preceded the emergence of capitalist economic systems. They also dismiss accounts of racism as rooted in psychological and cultural attitudes and beliefs, viewing these as, at best, intervening variables. They instead understand modern racist doctrines primarily as instruments employed, both consciously and unconsciously, to advance and defend capitalist-rooted inequalities. As Adolph Reed Jr. has recently put it, "white supremacy" has basically been an ideological "cover story" for American political orders that have been "clearly racial but that most fundamentally stabilized and reinforced the dominance of powerful political and economic interests" (Reed 2022, 137; cf. Fields 1990). This perspective points toward analyzing racial politics chiefly in terms of the underlying power structures of a capitalist political economy, for which inegalitarian racial conceptions have often served to "reify inequities organic to capitalism" and have provided what might be termed emotional accelerants and lubricants for the capitalist engine that drives most politics (Reed 2020, 164). In their most extreme versions, capitalist-focused views anticipate that racial ideologies and injustices will diminish dramatically or disappear entirely when an egalitarian socialist order is achieved. As the Black sociologist Oliver Cromwell Cox once put it pungently in his first major book, there "will be no more 'crackers' or 'n-----s' after a socialist revolution because the social necessity for these types will have been removed" (Cox 1959 [1948], 537, expletive modified).

Consequently, scholars and activists in this camp often regard political appeals and policies that primarily aim at condemning and altering racist attitudes, feelings, and beliefs, rather than achieving structural changes in the nation's political economy, as focused on the wrong target. At the same time, most if not all strongly support governmental efforts to combat harmful racially discriminatory conduct. Some also endorse race-based affirmative action programs as blunt but effective antidiscrimination measures, though others like Richard Kahlenberg have long opposed them, believing that once they are ended "class will be the only game in town" (Hartocollis 2023). All agree, however, that what they see as "race reductionist" emphases on "white privilege" and "identity politics" only serve to hamper the building of the broad-based coalitions needed to overturn capitalism and advance social justice, including racial justice, for all (e.g., Reed 2020; Silver 2022; Hartocollis 2023).

We strongly agree that analysts must always consider how far racial ideologies serve economic and political power goals. Our framework is, however, more open than most capitalism-focused accounts to the possibility that racial ideas and commitments may be constitutive elements of racial institutional orders, defining their ultimate ends as well as serving as means. If we accept that conceptions of group identities and interests are in significant measure politically and social constructed, it is readily conceivable that the self-conceptions of groups who see themselves as sharing core interests may in some times and places treat their racial identities and traits as definitive of those interests, in ways that might sometimes survive socialist economic transformations. Some scholars in fact argue that in modern socialist societies, racism and racial inequalities did not disappear with the establishment of socialist political economies (e.g., Wright 2022). As the capitalism-focused historian Touré Reed has acknowledged, "given racism's cultural imprint, it is safe to assume that if we were somehow able to end economic inequality next Tuesday, racial prejudice would not likely disappear on its own by next Wednesday" (Reed 2020, 121).

Perhaps, however, racial prejudice would fade away over time, as both the experiences of participating in interracial coalitions and the benefits of broadly beneficial new economic policies and institutions fostered more inclusive and solidaristic senses of shared identity. Perhaps not. Analyses of institutional orders cannot offer definitive answers. But if scholars conduct and knit together studies of the relationships of economic orders to racial orders in many settings, informative patterns may well emerge. We expect that much of this empirical research will affirm that class interests have sometimes driven ideologies and structures of racial inequality, and perhaps that they almost always have, as many capitalism-focused scholars believe.

The evidence in this book, however, renders that conclusion unsettled. We will certainly see in the ensuing chapters that modern corporations have long resisted heightened governmental regulatory, tax, and redistribution policies, much less public ownership, and so they have often opposed race-targeted as well as universal assistance programs, consistent with capitalism-focused accounts. Nonetheless, in recent decades many businesses did adopt diversity, equity, and inclusion initiatives and support for race-conscious policies in employment and education, sometimes even in public contracting. Today, some corporations are funding private initiatives favored by racial justice supporters, and wealthy individuals are donating to social justice groups so extensively that some groups report that they no longer worry about funding. As a result, in a sharp departure from the Reagan era and indeed much of US history, many conservatives today attack "woke" corporations as fiercely as they denounce political, media, and academic elites.

Capitalism-focused analysts can rightly reply that these corporate positions fall far short of the kinds of massive economic transformations that proponents of democratic socialism, and many supporters of Repair initiatives, regard as necessary. Many corporations support policies that critics deride as "multicultural neoliberalism," beneficial to small, wealthy subsets within many racial, ethnic, and cultural groups but not to most working and poor people in those groups. Our evidence complicates but does not refute judgments that so long as corporate interests are able to preserve capitalist systems that generate great material inequalities, racial inequalities will also persist—and those inequalities will probably be defended through racial as well as economic ideologies. We believe our findings here do demonstrate, however, that social science inquiries examining the relationships of economic and racial institutional orders are valuable, if not in fact necessary, for informing not just academic understandings of racial politics but also activist judgments on attractive political strategies and official decisions on appropriate policies.

We take the same basic view of how our framework relates to the second, *white hegemony* camp, though we have different agreements and disagreements with its proponents' premises. The foundational concern of white hegemony analysts is with what its members take to be the original, enduring, and perhaps unalterable racial ordering of the United States and, to a large degree, the prevailing international system. Most white hegemony scholars maintain that ever since its creation as a white settler-colonial nation, the US has been a fundamentally unitary state with a single white supremacist racial order. They argue that, as the historian Roxanne Dunbar-Ortiz has put it, "white nationalism was inscribed in the founding of the United States as a European settler-colonial expansionist entity, the economy of which was grounded in the violent theft of land and in racial slavery" (Dunbar-Ortiz 2021, xx). Most also contend, in agreement with the immigration law scholar and activist Monika Batra Kashyap, that the US remains "a present-day settler colonial society whose laws and policies function to support an ongoing structure of invasion called 'settler colonialism,' which operates through the processes of Indigenous elimination and the subordination of racialized outsiders" (Kashyap 2019, 548). In many of these formulations, the emphasis is on how settlers deeming themselves white, Christian, and civilized then conquered, displaced, robbed, and exploited people deemed non-white and savage in order to advance their own race, religion, and culture, as well as their economic interests. Consequently, the structures of power and the practices of everyday life they fostered express and reinforce pervasive systems of racial, religious, and cultural inequality that many white hegemony analysts see as separate from economic systems, and as patterns and structures to which those whom they benefit are often staunchly committed.

Many of the white hegemony scholars who depict the US as a "racial state," a "racial regime," or a "racial capitalist" society also portray the domination of its white ruling class as having historically faced significant opposition only from those groups it has exploited, marginalized, and excluded. These analysts generally speak of American society as displaying a single "racial order," intertwined with its "capitalist order," that controls "the state" or the "regime" and deploys it against transformative social movements (e.g., Omi and Winant 1986, 1994, 2014; Goldberg 2002; Hanchard 2018). Some insist, like the Afropessimist philosopher Tommy J. Curry, that this racial order is so ineradicably constitutive of American identity, institutions, and practices that "America is not capable of moral transformation concerning racism, because racism is a permanent and necessary feature of our American society" (Curry 2011, 125). Curry does not rule out, however, that forces other than moral suasion may ultimately compel the radical transformations in America and around the world that he supports (137–38).

Like Curry, virtually all in the white hegemony camp agree that America's white settler-colonial identity and its racial politics must be analyzed not just in their origins but throughout history as part of an evolving global system of European imperial conquests and colonization that still structures much of our allegedly "postcolonial" world (e.g., Dawson 2016, 149; Fraser 2016, 173–77; Schmidt 2020, 47). They display less agreement, however, on just how American and global racial and capitalist systems of inequality have been and are related, and whether they can ultimately be disentangled. Many take no clear position, focusing instead on opposing both; and the positions of some leading figures have shifted over time.

For example, in their seminal statements of racial formation theory, Omi and Winant argued that "(r)acial dynamics must be understood as determinants of class relationships and indeed class identities, not as mere consequences of these relationships"—phrasing that presented race as more fundamental than class (Omi and Winant 1994, 34). But in response to criticisms from intersectional scholars, they have more recently contended that "the literature on intersectionality has clearly demonstrated the mutual determination and co-constitution of the categories of race, class, gender and sexual orientation." They sometimes still insist that "*race is a master category*" (italics in the original) that "has become the *template* of both difference and inequality," shaping how all the intersecting regimes of domination and inequality are constructed (Omi and Winant 2014, 106). Most often, however, Omi and Winant, like most others in the white hegemony camp, simply assert that "racialization" and "capitalist exploitation" are "mutually constitutive," in the United States and throughout the world, without assigning explicit priority to either (cf. Burden-Stelly 2020).

In a much-discussed exchange, Michael Dawson and Nancy Fraser agreed to formulate this mutual constitution as arising from the fact that historically, capitalist systems in the US and elsewhere could not sustain themselves economically or politically by *only* exploiting wage laborers—profiting from their work while paying near-subsistence wages set in what were claimed to be "free" contracts. Such low-wage labor often proved insufficient to satisfy capitalist profit imperatives. Consequently, capitalist colonists especially also directly expropriated the wholly uncompensated labor and resources of Indigenous, enslaved, colonized, and imprisoned populations, in ways they generally justified through racialist ideologies (Dawson 2016; Fraser 2016). But unlike those in the capitalism-focused camp, these scholars contend, as Dawson said in relation to the Black Lives

Matter movement, that given "the evolution of racialized capitalism, they, and we, have no choice but to simultaneously fight white supremacy and economic injustice" (Dawson 2016, 160).

For many in the white hegemony camp, this conclusion means that the Left must engage in substantial political activism focused on what they see as racist attitudes, feelings, beliefs, symbols, discourses, language, and customs, as well as racial material disparities. Again, many in the capitalism-focused camp regard these initiatives as unproductive or counterproductive and believe they effectively place race above class as the central theme of progressive political organizing (Omi and Winant 2014; Reed 2020). While the evidence in this book cannot decisively resolve these disputes, we will see that in the agendas of those Repair groups who most stress the themes of white hegemony analyses, racial initiatives are indeed much more extensive and more fully specified than anti-capitalist proposals.

The agreements of our racial institutional orders framework with these white hegemony accounts are, however, as important as our disagreements with them. In addition to sharing the premise that racial identities and statuses are extensively politically constructed, we have no doubt about the white settler origins of the United States, or the pervasive persistence of many consequent forms of racial inequality. We also accept with Stuart Hall that many of these inequalities can be deemed products of "systemic" or "institutional racism," because any institutional system that deepens or simply perpetuates racial disparities that are traceable to past and present forms of racial discrimination can legitimately be called "racist," whether or not its particular policies result from intentional efforts to construct and maintain racial hierarchies (Hall 1999, 194). We agree as well that American racial politics must be analyzed as parts of transnational, indeed global developments, and the ensuing chapters will present much evidence of how both Protect and Repair advocates in the US are in communication and collaboration with their counterparts on other continents, at least as much as such advocates have ever been, and probably more so. We will note other transnational political, economic, and social pressures that affect domestic racial politics in the United States as well.

As we have already suggested, however, our framework resists the portraits of the US as a fundamentally unitary white supremacist state, opposed only by social movements of people of color, of the type that many white hegemony accounts present. We stress that America's origin as a *revolutionary* white settler colony, one that proclaimed commitments to universal human rights and republican self-governance even as it practiced enslavement and genocide, has made profound contestation over systems of racial inequality, not simply white domination, central to it from its inception, driving much American political development (Carpenter 2021).[14] To grasp America's evolving racial politics, we think it necessary to recognize that America's revolutionary ideologies have provided much of the rhetoric and the program of coalition-building for what we have termed the transformative racially egalitarian orders in US history—anti-enslavement, anti-Jim Crow, anti-color-blindness, and today, anti-white protectionism. These coalitions have generally been interracial, including reform-minded white individuals and groups as well as people of color, even though they would not have originated or been sustained without great pressure and vital intellectual and political leadership from the nation's oppressed communities.

We therefore do not believe that American racial politics can be understood *simply* as constituting an enduring coercive white racist regime in which "racism adapts rather than arrests, and evolves rather than subsides over time," even though such adaptations have undeniably occurred (Curry 2011, 133). Actions by parts of America's complex structure of governing institutions, generally administered by whites responding to a variety of political, economic, and ideological concerns, have also been forces for reform and change (King and Lieberman 2017). This duality is an unignorable American paradox. The great intellectual and reformer Frederick Douglass could both reject the easy celebration of July 4th and cite political principles from the founding documents to be realized as civil rights for all. As Jack Turner has noted, Douglass in fact systematically analyzed the issues of his day by whether they advanced "the spirit of slavery" or the "spirit of liberty," seeing American politics as divided between these two rival forces, much as we do (Turner 2018, 205–6). We think it vital to understand the ideas, interests, and actors, many directing governmental institutions, that have worked against state impositions of racial hierarchies, as well as those that have worked for them—especially since some real successes have been achieved over time. It is important to learn from, not dismiss, these successes, limited though they have been. Consequently, though white hegemony analyses of the US as a unitary "racial state" capture significant features of American political reality, we believe a framework of conflicting racial institutional orders captures still more.

Our emphasis on contestation does not rule out hypothesizing (to use institutionalist terminology) that racial hierarchies have been among the "cornerstone institutions" of the United States, of significance comparable to or perhaps even greater than the family, community, state, religion, market, professions, and corporations. It does insist that countering institutions must be acknowledged and assessed. Much scholarship suggests that this is also true of other Western societies and of the current global system of nation-states that emerged from a world dominated by primarily European and American imperialism. In assessing how ineradicably white-dominated both the US and the contemporary international system are, we believe that examinations of clashing racial institutional orders, as well as other institutional orders, are essential.

We also believe, however, that these examinations are likely to produce evidence that supports many core claims of white hegemony accounts. Contentions about "systemic" and "institutional racism," for example, can be richly explored by examining how racial orders have interacted with those structuring health systems, housing systems, educational systems, labor systems, media systems, and many more. We believe these studies will often show how policies fostering systemic inequalities arose not by chance but by the purposeful advocacy of active participants in the conservative racial policy alliances of different eras, including those favoring enslavement, those favoring racial segregation, those favoring color-blind policies, and those favoring Protect policies in more recent years. Our previous research has made us confident that if scholars investigate how competing racial orders shaped and reshaped real estate policies of redlining, criminal justice policies of incarceration, public education enrollments, corporate and labor union recruitment practices, and more, they will be able to identify the actual mechanisms by which many institutional systems have sustained multiple forms of racial inequality in some eras, and have sometimes been restructured to diminish them in others. The results will often support the claims of those empirical scholars who emphasize "white people's protectiveness of their racial group interests," and they can aid judgments of just how intractable American racial inequalities are (Yancy 2022, 10).

In the chapters that follow, we will see evidence that today's conservative Protect alliance still enjoys many advantages from the structures of American political systems and from the predominant views in American public opinion, suggesting that this alliance may continue to hold much more governing power than its Repair alliance rival in the years ahead, just as conservative racial policy alliances so often have in the nation's past. In the era we see as now ending, proponents of color-blind policies were able to do far more than were advocates of race-conscious measures to shape and limit the timing and degree of racial integration in existing American institutions. Again, we insist that it is nonetheless always vital to explore all aspects of the contestation of America's racial orders, recognizing that, for example, while Obama sometimes spoke in neoliberal tropes and did enact policies that merit that appellation, his administration, particularly his Justice Department, nonetheless pursued many race-conscious initiatives more aggressively than had any previous administration (King and Smith 2011, 132–43). Still, we agree that the evidence shows that America's *predominant* racial order from the 1980s through the Obama years was the color-blind policy alliance, and that the result was a strongly antiregulatory, anti-redistributive cast to American policies with racial dimensions that could fairly be described as a far from transformative "neoliberal racial order" (Dawson and Francis 2016).

We will also see in this book that a significant consequence of that era has been the increased prominence today of neoliberal politicians of color like South Carolina Senator Tim Scott and Kentucky Attorney General Daniel Cameron, supporters of many conservative Protect alliance policies who often present themselves as proof that in America no systemic changes are needed, because everyone can pull themselves up by their bootstraps (Dawson and Francis 2016; HoSang and Lowndes 2019; Weisman and Gabriel 2023). When we turn in chapter 10 to the possible scenarios for America's future that the clash of its new racial orders will shape, we will see that it is highly plausible that a conservative multiracial alliance united by the kinds of beliefs these actors uphold will prove predominant in American politics in the near- to medium-term future. If so, many of the most pessimistic white hegemony analysts will be able to adhere to their contentions that in America, nothing fundamental to racial justice is really changing. We will also see, however, that the evidence makes other scenarios clearly imaginable.

At this point, the potential contribution of an institutional orders approach for *intersectionality* theories and research will be plain. Recognition of societies as composed of multiple interacting institutional orders prompts awareness of how, even as the early American state privileged those it labeled "white," from its inception its institutions also gave preeminent status and power to Christianity, to patriarchal gender roles and identities, to heterosexuality, and to ableist conceptions of human fitness, as well as to private property owners. Whatever the viability of the intersectional camp's political and policy strategies may prove to be, our framework strongly affirms its insistence on greater attention to the complexities these historical interactions have generated. We see the rise of intersectional analyses that study the interrelationships among, and the consequences of, multiple systems of inequality as one of the most important intellectual developments in the last generation; and we believe that examinations of the interactions of institutional orders as we have defined them here are highly promising for further advancing those analyses.

As Ange-Marie Hancock notes, there have been two chief "dimensions of intersectionality's intellectual project": "a commitment to visibility or inclusion and a reconstitution of relationships among categories of difference" (Hancock 2016, 23; Kelley 2022). Numerous resulting works in many disciplines have indeed made visible an impressive variety of empirical phenomena, such as the noxious brew of racial, gender, and class stereotypes in the imagery of "welfare queens," and the simultaneous burial of the role of Black women's organizations in providing financial resources and administrative leadership for civil rights mobilizations (e.g., Hancock 2004; Simien 2007; Vickery, Trent, and Salinas 2019; Powell and Rich 2020). These analyses display the extraordinary variety of ways in which discourses, practices, and policies fostering and maintaining diverse systems of inequality can and have operated and interacted in different venues and at different levels of government, and they map how so often the results have preserved or even extended inequitable patterns, even as those inequities have frequently spurred resistance and reforms.

Leading proponents of intersectional analyses acknowledge, however, that theoretical accounts explaining the "how and why" of the relationships among categories of difference and inequality remain less definitive than the many compelling empirical studies guided by intersectional concerns. Because few intersectional theories specify hypotheses about when distinguishable systems of inequality will intersect in either reinforcing or conflictual ways, they provide less reliable guidance for intersectional empirical research than many seek (Hancock 2007; Cho, Crenshaw, and McCall 2013; Bauer et al. 2021).

Though we also cannot offer any universal explanatory theory of intersectionality, our framework does help illuminate how, in the politics of the American revolution and founding, the values and interests of the governing coalition of propertied white Christian heterosexual men who led those endeavors came to structure most if not all of the institutional orders of the new nation. That coalition was itself a result of historical processes that had long linked patriarchy, Christianity, and commercial property interests in the identities and values of leading European, and then European-descended, American-born colonists. Those colonists went on to build multiple intersecting institutional orders that expressed and enforced their concerns. Recognizing this construction makes it easier to see how and why, even though those orders have often embodied some conflicting interests and imperatives, those who have benefited from them—especially white, propertied Christian men—have usually found it politically feasible to make common cause with each other on issues they have seen as vital to preserving the "true" character of "their" America.

Just as in the case of racial and class orders, moreover, empirical research into the interactions of racial policy alliances and institutional orders with other institutional orders, such as corporate and labor institutional orders; those governing gender and sexuality; the institutional order of religion; the institutional structuring of disability policies, practices, and identities; and more, should yield both specific contextual accounts and broader theoretical explanations of many intersectional political and social phenomena. It is in fact an understatement to say that an institutional orders framework can aid intersectional analyses. Research premised on the centrality of institutional orders for social and political development clearly *must* focus on the intersections of at least some such orders; conversely, we think intersectional studies can and should often be structured as studies of intersecting institutional orders.

Such research is demanding, and our execution of it in this book is unavoidably partial. It has, however, also been inescapable, because though we have heretofore foregrounded only rival *racial* institutional orders, it is a striking feature of Black Lives Matter and of many other groups in today's Repair alliance that their aspirations and strategies are explicitly intersectional. Most self-consciously seek to forge alliances with both domestic and international groups that feature a variety of non-racial identities— LGBTQ+, the poor, working people, disabled persons, Indigenous peoples, and more. These Repair groups are striving to unite around intersectional analyses, intersectional coalition-building, and intersectional policy reforms. The quest to understand American racial politics today is therefore necessarily a quest to understand intersectional politics (as, indeed, it always should have been).

And while the scholarly challenges posed by the complexity of intersectional analyses can never be eliminated, they are likely to be made more manageable by the cumulative results of related studies of distinctive institutional orders. It may prove possible to combine separate analyses of the interactions of two or three institutional orders in specific contexts, such as those of race and class or gender, with studies of other institutional orders, such as those of religion and partisanship, that have also intersected in those contexts. Employing cognate institutional orders frameworks in their examinations of different dimensions of political life might well help scholars to achieve collectively a fuller grasp of intersectional social and political phenomena.

That grasp is vital, because even as Repair groups build broad coalitions through embracing intersectional goals, conservative protectionists are similarly strengthening their bonds with religious traditionalists, with economically neoliberal opponents of government aid for racial minorities, with militant nationalist opponents of many forms of globalization, and others (Jardina 2019; National Conservatism n.d.). Though the evidence and analysis of these emerging racial institutional orders this book provides cannot settle the question of how much change, in either direction, will occur in the years ahead, it does provide a robust basis for judging that, alongside the potentially catastrophic consequences of climate change, the clash of today's racial policy alliances is perhaps the most momentous issue of modern American life.

Conclusion

This chapter has mapped an extensive terrain, delineating our elaborated account of racial policy alliances, racial institutional orders, and racial policy regimes; comparing and contrasting it with important academic and activist perspectives on racial politics; and indicating what our framework seeks to contribute to theoretical and practical debates over what drives racial inequalities and how to address them. It is time now to take a closer look at the Protect and Repair alliances, the new inhabitants of contemporary America's rugged and dangerous political landscape.

PART 2
The Protect Alliance

CHAPTER THREE

The Rise of the Protect Policy Alliance
New Actors, New Money, Resurgent Causes

CRT is dividing and embittering the American population. By injecting the phantom concept of widespread racial discrimination in 21st-century America, CRT is creating real-world problems among the American population where they otherwise did not exist. —Center for Equal Opportunity (n.d.-b)

On November 2, 2021, first-time Republican candidate Glenn Youngkin ended former Virginia Governor Terry McAuliffe's bid to regain his old office, winning by close to 2 percentage points in a state Joe Biden carried by 10 points the year before. Though he had Donald Trump's endorsement, Youngkin did not associate himself with the locally unpopular former president, nor did he endorse Trump's claims that Democrats stole the 2020 election. Like most traditional Republicans, the wealthy Youngkin ran partly against high taxes. Dominating his campaign, however, was a promise to "ban Critical Race Theory" from Virginia public schools and to restore "parental rights" over education "on Day One" of a Youngkin administration (Laughland 2022).

Just a couple of years before, few outside of academia knew the term "Critical Race Theory." By late 2021, however, articles by a Manhattan Institute Senior Fellow, Christopher Rufo; a long report by the Heritage Foundation; abundant critical coverage by Fox News and other conservative media outlets; and activism by a wide range of conservative groups placed the phrase at the heart of impassioned national discourse over the future of public education and of America itself (Bailey, Cox, and Bajak 2021). To "protect our history and our students," policy advocates at institutions like the Texas Public Policy Foundation argued, America needed "Critical Race Theory bans" (Sylvester and Swain 2021).

These calls to protect Americans from threats posed by liberals and those further left, dangers said to include but to go well beyond the teaching of Critical Race Theory, represented a new emphasis for many conservative contributors to American policy debates.

Through the first decade of the twenty-first century, apart from some white supremacist proclamations by a racist radical fringe, the predominant racial policy theme of conservative groups remained what it had been for four decades: American public policies should be color-blind. Abandoning their post-Reconstruction insistence that *de jure* segregation was best for both races, by the 1970s American racial conservatives accepted, publicly at least, that American public institutions should be open to all, in ways that would produce some measure of racial integration. They worked instead to defeat public policies mandating rapid integration and, more broadly, to prevent the long history of public policies explicitly favoring whites from giving way to an era of measures favoring people of color. In these efforts, many conservatives employed "dog whistles," using imagery like "welfare queen" and "bucks" that most commentators thought summoned up negative racial stereotypes (Mendelberg 2001; Kelley 2022). But in mainstream American politics, at least, the overt public appeals to white supremacy commonly heard into the 1950s appeared to have become part of the nation's unhappy past.

This new opposition to liberal race-conscious policies on the part of many conservatives who had once supported illiberal racial laws fit comfortably with conservative opposition to government spending, taxes, and mandatory regulations in general. Indeed, economic themes predominated in the vast network of conservative think tanks, university centers, litigation groups, and advocacy and constituent mobilization organizations built by wealthy conservatives from the 1970s through the first decade of the twenty-first century. Although most conservatives opposed affirmative action, and some expressed alarm at the rise of ethnic studies programs in higher education, while in the 1990s an intense controversy raged over the results of the Republican-initiated effort to create a set of National History Standards, these issues stayed on the back burners of most conservative organizations' agendas (Silverstein 2021). Few gave priority to what was taught in public schools, commemorated in museum exhibitions and public monuments, or portrayed in Hollywood movies and television, or indeed to other "cultural" issues.

But in one of the most striking moments in our interviews, a senior policy analyst at a preeminent conservative think tank told us with some dismay that up through 2015, that institute's donors and board members had overwhelmingly urged its scholars to focus primarily on economic concerns. By 2021, however, they were exhorting all to write almost exclusively about race-related cultural issues, such as the teaching of Critical Race Theory and the place of race in American museums, monuments, and other media. Though this scholar had long been a leading voice on cultural issues, he examined what his own children were being taught in DC area schools, and he found this new emphasis excessive, even obsessive. He concluded that the donors and board members had come to fear not just restrictions on their wealth and economic liberties, but even more, the loss of what they understood to be their country.

This shift in conservative advocacy priorities is visible across many, though not all, of the older conservative groups created after 1970, as well as the newer organizations emerging in the twenty-first century that belong to the loose network of right-leaning groups and government agencies that we see as the conservative Protect policy alliance. Unsurprisingly, this development is most prominent in the deep Red states of the South and the Great Plains, but it is also visible in most rural and many suburban regions in battleground and even predominantly Blue states. In the eyes of many conservatives across the country, late twentieth-century racial policy debates centered on the means and extent to which government should aid racial integration into existing American institutions have given way to twenty-first-century debates in which the interests and the identities of white American and other traditionalist Americans, and the very legitimacy of America itself, are under radical attack.

Reagan-Era Conservative Groups and Protect Policies

The examples of this shift in focus among older conservative groups are legion. The Phoenix-based Goldwater Institute, founded in 1988 with the blessing of the father figure of the post–World War II American conservative movement, has always presented itself as "a free-market public policy research and litigation organization dedicated to advancing the principles of limited government, economic freedom, and individual liberty," the primary agenda of most similar conservative groups during the era in which it originated. But in the fall of 2022, the top issue its website listed was "Education," and the "Featured Story" on that web page was "Teacher Blows the Whistle on Critical Race Theory in California Schools" (Goldwater Institute 2023a, 2023b).

Similarly, the Texas Public Policy Foundation, founded in 1989 to defend "liberty, personal responsibility, and free enterprise," issued a report in 1990 that complained about the high levels of "inefficient" spending and regulations for Texas public schools. It contended: "Texas teachers are subjected to a myriad of specific regulations—telling them what to teach and when to teach it. Our teachers are enduring more harassment from the educational bureaucracy than at any time in our past" (Davis and Hayes 1990). The dangers that alarmed the Foundation then were government spending and regulation, not what teachers were teaching. In 2021, however, senior fellows at the Foundation wrote enthusiastically for a proposed state regulatory law preventing teachers from exposing students to what the Foundation scholars saw as versions of Critical Race Theory (though the bill they endorsed was far less restrictive than legislation proposed in many other states) (Sylvester and Swain 2021).

The leading female champion of conservatism in the late twentieth century, the longtime activist Phyllis Schlafly, formed the Eagle Trust Fund in 1968 to finance her preferred causes. The Fund focused on national security, anti-Communism, and the championing of free enterprise. In response to congressional endorsement of the Equal Rights Amendment in 1972, Schlafly reorganized the Fund to become what she eventually named the Eagle Forum, based in Illinois but with chapters elsewhere, and famously dedicated to defeating the ERA and promoting what it deemed "pro-family" policies. Today, however, the Eagle Forum—which splintered after Schlafly's death in 2016—is focused on the dangers of Critical Race Theory, accusing its proponents of espousing "the racist assumption that Americans are either guilty of racism or incapable of success because of their skin color." The Forum urges grassroots activism to "***fight back against Critical Race Theory***" (Eagle Forum 2023, italics and bold in the original).

A parallel shift is visible in the work of the Center for Equal Opportunity, founded in Washington, DC, in 1995 by former Reagan official Linda Chavez. From the first, the Center has defined its mission explicitly as to "study, develop and disseminate ideas that promote colorblind equal opportunity and nondiscrimination in America" (Center for Equal Opportunity n.d.-a). This mission originally meant chiefly opposition to affirmative action programs in education, employment, and public contracting, efforts to advance racial integration that the Center depicted as unjust to whites and Asian Americans. The Center continues that opposition today, but now its "core topics" begin with its role in opposing all forms of "identity politics," and particularly "Critical Race Theory," where it claims to be "in the forefront" of the fight. It is now Critical Race Theory, the Center contends, that "is dividing and embittering the American population. By injecting the phantom concept of widespread racial discrimination in 21st-century America," CRT creates "real-world problems among the American population where they otherwise did not exist" (Center for Equal Opportunity n.d.-b).

This shift to Protect themes is not, to be sure, universal, as can be seen by reviewing the websites of the sixty-four think tanks that are members of the State Policy Network (SPN). Originating in the mid-1980s and restructured and expanded in the 1990s to reach the entire nation, and long led by the wealthy South Carolina businessman Tom Roe, the primarily (but not exclusively) state-focused think tanks in this association all profess the sorts of commitments to limited government, free enterprise, and individual liberty long advocated by the Goldwater Institute and the Texas Public Policy Institute (two early members, and among the wealthiest in the SPN network—State Policy Network n.d.). The SPN members vary, however, in the extent to which they embrace the new Protect alliance themes. The South Carolina Policy Council, founded by Roe, has expressed *opposition* to a bill aimed at "the teachings of critical race theory," seeing it as likely to produce so many challenges to so much classroom instruction that it "would do more harm than good" (South Carolina Policy Council 2021). And while the SPN think tank Empower Mississippi noted with little comment the successful passage of a bill to ban CRT in that state, its "Education" section stresses, much like the Texas Public Policy Foundation once did, that "teachers know their students better than anyone in the State Capitol or Washington, D.C. Yet too often their hands are tied by top-down controls that prevent them from meeting the needs of their students" (Empower Mississippi 2023).

More typical, however, are statements like the Washington (State) Policy Center's attacks on the "dehumanizing concept known as 'Critical Race Theory,'" and the contention posted on the Florida-based Foundation for Government Accountability's website that parents "are fed up with the leftist political propaganda aimed at children" (Washington Policy Center 2021; Buhajla 2022). Some SPN think tanks more neutrally note the controversy over Critical Race Theory as strengthening arguments for school choice, a neoliberal policy the SPN organizations universally endorse. The think tanks who are not so stridently anti-CRT, however, often advocate Protect goals for numerous other policy regimes, such as election laws, immigration and crime enforcement policies, and protection of conservatives' religious liberties and freedom of speech. Consequently, while some of the sixty-four State Policy Network members and ninety-nine associate members cannot be classified as belonging to the recently emergent Protect policy alliance, a large number can.

Similarly, some older conservative litigation groups like the Pacific Legal Foundation and the Atlantic Legal Foundation continue to sue governments in the name of "individual liberty," chiefly economic liberties and property rights, as they have done since their founding in the 1970s. Today, however, even as they champion school choice, many of them also now stress the need to guard against the educational dangers posed by both the *New York Times*'s 1619 Project and Critical Race Theory, each seen as advancing a leftist analysis of race in America which the Pacific Legal Foundation says has "woven itself into almost every facet of our society," endangering "preservation of the Fourteenth Amendment promise of equality before the law" (Hunter 2021; Atlantic Legal Foundation 2021). FreedomWorks, a conservative advocacy group originally funded by the Koch brothers and associated with the Tea Party movement, also continues to stress primarily an economic libertarian agenda. However, under the heading of "Educational Freedom: Curriculum," it now champions not just school choice but efforts to prevent teaching Critical Race Theory and the 1619 Project that are far less libertarian (FreedomWorks 2022).

The National Tea Party, one of several organizations claiming to represent the Tea Party movement, is now less libertarian even on economic issues than it once was, instead serving chiefly an advocacy group for Donald Trump. Consequently, it has shifted still more strongly to Protect themes. The group celebrated Trump's meeting with Kyle Rittenhouse after Rittenhouse's shooting of protesters in Kenosha, Wisconsin, was judged to be self-defense. The Tea Party then enthusiastically celebrated Representative Marjorie Taylor Greene's proposal that Rittenhouse receive the Congressional Gold Medal because he had gone to Kenosha "to protect it from crazed radicals" during "a riot put on by BLM" (Black Lives Matter) (TeaParty.org Exclusive 2021).

This broad conservative shift to advocacy of Protect agendas for many policy regimes is, to be sure, far from a complete break with the past. In the era of rival color-blind/race-conscious policy alliances that is now ebbing, liberal critics including ourselves frequently argued that color-blind policies worked to protect the advantages possessed by, especially, more affluent whites. We suspected that for many in the conservative racial policy alliance, this protection was always the strongest motive for their support of color-blind policies, even if leading affirmative action opponents like Chavez and the mixed-race businessman Ward Connerly saw them as required by principles of justice.

For decades after 1970, however, only an extremist fringe on the American right argued openly that public policies should once again favor white Americans over people of color. In political practice, even those white supremacist groups operated effectively, when they were effective at all, as part of the color-blind policy alliance. They joined efforts to oppose government initiatives for mandatory integration and for enhanced opportunities and benefits for non-white Americans by endorsing the idea that neighborhood schools, parental choice, and merit, not race, should be the governing standards.

To be sure, many white conservatives may have longed to elect figures like David Duke, the former Klan leader and Louisiana state legislator who twice carried the white vote for statewide offices in his home state (Klinkner with Smith 1999, 307–8). With the broader franchise after the Voting Rights Act of 1965, however, overt supporters of white supremacy like Duke rarely won office, even in the Deep South. Consequently, their supporters settled for voting for Ronald Reagan, whose Justice Department pledged its commitment to color-blind policies but did far less than many hoped or feared to dismantle affirmative action programs. The journalist Christopher Caldwell suggests that the resulting disappointments "created conditions under which the next populist movement that arose would be satisfied only with deeds, not words" (Caldwell 2020, 124).

Trump-Era Conservative Groups in the Protect Policy Alliance

Those intensified demands for deeds are central to the new Protect alliance. By 2020, even as older conservative organizations were altering their emphases, new groups had emerged and were continuing to emerge that advanced protection-centered themes with even more ferocity, with less talk of color-blind principles or merit, with much more talk of white victimization, and with explicit rejection of some traditional conservative stances on trade, immigration, and now-ubiquitous cultural issues.

Perhaps the most high-powered of these new groups is the American

First Policy Institute (AFPI), headed by Brooke Rollins. A celebrated former leader of the flourishing Texas Public Policy Foundation, Rollins became the director of Donald Trump's Domestic Policy Council before heading the Institute (AFPI 2022a). The AFPI launched in 2021 with a $20 million budget and thirty-five employees, with plans to more than double both within a year (Allen 2021). Encompassing twenty centers and including former Trump officials such as Larry Kudlow, Linda McMahon, and Rick Perry, with other conservative luminaries like former governors Bobby Jindal and Phil Bryant, the AFPI seeks to advance the broad policies and priorities of the Trump administration.

In July 2021, for example, Rollins joined in support of Trump's class action lawsuit demanding greater regulation of the Big Tech companies, Facebook, Google, and Twitter. These companies had, she contended, achieved a "monopoly on our public town square," determining "whose voices get to be heard on issues like critical race theory, on issues like illegal immigration, on issues like COVID and mask-wearing and hydroxychloroquine" (Fitzgerald 2021). Rather than championing these successful businesses as proof of the virtues of a free enterprise system, Rollins instead portrayed them as in need of national governmental regulation to protect against what she saw as dangers to "the American people."

Similar themes dominate the priorities of most of the AFPI Centers. Their websites decry "DC and global corporate elites" who, "in the name of free trade orthodoxy, allowed markets and market efficiencies to be an overwhelming influence on policy decisions." They call for an end to economic policies "for the sake of big finance and big business," and declare America's workers, not its capitalists, to be the "class of Americans who made our Republic the greatest Nation on earth" (AFPI 2022b). Additionally, in contrast to the past receptivity of economic conservatives to immigrants sought by American employers, the AFPI Center for Homeland Security and Immigration "is devoted to protecting the American people" against unwanted immigrants by prioritizing "border security and the value of citizenship" (AFPI 2022c).

Other AFPI Centers promise to battle against "academic elites and demagogues" who "embrace identity politics, division, and submission" instead of working to "affirm and celebrate America." They promise to litigate to protect "the American way of life" against "Big Government, Big Tech, and Big Media." They profess allegiance to Dr. Martin Luther King Jr.'s "classic American view" that character, not "the color of your skin," should matter in American life. However, they exemplify this view not by stressing the dangers of racial bigotry and economic injustices, as King did, but by emphasizing their opposition to abortion and their commitment to "the sanctity of life," from "the womb to the tomb!" (AFPI 2022d).

In sum, like many older conservative policy organizations, the America First Policy Institute has not abandoned all rhetorical commitments to color-blind policies. It gives overwhelming emphasis, however, to protection against the dangers Brooke Rollins highlighted: the cultural agenda of Critical Race Theory and identity politics, the transformations threatened by unauthorized immigration, and "woke" regulatory policies, all traced to the un-American views of academic elites and Big Government, Big Tech, and Big Media. Though this Protect agenda is not concerned to defend only white Americans, there can be no doubt that Critical Race Theory, identity politics, and immigration are widely understood to threaten whites most of all. The African American political scientist Carol Swain, recently the Distinguished Senior Fellow for Constitutional Studies at the Texas Public Policy Foundation, is among many conservatives who maintain strongly that it is now white men who are most discriminated against in modern America, with conservative Christian white men the most vilified of all.[1]

Along with AFPI, numerous other groups also employ the "America First" label Trump popularized. Most elevate this sense of threat. Some collaborate with the AFPI and overlap in personnel, like America First Works, a 501(c)4 organization that can engage in partisan politics, unlike AFPI, a 501(c)3. America First Works also funds the America First Political Action Committee and a variety of other new conservative groups (Schwartz 2021). Different former Trump administration officials lead other, formally unaffiliated America First groups, notably Stephen Miller and Mark Meadows, who head America First Legal. Perhaps because Meadows faced investigation and eventual indictment in Georgia for his role in efforts to overturn the result of the 2020 presidential election, Miller has been the face of America First Legal since its creation (Wiessner 2023; Swan et al. 2023). The organization promises to turn "the legal tables on the radical activist left" which is "using its power inside and outside the government to destroy our country" (America First Legal 2022). America First Legal is one of a number of organizations launched with the aid of the Conservative Partnership Institute (CPI). The CPI was created in 2017 deliberately to "form and lead coalitions" of conservative activist groups that will work to combat, among other dangers, "Big Tech," "open borders," "race-based loan forgiveness," and "critical race theory" (Conservative Partnership Institute 2023). It is seeking to establish a network of like-minded "State

Freedom Caucuses" in every state, though as of 2022 only seven were in existence, and none reported robust funding (State Freedom Caucus Network n.d.). While sharing all of CPI's positions, America First Legal underscores a promise to defend the civil rights of all Americans, "regardless of race, color, religion or creed."

The former Trump advisor Sebastian Gorka, in turn, uses the America First brand for all his many broadcasts, podcasts, and publications. Gorka regularly contends in these multiple venues that "the extremists of the 1960s and 1970s, have become the 'mainstream'" of the Democratic Party, through which they seek "to abolish America." He prods his audience: "What are you prepared to do to protect our country?" (Gorka 2019). As examples of the battles in the Left's efforts to abolish traditionalist America, his website highlights controversies over a withdrawn Smithsonian "whiteness" display and President Trump's defense of the Confederate flag.[2]

Women for America First, a nonprofit organization founded in 2020 by a former Tea Party leader, Amy Kremer, started a "Stop the Steal" Facebook group the day after the 2020 presidential election and subsequently hosted "Save America" rallies, activities that have led to federal investigations about their possible connections to various kinds of unlawful actions.[3] Women for America First received a donation of $300,000 from the heiress Julie Fancelli, who leads the George Jenkins Foundation named for her father, founder of the Publix grocery chain. Fancelli's contributions helped orchestrate both the January 6 pre-insurrection rally and a previous pro-Trump rally in DC in mid-December 2020, overseeing caravans of Trump supporters from across the nation. Fancelli also donated to the Republican Attorneys General Association, which funded robocalls touting the march (Reinhard, Alemany, and Dawson 2021).

Although some Silicon Valley billionaires support left-leaning groups, a significant number fund many other influential conservative think tanks and events. Prominent examples include Peter Thiel's generous financing of the National Conservatism Conference, organized in part by the Conservative Partnership Institute to provide a still more Trumpist alternative to the older Conservative Political Action Conference (CPAC) (Dwoskin 2022). The National Conservatism Conference is one of a set of international meetings sponsored and promoted by the Edmund Burke Foundation, created in 2019 with David Brog, former executive director of Christians United for Israel, as its president, and Yoram Hazony, the

American-educated president of the Herzl Institute in Jerusalem, as its chair (Edmund Burke Foundation 2023a).

The annual National Conservatism Conference has quickly become influential among conservative thinkers. According to the journalist David Brooks, its attendance is composed of long-standing conservatives aged over fifty who have been further radicalized and embrace populism; younger politicians such as Senators Josh Hawley and J. D. Vance who seek to hone their populist skills and credentials; and still younger people who have been turned off of liberalism by elite university professors' sermonizing (Brooks 2021). In 2021, Hawley warned those attending the National Conservative Conference of the Left's "grand ambition . . . to deconstruct the United States of America"—rhetoric that made clear that conservatives must offer protection instead (quoted in Brooks 2021).

Most notoriously, in May 2020, Nicholas Fuentes launched the America First Foundation, claiming inspiration from Trump to "advocate for conservative values based on principles of American Nationalism, Christianity, and Traditionalism" (America First Foundation 2020–2023a). Railing against "establishment Republicans," Fuentes initiated an "America First Political Action Conference" to rival both the almost half-century-old Conservative Political Action Conference and the new National Conservatism Conference. The America First Foundation says it seeks to oppose "mass immigration, foreign wars, and social decay," and to build a "populist, nationalist movement, reviving working-class patriotism against the globalist agenda desperately trying to bury it" (America First Foundation 2020–2023a). On these points, it clearly promotes the same agenda as the other America First groups. Addressing AFPAC on February 27, 2021, however, Fuentes fired up the crowd by contending that if the nation "loses its white demographic core . . . then this is not America anymore" (Steakin 2021).

This statement and many like it clearly represented racial messaging that was far more explicit than "dog whistles." Survey experiments suggest that in recent years, political actors have in fact found it much less necessary to convey messages disparaging racial minorities implicitly: those who are receptive to those messages are now rarely disturbed when they are openly stated (Valentino, Neuner, and Vandenbrook 2018). In the case of Fuentes's speech, although some conservatives backed away, many powerful voices on the right endorsed his call to protect America from demographic, and inevitably racial, transformations. A few weeks after Fuentes spoke, on April 8, 2021, Tucker Carlson stated on Fox News that the Democratic Party was "trying to replace the current electorate, the voters now casting ballots, with new people, more obedient voters, from the third world." Less than a week later, Pennsylvania Republican Representative Scott Perry said at a US House Foreign Affairs Committee meeting that, "for many Americans . . . what appears to them is we're replacing . . . native-born Americans to permanently transform the landscape of this very nation" (Cillizza 2021).

The "replacement theory" Carlson and Perry invoked came from the French ideologue Renaud Camus. It is embraced by white nationalists in many countries, including participants at the 2017 Unite the Right rally in Charlottesville, Virginia, who chanted "You Will Not Replace Us" (Charlton 2019). The doctrine exemplifies how global political developments are shaping American movements for protectionism, providing reinforcing sources of energy and ideas. After an eighteen-year-old teenager professing allegiance to replacement theory shot ten people in a Buffalo supermarket on May 14, 2022, Carlson claimed not to know what replacement theory was, despite numerous videos of him invoking it, and despite his continuing confident endorsements of its core contentions (Bump 2022).

In parallel fashion, when the bizarrely pro-Nazi Black rapper Ye (formerly Kanye West) brought Nicholas Fuentes and another longtime Trump supporter to dine with Trump at Mar-a-Lago on November 22, 2022, provoking an avalanche of criticism of Trump for associating with a prominent anti-Semitic white supremacist, Trump simply claimed not to know Fuentes, without discussing or disavowing Fuentes's views (Caputo 2022; Lowell 2022b). Trump had previously heartened Fuentes by retweeting a video from one of Fuentes's America First clip accounts (Petrizzo 2020). Still, given Trump's well-known focus on himself at the expense of attention to others, his claim of ignorance may have been true; and many leading Republicans as well as others across the political spectrum quickly stated emphatically that Fuentes should be repudiated. Though House Republican leader Kevin McCarthy refused to criticize Trump, he condemned Fuentes's ideology and said it had "no place in this Republican party" (Jones 2022b).

We should therefore reiterate that, like all policy alliances and institutional orders, the new Protect racial policy alliance is a loose network of groups working in broadly similar policy directions, sometimes through active collaboration and networking, but often with differences, tensions, and conflicts among the various participants. Though all these groups warn of the dangers of immigration, many make no explicit reference to "replacement theory" or America's "white demographic." The America First Policy Institute is entirely separate from Fuentes's America First Foundation; and unsurprisingly, Jewish Trump supporters like the conservative activist Ben Shapiro and the head of the Zionist Organization of America, Morton Klein, have denounced Fuentes for his anti-Semitism, before and after the dinner with Trump (Boyer 2019; Weisman 2022).

In public discussion, however, the lines between the many different versions of "America First" often blur, with the blurring sometimes performed by Donald Trump himself. Fuentes's February 2021 AFPAC meeting featured an appearance by the controversial Arizona Congressman Paul Gosar, whom the House of Representatives censured for posting an animated depiction of himself killing fellow Representative Alexandria Ocasio-Cortez. The day after the House censure, former President Trump pointedly endorsed Gosar as "a loyal supporter of our America First agenda" (LeBlanc 2021). Fuentes's February 2022 AFPAC featured not only a return appearance by Gosar but also appearances by Trump favorites Representative Marjorie Taylor Greene and former Arizona Sheriff Joe Arpaio (America First Foundation 2020–2023b). After the controversy over the Mar-a-Lago dinner, Greene said she did not know much about Fuentes when she appeared at his conference, and she condemned his "racist anti-Semitic ideology," dismissing the significance of her smiling photographs with him (Lewis 2022). The incident dramatized the reality that prominent Trump supporters have often not been careful about associating with and thereby aiding white nationalists, whether knowingly or not.

Appendix B provides an illustrative list of 315 conservative groups, both old and new, that we see as loosely aligned in support of the newly ascendant agenda to protect more traditionalist Americans against the radical Left, despite inevitable differences on some specific policy regimes. As elaborated in appendix A in our discussion of our methodologies, the list is derived from analyzing the members of organizations that seek to link conservative groups, like the older State Policy Network and the newer Conservative Partnership Institute; the signatories to briefs in legal cases involving racial issues, such as *Students for Fair Admissions v. Harvard*; and respondents to our surveys of groups engaged with racial policies. When possible, we have tried to provide each group's age and financial status by citing their founding year or the year they received IRS recognition, as well as financial data on gross receipts, expenditures, or endowments available from the IRS, GuideStar, Charity Navigator, and similar online sources.

We have built on but modified the categories in which Alexander Hertel-Fernandez, Theda Skocpol, and Jason Sclar placed the groups constituting what they describe as the "Koch network" of conservative political organizations that predated the rise of the contemporary Protect policy alliance (Hertel-Fernandez, Skocpol, and Sclar 2018, 161). For our purposes, it makes sense to divide Protect organizations into:

1. *Think tanks*, who primarily generate ideas through research and publications;
2. *Policy advocacy groups*, who seek directly to influence officeholders and media debates;
3. *Constituency mobilization groups*, who focus more on voter information and energizing grassroots activism and turnout;
4. *Litigation and legal advocacy groups*, who generally stress constitutional issues;
5. *Religious groups*, whose mobilization has been central to the Protect alliance, and who in some cases are growing more militant;
6. *Racial and ethnic groups*, who can temper but can also reinforce the Protect alliance's focus on white victimization;
7. *Armed protectionist groups*, some of whom have made political violence a clear and present danger; and of course
8. *Funding groups*, who sustain the activities of all the others.

Though these eight categories define the main members of the Protect policy alliance, they are far from fully distinct. Some groups calling themselves think tanks, like the Texas Conservative Coalition Research Institute, engage in extensive policy advocacy (TCCRI n.d.). Some policy advocacy groups, like the Californians for Equal Rights Foundation, engage in extensive constituency mobilization, and of course most constituency mobilization involves policy advocacy, as provided for example by Heritage Action for America (CFER Foundation 2023; Heritage Action for America 2023). Some religious groups, like the Christian Legal Society, could as easily be classified as litigation groups, as could ethnic groups like the Asian American Legal Foundation (Christian Legal Society 2023; Asian American Legal Foundation 2022). Our particular categorizations are less important than the identification of these groups as endorsing one or more goals of the Protect policy alliance. When reviewing the think tanks that are members of the State Policy Network and other such associations, we have included only those that explicitly take Protect positions in one or more of the following policy regimes: race-related curriculum and book-banning in schools; voter restrictions; immigration control; criminal justice; abortion; LGBTQ+ rights; religious and expressive liberties; and cultural representations in museums, historic sites, names of public monuments, military bases, parks and buildings, and so forth. We have not listed those that appear to focus almost exclusively on libertarian economic policies, in the mode predominant in the 1970s and 1980s, important as those still very much are for the issues they address.

Although the list of groups provided in appendix B can thus make the concept of a Protect conservative policy alliance more tangible, it is not remotely exhaustive. In light of shifting political winds, we have not sought to include the local, state, and governmental agencies enforcing Protect policy regimes who make this alliance a governing, albeit contested, institutional order. In most categories, moreover, there are far more groups than we can easily identify, much less include: conservative churches that help mobilize their members to uphold traditionalist values undoubtedly number in the tens if not hundreds of thousands in America. Many conservative group leaders also appear reluctant to respond to surveys or interview requests from scholars suspected, rightly in our cases, of favoring progressives. As explained in appendix A, many of these groups' websites also prevent the crawling that software systems use to map networks.

The list is more than long enough, however, to convey that this policy alliance is formidable throughout the nation, even though it is more present in Red and rural regions. It has many recently created members, as well as increased support in recent years from older conservative organizations. And many of these groups also benefit from immense funding. Moreover, the categorizations, however inexact, are revealing. It is clear that while the 1970s and 1980s saw the creation of many conservative think tanks, most of the new groups of the twenty-first century focus less on producing scholarly white papers, and more on policy advocacy and constituency mobilization through use of new social media and grassroots organizing, as well as more traditional media outlets. It also appears that the bulk of the explicitly ethnic organizations working for Protect goals are Chinese American, in contrast, we will later see, to the many Japanese American groups that support Repair policies. Hispanic groups are largely absent from the Protect alliance when the issue is affirmative action, which many of them support. We will see that they are also, however, often absent from the Repair policy alliance when issues are labeled reparations, expecting the beneficiaries to be primarily or exclusively African Americans. In the new era of American racial politics, Hispanics are thus increasingly a swing constituency, rather than a solidly Democratic bloc.

Unsurprisingly, few organizations announce their goals explicitly in terms of protecting white Americans, though some, like the Council of Conservative Citizens, openly deride what they call mainstream conservatives' failure to combat "systemic anti-whiteness" aggressively (Mercer 2021). There are also comparatively few Black organizations who endorse Protect policies. Those that do endorse protectionist goals like restricting abortion and upholding conservative expressive and religious liberties, such as the Black Conservative Federation (BCF), often do so in moderate language (BCF 2022).

Like appendix B as a whole, these observations are partial and preliminary. More study is needed to identify conservative racial and ethnic groups and map their policy positions definitively. Even so, in the remainder of this chapter we give closer attention to three types of groups that are particularly important, and particularly controversial, for the Protect racial policy alliance: Christian nationalists, armed protectionist groups, and funders.

Christian Nationalists and Protect Policies

Even more than the Reagan coalition and the color-blind policy alliance of the late twentieth century, the contemporary Protect alliance includes a wide range of religious groups, old and new, that are overwhelmingly but not exclusively Christian. Though some operate on limited funding, many have multi-million-dollar budgets (appendix B). A large number are aided by the National Christian Charitable Foundation, a donor-advised fund which distributes more than $1.2 billion annually and favors conservative advocacy and think tanks, whether or not they are religiously affiliated (InfluenceWatch n.d.-c). Although observers have frequently puzzled over the allegiance of many religious conservatives to the often boastfully promiscuous and relentlessly mendacious Donald Trump, in fact deeply held traditionalist religious commitments probably do more than any other single factor to inspire belief in the validity of the Protect alliance cultural goals Trump has championed. For many alliance members, their faith that they are engaged in a righteous cause, even if it includes lawbreaking and acts of violence, stems from passionate convictions that they are serving the higher law of God and combating what they see as massive sinfulness in an increasingly secular modern America, including the killing of those they regard as unborn persons, and the proliferation of illicit sexuality and sexual orientations and gender identities.

In recent years, as cultural conflicts resulting from resurgent nationalistic conservatism on the one hand and heightening calls for systemic Repair transformations on the other have intensified, many more religious conservatives have openly embraced Christian nationalism, the belief that an America besieged by Godless secularism must now see itself and govern itself as an explicitly Christian nation. Various research projects, including a prominent collaborative study by the Baptist Joint Committee for Religious Liberty (BJC) and the Freedom from Religion Foundation (FFRF), found that Christian nationalists especially contributed to the January 6 insurrection, many contending that God calls for Christians to establish "dominion" over the United States, with Donald Trump as His tribune (BJC and FFRF 2022; Armaly, Buckley, and Enders 2022). Though many religious conservatives would not go so far, Religious Right groups that predate Trump's candidacy, such as the Faith and Freedom Coalition founded in 2009 by the longtime conservative activist and Christian Coalition founder Ralph Reed, and the Family Research Council led by the conservative radio host Tony Perkins, readily embraced Trump as the instrument of conservative religious causes, even supporting his claims that he was illegitimately denied victory in the 2020 presidential election (Stewart 2020, 14, 25, 60, 73–74, 178).

As a result, many data sources show that from 2016 on, the most ardent supporters of both Trump and a Protect agenda have been white Christian evangelicals and newly emboldened Christian nationalists (P. Miller 2022, 202–7; Gorski and Perry 2022). They have provided the Protect alliance with what the journalist Katherine Stewart depicts as an extensive "national infrastructure" that "consists not only of organizations uniting and coordinating its leadership, and a burgeoning far-right media, but also in large part the nation's conservative houses of worship" (Stewart 2020, 7). Almost all Christian traditionalists wanted a conservative Supreme Court committed to overturning *Roe v. Wade* and advancing other conservative Christian priorities, such as religious access to school funding and exemptions from antidiscrimination laws, privileges they claimed were required for religious liberty. When Trump did more than any prior Republican president to populate the Court with a super-majority of Christian conservatives (almost all Catholic), white evangelical Protestants increased their vote share for him from 77 percent in 2016 to 84 percent in 2020 (Igielnik, Keeter, and Hartig 2021).

The manner in which Trump's leadership fortified Christian nationalists within the Republican Party was exemplified when, addressing the "Patriots Arise for God, Family, and Country" conference in April 2022, the soon-to-be Republican nominee for the governorship of Pennsylvania, Doug Mastriano, dismissed the separation of church and state as a "myth," and joined with other ardent Christian Republicans to fuse conspiracy theories about American elections with religious principles (Kaylor and Underwood 2022). Trump-allied Congresswoman Lauren Boebert similarly told a Colorado Christian gathering that "the church is supposed to direct the government, the government is not supposed to direct the church" (Dias 2022). Electorally, these militantly Christian Republican candidates had only limited success outside intensely conservative areas in 2022. Mastriano lost handily and Boebert barely won an unexpectedly close race. Yet in the many deeply Red regions of the country, kindred spirits like Marjorie Taylor Greene, whose campaign merchandise proclaimed "Proud Christian Nationalist," cruised to victory, riding on the Trumpian heady mixture of the politics of faith, cultural traditionalism, and QAnon-style conspiracy theories, but above all a singular conviction that the US is a Christian nation and should be protected as such. In Montana, a state known for ticket-splitting, a surging Christian Right contingent helped Republicans win a super-majority of the state legislature in 2022, reinforcing evangelical Christian Governor Greg Gianforte (Streep 2023). Worried that Trump was nonetheless losing his capacity to win a national election, a number of prominent evangelical leaders began to distance themselves from him after the 2022 election results were known (Ecarma 2022). But given traditionalist Christianity's strength in many locales, especially rural areas and the South, analysts of the Christian national movement do not expect the militant faith of most of its adherents in the religious and cultural goals of the Protect alliance to be given pause by electoral evidence that a majority of Americans do not agree with them (Joyce 2022; Perry and Whitehead 2022).

This foundational assumption, merging patriotic American and faithful Christian identities, does not have to mean that these conservatives see only white Christians as true Americans. Many traditionalist evangelicals have sought, with some success, to include Black and Hispanic pastors and congregations in their ranks (Stewart 2020, 27, 98). Even so, the interlocking of race and religion among Protect conservatives is substantial. By a large margin, Christian nationalism is far more favored by conservative white Christian evangelicals than by other religious believers, much less secular Americans; and white Christian nationalists are also far more likely to believe that whites are facing mounting discrimination in America (Gorski and Perry 2022, 17–28). Similarly, white Americans conflate being American with being Christian much more than do Black and Hispanic respondents, among whom the identification of the two is virtually nonexistent (Perry and Schleifer 2022). White Americans, and especially white Christians, also disproportionately signal that American identity means being white (Devos and Mohamed 2014; P. Miller 2022, 180–87, 192–94). And though conservative Christians often stress that "we are comprised of all ethnicities and races," many explicitly interpret the Left's "assault on 'White America'" as "a widespread assault on the conservative, Christian community" (Mirahmadi 2021).

Armed Protect Groups

After the January 6, 2021, attack on the Capitol, a harsh reality must be fully acknowledged: at its extremes, but in ways that have proven to be none too distant from its center, the contemporary Protect policy alliance also includes members who are willing to wield armed force to provide "protection." The violence on January 6 exposed an underworld of shadowy militia and paramilitary groups dedicated to defending their vision of the United States and the Constitution and resolved to take brutal action to advance this goal. Some of these groups predated the rise of the MAGA (Make American Great Again) movement, with a number formed in opposition to Barack Obama's election, including the Three Percenters, founded in 2008, and the Oath Keepers, created in 2009 (ADL 2009). Others, such as the Proud Boys, founded in 2016, emerged with Trump's candidacy; and all were energized by his political career (Center for International Security and Cooperation n.d.). They became a much more visible and, given Donald Trump's promise to issue pardons if he regains the presidency, a much more openly accepted part of the Protect policy alliance than they or their white supremacist predecessors were of the color-blind policy alliance (Cawthorne 2022).

The violent Unite the Right rally in Charlottesville, Virginia in August 2017, in which militants displayed both Confederate and Nazi flags, proved to be a crucible for newly intense confrontations in American politics, foreshadowing the attack on the Capitol on January 6, and also mobilizing Left racial justice groups, as we shall see.

As tensions mounted in Charlottesville, anti-racist protester Heather Heyer lost her life to a right-wing rioter who deliberately drove into her, confirming for both sides that threats of violence were not just talk. Then on January 6, 2021, in Washington, seven more people died.

As the court cases arraigning and sentencing the perpetrators soon showed, the rioters, mostly but not exclusively white men, came from middle-class as well as working-class America, and included doctors, lawyers, teachers, military veterans, and some law enforcement professionals (Miller-Idriss 2022). After that day, the Proud Boys, Three Percenters, and Oath Keepers became household names. The less well-known 1st Amendment Praetorian, founded in the fall of 2020 to protect Trump supporters at rallies, was active after November 2020 in providing armed guards for "Stop the Steal" events, and its "Praetorian guards" also participated in the January 6 attack (Goldman, Benner, and Feuer 2021; Feuer 2022a). A New England white nationalist group, the Patriot Front, formed in the wake of the Charlottesville clashes and in ensuing years heightened its pace of demonstrations, violent confrontations, and intense recruiting efforts, especially on predominantly white college campuses (Crimaldi, Arnett, and Milkovitz 2023).

By early 2023, more than one thousand people had been charged with crimes for their actions on January 6; more than six hundred had been convicted for crimes on that day or in the days leading up to it; and both the founder of the Oath Keepers, the Yale Law–educated Stewart Rhodes, and the former leader of the Proud Boys, Enrique Tarrio, had been convicted of seditious conspiracy, along with others (US Department of Justice 2023; Feuer and Montague 2023; Anderson and McMillan 2023). Tarrio's conviction came despite the fact that he had periodically served as an FBI informant (Roston 2021). Rhodes got a tough eighteen-year sentence. In court he declaimed: "I'm a political prisoner, and like President Trump, my only crime is opposing those who are destroying our country" (quoted in Barber 2023).

At this writing it is too soon to judge the full impact of these criminal processes. While the Oath Keepers fragmented after Rhodes's indictment and conviction, the more decentralized Proud Boys have only expanded their political activities in support of Protect alliance goals (Wolfe 2023b). Since 2021 they have been even more visible in many grassroots venues, conspicuously attending local school board meetings, town council gatherings, and local health departments' question-and-answer sessions. One Proud Boy in North Carolina, Jeremy Bertino, explained that "the plan of attack if you want to make change is to get involved at the local level," and these groups undertook energetic local recruitment campaigns (Frenkel 2021). In the Pacific Northwest especially, the Proud Boys, Oath Keepers, and other right-wing groups have been pursuing the "precinct strategy" of gaining positions in local Republican organizations, with significant successes (Levinson 2023). A number of militia groups have also expanded their online activity markedly, sometimes using the encrypted messaging app Telegram to grow local groups under the radar of the national media and law enforcement authorities (De Vynck and Nakashima 2021).

Many January 6 participants ran for public office in 2021 and 2022, though most denied having entered the Capitol (Settles 2021; Edmondson 2022). In the 2022 midterms, half of the twenty identified participants who made it onto the November ballot were elected, half defeated. Derrick Van Oden of Wisconsin and George Santos of New York won election to Congress (though Santos was soon revealed to have falsified most of his life story and credentials), and seven others were elected to state legislatures. Kenneth Paxton was reelected attorney general of Texas, even though he was subsequently impeached by his fellow Republicans for a long list of offenses (Bickerton 2022; Bogel-Burroughs and Goodman 2023).

Not all of these candidates, and not all other members of the still emerging Protect policy alliance, have openly promised to protect the nation's "white demographic" against many dangers including ultimate "replacement," much less to support doing so through armed violence. Nonetheless, in our interviews several more moderate conservative leaders ruefully acknowledged that themes some politely termed "ethnonationalist," and others more bluntly called "white Christian nationalist," are now much more visible in American conservatism than in the decades when color-blindness was the racial conservatives' byword. Our interviewees believe this is so in part because many young conservatives find these "blood and soil" themes more exciting than low taxes and deregulation. Most also agree that, as Caldwell writes, those "who lost most from the new rights-based politics" of the 1960s "were white men" (Caldwell 2020, 276). Even these moderate conservatives, moreover, fully concurred with those explicitly championing the nation's "white demographic" that today conservatives must protect America forcefully against a cultural Left more militant and dangerous than ever before.

Protests and Armed Protectionists

In recent years, protests that spill over into violent confrontations have illustrated both the urgency many conservatives now feel to protect against radicalism in America, and the dangers impassioned protectionism can produce. Protest activity on both the right and the left rose sharply after 2015, and in 2020 over eleven thousand protests associated with Black Lives Matter occurred, most following the killing of George Floyd (ACLED 2021). Though analysts have categorized over 94 percent of the protests as peaceful, at many extreme right-wing groups showed up to engage in counterprotests, support the police, and (officially) protect against violence. In roughly a quarter of those cases, violence and destruction of property ensued (ACLED 2021). Over ten thousand protesters were arrested, and property owners claimed $2 billion in damages, though most of the arrests were for low-level offenses, not violent crimes or major property destruction (Pavilonis 2022). The far-right counterprotesters included overtly white nationalist groups like the Klan, as well as fellow travelers including the Groypers who follow Nicholas Fuentes, and some factions of the Proud Boys, whom President Trump urged to "stand back and stand by" at protests, but not to stay away (though he did subsequently issue a statement condemning them if they supported white supremacy) (LeBlanc 2020; ACLED 2021).

On August 24, 2020, speaking at the COVID-constrained Republican National Convention, Charlie Kirk, the founder of Turning Point USA, an organization set up in 2012 to promote conservatism among young people, underscored modern conservatives' perception of left-wing protests as existential threats to the nation. "Trump," Kirk proclaimed, "was elected to protect our families from the vengeful mob that seeks to destroy our way of life, our neighborhoods, schools, churches and values" (Bump 2020). The next day, the perils of militant protectionism were dramatized when Kyle Rittenhouse, a seventeen-year-old from Antioch, Illinois, drove to Kenosha, Wisconsin, along with others, armed with a semiautomatic rifle, in order to aid the police and protect property in demonstrations over the shooting of yet another Black man, Jacob Blake. Rittenhouse subsequently told interviewers: "Part of my job also is to protect people. If someone is hurt, I'm running into harm's way" (BBC News 2021). In this case, his doing so resulted in his killing two men and injuring a third, in what a jury determined to be self-defense under Wisconsin law.

The heightened efforts of militant right-wing groups to win offices in the Republican Party, on local school boards, and at higher levels of government have not meant any reduction in these protest confrontations that sometimes turn violent. The exclusively male Proud Boys participated in at least 145 protests and demonstrations in 2021, according to the Armed Conflict Location and Event Data Project (Frenkel 2021). Their protest activities then rose to almost weekly frequency in 2022, and increasingly focused on LGBTQ+ targets, especially drag performers (Italiano 2023). Even though only a small percentage of the demonstrations in recent years erupted into violent clashes, the large number of protests has both heightened conservatives' sense of embattlement and made the militant Right of the Protect policy alliance visible, increasing the risks that efforts to protect will instead spur grievous clashes.

Funding the Protect Policy Alliance

Numerous writers have detailed how, during the first Nixon administration, when the foreign policy-minded president appeared willing to let Great Society liberals continue to set much of the nation's domestic policy agenda, the conservative Virginia lawyer Lewis Powell—soon to be confirmed as a Nixon-nominated Supreme Court Justice—wrote what proved to be a historic memorandum for the US Chamber of Commerce. In it, Powell called for corporate America to conduct long-term "guerrilla warfare" against the perceived liberal domination of the media, the universities, and American politics.[4] The Powell memo circulated widely among America's corporate elites, reinforced by similar calls from many other conservative analysts and business and political leaders to step up defense of the "American Free Enterprise System," as Powell framed the task.

A number of America's wealthiest conservatives soon responded, including the oil-rich Koch brothers, Charles and David; Richard Mellon Scaife, heir to the Mellon banking fortune; John M. Olin, head of a munitions and chemical manufacturing empire; the Coors Brewing family; and the DeVos family, founders of Amway marketing, among others. Beginning in the early 1970s, these members of the nation's super-rich elite created a network of institutions comprising what is now deemed the "legacy" conservative infrastructure, including the Heritage Foundation, the American Enterprise Institute, Americans for Prosperity, the Cato Institute, the American Legislative Exchange Council (ALEC), the Pacific Legal Foundation, and countless other think tanks, policy advocacy nonprofits, conservative litigation groups, and right-leaning programs and centers within higher education institutions. These new entities collectively provided fresh ideas for new conservative policy regimes, including new legislative proposals, new legal arguments, and new campaign techniques, imagery, and expertise. These innovations were all fundamental to the era of the Reagan Revolution in American politics, which many date from 1980 through the election of Barack Obama in 2008, if not beyond.

As we have observed, their predominant emphasis in the late twentieth century was on libertarian economic policies. The rise of the "law and economics" movement in the early 1970s as a new pro-market school of jurisprudence was, for example, greatly aided by funding from the Olin Foundation, the Indiana entrepreneur Pierre Goodrich, and others. They paid for new academic initiatives and positions in leading law schools, and for junior scholars to participate in those programs (Teles 2008, 90–134; MacLean 2018, 122–26).[5]

The funding provided by the super-wealthy was, moreover, reinforced by developments that aided the abilities of many more Americans of all perspectives to target whatever philanthropic capacity they had to their preferred purposes. As wealth managers know, though most Americans have little reason to do so, the Tax Reform Act of 1969 requires private family foundations to give at least 5 percent of their assets to others annually. This mandate has meant that if those with high incomes or financial windfalls choose to obtain the tax benefits of creating what are often small family foundations, they must donate to what they consider worthy causes. They cannot use their foundations simply to shelter funds from taxes or for other private purposes. For some, this obligation has increased their giving to nonprofit groups that are officially aimed at serving the public interest but that often have a clear right or left tilt. For many others, the 1969 requirement has created an incentive to give to donor-advised funds, instead of establishing their own philanthropic entities. They can thereby save on administrative overhead, while still being able to designate when and to whom their donations will be re-granted (White 2017).

Consequently, in the twenty-first century the nation's largest charities are no longer the major foundations created by industrialists like Ford, Rockefeller, and Carnegie. They have instead become the leading donor-advised funds, Fidelity Charitable and Vanguard Charitable, which enable donors to give to a wide range of policy education and public interest organizations, though not directly to candidates. Additionally, tax laws have fostered the creation of not only 501(c)3 organizations like most foundations and think tanks, which are mandated to serve charitable purposes and donations to which are tax deductible. They have also fostered the growth of 501(c)4 organizations, which are also supposed to serve the public interest but which can engage in partisan political advocacy in their efforts to serve "social welfare" goals. Donations to 501(c)4 organizations are not tax deductible. Those groups can, however, often conceal the identities of the donors who are helping them work for controversial political causes, and so 501(c)4 spending in particular has come to be referred to as political "dark money."

These transformations in American tax laws and American philanthropy have made it easy for all those with some surplus wealth to donate in one way or another to their favorite political causes. As we will see, both very liberal and very conservative groups have benefited, to the consternation of some on the right (Vogel and Goldmacher 2022a). When they have sufficient resources, today liberal and conservative 501(c)3 bodies often establish, in addition to their core operations organization, a legally distinct but functionally linked 501(c)3 endowed foundation to provide a secure financial base, and a 501(c)4 advocacy group that can aid candidates. This three-part structure enables groups to pursue their aims in varied ways, while also reducing their tax liabilities and preserving and extending their funding.

While this restructuring of philanthropy and advocacy entities is being deployed on both the left and the right, those wealthy enough to take advantage of these opportunities generally lean toward conservative positions, certainly on economic issues, and increasingly on Protect cultural concerns. According to one analysis, donors to the Donors Trust, a donor-advised fund that explicitly solicits conservative libertarian donors, and to three more inclusive funds—Schwab Charitable, Fidelity Charitable, and Vanguard Charitable—collectively allocated $11 million between 2014 and 2017 to thirty-four groups identified by the Southern Poverty Law Center as anti-LGBTQ+, anti-Muslim, anti-immigrant, or in one case white nationalist (Kotch 2019). Whether or not these groups should be labeled "hate groups," as the Southern Poverty Law Center does, they undeniably pursue Protect goals with great intensity.

Scholars have shown convincingly how the extensive new conservative intellectual and advocacy infrastructure created in the 1970s and 1980s with the aid of these tax policies fueled the successes of the conservative legal movement, including making Federalist Society credentials a virtual necessity for federal judgeships under Republicans, and enacting at all levels of government conservative policy regimes limiting taxation, business regulation, and public aid, often with the support of neoliberal Democrats (Teles 2008; Hollis-Brusky 2015). The influence of these groups has only been enhanced by the fact that legislative and judicial successes of conservatives after 1980 included winning new limits on the constitutionality and administrative enforcement of campaign finance monitoring and restriction programs (Garrett 2021). In the landmark *Citizens United v. Federal Elections Commission* decision in 2010, the US Supreme Court vastly broadened the scope for anonymous donations, including corporate spending, and it also permitted the fiction that candidate-favoring 501(c)4 super PACs (Political Action Committees) could be set up in parallel but distinct from a candidate's official campaign (La Raja 2012).

As we and others have long documented, the broad range of anti-regulatory goals pursued by the extensive network of conservative groups created since the early 1970s frequently included opposition to vigorous administration of civil rights regulations, to explicitly race-targeted initiatives such as affirmative action in employment and in educational admissions, and to aid programs that do not use racial categories but appear designed to aid racial and ethnic minorities, all attacked as fostering a divisive race-conscious America instead of an increasingly color-blind one. Because most of the now older conservative litigation and civil rights advocacy groups funded by the mobilized right-leaning donors of the 1970s and 1980s emphasized those goals, the debate over color-blind versus race-conscious policy regimes was central to that era's clash of racial policy alliances.

Today, however, even as the extensive, abundantly funded conservative advocacy infrastructure created in the last quarter of the twentieth century continues to thrive, with many shifting their focus to supporting Protect causes and organizations, new funding sources have arisen, many even more strongly oriented toward contemporary Protect goals. Appendix B includes only a handful of these funding bodies, mainly to illustrate their range, from those operating only in the hundreds of thousands to those with hundreds of millions or even billions to bestow. For example, the hedge fund billionaire Robert Mercer and his daughter Rebekah Mercer have been major supporters and funders of first Steve Bannon, introducing him to Donald Trump, and then Trump himself, richly financing pro-Trump PACS during his presidential campaigns. In 2018 Rebekah Mercer also secretly co-founded Parler, an "alt-right" social media platform designed to compete with Twitter, and she now heads the Mercer Family Foundation, through which the Mercers assist Trump-aligned policy advocacy, among other causes (Jopson 2018; Benveniste and Yurieff 2020). In 2020, Leonard Leo, longtime co-chair and executive vice president of the Federalist Society, stepped back from his executive role there in order to help create and lead a company called CRC Advisers, which raises funds and aids groups seeking to help win elections and appointments for conservative, generally pro-Trump officials and judges. Leo works with a network of groups such as the Rule of Law Trust, the Concord Fund (previously the Judicial Crisis Network), the conservative Donors Trust donor-advised fund, and others, and collectively they reportedly spent $122 million in 2020, chiefly on conservative political advocacy (Vogel and Goldmacher 2022b).[6] Leo explained in an interview that he envisaged the network "funnel[ing] tens of millions of dollars into conservative fights around the country" (Perez, Kroll, and Elliott 2022). His work across the nation has included vetting state Supreme Court nominees for Governor Ron DeSantis (Reinhard and Dawsey 2023).

The watchdog group Campaign for Accountability has contended that in the Trump years, Leo also funneled over $70 million to his own for-profit businesses, making himself a wealthy man (Shah 2023). Whatever the accuracy of those calculations, Leo has only continued to expand his multifarious political activities. He also heads the Marble Freedom Trust, a 501(c)4 tax-exempt nonprofit that received $1.6 billion from Barre Seid, a ninety-year-old Chicago electronics executive. The Trust targets state and local politics, funding conservative candidates for governorships and state legislatures; supports conservative efforts to make voter ID rules tougher; and promotes bills that aim to ban Critical Race Theory teaching in schools (Perez, Kroll, and Elliott 2022). Leo also chairs the Teneo Network, which has twenty regional chapters and annual revenues in the range of $2 to $5 billion, and seeks, in Leo's words, to "crush liberal dominance" in "lots of areas . . . of American culture and American life where things are really messed up right now" (Kroll, Bernstein, and Surgey 2023). Leo portrays all these efforts as necessary responses to the recent increased number and activity of wealthy liberal donors, who reportedly enabled Democrats to raise and spend more dark money in the 2020 elections than Republicans did (O'Brien 2023). Leo has therefore proclaimed: "it's high time for the conservative movement to be among the ranks of George Soros, Hansjorg

Wyss, Arabella Advisors and other left-wing philanthropists, going toe-to-toe in the fight to defend our Constitution and its ideals" (Vogel and Goldmacher 2022b).

The funding network for contemporary conservative Protect groups is in fact far more extensive than we can convey here, in part because it is not easily tracked. The rise of vehicles for vast "dark money" funding of political causes, including 501(c)4 organizations and donor-advised funds, has both facilitated huge increases in political spending and made many of the donors unidentifiable. Ironically, this spending has been aided by tax policies that effectively impose a greater share of the tax burden on those without sufficient resources for tax-deductible philanthropy, even as the tax laws encourage massive expenditures by the nation's wealthiest citizens to influence every form of political decision-making at every level and in every branch of American government.

In sum, while the Protect policy alliance is still too new to have constructed the extraordinarily extensive network of think tanks, advocacy and mobilization groups, media outlets, litigation entities, academic centers, and funding organizations created by conservative billionaires in the decades following Lewis Powell's memo to the US Chamber of Commerce, it has converted many members of that network to Protect policy agendas, along with many leaders of what was formerly the Republican Party establishment. Aided by new organizations, new funding, and a deeper alliance with a religious Right now more often openly embracing Christian nationalism, and reinforced as well by similar national conservative movements in many other countries, the contemporary Protect policy alliance both seeks and has prospects of achieving greater victories on behalf of conservative policy regimes, including conservative racial policies, than the preceding color-blind alliance ever managed to do.

Yet important as all these elements are, in the eyes of many of its leading adherents the greatest strength of this still emerging racial institutional order is its compelling story of why traditionalist Americans, particularly virtuous religious white Americans, today need to be protected. To that story, and to the political vision of America and the world that it conveys, we now turn.

CHAPTER FOUR

The Conservatives' Story

Who and What to Protect

The greatest danger we have ever faced: the militant left wing in our country has become the enemy within. —Senator Rick Scott

Shared Themes in Conservative Narratives

Why do conservatives believe that the Left in America today has become even more threatening than the race-conscious policy alliance they long opposed, to such an extent that some see armed resistance as necessary, even a divine duty? What, in their view, went so terribly wrong over the last half century? Why did Florida Senator Rick Scott warn his fellow conservatives in a speech at the Conservative Political Action Conference in 2022 that the American Left is today "the greatest danger" that the country has ever faced (quoted in Smith 2022)?

There is no single authoritative answer. Unsurprisingly, conservative intellectuals and politicians offer accounts that vary in some particulars from each other. Some of the differences are both philosophically and politically important, particularly in their policy implications. Even so, in interviews, writings, broadcasts, and podcasts, and on their websites, most American conservatives converge on a reasonably consistent story of how America has gone badly astray and who is to blame. It is likely that beliefs in the fundamental veracity of this account, and the deeply felt emotions it both expresses and stirs, do more than any particular policy position to inspire support for the Protect policy alliance.

The basic themes of this story of America's modern decline are as follows. Most racial conservatives believe that, though America's problems can be traced further back, the main roots of today's dangers were planted in the 1960s. The nation ended de jure segregation then, and few if any conservatives today, however extreme, explicitly urge its return. Most believe, however, that the nation tragically failed in those years to commit fully to color-blind policies, and that it only temporarily discredited the most radical voices on the American left, including the Black Panthers, Black Power advocates like Stokely Carmichael (later Kwame Ture), Black Marxist feminists like Angela Davis, and Black LGBTQ+ advocates like the poet and activist Audre Lorde—all energetically supported by many in Students for a Democratic Society and other groups in the predominantly white New Left. While these radicals suffered some eclipse in the 1970s, conservatives believe, they and their successors—Black, white, Latinx, Indigenous, and others—nonetheless went on to pursue careers in academia, in the media, in nonprofit organizations and philanthropies, in K-12 education, and even in corporate America.

From the late twentieth century to the present, conservatives say, these now institutionalized radical voices have again and again made false or exaggerated claims to have exposed systemic racism in all sectors of American life. Consequently, the radicals, calling themselves sometimes liberals or more often progressives, have pushed for a sweeping variety of diversity, equity, and inclusion initiatives that by the early twenty-first century had come to feed and be fed by a massive and still growing DEI industry of consultants, organization officers, and advocates. Because that industry has placed proponents of what conservatives see as discriminatory woke policies in major corporations, media companies, educational institutions, foundations, and nonprofits, radical ideas have become signally fused with the self-interest of powerful people in almost every major institution.

And as radicals have gained more and more institutional and cultural power, conservatives believe, they have aggressively sought to shame and silence all voices championing traditionalist religious and cultural beliefs and practices, to promote people of color over more deserving whites in almost every venue, to lobby for open borders and a weakening of police forces, to confiscate guns, to offer abortions on demand, to celebrate polymorphous forms of sexuality and gender identities, and to support the globalist economic and immigration policies of many political and corporate elites who endorse their cultural values. Through tearing down monuments and commemorations valorizing American conservatives, especially white men, and through educational curricula and media presentations fostering white guilt and a sense of hopelessness among people of color, today's

Left is, conservatives believe, ultimately trying to get as many people as possible to share their core anti-American premise: that the USA is an irredeemably evil white supremacist, patriarchal, capitalist, heterosexist, traditionally religious imperialist nation that must be radically transformed in virtually every aspect.

Consequently, as the twenty-first century has unfolded, more and more conservatives have concluded that the most important task of conservatism today is not to promote color-blind public policies, but to take vigorous actions to protect traditionalist Americans, their values, their customs, and their institutions from these wide-ranging Left assaults. Christopher DeMuth is a Distinguished Fellow at the Hudson Institute and a former president of the American Enterprise Institute, both institutions that were for many years bastions of the economically and national-security-focused conservatism of the 1970s. But DeMuth is now chair of the Trump-era National Conservatism Conference, and he has articulated pellucidly the lessons that many contemporary conservatives draw from their story of modern American decline. He argues that a new, more uncompromising conservatism is needed now because when "the American left was liberal and reformist," conservatives could simply be "moderators of change." But, he insists, today's "woke progressivism isn't reformist. It seeks not to build on the past but to promote instability, to turn the world upside-down." Against this "radicalism . . . moderation is futile." And like many, he adds that today's conservatism must be aggressively nationalist, because "almost every progressive initiative subverts the American nation . . . opening national borders . . . transferring sovereignty to international bureaucracies . . . elevating group identity above citizenship; fomenting racial, ethnic, and religious divisions . . . defaming our national history as a story of unmitigated injustice" (DeMuth 2021).

To be sure, not all contemporary conservatives are so strident. Yuval Levin, director of Social, Cultural and Constitutional Studies at the American Enterprise Institute, does not see anti-American Left views as quite so hegemonic in America as some other conservatives do. Like many others, however, he is concerned that more radical Left positions have gained greater credibility and broader support since 2013, because videos of white police officers and vigilantes killing African Americans, and the ensuing massive protests, have made narratives of systemic, institutional racism in America more plausible, especially among young voters.[1] Even if radicals are not actually ruling America now, most conservatives see real dangers that young Americans will embrace their views.

While conservatives regularly accuse today's radicals of being Marxists, most who advance this story of how America has gone wrong do not see the Left as currently prioritizing any deeply threatening economic agenda. Consequently, most conservatives stress what they see as a far more pressing goal: recapturing control of America's cultural institutions. Many advocacy groups on the right focus on protecting freedom of speech for conservatives in the academy and the media, while at the same time they champion the rights of conservative parents to protect their children in K-12 public schools from what they see as offensive teachings derived from Critical Race Theory and celebrations of LGBTQ+ lifestyles.[2] Relying heavily on these cultural themes, conservatives believe those promising to be protectors of traditionalist America have great potential to win elections, because the globalist leaders of both parties have discredited themselves in the eyes of millions of Americans. To succeed, however, Protect conservatives must overcome "the corporate elite, the media elite, the political elite, and the academic elite," whom they see as having "coagulated into one axis of evil, dominating every institution and controlling the channel of thoughts," as the journalist David Brooks sums up the new conservatism (Brooks 2021).

It will be clear that this conservative story places the blame for the nation's heightening polarization on racial policy issues firmly on the rise of this radical "axis of evil," which they believe leaves conservatives with no real choice but to respond aggressively. Though (as we have indicated) we instead see the Protect and Repair alliances arising roughly simultaneously and in continuing interaction with each other, and we do not perceive progressives to be nearly so culturally dominant as some conservatives claim, it is not our aim here to evaluate the motivational stories found on either side of today's political divides—only to report them as accurately as we can. Nor can we judge with any certainty whether most conservatives are truly convinced of their account, or whether many are simply using it to fire up their constituencies, providing villains to blame for people's often very real troubles, in order to gain prominence and political power and to advance their economic interests, as progressives charge. It seems likely that many conservative intellectuals and policy advocates may well believe this story is basically correct, while some politicians and wealthy donors may well have more instrumental motives for endorsing these themes.

It is crucial to recognize, however, that tens of millions of Americans and many more people around the world find the basic claims of this conservative story, and the evidence used to support them, persuasive and enraging.

It is therefore important to understand its contents, its elaborations, and its variations in some detail. We begin with versions advanced by conservative intellectuals and activists, and then turn to the account popularized by its most influential American political voice, Donald J. Trump, along with other politicians, and by the new "National Conservatives" that Trump-style politicos have inspired.

Significant statements of this conservative narrative have been provided by two public intellectuals, the journalist Christopher Caldwell and the editor and academic Charles Kesler, both associated with the Claremont Institute. Longtime activists on behalf of color-blind policies including Ward Connerly and US Civil Rights Commissioner Gail Heriot reinforce these accounts, as do many newer, often more militant conservative leaders such as Christopher Rufo. Caldwell laid out his account forcefully in his 2020 book, *The Age of Entitlement*. Kesler provided his distinctive but ultimately overlapping narrative in his 2021 book, *Crisis of the Two Constitutions: The Rise, Decline, and Recovery of American Greatness*.

Conservative Intellectual and Activist Narratives: "It's the 1960s, Stupid"

Caldwell is among the many conservatives who take the upheavals of the 1960s as their starting point. He argues that the civil rights laws of that era initially aimed at the integration of, primarily, African Americans into the many American public institutions from which de jure segregation laws had long excluded or marginalized them. Caldwell believes, however, that the pursuit of racial integration soon "turned into" an "all-embracing ideology of diversity" that informed "not just a major new element in the Constitution" but "a *rival* constitution" (Caldwell 2020, 5–6). For Caldwell, the "increasing necessity that citizens choose between these two orders"—the true, color-blind Constitution and the new diversity Constitution—is the source of "the poisonous conflict" tearing America apart (5–6).

Veterans of the civil rights contests of the 1960s such as the businessman and activist Ward Connerly agree with Caldwell's view of the 1960s reform era as a lost opportunity.[3] Connerly supported civil rights initiatives in the early 1960s, but he opposed the rise of affirmative action programs, and decades later he became the chief architect of Proposition 209, the 1996 California referendum that prohibited the use of race, sex, or ethnicity in state public employment, public contracting, and public education programs. Like Caldwell, Connerly sees the mid-1960s as a moment when the nation might have embraced principles of color-blindness. He laments that instead legislators adopted measures that ended up making American public institutions and policies pervasively and perversely race-conscious. Caldwell specifies that it was some provisions of the 1964 Civil Rights Act, and even more Lyndon Johnson's executive orders and the ensuing regulations of federal agencies, all reinforced by liberal decisions of the Supreme Court, that prompted large employers and educational institutions to set up affirmative action programs for hiring, promotion, and educational admissions in order to avoid public and private lawsuits (Caldwell 2020, 31–33, 146). These institutions also began creating staff positions with diversity, equity, and inclusion responsibilities, initially to oversee affirmative action programs. Over time, these DEI officials have successfully advocated for more and more extensive and invasive race-conscious policies.

According to US Civil Rights Commissioner Gail Heriot, another long-time leader of efforts to end racial preferences, they did not do so on their own. Heriot agrees that in championing Critical Race Theory and calling for expansive transformations to defeat institutional racism the American Left has "hardened" its agenda in recent years.[4] She stresses, however, that the road to this radicalism was paved in part by the failure of Republican politicians to oppose race-conscious policies vigorously over the past half century. She calls particular attention to George H. W. Bush's support for the 1991 Civil Rights Act, which she faults for failing to override judicial interpretations of Title VII of the 1964 Civil Rights Act holding that employers could sometimes be liable for the disparate impact of their policies on racial minorities and women, even if no intentional discrimination had occurred (Heriot 2019). Heriot also emphasizes that for the first time, the 1991 law permitted litigants who could show intentional discrimination to recover damages for "emotional pain," not simply "pecuniary losses" (93n201).

These civil rights policies, Heriot believes, helped foster an environment in which many racial minorities and white liberals see all racial disparities as demonstrating the need for transformative systemic changes, and in which many interpret all experiences of emotional pain as the unjust results of racist "microaggressions" institutional policies must prohibit and punish. Heriot and other conservatives suggest that the resulting perceptions of systemic racism and pervasive discrimination, constantly highlighted by those who work in the DEI industry, have emboldened the cultural Left to push for more massive changes on more fronts than many earlier supporters of race-conscious policies envisioned.

Inevitably, there are some variations in these accounts. In our interviews, a surprising number of conservatives did not assign great significance to the election of Barack Obama as a catalyst for a more militant Right, even on racial issues. Some believe, like many of Obama's Left critics, that he did not feature racial policies very prominently, and they minimize the significance of the formation of armed right-wing groups like the Oath Keepers and Three Percenters in response to Obama's election. Others like Caldwell insist that it "was a shock," and an alienating shock, to most Americans when "Obama governed in such a race-conscious way" (Caldwell 2020, 188). They see his presidency as a major source of perceptions that white men, in particular, need greater protection against self-described progressives in modern America.

Christopher Rufo, the Manhattan Institute-affiliated journalist whose articles and media appearances catalyzed the uprisings against Critical Race Theory in 2020 and 2021, attaches less significance to the Obama presidency per se. He has, however, added to these accounts by elaborating on how the DEI and CRT advocates who became more prominent in the first two decades of the twenty-first century, especially during the Obama years, derive their basic ideas from late-1960s Black and white radicals who were significantly to the left of the pacifist democratic socialists of the early SDS. In his interview with us, Rufo recounted how he had traced many tenets of today's Left racial justice proponents to the Black Panther Huey Newton, whom he credits with first using "institutional racism"; to Noel Ignatiev, a former Communist and member of the Sojourner Truth Organization, an SDS offshoot, who coined the term "white privilege"; to Angela Davis, whose Black Marxist feminist ideas helped generate the Critical Race Theory focus on intersectionality; and to others in the more revolution-minded wing of the 1960s New Left. Rufo notes correctly that scholars sympathetic to critical theory perspectives like Isaac Gottesman, the author of *The Critical Turn in Education: From Marxist Critique to Poststructuralist Feminism to Critical Race Theories*, have mapped out similar intellectual and political histories (Gottesman 2016).

Rufo argues that these radicals never supported mainstream mid-1960s civil rights ideals of promoting integration within existing institutions, and he concedes that they discredited themselves with most of the American public by engaging in political violence in the early 1970s. But he sees them as nonetheless defining the agenda of the Left today, after they turned to careers in academia and nonprofits and eventually adapted their revolutionary views into the themes of CRT scholarship and the DEI movement in education, corporations, and government bureaucracies.[5] Reihan Salam, president of the Manhattan Institute where Rufo is a Senior Fellow, argues that under the influence of these radical perspectives "the definition of what counts as racist" has grown "ever more expansive and totalizing," with the American Left treating all who dissent from "elite progressive opinion" on virtually any issue as "guilty" of "multiracial whiteness" (quoted in Kang 2022).

Liberalism's Unendurable Longue Durée

Charles Kesler agrees with the critiques of the 1960s advanced by Caldwell, Connerly, Heriot, Rufo, Salam, and many others, but he places them within a more long-term story. Kesler sees the 1960s as the last of "three waves" of liberalism: first Woodrow Wilson's Progressivism, then FDR's New Deal, and then the Great Society and the New Left of the 1960s. Kesler believes activists in all three waves sought "not merely to reform but to *transform* the country" into something liberals saw as "freer, fairer, and more fulfilling" (Kesler 2021, 144). Each wave was, however, significantly more radical than its predecessor, even if liberals were simply working out what was always implicit in the Progressives' rejection of "natural-rights individualism" and their embrace of a "living Constitution" (150). The New Deal pushed further than the Progressives toward economic "entitlement" liberalism, while the 1960s fostered the "multicultural" or "diversity liberalism" that Caldwell depicts and that contemporary conservatives perceive as still more radically threatening (152, 158).

Kesler sees his third wave of liberalism as unfolding in two stages, with an "Old New Left" of the early 1960s that accused America of hypocrisy in living up to its principles giving way over time to a "New New Left" centered on "identity politics," "Critical Race Theory," and "intersectionality." He agrees with Rufo that today's "New New Left" has been inspired by late-1960s Black Power advocates, Black Marxists and feminists, and their white allies, along with Left groups representing other people of color. He maintains, moreover, that this yet more radical New New Left rejects American principles, "the American creed," altogether, because it sees these principles as always resting on a deeply-rooted racism that most white Americans now seek to deny and conceal (Kesler 2021, 279, 282–83, 367). Kesler also contends that in recent years many of these New New Left beliefs have been adopted even by Democrats who once were more centrist, like President Joe Biden. To Kesler, "the worst thing about Biden" is his embrace of the left-wing moral critique of America which presumes "that it's a racist country, in its DNA, that it has always been basically unjust, that it's been a kind of petty tyranny, intellectually, morally and spiritually, and it has never really risen above the crassest kind of self-interest, whether along class lines or racial lines or any lines of possible expression" (quoted in Zerofsky 2022).

Kesler edits the *Claremont Review*, published by the Claremont Institute, a conservative think tank founded in 1979. For many years the Institute was treated as esoterically academic and politically marginal, intensely reverential toward the American founding while consistently interpreting its principles as supporting very conservative political positions. Its influence soared, however, with the Trump presidency. As we will see, some of its themes also shifted; though because the Institute's scholars have warned about America's decline since the 1960s, Thomas Klingenstein, the chair of the Claremont Institute's board, asserted in 2022 that the modern conservative movement's "intellectual justification" for embracing Trump "comes from Claremont" (quoted in Zerofsky 2022). In appreciation, Trump awarded the Institute the National Humanities Medal in 2019, and the Institute's ideas have also influenced leading GOP conservatives such as Florida Governor Ron DeSantis and Supreme Court Justice Clarence Thomas. The lawyer John Eastman, a chief architect of plans by Trump allies to overturn the 2020 election, has been affiliated with the Claremont Institute for several decades. Though Kesler and others there reject Eastman's election claims and the January 6 invasion of the Capitol, Eastman continues to direct the Institute's Center for Constitutional Jurisprudence, pending the outcome of the multiple legal cases against him (Goffard 2023).

Dominated overwhelmingly by white males with a firm grasp of the sense of grievance of many in that demographic, in 2016 many Claremont Institute scholars quickly saw that a Trump-led conservative disruption had the potential to reverse much of the racial and cultural liberalism that had gained ascendancy since the Great Society years. Some hoped the Institute could be for Trump what the Heritage Foundation and the American Enterprise Institute were for Ronald Reagan: an abundant supplier of both ideas and personnel. Institute leaders have described America as in a "cold civil war," caused by progressives' assaults on the Constitution, and many hoped that Trump's rise would give the Institute the chance to become a new conservative strategic command center (Kang 2022). Though it did not quite play that role, the Institute did benefit greatly from the flow of funds to right-leaning think tanks during and after the Trump years, and many scholars, journalists, activists, and politicians with ties to it have provided leadership in efforts to articulate the more militant conservatism they believe America needs to defeat the radical New New Left.

The Enemy Within: CRT and BLM

It is perhaps not surprising that almost all the versions of the conservative story advanced by academics, journalists, and public intellectuals give a prominent place to radical ideas, especially the development of Critical Race Theory and related theories of intersectionality advanced by the law professor Kimberlé Crenshaw, her mentor Derrick Bell, and others, including scholars in graduate schools of education as well as law schools. Conservative activists like Rufo fully recognize that public school teachers are not assigning CRT law review articles; but they argue plausibly that CRT themes have influenced what many teachers who see themselves as progressives present in the classroom.

Rufo defines these themes as follows: First, the existence of "whiteness" as an almost mystical driving force in American life. Second, the claim that not only do some forms of "institutional" or "systemic" racism exist in America, but that America simply *is* systematically racist. Third, the claim that American racism is "intersectional," establishing a hierarchy of oppression with affluent white heterosexual males at the top, poor people of color, some with nonconforming sexual orientations and/or gender identities, at the bottom. Fourth, that people viewed as white in America all possess "white privilege," a panoply of unjust advantages that most whites take for granted as the natural order of things. And fifth, that the goal of racial justice requires "abolition," understood not simply as the end of racial discrimination and greater integration, but as revolutionary, radical transformation in all major American institutions.

These five themes, Rufo contends, are pervasive in progressive American education and in diversity, equity, and inclusion training programs of the sort Donald Trump, when president, banned after seeing Rufo on a Fox program.

Rufo and many other conservatives see the same ideas as dominant in most of higher education, in Hollywood movies, in much television, in popular music and plays, in leading newspapers and magazines like the *New York Times* and *Washington Post*, and in the social media operated by the new Big Tech companies, as well as in presentations at museums and historical sites and in all too many fiction and nonfiction texts. Bestsellers like Robin DiAngelo's *White Fragility* and Ibram X. Kendi's *How to Be an Antiracist*, and controversies over conservative speakers on numerous campuses, persuade conservatives that US public life has become dominated by social justice warriors trumpeting wokeness and subjecting all who do not embrace it to a repressive "cancel culture."

Like many on the left, conservative thinkers often credit Ta-Nehisi Coates's 2014 article in *The Atlantic*, "The Case for Reparations," as galvanizing civil rights calls for more radical change. Many more, however, stress the rise of Black Lives Matter and the mass protests it helped spark after the many killings of Black Americans from Trayvon Martin through Michael Brown and then, in May 2020, to George Floyd. Most conservatives agree with Yuval Levin that BLM and kindred protest movements have worked to broaden and embolden support for sweeping and occasionally violent challenges to a wide range of American institutions. Caldwell insists that the Black Lives Matter movement has linked angry "inner-city residents" and "idealistic college students" with "billionaire managers of foundations" and the "Democratic donor class," bringing "together these establishment and anti-establishment elements in an extraordinary ferment" (Caldwell 2020, 264). In interviews, many conservative leaders now casually use "BLM" to refer to the worldview of the radical Left they see themselves as combating. Though a number concede that American policing does need to improve, they dismiss, or sometimes gleefully celebrate, calls to "defund" or "abolish" the police and the Immigration and Customs Enforcement agency (ICE) as messages that only persuade most Americans that they do need protection against the policies of America's new cultural Left.

There are other differences in the various iterations of the conservative story, though the agreements are far more extensive and fundamental. Some conservative analysts trace the anger and alienation many Americans feel chiefly to liberal and "globalist" economic, immigration, and drug policies, all said to have fostered the Great Recession, the opioid epidemic, and the "deaths of despair" so many working-class Americans have suffered. Most conservative writers and activists, however, stress what they see as the Left's racial and cultural radicalism. Some conservatives think it is important that America's cultural Left is part of worldwide movements, but many do not think initiatives in other countries for reparations and other racial justice reforms have much resonance or impact in the United States. Some express deep anxiety about the mounting rage of many on the right, sometimes culminating in violence. Others, believing that America is in greater danger than ever before, unreservedly fuel it.

The Politicians' Stories: Trump's Seminal Protect Narrative

When we turn to the accounts conservative politicians have advanced about why and how the nation has fallen into such danger, it is reasonable to suspect that they may be more disingenuous than most conservative intellectuals and activists. Politicians, after all, seek power and often say and do whatever seems useful to obtain it. As an important example, one of the most distinctive features of contemporary conservative racial policy discourse is the ferocity with which some politicians are attacking "woke" corporations for their DEI initiatives, in apparently sharp contrast to the celebration of American businesses and American capitalism called for in the Lewis Powell memo to the US Chamber of Commerce. Florida Senator Marco Rubio, for instance, bluntly proclaimed to the National Conservatism Conference that "Big Business is not our ally. . . . They are eager culture warriors who use the language of wokeness to cover free-market capitalism" (Brooks 2021). Florida Governor Ron DeSantis has gone even further, taking billions in state assets away from the mammoth investment firm BlackRock for its socially conscious "ESG" (environmental, social, governance) investment policies, championing what he labeled the "Stop WOKE Act" to restrict diversity training in businesses and educational institutions, and getting into a barbed war with the Disney Corporation because it criticized Florida's "Don't Say Gay" bill (Guynn 2023). Yet many believe that despite their rhetoric, these conservative politicians are much more likely to advance than to oppose the power and the interests of major American businesses and their wealthy owners, as their voting records in Congress largely confirm. Though new conservative think tanks like the America First Policy Institute regularly attack "corporate elites" and "big finance and big business," they favor the low taxes, deregulation, and privatization policies that economic conservatives have long defended.

These conservative politicians are, moreover, widely thought to be trying to steal a share of the staggering appeal of the need to "Make America Great Again" story told by the nation's leading Protect politician, Donald Trump. Indeed, at this point it is reasonable for readers to wonder just how much, and in what ways, the rise of what we are calling the Protect policy alliance is really just the rise of a Trump alliance. Is Protect-ism simply Trump-ism, a political phenomenon so tied to his charismatic leadership that its political fate is ultimately dependent on his? And if it is really a Trump alliance, is it more expressive of Trump's personal ambitions than of the kinds of ideological positions emphasized by many conservative intellectuals and activists?

Most conservatives, including the politicians repeating and embellishing Trump's narrative, do not think so. As we have seen, they believe the appeal of promises to protect against radical policies fundamentally stems from the positions of contemporary American liberals that many traditionalist Americans find at best insultingly condescending, and at worst deeply threatening. Quite plausibly, they think that Donald Trump has been far more a vehicle than an instigator for the mounting popular anger against those policies.

Yet as shown by the plethora of new conservative organizations adopting Trump's America First label, along with many of his policies challenging older forms of conservatism, the significance of Trump's meteoric political rise and his tumultuous presidency cannot be disregarded. This contrast is revealing: in 2002, a Christian fundamentalist computer programmer in Mississippi, John Pittman Hey, and other Pat Buchanan supporters organized an America First Party with a platform that included many of the positions on immigration, trade, and other issues that would be central to Donald Trump's 2016 campaign (America First Party 2022). Although this America First Party for a time had chapters in a number of states, it never gained much visibility, and today it is almost wholly eclipsed by Trump. With a popularity long unnoticed or underestimated by many academic, media, and political elites, Trump has undeniably tapped into long-standing resentments against the values and policies of those elites; and his success with voters has persuaded the overwhelming majority of Republican politicians and many committed conservatives to embrace his version of American protectionism, whether opportunistically or sincerely.

Trump formulated his Protect narrative in his historic first presidential campaign (Smith and King 2020). When he announced his candidacy for president, Trump was an experienced public speaker but an untested politician. His message evolved during the course of the 2016 campaign, often in response to what his audiences cheered—consistent with the view that his story has been motivated as much or more by his desire for attention and acclaim as by deep ideological conviction. Still, his June 16, 2015, speech announcing his candidacy made plain the two themes that guided and justified his subsequent aggressive Protect policy agenda.

Once, Trump said, America "used to have victories," but "(w)e don't have victories anymore"; and he ended with his trademark promise, "we will make America great again" (Trump 2015). He urged a foreign policy designed "to reinvigorate Western values and institutions" by "promoting Western civilization and its accomplishments" (Trump 2016a). To many on the contemporary right as well as the left, "Western" civilization means "white" civilization (Hood 2019). Trump maintained that "our American culture is the best in the world," and he insisted that "(p)ride in our institutions, our history, and our values should be taught by parents and teachers and impressed upon all" (Trump 2016d).

To counter criticisms of American racial inequalities, Trump blamed the modern difficulties of America's racial minorities on Democratic leaders, not on centuries of unjust treatment. Instead of needing to be rectified in any way, traditional "American values and cultures," Trump contended, must be "cherished and celebrated once again" (Trump 2016f). In so arguing, Trump foreshadowed the attacks on Critical Race Theory and the efforts to remove conservative monuments and rename American institutions that he and many other Protect conservatives would soon portray as threatening America with decay and destruction.

Trump's second theme was a jeremiad proclaiming that this once great America had been dragged down in recent decades by a corrupt ruling class. In his announcement speech, Trump attacked China, Japan, and especially Mexico and Islamic terrorism; but he contended that America's "leaders," who were "stupid . . . losers . . . morally corrupt," were the nation's biggest problem (Trump 2015). Though then and thereafter Trump often preferred to berate what he saw as the stupidity and corruption of all his opponents, he did also attribute to them a nefarious ideology. In a refrain that by 2020 would be ubiquitous among conservatives, Trump accused recent leaders of both parties of surrendering the country to "the false song of globalism." Contending that the "nation-state remains the true foundation for happiness and harmony," he promised that "America first" would be his "overriding theme" (Trump 2016a). But in the US, Trump said, there were now "two Americas: the ruling class and the groups it favors, and then everyone else" (Trump 2016b). The "Washington establishment, and the financial and media corporations that fund it," were the "central base" of a "global power structure" that rewarded America's "corrupt political establishment" for welcoming cheap illegal immigrant labor, helping companies move jobs overseas, and cutting deals with countries that sponsored Islamic terrorism (Trump 2016k).

As his campaign proceeded, Trump increasingly insisted that liberal social and policing policies had added cultural and violent physical victimization to the economic victimization many Americans were experiencing. He did not explicitly attack race-conscious policies like affirmative action, one of many issues on which he had made conflicting statements prior to his candidacy. But Trump, who generally portrays issues in zero-sum terms, repeatedly made clear that he saw most efforts to assist long-discriminated-against minorities not as means to promote equality but as dangers to those whom America should protect (Schnurer 2017). He complained that concerns about "racial profiling" and calls for limits on severe policing and immigration measures meant that "political correctness has replaced common sense" (Trump 2016d). He excoriated "those peddling the narrative of cops as a racist force in our society" for "hurting" law-abiding Americans (Trump 2016e, 2016j). He tweeted accounts of, especially, white victims of crimes perpetrated by Blacks, twice retweeting from a Twitter user called "WhiteGenocideTM" (Kopan 2016; Confessore 2016; Holmes 2017). What Trump termed his "new civil rights agenda for our time" featured strong policing, school choice, and deregulation to promote jobs—all policies presented without reference to race, thereby nominally eschewing explicit white nationalism, but all promising greater protection as well as greater freedom (Trump 2016h). His proposals consistently presumed the "American people" needed to be defended against race-conscious measures and other liberal policies that allegedly only served globalist elites.

Trump also promised to protect Social Security and Medicare, social programs more commonly perceived by whites as beneficial to them than as aid to minorities (Jardina 2019, 4, 191–94, 202, 234, 258; *On the Issues* 2016). Trump's most specific calls for protection, however, came on behalf of conservative Christians. His nomination acceptance speech criticized the 1954 Johnson amendment for depriving "religious institutions" of their tax-exempt status "if they openly advocate their political views," saying their "voice has been taken away" (Trump 2016c). He went on to tell Christian groups: "Christian faith is not the past but the present and the future" of America. He contended that "our media culture often mocks and demeans people of faith," and that "our politicians have really abandoned you." Trump promised that in his administration, "Christian heritage will be cherished, protected, defended, like you've never seen before" (Trump 2016g, 2016i).

Whom to Protect?

With greater consistency and scope than many analysts initially appreciated, Trump's speeches and tweets thus advanced a specific and, for many, a galvanizing narrative of the state of modern America. A wide variety of studies, including experimental research, public opinion surveys, analyses of voting statistics, and panel studies, show that this narrative connected powerfully with those who had strong attachments to traditionally socially dominant identities, including white, Christian, and male. Using panel data for 2012 and 2016, Diana Mutz found that people whose orientation in favor of socially dominant groups (SDO) increased during those years judged whites more discriminated against than racial minorities, Christians as more discriminated against than Muslims, and men as more discriminated against than women. Their sense that "the American way of life is threatened" was strongly associated with voting for Trump (Mutz 2018, E4332, E4334–36). Though Trump spoke most explicitly to those who believe in a dominant place for Christianity in America, recent scholarship shows that those like Nicholas Fuentes who identify being Christian with being an American "are also more likely to hold racial attitudes that bolster white supremacy" (Perry and Whitehead 2019, 5). Conversely, white identifiers are more likely to believe that "being Christian is important to being American" (Jardina 2019, 107, 125). One 2018 survey found that 54 percent of white evangelical Protestants thought it would be bad for America to become a non-white nation. They represented a significant proportion of the slight majority of white Americans who then said the US was better in the 1950s than today; the 56 percent of whites who wished to limit immigration; and the growing number of Republicans who say America is a Christian nation (PRRI 2018).

We should underline that Trump has never explicitly endorsed white nationalism and has on occasion distanced himself from it. But he is often accused of (or praised for) favoring it, because his Protect rhetoric quickly gave both white nationalists and believers in a Christian America a renewed sense of legitimacy and opportunity from 2016 on (Lopez Bunyasi 2019). White supremacist posts accelerated on a leading right-wing website,

4Chan, after Trump announced his candidacy (Thompson 2018). Overt white nationalists like Richard Spencer and Jared Taylor soon rallied to Trump's cause. Spencer said that though Trump was not a self-conscious white nationalist, he was expressing "an unconscious vision that white people have—that their grandchildren might be hated in their own country" (Osnos 2015). He contended that Trump was "bringing identity politics for white people into the public sphere in a way no one has" (Confessore 2016). In 2016, Andrew Anglin of the neo-Nazi website *Daily Stormer* celebrated Trump's retweeting from the WhiteGenocide account by proclaiming, "Our Glorious Leader and ULTIMATE SAVIOR has gone full-wink-wink-wink to his most aggressive supporters" (Anglin 2016). As 2016 proceeded, champions of white identity including William Johnson, the chair of the American Freedom Party, and the former Klan leader David Duke contributed robocalls and other forms of vocal support for Trump (Confessore 2016; Sides, Tesler, and Vavreck 2018). Rachel Prendergraft, an organizer for the Knights Party (a successor to the KKK), maintained that the "success of the Trump campaign just proves that our views resonate with millions. . . . They may not be ready for the Ku Klux Klan yet, but as anti-white hatred escalates, they will" (Lopez 2019). Although many white supremacists wished Trump would go still further, most celebrated his election and many became more outspoken.

Trump's Inaugural Address

If Trump's announcement speech first made the themes of his campaign clear, his brief but revealing Inaugural Address, reportedly written chiefly by Trump's most ideological aides, Stephen Bannon and Stephen Miller, gave a crystal-clear statement of the Protect alliance's conservative story (Greenwood 2017). After the customary courtesies, Trump said that his inauguration had "a very special meaning" because it represented a transfer of power, not from one party to another, but "from Washington, DC . . . to the American people." In explanation, Trump told the tale of America's recent past as one in which "a small group in our nation's Capital has reaped the rewards of government," while "the people have borne the cost. . . . The establishment protected itself, but not the citizens of our country." For too many citizens, the results of this lack of protection were poverty, failing schools, crime, drugs—in sum, "American carnage" (Trump 2017a).

But, Trump announced, "January 20, 2017, will be remembered as the day the people became the rulers of this nation again." Rejecting what he portrayed as globalist policies that served other countries more than the American people, Trump promised that from "this day forward, a new vision will govern our land. From this day forward, it's going to be only America first. America first."[6] Every "decision on trade, on taxes, on immigration, on foreign affairs, will be made to benefit American workers and American families."

His America First vision, Trump said, invoked the conviction that since "a nation exists to serve its citizens . . . it is the right of all nations to put their own nation first." "America First" was therefore a political philosophy that Trump suggested all nations could and should emulate; but its own terms meant that whether or not they did so was their choice. Americans, Trump maintained, "do not seek to impose our way of life on anyone, but rather to let it shine as an example for everyone to follow."

Though he did not refer directly to racial policies, Trump also stressed that his vision encompassed "all the citizens of America." Americans, he said, form "one nation," sharing "one heart, one home, and one glorious destiny," with "no room for prejudice." Instead, all Americans should know "that whether we are black or brown or white, we all bleed the same red blood of patriots." That meant, however, that Trump's America First philosophy did not embrace all kinds of diversity. Instead, Trump asserted, "the bedrock of our politics will be a total allegiance to the United States of America, and through our loyalty to our country, we will rediscover our loyalty to each other." Trump reminded his audience that the Bible urged "God's people" to "live together in unity," and he promised that if Americans did so, "we will always be protected," by the military, by law enforcement, and most importantly, "by God."

Though proudly and fiercely nationalist, Trump's account gave no voice to white nationalism, and only moderate expression to religious nationalism, of a sort not unusual in inaugural addresses. Even so, Trump's story of modern America's corruption by self-serving globalist elites logically implied that everything the government might see as endangering "total allegiance to the United States" could be seen as dangerously disloyal and destructive of the protection he promised. It therefore set the stage for the cultural conflicts that Trump and other conservative leaders would subsequently emphasize more and more, as they increasingly portrayed today's Left as not simply lacking "total allegiance," but as militantly anti-American.

Playing with Fire

While in his Inaugural Address Trump promised racial inclusiveness for all who pledged allegiance to his vision, once in office he regularly made inflammatory race-related statements that received wide publicity—which some believed helped to stimulate further airings of prejudice by myriad others (Williamson and Gelfand 2019). The Trump White House, to be sure, consistently denied that he claimed that immigrants from Haiti have AIDS; that Nigerians come from huts; and that America needs immigrants from Norway, not "shithole [African] countries"—though former Trump aides confirmed these stories (Lopez 2019). To admirers, Trump's criticisms of African American football players protesting police killings of young Black men, and his characterizations of MS-13 gang members as "animals," expressed only support for law and order (Hayes 2018). Some regarded even his most controversial comments—his claims that there were "some very fine people" on both sides at the Charlottesville Unite the Right white supremacy rally, and that "both sides" were to blame for the ensuing violence—as simply displaying his commitment to resisting the demonization of traditionalist Americans.

But it is incontrovertible that Trump fiercely supported Senate candidate Roy Moore in Alabama, despite Moore's stating that America had been great in the days of slavery, because "families were strong, our country had direction" (Bump 2017). Trump praised Arizona Sheriff Joe Arpaio for keeping "Arizona safe" and pardoned him after Arpaio was found guilty of criminal contempt for racially profiling persons he suspected of being illegal immigrants (Davis and Haberman 2017). In both instances Trump had partisan motives, but his actions identified him with judicial and law enforcement figures widely perceived as determined to protect whites against dangerous people of color and their white liberal allies. Trump also won white nationalist applause when he tweeted that he had instructed Secretary of State Mike Pompeo to "study the South Africa land and farm seizures . . . and the large scale killing of farmers," giving credence to false claims that the South African government was murdering white farmers (Sankin and Carless 2018). When Trump later tweeted that four first-term representatives, all women of color, two Muslim, should "go back" to the "totally broken and crime infested" countries "from which they came," even Ted Cruz demurred from his "overheated" racial and religious rhetoric (Summers 2019).

Even so, as his failure to control the public health and economic ravages of the COVID-19 crisis caused him to plummet in the polls in the summer of 2020, Trump responded by ratcheting up his Protect rhetoric, promising not new public health initiatives, but instead safety against BLM protesters and against policies that might promote suburban integration. Over the July 4, 2020, weekend, Trump promised to defeat what he termed "a new far-left fascism" that sought to destroy not just the narrative, but the symbols of "our national heritage," like statues of his hero Andrew Jackson (Trump 2020a). He called painting "Black Lives Matter" in front of Trump Tower in New York City a "symbol of hate" (Liptak and Holmes 2020). He attacked Obama-era efforts to promote low-income, racially integrated housing in America's suburbs, contending that he was protecting "the American dream" of neighborhoods free from the poor and from unwanted racial diversity (Karni, Haberman, and Ember 2021). He threatened to veto plans to remove the names of Confederate generals from military bases—plans that even most Republicans supported (Edmondson and Broadwater 2020). Again and again he sought to mobilize racial conservatism not around color-blindness, but around what most understood to be white protectionism.

When these themes did not prevent his 2020 electoral defeat, Trump shifted to calls for aggressive protests and action to protect against what he claimed was a stolen election, including his incendiary speech on January 6, 2021, to a crowd that went on to storm the Capitol. In that speech Trump urged Vice President Mike Pence to send the 2020 presidential election results back to the states for recertification, saying "(w)e're supposed to protect our country, support our country, support our Constitution, and protect our Constitution." He said the proponents of "cancel culture" were out to rename the Washington, Jefferson, and Lincoln memorials, and he railed against the media, Big Tech, and "weak Republicans" as well as "radical-left Democrats," before calling on the crowd "to fight like hell" or "you're not going to have a country anymore" (AP News 2021).

All these statements, including Trump's January 6 speech, reiterated the two great narrative themes of Trump's campaign: first, that America was great in the old days (when it was an exclusively white Christian male-governed nation); and second, that good Americans, especially Christians, now faced assaults from dangerous immigrants, foreign nations and religions, and most of all from unpatriotic, corrupt globalist American elites, against whom good traditionalist Americans must be protected. Having won power on this narrative of victimization, Trump never ceased to promote it, in governing deeds as well as campaign words (Brownstein 2019). In so doing, he not only seized near total control of the Republican Party; he also elevated protection of traditionalist Americans and America, including protection of white Americans against the impacts of "radical" Left cultural and social policies, to the center of the modern conservative racial policy alliance. Although the emergence of the Protect alliance is not simply the emergence of Donald Trump, it is unlikely that it could have become as hegemonic among conservatives as it has without his successful presidential candidacy and ensuing administration.

The Next Chapter of the Conservative Story?

Trump's narrative of America's decline and those responsible for it proved so influential that most conservative politicians came to echo it in most regards. There are nonetheless important differences among conservative intellectuals, activists, and politicians about the story's implications, about how Americans should write the next chapter of their national story, in which they will make their country great again.

The extreme right wing of the modern Protect alliance, represented by figures like Nicholas Fuentes, clearly does long for a white-governed Christian America. Though Fuentes remains too incendiary to be embraced by most Republican leaders, more candidates are emerging on the right who are also willing to suggest that protecting American national traditions requires preserving the nation's predominantly white and predominantly Christian demographic core. Newly Trump-aligned candidates in 2022 included a number of figures like congressional candidate Joe Kent, who after gingerly distancing himself from Fuentes's explicit white nationalism told the American Populist Union (since renamed America Virtue) that he nonetheless agreed that whites were the most discriminated against people in America and that he saw whites as a legitimate "interest group," though he preferred to attack the "administrative state" (M. Goldberg 2020). While it is wrong to suggest that the Protect alliance centers on white supremacists, it cannot be denied that white identity concerns are a significant and influential presence in the alliance's vision for America.

Older Claremont Institute conservatives like Charles Kesler have instead long valorized what they see as the "natural-rights individualism" of America's founders, and they largely call for a return to it, though not to the founders' practices of enslaved labor and white supremacy. To the contrary, they oppose all race-targeted public policies, and thereby might well provide a measure of protection for those advantaged by the continuing impacts of policies, institutions, and practices originally constructed to favor whites. They would, however, reject what Kesler has termed the "ethnonationalist," Fuentes-style conservatism that, to his chagrin, many young conservatives find appealing.[7] Many also oppose what Jonah Goldberg, the former editor of *National Review*, has condemned as the tendency of the most militant younger conservatives "to think that it's a sign of courage and strength to be coarse or bigoted" and to feel "an *investment* in the politics of obnoxiousness" and "conspiracy mongering" (J. Goldberg 2023).

Other leading figures like Christopher Rufo say they are developing a new "multicultural conservatism," favoring low-tax, low-regulation market economies and certain widely shared family and religious values, but otherwise embracing considerable cultural diversity, with more traditionalist East Asians, South Asians, Hispanics, and African Americans all included. Consequently, the Manhattan Institute's Reihan Salam contends that there "is definitely a contest for the future of the center right" between "an emerging right-of-center politics that is deeply pessimistic about the prospect of a diversifying America" and his own hopes for America to become a "successful multiethnic democracy" in which all voices are heard. He insists with Rufo that this "multicultural right" is much more genuinely inclusive than the woke ideologues of the Left, who instead "freeze a lot of people, including a lot of people of color, out of the conservations" (quoted in Kang 2022).

Important as these voices are, at this writing the vision for America's future that most Protect conservatives share or are coming to share appears to be "National Conservatism," as defined by the sponsors of and participants in the National Conservatism Conferences, chiefly organized beginning in 2019 by the Edmund Burke Foundation and the Conservative Partnership Institute. In 2022, the "NatCons," as they are often called, issued a National Conservatism Statement of Principles signed by an extraordinary range of leading conservatives in the United States and other nations. Shaped in part by Trump administration alums, the statement is at once a significant summary of what the Trump movement sees itself as seeking to create and a revealing indication of what may well prove to be the enduring core positions of the Protect policy alliance.

The statement's preamble proclaims: "we see a world of independent nations—each pursuing its own national interests and upholding national traditions that are its own—as the only genuine alternative to universalist ideologies now seeking to impose a homogenizing, locality-destroying imperium over the entire globe" (Edmund Burke Foundation 2023b). "National Independence" is therefore the statement's first principle, including a call for each nation to "maintain its own borders" and adopt "a policy of rearmament"—clearly Trump-style Protect positions. It then rejects both imperialism and globalism, particularly opposing "transferring the authority of elected governments to transnational or supranational bodies." Ironically, while it calls for each nation to "chart its own course in accordance with its own particular constitutional, linguistic, and religious inheritance," its principles for structuring a "national government" simply paraphrase the preamble to the US Constitution. It also endorses "the federalist principle," while cautioning that "in those states or subdivisions in which law and justice have been manifestly corrupted," the "national government must intervene energetically to restore order" (Edmund Burke Foundation 2023b).

The statement's fourth principle is especially controversial: the "Bible should be read as the first among the sources of a shared Western civilization in schools and universities." Furthermore, where "a Christian majority exists, public life should be rooted in Christianity and its moral vision, which should be honored by the state and other institutions both public and private," though "Jews and other religious minorities are to be protected in the observance of their own traditions." The statement goes on to endorse the rule of law, denouncing "rioting, looting, and other unacceptable public disorder." It also favors "free enterprise," while insisting, with Trump and with the new anti-corporate conservatives, that "the free market cannot be absolute. Economic policy must serve the general welfare of the nation," at times through protectionist measures. "Crony capitalism, the selective promotion of corporate profit-making by organs of state power, should be energetically exposed and opposed" as well.

The NatCons urge public research to aid defense and manufacturing capabilities, but they condemn "most universities" as "partisan and globalist in orientation and vehemently opposed to nationalist and conservative ideas," and argue that those higher education institutions therefore "do not deserve taxpayer support." They also want "much more restrictive" immigration policies, even a moratorium, until countries "establish more balanced, productive, and assimilationist policies." Protecting and strengthening the "traditional family, built around a lifelong bond between a man and a woman," should moreover be a priority "of the highest order"—a position obviously hostile to many LGBTQ+ rights (Edmund Burke Foundation 2023b).

Most pertinently here, the final principle of the National Conservatism Statement is that "all men are created in the image of God," so that no "person's worth or loyalties can be judged by the shape of his features, the color of his skin, or the result of a lab test. The history of racialist ideology and oppression and its ongoing consequences require us to emphasize this truth." The National Conservatives call for pervasively color-blind policies, condemning "the use of state and private institutions to discriminate and divide us against one another on the basis of race." They contend that the "nationalism we espouse respects, and indeed combines, the unique needs of particular minority communities and the common good of the nation as a whole" (Edmund Burke Foundation 2023b).

These statements show that these National Conservatives explicitly reject white nationalism, even as they oppose private as well as public diversity, equity, and inclusion initiatives as discriminatory and divisive; even as they implicitly challenge natural rights doctrines of universal individual rights; and even as they express support for at least a mild form of Christian nationalism. The signers are an impressive variety of older and new conservative voices. They include not only Yoram Hazony of the Edmund Burke Foundation and Mark Meadows and the former senator and Heritage Foundation president, Jim DeMint, of the Conservative Partnership Institute, but Kirk of Turning Point USA; Rufo of the Manhattan Institute; Swain of the Texas Public Policy Foundation; fellows of the Claremont Institute, the Hudson Institute, the Intercollegiate Studies Institute, and the Hoover Institution; and leaders of Hillsdale College and the Center for Immigration Studies, among others. Among that broad range of supporters is the formerly libertarian billionaire Peter Thiel, whose resources alone provide the National Conservatism movement with a robust financial foundation.

Emerging Struggles over National Conservatism

Impressive as those supporters are, it is important to recognize that some conservatives who support many of the same Protect policies nonetheless find the Statement of Principles objectionable (Berkowitz 2022). In August 2022, a number of conservative thought leaders, most in the UK but some in the US, signed an "Open Letter Responding to the NatCon 'Statement of Principles'" in *The European Conservative*, which had previously published the National Conservatism Statement. While applauding the Statement's "critique of destructive globalization" and "its call for the renewal of national culture and traditions," these conservatives challenged its assault on universalist ideologies, contending that "a universalist ethical, spiritual, and yes, political vision" underpinned "Western, European, and Christian civilization" (Blond et al. 2022). They refused to "uncritically embrace the nation-state as the one true political form," contending that "the natural law that is written on the heart of every man and woman in every nation" means that the "absolute sovereignty of the nation-state" must be regarded as "a modern myth" that "can lead to terror and tyranny" (Blond et al. 2022). Thus, for many conservatives who maintain belief in natural law and natural rights on the one hand, and for many Christian conservatives who urge guidance by what they believe to be divine law on the other, National Conservatism seductively offers the sovereign nation as a false idol. Some also question whether rooting American public life "in Christianity and its moral vision" is really consistent with American national traditions that largely separate church and state, or with genuine opportunities for non-Christian faiths and cultures to flourish, or indeed with Christianity itself, as Roger Williams and other Christian leaders have long understood it.

Many more libertarian economic conservatives prefer a more full-throated endorsement of free markets than the statement provides. In July 2023, a large number of such conservatives, including Jeb Bush, Jonah Goldberg, Grover Norquist, Karl Rove, George Will, and some members of the State Policy Network, joined in issuing a ten-point manifesto titled "Freedom Conservatism: A Statement of Principles" which was clearly intended to rival the National Conservatism statement (Freedom Conservatism 2023). Yet while the NatCons represent only a portion of the Protect policy alliance, it is striking that even many conservatives who have long celebrated the natural rights understandings of America's founding, like those associated with the Claremont Institute and Hillsdale College, have signed the National Conservatism Statement of Principles denouncing "universalist ideologies," as have many affiliates of institutes long associated with libertarian economic policies and more interventionist national security policies. Still more importantly for current purposes, most of the conservatives who have so far refused to endorse the statement fully share its conviction that contemporary progressive racial policies, especially as they have shifted to embrace transformative Repair goals, represent destructive dangers against which conservatives must unite to protect the country. Various conservatives may defect from the dominant positions of the Protect policy alliance in a few policy regimes—in some cases trade, in some cases immigration, in some cases religion. But when confronted by the policies of the Repair alliance, they know on which side they belong.

Both conservative proponents and opponents of the Statement of Principles acknowledge that young conservatives eager to act are far more fired up by National Conservatism, which they believe mandates strong national government actions against threatening progressive initiatives, than they are about the limited government visions that predominated among conservatives in the Reagan era, including many who signed the "Freedom Conservatism" statement. A number of our interviewees commented on the ironic fact that the contemporary Right and Left both see their own side as unduly passive, lacking in unity and self-confidence in their pursuit of their vision, while they see their opponents as strongly united and energetically militant. For many on the right, National Conservatism promises to change that. Nonetheless, for the NatCons and the Protect alliance more broadly, the most important driver of heightened activity remains their belief that unrestrained radical progressives are the ultimate source of injustice and moral corruption in America, which some fear has already gone too far to correct, at least without radical actions by the Right.

Most contemporary conservatives, to be sure, still hope that those actions can take the form of the kinds of governmental policies they see as urgently needed today, rather than vigilante violence. Their embrace of the Protect story of national decline leads them to seek to enact a great variety of policy regimes that will work to restore to American life the kinds of order that they believe should never have been lost. The "ordering" that has been and is being done by the Protect alliance includes but goes beyond the policies of the Trump administration, because supporters of Protect positions have held and continue to hold official power in many states and localities, as well as in the national government. Nonetheless, in policies as in rhetoric, the Trump administration has played the most prominent role in giving definition to the Protect agenda and gaining popular support for it. Those Protect policies are so extensive that it can be easy to fail to grasp their range and impacts, especially as America First conservatives continue to introduce new measures frequently and at virtually every level of government. In chapter 5, we seek to convey that range by providing an overview of the Protect policy agenda as it stood in 2023.

Yet important as they are, policy agendas shift with changing circumstances. This chapter has explored a subject that is in many respects more fundamental and perhaps more enduring: the story of who Americans truly are and should be, and what their core values and challenges are, that motivates the modern conservative movement. It is a story millions of Americans have clearly wanted to hear: that America at its birth and in its core was always exceptional, but now radicals are destroying it, so strong leaders must protect the nation's good people against those radicals on every front if America is even to survive, much less to be great again.

CHAPTER FIVE

The Protect Alliance at Work

Policies and Reforms

Trump was elected to protect our families from the vengeful mob that seeks to destroy our way of life, our neighborhoods, schools, churches and values. —Charlie Kirk, Turning Point USA

Donald Trump began his administration in January 2017 by providing in his Inaugural Address a succinct exposition of his America First vision and agenda, in ways that foreshadowed the National Conservatism Statement of Principles. He ended it in January 2021 with public and private incitement of his followers to take insurgent actions against the nation's elected political leaders. In between, despite the president's often erratic behavior, his administration put policy flesh on the bones of his Protect themes with a breadth and intensity that helped persuade many conservatives that resistance to progressivism in the service of national conservatism could succeed.

Conservative promises became practice.

To be sure, many of Trump's policies were not new. They were rather policies freshly and energetically implemented. In his four years in the White House, Trump came to lead and define the agenda of the modern Protect policy alliance by building on forms of conservative resentment and activism that had been rising for years to enact Protect measures across a striking range of policy regimes.

During the Trump years and since, these policies have been picked up and emulated by his GOP allies at state and local levels. Since 2020, their efforts have proliferated rapidly, especially in the areas of election law, public education, and protest regulations. Though Protect policies are very much Trump policies, they may prove to have even more significant, sustaining support from the plethora of local, state, and national officials and agencies that have made the Protect racial policy alliance very much a powerful, governing institutional order.

Yet as we specify what the new Protect policy regimes are and will be, the policies of the Trump administration are still the best place to start.

Trump Administration Actions and Policies

Once ensconced in the Oval Office, Trump pursued measures that went even further than his campaign rhetoric did to protect traditionalist, predominantly white Americans. In so doing, the Trump administration cemented the shift of racial conservatism from upholding color-blind principles to installing Protect policies. This change intersected with Trump's shift away from some older Republican economic policies, chiefly from a receptivity to immigrant labor to immigration bans, and from free trade to protectionist tariffs. Indeed, Trump's rallies often suggested that the chief audience for his economic protectionism was traditionalist white workers.

Trump implemented his Protect agenda in two ways: through his appointments of executive officials and judges, and through his executive orders and the policies of the agencies his appointees led. At the national level, both transformed the Protect policy alliance into a Protect institutional order.

Appointments

Despite unprecedented turnover among Trump's appointees due to legal troubles, other scandals, or perceived disloyalty to the president, Trump consistently appointed opponents of policies of aid for communities of color to key positions within cabinet agencies and the federal judiciary. His first attorney general, Jefferson Sessions, had previously used his position as Alabama's attorney general to defend that state's post-*Brown* de facto segregated education system (Sugrue 2016). Prior to that, Sessions frequently criticized the NAACP and the Southern Christian Leadership Conference as "Communist-inspired," and he went on to denounce affirmative action and to sound alarms about vote fraud, without evidence of any such fraud (Sugrue 2016; Levine 2016). In a 2015 interview with Stephen Bannon, Sessions also praised the race-based national origins quota system the nation adopted in 1924 and ended in 1965 (Serwer 2017). Though Trump fired Sessions for refusing to stop the FBI investigation into Russian interference with the 2016 election, and Sessions's successor as attorney general, William Barr, also eventually broke with Trump, in office Barr echoed his predecessor's condemnations of older civil rights groups by calling the Black Lives Matter movement "Bolsheviks" with "fascistic" tactics and accusing one of its members of "treason" (Miller 2020; Peiser 2020).

Steve Bannon himself was only briefly a Trump White House speechwriter and adviser, but he thereafter continued to be a Trump consultant and confidant. Like the former president, he professes to be anti-globalist but not a white nationalist. Even so, in his earlier stint as chief executive of Breitbart News Bannon oversaw frequent publication of white nationalist writers (Smith 2017). By fall 2023, though he was facing a sentence of four months in prison for contempt of Congress after he refused to appear before the committee investigating the January 6 insurrection, and while he was confronting other legal troubles for alleged financial fraud, Bannon continued to maintain an outsize presence in US politics by hosting a radio program, "War Room." There he and his guests championed Protect themes, both for the US and for other nations (Lowell 2022a). Bannon also sought with limited success to create a Brussels-based group, "The Movement," to mobilize European nationalists, and he went on to deny the legitimacy of the 2022 Brazil election and to cheer the Bolsonaro supporters who stormed the governmental buildings in Brasilia (Nguyen 2019; Palmer 2023). In office and out, in the US and abroad, Bannon relentlessly pressed for a militant Protect agenda.

Trump's African American secretary of Housing and Urban Development, Ben Carson, an indefatigable proponent of neoliberal economic policies, opposed a range of affordable housing and antidiscrimination fair housing initiatives, despite having benefited from public housing when he was growing up (Andrews 2020). Under Carson, HUD added Eric Blankenstein to its general counsel's office, even though Blankenstein had previously been compelled to leave the Consumer Financial Protection Bureau after racist blogs he authored years before surfaced—blogs he dismissed as irrelevant to his duties (Fadula and Thrush 2019).

Among all of Trump's appointees, no figure was more important in shaping the administration's Protect policy regimes, including on immigration and a range of related issues, than Stephen Miller, now co-founder of America First Legal. Miller has a long history of denouncing immigrants, and leaks of Miller's emails in the years immediately preceding his joining the Trump campaign show that like Bannon, Miller often publicized white nationalist views. These revelations draw sharp criticisms, but not from

Donald Trump (Holpuch 2019; Garcia-Navarro 2019; Rogers and DeParle 2019). In office, Miller was an insistent voice for an extraordinary range of severe immigration restriction measures, including the "Muslim ban" and, most notoriously, family separations (Rogers and DeParle 2019; *Hatewatch* Staff 2018). Due in no small part to Miller's advocacy, the Trump administration eventually implemented over four hundred changes to the US immigration system, drastically reducing quotas for refugees, posing new barriers to naturalization, heightening deportations with limited due process, especially during the pandemic, and more (Fox 2020; Anderson 2020; Guttentag and Bertozzi 2020).

Although most Trump-appointed judges' responses to his evidence-free challenges to the 2020 election disappointed him, on balance Trump's large number of judicial appointments have advanced Protect alliance goals across many policy regimes, including religion, abortion, immigration, election law, policing, and regulatory and economic issues. Trump-appointed judges have thereby bolstered the establishment of a potent Protect institutional order that encompasses all three branches of the federal government, not simply numerous executive agency appointees and legislative allies. These judicial appointments, abetted by the ruthless legislative maneuvering of Senator Majority Leader Mitch McConnell, are as significant as Trump's appointments to the White House staff and executive agencies—indeed, given their endurance beyond the Trump years, probably more so. Though in his first two years Joe Biden would exceed his predecessor's pace in making appointments at the lower federal court levels, in his one term Trump appointed nearly the same number of appellate judges (54) as Obama did in two (55), and he appointed 226 federal judges overall (Gramlich 2021). He flipped three circuit courts (the 2nd, 3rd, and 11th) to majority Republican appointees, and made Republican appointees a majority of all circuit court judges (Wheeler 2020, 2021; Itkowitz 2019).

Trump also, of course, far surpassed what Biden would be able to do by appointing three Supreme Court justices, creating a super-majority on an already conservative high bench that quickly swung sharply and aggressively further to the right (Thomson-Deveaux and Bronner 2022). Over two-thirds of Trump judicial appointees were white men, and 84 percent were white (Ruiz et al. 2020; Chemerinsky 2021). Trump appointed only one Latina appellate court judge, and remarkably, not a single Black judge (Gramlich 2021; Johnson 2020). Many of Trump's judicial nominees had questionable credentials: three nominees deemed unqualified by the ABA won confirmation for the first time since the 1970s (Ruiz et al. 2020). Most of these appointees went on to vote frequently in favor of strongly conservative rulings on Protect policies (Ruiz et al. 2020; Sherman, Freking, and Daly 2020; Hurley 2021).

The judicial reticence of many Trump-appointed judges to deny the validity of the 2020 vote was not shared by GOP election hopefuls post-Trump. By the midterm elections in November 2022, a majority of Republican candidates on the ballot for Senate, House, and statewide offices had either challenged or outright denied the result of the November 2020 presidential election. Such candidates ran in every state and every region of the United States, and in four states voters had a full slate of election deniers as their GOP candidates. The *Washington Post* analysis calculated that of the 299 election deniers, 174 were candidates in safely Republican seats (Gardner 2022). Although on the whole election denier stances proved detrimental in the midterm elections, especially in battleground states, in the nation's many Red regions a large proportion did win, placing Protect partisans in charge of many local and state as well as national legislative, administrative, and judicial institutions (Blake 2022).

Policy Regimes

As shown in table 5.1, Trump and his executive and judicial appointees were by no means evenhanded in whom they sought to protect, just as the conservative story would lead one to expect. They ratcheted up conservative efforts to end affirmative action, a central, never-attained goal of the color-blind policy alliance. Still more strikingly, they weakened antidiscrimination civil rights policies that many color-blind proponents had professed to support and had sometimes helped to create. Most centrally, they promoted immigration, naturalization, and voting and election policy regimes that operated to keep the "white demographic" predominant, both in the American citizenry and in American elections. At the same time, the Trump administration, despite occasionally promising to do otherwise, cut back on efforts to monitor white nationalist groups for terrorist violence and other criminal activities, even as the FBI reported that such activities were on the rise.

With only very limited exceptions, the Trump positions summarized in table 5.1 include all the major racial policies as well as most of the initiatives in other policy regimes preferred by most conservatives, particularly those policies that serve Protect goals. In many cases, administration actions went beyond what Trump said in the campaign or his later proclamations of his achievements in office. Throughout, Trump's officials offered

TABLE 5.1 **Trump Administration Protect Policies**

Affirmative Action

Justice Department initiated investigations of affirmative action policies at Harvard, Yale, and other universities (Savage 2017); sided with litigants challenging Harvard's affirmative action program (Alexander 2018). The Supreme Court ruled against affirmative action in 2023 (Gersen 2023).

Departments of Education and Justice issued joint letter to universities rescinding seven Obama affirmative action guidelines for advocating "policy preferences and positions beyond the requirements of the Constitution" (Green, Apuzzo, and Benner 2018).

Administration challenged constitutionality of HBCU Capital Investment Fund & reduced support for low-income students, even while extending overall funding for HBCUs (Camera 2019).

Civil Rights Enforcement

Justice Department prioritized religious freedom over other civil rights (Sessions 2018).

Equal Employment Opportunity Commission ended the rule requiring companies to report employee pay by sex, race, and ethnicity to identify discriminatory pay patterns (Mann 2017).

Consumer Financial Protection Bureau's Office of Fair Lending and Equal Opportunity lost enforcement powers against discrimination in lending, reduced lenders' reporting requirements (Berry 2018; McCaskill 2020).

Funding cut for investigations of white nationalist groups; FBI investigations of white nationalists reduced despite increases in white supremacist crimes (Beinart 2018; Einbinder 2019).

Education Department delayed Individuals with Disabilities Education Act rule limiting disproportionate treatment of minority students with disabilities (Office of Special Education and Rehabilitative Services 2018).

Veterans Affairs diversity officer told not to condemn white nationalists (Rein 2018).

Justice Department held 1964 Civil Rights Act does not protect against workplace discrimination against transgender persons (Supreme Court disagreed) (Moreau 2018).

Justice Department sought to restrict enforcement of Title VI of the 1964 Civil Rights Act to intentional discrimination, not racially disparate impacts in housing, employment, education, health care, and other programs (Benner and Green 2021).

Cultural Conflicts

President banned racial sensitivity training, including Critical Race Theory, for federal government employees, the US military, federal contractors, and federal grant recipients (Guzman 2020).

Created 1776 Commission to provide guidelines for patriotic education countering the *New York Times*'s 1619 Project and Critical Race Theory (Autry 2021).

President vetoed bipartisan bill to rename military bases now named for Confederate leaders (Congress overrode veto) (Edmondson and Broadwater 2020; Daly 2021).

President engaged in federal, state, and local struggles over monuments and statues (Burch 2022).

Immigration

President imposed travel ban on predominantly Muslim nations (Gladstone and Sugiyama 2018).

President shut down government, transferred funds to try to construct wall using emergency powers (Paletta, DeBonis, and Wagner 2019; Fox 2020; Weissert and Woodward 2020).

Imposed new fees, other requirements on asylum seekers (Sacchetti, Sonmez, and Miroff 2019).

(*continued*)

TABLE 5.1 *(continued)*

Immigration

Cut Obama refugee ceiling from 110,000 to 18,000, contributing to 49 percent reduction in legal immigration in Trump years due to presidential proclamations, not new laws (Anderson 2020).

Imposed case quotas for immigration judges to facilitate deportations (Sacchetti 2017).

Pardoned former Arizona Sheriff Joe Arpaio (Davis and Haberman 2017).

Rescinded DACA program (National Immigration Law Center 2019).

Curbed grants to sanctuary cities, with threats of further sanctions (Leadership Conference on Civil and Human Rights n.d.).

Terminated Temporary Protected Status for Nicaraguans, Haitians, Salvadorans, Nepalese, and Hondurans in the US (Leadership Conference on Civil and Human Rights n.d.).

Terminated eligibility of Haitians for H2-A and H2-B visas (Torbati 2018).

Increased denial rate for H1-B, high-skill visas from 5 percent to 30 percent (Anderson 2020).

Deported H1-B visa holders laid off during the pandemic (Jordan 2020).

Created a Denaturalization Section in the Justice Department to increase denaturalizations of immigrants even in cases of clerical errors (Benner 2020).

Increased denials of military naturalizations from 7 percent in 2016 to 17 percent in 2019 and increased fees by 80 percent for all naturalizations (Anderson 2020).

Deployed military troops to prevent immigrant caravans (Gutierrez 2018).

Used the pandemic to heighten deportations, including children, with very limited due process (Guttentag and Bertozzi 2020).

Voting

Created unsuccessful commission to find evidence of vote fraud (Ingraham 2016).

Justice Department supported state efforts to enforce tougher voter ID requirements (Public Interest Legal Foundation 2018a).

Justice Department supported Ohio's registration roll-clearing law; sued Kentucky to compel it to purge its rolls (Liptak 2018; Sanders 2018).

Proposed new citizenship question on census, risking accuracy, through procedures Supreme Court deemed improper (Public Interest Legal Foundation 2018b).

Trump-appointed Supreme Court justices provided the majority upholding Arizona voting restrictions and weakening enforcement of Section 2 of the 1965 Voting Rights Act against other new state restrictions (Levine 2021).

Made extensive claims about "voting stealing" and fraudulent balloting in 2020 presidential election, though none were upheld in court (Holmes 2023).

Administration supported state and local conservative reforms to election rules, ID requirements, and eligibility (Brennan Center for Justice 2021b).

Policing

Justice Department sought to reverse consent decrees reforming practices of twenty city police departments (Bosman and Smith 2017).

Attorney general curbed further use of reformist consent decrees (Benner 2018; Ray and Gilbert 2020).

Attorney general ended ban on transfer of military equipment to police forces (Viswanatha 2017).

Policing

Justice Department stopped new investigations into police shootings (Lowery 2018).

Justice Department's Civil Rights Division's Special Litigation Section, responsible for police investigations, downsized (Reilly 2019).

President expressed support for stop-and-frisk by police in US cities (Rucker 2018).

Office of the Community Oriented Policing Services (COPS) closed (Reilly 2019).

President sent federal armed forces into cities to combat protests against police violence (Smith 2020).

President signed bipartisan First Step Act, based on bill by Democratic Senator Cory Booker, providing sentencing relief, rehabilitation programs to reduce mass incarceration (Trump 2019; Ray and Gilbert 2020).

President engaged in state and local defunding battles (Gittelson 2020).

Housing

Justice Department and HUD stopped Fair Housing Act disparate impact suits (Arpey 2017).

HUD proposed rule change to preclude disparate impact review (Furman Center 2019).

HUD suspended Obama-era "Affirmatively Furthering Fair Housing" rules promoting remedies to barriers to housing choice (Arpey 2017; Furman Center 2018).

HUD suspended programs varying rent subsidies with regional wealth (Hall 2017).

Schools

Education Department created grant program to promote private school vouchers (Strauss, Douglas-Gabriel, and Balingit 2018).

Justice Department limited federal monitoring of integration plans and urged releases from court desegregation orders (Hannah-Jones 2017; Felton 2017).

Justice Department and Education Department revoked Obama-era guidance for promoting diversity in public school student populations (Anderson and Balingit 2018).

Education Department revoked guide for reducing racial biases in school discipline (Ujifusa 2018).

Education Department rescinded guides for addressing campus sexual misconduct and protecting transgender students, students with disabilities (Bayer 2017).

Economic Aid

Proposed work requirements for Medicaid and SNAP program recipients, with some exemptions for primarily rural white counties (Covert 2018).

Executive order imposed other new work requirements, called for developing more (Andrews 2018).

FCC sought to limit providing phone and internet to low-income and tribal areas (Morris 2018).

Trump Small Business Administration "Pay Protection Plan" denied funding to over 90 percent of Black-owned business applicants during the COVID-19 pandemic (Ray and Gilbert 2020).

Proposed two-page "Platinum Plan" to provide access to capital to Black businesses, churches, and communities in September 2020, but after election did not include plan in final measures (Donald J. Trump for President 2020).

invigorated defenses and accommodations for anxious and angry members of his base, especially native-born white Christian Americans. Voters and activists who cared most about these policies surely took note. Those who hoped not just for color-blindness but for policies that would bolster the position of traditionalist Americans, especially whites, against unwanted changes had ample reason to feel satisfied.

AFFIRMATIVE ACTION

A closer look at the policy regimes listed in table 5.1 shows why. Though Trump did not campaign against affirmative action programs, his Justice Department's Civil Rights Division soon prepared an initiative to sue universities suspected of emphasizing race in their admissions policies, including Harvard and Yale (Savage 2017). Attorney General Sessions assisted the longtime affirmative action critic Edward Blum in marshaling a lawsuit against Harvard's program (Alexander 2018). Though Harvard won at the district court level, Blum appealed to the Supreme Court, confident of a favorable reception from its Trump-tilted bench (Hartocollis 2019). In June 2023, his efforts were rewarded when the Court overturned the affirmative action admissions policies at Harvard and the University of North Carolina (Gersen 2023). Blum and others now have their sights set on the use of affirmative action-style programs in the corporate world, including law firms (Francis and Weber 2023; Mark and Tan 2023; Miller 2023). Similarly, Kenneth Marcus, after 2018 the head of civil rights enforcement in the Department of Education, previously worked with groups filing briefs against affirmative action (Green, Apuzzo, and Benner 2018; Chen 2018). Both the Justice Department and the Education Department under Trump rescinded Obama-era guidelines for legally achieving greater diversity and prodded educational institutions to abolish many such policies. The Trump administration briefly challenged the constitutionality of the HBCU Capital Initiative Fund, before deciding to extend funding for HBCUs for ten years while reducing funding for low-income students at all higher education institutions (Camera 2019). Though many leaders of HBCUs celebrated the funding guarantees, the policies were consistent with the administration's refusal to pursue racial integration goals.

CIVIL RIGHTS ENFORCEMENT

In civil rights enforcement more generally, the Trump administration's stance mirrored Trump's campaign theme that religious Americans, especially traditionalists who are predominantly white, are the greatest victims of discrimination today. Attorney General Sessions made mistreatment of religious groups the Justice Department's highest priority. The DOJ provided guidelines for all executive agencies to insure they did not violate "religious liberty protections"; forcefully pursued litigation on behalf of religious groups; and created a Religious Liberty Task Force, so that "our employees know their duties to accommodate people of faith" (Sessions 2018). A "Conscience and Religious Freedom Division" in the Office of Civil Rights sought to permit health care providers to refuse treatment to certain patients on religious grounds (Leadership Conference on Civil and Human Rights 2023). Attorney General William Barr continued Sessions's prioritization of religious liberty, contending that "secularists" had been using law "as a battering ram" in "an unremitting assault on religion and traditional values" in multiple ways that the Justice Department was "ready to fight" (Barr 2019).

This agenda did not always succeed. Though Trump boasted that he ended the Johnson Amendment by executive order, in fact the legislative ban on endorsing candidates remained. The Trump administration mobilized religious leaders to get Congress to overturn the law, but was unsuccessful (Dias 2017). Religious conservatives cheered when Trump's Justice Department urged the Supreme Court to rule that the Civil Rights Act does not protect transgender persons (Moreau 2018). Trump-nominated Justice Neil Gorsuch disappointed them on that issue when writing for the Court in *Bostock v. Clayton County* in 2020. Nonetheless, in many other cases Gorsuch, Brett Kavanaugh, and Amy Coney Barrett have proven eager to support claims that the religious liberties of conservative Christians face abuse, as well as other Protect priorities (Weber 2019; Salozar 2019; Biskupic 2021).

The Trump administration also ended federal grants to groups working to oppose white nationalism (Raymond 2017; Beinart 2018). Although Trump announced that monitoring of anti-white nationalists would increase after a white supremacist perpetrated shootings in El Paso, Texas, in fact it continued to decline (Einbinder 2019). Instead the Trump administration made domestic anti-terrorism efforts on Muslim groups its main focus, even though most analysts accept that white supremacists committed more than three times as many violent crimes and murders in the US as Muslims did during the Trump years (Reitman 2018). A Veterans Administration official even discouraged the agency's diversity officer from condemning white nationalists (Desjardins 2017).

Trump officials eliminated an Equal Employment Opportunity Commission requirement for large companies to disaggregate employee pay scales by sex, race, and ethnicity, hampering antidiscrimination efforts, though a federal court overturned that action and the Biden administration restored the Obama-era standard (Schmidt 2019; Smith and LaBrecque 2021). Other Trump appointees cut back on the enforcement authority of the Consumer Financial Protection Bureau's Office of Fair Lending and Equal Opportunity and delayed the implementation of a rule to protect racial and ethnic minority students with disabilities against denials of loans and employment disproportionate to the treatment of similarly disabled white applicants. At the very close of the Trump administration, the Justice Department sought to end all enforcement of rules focused on racially and ethnically disparate impacts in every area covered by the 1964 Civil Rights Act and its amendments, including employment, education, housing, health care, and more (Benner and Green 2021). The Trump administration did not eliminate the offices of civil rights created in most federal agencies in the late 1960s, which monitor hiring, promotions, and discrimination among employees. However, it shifted authority in these offices from career civil service employees to political appointees, changing the ethos of enforcement (Savage 2017).

CULTURE WAR

As his term proceeded, Donald Trump accompanied his almost incessant rhetorical heightening of "culture war" conflicts with some controversial actions. After watching the Fox News interview in which Christopher Rufo attacked diversity training, Trump acted with alacrity.

He issued two bans on all "racial sensitivity" training for federal employees, including all serving in the US military, as well as in the activities of federal grant recipients and federal contractors. He called all such training using concepts like "white privilege" and Critical Race Theory forms of "divisive, anti-American propaganda" (Schwartz 2020). On January 20, 2021, Joe Biden rescinded those bans (Williams 2021). Conservative Republicans in Congress, however, continue to propose bills to curb diversity training in federal programs as well as any teaching of Critical Race Theory (Iati 2021; Stein 2021; Sprunt 2021).

In November of 2020, Trump took a further step to counter what he termed "a radicalized view of American history" that "vilified our Founders and our founding," views he associated with both Critical Race Theory and the *New York Times*'s 1619 Project, which stressed the importance of slavery in shaping American development (Autry 2021). The president created a 1776 Commission that quickly prepared a report on how to provide a superior "patriotic education" stressing the nation's founding commitments to natural rights, liberty, and limited government (Trump 2020b; President's Advisory 1776 Commission 2021). The Commission presented a traditionalist narrative of American political development but began with the 1770s, ignoring the seventeenth- and most of the eighteenth-century establishment and expansion of white settler colonies on the lands of Indigenous tribes. Its account of civil rights recognized the evils of both slavery and the invidious post-Reconstruction segregationist regime, and it celebrated the triumph of the Martin Luther King-led reforms in the 1960s. But the authors then turned their ire to contemporary "identity politics," ascribed—in harmony with conservative accounts discussed in chapter 4—to a corruption of the civil rights laws in the same decade. The Report contended:

> The Civil Rights Movement was almost immediately turned to programs that ran counter to the lofty ideals of the founders. The ideas that drove this change had been growing in America for decades, and they distorted many areas of policy in the half century that followed. Among the distortions was the abandonment of nondiscrimination and equal opportunity in favor of "group rights" not unlike those advanced by Calhoun and his followers. The justification for reversing the promise of color-blind civil rights was that past discrimination requires present effort, or affirmative action in the form of preferential treatment, to overcome long-accrued inequalities. Those forms of preferential treatment built up in our system over time, first in administrative rulings, then executive orders, later in congressionally passed law, and finally were sanctified by the Supreme Court.... Identity politics makes it less likely that racial reconciliation and healing can be attained by pursuing Martin Luther King, Jr.'s dream for America and upholding the highest ideals of our Constitution and our Declaration of Independence. (President's Advisory 1776 Commission 2021, 15–16)

Again, immediately upon taking office, President Joe Biden ended the Commission and ceased distribution of its report, confirming to many conservatives that the new administration was captive to the radical Left progressive agenda (Somvichian-Clausen 2021).

In December 2020, Trump fulfilled a campaign promise by vetoing the National Defense Authorization Act because it included an amendment, passed with bipartisan support, to set up a commission to consider the renaming of military bases honoring Confederate leaders (Edmondson and Broadwater 2020). Trump insisted that renaming those bases would dishonor those who had served on them, and he linked the bill to efforts to take down statues and change place names honoring a wide range of other American historic figures. Congress overrode his veto in January 2021 (Reuters 2021). However, both the 1776 Commission and the base naming veto fueled passionate activism by the Protect policy alliance in the wake of Trump's defeat.

As we have seen, Critical Race Theory agitations especially gained fervent local and state attention. Numerous conservative advocacy organizations, local, state, and national, joined with conservative media coverage to help get parents and school boards to organize against what they portrayed as divisive, race-inflaming, anti-American teaching in the public schools. In sounding the charge against CRT, Christopher Rufo acknowledged intentionally using the term broadly to refer not just to a specific set of legal academic writings but to "woke" instruction more generally (Wallace-Wells 2021). In 2021, Fox News mentioned Critical Race Theory 1,300 times in the first four months, and the messages of Rufo, Fox, and many other leading conservative voices began to influence state and local policies and legislation (Ray and Gibbons 2021).

In part because the Repair policy alliance is in fact potent in public education, there are strong countercurrents. In 2020 and 2021, seventeen states initiated programs to include anti-racist historical narratives in their schools, with Connecticut mandating the inclusion of African American and Latino American history, and Illinois including Asian American history. Yet in contrast, in those years, twenty-six states introduced measures restricting such topics, a number that rose to forty-four by early 2023 (Lepore 2022; Schwartz 2023). Of the eighteen states that had by then enacted constraints on teaching "divisive concepts," most acted via legislation, though some state boards of education took action (Headley 2021; Lepore 2022). Arkansas's ban did not go far enough for the state's new governor, Sarah Huckabee Sanders, Trump's former press spokesperson. On her first day in office in January 2023, she issued an executive order explicitly banning Critical Race Theory in public schools (Pandolfo 2023).

Though many of the new restrictive laws did not specifically mention Critical Race Theory, they did ban teaching that the United States is a systemically racist country, or that unconscious bias may result in discriminatory behavior, or that whites have reasons for guilt and that people of color face enormous obstacles to achieving success in America, among other concepts. The movement has not been uniformly successful. An Arizona court overturned that state's law on technical grounds of containing too many issues within one bill, and legislation in many other states stalled.

Still, through 2023, conservative groups remained confident they were winning over American voters by promising to protect their children against what they judged to be false, malignant teachings about their nation.

Most felt vindicated by the November 2021 elections, in which opponents of Critical Race Theory won school board elections even in Biden-leaning suburban districts like Montgomery County, outside of Philadelphia. The 1776 Project Political Action Committee, formed in the wake of the demise of Trump's 1776 Commission, claimed to have won 75 percent of the school board races in which its candidates competed (Hutchinson 2021). In our interviews, many progressive activists acknowledged that they had not seen the furor over Critical Race Theory coming and had never prepared to compete in school board elections. The success of the Protect conservatives also came in part from parents' anger over the failure of many public schools to cope well with the COVID-19 crisis and the challenges it posed for conducting classes. Even so, as Glenn Youngkin's victory in Virginia showed, conservatives appeared to be succeeding in presenting both Critical Race Theory and the schools' pandemic struggles as similarly destructive products of progressive activism that overrode parental rights and endangered their children.

School board elections in the spring of 2023 in Wisconsin and Illinois, however, produced different results. Having learned from their recent defeats, Democrats and teachers' unions focused much more on these local contests, and they boasted that they "trounced" cultural conservatives in many places. Conservative education groups did not dispute that their candidates had losing records in the spring contests, but many remained confident that they would perform better in subsequent school board elections (Perez 2023).

Conservative Republicans aligned with Trump then turned to reducing public university autonomy. Florida's Ron DeSantis approved laws to require annual "viewpoint diversity surveys" from faculty and students to determine whether conservatives were adequately represented and fairly treated, along with measures to weaken tenure and shift the state's universities out of some national accreditation frameworks. He also appointed Christopher Rufo and Matthew Spalding, a dean at Hillsdale College, along with four others as trustees of the thirteen-member board of the New College, a respected Florida institution with progressive traditions, to transform it into a public Hillsdale, featuring a "patriotic education" (M. Goldberg 2023). Another DeSantis law, the "Stop the Wrongs to Our Kids and Employees" or "Stop WOKE Act," imposes rules for both schools and universities about the content of teachings on race and identity. In November of 2022, its implementation was temporarily stayed by a court order (Migdon 2022). Nonetheless, higher education faculty in Florida canceled courses that they feared would jeopardize their employment and careers (Golden 2023). At this writing, Texas and Tennessee have comparable draft bills to reform universities under review, and Tennessee also has laws planned to prohibit books about racism and sexuality in schools (Kasakove 2022).

In many other parts of the country, the new laws restricting what teachers can teach, along with pressures from conservative groups who must be seen as members of the Protect policy alliance, have similarly resulted in banning books from school libraries and public libraries. Tracking book bans from the summer of 2021, the free speech organization PEN America had identified more than four thousand instances of books being removed from libraries by spring 2023. Other groups such as the American Library Association had like findings. The banned books were often by and about LGBTQ+ people and people of color, portrayed in ways that conservatives deemed threatening to traditionalist Americans (Alter 2023).

IMMIGRATION POLICY

The Trump administration's immigration policies signaled a key Protect theme: working to limit the growth of the nation's non-white population. Against both Democrats and some libertarian conservatives who broke from the Protect alliance in this policy regime, Trump fervently pressed to build a wall along the nation's southern border, even if this effort required shutting down the government or making disputable constitutional claims to emergency powers. That quest had limited success, and litigation stalled Trump's effort to rescind the DACA program benefiting some unauthorized immigrant children—though in July 2021 a Texas district court judge held that the Obama administration had created the program without proper procedures (National Immigration Law Center 2019; Garcia and Healey 2021). In October 2022 a Circuit Court of Appeals panel agreed, though it allowed the program to persist pending further litigation (García 2022).

Trump did arrive at a judicially acceptable executive order restricting travel to the US by citizens of six predominantly Muslim nations. His administration also terminated temporary protected status for persons from four Central American nations as well as Nepal, and it ended the eligibility of Haitians for H2-A and H2-B visas, used primarily by low-skilled workers, while increasing denials of H1-B visas for high-skilled workers sixfold and increasing their deportations when they lost jobs during the COVID-19 pandemic (Anderson 2020; Jordan 2020). Singularly unreceptive to refugees requesting asylum, the administration collapsed the ceiling for their admission from 110,000 to 18,000. Collectively its measures resulted in a nearly 50 percent reduction in legal, not simply unauthorized, immigration during the Trump years (Anderson 2020).

Trump also deployed 5,200 military troops to the southern border, and Stephen Miller reportedly sought during the pandemic to have 250,000 troops sent there—more than half of the active US Army forces (Sanger, Shear, and Schmitt 2021). Trump's Justice Department also created a Denaturalization Section to facilitate withdrawal of naturalizations from foreign-born Americans, even in cases of minor errors or misstatements in naturalization documents (Benner 2020). These measures all signaled that most Hispanic and Muslim immigrants were not welcome in Trump's America.

POLICING

Along with immigration, policing is the policy regime that most clearly invokes Trump's promises of protection for Americans portrayed as victims of violence. Here, too, the administration's policies made even clearer than Trump's rhetoric did just who was to be protected. Attorney General Sessions first ordered a sweeping review of federal studies of twenty city police departments' practices, hoping to reverse court-ordered consent decrees designed to limit racially discriminatory police abuses (Bosman and Smith 2017). Sessions also declined to open new investigations into police misconduct, despite continued police shootings of Black people (Lowery 2018). He restored the transferal of surplus military equipment to local police forces, enabling them to create paramilitary units, as in Ferguson, Missouri (Viswanatha 2017). On his last day in office, Sessions issued a memo to prevent the Justice Department from using consent decrees to reform local police misconduct (Benner 2018). When the police killing of George Floyd and violence against other African Americans sparked protests in the summer of 2020, Trump responded by ordering a variety of armed federal agents into cities, often against the wishes of city officials because tensions between protesters and counterprotesters then frequently escalated (Smith 2020).

Following persuasion by Kim Kardashian and Kanye West, and faced by overwhelming bipartisan support that included both the ACLU and the Koch brothers, Trump did endorse and sign the First Step Act (Bennett

2018). Based in part on a bill originally introduced by Democratic Senator Cory Booker, it gave sentencing relief for elderly inmates and those who received mandatory minimum sentences, and authorized rehabilitation programs. In 2020 Trump repeatedly cited it, along with historically low African American unemployment, as evidence of his commitment to aiding all Americans (Camera 2019; Trump 2019). After it failed to generate the African American votes he hoped to gain in the 2020 election, however, Trump ceased to discuss it, and in the 2022 midterm campaign leading Republicans denounced the reform (McGraw 2022). In all other regards, Trump himself never retreated from his "tough on crime" rhetoric, which included urging police to use stop-and-frisk tactics, often deployed in racially discriminatory ways (Rucker 2018). His message was that police should have greater freedom and greater weaponry to engage in the most controversial forms of policing.

Although in the immediate wake of George Floyd's death many Republicans initially supported local laws to restrict police uses of forces like chokeholds, most conservatives soon swung over to resistance to police reforms, especially efforts to shift responsibilities and funding from police forces to social service and health agencies. Missouri, Florida, Georgia, and Texas passed laws making it easier for dissident officials and citizens to sue their city governments for cutting police funding (Beaumont 2021). Texas, Iowa, Arizona, Wisconsin, and other states considered proposals to cut state funding for any cities that reduced their police budgets (Crampton 2021). Often the proponents of preserving police funding insisted that strong police forces were necessary to protect against the violence of radical Left protesters and activists, as well as against progressive policies that indulged and therefore encouraged criminal behavior. Federal reforms to policing also stalled. For many Republicans and also Democrats the issue has reverted to increasing funding for police forces, not any form of defunding (McWhirter 2022). Indeed, President Biden's proposed budget for 2023 included a marked uptick in funding to fight violent crime, a central priority of Biden's when he was in the Senate (Downey 2022).

HOUSING

Trump's appointment of Ben Carson as secretary of Housing and Urban Development placed in his cabinet a prominent example of the Americans of color who join the Protect policy alliance because of their belief in traditional American economic and social values and their confidence that anti-Black discrimination has declined. Under Trump and Carson, HUD moved swiftly to end Obama-era efforts to promote racial integration in housing, and to reduce public housing services more generally. The Justice Department and HUD made clear they would no longer file disparate impact suits to advance the Fair Housing Act's aim of fighting racial discrimination (Arpey 2017). HUD went further in 2019, proposing rules that would make it difficult if not impossible for regulators to find violations based simply on demonstrated disparate impact without evidence of intentional discrimination (Vadum 2019). Carson's incumbency at HUD targeted reversal of the Obama "Affirmatively Furthering Fair Housing" rule. This measure required localities to evaluate obstacles, including racial barriers, to housing choice in their jurisdiction, and to specify remedies as a condition of receiving federal funds. HUD suspended the rule in 2018 (Arpey 2017; Furman Center 2018). The upshot of these initiatives was to turn the agency away from the pursuit of racially integrated housing and housing aid to the poor.

EDUCATION

Before and continuing through the culture war over CRT in public education, most modern conservatives have sought to find ways to use public funds to finance schools that conservatives and religious traditionalists can administer, whether charter schools or private schools. Often they contend that these initiatives benefit children of color who are ill-served by underfunded public schools, even as they propose diverting funding from those schools. In his 2016 campaign Trump championed vouchers for school choice as central to his civil rights agenda, though most leading civil rights groups oppose them. He made Betsy DeVos, a prominent proponent of school choice, private schools and weaker federal regulation, his secretary of education. His Education Department then created a grant program to promote vouchers. It rescinded guidance documents designed to prevent racial biases in school discipline, campus sexual misconduct, and discrimination against transgender students and students with disabilities. The Trump Justice Department simultaneously rescinded Obama-era guidelines for how public school districts could permissibly promote diverse student populations in their school, and it cut back on efforts to continue court-ordered school desegregation (Anderson and Balingit 2018).

SOCIAL WELFARE

Scholars have argued for decades that racial conservatism, along with economic conservatism, is strongly associated with opposition to social welfare programs, some of which are seen as chiefly benefiting poor people of color (Gilens 1999). Here too the Trump administration sought to satisfy its base. It promoted state and national work requirements for benefits including Medicaid and SNAP, with some exemptions for areas predominantly populated by rural whites (Covert 2018). Its Federal Communications Commission sought to limit Lifeline, a program that assists low-income people, often people of color and disabled persons, in obtaining phone and internet service. Lifeline has been vital for many tribal lands (Morris 2018).

The pandemic crisis compelled the Trump administration and Congress to support major economic relief bills, including the $2 trillion CARES Act in March 2020 and a $900 billion aid package in December 2020, passed over Trump's objections (Gonyea 2020). Much of that spending, however, went to white Americans. In particular, the Small Business Administration's "Pay Protection Plan" turned down over 90 percent of the applications for aid coming from Black-owned businesses (Ray and Gilbert 2020). Late in the 2020 campaign, Trump tried to gain Black support by issuing a two-page set of bullet points called the $500 billion "Platinum Plan," promising capital assistance to Black businesses, churches, and communities (Donald J. Trump for President 2020). Yet unlike Trump's December 2020 veto of the Defense Authorization Act to prevent removing Confederate military base names, or his Justice Department's last-gasp effort in January 2021 to end all governmental actions to address racially disparate harms, Trump never tried to implement his Platinum Plan promises after losing the November 2020 election.

VOTING RIGHTS AND ELECTION SYSTEMS

Similarly, Trump's message of protection for some shaped his policies on voting rights. Trump appointed Kansas Secretary of State Kris Kobach, a leading alarmist about alleged vote fraud and an architect of anti-immigration laws, to head a commission to investigate fraudulent voting (Ingraham 2017). It found little evidence of any. Disbanded in January 2017, the commission's mandate was transferred to Homeland Security (Ingraham 2017; Tackett and Wines 2018).

The Trump Justice Department also frequently filed briefs in support of the numerous new state measures restricting voting. In *Brnovich v. Democratic National Committee* in 2021, the three Trump Supreme Court appointments provided the majority needed to sustain two such laws adopted in Arizona. The ruling signaled that the Court would probably uphold other restrictive laws as well. The Court held in *Brnovich* that Section 2 of the Voting Rights Act could not be used to invalidate laws that made it harder for racial and ethnic minorities to cast ballots unless both the difficulties and their disparate impacts were substantial, going well beyond "mere inconvenience." Justice Elena Kagan, in dissent, contended that the majority gave "a cramped reading to broad language ... to uphold two election laws from Arizona that discriminate against minority voters" (Liptak 2021). Though the Court later ruled that precedents might still require states to create majority-minority districts to comply with Section 2, and lower federal court judges then rebuked Alabama's repeated refusals to do so, few analysts expected vigorous enforcement of the VRA to resume (Hasen 2023; Wang 2023).

The Trump administration also urged, with great effect, aggressive purges of voter rolls by state election boards, the redrawing of political boundaries in ways that often diluted the impact of African American voting, and stringent photo ID registration and voting requirements. It joined a suit against Kentucky to compel the state to cull rolls of voters who had moved, and supported a similar effort in Ohio (Wines 2018). The Justice Department and the Immigration and Customs Enforcement agency also coordinated requests to states for data on voter records, seeking to identify noncitizen and other fraudulent voters: millions of North Carolina records, for example, were subpoenaed from the state elections board and forty-four county elections boards, including many with low-income voters of color (Faussett and Wines 2018). Political appointees, not career lawyers, led these actions.

A related controversy heightened the significance of such efforts to prevent any increase in non-Republican, non-white voters. Secretary of Commerce Wilbur Ross ordered that a citizenship question be added to the census for the first time in half a century. Critics contended this move would diminish participation in the census, harming its accuracy while also curtailing representation for areas with many immigrant residents and possibly abetting deportations. The administration suspended its effort after the Supreme Court required further justification (Liptak 2019). It then, however, used statistical estimates of unauthorized immigrants to seek to reduce the number of seats in the House of Representatives for states thought to have many such residents (Liptak 2021). A federal court overturned Trump's order requiring that only citizens be counted for apportionment purposes (Wines 2020a). The administration then ended the census count a month earlier than originally planned, provoking charges that it sought to undercount hard-to-reach, predominantly non-white Americans and to maintain control over the apportionment of House seats (Wines and Fausset 2020).

Voting is, of course, intensely contested at the state and local as well as the federal level. Dating back to the Richard J. Daley machine in Chicago in the mid- twentieth century and Tammany Hall in New York City in the nineteenth century, Republicans have long held as a central article of their faith that Democrats cheat to win elections. There is little doubt, moreover, that historically, cheating and other forms of political corruption have indeed occurred in many American locales, though vote rigging has generally been small-scale and often done by both sides. Consequently, with the massive exception of the disfranchisement of racial and ethnic minorities, it is not clear that cheating has often determined outcomes (Campbell 2005). Election experts agree that the professionalism and integrity with which American election administrators do their work have improved in the last decade, though the decentralized structure of American elections has meant that many problems persist (Campbell 2005).

Nonetheless, as the 1965 Voting Rights Act and the 1965 Immigration Act began to foster a more demographically diverse American population and electorate in which non-whites strongly leaned Democratic, Republicans began ramping up concerns about election integrity. When Democrats briefly returned to power in 1993, twelve years after the start of the Reagan Revolution, they passed the National Voter Registration Act of 1993, the "Motor Voter" bill designed to achieve near-universal registration of American voters (Minnite 2010). Republicans immediately contended that the act endangered election integrity and began passing new state voter ID requirements that often particularly burdened poorer voters of color. They have gone on to support innumerable new laws aimed at remedying allegedly massive vote fraud, despite repeated failures to find any evidence of such crimes. The many Republican-controlled state legislatures pursued this agenda ever more ardently after the Supreme Court hobbled enforcement of the Voting Rights Act in the *Shelby County v. Holder* decision of 2013 (Davis 2020). They were active during the Trump administration; and they have been still more active in the wake of the 2020 election. The measures include a startlingly wide array of policies that disproportionately hinder poorer minority voters in comparison with more affluent white voters. Examples are stricter voter ID laws; new requirements to prove citizenship; restrictions on opportunities to register to vote; curbs on early and absentee voting via mail-in ballots; newly limited voting hours;

bans on the use of ballot drop-boxes; reductions in the number of polling places, especially in Democratic-leaning areas; purging of voter rolls if any uncertainty about a voter's status exist; bans or fees imposed on voting by ex-felons; and much more (Morris and Perez 2018; Brennan Center for Justice 2021b).

Between January 1 and September 27, 2021, 49 state legislatures considered more than 420 bills imposing such voting restrictions, and 19 states enacted 33 new laws doing so (Brennan Center for Justice 2021b). The trend has since continued: as we completed this book in spring 2023, the Brennan Center reported that since the beginning of that year state legislators had introduced roughly 150 restrictive voting laws in 32 states, and 27 bills had been introduced in 10 states to enhance the powers of legislatures and prosecutors to interfere with election administration. Democrats, to be sure, continued to fight energetically to expand access to voting: 274 bills seeking to do so in various ways had been introduced in 34 states in that same period (Brennan Center for Justice 2023).

Many Republican measures seemed consciously to target minority voters, such as bills to reduce the number of polling sites and impose other restrictions in urban areas with more than one million in residents in Texas, thereby limiting voting access in heavily Democratic Houston precincts with many citizens of color, and proposals to ban Sunday voting, traditionally an occasion when Black churches help move "souls to the polls" in Georgia (Corasaniti 2021). Other novel initiatives include fresh financial and criminal penalties imposed on election administrators accused of dereliction of duty, and empowering state legislatures or other partisan elected officials to take over election management from such administrators. These measures have led to mass resignations of experienced poll workers and other election officials (Wines 2020, 2021a, 2001b, 2021c).

In addition, Republican majority state legislatures have used the redrawing of state electoral maps to limit the likely impact even of high African American turnout rates. Disputes are unresolved at this writing. For example, the Supreme Court first provisionally upheld, then struck down an Alabama congressional districting plan that created only one Black majority-minority district (Liptak 2022; Totenberg 2023). The Alabama state legislature responded by adopting another plan which still created only one such district, despite claims that the result was to restrict the power of Black voters. Federal judges rejected that plan as well, and the state sought to appeal back up to the Supreme Court (Bohannon 2023; Wang 2023).

Many more such disputes are likely in the years ahead. Gerrymandering across the US is, to be sure, a two-party practice, a result of both Democratic and Republican measures to create districts dominated by one party and to reduce the number of competitive congressional seats (Klaas 2017). However, for many Republicans partisan goals involve racial Protect measures. Across the United States in 2021, overwhelmingly white Republican lawmakers redrew maps to the disadvantage of black Democrats (Corasaniti and Epstein 2021). Partisan gerrymandering has fused with racial gerrymandering in North Carolina, Ohio, Georgia, and Texas as African American elected officials either found their districts redrawn to their disadvantage or were placed in new districts that required a primary contest with fellow Democrats. For example, after losing Pitt County, which is 35 percent African American, from his district, North Carolina Representative G. K. Butterfield, a former chair of the Congressional Black Caucus, quit, observing "I just didn't see it coming. Let's call it a five-alarm fire [since I] did not believe that they [Republican state lawmakers] would go to that extreme" (quoted in Corasaniti and Epstein 2021). Because of this case and many others affecting African American state legislators and county officials, civil rights groups are litigating against North Carolina. The pattern is, however, replicated in many parts of the nation, leading NAACP Legal Defense and Educational Fund deputy director Leah C. Allen to conclude that the racial distortion effects of redistricting in 2021 were "worse than . . . in any recent decade." Allen added: "we have so much to contend with and it's all happening very quickly" (quoted in Corasaniti and Epstein 2021).

As Alabama's experience shows, not all these partisan efforts with substantial racial impacts have survived judicial scrutiny, though in states with judicial elections rulings sometimes swing back and forth rapidly. Two months after North Carolina's legislature enacted new districting maps, the state's Supreme Court, in a 4–3 party-line decision, threw the maps out as partisan violations of the State Constitution (Chen 2022). But Republicans gained a 5–2 majority on the North Carolina Supreme Court in the November 2022 election, and in April 2023 the Republican majority overturned the Court's earlier decision, holding that judges have no manageable standards to assess districting plans. The majority also paved the way for reinstatement of the Republicans' voter ID law (Marley and Barnes 2023).

In other states, such as Ohio, courts rejected new districting plans as partisan and racially biased in rulings that still stood as of spring 2023. Consequently, Republicans sought to insulate districting from judicial review, advancing an "independent state legislature" theory that state courts have no power under the Constitution to overturn a state legislature's plans. In *Moore v. Harper*, decided in June 2023, a 6–3 majority of the Supreme Court rejected that claim, though it said the scope of state judicial power over districting was subject to federal judicial scrutiny. The decision, arising out of the districting disputes in North Carolina, had no immediate impact since the altered North Carolina Supreme Court had recently restored the disputed Republican districting plan (Liptak 2023).

Democrats have also sought to protect what they regard as fundamental voting rights through a variety of national legislative initiatives. But in the Senate, Republicans have remained united in opposing voting reforms to reinstate the federal powers removed in *Shelby*. The "For the People Act" was passed by the House in 2021, but then squashed by the GOP in the Senate (DeBonis 2021). In the wake of that outcome, in August 2021, Texas legislators and Governor Greg Abbott enacted new restrictive voting rules ending twenty-four-hour and drive-through voting, restricting the use of absentee ballots, and imposing new ID requirements, among other measures. A walkout by Democratic state lawmakers failed to stall the bill. Trump Republicans also responded to the fact that, aided by major gifts from Facebook's founder, Mark Zuckerberg, and others, many nonprofit organizations gave valuable aid to embattled and underfunded local election administrators in the 2020 election. In 2021, five states—Arizona, Florida, Georgia, Kansas, and Tennessee—enacted new restrictions or bans on acceptance of such assistance (Brennan Center for Justice 2021a).

In many other respects, Trump's onslaught on the veracity of the 2020 election results achieved remarkable momentum up through the 2022 midterm elections. Trump supporters began energetically seeking appointments or running for election administration offices so that they would be in command in many jurisdictions when future election disputes arose (Gardner, Hamburger, and Dawsey 2021). Over 160 Republicans seeking office in statewide positions which hold the authority over how elections are run signed on to the false election claim, and many Republican officeholders and candidates for other offices also endorsed the "Big Lie" articulated by the former president's team (Parker, Gardner, and Dawsey 2022). The party eliminated the ten GOP House members who voted for Trump's impeachment; some chose to retire after censures by local party organizations, and most were voted out in primaries, notably former House Republican Conference Chair Liz Cheney in Wyoming. Like Cheney, even

Republicans who voted overwhelmingly for Trump administration policies were often condemned as RINOs, "Republicans In Name Only," if they expressed any doubts about whether Trump had won the 2020 election (Muravchik and Shields 2022). Campaign funds poured into the coffers of conservative candidates pledging allegiance to Trump and his stolen election narrative. Since 2020, polls have consistently found a substantial majority of Republicans agreeing that Trump was the lawful victor and believing that electoral fraud was a serious concern throughout the United States. "Stop the Steal" undeniably proved a successful mobilizing mantra.

The story is not all one-way. Election denier candidates did not just fare poorly in battleground states in the 2022 midterms. After the 2020 election, some states adopted omnibus voting bills that combined restrictive measures with provisions that eased access to voting, so that their overall impacts are unclear. By October 2021, twenty-five states had enacted sixty-two laws that in important respects facilitated rather than hindered voting (Brennan Center for Justice 2021b). Nonetheless, how such laws would be implemented often proved a matter of further, fluctuating contestation. In November 2018, for example, Florida voters approved a constitutional amendment to restore voting rights to over a million ex-felons. However, the state's Republican governor and legislature blocked its full implementation by requiring ex-felons to pay all outstanding fees they owed to the state before they could vote. A federal court sustained the state law against initial challenges, though other litigation continued (Mazzei 2019; Stein 2018; Stofan 2021).

How successful these voting restriction initiatives can be is debated. Many suppression measures impose obstacles on some likely Republican voters as well as Democratic voters. They also can spur outrage that may increase voter turnout, as perhaps happened in both 2020 and 2022 in a number of states. Nonetheless, the restrictions represent efforts to protect American elections against what conservatives see as corrupting influences, in ways that pose barriers chiefly to Democratic-leaning voters. Since in the last generation there has been no evidence of any substantial vote fraud, only increases in the proportions of voters who are non-white, it is hard to escape the suspicion that it is this group of voters whom these new conservative laws primarily seek to protect against.

SECURING PROTECT POLICY REGIMES

This overview of federal, state, and local policies and initiatives advanced since 2016 conveys the scale of the Protect policy agenda. As we have stressed, the Protect policy alliance is not a seamless, coherent network of tightly interlinked groups. It is much looser. But it is a network with ideas exchanged across groups, elected politicians and activists who are united in a commitment to the broad goals of the policies they have enacted or proposed. Some libertarians may defect on immigration or policing issues. Some Black conservatives may support more vigorous antidiscrimination enforcement. But for the most part, today's Protect policy alliance, including those whose governmental offices make it a potent institutional order, act cohesively and aggressively.

One additional set of measures dramatizes the alliance's ferocity about its Protect aims, especially when there are perceived dangers to conservative white Americans: the new, aggressive penalties that many states and localities have been adopting for protests. Conservative officeholders throughout much of America responded to the wave of protests that swept the country in the summer of 2020 after the killing of George Floyd by adopting numerous and varied state measures to restrict protest activities, as called for in the NatCon Statement of principles, and repeatedly by Donald Trump (Epstein and Mazzei 2021). In the fall of 2021, the International Center for Non-Profit Law's "US Protest Law Tracker" reported that 45 states had recently considered 230 anti-protest bills, with 36 enacted and 50 pending (ICNL n.d.). At least 11 states considered proposals to impose more severe penalties for defacing public monuments and statues, including Alabama, Arkansas, Florida, Georgia, Mississippi, and North Carolina, all boasting public commemorations of their former Confederate leaders and southern slaveholders. Arkansas, Florida, and Iowa enacted such laws, with Arkansas declaring damaging such monuments "acts of terrorism"; efforts to pass other such laws have since continued in many states (ICNL n.d.).

The most widely adopted measures added penalties for protests near oil and gas lines or other forms of critical infrastructure, and a few states added penalties for disrupting government activities through camping on, protesting near, or otherwise trespassing on government buildings and properties. A number of states considered, and West Virginia enacted, reductions in police liability for harms inflicted on protesters, while Oklahoma and South Dakota each made organizations that aided protesters liable for civil penalties. Missouri limited the rights of public employees to engage in protest.

Perhaps most menacingly, many states considered, and Iowa and Oklahoma enacted, laws granting drivers immunity from civil liability if they injured protesters who were blocking public roads (ICNL n.d.). Conservative advocates and government officials in a number of other states also appeared to encourage private citizens to use force against those they perceived to be dangerous radicals. In Virginia, new militias began forming in 2020, successfully claiming a right to do so under the Virginia state constitution and promising to "protect themselves and their communities" if volatile political protests posed dangers and if the "defund the police" movement had any success (Martin 2020). Some did seek approval from their County Board of Supervisors and sheriff before acting. In Michigan, one local sheriff praised and shared a stage with the Wolverine Watchmen, a militia group including some members later convicted of plotting to kidnap Michigan Governor Gretchen Whitmer (Sidner 2020). A video taken in Kenosha, Wisconsin, similarly showed police praising and aiding militia members who arrived to protect against what they saw as dangerous radical protests, leading to charges that the police had effectively "deputized" armed vigilantes like Kyle Rittenhouse (Brooks 2020; MacFarquhar 2020).

All these developments conveyed a message. Whether or not Donald Trump was president, the conservative racial policy alliance, now an increasingly powerful institutional order that included a wide range of local, state, and national officials supported by advocacy and litigation groups and armed militia, stood prepared to protect against dangers that most associated with Black Lives Matter and other proponents of radical change in America. The substantial record, spanning numerous policy regimes, compiled during and after Trump's White House years provided abundant evidence that conservative promises of heightened protection had been and would be embodied not just in politicians' words but also in government deeds that would play a major role in ordering the lives of all Americans.

PART 3
The Repair Alliance

CHAPTER SIX

The Rise of the New Repair Groups

The 21st century will be the century of global reparatory justice. —Sir Hilary Beckles

The Waning of the Twentieth-Century Civil Rights Movement

In 1903, W. E. B. Du Bois famously declared that "the problem of the twentieth century" was the "problem of the color line." The ensuing decades did see major conflicts over segregation and race-justified imperialism, resulting in the formal repudiation of both in the US and around the world, though without radical transformations in many of their enduring impacts. However, just as in the case of enslaved labor in the nineteenth century, the ending of the era when the nation's racial policy debates centered on the legitimacy of de jure segregation was a historic development.

The nation's competing racial orders, and its overall racial structuring, were fundamentally changed.

In contrast, one hundred years later in 2003, it seemed to many that the twenty-first century might prove to be the "century of civil rights stagnation." In America, the decades-old clashes between proponents of purely color-blind public policies and champions of race-targeted measures had reached a stable equilibrium, or perhaps simply a dreary gridlock. Affirmative action programs in education and employment and school desegregation mandates survived in many places and at all levels of government, but many agencies and institutions had trimmed them back substantially under pressure from Supreme Court decisions and, in a growing number of states, legislation and popular referenda requiring color-blind programs in many policy regimes. At the same time, what would come to be known as diversity, equity, and inclusion initiatives and offices were proliferating in both private and public institutions, fueling and fueled by the mushrooming of DEI consultants and specialists. In the eyes of many observers, however, the rise of the DEI industry simply meant that the neoliberal policies of the decades following the 1980s Reagan Revolution included mild "multicultural" features that did benefit some people of color, but left most systemic inequalities intact, and some exacerbated.

Overall, by the dawn of the twenty-first century, civil rights issues had receded measurably from political and partisan discourse, especially because Democrats were reluctant to trumpet support for race-conscious measures in a political climate where expressions of commitments to color-blindness predominated, all too often shadowed by overt hostility toward aid to racial and ethnic minorities. Although the 2000 Democratic Party platform promised that the Democratic presidential nominee, Al Gore, "strongly opposed efforts to roll back affirmative action" and endorsed the creation of a commission "to examine the history of slavery, discrimination, and exclusion suffered by all minorities" and make "appropriate recommendations," both that platform and the candidate proposed no specific new civil rights initiatives. Each instead stressed issues of the economy, the environment, health care, and education (American Presidency Project 2022).

Some figures on the left of the Democratic Party and beyond wanted a more aggressive racial justice agenda. As noted in chapter 1, in that election year the activist Randall Robinson published *The Debt* and the law professor Charles Ogletree formed the Reparations Assessment Group, both stirring renewed interest in the case for reparations. Their efforts also encouraged many to begin defining what transformative reparations might entail, advancing beyond one-time checks to compensate for proven damages. Building on an idea from Robert Westley, Robinson proposed the creation of a trust fund, primarily financed by companies that had benefited from enslaved labor and discriminatory policies, to pay for K-through-college education for African Americans, with funds also for Black political organizations, civil rights advocacy, and aid to African and Caribbean communities damaged by American support for slavery (Robinson 2000, 244–45). The Democratic Party platform's endorsement of a reparations study commission modestly reflected this renewed and revised focus on reparations. It also came in response to how, beginning in 1989, in each congressional session Representative John Conyers of Michigan had introduced HR 40, the bill to create a national commission to study the feasibility of reparations for African Americans injured by legacies of enslavement and Jim Crow segregation.

Although today's Repair alliance extends beyond support for reparations, and indeed includes some who oppose the concept, the idea of reparations for Blacks has a long history in the US. In the wake of the American Revolution, some repentant slaveholders and the Massachusetts state legislature provided some formerly enslaved individuals with land, schools, and at least one pension (Coates 2014, 61). During and after the Civil War, emancipated African Americans insisted they were entitled to many of the lands their labor had made fruitful. Their demands briefly appeared to have a chance of being met by a Radical Republican-led Congress, until President Andrew Johnson's truculent resistance aided renewed efforts to keep property in white hands (Franke 2019, 15, 18, 104; Darity and Mullen 2020, 16–17). In the early twentieth century, Callie House and others formed the National Ex-Slave Mutual Relief, Bounty, and Pension Association (MRBP) to lobby for pensions for all ex-slaves, among other demands, and formerly enslaved Americans also sued unsuccessfully for a share of the taxes on profits from the crops they had grown (Franke 2019, 118; Darity and Mullen 2020, 19–20). In the 1950s, Queen Mother Audley Moore created the Committee for Reparations for Descendants of US Slaves, appealing to the new United Nations and international human rights declarations for support (Kelley 2022, 118–20). The Committee's demands were then echoed and elaborated in the Black Manifesto advanced in the 1960s by James Forman and the League of Revolutionary Black Workers. Their advocacy helped inspire the Yale law professor and tax expert Boris Bittker to write a tantalizing how-to guide, *The Case for Black Reparations*, in 1973. In the 1980s, several Black organizations joined in founding the National Coalition of Blacks for Reparations in America (N'COBRA), establishing chapters internationally and working with Rep. Conyers to develop his HR 40 proposal to establish a "Commission to Study and Develop Reparations Proposals for African Americans" (Darity and Mullen 2020, 21–24). Then Robinson, Ogletree, and others added their advocacy, roughly a decade after Conyers first introduced his bill.

For more than thirty years, however, HR 40 never made it out of committee. Though there had been periods of greater and lesser receptivity to reparations proposals in the course of American history, the truth is that ever since the defeat of Radical Reconstruction, reparations advocacy was generally dismissed as utopian and extremist and remained marginal in American politics (Michelson 2002). Even though many civil rights supporters gave formal support to HR 40 after its introduction in 1989, for the next quarter-century reparations did not come to the fore of the agendas of the nation's most prominent social justice organizations and political leaders. Nor, however, did they rally around any other galvanizing, unifying racial justice issue, as opponents of de jure segregation had once done. In 2003, Chicago did pass a Slave Era Disclosure Act, modeled on a narrower Los Angeles ordinance. The Chicago law required all companies doing business with the city to disclose whether they had benefited from the use or sale of enslaved labor. Not only did that initiative fail to catch on in other locales; two decades later, Stephanie Coleman, the chair of the Chicago Board of Aldermen's new Subcommittee on Reparations, reported that it had never been enforced (Cherone 2022). The reality is that by the early twenty-first century the powerful anti-segregation civil rights movement driving major legislative victories in the 1960s appeared long dormant and unfocused, or at least significantly less mobilized as an identifiable national force.

Beginning around 2001 a mentee of Queen Mother Audley Moore, the veteran activist Dr. Ron Daniels, who was also a longtime member of N'COBRA, and key contributor to Jesse Jackson's presidential campaigns in 1984 and 1988, concluded that civil rights efforts had become too fragmented and siloed.[1] In the 1980s and 1990s pre-social media era, thousands of local groups were active in America and elsewhere, but they were disconnected, only remotely aware of each other's work. That year Daniels aided in convening in Atlanta a "State of the Black World" conference, attended by over 2,500 delegates, which led to the creation of the Institute of the Black World 21st Century (IBW21) under his leadership (IBW21 n.d.). The new advocacy organization was especially keen to connect and mobilize grassroots and community action-oriented groups, domestically and internationally, in working for racial justice reforms on a range of issues, including reparations. Today the IBW21 continues to strive to be both a resource center for activists, offering policy analyses and options, and a coordinating organization helping local groups build capacity for the empowerment of communities of color, in line with its commitments to "principles of self-determination, African humanism and social justice" (IBW21 n.d.). It has thereby strengthened connections among the participants in today's left-leaning racial policy alliance, as illustrated in the network figure in chapter 2, and along with other factors it has contributed to the shift in the agenda of that alliance toward Repair policies, including but not limited to reparations.

Daniels and the IBW21 did not do so, however, alone or overnight. While the Institute communicated and met regularly with older civil rights groups like the NAACP and the Leadership Conference on Civil and Human Rights, those organizations—all supporters of HR 40—placed talk of reparations low on their advocacy agendas. The election of the racially cautious Barack Obama to the presidency in 2008 was a historic triumph in a nation that had disenfranchised Blacks for so long, but it did not alter that pattern. Despite the Obama administration's expansion of health care through the Affordable Care Act and its heightened civil rights enforcement, which angered conservatives, to many on the left the Obama years ultimately seemed more an accommodation to the era's dominant neoliberal multiculturalism than a challenge to it. Moreover, the fact that Blacks had been disproportionately sold subprime mortgages meant that the housing crisis of the Obama years led to an overall decline in Black home-owning and wealth, demoralizing many Black Americans, including activists (Jilani 2017; Davies 2021). Few, however, wanted openly to oppose the nation's first Black president. According to some N'COBRA leaders, even Conyers himself felt reluctant to push HR 40 too intensely in the Obama years. By 2013, the possibilities for truly radical racial change seemed so remote that Ron Daniels and many others wondered whether the repeated introduction of HR 40 served any purpose.[2]

The Rise of a Repair Alliance

But then racial justice causes gained robust new life—more so, we submit, than many analysts recognize. This development is not so visible in public opinion data, which show that the spike in activists' optimism excited by the massive demonstrations that followed the killing of George Floyd in the summer of 2020 soon receded, and that not only most whites, but even two-thirds of white Democrats, oppose reparations and other more sweepingly transformative racial justice proposals (Conroy and Bacon 2020; Reichelmann and Hunt 2021). Attention to the proliferation, the agendas, and the actions of both public and private institutions concerned with racial issues reveals, however, that much more has occurred since 2020 than public opinion data would predict. New governmental bodies, private organizations, and individuals have joined many older agencies and civil rights advocacy groups in undertaking a wider variety of better-funded racial justice initiatives than the nation has witnessed in many decades, including initiatives that many today are comfortable calling forms of reparations.

The main catalysts of these developments include the formation of

Black Lives Matter in 2013 after Trayvon Martin's killing, an event repeatedly reinforced by all too many subsequent killings of Black people; the massive numbers of protests those events spurred; and the accompanying rise in calls for new racial justice initiatives in mainstream media, including Ta-Nehisi Coates's 2014 *Atlantic* article and the inspiring writings of the journalist and architect of the *New York Times* 1619 Project, Nikole Hannah-Jones (e.g., Hannah-Jones 2012). In interviews, activists on both the right and the left strongly affirm the importance of all these factors, stressing how they bolstered the credibility of the long-standing, but previously treated as radical, critiques of America that called for transformative racial equity reforms. And as proponents of white settler-colonial accounts of America rightly argue, the international context of the early twenty-first century has mattered greatly, exposing the limits of a solely national silo.

For just as America's exploitation of enslaved labor up to the nineteenth century and its elaborate new systems of racial segregation in the early twentieth century claimed legitimacy from the related practices of European empires and other European settler nations, a changing international political climate widened acceptance of the need for transformative racial measures as the twenty-first century unfolded. "Reparations for Native Genocide and Slavery," the report of the Caribbean Reparations Commission created by the Caribbean Community and Common Market (CARICOM) in 2013, emboldened and inspired many advocates, as did the transnational conferences and networking it fostered (Caribbean Community Secretariat 2015). Founded in 1973 and currently consisting of fifteen member states and five associate members, in 2014 CARICOM adopted a "Ten Point Plan for Reparatory Justice" that moved Ron Daniels and the IBW21 to host an International Reparations Summit in New York in 2015, attended by reparations advocates from twenty-two countries (Caribbean Community Secretariat 2023). The conference prompted the establishment of a Global Reparations Committee whose work is modeled on CARICOM's Ten Point Plan. CARICOM also launched a lawsuit against Britain, targeting Spain, Norway, Portugal, Sweden, and Denmark too, to win reparations for enslavement and for resources extracted from Caribbean states when they were European colonies. The suit invokes the defendant nations' commitments under the International Convention on the Elimination of All Racial Discrimination, as well as the precedent of litigation in the British High Court that prompted the British government in 2013 to award almost £20 million to Kenyan survivors of British torture during the 1950s Mau Mau uprisings (Mullins 2013).

CARICOM's initiatives also built on the 2012 publication of *Britain's Black Debt: Reparations for Caribbean Slavery and Native Genocide*, a searing account of the debts from enslavement owed by Britain to the Caribbean nations, written by the Caribbean Reparations Commission's chair, Professor Sir Hilary Beckles, a distinguished historian and university administrator (Beckles 2013). Beckles's work was buttressed by the research of the University College London (UCL)'s "Legacies of British Slave-Ownership" project (2009–2012), now housed at the UCL Centre for the Study of the Legacies of British Slavery, directed by the sociologist Paul Gilroy (Center for the Study of the Legacies of British Slavery 2023). The project documented the shockingly generous payments Britain made to owners of enslaved people when slavery was abolished in the British empire, and the continuing bounty of that compensation. Its researchers calculated that in today's prices, £17 billion, or almost $20.5 billion, were paid to forty-six thousand British owners of enslaved persons after slavery's abolition in the 1830s. Those who were victims of enslavement received nothing. In light of those indefensible inequities, Beckles has refashioned Du Bois to rebut pessimists by contending that "the 21st century will be the century of global reparatory justice" (Caribbean Community Secretariat 2015).

These Caribbean reparations developments have had especial significance for many Black activists in the US due to long-standing personal and political ties. They are also, as the 2015 New York conference showed, part of a modern global context that displays a burgeoning multiplicity of demands for various kinds of redress of harms done by European states, their colonial settler offspring, and their major institutions, including churches, universities, and private corporations. Some are cast as calls for reparations, others as different sorts of equity initiatives. Examples include the conference convened in Abuja, Nigeria, in 1993—which resulted in the Abuja Proclamation, calling on heads of government in Africa and the African diaspora to seek reparations for the continent's former pillage—and the United Nations World Conference against Racism, Racial Discrimination, Xenophobia and Related Intolerance convened in South Africa in 2001 (Howard-Hassmann 2004).

New efforts continue to be initiated. In the summer of 2023, King Willem-Alexander of the Netherlands formally apologized for his country's and his ancestors' role in slavery, following on a similar apology by Dutch Prime Minister Mark Rutte in December 2022, and Rutte's government has added that it will create a fund of 200 million euros, or roughly $218 million, to "increase awareness and involvement and follow-up"

(Moses 2023). Also in 2023, the Church of England committed £100 million from the Church Commissioners' funds, which a Church report showed to have been substantially enriched through investments in enslavement, for use in part as an "impact investment fund" designed to aid communities injured by enslavement's legacies (Wright 2023; Church Commissioners for England 2023).

Beyond reparation for the harms of enslavement, kindred initiatives have included the Transnational Justice program employed in postwar countries such as the Balkan states; the National Commission on the Disappearance of Persons (CONDADEP) on the disappeared in Argentina during the 1976–1983 military junta, chaired by the novelist Ernesto Sabato, with its tally of thirty thousand victims; the Truth and Reconciliation Commission, chaired by the late Desmond Tutu, recording and trying to settle the malign legacies of apartheid violence in South Africa; the successful demands of Indigenous children in Canada for compensation for forced time in residential schools; the Mother and Baby Homes Commission on the Magdalene Laundries scandal in Ireland; and the myriad Catholic religious orders compelled to compensate children abused by priests and nuns, some of whom got jail time for their behavior, faithfully depicted in the film *Spotlight*.[3]

For many American activists, Germany's policies have been among the most salient international precedents. Having long made substantial contributions to Israel because of Nazi Germany's Holocaust against Jews, in 2021 Germany also compensated Namibia for the genocide German soldiers and politicians inflicted on the Herero and Nama peoples there between 1904 and 1908, in which they exterminated 80 percent of the population. After six years of negotiation between the two states, Germany agreed to go beyond a formal apology and to pay the Namibian state £940 million, on top of its existing aid programs. While conceding that its previous regime had committed genocide, the German government refused to use the term "reparations" in the agreement, partly due to pressure from other formerly imperial countries to avoid setting a legal precedent for claims from their former colonial peoples (Oltermann 2021). Many activists around the world nonetheless perceive Germany's payment as a political precedent.

Proponents of reparations in the US, including N'COBRA and BLM activists, also often stress the precedent of congressional payments to survivors of the nation's World War II Japanese internment camps. For example, Trahern Crews, a leading figure in BLM Minnesota and also co-chair of the

US Green Party's Reparations Working Group, argues that the federal government should pay reparations owed to African American descendants at least mirroring payments totaling $1.6 billion given to Japanese American internees (Rogers 2021; Clarion Staff 2022). Like many contemporary reparation proponents, Crews calls for major public investments in housing, education, and health care in communities of color (Janzer 2021).

Taken alone, however, the precedent of payments to Japanese and Japanese American World War II internees would probably never be enough to make the case for African American reparations and related racial equity programs, which would cost far more. Canvassing various calculations, William Darity Jr. and Kirsten Mullen have estimated the cost for descendants of enslaved Africans in America alone at $10 to $20 trillion (Darity and Mullen 2020, 256–59). If such sums are ever to be politically conceivable, the twenty-first century's increasingly wide array of relevant international developments will surely have to matter even more than it has already. Many of the Repair activists with whom we spoke, from local group leaders to prominent national organization heads, stressed how they and their groups had studied many of these redress initiatives in other countries, taken inspiration from them, and communicated to make connections with their participants. They have thereby made the modern American Repair policy alliance an active part of international movements, just as is true of the traditionalist conservatives leading the nation's opposing Protect alliance. Consequently, contemporary analysts who see racial justice movements as aspects of global struggles against white colonialism and imperialism, and therefore as having truly radical potential, have good reasons to do so. These international alliances also mean that the resilience of the Repair movement in the US does not depend on domestic politics alone.

The BLM Surge

Even so, the most direct contributors to the shift toward a Repair agenda have been the new social activists and grassroots movements created in the 2010s, initially in respect to police and white vigilante killings of African Americans. These new groups are now often generically referred to as the Black Lives Matter movement, especially by conservatives, and it is an affiliation most in the new groups are happy to affirm, even if they are not actively collaborating with the original Black Lives Matter organization. That organization has experienced some internal disputes, but its extraordinary story nonetheless provides rich evidence of how new technologies, new actors, new perspectives, and new funding have reshaped American racial politics and policy debates.

The BLM label emerged from Alicia Garza's July 13, 2013, message of outrage on Facebook after the acquittal of George Zimmerman, the killer of the young Black Floridian Trayvon Martin. Patrisse Cullors shared Garza's message across the internet under the hashtag #BlackLivesMatter. Opal Tometi then designed a Black Lives Matter web platform in yellow and black colors. The label and movement had immediate global resonance, sparking protests in over sixty countries, with politicians, public figures, celebrities and sportspeople, and even many corporations rallying to the cause's imperative. Though much has since happened involving the founders of BLM, their initial invigorating message—that community-based organizing and protests via local chapters and individual actions can have political traction for major change—has been widely embraced.

Still more pertinently for our purposes, so has their sweeping vision of the changes needed. The younger activists maintain, as the political scientist Fredrick Harris has noted, that this "is not your grandmamma's civil rights movement" (Harris 2015, 35). We examine their vision in more detail in chapter 7. Here it is sufficient to note that from the start, the BLM website covered not only many aspects of the criminal justice system, but a wide range of other issues, including education, health care, housing, immigration, and other areas that all displayed what BLM organizers saw as systemic racism. These concerns point to a broadly transformative Repair agenda, with reparations increasingly becoming an umbrella term encompassing many of its parts. The original BLM organizers were also well positioned to articulate this agenda in the newly prominent language of intersectionality and transnationalism. Tometi is the daughter of immigrants from Nigeria, and Garza and Cullors self-identify as queer (Jones 2020). Through their advocacy and that of many other activists, intersectionality became not just a concept in academic analyses but a guide for political coalition-building and policy construction. Its embrace has helped include under the label "BLM" a far greater range of social justice endeavors, involving many more groups, than the term "Black Lives Matter" alone conveys.

The scale and importance of this broad-based, organizationally decentralized social movement and its expansive agenda ballooned after the killing of Michael Brown on August 9, 2014. Loosely assembled under the

BLM label, protesters and activists immediately converged on Ferguson, Missouri, joining in large demonstrations and activist mobilizing sessions. As well-publicized killings of African Americans nonetheless persisted, media coverage and political and academic discourse also continued to link most of the ensuing protests to BLM, regardless of their specific organizational origins. Though generally focused on criminal justice concerns, participants and observers alike interpreted the protests as aimed at comprehensive systemic reforms (Roberts 2018; Campbell 2021).

The surge of racial justice protests then reached unprecedented heights in both numbers and intensity following the murder of George Floyd on May 25, 2022 (New York Times Staff 2021). Captured on a brutal and brutalizing nine-minute video, the handcuffed Floyd's death at the knee of Derek Chauvin, the officer exercising excessive force, prompted at first disbelief, then anger, and then enraged mobilization in Minneapolis, across the US, and around the world. By July 2020, the *New York Times* published a story under the headline "Black Lives Matter May Be the Largest Movement in U.S. History," noting that half a million people had demonstrated in 550 places on June 6 alone, and that 15 to 26 million people had participated in protests so far that summer (Buchanan, Bui, and Patel 2020). These protests unfolded despite the fact that the nation was in the middle of a pandemic.

In this new BLM era of visible and mounting public demands for racial justice, and especially after what the courts judged to be Floyd's murder, a fast-growing multitude of businesses, universities, and NGOs rushed to pledge their commitment to addressing racial inequalities across many policy regimes. Civil rights advocacy groups renewed their resolve to win voting reforms, policing and criminal justice reforms, and other systemic changes, often now presented as aspects of a meaningful engagement with reparations. Citizens and foundations donated copiously to civil rights advocacy groups. Corporations including Bank of America, PepsiCo, Apple, and many others pledged millions for racial justice. Many sponsorships for sports and other events and advertisements for products were withdrawn, reallocated, or restated because of lingering racist motifs. The Cleveland professional baseball team became the "Guardians" rather than the "Indians," and the Washington, DC, football team became the "Commanders," not the "Redskins." Emulating the much-publicized example of the American football quarterback Colin Kaepernick, numerous sports players began taking a knee during the national anthem as a means to express solidarity with victims of racism and a commitment to reform. A host of symbolic and material expressions of America's history of enslavement, especially the names of public and private institutions, statues, paintings, and museum exhibits, faced scrutiny and removal. For a time at least, intense national conversations about America's road to racial justice surged, as books on race history, anti-racism, and whites' responsibilities flew off the bookshop shelves (Harris 2021).

Through all of this, BLM itself grew at a startlingly rapid rate, eventually encountering some of the difficulties that often accompany rapid growth. The protests following Michael Brown's death in Ferguson prompted the establishment of BLM chapters across the US, from Boston to Birmingham, Alabama, and from Chicago to Long Beach, California. Organizationally, both BLM and the umbrella organization M4BL opted for decentralized structures—partly for reasons of personal safety for their leaders, but also in order to enhance democratic participation (Waldmeir 2020). The range and diversity of efforts enabled by this structure led Fredrick Harris to characterize the activities under the BLM banner as a "movement" and not just a "moment," comparable to the energy unleashed after Emmett Till's murder in August 1955, with prospects of becoming an engine of "real change" (Harris 2006, 2014).

By the end of the 2010s, BLM had developed into the three kinds of groups characteristic of many advocacy organizations today: BLM Grassroots, the BLM Global Network Foundation, and the BLM Political Action Committee, each ardently engaged in different forms of public advocacy and community and grassroots activism (Black Lives Matter 2020). There are also several separate, unrelated Black Lives Matter Foundations that have been criticized for raising funds while not being affiliated with the core Black Lives Matter organizations (Mac and Sacks 2020). In the wake of Floyd's killing, the BLM Global Network Foundation alone received over $90 million in donations—followed, perhaps not surprisingly, by some painful disputes among local BLM groups and national leaders over the use of the funds (Morrison 2021; S. Levin 2022). Even so, in less than a decade BLM had gone from a Facebook post to a driving force in a new era of racial politics. Its name had come to symbolize a movement that had mobilized a stunning array of older and newer groups, organizations, and individuals, many with substantial financial resources, who despite inevitable internal differences were joined in deploying new technologies, tactics, and discourses to advance what they and their opponents saw as a substantially more radical Repair agenda.

Revision and Revival of HR 40

The emergence of BLM and the ensuing rising tide of protests, the Coates article, the CARICOM actions on reparations, and related international developments all encouraged longtime reparationist activists to renew and intensify their efforts as the Obama years were coming to an end. Along with organizing the International Reparations Summit in 2015, Dr. Ron Daniels and IBW21, working with N'COBRA, recruited a number of leading professionals in law, medicine, journalism, academia, and social justice advocacy into a new National African American Reparations Commission (NAARC). Building on CARICOM's 10 Point Plan, NAARC promulgated a "Preliminary Ten Point Reparations Program" to "guide the struggle for Reparations for people of African descent" in the US (NAARC 2023a). In an ensuing presentation to the Congressional Black Caucus, which at one time was reluctant to support reparations, NAARC brought in the Caribbean leader Sir Hilary Beckles to link the American Repair agenda with the efforts of the CARICOM Reparations Commission.

At the same time, Kamm Howard, co-chair of N'COBRA and a standing NAARC member, worked with John Conyers to prepare a new, bolder version of HR 40. Instead of focusing simply on the eras of enslavement and Jim Crow segregation, it now urged study of and recommendations for reparations against the many forms of discrimination that its proponents maintain characterize America through the present day. This addition implied the kind of expanded definition of reparations that the BLM movement was also coming to adopt: rather than focusing on cash payments to descendants of enslaved Americans or even victims of Jim Crow laws, "appropriate recommendations" might well include transformative efforts targeted at what advocates see as enduring systemic or institutionalized racism in many arenas, including employment, education, housing, health care, lending and credit provision, environmental protections, and more, of course including the criminal justice system. Reparations thus became, if not synonymous with, at least a pathway into a broader Repair agenda. Conyers adopted this new, more ambitious HR 40 enthusiastically.[4] After he then resigned his seat in 2017 due to allegations of sexual harassment, Texas Representative Sheila Jackson Lee eagerly took up sponsorship of the reformulated bill. Senator Cory Booker of New Jersey served as the lead sponsor of the Senate version of the House bill.

They did so when, as a result of the convergence of forces just described, prominent calls for reparations were multiplying across the country, including Nikole Hannah-Jones's post–1619 Project advocacy of cash payments and William A. Darity Jr. and A. Kirsten Mullen's prominent book-length treatise titled *From Here to Equality: Reparations for Black Americans in the Twenty-First Century* (E. Goldberg 2020; Hannah-Jones 2020; Darity and Mullen 2020). In his interview with us, N'COBRA co-chair Howard argued that the new prevalence of videos showing police abuse (as in the case of George Floyd) and the power of modern "big data" were providing rigorous demonstrations of America's racial inequalities and strengthening the case for reparations, broadly conceived, in the public mind. Howard stressed that the scientific quantification of disparate impacts helped people "see what has happened," how intentional governmental policies in areas such as housing and credit had fostered segregation and later, loss of homes, maltreating the African American community while benefiting some parts of the private sector, with entrenched racially unequal effects.[5] He noted that researchers and institutions like CitiBank that were not tied to reparations advocacy were using newly available quantitative data to calculate the costs of racial disparities to the national economy as a whole, as well as the likely positive economic benefits of racial equity initiatives, in ways that gave further credibility to reparations—because even though the debts were in the trillions of dollars, the benefits were much greater (Peterson and Mann 2020).

Perhaps more notably, beginning in 2020, a growing number of politicians also embraced reparations and related calls for robust racial justice initiatives. Senatorial candidates including Andrew Romanoff in Colorado, congressional candidates including Jamaal Bowman in New York, and presidential candidates including (most prominently) Joe Biden all supported at least the study of reparations in the near future, and some called for much more (E. Goldberg 2020; Freking 2021a). Even some notable conservative pundits like the *Washington Post*'s Gary Abernathy embraced the movement, citing the scholarship of Darity and Mullen and Randall Robinson's *The Debt* (Abernathy 2021). This escalated political advocacy and energy—rewarded in broader and deeper support for HR 40—is one of the forces that made a Repair agenda a more credible national priority by the third decade of the twenty-first century, along with nationwide protests; mounting piles of journalistic, think tank, and academic studies of the wounds of America's racial hierarchies; and international pressures.

As a result of all these forces, on June 19, 2019—Juneteenth, the date African Americans commemorate the end of enslavement—the House

Judiciary Committee convened hearings about HR 40. It was the first such hearing in over a decade, and compared to previous iterations, it was a triumph. After three decades, the committee at last voted the bill to the House for floor debate.

Representative Sheila Jackson Lee introduced HR 40 by saying that "the basis of this commission" was "to be able to look globally at the issue of slavery as the original sin and the brutality of it, and to then take the journey as it looks at the stark disparities in the African American community. I hope we will not take the opportunity to point blame or to cast any actions of racism as one party or the other. It was America's sin" (Sotomayor 2021). At the ensuing hearings, Ta-Nehisi Coates argued that reparations allowed America "to say that a nation is both its credits and its debits." In his appearance, the actor and activist Danny Glover recalled his family lineage including an enslaved great-grandmother and sharecropper grandparents. For Glover, national reparations constituted "a moral, democratic, and economic imperative" (Goodman 2019). Jerrold Nadler, the Democratic chair of the House Judiciary Committee, commended HR 40 as "legislation . . . long overdue." Nadler outlined how "H.R. 40 is intended to begin a national conversation about how to confront the brutal mistreatment of African Americans during chattel slavery, Jim Crow segregation and the enduring structural racism that remains endemic to our society today"—thereby noting all three targets of study in the revised HR 40 proposal (Freking 2021b).

But consistent with partisan polarization in general and especially over racial and economic policies, the bill's vote received all Democratic committee members' yeas, and not a single Republican committee member's support. Instead, GOP members of the committee brought in witnesses, mostly African Americans like the American football star, Trump ally, and later failed Republican Senate candidate Herschel Walker, to endorse their opposition. Utah Representative Burgess Owens, the ranking Republican member on the Judiciary subcommittee and an African American, dismissed reparations as "impractical and a non-starter." Owens said it was "unfair and heartless to give Black Americans the hope that this is a reality" (Blitzer 2021).

Because of this adamant GOP opposition, because the Senate was divided 50–50 between the two major parties, and because HR 40, not involving spending, could not be made filibuster-proof through enactment as a reconciliation bill, it did indeed have no chance of ultimate passage. Largely in consequence, the House as a whole did not act on it. Supporters of the bill then urged President Joe Biden to go beyond his support for the legislation to create the reparations commission by executive order, which Biden refused to do (*Why We Can't Wait* Coalition 2022b). Despite the ensuing acrimony, the proposal's emergence from committee for the first time, with presidential backing, still indicated that reparations now had greater support than ever before.

Old and New Groups in the Repair Policy Alliance

Although, like other political coalitions, racial policy alliances are always experiencing processes of change, and in many respects the Repair alliance is still emerging, an overview of its composition in the early 2020s provides abundant evidence that it is broader, deeper, and more varied than many commentators yet acknowledge. One place to begin mapping the network of groups, organizations, agencies, and individuals that support Repair agendas is with those who have officially endorsed HR 40—though the Repair alliance is in fact far larger. In July 2020, the members of the recently formed *Why We Can't Wait* Coalition issued a statement urging passage of HR 40 that was signed by 359 organizations. In February 2022, N'COBRA, NAARC, Human Rights Watch, the NAACP, the other groups that comprise the *Why We Can't Wait* Coalition, and a total of 365 organizations in all, along with over forty "leaders, activists, and celebrities," sent to the House leadership of both parties a letter urging that HR 40 be brought before the full House. Its signatories included 134 groups that had also signed the 2020 letter (*Why We Can't Wait* Coalition 2022a). Then in August 2022, the *Why We Can't Wait* Coalition organized a subsequent letter that protested Biden's failure to use his executive powers to create a commission unilaterally. It was signed by 109 organizations as well as thirty-five prominent individuals (*Why We Can't Wait* Coalition 2022b). The August letter featured 50 new organizations as signatories. It is reasonable to see the 640 organizations who signed one or all of these statements as at the core of the Repair alliance, even though it includes racial equity supporters who oppose the language of reparations, and abolitionists who see HR 40 as not radical enough. Because the signatories do include some local and state governments that have taken concrete reparation initiatives, they provide evidence that the Repair alliance is in the incipient stages of becoming an institutional order.

Nonetheless, we stress that the HR 40 signatories are only a small subset of the larger Repair policy alliance. The list of signatories does not include a host of other individuals and institutions active on racial equity initiatives, notably a number of the cities and states that have undertaken their own independent reparations programs. Many of the signatory groups, moreover, have scores of chapters, some of which signed in their own names though most did not. Many are themselves coalitions—sometimes very large groups, like the Leadership Conference on Civil and Human Rights with more than 230 members (some of which again signed separately, though most did not). None of the three Black Lives Matter organizations signed directly, though the Movement for Black Lives, the umbrella group to which BLM belongs, did so.

Some groups, like the American Descendants of Slavery (ADOS), founded in 2016, and the National Assembly of American Slavery Descendants (NAASD), founded in 2019, believe as their names suggest that reparations should be confined to descendants of persons enslaved in America (Cokely 2020; NAASD n.d.). These groups generally keep their distance from proponents of broader conceptions of reparations, who criticize their goals as insufficiently attentive to continuing discrimination against all people of color. Like Black Lives Matter, ADOS began via a hashtag, #ADOS, promulgated by radio co-hosts Yvette Cornell (a former aide to Democratic officeholders) and Antonio Moore (a Los Angeles defense attorney). They have built support for ADOS through frequent advocacy on radio, in print, and on social media, ultimately leading to the creation of the ADOS Advocacy Foundation in 2020 with Cornell as president. ADOS has been controversial because its leaders have argued that affirmative action should be confined to Black Americans and have insisted that immigration policies must be judged by their impact on Black American communities (ADOS Advocacy Foundation 2023b). Like other reparations advocates, however, the ADOS Foundation advances both a specific reparations agenda and a broader "Black Agenda" that, as detailed in chapter 7, addresses policy regimes in numerous areas including business, agriculture, drug policy, environmental policy, education, health care, criminal justice, housing, employment, immigration, infrastructure, and more (ADOS Advocacy Foundation 2022a, 2022b).

Similarly, the NAASD, which became a 501(c)3 organization in 2022 and has seven chapters in eight states, pursues a broad agenda it labels "R.E.P.A.I.R.," which includes "Reconciliation" pursued through a reparations commission created by executive order; "Equity" initiatives focused on voting rights, mass incarceration, and education; "Protections" including a new Freedmen's Bureau and credit, housing, medical, and environmental protection; "Atonement" via formal apology, museum commemorations, and other measures; "Investment" in Black-owned businesses, HBCUs, farming, and infrastructure; and "Remuneration" in the form of direct cash payments, homeownership aid, medical coverage, and free college and trade school educations (NAASD n.d.). Despite the significant differences between ADOS and NAASD and most other racial justice groups on important specific issues, it is undeniable that they and many other groups that did not sign the HR 40 statement all often act as members of the new Repair policy alliance.

Appendix C includes a complete list of the organizations that have signed statements in support of HR 40, as well as their breakdown into sixteen categories—though some signatories, such as the Black Women's Leadership Forum or the USC Shinso Ito Center for Japanese Religions and Culture, could reasonably be placed in categories other than those to which we have assigned them, precisely because they are intersectional in character. The categories do not mirror the eight classifications used for the Protect alliance in chapter 3, because the types of groups in the rival racial policy alliances are significantly different, reflecting the coalitions' substantive contrasts. The Repair alliance consists of many more groups explicitly focused on an intersectional variety of distinct but related "identity politics" goals, such as LGBTQ+ rights, immigrant rights, disability rights, and more. In contrast, the Protect alliance includes many more think tanks and policy advocacy and constituent mobilization organizations that structure themselves around conservative ideological goals, not identity groups. Consequently, while Progressives have thus far failed to match the extensive, well-funded network of conservative organizations built up since the 1970s via the mobilization spurred by the Powell memorandum, HR 40 supporters fall into sixteen categories—twice as many as the Protect alliance—as can be seen in table 6.1.

The largest category of HR 40 endorsers is, unsurprisingly, racial justice organizations, with 137 members. These include 13 N'COBRA chapters and the Institute for the Black World 21st century; legacy civil rights groups such as the NAACP, founded in 1909, the National Urban League (1910), the Leadership Conference for Civil and Human Rights (1950), and newer groups such as Color of Change (founded in 2005), NAARC (2015), and FirstRepair (2021). It includes both Black groups like I Love Black People (2015) and white groups supporting Black reparations like Showing Up for Racial Justice (SURJ) (2009) and the Fund for Reparations NOW! (2019).

TABLE 6.1 **Organizations Signing In Support of HR 40, 2020–2022**

Racial Justice	137
Religious	127
Social Justice	97
Business Sector	72
AAPI	70
Civic and Cultural Education Organizations	44
LGBTQ+	21
Women's Organizations	14
Criminal Justice	13
Legal Advocacy and Legal Services	12
Immigration	11
Professional Associations	7
Local and State Governments	6
Disability	4
Hispanic/Latinx and Indigenous	4
Environmental	1
Total	**640**

More surprising, perhaps, is the magnitude of the other categories of signatories. The second largest category is religious groups, with 127 signatories, showing that there is scope to the religious Left, even if it does not mobilize nearly so many voters as the religious Right. The religious bodies include predominantly Black and predominantly white groups; Catholic, Protestant, Jewish, and a few Muslim groups like the ICNA Council for Social Justice; international organizations such as the Sisters of Bon Secours; national denominations and associations like the American Baptist Churches USA and the National Council of Churches; and local congregations such as the Meriden Congregational Church in New Hampshire and the First Unitarian Society of Denver, Colorado.

Next in magnitude are the ninety-seven organizations with social justice agendas, like People for the American Way, the Global Human Rights Clinic, and the Gandhi Institute for Nonviolence. We have included here some organizations whose primary focus is on a single other issue—for example, the National Coalition against Domestic Violence—when they link that issue to kindred social justice concerns, including racial equity goals. Once again there are older groups, like the National Consumers League (1899!) and Community Change (1968), newer organizations like the Next

Generation Action Network (2014) and the University Network for Human Rights (2019); and international, national, and local organizations like the international UNESCO Inclusive Policy Lab, the national Southern Poverty Law Center, and the local Peace Builders of Orange County.

Strikingly, the next two largest categories are business groups, with seventy-two members, and Asian American and Pacific Islander organizations, with seventy. The businesses primarily fall into two subsets. Some are minority-owned businesses like Bethel Business Machines, or businesses with liberal white owners like The Chocolate Factory, who are simply expressing support for racial justice initiatives. Others are businesses like Common Talks Consulting in Wisconsin and Racial Literacy Groups in New York City who are themselves part of the burgeoning DEI industry. As noted below, they are joined in the broader Repair alliance by the many large firms and the individual socially conscious tech billionaires who did not endorse HR 40 but who are donating hundreds of millions of dollars to racial justice initiatives capaciously defined, leading to the widespread denunciation of woke corporations by many conservatives.

We do not wish to overstate the novelty of this development. On the one hand, many businesses, and not only minority-owned businesses, long supported race-conscious policies; on the other, few if any corporations are supporting radical systemic economic transformations. Even so, contributions from companies and individuals who are on the fortunate end of the vast range of economic inequality of the twenty-first century do mean that many organizations supportive of Repair initiatives are far better funded today than they have ever been, as detailed below. While many are small, shoestring operations, a number are more financially secure than many leading organizations were in the heyday of the civil rights movement and the era of race-conscious advocacy. Some of those older organizations, in turn, are now better funded than in most if not all of their histories.

Of the Asian American and Pacific Islander groups, many are Japanese American organizations understandably committed to the legitimacy of reparations like those from which some Japanese Americans have benefited. As noted in chapter 3, they greatly outnumber Chinese American groups signing on in support of HR 40. Still, the signatories represent a wide variety of other Asian and Pacific Islander groups, including seven chapters of the Asian Pacific American Labor Alliance, AFL-CIO and the Chinese American Planning Council. This Japanese-tilted Asian American support stands in sharp contrast to Latino and Indigenous organizations. Only three Latino groups and one Indigenous body were signatories, though all four are part of broader networks. Moreover, the Indigenous Solidarity Network is an alliance of predominantly non-Native American supporters of Indigenous rights that developed out of the white pro-reparations organization SURJ.

The low representation of, especially, Hispanic/Latinx organizations was decidedly not true of the race-conscious policy alliance we delineated in 2011 (King and Smith 2011, 118, 155, 178, 200, 210, 225, 242, 244, 261). That alliance contained many such organizations, including the League of United Latin American Citizens (LULAC), the Mexican American Legal Defense and Education Fund, the National Coalition of Latino Clergy and Christian Leaders, and the Hispanic National Bar Association, all of which strongly supported affirmative action, as well as the National Council of La Raza, which did sign in support of HR 40. Today some Hispanic groups form an increasing presence in the conservative Protect alliance, though most are still not aligned with it. It is not surprising that many Hispanic groups were more favorable to race-conscious policies, from which many of their constituents benefited, than they are to a reparationist agenda, which might well offer comparatively little to them, since few had ancestors who were enslaved or even subjected to formal segregation laws (though Black Hispanics certainly were). The leading call for reparations for Latinos, by the UCLA law professor Laura Gómez, does not focus on enslavement. She instead emphasizes "reparations" for unjust discrimination against Hispanics and suggests they take the distinctive form of greater access to immigration, legalization, and naturalization (Savage 2020; Gómez 2020). While eleven immigrant advocacy groups signed on in support of HR 40 and most Repair advocates (though not ADOS) also champion immigrant rights, often as part of their opposition to an imperially forged global system of sovereign nation-states, immigrant concerns are still not often central to Repair agendas. For these reasons, the shift of civil rights advocates toward greater support for reparations may well be a source of the much-noted decline in Hispanic voters' support for progressive candidates, though a majority still lean Democratic (Cadava 2022). Indigenous rights groups certainly support reparations in the form of restoration of Native American lands, resources, and self-governance. Campaigns for land grant universities and other American institutions to recognize their debts to Indigenous communities and provide some form of compensation have multiplied in recent years, and some advocates see the causes of Black reparations and Native American reparations as allied (Hatzipanagos 2023). Others, however, see reparationist initiatives like HR 40 that are focused on African Americans as chiefly valuable for a rival settler population, even if it is one that has endured great injustices.

Lack of Hispanic/Latino backing and limitations in Indigenous support may therefore prove a major political liability for the Repair alliance. However, the alliance has other strengths. Many other groups that we found to be prominent in the race-conscious policy alliance now give more support to transformative Repair initiatives than they have in the past, including the NAACP, the United Church of Christ, and the American Civil Liberties Union (though the ACLU was not a signatory on these HR 40 statements). There are many more Asian American activist groups in the 2020s than there were even in the early 2000s, and as noted, while Chinese organizations are divided, a large number of AAPI groups favor reparations. The business sector is also a more prominent component of the Repair alliance than it was of the race-conscious coalition. Although major corporations' support for affirmative action was a critical factor in keeping it alive after 1980, and many businesses always contributed to civil rights organizations, the expansion of DEI corporate offices and policies, and greater national awareness of racial abuses and hardships, have heightened business engagement with racial justice organizations, even as many of those groups have moved to more demanding agendas.

It is also notable that the HR 40 signatories include twenty-one LGBTQ+ groups, a stronger presence than we found in the older race-conscious policy alliance, both because the number of such groups has grown with the advances of the gay rights movement and because many Repair advocates, including the BLM leadership, have explicitly included LGBTQ+ issues in their broader goals. In addition, displaying the deeper institutionalization of DEI concerns in academia and the nonprofit sector, there are many more civic and cultural educational organizations in higher education and more nonprofits attending to racial and social justice issues now, with forty-four such groups having signed in support of HR 40. These organizations are joined by a diverse but increasingly interconnected array of other advocates, including women's groups; professional associations, primarily for Black professionals; criminal justice advocacy organizations; and some immigrant, disability, and environmental advocacy groups, along with some state and local governmental bodies. They collectively comprise a racial policy alliance with a depth and breadth too extensive to be dismissed.

That depth and breadth are all the more evident when we look beyond the signers of the HR 40 statements. Many groups in the private sector and some local and state governments are focused on making reparations to those they believe they have directly harmed, rather than on national legislation. Other groups and individuals feel that whether or not they have been direct beneficiaries of profits from enslavement or other injustices, they should make some financial sacrifices to help people overcome the debilitating legacies of past and present racial discrimination. We cannot provide a comprehensive catalogue of these efforts, many of which are done without publicity; but examples from a number of categories can serve to indicate their variety and range.

The Broader Repair Alliance: Group-Facilitated Individual Donations

The hardest category of racial equity initiatives to research is personal donations, but many sources suggest that these have become significantly more prevalent in recent years, aided by facilitating groups and online sites. Some individual donors are spectacularly wealthy, such as Mackenzie Scott, the ex-wife of Amazon founder Jeff Bezos, who has been prominent in channeling tech-sector riches toward racial justice efforts (Hadero 2021). Scott reportedly donated over $6 billion in 2020 for a wide range of causes, and Scott stated that in the first half of 2021 alone she gave another $2.7 billion to 286 different organizations (Scott 2021). Aided by the philanthropic nonprofit consultant Bridgespan, Scott has made major donations to HBCUs like Prairie View A&M in Texas, the African American Cultural Heritage Fund, and other primarily educational and cultural organizations. She has also contributed substantially to a number of social justice organizations like the Borealis Philanthropy, which in turn re-grants to the Black-Led Movement Fund, aiding the Movement for Black Lives, and to a wide range of other grassroots activist groups. Borealis has reportedly donated over $100 million to these varied social justice organizations (Borealis Philanthropy 2023). Scott has also made major gifts directly to civil rights advocacy groups like Community Change, founded in 1968 in honor of Robert F. Kennedy and currently consisting of a core Center for Community Change 501(c)3 organization; a 501(c)4 called Community Change Action, which can take a more active political role; and a Community Change Political Action Committee that supports particular candidates. Aided by Scott's largesse, Community Change reported over $64 million in assets in 2021 and felt no need to make fundraising a priority (GRF 2021).[6]

It has instead initiated and funded a Black Freedom Collective that links twenty-five Black grassroots groups focused on racial justice issues—none HR 40 signatories, but all part of the larger and growing number of reliably resourced organizations favorable to an aggressive Repair agenda (Black Freedom Collective 2022).

The super-rich are, however, not the whole story of individual donations. As protests over police killings proliferated, a growing number of white people began using cash payment apps like PayPal to make modest transfers directly to Black colleagues and friends as a form of small-scale reparations. For example, Freeskewl is a platform for a variety of hybrid online/in-person movement classes, performances, and discussions. Since 2020 its white teachers have transferred from 5 to 40 percent of their Freeskewl earnings to a fund that goes to Black and Indigenous Freeskewl instructors (Skewl n.d.). Some activists use Twitter to propose such transfers to Black recipients through Venmo and Cash App, and one study found over ninety-one thousand such tweets, with 30 percent sent on the first official national Juneteenth holiday in 2021 (King 2021). Multiple Black-run organizations have received spontaneous gifts from anonymous white donors, who often seek to pay reparations in rectification for their family's slave ownership (Chappell 2021).

These developments have stimulated a number of new organizations to use crowdfunding for community racial justice endeavors (Moscufo 2021; King 2021). Reparations Roundtable (RR) is a Louisville-based set of grassroots activists who host a Facebook page and encourage white Americans to set up monthly payments toward reparations for needy beneficiaries selected by the organization, such as a single parent who had been evicted with her five children. To join the RR Facebook account, contributors agree to pay $25 a month and accept the RR community guidelines in order to overcome "white supremacy" (Reparations Roundtable 2023). Though some deem these donations charity, Liz Cardenas, who administers the RR Facebook page, explicitly justifies them as racial justice Repair measures: "When there is a wrong that is committed by one group of people against another, there needs to be some repair" (Moscufo 2021).

Change Today, Change Tomorrow, also based in Louisville, assists marginalized communities across Kentucky, especially communities of color (CTCT 2022). Typical of the experiences of many of these groups, CTCT received an unexpected donation from an anonymous resident who discovered that his inherited family wealth had its origins in enslaved labor. This donor too called his gift "reparations." According to Nannie Grace Croney, the group's deputy director, the donor found "their great-grandfather had enslaved six individuals in Bourbon [County], Ky," and told the nonprofit that "as white people we all unfairly benefit from racism. We have to be willing to part with what was stolen, and do so without expectations of praise or control over how the money will be spent." The founder and executive director of the NGO, Taylor Ryan, was blunt about the justice of such payments: "it is a blessing for us but also definitely owed" (quotations in Chappell 2021).

Other examples include a Facebook group, launched by a conceptual artist in Seattle in 2016, called Reparations: Requests and Offerings, as well as Tucson Reparations, a "Black, queer, trans and disabled led organization" established in 2018 to serve that city's Black community (Reparations: Requests and Offerings n.d.; Tucson Reparations 2022). After Floyd's killing, Reparations: Requests and Offerings saw their Facebook group increase its membership from fifteen thousand to over twenty-one thousand within a matter of weeks, and received such an upsurge in donations that it temporarily suspended disbursement of funds, recruited forty additional volunteers, and reformed the leadership structure to bring local African American leaders into decisions about how to distribute its expanded resources (Moscufo 2021). Similar reparations nonprofits have been reported in Austin, Brooklyn, Cleveland, and Philadelphia, as well as other locales (Moscufo 2021).

There are also many related efforts that do not rely primarily on online crowdsourcing. The Denver Black Reparations Council solicits white donors to fund efforts to repair and reenergize "institutions, religions, languages and traditions" of the city's Black community and throughout Colorado (DBRC n.d.). The Reparations Legacy Project is a nationwide initiative, though it works most extensively in the St. Louis area, created by a white organization, the Uhuru Solidarity Movement, formed in turn by the African People's Socialist Party. Its aim is to organize "white people with access to financial wealth to take a stand in repairing the damage of slavery and economic injustice through the redistribution of resources" toward "Black self-determination programs" (Uhuru Solidarity n.d.). Reparation Generation is a Black-founded national organization that solicits funds from individuals, corporations and foundations to distribute to Blacks for "wealth-building" endeavors under the headings of home ownership, entrepreneurship, and education (Reparation Generation n.d.).

It is reasonable to doubt how transformative these kinds of donations can be, even if facilitated by modern social media and technology. William

Darity and Kirsten Mullen have repeatedly criticized individual, nonprofit, and municipal reparations initiatives as perhaps commendable forms of charity, but as too tiny and diffusely structured to warrant being called "reparations," and have expressed the fear that such initiatives may impede efforts to win the multi-trillion-dollar national program they believe to be necessary (A. Brown 2021). In interviews, all Repair activists agree that a large-scale national initiative is needed, but they believe smaller-scale efforts can foster a political climate more favorable to national action.

The broader political climate is of course shaped by a wide variety of media, cultural, educational, and social institutions. New efforts to rectify their past sins of omission and commission through diversifying their work forces and content are occurring in many venues, often with attendant controversies. By 2022, the Museum of Fine Arts in Boston; the Metropolitan Museum of Art, the Guggenheim Museum, and the Juilliard School in New York; the Art Institute in Chicago; the Minnesota Alliance for Volunteer Advancement in Minneapolis (which advocates for policies governing museum volunteers); the Museum of Fine Arts in Houston; and the LA County Museum and the leading paper, the *Los Angeles Times*, in Los Angeles had all announced they were seeking to sever their complicity in white supremacy (Powell 2020; P. Brown 2021; Hernandez 2021; Pogrebin 2021; Bottum 2021). Everywhere, however, reforms have been met with intense opposition and denunciations, and so the nature and extent of the cultural transformations underway, and how favorable they may prove to be to Repair policies, are uncertain.

Secular and Religious Universities

Educational institutions—public and private, religious and secular—are also among the major forces shaping the nation's political culture. While battles at the K-12 level have focused on curriculum, some institutions of higher education have begun to strive to lead by example, undertaking reparations actions. In so doing, they have contributed to understandings of reparations as involving much more than cash payments. Though some universities, especially HBCUs (Historically Black Colleges and Universities), have publicly endorsed HR 40, others have simply sought to redress their own connections to enslaved labor and racial discrimination.

Georgetown University has confronted a grim history. In 1838 the university avoided financial collapse when its leaders sold off 272 enslaved laborers to Louisiana plantation owners to raise capital. When the story emerged, the university delivered a formal apology and instituted a program of reparations. Prodded by a student vote to tax themselves to raise funds, the university committed to fundraising by other means to aid the direct descendants of those sold, with eight thousand identified so far. The descendants are also receiving enhanced access to university admission (Ebbs 2019; Desai 2109). The university has sought to pay up to $400,000 a year by drawing on the commitment of its founding Jesuit order to raise $100 million, eventually to rise to $1 billion, for descendants of those the order held as slaves. So far, however, fundraising has flagged, with a major land sale delayed and only $180,000 raised via small donations by the summer of 2022 (Swarns 2022).

In response to a report on its historical complicity with enslaved labor and racial discrimination, Harvard University similarly committed in April 2022 to establishing a $100 million endowment fund, to be spent to aid descendants of those whose enslaved labor had benefited the university, and to address racial inequities more broadly (Moscufo 2022). Given Harvard's vast resources, funding for the endowment appears secure.

Harvard and Georgetown are hardly unique. Apart, perhaps, from a few abolitionist-founded institutions, virtually all American colleges with antebellum roots benefited from chattel enslavement in one form or another (Wilder 2013; Harris, Campbell, and Brophy 2019). Some are seeking to respond in cooperation with the HBCUs created after the Civil War. In 2020, Columbia University's School of International Affairs and Institute for the Study of Human Rights partnered with the Thurgood Marshall Civil Rights Center at Howard University to create the African American Redress Network, a broad initiative that aims to provide over one hundred forms of reparations, including scholarships and cash payments (African American Redress Network 2023a). The Princeton Theological Seminary did not itself own slaves and was not built with slave labor, but many of its founders, leaders, and donors were slave-owners, and for a time it kept its endowment in southern banks financing the westward expansion of slavery. Consequently, it set aside $27.6 million of its $1.2 billion endowment for scholarships for descendants of enslaved people and for changes in its curriculum, faculty, and campus commemorations (Kaur 2019). Seminary leaders present their steps as "an act of confession. These responses are intended as acts of repentance" (Pride 2019).

The Virginia Theological Seminary in Alexandria, Virginia has created a more modest $1.7 million reparations fund, which it is dispensing as annual cash reparations payments of $2,100 to African Americans identified as descendants of the enslaved people who worked in the seminary before and after the Civil War. The president of the seminary, the Rev. Ian S. Markham, explained that the seminary "wanted to make sure that we both not just say and articulate and speak what's right, but also take some action" (W. Wright 2021).

Similarly, in 2020 the Union Presbyterian Seminary in Louisville, Kentucky, a city notable for reparations activism, created a $1 million endowment "to recognize and repent the resourcing provided to the seminary through the labor of enslaved persons." It raised funds in part by developing the seminary's Westwood Tract, land once owned by the slaveholding doctor to Confederate General Stonewall Jackson. The endowment is being used chiefly to support the seminary's Katie Geneva Cannon Center for Womanist Leadership, whose director, Rev. Melanie C. Jones, contends that the seminary's historic role in the Confederacy demands "repentance, restoration, and reparation" (Union Presbyterian Seminary 2020).

At this point, however, statements of repentance are more common than acts of reparations at the university level. Brown University, for example, created a Center for the Study of Slavery and Justice in 2012 in recognition of its founder's significant role as an owner of enslaved people and in response to a university commission on enslavement that issued a major report in 2006 (Simmons 2004; Brown University n.d.). Brown students, like those at Georgetown, voted overwhelmingly in favor of the university paying reparations to the descendants of those it had enslaved. So far, however, the university has made no commitment to do so, though it has created a Fund for the Education of the Children of Providence and its Center for the Study of Slavery and Justice (Paxson n.d.; McDermott 2021).

The University of North Carolina has built a memorial intended to recognize the roles of enslavement work and profits in the university's founding and past funding, and in October 2018 the UNC chancellor apologized for the university's historical involvement in slavery (Fortin 2018). Like Brown, however, the university has yet to make a financial commitment to reparations. The University of Virginia, founded by Thomas Jefferson, was unsurprisingly long awash in enslaved labor. Under pressure in 2007, the university's president established a Commission on Slavery and the University, which led to the installation of a Memorial to Enslaved Laborers documenting the chronology of enslaved people at the institution from the early seventeenth century to 1889, the date of the death of a former enslaved woman, Isabel Gibbons, who wrote about her experiences there

(Cotter 2020). However, in 2023, anti-CRT Virginia Governor Glenn Youngkin appointed UVA alumnus Bert Ellis—head of the Jefferson Council, a group opposed to the university's DEI initiatives—to the university's Board of Trustees. Ellis was expected to resist further racial equity changes and to seek to roll back some recent measures (Saul 2023). Similarly, the very name of Washington and Lee University in Lexington celebrates the Confederacy's leading general. In July 2020, almost 80 percent of the faculty voted to excise Lee's name, but the Board of Trustees did not comply (Golembeski 2021).

Like a number of other universities, Penn State announced it would create a Center for Racial Justice after George Floyd's murder. It did not, however, undertake the raising of funds to pay for any forms of material reparations. After a new president, former University of Louisville President Neeli Bendapudi, took office in May 2022 in the midst of a still COVID-constrained financial environment, she canceled the Center, arguing that it made more sense to invest in the anti-racist efforts of existing faculty and university programs, including DEI initiatives. To its critics, the cancellation was another sign that American institutions were once again retreating from the racial reckoning that seemed underway in the summer of 2020 (Anderson 2023).

There are indeed reasonable grounds to question how significant the recent higher education reparations and racial justice initiatives will prove to be. Yet despite and in part because of the disagreements they generate, these efforts make Repair initiatives far more prominent in American political discourse in the second decade of the twenty-first century than at any point in the preceding century and a half.

Religious Groups

Given the vast number of religious congregations and organizations in the United States, it is not surprising that even though many signed statements in support of HR 40, there are a great many others that did not do so but are nonetheless undertaking significant Repair initiatives of their own. Many religions, including both African American and white churches, have doctrines emphasizing social and racial justice missions, some taken directly from the Black church and Social Gospel traditions espoused by the Rev. Dr. Martin Luther King Jr., even if these traditions are less visible in mainstream media today than conservative creeds of Christian nationalism. Although Black churches are not so central to the Repair alliance as they were to its anti-segregation predecessor, it is wrong to think that they are no longer a tremendous force working for racial justice, in ways that summon extensive support from many predominantly white as well as Hispanic and Asian religious groups. The Poor People's Campaign, co-chaired by two charismatic leaders, the Rev. Dr. William J. Barber II and the Rev. Dr. Liz Theoharis, stresses that it is carrying on the fight for economic justice for all that Dr. King championed in his final years. At the same time, it describes its agenda as a "Third Reconstruction," aimed at the "interlocking injustices of systemic racism, poverty, ecological devastation, the war economy/militarism and the distorted moral narrative of religious nationalism"—thereby endorsing the central concerns of the racial Repair alliance (Poor People's Campaign n.d.).

The Jesuits' as yet unfulfilled commitment to raise $100 million for reparations is the largest initiative of any American religious group to date, but other Catholic groups have embraced Repair obligations. These include the American branch of the French-originated Society of the Sacred Heart, also known as the Religious of the Sacred Heart of Jesus, which in 2018 acknowledged its convents had owned roughly 150 enslaved people in Louisiana and Missouri who labored in its schools in those states. It has created the Cora Unum Scholarship fund to provide tuition aid to African Americans attending its school in Grand Coteau, Louisiana, and to advance other Repair goals (Mogannam n.d.).

The Society was an HR 40 signer, as was the Episcopal Church, which at this point appears to have the most congregations funding Repair initiatives (Powers and Gibbons 2022). At least seven Episcopal dioceses have made significant financial commitments. The largest so far came in 2020, when the Episcopal Diocese of Texas, with $1.8 billion in assets, announced it would devote $13 million to "repair and commence racial healing for individuals and communities who were directly injured by slavery in the diocese" (Michael 2020; Powers and Gibbons 2022). The funds are to go to students at the Austin, Texas, Seminary of the Southwest, to HBCUs in the diocese, and to African American churches and local church-based initiatives.

In 2022, The Episcopal Diocese of Virginia voted to commit the next largest amount, $10 million, for reparations to Black and also Indigenous communities, though it had not yet made decisions on how the funds would be spent (Boorstein 2022). In 2019, the Episcopal Diocese of New York committed to spend $1.1 million and established a task force to determine how the money could best be used (Millard 2019). In 2020, under the leadership of the African American Bishop Everett Taylor Sutton, the Episcopal Diocese of Maryland made a $1 million commitment, more than 20 percent of its annual operating budget, to seed a fund for programs that would aid African Americans in Baltimore and beyond. Bishop Sutton stated: "We've benefited from racist institutions, and now we're going to invest financially" (Pitts 2020). Within the diocese, the Memorial Episcopal Church of Baltimore, after discovering that several of its founders were slaveholders, committed in 2021 to giving out $500,000 over the next five years to local groups such as Black Women Build, which turns abandoned housing into affordable homes (CBS News Baltimore 2021). In 2019, the Episcopal Diocese of Long Island announced that roughly $500,000 from a pending sale of church real estate would be used to establish a reparations fund (Episcopal Diocese of Long Island 2019). The diocese has since established a reparations committee that, among other activities, oversees the Barbara C. Harris Scholars Program for Truth and Reparations, awarding scholarships and union fees to African descendants of slavery in the US. The program is named for the first African American woman to become an Episcopalian bishop (Episcopal Diocese of Long Island 2021). In 2020, the Episcopal Diocese of Georgia committed 3 percent of its unrestricted endowment to create a center for racial reconciliation, and the Minnesota Council of Churches, which includes the Episcopal Church along with twenty-four other denominations, launched a decade-long "truth and reconciliation" initiative to engage in education and fundraising to aid both African Americans and Native Americans (Crary 2020).

Churches and faith-based groups also often partner with other agencies in cities in which Repair initiatives are underway. The municipal reparations program in Evanston, Illinois, discussed below, is complemented by the work of a nonprofit organization, the Reparations Stakeholders Authority of Evanston, funded by local groups including the Evanston Community Foundation. In 2021 members of the First United Methodist Church of Evanston donated $50,000 via the Community Foundation to the Reparations Stakeholder Authority (Kromash 2022). The city of Denver is home to a number of reparations initiatives, including the Denver Black Reparations Council and its white-led partner, the Reparations Circle Denver, which had together raised $230,000 by 2022, and which seek to award $100,000 annually (Reparations Circle Denver n.d.). Members of the predominantly white First Unitarian Society of Denver helped prepare the way for those and related initiatives by undertaking, after 2015, a Racial Justice Project that explored the damaging consequences of redlining in its own neighborhood; consulted with Black church leaders; studied reparations efforts elsewhere; and then helped create the Society's own Reparations Fund, to be expended locally.[7] The Black church leaders consulted included Rev. Tawana Davis and Rev. Dr. Dawn Riley Duval, who co-founded Soul 2 Soul Sisters, a Denver racial justice nonprofit shaped by womanist theology (Soul 2 Soul Sisters n.d.). The First Unitarian Society was also conscious of the heightened concern for both Native Americans and the complex legacy of Indigenous enslavement in Colorado (P. Brown 2021). In Denver as elsewhere, these different currents have raised questions about what the priorities for reparations should be. Like many other predominantly white reparations organizations, the First Unitarian Society in Denver resolved that the city's Black community should decide on how reparations funds would be used.

Municipalities

Though most in the Repair policy alliance hope ultimately for major national initiatives, its claim to be an incipient institutional order that includes governing bodies now rests primarily on the growing number of cities that are undertaking reparations programs. The leading example is Evanston, Illinois, located north of the Chicago metropolitan area. On March 22, 2021, the Evanston City Council approved a new "Local Reparations Restorative Housing Program" designed to help compensate for some of the city's historical discriminatory housing policies and practices, which sustained segregated residential patterns throughout the twentieth century (Perry and Ray 2021; Bosman 2021; King 2007). The council allocated the first $10 million raised by the city's new tax on cannabis to provide aid to the city's African American residents in purchasing housing. Those households assessed to be eligible could receive $25,000 grants for repairs or down payments on homes. Though critics like Darity and Mullen dismiss Evanston's reparations initiative as too modest and too convoluted to qualify as reparations, one of its champions, Alderwoman Robin Rue Simmons, argued the program was "the start" of more sweeping efforts (Mullen and Darity 2021; Bosman 2021). She acknowledged that the program alone "is not enough. . . . But we all know that the road to repair injustice in the Black community will be a generation of work" (Guarino 2021b). Another Evanston alderman, Peter Braithwaite, hoped the scheme would be a model: "I hope that this first step will provide other local municipalities the confidence, as well as a path, to creating local reparations to help improve and repair the conditions of those injured in our other Black communities" (Bosman 2021). Speaking as a major architect of the resurgent national reparations movement, Dr. Ron Daniels declared that "right now the whole world is looking at Evanston, Illinois. This is a moment like none other that we've ever seen, and it's a good moment" (Guarino 2021b).

Soon thereafter, on July 14, 2021, the Asheville, North Carolina, City Council unanimously passed a motion in support of reparations for African American residents of the city, instituting a process for deciding on specific measures (Blackburn 2021). The result was the creation of a twenty-five-member Community Reparations Commission, with fifteen of the members appointed from neighborhoods historically impacted by racial discrimination. The Commission is charged with addressing five focus areas: criminal justice, economic development, education, healthcare, and housing. As in Evanston, Asheville is not planning on cash payments to individuals, which might be subject to taxation. Instead its focus will be on efforts to address what its leaders perceive as the legacies of systemic racism in these areas (Kim Miller 2022). Many Black residents have been skeptical about how much will be accomplished, but Asheville's efforts continued to move forward through 2023 (Durr 2021).

At least nineteen other cities have launched similar initiatives, though none are as yet making actual reparations expenditures as Evanston has done. Burlington, Vermont, voted to create a Reparations Task Force in 2020 that was still getting underway in 2022 (Redell 2020). Providence, Rhode Island, created the Providence Municipal Reparations Commission in 2020, and it has proposed funding a wide variety of initiatives, including home repairs, financial literacy programs, aid to Black and Indigenous groups, criminal justice reform, health equity, and more. The city has earmarked $10 million in federal COVID pandemic funds for reparations-related work (Marcelo 2022). Amherst, Massachusetts, also resolved in 2020 to "End Structural Racism and Achieve Racial Equity for Black Residents," and in 2022 the Amherst Town Council voted to create a $2 million reparations bank, to be funded as in Evanston by a tax on cannabis (Russell 2022). It, too, still needed to decide on specific criteria for expenditures. Philadelphia, Pennsylvania, created a Mayor's Commission on Faith-Based and Interfaith Affairs in 2020 that has undertaken a "Rise Up for Reparations" campaign, convening, for example, more than eighty faith leaders in 2023 for a course on reparations, though specific programs and expenditures remained only possibilities for discussion (File 2023). Iowa City, Iowa, authorized a Truth and Reconciliation Commission in 2020 that might have led to Repair recommendations, but it has struggled due to clashes with the mayor and controversies over its chairs (Perreault 2022).

In February 2021, Athens-Clarke County commissioners voted unanimously to pursue some form of reparations for Black residents of Linnentown, a Black community whose lands and homes were appropriated in the 1960s to create housing for students at the University of Georgia, located in Athens. They also hoped to use federal pandemic recovery funds for that purpose, as well as contributions from the university, which has so far resisted any commitment (Solomon 2021). In November 2021, Detroit voters overwhelmingly approved the creation of a Reparations Task Force, and in 2022 its work was just getting underway (Rahal 2022). In December 2021, the St. Petersburg, Florida, City Council approved a reparations initiative that involves investments in affordable housing, educational programs, and economic development for Black residents (C. Wright 2021). In April 2022, St. Louis Mayor Tishaura O. Jones signed a bill permitting local taxpayers to donate voluntarily to a reparations fund as a "first step" toward a city reparations initiative (Schlinkmann 2022).

Already in 2015, the city of Chicago passed a more specific reparations ordinance, designed to redress more than 125 African American victims of police torture from the 1970s through the 1990s under former Police Commander John Burge. Burge's reign ended in 1993 and he was later sentenced to over four years in prison. The law authorized $5.5 million for compensation to survivors and their families, and it waived tuition to city colleges, reformed the public school curriculum to acknowledge the torture, and provided for building a public memorial, among other steps (Jaffe 2020). Then in 2020, the city council created a Subcommittee on Reparations, which recommended in June 2022 that the city provide a guaranteed annual income to Black men. Chicago has not, however, yet made any monetary reparations, and many maintain that the promises of 2015 and 2020 still need to be fulfilled (Spielman 2022; Mayer 2022). In March 2023, the San Francisco Board of Supervisors accepted a report recommending a range of reparations measures, including payments of $5 million to Black residents of the city. That approval only authorized further deliberations and planning that are still underway, however, and the San Francisco chapter of the NAACP indicated its opposition to one-time cash payments and preference for more systemic transformations (Har 2023; Rucker and Chamberlain 2023).

Still more ambitiously, though also without concrete results so far, in 2021 the outgoing mayor of Los Angeles, Eric Garcetti, set up a multi-city initiative, Mayors Organized for Reparations and Equity (MORE), co-chaired by Garcetti and Denver Mayor Michael Hancock (MORE 2021). By 2022, MORE had been embraced by twelve mayors and one former mayor, including the mayors of Providence, Asheville, and St. Louis, and also Austin, Texas; Durham, North Carolina; Carrboro, North Carolina; Kansas City, Missouri; Sacramento, California; St. Paul, Minnesota; and Tullahassee, Oklahoma. Participating mayors and cities had all created or were working to create Black advisory committees and city commissions to hold hearings and determine what reparationist measures would be most appropriate to local circumstances. In Los Angeles, Garcetti allocated $500,000 for two years for the Los Angeles Reparations Commission, which had seven members, four selected by the mayor, the rest nominated by African American city council members. The commission is charged with considering reparations to Chinese Americans as well as African Americans, given the city's history of anti-Asian violence, which includes the notorious killing of eighteen Chinese men in 1871 (Miranda 2021). Mayor Garcetti explained that the city-level initiative has national aspirations: "Cities will never have the funds to pay for reparations on our own. When we have the laboratories of cities show that there is much more to embrace than to fear, we know that we can inspire national action as well" (Beam 2021).

State Legislatures

In the wake of the killing of George Floyd, the California General Assembly created a California State Reparations Task Force that issued an interim report in 2022, with a final report provided in 2023. The interim report said that the task force would ultimately recommend a "comprehensive reparations scheme" that could involve individual compensation as well as initiatives in voting rights, housing, education, environmental and infrastructure investments, entrepreneurial aid, criminal justice reform, and more, including the creation of a California African American Freedman Affairs Agency (Bonta 2022). Task force chair Kamilah Moore noted that since California had a $97.5 billion budget surplus, significant expenditures were credible—though by 2023, declining tax revenues amid tech-industry woes had reversed the state's finances to a deficit of over $22 billion (Cineas 2022; Walters 2023). If funded, reparations would be confined to descendants of either enslaved African Americans or a "free Black person living in the United States prior to the end of the 19th century." Even so, roughly 2.5 million Californians would be eligible for aid; and the Task Force estimated that based on housing discrimination between 1933 and 1977 alone, each person merited compensation of $223,000, or $569 billion altogether (Lee 2022). Critics were quick to deride that figure as almost doubling the state budget, but the Task Force proceeded in its work nonetheless (Frank 2022).

Though legislators have advanced reparations proposals in a number of other states, including Maryland, New Jersey, New York, Vermont, and Oregon, they have not won approval (Wiltz 2019; Blackburn 2021; Beam 2021; Simpson 2022). Proponents of these state measures regularly acknowledge that, as Vermont State Representative Sarah Copeland-Hanzas argued in 2019, "the scope of the conversation is best done at a national level, given that the impacts of slavery and post-slavery discrimination have been felt by people of color from around the country and not just the folks living in Vermont" (Wiltz 2019). Most agree, however, with Oregon State Senator Lew Frederick, who contends that "it's going to take a lot of states saying that this is something we have to do before we actually get something done at the national level" and has vowed to keep trying to create an Oregon Reparations Task Force (Blackburn 2021).

Some states have acted to redress racial injustices inflicted in their cities. In 1994, the Florida state legislature authorized a payment of $2 million to survivors of a 1923 massacre in Rosewood, Florida, when an unknown number of African Americans were killed by hundreds of rampaging whites who burned the city to the ground. The legislators also created a Rosewood Scholarship fund for descendants of those killed (Garrett-Scott 2021). Although the State of Oklahoma has not authorized reparations for the now notorious Tulsa Massacre of 1921, which killed three hundred African Americans, left ten thousand homeless, and destroyed the valuable properties that constituted Tulsa's "Black Wall Street," in 1997 the state legislature did establish a study commission which concluded that reparations should indeed be made (Goble 2022). With no aid coming from the state, in 2021 three survivors of the riot—Viola Fletcher, 107; her brother, Hughes Van Ellis, 100; and Lessie Benningfield Randle, 106—also joined in a public nuisance lawsuit against the City of Tulsa and other defendants, which the Oklahoma Supreme Court agreed to hear in August 2023, after contradictory rulings by lower state courts (Campo-Flores and Calfas 2023; McCarthy 2023).

California's positioning far out in front of other states on racial justice issues has been reinforced by Governor Newsom's establishment by executive order of a Truth and Healing Council, initially funded with $500,000, to apologize for and find ways to redress the state's treatment of Native Americans (Governor's Office of Tribal Affairs 2023). Newsom's 2018–19 state budget also allocated $100m to the fifty-one-acre California Indian Heritage Center in West Sacramento (Wiltz 2019). Then in December 2021, the California State Assembly passed a law returning to the family of Charles and Willa Bruce the land from which the city of Manhattan Beach had evicted them in 1924, an eviction designed to prevent them from providing valuable beachfront access to African Americans (J. D. Brown 2022). The advocacy group Where Is My Land played a major role in this success, and it currently has dozens of other cases of unfair land seizures that it is pursuing (Brownlee 2021; Burch 2023).

This flurry of state action has nonetheless produced meager results overall so far, and critics can legitimately doubt how much will ever be achieved through these means. It is undeniable, however, that states have never before shown as much interest in racial equity initiatives as they have in recent years, and efforts continue to multiply.

Congressmembers

At the federal level, the center of activity for reparations has of course been HR 40. It is worth noting, however, that the Congressional Black Caucus (CBC) had grown to fifty-seven members by 2021, with many of the new members elected in 2020, such as Cori Bush of Missouri and Jamaal Bowman of New York, proudly identifying with the Black Lives Matter movement and with the cause of reparations. In contrast to the past, CBC members now overwhelmingly support HR 40, and many favor other substantial Repair initiatives. Georgia Representative Hank Johnson has introduced the Tulsa-Greenwood Massacre Claims Accountability Act, designed to assist the survivors and descendants of those infamous attacks in gaining some form of reparations (D. Brown 2021a).

The New Funding Environment

Probably the single most striking and underappreciated fact about the many groups that are now supporting racial equity measures in one form or another is that many are bounteously funded—though far from all, and still less in aggregate than their conservative opponents, in all probability. A number of factors have converged to make this surge in financial resources for progressive groups possible.

First, as we have noted, the rise of social media has enabled the widespread publicizing of racial injustices and the collection of donations online, literally capitalizing on the emotions stirred by horrifying events like the killings of Trayvon Martin, Michael Brown, Breonna Taylor, George Floyd, and all too many others. Commentators have noted that racial justice organizations can have their agendas shifted by donor preferences, and this undoubtedly remains an anxiety (Francis 2019). Soliciting donations online can, however, make it possible to limit dependence on a few donors or a single type of donor. Conscious of how these new media are facilitating organizing and fundraising, moreover, new nonprofits have formed, such as Allied Media Projects, based in Detroit but with a global network, that aid other groups in developing the skills and strategies to deploy social media effectively (Allied Media Projects 2022). There is little doubt that these initiatives will continue to proliferate.

Second, the munificent wealth generated by the "new Gilded Age" economy of the twenty-first century, along with the growth of a business culture oriented to diversity, equity, and inclusion values, has meant there are many more businesses as well as individuals with incredibly deep pockets who are willing to contribute to racial justice organizations and causes. A 2021 *Washington Post* study found that America's fifty biggest corporations and their foundations, many prominently proclaiming that "Black Lives Matter," pledged after George Floyd's death to spend at least $49.5 billion on efforts to address racial inequities. Only $4.2 billion of those commitments were to outright grants, however. The other $45.3 billion was for loans and investments in efforts to advance Black economic mobility through homeownership, education, health care, and entrepreneurship, many representing funding from which the corporations could hope ultimately to profit. JPMorgan Chase and Bank of America accounted for most of those commitments, with companies like PayPal and Google contributing in the tens of millions, rather than billions. Companies did, however, give directly to Black Lives Matter, as well as to older civil rights groups like the Urban League, the NAACP and the NAACP Legal Defense and Education Fund, and HBCUs (Jan, McGregor, and Hoyer 2021). Two years after its announcement JPMorgan's $30 billion had been used for mortgages, loans to small businesses, and loans for development. The president of the National

Urban League, Marc Morial, welcomed the bank's $30 billion commitment as "a down payment" (quoted in Flitter 2022).

WarnerMedia pledged to give free on-air advertising to the civil rights advocacy organization Color of Change, as well as to the NAACP Legal Defense and Educational Fund (Friedman 2020). The Walmart Corporation's foundation promised to spend $100 million over five years through a newly created Center for Racial Equity, with special attention to finance, health, education, and criminal justice and with the aspiration to "change society's systems that perpetuate racism and discrimination," according to the Center's senior director, Kirstie Sims (Walmart 2021). Amazon, Apple, Uber, and the luggage brand Away donated to Bryan Stevenson's Equal Justice Initiative, devoted to aiding the wrongly incarcerated; AirBnB and the beauty company Glossier donated to Black Lives Matter; Nike announced a commitment of over $40 million "to support the Black community" in America; Mark Zuckerberg said Facebook would donate $10 million to "racial justice groups"; and the eyeglass company Warby Parker promised to give $1 million to organizations "combating systemic racism," among many other examples (Wellemeyer 2020).

Both older and newer philanthropic foundations have similarly increased their contributions to racial equity causes. Some, like the Andrew W. Mellon Foundation, have focused more on cultural dimensions of racial issues. Mellon allocated $250 million over five years to "The Monuments Project," an effort to replace the commemoration of Confederate leaders and other oppressive images immortalized in statues, museums, and street-level artifacts with installations celebrating racial equality and inclusion (Schuessler 2020). Other philanthropic foundations, including Ford, Kellogg, Rockefeller, and Kresge, are also giving gifts to fund removing and replacing Confederate monuments, but most are also aiding initiatives in, especially, criminal justice, housing, and economic development. To heighten its contributions but protect its endowment, in 2020 the Ford Foundation adopted a plan to borrow $1 billion in "social bonds" that it would use to increase its grants to US racial justice and civil rights groups by $180 million, bringing its commitments in the civil rights arena to $330 million (McGirt 2020).

Aided by wealthy individuals as well as corporations, foundations, and personal contributors of smaller donations, many racial justice organizations today tell positive stories of robust finances and expanding activities. DeRay McKesson, the prominent Black Lives Matter protester who now leads Campaign Zero, another major NGO focused on criminal justice reforms, reports that with an endowment of roughly $40 million, his group no longer devotes any time or effort to fundraising, though they continue to accept unsolicited donations.[8] Although Black Lives Matter itself continues to fundraise, it is even more substantially resourced. In its annual report for 2020, the BLM Global Network Foundation not only stated that its endowment campaign had already raised over $90 million, against administrative expenses of $8.4 million (Black Lives Matter 2020). It also committed $21.7 million in grant funding to eleven BLM chapters and thirty Black-led local organizations. Though some chapters rejected funding, finding the Foundation's decision-making insufficiently transparent, and some complained about its emphasis on Black LGBTQ+ groups, the foundation's resources and those of the other BLM groups insured that BLM would remain a powerful participant in racial justice struggles well into the future (Manfredi 2021).

These fortunate financial circumstances for many racial justice organizations have arisen in part because of a third factor: the proliferation in the twenty-first century of progressive philanthropic mediators—organizations that channel individual, foundation, and corporate donors to racial justice advocacy and service groups that donors might not otherwise discover. Some of these organizations primarily play advisory roles, but many receive substantial gifts themselves with the understanding that they will re-gift them for progressive purposes. This new and fast-growing philanthropic infrastructure, which scholars are just beginning to map comprehensively, is a significant reason we believe that reparations activism may have more staying power than many commentators recognize.

A model for and a funder of many of the newer organizations in this space is the Tides Foundation, created in 1976 to provide donor-advised funding services and later to incubate progressive nonprofit organizations, primarily through seed money. It has since formed a number of Tides-affiliated organizations. In 2020, the Tides Foundation alone had total revenues of over $1 billion and made grants totaling $619 million (GuideStar 2022). Tides Nexus, the set of Tides nonprofit organizations as a whole, received over $1.5 billion, and granted over $975 million (InfluenceWatch n.d.-a). Tides has received support from major mainstream foundations including Kellogg, Rockefeller, Hewlett, Ford, Packard, MacArthur, and many more, and it has donated to a very wide range of groups, many focused on non-racial progressive causes but others working specifically on racial justice issues, including Black Lives Matter, the NAACP, and many others (Tides 2022).

Perhaps the most prominent of the more recent philanthropy mediating organizations, due to its work with Mackenzie Scott, is the Bridgespan Group, founded in 2000 to aid "social change leaders," including NGOs, other nonprofits, philanthropists, and "impact investors," with racial equity "central" to its work and mission. Bridgespan was created to provide consulting services, and it has done so with innumerable moderately to extremely liberal foundations and social justice groups, including the Gates Foundation, the Ford Foundation, the Robertson Foundation, and many more. Today, however, Bridgespan facilitates social justice philanthropy and activism in many other ways as well. Its annual report for 2020 indicated it had over $115 million in net assets (Bridgespan Group 2022).

The Borealis Philanthropy, founded in 2015, is perhaps the most prominent of the new mediating groups that focuses especially on new racial justice organizations. It stated in its report for 2021 that it had in that year alone received $82.3 million in gifts and in turn donated $31.7 million to 329 grantees, through not only its Black-Led Movement Fund (which aids Black Lives Matter), but also its Communities Transforming Police Fund, its Emerging LGBTQ Leaders of Color Fund, its Racial Equity to Accelerate Change (REACH) Fund, its Racial Equity in Journalism Fund, its Racial Equity in Philanthropy Fund, and others (Borealis Philanthropy n.d.).

There are numerous other nonprofit philanthropic consulting and donor-advising organizations that provide similar services on smaller, often regional or local scales. Resource Generation, created in 2000 out of earlier efforts funded in part by the Tides Foundation, and later supported by the Ford Foundation, aids wealthy younger people (between the ages of eighteen and thirty-five) to donate to social justice initiatives, with a strong emphasis on racial justice (Resource Generation n.d.). According to InfluenceWatch, in 2021 its members donated $98.3 million to "critical race theory-influenced social justice movements," including Black Lives Matter and the Movement for Black Lives (InfluenceWatch n.d.-b). Resource Generation is a member of Funders for Justice, a "national network and organizing platform of funders" created to assist Black Lives Matter and now seeking to help donors provide "resources to BIPOC grassroots organizations working at the intersections of racial justice, gender justice, ending criminalization, and building models for community safety & justice" (Funders for Justice 2012–2021). The Solidaire Network and its companion organization, Solidaire Action, formed in 2013, are associations of donor organizers based in the San Francisco Bay Area with some three hundred members wealthy enough to provide $50,000 each. According to Solidaire Network's 2021 report, it had income of over $35 million and net assets of over $10 million (Solidaire 2022). In 2020 and 2021, its Janisha R. Gabriel Movement Protection Fund directed roughly $3 million to majority Black-led organizations, and it then launched a Black Liberation Pooled Fund that sought to move $14 million to Black-led groups and projects over the next two years. Recipients have included local Black Lives Matter chapters, the Black Feminist Project, the BlackOUT Collective, and many others. Its website states that it is committed to a "more radical vision and model for giving" to "the frontlines of intersectional movements for racial, gender, and climate change" (Solidaire n.d.). On the other side of the country, the Brooklyn Community Foundation provides services that donors can elect to finance and supports a community fund that has a strong emphasis on grant-making to Brooklyn nonprofits that are "addressing racial justice issues." It has provided over $75 million to local nonprofits since its founding in 2009 (Brooklyn Community Foundation 2016).

Many more examples from this part of the nonprofit sector could be added. The existence of these varied and substantial funding sources shows that the ways in which the institutions that comprise America's economic order, broadly defined, interact with its racial policy alliances are not simple and straightforward. There are certainly many wealthy, strongly pro-capitalist corporate interests funding racially conservative groups and initiatives, and few if any wealthy funders of left-leaning groups are prepared to overthrow capitalism in its entirely. Nonetheless, a variety of social justice groups that are in many cases expressly anti-capitalist, including reparations groups, are being funded through capitalist-acquired wealth at levels abundant enough to enable them to undertake a wide range of initiatives for years to come.

The clash of the emerging racial policy alliances therefore does not appear simply to be driven by the capitalist economic order in any straightforward away, even if that order may well constrain the scope of attainable changes; and today's racial policy disputes will probably not be settled, insofar as they can or ever will be, by changes in funding alone. On both sides of today's racial policy divide, many individuals and groups demonstrate a willingness to put their money where their mouths are.

Violence on Behalf of Repair Goals

An account of the emerging Repair alliance would be incomplete without including groups who are willing to engage in violence to combat what they see as systemic racism. Yet it is more difficult to document militant members of the progressive Repair alliance than it is such members of the conservative Protect alliance, which includes armed groups explicitly calling themselves militias. On the Left, there are no self-proclaimed "militias," and although there are armed activists, the groups or simply individuals who sometimes threaten violence are less visibly organized.

Moreover, most analysts argue that although racially and ethnically motivated violence is the leading category of extremist violence in America, it has long been far more common on the gun-valorizing American Right than on the Left (Program on Extremism and NCITE 2021; Jasko et al. 2022). The Anti-Defamation League (ADL) contends that in 2020, for example, of seventeen extremist murders, sixteen were inflicted by right-wing extremists, and only one by a leftist—a pattern it says has held for at least a decade (ADL 2022). Many conservatives fiercely insist, however, that liberal media and advocacy groups minimize or deny the violence perpetrated by "Antifa," leftists presenting themselves as anti-fascist. The *Business Insider* reporter Anthony L. Fisher has argued that the widely used ADL numbers include right-wing extremists involved in killings over domestic conflicts or drug deals that are not clearly motivated by political views, though he acknowledges that it remains true that "ultrarightist groups" account for "a disproportionate number of hate crimes and acts of terror" (Fisher 2020). It is also undeniable that for decades groups and individuals on the right have engaged in major acts of planned violence, including Timothy McVeigh's 1995 bombing of the Oklahoma City federal building, the 2020 plot to kidnap Michigan Governor Gretchen Whitmer, and of course the January 6, 2021, attack on the US Capitol. Since the early 1970s, there have not been comparable conspiracies by what appear to be the far fewer violent groups on the left.

Nonetheless, there have always been and there remain Left groups who defend use of arms and engage in acts of violence to advance their cause. Many were formed or became more prominent after the clashes at the 2017 Unite the Right rally in Charlottesville. In contrast to the more organized radical Socialist and Communist Left of the twentieth century, contemporary violent Left activists tend to be bound together at most by a general anti-fascist and anti-racist ideology that is open to many interpretations and strategic choices (Counter Extremism Project 2023a, 3–5). But Antifa groups in New York, Philadelphia, and Portland, Oregon (called Rose City Antifa), all have websites, indicating some measure of institutionalization.

The NYC Antifa website has links to thirty-six other organizations in the US as well as many overseas, and it features detailed information on those it terms fascists, which could facilitate violent attacks on the groups it names (NYC Antifa n.d.). Rose City Antifa formed in 2007 to resist what it terms "a neo-Nazi skinhead festival called Hammerfest," and says it seeks not only to "prevent fascist organizing" but to "provide consequences to fascist organizers" (Rose City Antifa n.d.). It has been involved in the multiple violent clashes in Portland protests that occurred after George Floyd's murder, and its website, like NYC Antifa's, identifies in some detail those it sees as fascist enemies, possibly facilitating attacks on them. The Antifa group in Philadelphia says it is in "direct conflict with Racism, Homophobia, Sexism, Anti-Semitism, Islamophobia, Transphobia, and all other flavors of fascism" (Philly Antifa 2022). It has been described as violent, and responsible for vandalism as well as confrontations with pro-Trump crowds, though what specific acts of violence its members have been responsible for and have suffered are disputed (Phillips and McCoy 2017; Palmer, Rowan, and Roebuck 2021).

The Redneck Revolt, founded in 2016, describes itself as a "national network of community defense projects" that are "pro-worker, anti-racist," seeking to rally working-class white people especially to oppose white supremacy. Its principles include commitments to "organized defense," and it has fostered John Brown Gun Clubs for "armed community defense" in various states (Redneck Revolt n.d.-a). It provided protection for Left protesters at the Charlottesville rally. Redneck Revolt appears to rely on online fundraising through its website. It is not clear how well resourced and extensive its network is (Redneck Revolt n.d.-b).

Of the John Gun Brown Clubs Redneck Revolt has fostered, the most active is the Puget Sound John Brown Gun Club, though that club has cut ties with its parent organization. The Puget Sound club professes its commitment to "**active resistance** to the corrosive and destructive social effects of white supremacy, sexism, bigotry, and economic exploitation" and it offers "support upon request to those in our communities targeted by white supremacists and other agents of oppression and exploitation," including "trainings, security, and concealed pistol license assistance" (Puget Sound John Brown Gun Club n.d.). It, too, has reportedly been involved in violent clashes during the many racial protests in the Northwest, especially in Portland and Seattle.

Also noteworthy is Black Bloc, an international group with no formal organizational structure, website, or funding that nonetheless is credited with playing a significant role in demonstrations at the World Trade Organization, protests at Donald Trump's inaugural, confrontations with the Proud Boys at rallies against police violence, and other similar events. Although some activists who identify with Black Bloc invoke the Black Panthers and Malcolm X, it is an international movement that began in Germany in 1970, and the backgrounds of its American participants are murky. Linked chiefly by a broad anti-capitalist, anti-racist, anti-fascist ideology and by tactics that include appearing at demonstrations organized by others, Black Bloc members are often dressed in black and masked or helmeted to disguise their identities. Black Bloc protesters have especially been associated with violence in Europe, but observers credit them with heightening confrontations at racial justice protests in the United States as well (Counter Extremism Project 2023b).

In sum, conservatives are not wrong to say that there are some groups on the left willing to use violence to overturn what they see as pervasively unjust, racist American institutions, even if many right-wing media accounts of the harms these groups have inflicted are overblown and unsubstantiated. Though they appear much less numerous and organized than the militia of the Right, these armed Left groups also contribute to the dangers in America that race-related battles present today.

As this chapter has shown, conservatives are also not wrong to see what we are terming the Repair alliance as growing, as well-funded, as committed to more sweeping transformations than many earlier civil rights advocacy groups, and as already inspiring many new racial equity initiatives by increasing numbers of cities, states, churches, universities, museums, corporations, and individuals. The evidence is clear that the Repair policy alliance has already become a significant force in American politics, and its growth has not been ended by the fading of public opinion support for protests and for BLM after the summer of 2020. Whether this means that today's Left is pursuing a racial agenda so threateningly radical as to foster unbridgeable divides in American politics depends, however, on a grasp and an assessment of the Repair alliance's story of America and its driving political vision. These are the topics of chapter 7.

CHAPTER SEVEN

The Repair Story and Transformative Visions

Today, 160 years after the abolition of slavery, its badges and incidents remain embedded in the political, legal, health, financial, educational, cultural, environmental, social, and economic systems of the United States of America. Racist, false, and harmful stereotypes created to support slavery continue to physically and mentally harm African Americans today. Without a remedy specifically targeted to dismantle our country's racist foundations and heal the injuries inflicted by colonial and American governments, the "badges and incidents of slavery" will continue to harm African Americans in almost all aspects of life. —California Task Force to Study and Develop Reparations Proposals for African Americans (2022, 6)

The Repair Story

As we saw in chapter 4, conservatives believe that a more radical racial justice movement has emerged chiefly because extremists of the "New New Left" managed to gain control of educational institutions, many popular media, and even corporate human resources departments, aided by the growth of the DEI industry they helped to create. Conservatives differ on various particulars, such as the extent to which these developments were rooted in intellectual and moral changes dating back at least to the Progressive era, and how significant the presidency of Barack Obama and international reparations movements have been. They wholeheartedly agree, however, that the contemporary Left has embraced and extended the most radical views of the 1960s in ways that have made it necessary to protect traditional American values, institutions, and citizens aggressively.

Similarly, as we saw in chapter 2, there are differences among Left analysts and activists in their views on the origins of racial ideologies, attitudes, and inequalities; on the relationship of racial inequities to those of class, gender, and many other dimensions of human social structures and identities; and on what forms of political organizing, messaging, and policies should be adopted to achieve a more just society and world. Yet Repair proponents also converge on an overarching Left narrative of how the nation's current racial politics arose that has some overlaps with the Protect story, but is fundamentally distinct.

The key difference is that Repair advocates do not believe that modern racial justice demands arise from a misguided revolt of twentieth- and twenty-first-century liberals, progressives, and radicals against the Constitution and its framers. They see today's racial justice movements as primarily building not on modern American liberalism but on a long history of Black resistance to the different forms of white supremacy in America that date back to the colonial era, as well as on struggles of African-descended peoples against white European imperialism more generally. That resistance arose, they argue, because the American constitutional system was all too complicit in racial injustices from the start, whether due to economic, political, or cultural motives, or some combination.

As the reparations advocates William Darity Jr. and A. Kirsten Mullen put it, the core problem is that "racism and discrimination have perpetually crippled black economic opportunities," "freedom," and "citizenship"; and while at "several historic moments the trajectory of racial inequality could have been altered dramatically," beginning with the very "formation of the republic," those roads were not taken (Darity and Mullen 2020). The California Task Force to Study and Develop Reparation Proposals similarly argues that "the effects of slavery infected every aspect of American society over the last 400 years" because "to maintain slavery, government actors adopted white supremacist beliefs and passed laws to create a racial hierarchy and control enslaved and free African Americans. After the end of slavery . . . the government failed to give them the full rights of citizenship and failed to protect African Americans from widespread terrorism and violence . . . direct federal, state, and local government actions continued to enforce the racist lies created to justify slavery. These laws and government-supported cultural beliefs have since formed the foundation of innumerable modern laws, practices, and policies across the nation" (California Task Force to Study and Develop Reparation Proposals for African Americans 2023, 3). In agreement, the history sketched in the "M4BL Reparations Toolkit" that the Movement for Black Lives published in 2019 condemns "the long history of colonialism, genocide, land theft, enslavement, anti-Black racial terror, racial capitalism, structural discrimination, and exclusion that have been foundational to the establishment and economic growth of the United States, and their ongoing impacts" (Ritchie and Stahly-Butts 2019).

Unsurprisingly, then, few of the Progressive thinkers and politicians like Woodrow Wilson that conservatives see as paving the way for today's radical perspectives appear in Repair narratives of their roots. Only W. E. B. Du Bois is a shared touchstone. In the Toolkit's overview of the history of racial justice demands in the United States, white Progressives and New Dealers receive no mention, though the systems of segregation they helped to create and perpetuate are prominent. Instead, the Toolkit's narrative features developments that conservatives largely ignore, especially the calls of Thaddeus Stevens, Charles Sumner, and other Radical Republicans for land redistribution to newly emancipated slaves during Reconstruction. Darity and Mullen give special attention in this regard to Frederick Douglass, portraying him not as the advocate of color-blindness that many conservative narratives depict, but as a leader with evolving ideas and analyses, who came to recognize that land redistribution to emancipated Black Americans was imperative (Darity and Mullen 2020, 14). The Toolkit, Darity and Mullen, and many others also highlight Callie House's late nineteenth-century Ex-Slave Mutual Relief and Bounty and Pension Association and Queen Mother Audley Moore, termed "the mother of the modern-day reparations movement" and a mentor to members of the Black Panthers and the Republic of New Afrika during the 1960s, among many other historical racial justice advocates (Ritchie and Stahly-Butts 2019, 54; Darity and Mullen 2020, 15, 22).

The Protect and Repair narratives are in more agreement on the importance and continuing influences of the new elaborations of racial justice ideas advanced by both white and Black radicals in the 1960s. Building on Du Bois, the SDS leaders Ted Allen and Noel Ignatin (later Ignatiev) began arguing in the mid-1960s that working-class whites must be persuaded to recognize and repudiate their "white-skin privilege" before an interracial political movement capable of overcoming capitalist and imperialist inequalities could be formed (Ignatin and Allen 2011). Many Repair advocates concur with conservatives like Christopher Rufo that versions of these arguments eventually became central to influential formulations of "whiteness" studies, Critical Race Theory, and critiques of "racial capitalism."

Many on both sides also give great weight to how almost simultaneously in 1966, the Black Panther Party adopted a ten-point "Platform and Program," subsequently amended in 1972 to include all people of color and oppressed groups along with Blacks, that anticipated many of the arguments and demands of the Black Lives Matter movement, NAARC, N'COBRA, and other Repair advocates today, as well as CRT themes (Gaiter 2015). The Panthers called for:

1. Black self-determination, full control of the institutions in their communities;
2. Federal provision of full employment or guaranteed incomes to all people;
3. An end to the "robbery by the capitalist" of Black and oppressed communities, with federally mandated "restitution for slave labor and mass murder of black people" in the form of currency to pay "the overdue debt of forty acres and two mules";
4. Aid in acquiring decent, possibly cooperatively owned housing and land;
5. An educational system supportive of Black self-knowledge and awareness of "the true nature of this decadent American society";
6. An exemption from military service for Black men, to which the Panthers subsequently added a call for an end to all American wars of aggression against people of color around the world;
7. An end to "police brutality and the murder of Black people" and recognition of their right to bear arms in their self-defense, later expanded to include other people of color and all oppressed people inside the United States;
8. The release of "all Black People" incarcerated in all the nation's prisons and jails, again later extended to all oppressed people;
9. Trials by juries of their peers and attorneys of their choice henceforth, in accordance with the Constitution; and
10. Access to "land, bread, housing, education, clothing, justice and, peace," demands the Program justified by citing the Declaration of Independence (BlackPast 2018; Gaiter 2015).

In 1972, the Panthers also added "people's community control of modern technology" to their tenth point, along with a call for government-provided health care (Gaiter 2015). The Panthers argued for advancing their goals via a UN-supervised plebiscite through which America's Black "colonial subjects" would decide their destiny. Their framing of racial justice initiatives in the context of resistance to racist white settler colonialism, and in association with demands across a range of policy regimes that included obtaining decent housing, employment, and income; culturally responsive education; policing and criminal justice reform; and health care all became themes of most modern Repair proponents.

In contrast to Protect narratives, when discussing the 1960s Repair advocates contend that the Rev. Dr. Martin Luther King Jr., like Frederick Douglass, was not the moderate champion of color-blind principles that conservatives sometimes make him appear to be. They portray King as a far more radical figure on issues of race, economics, and imperialism. The M4BL Toolkit presents the SCLC leader as a reparations advocate, and it also celebrates the 1960s call for reparations included in James Forman's Black Manifesto, issued when he was prominent in the Student Non-Violent Coordinating Committee as well as the Black Panthers and the League of Revolutionary Black Workers.

Skipping over the discrediting of radicalism in the 1970s, the Toolkit's history then traces the creation of N'COBRA in 1987, the introduction of HR 40 in 1989, and the heightened racial justice demands that followed not only with the rise of Black Lives Matter and the Movement for Black Lives, but also from the appeal for US reparations made by the United Nations Working Group of Experts on People of African Descent in 2016 (Ritchie and Stahly-Butts 2019, 55–56). Unlike most conservative stories, the M4BL Toolkit narrative stresses the international context for racial equity demands throughout its history and policy discussions, arguing that reparations in particular is a robust concept under international law and citing examples of reparations made by Germany, Italy, Japan, Canada, South Africa, and even Iraq (Ritchie and Stahly-Butts 2019, 51–57).

Furthermore, in sharp disagreement with conservatives, few of today's racial progressives place much weight on the rise of the DEI industry as a driver of major changes, for good or ill. Nor do they see woke ideology, cancel culture, or Critical Race Theory as verging on anything remotely approaching dominance in most modern American institutions, or as frequently violating conservative freedoms. Though most Repair advocates support various DEI initiatives, many see them as at best mildly ameliorative of the nation's problems, at worst as mechanisms of cooptation that perpetuate its injustices, and not as potent means for the systemic transformations they seek.

For those very reasons, even as Repair advocates stress that their concerns have a long history, most do agree with contemporary conservatives that while in the early 1960s, many mainstream civil rights leaders stressed ending segregation and moving toward integration of African Americans into existing American economic, political, and social institutions, today's racial justice advocates more often contend, like the militant wing of the 1960s civil rights movement, that America needs more radical changes.

The M4BL Toolkit stresses that the "long-term systemic solutions" its authors seek require "thoroughly tending to the root causes of the problems, whereas non-transformative (often labelled reformist) change does not" (Ritchie and Stahly-Butts 2019, 49). Like most Repair advocates, the Toolkit also rejects the view advanced by both conservative advocates of colorblindness and class-focused progressives that to address those root causes, universal programs are most just and efficacious. It asserts repeatedly that race-targeted initiatives, whether or not they are termed reparations, "are owed to specific people and communities that have been harmed, and cannot be accomplished through generic social programs or investments in communities" alone, though it supports many such measures (Ritchie and Stahly-Butts 2019, 45).

Most Repair advocates do agree with today's nationalist conservatives that millions of Americans and billions around the world were harmed over the last four decades by the policies of neoliberal globalist elites. However, many reject the idea that today's conservative insistence on greater economic, social, and political protection for traditionalists stems chiefly from grievances against those recent policies, or that they have arisen as defensive responses to militant Left radicals. They instead see contemporary racial conservatism as a feverish reassertion, against what have so far been only modest changes, of the political, economic, social, and ideological interests that first created the United States and that have sustained it as a society dominated by wealthy white Christian men ever since. Most in the Repair alliance believe that the police killings, the stagnation and decline in Black wealth, and especially the rise of Donald Trump and the MAGA movement all show that it is the champions of those who have long sat atop America's economic, political, and racial hierarchies who have intensified their ruthless enforcement of their own advantages in recent years, in ways that have made it clear to more and more liberals as well as radicals that many American institutions, and America itself, are in need of fundamental repair.

In interviews as well as in their writings, Repair proponents also stress that although twenty-first-century racial justice movements do build on the more Left perspectives of the 1960s, they move beyond them in important ways. Many like NAARC's Kamm Howard agree with conservatives that reparations advocacy revived after 2010 in large part because new social media made people throughout America and around the world painfully aware of the series of police killings of Black people that seemed to accelerate, not decline, after the acquittal of George Zimmerman catalyzed the Black Lives Matter movement and innumerable protests.[1] Progressive activists, as much as some conservative analysts, believe that seeing videos of (especially) white police officers and vigilantes killing Black people, along with subsequent failures to punish the killers, enhanced the credibility of claims that America's criminal justice system suffered not just from a few bad apples, but from deeply institutionalized racism requiring major systemic changes. As the Black Panther Ten-Point Program shows, condemnations of police brutality were hardly new in racial justice advocacy; but from roughly 2012 on, millions felt newly engulfed by what seemed to be undeniable evidence of those realities. Because police did not appear to be killing whites so cavalierly, moreover, many accepted that changes had to focus on the special harms being done to African Americans.

Another lesson appeared to be that if the nation's systems of law enforcement displayed systemic racism, then it was plausible to think that American agencies were not vigorously enforcing antidiscrimination laws to defeat racism in many other venues of American life. It therefore made sense to see systemic racism as not just a problem of the criminal justice system, but as widespread throughout the country. While many Repair narratives also note the impact of a more favorable international climate and an expanded set of global allies, the institution-building of the Institute for the Black World 21st Century and N'COBRA, which together created NAARC in 2015, and the influence of both the Coates article and, later, the 1619 Project, in explaining the heightened Left calls for systemic change, most still give primacy to the impact of police killings, the accompanying protests, and the rise of the BLM/M4BL movement.

Most versions of the Repair story also stress much more than conservatives do that the rise of BLM and related new racial justice organizations has involved the strong embrace of certain ideas that either had not yet emerged or were far more marginal in the 1960s civil rights era, even among radicals. The most novel and significant of these ideas reflect discontents with how heterosexual, sometimes misogynist men dominated visible leadership roles through the 1960s, with figures like Martin Luther King Jr., Bobby Seale and Huey Newton, Stokely Carmichael, and later Jesse Jackson receiving more attention than women leaders like Dorothy Height and Ella Baker, the gay Bayard Rustin, or the would-be transgendered Pauli Murray.

First, as the historian and BLM participant Barbara Ransby has detailed, the Black Lives Matter movement has "championed [a] grassroots, group-centered approach to leadership," seeking as much as possible not to have its activism identified with one or two charismatic figures. Before DeRay McKesson went on to head Campaign Zero's police reform initiatives, for example, he faced criticisms from Patrisse Khan-Cullors and others in BLM because they perceived his growing prominence as having "celebritized the movement" (Ransby 2018, 102–3). Whereas in the 1960s media coverage referred to Martin Luther King Jr. much more than to the SCLC (Southern Christian Leadership Conference), and later to Jesse Jackson more than to the various organizations he headed and allied with, today references to BLM vastly outweigh attention to any one leader, consonant with this new theme. Groups like Community Change, moreover, today place greater emphasis than they did in the late twentieth century on funding and aiding grassroots local organizations, rather than simply advocating at the national level.[2]

In contrast to both their more mainstream and more radical 1960s predecessors, the BLM movement and many other contemporary Repair organizations are deeply shaped by the Black feminist and Black queer theorizing and activism that emerged largely after 1970. Accordingly, Repair narratives stress that today's racial justice alliance is far more strongly committed to intersectionality, as an analytical approach to political understanding, as a strategic approach to political organizing, and as a guide to policy design, than were its 1960s predecessors. The Preamble to the M4BL 2020 Vision for Black Lives insists that there "can be no liberation for all Black people if we do not center and fight for members of our communities who are living at the intersections of multiple and mutually reinforcing structures of oppression" (Ritchie and Stahly-Butts 2019). Proponents contend that through this focus on intersectionality, a Black-led movement that includes reparations specifically for Black Americans can nonetheless include and benefit all people. As Ransby puts it, "Black people are represented in all the categories of the oppressed in the United States. They are immigrants. They are poor and working class. They are disabled. They are Indigenous. They are LGBTQIA. They are Latinx and Afro-Asians. They are also Muslim and other religious minorities, and the list goes on. So to realize the liberation of 'all' Black people means undoing systems of injustices that impact all other oppressed groups as well" (Ransby 2018, 3–4).

The historical narratives of Repair-aligned analysts and activists highlight other new features of contemporary racial justice groups. Some stress their innovative reliance on social media for organizing (Roberts 2018). Some stress the rejection by many of their participants of older forms of "respectability" politics, in which leaders sought to present themselves as conforming to white bourgeois cultural standards (Ransby 2018; Harris 2014; Dazey 2021). Yet some within BLM and many other supporters of Repair policies do not stress social media use, ubiquitous as it has become among everyone in modern life, because they value in-person group deliberations and actions. Many also do conform to conventional standards of respectability; and in any case, the more radical activists of the 1960s rejected white bourgeois norms at least as much.

These variations do not undermine the core agreements in Repair stories about how and why today's racial justice activists have come to adopt policies and strategies beyond those of the 1960s, as well as how and why they see their conservative opponents as more intransigent and dangerous than in past decades. Virtually all Repair advocates tell their stories as involving continuity with Black historical struggles for racial justice, not with modern liberalism; heightened awareness of the need for transformative, systemic changes, especially against an unjustified renewed conservative militancy; and programs for change involving a fresh embrace of grassroots group leadership and intersectional agendas and coalitions, all energized to a considerable degree by massive modern evidence of police brutality. These elements feature prominently in the visions of what racial justice measures should entail and achieve advanced by leading members of the Repair policy alliance.

Visions of Racial Repair

We saw in chapter 6 that an extraordinary range of groups and individuals are pursuing agendas that seek to promote racial justice throughout the United States and at local, state, national, and international levels (African American Redress Network 2023b). Together they comprise the Repair policy alliance; but like all coalitions, including the contemporary Protect racial institutional order, the still emerging Repair alliance includes members with overlapping but partly distinct policy agendas and larger visions of what "reparations" entails.[3] Its participants are united chiefly by their conviction that rather than seeking to protect existing American institutions, practices, and group interests, the nation must begin pursuing a wide range of systemic transformations to place those victimized by past and present racial injustices in a position to thrive in the future. Even though many more are coming to apply the label of reparations to their agendas, most either include in or accompany their calls for reparations with advocacy for numerous initiatives aiming at racial equity, and in the more extreme cases at outright abolition of mass incarceration, of policing, of immigration enforcement, of national boundaries, of "racial capitalism," and perhaps even of capitalism—though this last position is far less frequently and concretely urged by today's Left than it was by Socialists and Communists in the early twentieth century.

In keeping with its emphasis on decentralized leadership, there is no figure comparable to Donald Trump at the center of the Repair alliance. The American Left's most prominent contemporary political leader, Senator Bernie Sanders, stands in the class-focused camp that endorses many Repair proposals but refuses to treat race as its central concern. Consequently, the contents and breadth of today's Repair visions can best be grasped by examining the positions of some of the most prominent racial justice groups, as well as allied governmental agencies and academic voices.

The Movement for Black Lives

In rhetoric and to a significant degree in substance, the M4BL platform, "Vision for Black Lives," first adopted in 2016 and then revised in 2020, is the most significant statement of the BLM movement's ideology and the fullest expression of the most novel and radical elements of the Repair alliance. M4BL began the 2020 iteration of its Vision by thanking "Black feminists and Black trans women" for deepening the presence in the Vision of "a Black queer and trans feminist lens and a disability justice analysis." It thereby underlined the movement's commitment to analyses and coalition-building involving all "who are living at the intersections of multiple and mutually reinforcing structures of oppression" (Ritchie and Stahly-Butts 2019; Movement for Black Lives 2023). In accord with Ransby's argument, the Vision's authors expressly sought to elevate an impressive array of "the most marginalized Black people, including, but not limited to, women, femmes, queer, trans, gender nonconforming, intersex, Muslim, disabled, D/deaf, and autistic people, people living with HIV, people who are criminalized, formerly and currently incarcerated, detained or institutionalized, migrants, including undocumented migrants, low and no-income, cash poor, and working class, homeless and precariously housed people, people who are dependent on criminalized substances, youth, and elders" (Ransby 2018, 3–4: Movement for Black Lives 2023).

The Vision statement adds that although "this platform is focused on domestic policies, we know that cisheteropatriarchy, ableism, exploitative racial capitalism, imperialism, militarism, and white supremacy and nationalism are global structures." Consequently, M4BL activists seek to join "with descendants of African people all over the world in an ongoing call and struggle for reparations for the historic and continuing harms of colonialism and slavery, including structural and systemic sexual and gender-based violence, and *we recognize and honor the rights and struggle of our global Indigenous family for reparations, land, sovereignty, and self-determination*" (Ritchie and Stahly-Butts 2019; Movement for Black Lives 2023, italics in the original). BLM activists also strive to work with progressives of all demographic backgrounds on an even wider array of issues through "The Rising Majority," a multiracial coalition consisting primarily of people of color, but also including progressive whites, that M4BL formed in 2017. The Rising Majority has sought to unite "labor, youth, and feminists; activists working toward abolition, immigrant rights proponents, economic and environmental justice; and activists working against climate change, war, and imperialism" in order to develop "an anti-capitalist, intersectional, and anti-racist strategy in the fight against neo-fascism" (Rising Majority n.d.).

Even more than most other Repair groups, the M4BL Vision presents a plethora of proposals for change. As noted in chapter 1, it organizes them under six headings, only one of which is "Reparations." The others are "End the War on Black People," "Political Power," "Community Control," "Economic Justice," and "Divest/Invest" (Ritchie and Stahly-Butts 2019; Movement for Black Lives 2023).

1. The "End the War" category encompasses many demands, including ending the war on Black Youth, Black Women, Black Trans, Queer, Nonconforming and Intersex People, Black Health and Black Disabled People, and Black Migrants, along with calls to end all jails, prisons, and immigration detention, the death penalty, the war on drugs, surveillance of Black communities, pretrial detention and money bail, the militarization of the police, and more.

2. Under "Political Power," the Vision demands "independent Black political power and Black self-determination in all areas of society," including a "remaking of the current U.S. political system to create a real democracy" through "public financing of elections and the end of money controlling politics through ending super PACS and unchecked corporate donations" and "electoral protection, electoral expansion and the right to vote for all

people" via "universal . . . automatic voter registration . . . and a ban on disenfranchisement laws," as well as other measures.

3. Under "Community Control," it calls for "democratic community control of local, state, and federal law enforcement agencies," an "end to the privatization of education and real community control by parents, students and community members of schools," and "participatory budgeting at the local, state, and federal level."

4. Notably, its "Economic Justice" provisions call not for the end of capitalism, but for its transformation through measures including a "progressive restructuring of tax codes at the local, state, and federal levels"; "federal and state job programs that specifically target the most economically marginalized Black people" as well as "compensation for those involved in the care economy"; rights to "restored land, clean air, clean water and housing and end to the exploitative privatization of natural resources"; enhanced rights for "workers to organize in the public and private sectors"; restoration of the Glass-Steagall Act and creation of a National Credit Union Administration to promote Black "banks, small and community credit unions, insurance companies, and other financial institutions"; a "renegotiation of all trade agreements to prioritize the interests of workers and communities"; support for "the development of cooperative or social economy networks to help facilitate trade across and in Black communities globally"; financial support for "low-interest loans" to promote the development of food, residential, and other cooperatives; "trusts and culturally responsive health infrastructures"; and protections "for workers in industries that are not appropriately regulated including domestic workers, farm workers, and tipped workers."

5. The Vison's "Invest/Divest" section calls for reallocating funds from policing and incarceration to "long-term safety strategies such as education, restorative justice services, and employment programs"; reparations for "the devasting impact of the 'war on drugs' and criminalization of prostitution"; universal health care; a "constitutional right at the state and federal level to a fully-funded education" with a "curriculum that acknowledges and addresses students' material and cultural needs"; divestment from "industrial multinational use of fossil fuels"; investments in "sustainable energy solutions"; and a "cut in military expenditures."

6. Finally, under "Reparations" the proposals include free access for "Black people (including undocumented and currently and formerly incarcerated people) to lifetime education," with "free access and open ad-

missions to public community colleges and universities" and "technical education," accompanied by "forgiveness of student loans"; a "guaranteed minimal livable income for all Black people"; "corporate and governmental reparations focused on healing ongoing physical and mental trauma, and ensuring our access and control of food sources, housing, and land"; mandated "school curriculums that critically examine the political, economic, and social impacts of colonialism and slavery, and funding to support . . . cultural assets and sacred sites"; federal and state acknowledgments of the lasting impacts of slavery; and immediate passage of HR 40 (Ritchie and Stahly-Butts 2019; Movement for Black Lives 2023).

The M4BL Vision thus aims at major domestic and international transformations of numerous institutions and policy regimes, on behalf of a kaleidoscope of identity groups. It is important to recognize, however, that not only is its agenda primarily domestic; many of its specific proposals are efforts to advance the goals of Blacks and their allies within the broad parameters of existing national political, economic, and social institutions and structures. The radicalism of the Movement for Black Lives and Black Lives Matter vision is, for many of their leaders and activists, not inconsistent with pursuing a wide variety of smaller, more immediate policy goals. Theirs is a panoramic vision for a still distant future more than an immediate legislative agenda, though its profoundly transformative aspirations are clear.

ADOS and NAASD

In contrast, the American Descendants of Slavery (ADOS) and the National Assembly of American Slavery Descendants (NAASD) occupy significantly more conservative places in the Repair alliance, seeking reparations only for Black Americans with ancestors who suffered enslavement, rather than a broad intersectional, international agenda. It is all the more striking, then, that the agendas they propose still go well beyond traditional notions of reparations and are also extremely wide-ranging.

For example, under the heading of "Reparations," the ADOS Advocacy Foundation urges a presidential executive order designating descendants of chattel slavery in the United States as a "protected category" and creating a federal "Office of ADOS" that will champion their interests (ADOS Advocacy Foundation 2022a). It also, however accompanies these two comparatively limited reparations demands with a "Black Agenda" of what may best be termed racial equity initiatives. That agenda includes proposals under twelve headings:

1. "Agriculture," seeking redistribution of farmlands granted to white homesteaders until at least 15 percent of the arable lands in the US are owned by Black Americans, as well as loans to Black farmers, among other measures.
2. "Black Business," demanding a "permanent White House Initiative on Black Americans' Economic Uplift and Full Economic Inclusion," a "National Program for Black American Business Enterprise," federal grants and loans, contracts for Black businesses, and other measures.
3. "Cannabis," urging presidential pardons for all federal prisoners convicted of "marijuana-related crimes" and a "40 percent rule" requiring that "40 percent of all licenses for the cultivation, sale, and distribution of cannabis must be set aside for Black Americans," among other steps.
4. "Climate Change," advocating for federal funding for all "clean or renewable jobs" to go only to sectors that have a 15 percent Black employment rate, and for FEMA to create a "special office that identifies and attends to the needs of Black Americans," along with other measures.
5. "Criminal Justice," calling for identifying ADOS as a "protected class" in the criminal justice system, so that they are judged in part by the effects of racial injustices on them; and urging a wide range of investments in communities hurt by mass incarceration.
6. "Education," demanding bans on school expulsions and $500 million in Department of Education funds for "specialists in race-based trauma," accompanied by new national race-conscious history standards and funding for HBCUs, formerly Black public elementary and secondary schools, and scholarships, and more.
7. "Environmental Racism," with heightened information-gathering on and enforcement against racially skewed environmental violations, as well as many kinds of aid for affected persons and communities.
8. "Health & Nutrition," demanding the creation of a White House Equity Task Force, $45 million to fund an "ADOS Healthcare Ombudsmen," and $2.25 billion for public health departments to "promote health equity," along with other steps.
9. "Housing," calling for grants and loans to Black homeowners and renters and $750 billion in federal funds to expand the affordable housing stock.
10. "Immigration," insisting that unless impacts on Black communities are considered in immigration laws, ADOS will oppose all immigration legislation.
11. "Infrastructure," urging the creation of a federal "Office of Inclusion of

Black Americans in Energy, Engineering, and Technology" and insuring that Black-owned businesses have at least a "fifteen percent stake in the natural resources, supply chains, production, manufacturing, and distribution of components and end-products in all industries" that build or form parts of the nation's infrastructure, as well as other actions.
12. "Unemployment & Labor," demanding a "permanent federal jobs preference for Black Americans that guarantees a living wage," a requirement that at least 15 percent of all federal contracts go to Black-owned businesses, and $20 billion in workplace development and STEM apprenticeship programs for ADOS workers, among other policies (ADOS Advocacy Foundation 2022b).

As noted in chapter 5, the National Assembly of American Slavery Descendants (NAASD) structures its proposals as a "R.E.P.A.I.R." agenda, with headings of Reconciliation, Equity, Protections, Atonement, Investment, and Remuneration. It advocates for a national acknowledgment of America's "original sin" of slavery and "Truth and Reconciliation" hearings for Black American Descendants of Chattel Slavery (BADOCS); affirmative action by executive order; an end to voting rights restrictions and mass incarceration and expanded pre-K–12 school funding; a new Freedmen's Bureau; the creation of BADOCS as a census category; stronger laws against hate crimes, predatory lending, housing discrimination, medical experimentation, and environmental injustices; presidential pardons for racial justice protesters; a program of cultural and historical preservation, monument restoration, and "de-Confederization" of public sites; small business loans, federal contracts, infrastructure initiatives, farming, and STEM programs for BADOCS, along with cannabis decriminalization; and direct cash payments, homeownership assistance, free college and trade school tuition, and free medical coverage for BADOCS (NAASD n.d.).

It will be obvious that even these advocacy groups with narrower definitions of reparations and reparations eligibility are nonetheless promoting numerous racial equity initiatives that make them full members of the Repair policy alliance across a very wide range of policy regimes. As part of those efforts NAASD, founded in Los Angeles, claims proudly to have significantly influenced the creation, the interim report, and the recommendations of the California Task Force to Study and Develop Reparation Proposals for African Americans (A. Brown 2022). ADOS Advocacy Foundation President Yvette Cornell has observed archly that the Task Force interim report places under "Reparations" virtually all the proposals ADOS lists as its distinct "Black agenda." While still supporting those recommendations, she has worried, like Darity and Mullen, that state efforts may provide excuses for shirking the federal reparations program she believes is needed (CBS News Bay Area 2022).

The California Task Force's policy recommendations do indeed include numerous proposals, far too many to list here, that draw on all the platforms and agendas reviewed so far (Felton 2023a). They are presented under the twelve headings of Enslavement; Racial Terror; Political Disenfranchisement; Housing Segregation & Unjust Property Takings; Separate and Unequal Education; Racism in Environment and Infrastructure; Pathologizing the African American Family; Control over Creative, Cultural & Intellectual Life; Stolen Labor and Hindered Opportunity; the Unjust Legal System; Mental and Physical Harm and Neglect; and The Wealth Gap, while proposing a California African American Freedman Affairs Agency to implement all the adopted recommendations (California Task Force to Study and Develop Reparation Proposals for African Americans 2023, 644–789; Lee 2023). Because the recommendations of the Task Force for the Study and Development of Reparation Proposals' do indeed encompass almost everything Repair alliance members are proposing as racial equity as well as reparations initiatives, they confirm that many Repair advocates now use "reparations" as an umbrella term for the entire Repair agenda.

From Here to Equality

This increasingly common blurring of the lines between "reparations," "racial equity initiatives," and even "abolition" arises because, as we have noted, most proponents of reparations now define them as concerned with problems traceable not simply to slavery, or to slavery plus Jim Crow–era segregation and disfranchisement, but also to a great variety of still present public and private policies racial justice advocates see as systematically inflicting unjust discrimination and disadvantages on Black Americans in most venues of America life. The California Task Force is something of an outlier in referring to all the later developments as "badges of slavery." More typical now is the M4BL Reparations Now Toolkit, which stresses that not just the legacies of "slavery" and "Jim Crow" but also "structural discrimination and exclusion from employment, housing, institutions and communities," which have sources beyond slavery, continue "to this day" (Ritchie and Stahly-Butts 2019, 16).

Darity and Mullen (2020) adopt a similar view in *From Here to Equality*, the most celebrated academic argument for reparations. Like ADOS, NAASD, and the California Task Force, they strongly favor the confinement of reparations to Black Americans who are descended from enslaved people in this country. Nonetheless, just as much as, for example, Kamm Howard and N'COBRA, Darity and Mullen insist that the case for reparations must be considered in light of all "three tiers of injustice — slavery, the regime of legal segregation and subordination, and current discrimination" (Darity and Mullen 2020, 11).

They do remain closer than many current Repair advocates to what might be termed the traditional, retroactive "tort model" of reparations, focused on financial payments to "repair" those who can be clearly identified, politically if not legally, as victimized by one or more of these three tiers of injustice. It is from this perspective that they would confine eligibility for reparations not only to US citizens who can show that they have at least one ancestor who was enslaved in the US after its formation as an independent republic, when it acquired responsibility for enslavement, but also to those who can prove that they self-identified as Black or some equivalent term at least a dozen years before the establishment of a reparations commission or program, in order to fence out opportunists (Darity and Mullen 2020, 252). Much like tort litigants, Darity and Mullen analyze a variety of legal and economic approaches to calculating the costs of reparations, far more thoroughly than most other advocates. In the end, they endorse a focus on what it would take to close the wealth gap between white and Black citizens, a gap produced by all three tiers of past and present racial injustices (257).

Yet by adopting this latter position, Darity and Mullen, like most current Repair advocates, move away from a precise calculation of the losses incurred by demonstrable unjust actions, as called for in a retroactive tort model. Their approach more closely resembles forward-looking tort relief provided via injunctions that seek to shape current and future activities, or what advocates now most often refer to as an "equity" or "empowerment" model. These positions take as their goal the achievement by persons of African descent of sufficient material resources, political governing power, and cultural recognition that they can see themselves, and be seen by others, as having genuinely equal status in the United States and the world. On such views, the culpability of American governments in fostering the unequal circumstances of Black Americans remains central to the case for reparations. Once significant state responsibility is established, however, the emphasis shifts to how to create equitable conditions, in which Blacks' opportunities to lead fulfilling lives are comparable to those of others.

In common with most of today's Repair alliance members, Darity and Mullen propose that instead of one-time, lump sum direct payments, financial reparations could take a variety of forms, some of which might dramatically transform existing systems of home-owning, education, economic entrepreneurship, and more. These include the establishment of a national reparations trust fund, much like what Randall Robinson urged in 2000, to which eligible Blacks could apply for "various asset-building projects, including homeownership, additional education, or start-up funds for self-employment, or even vouchers for the purchase of financial assets." They also suggest that historically black colleges and universities might receive much more funding (Darity and Mullen 2020, 258).

But in contrast to many other Repair advocates, while Darity and Mullen regard "institution building" as an appropriate use of reparations funds, they insist that for both *"symbolic and substantive reasons"* of public acknowledgment and economic efficacy reparations must still include some direct payments to eligible recipients (Darity and Mullen 2020, 258, italics in original). Even so, they suggest that a portion of a national reparations fund might be distributed competitively through a process that gives priority to eligible Blacks with low current wealth or income, perhaps favoring those who seek to develop new business enterprises, products, or technologies, without any tort-like calculation of whether those Blacks have in fact been the most harmed by racial injustices (261).

While Darity and Mullen are in many respects less radical than many other Repair alliance members, the price tag for what they propose is, as we have mentioned, daunting—from $10 to $20 trillion in various estimates. Their vision of reparations is only a step, but a Coltrane-like "giant step," removed from the efforts to achieve integration into existing socioeconomic and political American institutions that predominated among the leaders of the 1950s and 1960s civil rights movement, including those who came to urge affirmative action in education and employment.

NAARC and N'COBRA

Darity, Mullen, ADOS, NAASD, the California Task Force, and kindred groups are thus important though more conservative members of the contemporary Repair policy alliance, while the M4BL Vision for Black Lives captures well its more radical wing. If we seek to locate close to the center of the alliance a counterpart to the Ten Principles in the National Conservatism Statement discussed in chapter 3, it is probably the Ten Point Reparations Plan of the National African American Reparations Commission (NAARC 2023b). In sharp contrast to the NatCon Statement's opening principle celebrating "national independence," the NAARC Plan as posted in 2023 begins by calling for the US government to make a formal apology for its role in the institution of chattel slavery, and urges the creation of an African Holocaust Institute, to be called the "Maafa Institute," using the Swahili word for "great disaster."

Second, the Plan calls for the US government to fund an African repatriation program and an African Knowledge Program, based on a provision in the CARICOM Reparations Commission's Ten Point Plan, to aid Americans of African descent who wish to visit and to connect more fully with their ancestral lands and cultures.

Third, the NAARC Plan, like other reparations proposals, urges the creation of a National Reparations Trust Authority that is to gain control of lands worked by enslaved labor and devote parts of them to educational, business, and health institutions to aid persons of African descent, accompanied by funds to support Black agricultural development.

Fourth, NAARC calls for creation of a Black Business Development Bank, and also for a Board of Trustees appointed to use the National Reparations Trust to "develop an infrastructure of strategic financial, commercial, industrial, agricultural and technology-oriented business/economic enterprises for the benefit of Black America as a whole."

Fifth, NAARC proposes the creation of a system of Black-controlled Health and Wellness Centers, as well as funds to aid existing health organizations serving Black communities and Black medical schools.

The sixth proposal is funds for the national Board for the Education of People of African Ancestry, for historically Black colleges and universities, for the creation of an endowment to make education at those institutions free, and for developing a "Curriculum of Inclusion" for all educational institutions.

Seventh is the creation of an African American Housing and Finance Authority to plan and finance the construction of affordable housing "villages" and to issue grants and loans to homebuyers.

Eighth is funds to aid Black-owned media of all kinds, including a nonprofit national network featuring programming to aid Black America.

Ninth is the identification, preservation, and erection of Black Sacred Sites and Monuments throughout the US.

Tenth is criminal justice reforms, including the creation of a Black-controlled Agency for Returning Citizens to aid the formerly incarcerated; restoration of voting rights to ex-felons; exoneration of Marcus Garvey; and revisions in the Thirteenth Amendment so that its language cannot be used to legitimize forced labor by those convicted of crimes, among other particulars (NAARC 2023b).

Though these points include some distinctive features, they obviously echo many in Darity and Mullen's discussion of possible uses of a national reparations fund, as well as provisions in the ADOS Black Agenda, the NAASD R.E.P.A.I.R. program, the California Task Force's recommendations, and elements of the M4BL's Vision for Black Lives. Such agenda overlaps are consistent with these groups all acting as part of a broad Repair policy alliance, despite their differences.

Unlike Darity and Mullen, NAARC does not give any detailed attention to the various means of calculating what reparations are "owed" in dollar terms, nor does it stress direct cash payments to the descendants of those enslaved in America. Its ten points represent multiple and diverse forms of aid and investment in Black Americans and Black communities today, whether or not their ancestors were enslaved, because its proponents consider all Black people in America to be members of a pan-African diasporic population whose experiences have been shaped by the legacies of European imperialism, enslavement, segregation, and enduring forms of racial discrimination. In this, NAARC sides with the M4BL Reparations Toolkit, which contends that "Jim Crow segregation, redlining, and other forms of structural discrimination and exclusion, and racialized criminalization, have impacted all Black people in the United States, not just those who can prove that their ancestors were slaves." M4BL adds that far from being confined to cash payments, reparations "must take as many forms as necessary to address the many forms of injury caused by chattel slavery and its continuing vestiges" (Ritchie and Stahly-Butts 2019, 16, 18; Movement for Black Lives 2023). Here too NAARC is similar. But apart from its call for aid in "repatriation," NAARC's ten points do not place the same emphasis on intersectionality and internationalism that M4BL and the more left-leaning members of the Repair policy alliance do, even though NAARC leaders are sympathetic to those themes.

The logic of NAARC's centrist Repair alliance (not centrist American) vision of needed initiatives has been spelled out in part by N'COBRA, the organization that aided John Conyers in composing both versions of HR 40 and helped to create NAARC (in fact the organizations have shared some leaders ever since NAARC's founding). Having long worked internationally, N'COBRA invokes the United Nations' "Basic Principles and Guidelines on the Right to a Remedy and Reparation for Victims of Gross Violations of International Human Rights Law and Serious Violations of International Humanitarian Law" as guidance for Repair policies in America (United Nations 2005). Its focus is not on what specific American laws have been broken, but on what is required to make the experience of Black people in America, and America itself, humane and just by global standards. Since the American legal system actively structured massive racial injustices, N'COBRA and many other contemporary Repair organizations insist that ultimately the entirety of the American system of legal, political, economic, and cultural institutions must be repaired. In so doing, N'COBRA contends, in perhaps surprisingly patriotic fashion, "the nation as a whole will become stronger," as all will share in the benefits of living in a "just and peaceful society" (N'COBRA 2004).

N'COBRA does not have an agenda or platform on its website. But according to Kamm Howard, who holds leadership posts in both NAARC and N'COBRA, the latter group similarly demands that the US cease discriminatory policies and practices against Black people and prevent their recurrence; restore to Black people many kinds of resources of which they have been unjustly deprived; compensate Blacks for the resulting losses of economic and educational attainments, personal liberty, health benefits, and experiences of cultural self-determination they would have enjoyed; revise public place names, monuments, and curriculum to grant recognition to Black experiences and achievements; and provide rehabilitative services for those harmed by racial injustices.[4] In all these respects, even as Howard and other advocates speak of making Black people "whole," the overriding concern of their vision is not so much to calibrate legally required financial compensation according to tort law standards or to create the exact state of things that would have existed if injustices had not occurred. It is to create a nation and ultimately a world in which all have an equitable opportunity to flourish in the ways they choose today, unburdened by the disadvantages created over centuries of abuse. Many leaders of older civil rights groups like the Leadership Conference on Civil and Human Rights have now shifted similarly to stress their human rights commitments, not just nationally defined civil rights. Many fear that the assertive nationalism of Donald Trump and other conservatives may make national "civil rights" no bar to maintaining systems of white supremacy and privilege.[5]

As colossal and far-ranging as are the visions for reparations advanced by M4BL, ADOS, NAASD, the California Task Force, Darity and Mullen, NAARC, and N'COBRA, it is notable that they do not include specific proposals to end American capitalism. Instead, they all include many proposals to increase the participation in and ownership of businesses and private property by Black Americans and (especially in the case of the Movement for Black Lives) many other disadvantaged groups. Nor do any of these groups call for ending, rather than transforming, the American nation-state, though most do attack many aspects of the immigration policies and the global system of nation-states those policies help to sustain. And while most of these Repair organizations express solidarity with other oppressed communities, the M4BL vision most expansively, their focus remains either on Black American citizens or on all Black people in America.

Nonetheless, many readers encountering for the first time the radical rhetoric, the extraordinarily wide substantive scope, and the proposed price tags of these Repair initiatives may feel that all this goes much too far to ever be more than politically marginal, despite the successes of racial justice groups in mobilizing demonstrators and attracting funding. Repair advocates have many responses, including the conclusion of the 2020 CitiGroup report, *Closing the Racial Inequality Gaps: The Economic Cost of Black Inequality in the U.S.* That report held that if racial gaps in wages, housing, education, and investment had been closed in 2000, the US economy would have been $16 trillion larger than it was by 2020. The report also argued that spending to close gaps in 2020 could have a net benefit of $5 trillion over the next five years (Peterson and Mann 2020, 3). Conservative critics dismiss such economic analyses as pandering by woke corporate DEI proponents.

It is beyond our remit here to make a definitive case for or against either of the rival racial policy alliances we depict. We do, however, regard it as essential to recognize that while the vision of the most radical Repair advocates as described in this chapter may seem utopian, or in some eyes dystopian, it is nonetheless true that throughout the United States today groups in the Repair alliance are in fact pursuing a great variety of observable policies, with some real successes. Realization of their vision in its entirety is certainly a long way off, if it can be realized at all. But in part because millions of Americans find the Repair story of America's persisting unjust racial inequalities and resulting needs to combat systemic racism compelling, racial justice advocates are achieving many smaller but nonetheless significant reforms in the here and now. In assessing the political prospects and potential impacts of the expanding Repair policy alliance, the reforms its members are currently getting enacted in many policy regimes, as detailed in chapter 8, should be given prominent weight.

CHAPTER EIGHT

Today's Repair Alliance

Current Initiatives across Policy Regimes

Black Lives Matter has always been more of a human rights movement rather than a civil rights movement. BLM's focus has been less about changing specific laws and more about fighting for a fundamental reordering of society wherein Black lives are free from systematic dehumanization. Still, the movement's measurable impact on the political and legal landscape is undeniable. —Activist and writer Frank Leon Roberts (2018)

The partly distinctive but substantially overlapping programs of Repair alliance members make clear that its advocates urge initiatives in virtually every major American policy regime, with many proposals confined to Black Americans, but many that extend beyond that community. Some are meant to encompass only other disadvantaged groups; others seek to aid all the nation's residents. If and when the Repair policy alliance gains wider support and control of more public and private institutions, many of these proposals that are now on the back burner may become central to the twenty-first-century Repair agenda. Even so, believing that it is important for readers to recognize that this alliance is becoming a Repair institutional order, we focus here on measures that are currently being enacted, some by private groups and individuals but many by governmental agencies.

Housing

Although, as discussed in chapter 5, a number of municipalities are now undertaking Repair initiatives that many call "reparations," most have not begun distributing funds at this writing. Perhaps because of the well-documented roles of the federal government and many state and local agencies in fostering real estate redlining, subprime lending, and other practices contributing to substandard and effectively segregated housing opportunities for Blacks, and perhaps because home-owning is a major source of wealth for most Americans, housing is the primary sector in which public as well as private reparations payments have been made thus far. Though these circumstances make the focus on home-owning understandable, to critics this priority symbolizes how the Repair alliance is in practice often aimed at goals that reinforce rather than challenge the middle-class values of modern Americans.[1]

In any case, the amounts are not yet substantial. In the summer of 2022, Evanston, Illinois, began distribution of the much-publicized payments from its "Restorative Housing Fund" raised through a tax on cannabis: out of 122 applicants verified as eligible, 16 received $25,000 each, which could go toward home improvements, mortgage assistance, or house down payments (Abraham 2022). The City of Asheville, North Carolina, committed $2.1 million in its 2022 budget, and reserved $500,000 in its 2023 budget, for reparations, and the commissioners of Buncombe County, in which Asheville is located, added $2 million for 2022 and another $500,000 for 2023 (Nefzi 2022). Echoing Evanston, the Asheville City Council has identified housing aid as its leading priority for use of these funds, along with efforts to improve Black economic and educational opportunities, health care, and more; but at this writing it has not yet begun to award funding.

Notably, in both communities these public efforts are being complemented by recently created private "Reparations Stakeholder Authorities," which seek to extend reparations efforts over time and via other mechanisms, including individual cash payments, which public agencies can sometimes not legally provide. In Asheville, a local social justice fund named Tzedek initiated the Reparations Stakeholder Authority (Honosky 2022). In Evanston, the Evanston Community Foundation established the Evanston Reparations Community Fund, initially with $300,000, to aid Evanston's Reparations Stakeholder Authority. Robin Rue Simmons, who is founder and executive director of FirstRepair, a nonprofit that aids local racial justice initiatives, and who also chairs the City of Evanston's Reparations Commission, helped lead the creation of the private Reparations Stakeholder Authority (Honosky 2022). Similarly, the pilot project of the Berkeley- and Detroit-based social justice fund Reparation Generation, which includes John Conyers's son Ian among its board members, has made grants of $25,000 to Black Americans purchasing or improving residences in Detroit (Reparation Generation 2022). For these and similar public and private bodies, aid to home-owning, especially at a time when pandemic-induced construction delays contributed to housing shortages and high prices, has seemed the most attractive initial use of racial justice funding; but all express commitments to other Repair efforts as well.

Criminal Justice

At least until the national furor over Critical Race Theory, the policy regime with which Repair advocates were most associated was criminal justice reform, urged with the deliberately radical slogans of "defund the police" and "abolitionism," often advanced to demand the termination of ICE (the Immigration and Customs Enforcement Agency) as well as police forces. At the national level, much of this advocacy has focused on the BREATHE Act of the Movement for Black Lives, proposed in the House in 2020 by two members of the progressive "Squad," Representatives Ayanna Pressley and Rashida Tlaib (King 2020). The BREATHE Act would divest most federal funding from police and immigration enforcement and invest instead in a new Community Public Safety Agency, which would provide grants to local community bodies offering nonviolent security, health, housing, education, and employment services in order to reduce crime, among many other provisions (M4BL n.d.).

With the Biden administration focused instead on increasing police funding, the BREATHE Act met with a chilly reception in the House of Representatives, which certainly did not warm when the House flipped to Republican control in 2022. Similarly, local efforts to "defund" the police by transferring resources to new community public safety departments or agencies have failed so far, most visibly in George Floyd's Minneapolis, where voters rejected a ballot option to "create safety by changing the entire system" in this manner (Smith and Arango 2021). Though the Department of Justice later found the Minneapolis Police Department guilty of rampant discrimination, major changes remained elusive (Smith, Londoño, and Thrush 2023).

It is nonetheless important to recognize that many older reform groups, like the Leadership Conference on Civil and Human Rights, now agree that the long-range goal for criminal justice systems should involve "reimagining public safety," in the words of Sakira Cook, director of the Leadership Conference's Criminal Justice Program.[2] Repair activists contend that public safety is most effectively achieved not through coercion and incarceration, but by establishing a variety of well-funded, competently staffed community service and support programs, narrowing police responsibilities for social services, and adopting more extensive monitoring and accountability systems for police misconduct. DeRay McKesson of Campaign Zero argues that while there was a brief vogue among Left racial justice groups for publicizing this reimagining of public safety systems via the riveting rhetoric of "defund the police" and "abolition," most groups have in fact been working behind the scenes with organizations like his.[3] Campaign Zero focuses on curbing police violence through lobbying for an extensive range of attainable reforms, like new rules on use of force, body cameras, removal of barriers to investigations of police conduct, enhanced community oversight, and more.

Many of these reforms are not only attainable—they are actually being put into effect. For example, especially since the killing of George Floyd, members of a BLM offshoot organization, Black Lives Matter Grassroots, have joined with older police reform groups to win the creation of community policing review boards in a growing number of cities, striving for greater police accountability (Kutner, Macias, and Iovino 2020). In July 2020, the Connecticut General Assembly passed "An Act Concerning Police Accountability" that, along with other provisions such as improved police training, authorized all the state's cities and towns to create this kind of civilian-led review board (Yankowski 2020). Also in 2020, the city council of Alexandria, Virginia, condemned "police brutality and systemic racism," reaffirmed "that Black Lives Matter," and created the Alexandria Community Policing Review Board, to which it gave the authority to receive complaints and conduct independent investigations of police misconduct (City of Alexandria 2022).

While such civilian review boards have a range of supporters that predate the rise of BLM, and though their efficacy has long been disputed, the Repair alliance has reinvigorated efforts to establish and strengthen them. To cite instances from perhaps unexpected locations, BLM activists joined with the local NAACP in 2020 to win expansion of the membership and powers of the Springfield, Missouri, Police Civilian Review Board; other BLM groups have championed the Community Policing Review Board in Columbus, Indiana; and in Iowa City, Iowa, the Community Police Review Board has expanded and begun pushing for more substantial policy changes in recent years (KCRG News Staff 2021; Keegan 2020). Less surprisingly, perhaps, with aid from the local chapter of the white Repair group SURJ (Showing Up for Racial Justice), in March 2020 Los Angeles

County voters strongly approved Measure R, a referendum to enhance the subpoena powers of the Civilian Oversight Commission for the LA County Sheriff's Department and to promote alternatives to incarceration as punishment (Ballotpedia 2020).

Protests by BLM activists and others have spurred investigations that have sometimes led to what at least promise to be significant reforms. The leading example is the US Department of Justice investigation of the police force in Ferguson, Missouri, the site of Michael Brown's killing and of sizable BLM protests in August 2014. That investigation produced a sharply critical report that led to a sweeping decree agreement (US Department of Justice Civil Rights Division 2015). It included reforms to foster community policing and engagement; bias-free police and court practices; reduced stops, searches, and arrests; limitations on use of force; civilian oversight; municipal court reform; and more, with an independent monitor to assess the decree's implementation over a mandatory period of two years (US Department of Justice Office of Public Affairs 2016).

The publicity around police killings and racial justice protests has also created political opportunities, especially but not exclusively in urban areas, for the election of public prosecutors who embrace much of the "community public safety" vision of criminal justice reform. Miriam Krinsky, a former federal prosecutor, is the executive director of Fair and Just Prosecution, a group that she says represents "a new generation of elected prosecutors" engaged in a "transformational effort" to reform American criminal justice practices. Her group estimated that in 2021 there were seventy such progressive district attorneys in office across the nation, overseeing constituencies representing one-fifth of the US population, an increase from fourteen in 2016. Half were women and half were people of color (Krinsky 2021). One of these, Jose Garza, elected in 2020 in Travis County, Texas, which includes the university city of Austin, has contended: "(F)or 200 years in this country we have been electing one kind of prosecutor. People across the country have spoken up loudly and clearly . . . to say they want a new way of being policed" (Eder and Kirkpatrick 2021). Garza swiftly persuaded grand juries to issue a remarkable eleven indictments against officers in use-of-force cases, none of whom were charged by his predecessor.

Black Lives Matter activists have shown they care far more about the substantive criminal justice vision of prosecutors than about their race or gender. The frequent protests of BLM LA helped defeat Jackie Lacey Jr., Los Angeles County's first Black district attorney, when she ran for reelection in November 2020 (Elam and Kravarik 2020). These efforts have predictably aroused vehement conservative criticism. The Republican district attorney in neighboring Orange County denounced the election of "woke DAs" who, he said, are "utterly destroying police morale. They are making it impossible to recruit police" (Eder and Kirkpatrick 2021). But however one evaluates their conduct, these reform-minded district attorneys represent another of the significant impacts of the Repair policy alliance—along with other reformers—on American criminal justice systems.

Los Angeles is also home to a development that links criminal justice reform with educational reform. In February 2021 a local activist movement, "Students Deserve," which works in partnership with Black Lives Matter, successfully campaigned to get the Los Angeles Unified School District, the second largest in the nation, to reallocate $25 million from school policing to investment in "climate coaches," efforts to combat implicit bias, and achievement planning for African American pupils. School boards in Oakland, California, and Portland, Oregon, had previously removed police from school campuses and sought to promote student learning and safety through other means (Gomez 2021; Students Deserve n.d.). In many places, those other means include the adoption of curricular materials and counseling practices that, to conservatives, amount to the takeover of public education by proselytizers for Critical Race Theory. By 2022 some school districts, often under pressure from conservatives, had begun to bring police back (Morton 2022).

Education

As we have seen, virtually all leading Repair proponents stress the need to reform American curricular materials to do justice to the experiences and perspectives of African Americans and other historically marginalized groups. They urge greater funding for the institutions that primarily serve such groups. The most prominent progressive curriculum initiative is the effort to promote the use of materials created by the reparations advocate Nikole Hannah-Jones's 1619 Project, now being advanced chiefly through the Pulitzer Center's 1619 Project Education Network. The Pulitzer Center, not affiliated with Columbia University's Pulitzer Prizes, was created in 2006 to "raise awareness of underreported global issues" through aid to journalists and programs for education and public outreach (Pulitzer

Center n.d.). By 2021, the 1619 Project Education Network had forty-one teams, involving over 170 teachers and administrators from twenty-one states, creating 1619 Project curricular resources (Swan and Jamnah 2021).

Scholars and journalists have yet to track where and how extensively these resources, or those created by Hillsdale College to advance the rival narrative of the Trump administration's 1776 Commission, are being implemented. Doing so is challenging, since teachers often diverge from the curriculum they are officially assigned to teach (Sheasley 2022). Moreover, while Trump-aligned Republican governors in Tennessee, Florida, and South Dakota have sought to mandate the use of Hillsdale's 1776 curriculum in new charter schools and existing public schools, prominent state officials have not similarly sought to require the use of 1619 Project curricular resources (AP News 2022; Harris 2022; Adams 2022). It is likely that in many places they have not needed to compel teachers to do so. Indeed, when news media revealed that Hillsdale President Larry Arnn had been secretly recorded dismissing graduate schools of education and the teachers they produce as "dumb," teacher resistance to being compelled to adopt more conservative curricular materials appears to have heightened (D. Mitchell 2022). Many educators and activists have instead endorsed the 1619 Project's aims of giving fuller attention to how much enslavement influenced arguments made by the founders in Philadelphia during the Revolution and the adoption of the Constitution, and how fears of potential enslaved peoples' and Native Americans' insurrections weighed on them (Parkinson 2021).

In addition, especially since the protests of 2020, numerous student groups have demanded curricular reforms of the sort urged by Repair advocates—efforts that appear more extensive than those of any conservative student counterparts. Perhaps most notable is the 501(c)3 group #DiversifyOurNarrative, founded in June 2020 by two Stanford undergraduates and currently consisting of over 6,000 student organizers working in over 250 school districts, providing templates for curriculum change and recommending anti-racist texts, and often winning adoptions, at least by individual teachers (Natanson 2020; Diversify Our Narrative n.d.). There are many similar local groups. Students in Winooski, Vermont, lobbied to include an ethnic studies module in the school curriculum after pressuring the school district to do more to combat racism and teach anti-racism. At Belmont High School in Massachusetts, students petitioned successfully for the removal of a bell formerly used on a sugar plantation to summon enslaved workers. They had less success in getting the curriculum broadened, though the school adopted a diversity action plan intended to bring more multicultural curriculum into the school (Natanson 2020).

In sum, while many of the fears that students are being indoctrinated in Critical Race Theory are not based on studies of observed teaching practices, which generally aim at promoting critical thinking rather than proselytizing, there is little doubt that educators in many parts of the nation are being influenced by the advocacy for curricular reform urged by members of the Repair policy alliance, and that they are finding many new curricular materials to employ in working toward that goal. The political fires over radical teaching about race have surely been fanned by partisan pursuits of power, but they have not been without kindling.

That is hardly surprising, because while there are debates over how much and in what ways the themes of Critical Race Theory are featured in public K-12 education, there is no dispute that those ideas have a significant presence in most American institutions of higher education. Though Critical Race Theory originated in law schools, its proponents have actively sought to inform scholars and teachers in other disciplines through works such as *Critical Race Theory: An Introduction* by Richard Delgado and Jean Stefancic (now in its third edition), which includes classroom exercises, suggested discussion questions, and other teaching aids (Delgado and Stefancic 2017). Gloria Ladson-Billings, formerly the Kellner Family Distinguished Professor of Urban Education in the Department of Curriculum and Instruction at the University of Wisconsin and also a former president of the American Educational Research Association, played a prominent role in introducing Critical Race Theory into education schools and teacher training programs, as summarized in her book *Critical Race Theory in Education: A Scholar's Journey*. As we have noted, the education scholar Isaac Gottesman has also explored how the critical pedagogy developed by Ladson-Billings and others built on but modified critical Marxist thought emerging out of the New Left of the 1960s, as the subtitle of his book, *The Critical Turn in Education: From Marxist Critique to Poststructuralist Feminism to Critical Theories of Race*, shows (Gottesman 2016). Although it is hardly the case that America's graduate schools of education turn out only proponents of pedagogies informed by Critical Race Theory and other Left perspectives, or that their graduates are "dumb," it is true that many—perhaps most—American teachers have encountered critical theoretical perspectives as part of their pedagogical training, providing evidence of some institutionalization of the broader visions that inform and are advocated by the modern Repair policy alliance.

Transforming Public Memorials

These same perspectives have contributed significantly to movements to modify public monuments, statues, memorials, holidays, and museums, and to alter names of military bases and other public places in order to end celebration of supporters of white supremacy and to honor instead those who have fought against racial injustice. Again, these movements have already had significant successes.

Just as the killing of George Floyd spurred unprecedented protests and donations to racial justice organizations, it also accelerated efforts to remove statues of Confederate political and military leaders and other supporters of white supremacy throughout the nation (a pattern that was also emulated internationally). Those campaigns had already been fueled by, especially, the Confederate flag-wearing Dylann Roof's murder of nine African Americans who welcomed him into the Emanuel African Methodist Episcopal Church in Charleston, South Carolina, on June 17, 2015 (Burnip and Boroff 2020). After Floyd's death, some 230 Confederate monuments and memorials were taken down, sometimes by protesters, often by governmental action. Virginia had been given pause when the Charlottesville City Council's decision to take down a statue of the Confederate general Robert E. Lee prompted angry right-wing activists to organize the notorious Unite the Right rally that culminated in violence and Heather Heyer's death. But from 2020 on, the state removed sixty public Confederate symbols, and North Carolina took down eighteen—though more than two thousand remained across the nation, mostly in the South (Burch 2022; Seisdedos 2023). A group of Virginia-based scholars has shown that Confederate monuments are most prevalent in counties where lynchings once occurred (Henderson et al. 2021).

In a particularly striking example of these transformations in public commemorations, ten days after Floyd's murder Virginia Governor Ralph Northam announced his intention to take down another sculpture of General Lee, a towering twenty-one-foot bronze equestrian statue in the state's capital city, Richmond. Though removal was delayed by two lawsuits, the state's Supreme Court approved the decision in September 2021 (Tavernise

2021). When no white contractors would take the job, a Black owner of a construction business, Devon Henry, did so, fulfilling the prophecy the African American newspaper editor John J. Mitchell made when the statue was first erected in 1890, also by Black labor (Schneider 2023).

Henry went on to make a specialty of removing similar statues and monuments—some twenty-four in Virginia and North Carolina, including in Richmond as the city proceeded to take down all the Confederate statues along its historic Monument Avenue, which had long exclusively featured them. A founding member of the Virginia Defenders for Freedom, Justice and Equality, Ana Edwards, applauded the changes: "it's very difficult to imagine, certainly, even two years ago that the statues on Monument Avenue would actually be removed. It's representative of the fact that we're sort of peeling back the layers of injustice that Black people and people of color have experienced when governed by white supremacist policies for so long" (quoted in Rankin and Lavoie 2021). State Senator Jennifer McClellan, an African American, observed of the removal and destruction of the Lee statue: "I physically felt in the air hope . . . because I saw multigenerational, multiracial people chanting to take it down and demanding change" (quoted in Rankin and Lavoie 2021). These changes were supported by a diverse cohort of Americans, but they undeniably advanced an often urged and continuing goal of the modern Repair alliance.

In many cases, statues of slaveholders were removed from public pedestals but not destroyed—simply transferred to museum-type settings, with historical context added to their display. For example, the New York City Council voted in November 2021 to remove a seven-foot-high plaster replica statue of Thomas Jefferson from City Hall, where it had towered since 1834, and to deliver it to the New York Historical Society. The original Jefferson statue remains, however, in the US Capitol Rotunda (Mays and Small 2021; Smart 2021). In June 2021, a giant equestrian statue of Theodore Roosevelt standing outside the American Museum of Natural History in New York City, unveiled in 1940, was slated for removal to Medora, North Dakota, where a new Theodore Roosevelt Presidential Library is to open in 2026. The statue depicts an African American and a Native American standing submissively on each side of Roosevelt. A review by the New York City mayor's office had concluded that this public artwork deliberately exalted a colonial power relationship: "Roosevelt's statue on his noble steed visibly expresses dominance and superiority over the Native American and African figures." In the presidential library, the statue will be accompanied by descriptive content developed with Native American and African American advisors (Bahr 2021).

Once Donald Trump was out of office, similar steps accelerated at the federal level. The West Point Military Academy has received a recommendation from the Naming Commission set up in 2021, under the National Defense Authorization Act, to remove a plaque with the image of a hooded figure over the words "Ku Klux Klan" (Kaufman2022). The US Navy renamed two vessels whose names celebrated the Confederacy: the USS Chancellorsville, which commemorated a southern Civil War victory, will become the USS Robert Smalls, named for a formerly enslaved mariner who achieved heroic status in the Civil War; while the USS Maury will become the USNS Marie Tharp, named after a renowned ocean geologist (Schmail 2023). The nation's first Native American secretary of the interior, Deb Haaland, also established a task force to remove the term "'squaw'" from more than 650 geographic place names, observing that "racist terms have no place in our vernacular or on our federal lands" (quoted in Brulliard 2021).

But at times criticisms of commemorations of figures identified with American racism have been quieted by promises that have not been fulfilled. One major site of contention has been Georgia's Stone Mountain Park, the birthplace of the second Ku Klux Klan, which features mountainside carvings of Jefferson Davis, Robert E. Lee, and Stonewall Jackson that have long drawn the ire of African Americans and progressive activists. The Board of the Stone Mount Memorial Association unanimously voted in 2021 to modify the carvings, removing the Confederate flags it featured; but by late 2022, nothing had been done, with the Memorial Association's CEO acknowledging that they "just kind of put it on the back burner and left it there" (quoted in Estep 2022). In 2015, Virginia Military Institute, a state institution, ended its traditional instruction that all first-year cadets salute the statue of Stonewall Jackson when passing; under pressure from Governor Northam, a 1981 VMI graduate, and other state leaders, the statue was finally removed in 2020. VMI also appointed its first Black superintendent, Major General Cedric Wins, who undertook other diversity, equity, and inclusion initiatives. But alumni protested, and in April 2022 the VMI Board voted to retain all remaining statues and building names, while providing "contextualizing information" for those associated with slavery and the Confederacy (Sonnenberg 2022).

Yet some long and hard-fought battles have been won. In Franklin,

Tennessee, a local group of African Americans campaigned in vain for several years to get a statue (known as "Chip") commemorating Civil War Confederate heroes removed. In the end, they got an accompanying new bronze statue, "March to Freedom," in place. Unveiled in October 2021, the new statue features a life-size soldier from the US Colored Troops, an African American regiment in the Civil War. One of the advocates, the seventy-three-year-old African American Hewitt Sawyers, celebrated the new figure: "here is a Black man who was enslaved, who gave his life to go out to help free other people . . . what a powerful message." He added, "I ain't got time for Chip" (quoted in McGee 2021).

In 1894 the State of Mississippi adopted a state flag that featured the Stars and Bars, an emblem of the old Confederacy. In 2001, Mississippians voted on whether to retain that flag, and two-thirds favored keeping it. But in 2020, as Movement for Black Lives protests spread across the US, BLM activists, religious leaders including the Mississippi Baptist Church, sports organizations such as the National Collegiate Athletic Association and the Southeastern Conference, and many businesses all pushed for renewed scrutiny. In response, the Republican legislature and governor conceded the need for change. Mississippi voters then approved a new flag design with no reference to the Confederacy, though the effort did placate conservatives by including the slogan "In God We Trust" (Rojas 2020; Pettus 2020).

Few of the proposed alterations in public commemorations enraged Donald Trump more than the drive to overturn the naming of military bases for Confederate leaders; but this, too, proved to be a victory for progressive racial justice advocates. Using Confederate names was part of the early twentieth-century effort to restore unity between the North and the white South through a grand mythologizing of the latter's role in the Civil War as a noble if defeated "Lost Cause" (Blight 2001). The nine US military installations named for Confederates, including Fort Hood in Texas, Fort Bragg in North Carolina, and Forts Gordon and Benning in Georgia, were miserable places for Black recruits during both world wars: rigorously enforced racial hierarchy, segregation, and racism in the military ensured the message of white dominance (King 2007). Fort Benning was named for the Confederate General John Lewis Benning, a vigorous proponent of secession "to prevent the abolition of slavery." Fort Gordon commemorated John Brown Gordon, a Confederate general and later a leader of the Georgia KKK and energetic participant in the disenfranchisement of African Americans in the 1890s (Cameron 2022).

In June 2020, Trump nonetheless called the bases part of "a Great American heritage, a history of Winning, Victory and Freedom. The USA trained and deployed our HEROES on these Hallowed Grounds, and won two World Wars. Therefore, my administration will not even consider the renaming of these Magnificent and Fabled Military Installations. Our history as the Greatest Nation in the World will not be tampered with. Respect our Military" (BBC News 2020). As mentioned earlier, Trump vetoed a defense bill that included creating a commission to review the names. But military leaders spoke out in its support, and the bill was passed over his veto (Daly 2021). On taking office, President Biden appointed a Naming Commission to recommend changes, and it provided a preliminary set of recommendations in May 2022, estimating the costs of change at $21 million (E. Mitchell 2022). At this writing many changes appear unstoppable.

A similar victory in a long-standing campaign came when Congress recognized "Juneteenth," June 19, as a national holiday. The day had long been celebrated in communities of color as marking the end of enslavement, specifically commemorating its formal announcement in Texas in 1865.[4] Formal recognition of the holiday finally came in 2021, when new President Joe Biden signed the Juneteenth National Independence Day Act. He declaimed, "great nations don't ignore their most painful moments. I've only been president for several months, but I think this will go down for me as one of the greatest honors I will have had as president." The President was flanked by Congressional Black Caucus members and by ninety-four-year-old Opal Lee from Fort Worth, Texas, who had spent decades lobbying for Juneteenth to be recognized as a holiday (Kim 2021). The NAACP's president, Derrick Johnson, declared, "as we work towards substantive pieces of legislation to protect voting rights and create transparency and accountability in policing, we are encouraged by today's signing of the Juneteenth bill. It is a reminder that freedom is an ongoing fight" (Kim 2021). For conservatives like Montana Republican Representative Matthew Rosendale, however, the elevation of Juneteenth was only another part of the radical progressive campaign to make Critical Race Theory "the reigning ideology of our country" (quoted in Kim 2021).

These governmental efforts to transform the nation's public symbols embodied in statues, monuments, place names, holidays, and more have been accompanied by a wide variety of private initiatives, of which we can only provide a few examples. In Washington, DC, the National Cathedral commissioned a renowned artist to design stained-glass windows addressing racial justice that will fill the space previously occupied by windows honoring the Confederate generals Robert E. Lee and Stonewall Jackson (Public Arts Foundation 2021). An Idaho church similarly replaced a stained-glass window depicting Lee with one honoring the first African American woman elected a bishop of the United Methodist Church, Leontine T. C. Kelly (Banks 2021). The racial justice nonprofit Color of Change successfully protested the presentation of former slave plantations as idyllic event locations on online wedding platforms such as Pinterest and the Knot Worldwide. Color of Change advocates argued that "plantations are physical reminders of one of the most horrific human rights abuses the world has ever seen. The wedding industry routinely denies the violent conditions Black people faced under chattel slavery by promoting plantations as romantic places to marry" (Jabali 2019). HBO Max temporarily pulled *Gone with the Wind* off the air because of its glamorization of the white supremacist South during and after the Civil War (Victor 2020). The NASCAR auto racing organization has banned use of the Confederate flag at all of its events and properties (Romo 2020). Innumerable other protests on behalf of racial justice in professional sports and the entertainment industry have reflected the increasing cultural potency of the concerns driving the Repair alliance and reinforced conservative fears that a woke ideology is becoming or has become hegemonic throughout the major media and cultural sectors of American life.

And indeed, even as old symbols deemed racist and imperialist have been torn down, new projects have proliferated that try to provide the public narratives of America's racial injustices and struggles for reform that Repair supporters have demanded. In Washington, DC, the African American Museum of History and Culture opened in 2016, and in Montgomery, Alabama, the Legacy Museum and the National Memorial for Peace and Justice opened in 2018, remembering 4,400 African Americans lynched between 1877 and 1950. The driving force behind the National Memorial was the defense attorney Bryan Stevenson, whose 501(c)3 organization, Equal Justice Initiative, was founded in 1989 to tackle mass incarceration and injustice. The Initiative says its "community remembrance work is part of a larger movement to create an era of restorative truth-telling and justice that changes the consciousness of our nation" (Equal Justice Initiative n.d.). Toward those same ends, the International African American Museum, which aims to connect the local experience of African Americans in South Carolina with the global origins and connections of enslavement, opened in Charleston in January 2023 (IAAM n.d.). Even Virginia's Governor Glenn Youngkin, who campaigned on his opposition to Critical Race

Theory, has applauded Colonial Williamsburg's efforts to providing fuller representation of all the colonial site's inhabitants, including the restoration of its Bray School, which taught free and enslaved Black children in the 1760s and 1770s. Youngkin affirmed the need to "teach all of our history, all of it, the good and the bad" (Jay 2023).

Many more examples could be added. It is important to acknowledge, however, that while transforming public memorials and the official narratives of the nation's past and present is a key goal for the Repair policy alliance, most if not all of its members recognize that symbolic actions are far easier to win than material changes, but are also far from enough to achieve alliance goals. Many are frustrated when reforms go no further. Some boycotted instead of celebrating the opening of a new museum, Greenwood Rising, to commemorate Tulsa, Oklahoma's "Black Wall Street," destroyed in the infamous 1921 Tulsa Massacre. In 2021 the New Black Panthers, a separatist organization founded in 1989 in Dallas, went further, organizing an armed "Second Amendment March for Reparations" in Tulsa during which they shouted, "what do we want? Justice! When do we want it? Now! How we gonna get it? By any means necessary!" (D. Brown 2021b; Laila 2021). Although this "public memory" cultural arena is one where Repair advocacy has had an impact, few in the policy alliance see it as one in which the most needed changes have been or can be won.

Public Health and Environmental Justice

Many of the claims that systemic racism is visible in most if not all major institutional sectors of American life rely substantially on evidence that communities of color are disproportionately disadvantaged in almost every sector. While vigorous debates continue over the extent to which those disproportions are due primarily to class rather than racial inequities, and even more over whether the remedies should be race-targeted or more universal social and economic aid programs accompanied by systemic restructuring, few deny that racial disparities can readily be found. In a growing number of sectors, pressures from Repair advocates and others have persuaded some public agencies to adopt initiatives explicitly to end what the agencies affirm to be systemic racism. Prominent among these are the linked areas of public health and environmental justice—linked because environmental harms so often damage the health of the communities in which they occur.

The spread and consequences of COVID-19 confirmed the malign effects of environmental racism for many activists and researchers, manifest for instance in the higher prevalence of respiratory illnesses in the neighborhoods of communities of color, resulting from decades of poorer air quality (Lakhani and Watts 2020). Even prior to the pandemic, however, Repair activists had insisted with increasing success that public health agencies should regard racism as a chief hazard to the health of racial minority communities. In May 2019, Milwaukee County in Wisconsin became the first prominent public body to adopt a resolution declaring racism to be a public health crisis; it was soon followed by the City of Milwaukee; Cook County, Illinois; and Pittsburgh, Pennsylvania (Mendez et al. 2021). Adoption of such resolutions accelerated dramatically after the police killings of Breonna Taylor and George Floyd and the many Black Lives Matter-associated protests that followed.

Several counties in Michigan, for example, pledged to combat systemic racism in health care in the days after Floyd's murder. They complied with demands advanced by Black Lives Matter Michigan, which originated as Black Lives Matter Lansing and then fostered other BLM groups around the state (BLM Michigan 2023). In June 2020, the Board of Commissioners of Ingham County, home of East Lansing's Michigan State University, also officially declared racism to be "a public health crisis," and created a new advisory board to find "community-centered solutions to address the legacies of racial injustices," including health and housing inequities (Ingham County 2020). Almost simultaneously, the City Council of Flint, Michigan, and the Board of Health of Genesee County, in which Flint is located, each "declared racism a public health crisis" and initiated internal policy assessments to promote "racial equity" (Fonger 2020). The Health Department in Washtenaw County, home to both the University of Michigan and Eastern Michigan University, posted on its website a "WHP Statement on Racial Justice and Health Equity" proclaiming that the "Washtenaw Health Plan stands in solidarity with Black Lives Matter" and that "structural racism and discrimination permeate every aspect of our lives and that includes access to health care and public benefits." Consequently, the agency pledged to examine "our internal practices to make sure we are a vehicle to address structural racism and mistrust of our health system" for "years to come" (Washtenaw Health Plan Staff 2022).

One study found that by October 2020, state and local governments in a total of twenty-five states had adopted 128 resolutions, declarations, or laws presenting racism as a public health crisis, with Michigan, Wisconsin, and Nevada having state-level declarations. About three-fourths of the resolutions decried systemic racism, and over half cited disparate COVID-19 impacts (Mendez et al. 2021). Many of these resolutions were essentially hortatory. Seventeen percent included funding initiatives, though as of the date given in the study only four municipalities had specified funding. Long Beach, California, allocated $3.2 million for racial equity; San Luis Obispo, California, dedicated $160,000 to diversity and inclusion public health initiatives; Boston proposed reallocating $3 million of its $414 million police budget to public health and race concerns; and Lansing, Michigan, combined $100,000 from its police budget, $20,000 from the mayor's office, and $50,000 from its Human Relations and Community Service office to create an Equity and Anti-Discrimination Fund to address public health racial disparities (Mendez et al. 2021).

Similar initiatives have since continued in many places. By the summer of 2022, the American Public Health Association had identified over 250 such declarations, in 21 states, 89 counties, and 146 cities (Late 2022). In Chicago in 2021, a report from the city's Department of Public Health on the impacts of the COVID-19 crisis and other health disparities prompted Mayor Lori Lightfoot to declare racism a public health crisis in that city (CBS Chicago 2021). The report squarely tied contemporary public health inequalities—such as average life expectancies of 71.4 years for African Americans compared to 80.6 years for whites—to the city's history of segregation. Its authors found that the color of a person's skin could "determine how long they live [and] their quality of life." Alison Arwady, Chicago's public health commissioner, emphasized structural factors over individual behavior in explaining the disparities: "for a number of years we in public health have been particularly focused on the fact that it is not just access to health care that drives most health care outcomes. There's been a strong drumbeat that asks about the structural decisions that we have made as a society that have set up inequities. In the U.S., if you were to be honest about that, you have to start with race" (quoted in Guarino 2021a). The department then appointed its first chief racial equity officer.

In many places, concerns about racially disparate health harms traceable to public health and environmental policies go beyond the legacies of slavery, segregation, and other more distant discriminatory practices, and they do not focus on the recent COVID-19 pandemic. For the first two decades of the twenty-first century, raw sewage regularly flooded houses in the African American-majority city of Mount Vernon, New York, a short drive from Manhattan, inflicting misery on over one thousand families annually. These harms violated the Clean Water Act, Environmental Protection Agency orders, New York state law, and a federal court order. Inadequate federal investment in wastewater infrastructure was the larger cause of this environmental pollution, but quantitative analysis revealed a disproportionate impact on communities of color, consistent with claims of persistent structural racism (Flowers and Bernard 2021; Roesler 2021). Finally in 2022, Governor Kathy Hochul announced $150 million in funding in partnership with Mount Vernon and Westchester County to replace the city's century-old, often-collapsing clay pipe system (Greenfield 2022).

While the state and municipal resolutions on racism and public health in Michigan were part of a national trend, activists there were particularly focused on the links between public health policies and racial injustices because of the recent egregious case of water poisoning in Flint. When the city changed the source of its water supply in 2014, the new source was incompletely filtered, permitting lead to leach into drinking water. Michigan's Republican Governor Rick Snyder initially denied any ill effects, but the lead levels subsequently proved to exceed the Environmental Protection Agency's threshold for toxic waste. Because 57 percent of Flint's population was African American and the majority of the patients treated in hospitals were children of color, many saw both the initial failure and the efforts to deny it as part of a national pattern of callously permitting environmental public health damages to Black communities (Craven and Tynes 2016; Sampson and Winter 2016). In 2021, a court awarded $626 million to tens of thousands of claimants seeking compensation because the state had permitted children in Flint to be exposed to lead poisoning from tap water (Bosman 2020). Former Governor Snyder and other officials were also charged with the crime of willful neglect of duty, but the Michigan Supreme Court ruled that they could not be indicted under the old, little-used law on which prosecutors relied (White 2022a). In a separate civil suit for damages inflicted by Flint's polluted water, Snyder invoked his Fifth Amendment right to remain silent rather than incriminating himself, a position that a federal Circuit Court of Appeals affirmed (White 2022b).

At the national level, Congresswomen Ayanna Pressley and Barbara Lee and Senator Elizabeth Warren began in 2020 introducing an "Anti-Racism in Public Health Act," but it has not been adopted (Pressley 2021). The US House of Representatives also has a Black Maternal Health Caucus whose members have combined a dozen pieces of proposed legislation into the "Black Maternal Momnibus Act," which similarly has not won approval (Underwood 2021).

As in other areas, then, public agencies have thus far proven more willing to adopt condemnations of systemic racism in public health and environmental policy programs than to fund and implement concrete measures. Even so, the impacts in recent years of Black Lives Matter and other Repair proponents on public health and environmental justice mission statements have been widespread and accelerating, making it premature at best to dismiss them as inconsequential.

Immigration

We have observed that many of today's Repair advocates (though not ADOS) affirm solidarity with immigrants, including unauthorized immigrants. To be sure, few place immigration issues at the center of their advocacy, and for their part many first- and second-generation immigrants reject the notion that they should be obligated to share in the burden of paying public reparations. We saw in chapter 6 that although some immigrant rights groups are among the signers of statements supporting HR 40, they are not numerous. Even so, many social justice organizations that have endorsed HR 40 and other Repair initiatives do place strong emphasis on immigration issues. One example is Community Change, founded in 1968 in honor of the recently assassinated Robert F. Kennedy and long concerned with economic justice, with a heightened focus in the twenty-first century on the economic needs of minority communities. Concerned about how immigrants had been increasingly cut out of American welfare and social safety net programs, and about rising anti-immigrant sentiments following the 9/11 attacks, in 2003 Community Change founded the Fair Immigration Reform Movement, which today consists of more than forty groups, the majority led by women of color, and four national allied groups, working at local, state, and national levels to combat anti-immigrant laws and policies and support more inclusive measures (Community Change n.d.).

Their activism and that of many other groups allied around Repair efforts were particularly energized by the Trump administration's family separation actions and aggressive detention and deportation policies. Through 2018, when protests and judicial interventions prompted the administration to pause the practice, roughly 5,500 young children went to shelters while their parents were imprisoned awaiting deportation. In February 2021, shortly after taking office, President Joe Biden appointed an Interagency Task Force on the Reunification of Families; but he later rejected the idea that the government would pay over $400,000 in compensation to each family affected, and in December 2021 his administration withdrew from negotiations to reach a global settlement for all families, saying it would instead litigate each case individually (Fox 2021). Immigrant rights advocates have been sharply critical, and in January 2022, thirty-five groups signed a letter to President Biden and his top administration officials to "demand full measures of accountability, reparations, and restorative justice for all human rights violations related to the forced separation and detention of migrant families" by the US government. The signatories included several organizations, such as the National Network for Immigrant and Refugee Rights, the La Raza Centro Legal chapter of San Francisco, and the Japanese American Citizens League, who were also among the signers in support of HR 40 (Witness at the Border 2022; Pérez-Bustillo 2022).

So far, this advocacy has been unsuccessful; it would also be incorrect to say that Repair advocates and immigrant rights activists are working together to anything more than a limited extent, or that they have achieved great victories for victims of what they see as unjust immigration policies. Yet efforts to build solidarity as part of a broad intersectional alliance are real, and especially in municipalities receptive to immigrants they have helped achieve some positive results. Of note are efforts to extend voting rights in local elections to noncitizens. In December 2021, New York City passed legislation enabling noncitizens who are legally resident in the US to vote in the city's local elections, but not state or national elections, beginning in January 2023. The bill's primary sponsor, council member Ydanis Rodriguez, argued that "people who are looking to get elected to office will now have to spend the same amount of time in the communities affected by this legislation as they do in upper-class neighborhoods." The pool of eligible voters under this legislation would be close to 800,000, roughly 250,000 of whom would be either Chinese or Dominican citizens. One council member, Laura Cumbo of Brooklyn, therefore expressed fear that the innovation would weaken African American voting clout (Mays and Correal 2021). In any case, in late June 2022, a state supreme court judge on Staten Island struck down the law as violating the New York State Constitution, which refers to the voting rights of the state's citizens, thereby implying in the judge's view that the state only allows citizens to vote (Mays 2022). The fate of efforts to appeal that ruling is uncertain at this writing.

Even so, noncitizen voting rights, common in the nineteenth century in western states seeking to attract European immigrants, are attracting renewed support in other places. Eleven cities and villages in Maryland have allowed noncitizen voting in local or school board elections for some time; noncitizens in San Francisco have voted in school board elections since 2017; and in 2021, the Vermont legislature upheld city charters for Montpelier and Winooski, already approved by local voters, that extended the vote to noncitizens in city elections (Vasilogambros 2021). In January 2023, the Vermont Supreme Court upheld the legislature's action; in March, Burlington, Vermont, also permitted noncitizens to vote in its elections; and on March 14, 2023, Washington, DC, extended the vote to noncitizens (Roth 2023). Republicans in the US House of Representatives condemned the DC action as a "disgraceful" violation of "American sovereignty," and after 2020, five states — Alabama, Colorado, Florida, Ohio, and Louisiana — amended their state constitutions to ban all noncitizen voting, joining Arizona, Minnesota, and North Dakota among states with similar provisions, and more such conservative efforts are underway (Roth 2023). Noncitizen immigrant voting is thus another policy regime in which Repair and Protect advocates can now claim some recent victories in different political jurisdictions — and another one in which contestation is likely to be ongoing (Glover 2022; Roth 2023).

Voting Rights and Political Candidacies

At this point it will be obvious that state and national bills and judicial decisions affecting access to voting and the structuring of electoral systems and districts are among the most broadly and bitterly contested battlegrounds in contemporary American politics, with a panoply of partisan participants on both sides. As we have noted, even though by early 2023 Protect conservatives had already extended their long-standing efforts to limit voting by introducing 150 restrictive bills in 32 states, 274 bills to instead expand access to voting had been filed in 34 states (Brennan Center for Justice 2023). Due to the intensity of opposition to restrictive measures, Republicans in many states were proposing less sweeping, more incremental measures, and both sides continued to have some successes. By May 2023, 10 states had enacted a total of 18 restrictive laws, while 17 states and Washington, DC, had passed a total of 28 laws expanding voting access (Corasaniti and Berzon 2023). Repair activists were passionately at work in these struggles, alongside many others.

Repair proponents have simultaneously been providing strategic services and mobilizing voter support for racial justice candidates, many of whom explicitly pledge support for reparations. The Movement for Black Lives's Electoral Justice Project, for example, is co-led by Jessica Byrd, who also served as chief of staff to Georgia gubernatorial candidate Stacey Abrams and who founded Three Point Strategies to provide strategic consulting for progressive Black candidates, having advised Black women running in US House and Senate races and mayoral contests in major cities (Electoral Justice Project 2023). The Electoral Justice Project's other leaders are Rukia Lumumba, a lawyer who is the founder and executive director of the People's Advocacy Institute, whose projects include securing voting rights for two hundred thousand Mississippians it finds to be wrongly disfranchised; and Kayla Reed, director of Action St. Louis, a grassroots racial justice organization that seeks to build political power for Black communities in the St. Louis region, in part through its #WokeVoterSTL voter mobilization campaign (Electoral Justice Project 2023; People's Advocacy Institute n.d.; Action St. Louis 2022). These activists have numerous counterparts across the United States. To document their activities and to quantify their impacts would require a separate major study.

Suffice to say here that as in so many other regards, the year 2020 saw a turning point in the relationship of Repair advocacy to political campaigns. As racial justice protests and voter mobilization efforts escalated, candidates at all levels who sought progressive support showed greater receptivity than ever before to Repair proposals that once seemed extreme, including reparations. In the 2020 presidential primaries, Kamala Harris, Marianne Williamson, Elizabeth Warren, Julian Castro, and Beto O'Rourke all supported some form of reparations for African Americans, at least for those with ancestors who were enslaved. In keeping with Repair concerns for the multiple tiers of racial injustice and not just the direct legacies of enslavement, Warren supported special home-buying assistance to residents in communities of color who faced the legacies of redlining (Herndon 2019a). These endorsements broke with the positions of both Hillary Clinton and Bernie Sanders in 2016, and with the stance of Barack Obama when he was in the White House. As previously noted, although Joe Biden supported the creation of a reparations commission via HR 40, he refused to appoint a commission by executive order when HR 40 stalled after being reported out of committee.

Though various Black Lives Matter groups had campaigned for and against local, state, and national candidates many times before 2020, their efforts accelerated in that year. In October 2020, the BLM PAC worked vigorously for pro-reparations congressional candidates including Cori

Bush and Jamaal Bowman, both of whom won election and quickly became prominent (if controversial) voices for an aggressive racial justice agenda and other progressive causes. Bowman contended that the push for reparations came from his constituents, saying: "young people across races are very excited about it. Voters have been telling me this is long past due. For a very long time we've talked about the study of the need for reparations, but the data is already available" (quoted in E. Goldberg 2020). Later, when he was in office, Bowman argued that in addition to reparations—not just cash payments but also homeownership programs, higher education assistance, and much more—the nation needed to take a related step. He urged creation of a Truth and Reconciliation Commission that would promote greater understanding and healing among all Americans, building wider and deeper support for racial progress.[5] Both Bush and Bowman easily gained reelection in 2022, and as previously mentioned, Bush then introduced a resolution calling for $13 trillion in reparations initiatives. Even though Republicans narrowly gained control of the House in 2022, rendering Bush's resolution a symbolic act, other progressives expected to become allies of the proudly left-leaning "Squad" in the House also won, expanding the possible base for more substantial actions (Wells 2022).

However, many candidates who featured Repair policies in their campaigns did not win in 2020 or 2022. What remains to be seen is whether, by putting the case for Repair measures more forthrightly and prominently than in the past, even these unsuccessful aspirants to office have contributed to building support for their cause over time. Many of their arguments do appear in the Repair advocacy of a number of the groups we have reviewed. In 2020, for example, Shaniyat Chowdhury, a twenty-eight-year-old democratic socialist Democratic candidate for Congress in New York, responded to a question about what was the most urgent issue facing his district by singling out reparations, which he defined, as most reparations proponents now do, in both material and symbolic terms: "It's about more than a check. It's about improving the quality of life for black Americans. It's about addressing the sins of this nation over 400 years" (quoted in E. Goldberg 2020). Andrew Romanoff, who previously worked at the Southern Poverty Law Center, argued during primary debates in Colorado for the 2020 Democratic nomination to the US Senate that reparations was no longer just a pipe dream: "Like other big ideas, reparations is one arriving more swiftly to the realm of the possible. For a long time it was stuck in a debate over the mechanics and the money. How much would it cost? The first step is to recognize the moral obligation." He resisted the idea of reparations as "too extreme" or "too far left," contending that "if you agree it's the right thing to do, then the fact that it may not poll well isn't a concern. Consensus doesn't magically materialize, it has to be forged" (E. Goldberg 2020). Many advocacy organizations have echoed these themes ever since, showing that although a great deal of consensus-forging would need to be done for major Repair initiatives to gain enactment, since 2020 many Repair proposals, including direct reparations, have moved into mainstream political debate to a much greater degree than ever before—advanced by an advocacy infrastructure that is likely to endure.

Systemic Economic Justice

A striking feature of current racial policy debates is that conservatives almost universally identify the radical woke Repair ideology they oppose as a form of Marxism, even as many (not all) on the Marxist left reject it as a divisive form of "identity politics." There is some basis for both characterizations. Repair groups like the Movement for Black Lives do regularly denounce "racial capitalism" and insist they are seeking to build a coalition that is "anti-capitalist" as well as anti-racist, anti-fascist, anti-imperialist, anti-misogynist, anti-homophobic, anti-ableist, and more. But as chapter 7 showed, the economic proposals that are most emphasized by the leading Repair organizations do not include any wholesale restructuring of the American economic system along socialist or communist lines. Many emphasize race-targeted employment and job training programs; health, housing, and nutritional aid; and workers' rights, but very often Repair advocates also seek aid for Black entrepreneurship and business, land, and home ownership. If expansive enough, such initiatives could significantly transform America's political economy; but they would not by themselves create a socialist or even a social democratic economic system.

Repair advocates we interviewed did highlight and endorse the recent emergence of "Universal Basic Income" (UBI) programs in a growing number of American municipalities, frequently building on aid initiatives adopted during the COVID-19 pandemic.[6] In 2021, a group of mayors that has grown to over seventy members created Mayors for a Guaranteed Income, which states that its efforts are rooted "in Dr. King's Legacy" (Mayors for a Guaranteed Income 2023; LaPonsie 2022). Despite the UBI label, most of the programs so far, modeled on a pioneering effort in Stockton, California, provide $500 a month or similar aid only to low-income residents. The evidence thus far suggests that doing so helps many low-income people to gain, rather than to avoid, employment. In May 2022, the business magazine *Forbes* reviewed nine such programs: in Stockton, Compton, and Los Angeles, California; Denver, Colorado; Gainesville, Florida; Georgia (where it is a statewide initiative aimed at women); Chicago, Illinois; Shreveport, Louisiana; Newark, New Jersey; and New York City. The review further noted that Alaskans have been receiving regular annual payments from the federal Permanent Dividends Fund for years (Napoletano 2022). Subsequently, San Diego adopted a similar initiative, and as the existence of Mayors for a Guaranteed Income indicates, many other cities are contemplating doing so (Garrick 2022).

Most of these efforts, including the initial program in Stockton, have been aided by the Economic Security Project, funded and co-chaired by the wealthy Facebook co-founder Chris Hughes, along with Natalie Foster of the Aspen Institute and Dorian Warren, president of Community Change. By 2022 the Economic Security Project had helped launch one hundred guaranteed income pilot projects of various sorts, publicly and privately funded, in thirty states, reaching thirty-eight thousand recipients (Economic Security Project 2023). Although these economic initiatives cannot be attributed to the Repair policy alliance, a number of the alliance's members have worked to support them, and most Repair allies appear to view them very favorably. If these programs continue to gain traction, it is possible that more Repair advocacy may come to feature UBI initiatives of various sorts (including expansions of the federal Child Tax Credit) along with race-targeted proposals, thereby fostering a significantly more substantial American social welfare state. The Biden administration has quietly aided these developments through enhancements in the Child Tax Credit program (Manjoo 2022).

In its 2020 Vision, the Movement for Black Lives also endorsed reparations for Black farmers and Indigenous communities. This represented an intervention in a continuing controversy in which the Biden administration has struggled with Trump supporters over the legitimacy of agricultural reparations efforts (McFadden 2020; Rappeport 2022). Government investigations and reports have repeatedly acknowledged that Black farmers faced discrimination in loan and aid programs of the US Department of Agriculture (USDA) throughout the twentieth century and into the twenty-first, contributing to their decline from 14 percent of all farmers in 1920 to less than 2 percent today. In 1999, a settlement in the antidiscrimination case of *Pigford* v. *USDA* appeared to offer Black farmers $1.03

billion in restitution, but few were found eligible and most received only modest sums. Both litigative and legislative efforts to receive more sufficient restitution therefore continued.

Significant success appeared on the horizon when the Biden administration created an Equity Commission that included a Subcommittee on Agriculture and placed in the 2021 American Rescue Plan $5 billion for Black, American Indian/Alaskan Native, Asian American, Pacific Islander, or Hispanic farmers and ranchers who had experienced discrimination. But Texas white farmers and ranchers, aided by Stephen Miller's America First Legal group, claimed those provisions were illegally discriminatory and sued, thereby stalling payments. The subsequent Inflation Reduction Act of 2022 replaced the 2021 reparations plan with $2.2 billion for any farmers, ranchers, or forest landowners who faced discrimination before 2021, without specifying any racial or ethnic groups, along with $3.1 billion in Agriculture Department loans for farmers in financial distress. In light of past history and the continuing threat of litigation, how much funding Black or Indigenous farmers will in practice receive remains in doubt (Hayes 2021; Rappeport 2022).

In sum, despite much radical rhetoric, most of the economic initiatives advocated by Repair proponents represent efforts to include more people of color, especially Black Americans, in the forms of economic employment and ownership offered by the existing American capitalist system, or at most to provide a more substantial social welfare system accompanied by race-targeted programs of varying magnitudes. Most Repair economic initiatives, moreover, remain proposals and not enactments. These ideas are, however, contributing to legislative and litigative initiatives at all levels of government and to a wide range of nonprofit programs as well, with some recent successes especially in cities with substantial non-white populations. Though class-focused critics have reason to charge that much Repair advocacy may end up enhancing "Black capitalism" in neoliberal fashion rather than overturning "racial capitalism," many Repair initiatives seek to plant seeds of more substantial economic transformations. It is too soon to say whether those seeds will grow.

Continuing Litigation

We have stressed throughout this chapter that contemporary Repair advocates generally do not invoke a narrow "torts model" of reparations in which remedies for legally proved unjust discrimination against specific individuals and groups are tailored fairly precisely to try to place the victims of discrimination in the positions they would occupy if the discrimination had never occurred. Instead, most advocates simply make the case that significant public and private racial injustices have been inflicted, with wide-ranging consequences, and urge legislative as well as private institutional actions to produce transformative systemic changes in many policy regimes. A number of those changes appear to focus on winning recognition of people of color and their history, cultures, and traditions as having equal status with those of white Americans, rather than on making fundamental changes in American economic or political institutions, though many Repair advocates urge much more.

Yet even though legislative proposals now receive the greatest attention, lawsuits involving "tort model" concepts of reparations remain a route that many Repair proponents continue to pursue, as the continuing saga of Black farmers seeking restitution for USDA discrimination shows. Doing so may be wise. A number of racial conservatives with whom we spoke underlined that, if illegal discrimination could be proven in court (against any racial group, definitely including whites), they could support remedies in the form of reparations.[7] Some acknowledged that in light of America's history of discriminatory policies, there are indeed Black Americans who should win some such lawsuits. Frustrated by failures in other venues, some racial justice activists are therefore calling for renewed emphasis on litigation strategies (Coard 2021).

The obstacles presented by the litigation route remain great, however. A sobering though still unresolved example is the fate of Tulsa African Americans' efforts to win reparations in court for the enormous harms inflicted on them and their families in the 1921 Tulsa Massacre that devastated the Greenwood neighborhood of the city. In an early twenty-first-century lawsuit, survivors sued the police department, Tulsa, and the State of Oklahoma for negligence and conspiracy. Although there was considerable evidence for these claims, in 2005 the US Supreme Court dismissed the lawsuit without comment (IBW21 n.d.).

The story has, however, not ended. Three impressively long-lived massacre survivors, all over one hundred years old, have continued to sue for reparations in the Oklahoma courts, naming seven defendants including the City of Tulsa, the Tulsa County sheriff, the Oklahoma National Guard, and the Tulsa Chamber of Commerce. In May 2022, Judge Caroline Wall of the Tulsa County District Court ruled that the case could proceed, over objections that the injuries were too distant in time to be subject to current correction, and the Oklahoma Supreme Court subsequently agreed (Hauser 2022; McCarthy 2023). Whether that meant the plaintiffs would ultimately win a significant victory is not yet apparent.

Obviously, pursuing reparations via litigation that might result in direct compensation to only three persons more than a century after racial injustices occurred is not a viable means of achieving the eradication of systemic racism in all venues of American life that the Repair policy alliance seeks. Yet as in the case of the nation's Black farmers, litigation can sometimes generate pressures that bear some legislative fruit down the road. Any and all successes in particular legal decisions can also enhance the visibility and the perceived legitimacy of broader Repair efforts.

Conclusion

It must be acknowledged that the policy accomplishments of the Repair alliance, whose members include far fewer governing officials and agencies than the Protect alliance, remain limited on many fronts. We suspect, however, that many readers will not have been aware of many of the Repair-supported policies that have already been enacted, as we were not before we undertook this research. The range of policy regimes impacted is undeniably broad, even if in many areas the impacts are not as yet deep. Housing grants cast as reparations have begun. Community policing review boards have expanded. Reform prosecutors have been elected. Race-conscious, culturally responsive school curricular materials have been more widely adopted. Confederate statues and place names have come down, and new monuments and museums commemorating civil rights struggles have gone up, all across the country. Public health agencies have taken new steps to combat what they call systemic racism in their jurisdictions. Noncitizens, often non-white, have gained the vote in many locales, and new protections for voting rights have been enacted or are being pursued in many states. Support has grown for economic initiatives like Universal Basic Income.

When we add to this record the continuing growth of well-funded groups and individuals supporting Repair policies, the additional legislative and litigative initiatives now underway at local, state, and national levels, and the moral, intellectual, and political reinforcement for these efforts that international reparations movements provide, there are strong reasons to believe that while today's Repair policy alliance may not be as powerful as conservatives claim and fear, it is far from marginal. It is reasonable to conclude that the Repair alliance is and will be a significant force in American politics for many years to come.

What does the emergence of these two modern rival racial policy alliances reveal about the cogency of the different approaches to understanding racial politics that we reviewed in chapter 1? In what possible directions may their clash take life in America in the future? To those questions we turn in part 4.

PART 4
The Rough Roads Ahead

CHAPTER NINE

Lessons for and from Theories of Racial Politics

Philosophers have hitherto only *interpreted* the world in various ways; the point is to *change* it.
—Karl Marx, 11th Thesis on Feuerbach

Interpretation, Change, and Racial Orders

In parts 2 and 3, we have seen that in contemporary America there are large numbers of public and private organizations, agencies, and individuals striving to change the world, though in conflicting ways. The Protect alliance, to be sure, seeks in part to prevent many destructive changes that it perceives the contemporary radical Left as threatening to impose on all more traditionalist Americans. But its members believe that considerable rot has already set into most American institutions, due to pernicious influences that go all the way back to the Progressive era. Consequently, they are striving not simply to stop changes but to enact changes, to turn the clock back in important ways, to make America great again. The Repair alliance is obviously all about change. Its members are working passionately to achieve what they regard as truly fundamental transformations in all the major institutions, belief systems, and social practices of American life.

Strategies for change, however, depend on understandings of what needs to be changed. Karl Marx never denied that it was vital to interpret the world; indeed, he spent an enormous amount of time and energy doing exactly that, with great impact. In chapter 2 we laid out our historical institutionalist framework to guide studies of America's racial politics, and we juxtaposed it with three other schools of thought that have influenced our work. We indicated our belief that research structured in accordance with our racial institutional orders approach could help clarify what each of these other interpretive camps gets right, and where they may go astray, in the portraits they paint of what has driven and is driving American racial developments. Those clarifications could in turn aid in assessments of which strategies for change, on the right and the left, are likely to succeed.

This chapter considers what we have learned in these regards. In brief, we maintain that our evidence shows that when the three interpretive schools we reviewed are presented in the simplistic formulations they are sometimes given in political debates, none of them can claim to be strongly vindicated, either as explanatory theories or as guides to political strategies. If, however, we consider the articulations of these positions presented by their most thoughtful proponents, none can be said to be fully refuted, as theories or as strategies. Unsatisfying as that conclusion may sound, what the harvest of our studies provides is not a decisive victory for any one position, but instead a more informed grasp of where and how their accounts are strongest and weakest. As we seek to demonstrate in chapter 10, that grasp can assist judgments of what political stances and strategies are most likely to have success over the next five to ten years.

What About Those Conservative Theories of Race?

In chapter 2, we noted that we are not devoting the same attention to a range of conservative accounts of race in America that we have been giving, and will be giving in this chapter, to views associated primarily with progressive perspectives in American politics. As we explained, the common denominator of the positions we believe our racial orders framework can illuminate, and be illuminated by in turn, is that they all regard systems and patterns of racial inequalities as socially and politically constructed, as we do. They differ on who the key political actors are in those constructions and what their motivations are. By identifying and exploring the members of racial policy alliances, a racial orders analysis is well suited to aid assessments of these rival claims. It is not appropriate for assessing the particulars of those conservative views that trace racial differences and inequalities to deep structures of biology and/or group culture, rather than political causes. It would be worthwhile to pair a historical institutionalist account of how political factors may have contributed to American patterns of racial equality with accounts emphasizing biological and cultural factors. That would, however, require a separate and distinct major study.

Our framework is better suited to assessing those versions of the modern conservative story of America discussed in chapter 3 that focus on politics and political ideas. It shows that on some points they have considerable force. The evidence in both parts 2 and 3 demonstrates beyond doubt that Protect alliance members are correct to say that today, many ideas that were on the extreme left in the 1960s are now embraced by myriad members of the contemporary Repair alliance. Conservatives are also right that most if not all Repair advocates are consciously seeking major transformations in American institutions and practices, including changes most on the right fear. Through mapping the extent and character of the Repair alliance, we have seen many instances of how its perspectives truly are a substantial presence in American universities and public schools, in older and newer American media, in cultural institutions, in nonprofit organizations, in corporate DEI departments, and in some governmental agencies at all levels—even though the abundant contestation we also found suggests that they are not so powerful or hegemonic as conservatives often contend.

Our past and present research makes us more skeptical of two further claims often embedded in the explanations of American patterns of racial inequality advanced by most narrators of the modern conservative story. The first is the contention that, as figures like Charles Kesler, Christopher Rufo, and Richard Smith (the Queen Anne's County School Board president) all maintain, the United States has never been so systemically and massively racist as many versions of the Repair story presume. The second, argued vociferously by Donald Trump, is the insistence that insofar as unjust racial inequalities exist in America today, they are due to liberal policies that have harmed minority groups by fostering welfare dependence, socially and personally destructive conduct, political radicalization, and false beliefs that honest efforts by people of color will not be rewarded and so are not worth undertaking. These factors are said to have exacerbated for racial minorities the nation's overall economic and cultural decline under liberal leadership.

Our earlier works have made clear that we question the first claim because we see political coalitions actively seeking to establish and preserve systems of white supremacy as central players throughout American history, to a much greater degree than most conservative analysts acknowledge. To some degree this is admittedly a matter of interpretive emphasis;

but in light of the fact that through most of American history the racial institutional orders seeking to preserve or even extend American systems of racial inequality have been more powerful than their opponents pursuing egalitarian changes, we think an emphasis on the centrality of America's always contested racial hierarchies to the nation's development is warranted. We agree with many conservatives, however, that it is also vital to recognize how America's revolutionary republican origins generated transformative egalitarian ideologies that many groups have employed throughout US history in their battles against those powerful hierarchies, including the invocations of the Declaration of Independence not only by Frederick Douglass and the Rev. Dr. Martin Luther King Jr., but also by the Black Panthers.

This book's focus on contemporary racial politics has meant, however, that we have not sought to address the historical issues further here. Similarly, an analysis of the makeup of today's racial policy alliances is not helpful for determining what the actual sources of current racial inequalities are, so that is another task we have not undertaken in the present volume. We simply note that our prior analyses of America's massively repressive historical racial policies have left us dubious about claims that modern liberal programs and ideas are the heart of today's problems.

Our framework *is* highly appropriate, however, for considering whether the key conservative political actors in America's racial politics today are capitalist organizations, individuals, and interests, as the capitalism-focused camp claims; or whether they are groups primarily seeking to preserve systems of white privilege and domination, as the white hegemony camp contends; or whether all actors must be understood analytically and politically as intersectional entities, with gender and sexuality as well as other systems of identity and inequality always brought into the picture, as the intersectional camp maintains. Each of these positions implies perspectives on how racial institutional orders are related to other institutional systems, including those structuring the economy, gender and sexuality, religion, disability, immigration, the statuses of Indigenous peoples, and much more. It has not been possible within the confines of this project to examine in detail the many institutional orders that shape contemporary American racial politics and the relationships among them. Informed by these different interpretive camps, however, we have sought throughout parts 2 and 3 to take note of what the memberships of today's racial alliances suggest concerning claims about the roles of capitalist interests, commitments to white hegemony, and intersectionality. The results justify some conclusions.

Capitalism-Focused Theories

At contemporary progressive political rallies, and indeed in many academic settings, it is not at all unusual to hear speakers state without much elaboration that America's racial problems all stem from "capitalism" or "racial capitalism." Insofar as these statements imply that virtually every American capitalist and capitalist institution can readily be seen on one side of the nation's past and present racial policy divides, consistently fostering and sustaining the nation's racial inequalities, our evidence indicates that such claims cannot withstand scrutiny. We have seen that there are many wealthy individuals and corporations providing massive funding to organizations pursuing different aspects of the contemporary Repair agenda, and many others mobilizing their great wealth to instead support and expand the Protect cause. There are capitalist individuals and organizations that are spending hundreds of millions of dollars in efforts to purge racial disparities from the central institutions in American life, and capitalists providing almost bottomless funding to drive DEI initiatives out of those institutions. It is probable that the overall financial resources of the Right greatly exceed those of the Left, but the extent of the funding advantages Protect organizations working on racial issues have over Repair groups right now is less clear. The reality is that both sides have substantial financing, much of it from capitalists.

In assessing the significance of that fact, it is important to recall that while Repair groups like the Movement for Black Lives rhetorically condemn "racial capitalism" and sometimes simply "capitalism," their agendas do not call for the expropriation of the property of most capitalists and the establishment of systems of public ownership, as radical socialists once did. Instead, it is striking that the policy proposals of even the most radical Repair proponents include many that are designed to stimulate Black business and property ownership and entrepreneurship. Critics have, to be sure, sharply challenged what they see as a neoliberal, pro-capitalist turn in modern racial justice advocacy (Spence 2015). And building on the expanded Ten Point Program the Black Panthers adopted in 1972, some Repair groups do continue to call for the redistribution of land as well as wealth to the heirs of Blacks whose enslaved labor made American lands productive, and to Indigenous peoples who once made their lives upon them.

It nonetheless remains true that the extensive scholarly literature and media coverage contending that there has been marked growth of income and wealth inequalities in the United States since the 1990s have not made radical economic demands central to Repair advocacy in the twenty-first century. It is uncertain whether doing so would add to their appeal, since public opinion data indicate that among Americans as a whole, beliefs in individualist "rags to riches" ideologies that extol the opportunities provided by capitalism remain widespread (Hajnal 2020; Kim 2023). The alliances between working-class white and Black voters on economic issues that capitalism-focused advocates seek to build remain elusive, a phenomenon many "racial capitalism" and "white hegemony" proponents trace, with W. E. B. Du Bois, to white attachments to the "social and psychological wage" provided by America's systemic privileging of most whites in numerous regards (Du Bois 1935, 700).

Even so, the surprisingly brief, nonspecific radical economic advocacy in most Repair agendas, along with their numerous capitalist sponsors, make it reasonable for proponents of class-focused accounts to argue that, precisely because capitalists and capitalist enterprises can indeed be found on both sides of today's major racial policy divides, the clash of the Protect and Repair policy alliances as they are currently constituted will never extend to any major overhaul of American capitalism. While the interests shaped by the nation's economic institutional order may not be driving all the positions taken on racial issues by all Repair and Protect members, class-centered analysts can say, they may well impose outer boundaries to change, ensuring that capitalism itself is not in danger. Class-minded proponents can therefore cite the evidence we have reviewed in support of their core contention: that progressives need to reject identity politics and embrace a much more full-throated and single-minded attack on capitalist institutions and ideologies than most contemporary Repair advocates are providing. Class analysts can, and many do, interpret the continuing major wealth gaps among white and Black Americans as proof that racial economic inequalities are unlikely to be reduced until all capitalist economic inequalities are reduced, and that any white attachments to a racial "psychological wage" are likely to be intensified rather than overcome by forms of Repair advocacy that stress race-specific concerns rather than universal economic reforms.

At the same time, our evidence of how Protect advocates are promising to defend traditionalist whites against what they see as radical Left dangers allows many Repair proponents, including most who speak of "racial capitalism," to continue to claim credibly that it is necessary to discredit ideologies of whiteness and institutional policies and practices that effectively advantage whites in many policy regimes. Perhaps the anxieties stirred by figures like Nicholas Fuentes and Tucker Carlson about America losing its "white demographic core" and about the alleged proliferation of anti-white discrimination can be alleviated by a purely economic agenda that promises to benefit all but the super-rich. It is nonetheless understandable that many on the left conclude instead that it is necessary to fight fire with fire, that white identity politics must be countered by a politics that openly defends the identities, the values, and the needs of diverse people of color—especially since many of those people already cherish their racial identities and wish to see them recognized and upheld. More moderate members of the Repair alliance can also argue on the basis of our evidence that the willingness of many capitalists to fund Black entrepreneurs shows that it may actually prove possible to purge American capitalism of unjust racial inequalities, and to make it work for the prosperity of all.

Our research does not resolve these debates. Instead, it shows why they should be seen as unresolved, why dogmatism about the answers must be deemed premature. The fact that capitalist actors and funding can be found for both of the contemporary racial policy alliances means that it is not obvious whether it is necessary to overthrow capitalism to win support for policies that can end unjust racial inequalities along with economic injustices more generally, or whether the race-conscious policies most Repair advocates endorse can suffice to make America's economic institutions, whether they remain capitalist or not, broadly beneficial. Proponents of class-focused political strategies can take comfort in public opinion data showing that most Americans, and a super-majority of white Americans, are not prepared to support a radical reparations agenda, much less out-and-out abolitionism. But most Americans are not prepared to endorse a radical economic agenda, either; and once we turn from survey data to organizations and trace the tremendous surge in the numbers, members, and funding of Repair alliance groups in recent years, while also noting the limited but real successes of those groups in reshaping some policy regimes, it becomes much harder to assert that political strategies centered on class or universal economic concerns have greater political potential than Repair positions.

In sum, capitalist-centered accounts can still contend on the basis of our evidence that capitalist interests remain all too completely in control of both sides of today's racial policy alliances. However, their arguments that in response progressives should focus on purely anti-capitalist strategies, in both political organizing and policy-making, will need further support if they are to become more widely persuasive.

White Hegemony Theories

The evidence in the preceding chapters supports a similarly nuanced conclusion concerning those frameworks that see the United States as ineradicably a white settler regime, embedded in a global system largely constructed out of racist empires with deep continuing legacies, and inherently incapable of providing racial justice for all. Again, we have long differed with the simplistic political and academic versions of these accounts that portray America as a unitary, fully white-controlled state that historically has been challenged almost exclusively by social movements of people of color, with no truly significant change possible until and unless those movements finally either overthrow the current American state or secede from it. We do not think those narratives capture the full scope, contents, or participants in the series of major contests over American racial policies that have shaped American political development throughout the nation's history, and we believe the emergence of today's rival Protect and Repair alliances makes these simplistic accounts of white hegemony still less credible.

In considering the relationship of those policy alliances to "the American state" as a whole, it is important to bear in mind that, to a greater degree than most people appreciate, the US has an extraordinarily complex array of governing institutions at the national, state, and local levels. Their composition, powers, and occupants vary greatly across the different states and national regions, and across the large cities, smaller towns, and rural areas within states. Currently, Protect alliance members are largely in control of strongly Red states that vote overwhelmingly Republican, often now for MAGA Republicans, and they also command most rural regions within more divided states. At the same time, Repair alliance members are clearly powerful in many if not most major American cities, including in states like Texas and Mississippi where Republicans control the state legislature and seek to weaken Democratic officials' regulatory powers and authority to structure elections in cities like Houston and Jackson (Elbein 2023; Goodman 2023). Repair supporters also wield substantial influence in the governance of many Blue states, with some seeking to follow the examples of California and Evanston by establishing state and local reparations commissions, and most adopting some of a wide range of other types of racial equity initiatives.

In light of all these different government agencies in control of different political forces in different locales and at different levels of government, it sacrifices too much of the complex realities of political power and contestation to present "the state" in America as effectively unitary and as obviously, overwhelmingly committed to traditionalist forms of white hegemony. Analysts must acknowledge the great variations in national regions, states, cities, towns, and rural areas, and they must recognize that these variations provide diverse venues for the clashes of the nation's rival racial policy alliances, institutional orders, and policy regimes, fostering different outcomes in different places.

It is even more inadequate than it has been in the past to portray battles over racial policies as essentially consisting of whites in control of state institutions versus social movements consisting primarily of oppressed communities of color. Today's racial policy alliances display more internal demographic diversity than any of their predecessors. Many supporters of Protect policies that benefit traditionalist whites are themselves Black, like Utah Congressman Burgess Owens and former HUD Secretary Ben Carson. Many Repair proponents are white, like Asheville Mayor Esther Manheimer, Sacramento Mayor Darrell Steinberg, and the founder of Mayors Organized for Reparations and Equity, former Los Angeles Mayor Eric Garcetti, currently the US Ambassador to India.

When we include in the picture of the Repair coalition the still expanding array of private advocacy, litigation, service, and educational organizations and philanthropy groups, many of them predominantly white, that both influence public policies and provide mechanisms for private redistribution, it becomes impossible to deny that contestation between the contemporary rival racial policy alliances—both of which include Americans of all demographic backgrounds—runs through much of American life. It certainly remains true that the majority of whites largely favor Protect policies, while support for Repair initiatives comes most extensively from Black Americans and to lesser degrees from Hispanic and East and South Asian Americans, and Indigenous peoples, joined by progressive whites. But contentions that whites will never support fundamental transformations in America's white settler-colonial nation can only be made persuasively by taking the far from trivial white support for change into account, rather than denying or dismissing it.

At the same time, just as in the case of class-centered accounts, our evidence for these complex realities does not make it impossible to sustain more nuanced versions of white hegemony theories. Yes, contemporary America displays rival racial institutional orders that are more demographically diverse than in the past. But as we have noted repeatedly, the conservative whites who still largely comprise the Protect alliance undeniably enjoy structural advantages in the ways American governing institutions are constituted, advantages that make them even more powerful than their sheer numbers warrant.

The main pillars of these structural advantages are now familiar. Aided by partisan gerrymandering, districts that tend to vote conservative are notoriously overrepresented in many state legislatures and in the House of Representatives. The US Senate vastly overrepresents smaller, more rural states, providing a conservative tilt in the Electoral College that chooses the president—twice in the twenty-first century against the results of the popular vote, out of six presidential elections so far. Control of state legislatures often also enables conservatives to structure local, state, and congressional election processes and major aspects of many policy regimes, and we have seen throughout this book that today they are doing so more and more aggressively in support of Protect goals. As a result of these structural advantages, along with fervent opposition from traditionalist Americans, the Repair policy alliance and its nascent governing institutional order remain much less powerful than its contemporary rival.

We have argued throughout all our works that the historical clashes of America's evolving racial institutional orders have generated some major changes that represent steps toward greater racial justice, including the ending of legally authorized chattel slavery labor systems, the barring of de jure racial segregation, and the expansion of voting rights for Black Americans and many more citizens. Consequently, we are reluctant to conclude that today's Repair alliance has no prospects of ever achieving change of comparable significance. We acknowledge, however, that the evidence we have presented here is not sufficient to invalidate even extreme versions of white hegemony theories, including those Afropessimist accounts which contend that while some improvements can occur at times, achieving full racial equality is impossible in the United States because the nation has been too deeply constituted by its white settler origins for systems of white advantage ever to be truly overcome.

Much depends, of course, on how the goal of "truly overcoming" is defined and how progress toward it is measured. In assessing the history of a nation that began with most persons of African descent in the chains of chattel enslavement, but that by the twenty-first century boasted African American billionaires both male and female, a Black president, and accomplished Black leaders in almost every major American institution, we resist judgments that nothing has ever really changed in the course of American political development and that meaningful racial advances are therefore not truly possible in America.

We recognize, however, that there are two powerful types of evidence that make it reasonable to judge the changes that have occurred to be insufficient, and to doubt Americans can ever achieve full racial equality.

The first is the undeniable fact that progress toward greater material equality remains limited in many areas of American life. We have noted throughout how severe racial disparities persist in modern America in wealth, in income, in homeownership, in health outcomes and longevity, and in representation in many institutions, even though the sources of those disparities remain unsettled, with some on the left stressing racial discrimination and others economic causes, and some on the right blaming the ill effects of liberal policies and of Black cultural and biological traits. We have noted that many American Blacks were bitterly disappointed with how their economic positions in practice declined in the Obama years, fueling considerable political despair, though also support for Repair alliance activism (Davies 2021). Both reactions deepened when, after Obama, Donald Trump won the White House via his victory in the Electoral College. Although a majority of voters rejected him in his bid for reelection in 2020, the prospects that he or a Protect conservative with similar views will regain the White House in 2024 or 2028, and that similar conservatives will occupy many other powerful governmental offices, are quite real. It is therefore hard to dismiss the contentions of white hegemony theorists that Americans cannot expect to see much new material progress toward racial equality over the next decade, if ever under its current political system, and that instead further declines may occur in the years ahead.

That judgment is reinforced by public opinion data consistently indicating, as we have noted, that most white Americans, and substantial minorities of other American groups, oppose aggressive measures to reduce racial inequalities. It might be argued that the fact that only 18 percent of white Americans support reparations to the descendants of people enslaved in America means that it is politically hopeless to pursue the kinds of radical changes most people in the white hegemony camp favor (Blazina and Cox 2022). Few white hegemony proponents, however, believe that their aspirations will be realized through election victories. They agree that the opposition of white Americans to major changes in racial statuses is too widespread to be overcome through voting, so many of them pursue a more radical politics of protests, separate community-building, transnational alliances, and sometimes violence.

Though we are not Afropessimists, both public opinion data and our own evidence of the power Protect conservatives now wield, coupled with the structural advantages American governing institutions provide, compel us to argue in chapter 10 that the most likely scenario for the near future is one in which conservative policies will continue to prevail, bringing about no major changes in the nation's racial status quo. That is exactly what Afropessimists and other proponents of white hegemony theories of American politics predict, and nothing we have presented here can be said to prove them wrong, even if many particular "white hegemony" accounts of current racial policy contests can be enriched, and at times corrected, by the analysis of racial policy alliances we have provided.

We do maintain, however, that at a minimum our evidence of the breadth, depth, and growth of the Repair policy alliance and the incipient Repair institutional order casts doubt on contentions that meaningful transformative egalitarian changes are inherently impossible in America. We believe those doubts provide a reasonable basis for not ruling out political strategies that are more hopeful about achieving change by working through existing American institutions than many in the white hegemony camp accept.

Intersectional Theories

For intersectional accounts that address, as almost all do, systems of racial inequality, the lessons of our research are twofold. First, the analysis of the Protect and Repair policy alliances in parts 2 and 3 strongly supports the contention of intersectional scholars that it is necessary to study racial politics by employing an intersectional frame that is as inclusive as possible, difficult to do though that is. Second, our work nonetheless raises questions about how successful intersectional approaches can be as strategies for organizing and policy-making—though here, too, the arguments of intersectionality analysts and activists cannot be dismissed.

One of the most valuable insights our mapping of the kinds of groups that are now members of the Protect policy yields is that just as much as the Repair alliance, the contemporary conservative coalition on racial issues has been built through intersectional appeals. Rather than consisting of simply groups with capitalist economic interests or investments in white privilege, the Protect alliance includes a wide variety of groups that see themselves as having interests and identities the modern American Left endangers. Today's conservative racial policy alliance has been built not only through promises to protect whites from unfair, racially discriminatory progressive policies, but also through the championing of traditional religions, especially Christianity, against secular liberal measures; promises to defend the economic interests of working-class Americans against hostile global economic forces; efforts to protect the cultural and historical traditions of conservative Americans against anti-American revisionism; and concerns to uphold and enforce traditional sexual mores, roles, and identities against any egalitarian embrace of greater gender and sexual diversity, among other appeals (Bella 2021; Natanson 2022). Collectively these varied forms of traditionalist protection, including but not confined to white protectionism, inevitably make the Protect alliance an intersectional one. We have also seen, however, that many members of the Protect alliance agree that whites, especially conservative Christian white men, are now the most unjustly discriminated against group in the United States. Whether or not protection for whites is the core of modern conservatism, as some white hegemony theorists argue, the entire alliance agrees today that protection for traditionalist whites is badly needed. We doubt that the alliance could exist without this unifying element.

When we turn to the Repair alliance, our evidence shows that intersectionality as a multipurpose tool of analysis, organizing, and policy design is an even more obviously defining element of the rhetoric and writings of the alliance's proponents (Collins 2021; Curry 2021; Ghavami and Peplau 2012). As we have seen, the Movement for Black Lives platform explicitly seeks to build the most broadly intersectional coalition of disadvantaged and discriminated against groups that it can. It draws on Black feminist and queer theorizing as well as radical racial and economic thought, and many of its policy proposals address multiple forms of oppression and discrimination, not simply racial injustices. It is hard to find groups belonging to the Repair alliance that do not at least declare solidarity with one or more groups that include but go beyond Black Americans, such as Indigenous peoples, Hispanics, Asian Americans, women, LGBTQ+ persons, working-class and impoverished people, disabled persons, immigrants, and many more, even if some groups like ADOS limit their support to Americans.

These efforts to make the Repair alliance an intersectional alliance have, moreover, clearly had significant success. One empirical study, based on data collected by surveys of a random sample of activists who participated in the protests after George Floyd's killing, found that whereas once "participants at demonstrations focused on racial justice were predominantly people of color," after Floyd's death the marches and rallies became much more diverse (Fisher and Rouse 2022, 4). These researchers also reported from their fieldwork that many participants had what can reasonably be judged intersectional motives, with pro-women's and LGBTQ rights activists championing those causes in ways they intertwined with their opposition to systemic racism. It is therefore impossible to analyze today's rival racial policy alliances and institutional orders without recognizing them both as forms of intersectional politics, just as intersectional scholars insist.

When it comes to political strategies, however, it is necessary to recognize that success in building protest movements is not the same as success in gaining governmental power and designing and implementing the policies a coalition desires. The fact that both of today's racial policy alliances appeal to an array of intersectional identities suggests that the Left's more overt celebration of intersectionality may not necessarily translate into political victories over its rival. To be sure, there are significant challenges facing the intersectional coalition-building of each alliance. For example, older free trade, anti-regulatory libertarians are often wary of the economically protectionist, even mildly redistributive agenda of many national conservatives, who attack big corporations and promise to sustain Social Security and Medicare. Some of the former "neocons" who still believe America has a mission to spread democracy and capitalism around the world are sharply opposed to "America First" isolationism. Some color-blind-minded conservatives are equally averse to the overtly "ethnocultural," if not outright racist, messages of many militant contemporary conservative nationalists.

Still, the difficulties facing the intersectional coalition-building of the Repair alliance appear greater. We have already observed that the very fact that the United States was created largely by wealthy white Christian men has meant that those who hold one of those identities are long accustomed to working in harness with those who share one of the others—especially since many possess more than one of those identities themselves. Furthermore, virtually all varieties of traditionalist conservative can appeal to the nostalgic attachments of millions of Americans to the "imagined community" of the predominantly white Christian male-governed nation in which they were raised.

In contrast, efforts to build a sense of solidarity and a set of shared political initiatives among Blacks, Hispanics, Asian Americans, immigrants,

Indigenous peoples, LGBTQ+ Americans, disabled persons, and others are not only newer; they also confront three major difficulties. First, the agendas of these groups conflict on some important issues, such as who should be eligible for reparations funding and land redistribution and the desirability of immigration. Second, even the most ardent Repair advocates acknowledge that the collective costs of their racial equity initiatives across numerous policy regimes are extraordinarily high, in the tens of trillions of dollars. It is not surprising that for many taxpaying Americans, and for those of the wealthy who do not pay taxes but still despise all government spending, the price tag alone makes a good portion of the Repair agenda a nonstarter. Third, visions of the "imagined community" Repair proponents seek to build remain hazy and undefined even in comparison with the highly mythologized account of America's past that Protect advocates invoke to inspire efforts to make the nation "great again."

Though the original formulators of intersectional accounts would not be at all surprised to find that seeing the world through an intersectional lens often reveals barriers to change even more extensive than might otherwise meet the eye, it is nonetheless sobering for Repair proponents to recognize that intersectional political strategies are far easier to announce than they are to achieve. Proponents of class-centered and white hegemony approaches to the nation's racial inequalities do have grounds to argue that a politics that seeks to be fully intersectional, instead of focusing primarily on class or race, is more likely to experience fragmentation and intense political resistance than to meet with success. It is nonetheless crucial to recognize what our evidence shows about the newly emerged Repair policy alliance, with its much-heightened emphasis on intersectionality as a mode of analysis, organizing, and policy-making. It is far better funded, more extensive, and more active at more levels of American public and private life, including local, state, and national government agencies along with churches, educational institutions, foundations, and some corporations, and with more supporters among whites and Asian Americans as well as Blacks and other groups, than many analysts from all theoretical camps have often recognized. Its road ahead is daunting, but it is remarkable how much ground it has covered already.

Conclusion

The evidence we have compiled and analyzed using our framework of racial institutional orders provides, then, a basis for saying, first, that the contemporary racial policy alliances cannot be understood simply as "capitalist interests against their opponents," as less sophisticated versions of class-centered analysis suggest. Even so, the possibility that both alliances are in fact constrained by American capitalism in ways that reduce their capacities to provide justice for all remains highly credible. Second, our evidence confirms that viewing contemporary racial politics as fundamentally a battle between a unified, white hegemony-upholding American state and movements of oppressed peoples misses much of the complexities of contestation over racial issues—far too much, in our judgment. Yet there is no basis for dismissing, and much to support, expectations that America will remain far into the future a society in which whites are predominantly on the high end of the nation's extreme racial disparities, in comparison to most Black Americans and many other people of color. Finally, even though our work strongly affirms the necessity for intersectional analyses, the support it provides for intersectional political strategies is less clear, though again it documents significant achievements for those approaches to politics, as well as challenges.

We conclude that there is good reason to believe that the sorts of empirical investigations of institutional orders we have sought to exemplify in this book can illuminate, even if they cannot resolve, many of the debates between different accounts of racial politics, in ways that can inform political strategies. It is inevitably a more speculative venture to try to lay out the probabilities and possibilities for where the clash of the contemporary Protect and Repair alliances may lead. Even so, readers will naturally be curious, and so are we. Consequently, that is what we attempt in chapter 10.

CHAPTER TEN

Views from the Battleground

Paths and Prospects for America's New Racial Politics

White Americans find it as difficult as white people elsewhere to divest themselves of the notion that they are in possession of some intrinsic virtue that black people need, or want. . . . The only thing white people have that black people need, or should want, is power. —James Baldwin

The International Context

Will the Protect or the Repair coalition hold more power in America in the years ahead? To consider this question, we must bear in mind the criticism that too much American politics research, including ours, has focused parochially on domestic politics, neglecting potent transnational factors. Throughout this book we have sought to call attention to how both Protect advocates, particularly national conservatives, and Repair activist groups like the Movement for Black Lives are collaborating with like-minded associates in many parts of the world, and how the successes of conservative and progressive movements abroad often serve to inspire their American allies. Before we turn to some alternative scenarios of where the contestation between America's new racial orders may lead over the next decade, it will be useful to sketch this international context more fully. Judging global trends is even more difficult than assessing their domestic counterparts, but there can be no doubt that the intense zeal and the more extreme positions that have increasingly characterized American racial politics have powerful parallels around the world.

National Conservatisms and Ethnocentric Populisms

The global trends that favor the Protect alliance are the most visible. We noted in chapter 3 that the Conservative Political Action Conference (CPAC) was created in the early 1970s as part of the mobilization of conservatives partly stirred by the Lewis Powell memo, which contributed greatly to Ronald Reagan's rise. We discussed how CPAC has been rivaled in recent years by the pro-MAGA National Conservativism Conference and by Nicholas Fuentes's still more extremist America First Political Action Conference. In striking confirmation of how even older conservatives are shifting in the ideological direction of these newer alternatives, in both 2022 and 2023 the Conservative Political Action Conference held international conferences in Budapest, Hungary, with Hungarian Prime Minister Viktor Orbán as their keynote speaker. At these events CPAC members celebrated their solidarity with nationalist conservatives from many lands (Olsen 2023).

The 2023 conference dramatically displayed how national conservatism has become, somewhat ironically, a vibrant international movement. The speakers included the prime minister of Georgia; the chair of the Austrian Party for Freedom; Eduardo Bolsonaro, the son of former Brazil President Jair Bolsonaro; former prime ministers of Slovenia and the Czech Republic; the president of the Japanese Conservative Union; the president of the French National Rally party; the chair of the Portuguese Chega Party; the former head of Germany's Office for the Protection of the Constitution; the president of Italy's Nazione Futura think tank; the leader of Israel's Zionist Im Tirtzu party; the chair of the Estonian Eken Party; a Danish European Parliament member and a Croatian parliamentary member, both described as enemies of "gender propaganda"; a leading Polish conservative intellectual; the Slovakian minister of family affairs; a South African filmmaker called a "staunch defender of the Afrikaner community"; the Spanish vice president of the European Conservatives in the European Parliament; a Dutch member of the European Council; a Swiss National Council member; and many more, including a host of American conservative politicians, foundation leaders, and media personalities such as US Representative Paul Gosar, former Trump Chief of Staff Mark Meadows, and Kevin Roberts, president of the Heritage Foundation (CPAC Hungary 2023). Roberts soon joined Ohio Senator J. D. Vance, Israel's Yoram Hazony, and numerous other speakers, including many UK Conservative

Party MPs and British conservative media stars, at an ensuing National Conservatism Conference in London (National Conservatism 2023).

Despite the electoral defeat of two of their heroes, Donald Trump and Jair Bolsonaro, such events reveal an accelerating international networking of nationalist conservatives. To many analysts, the election of Giorgia Meloni as prime minister of Italy on an anti-immigrant platform, the enormous popularity of India's Narendra Modi, the successful consolidation of power in the service of fiercely nationalistic policies by both Russia's Vladimir Putin and China's Xi Jinping, the election of President Recep Erdoğan for a third term in Turkey, and the continuing successes of kindred candidates in many other countries all confirmed that in the third decade of the twenty-first century the much-discussed rise of often authoritarian populist nationalisms was still dominating the political agendas of many of the world's regimes and most of the world's population (Mylonas and Tudor 2023, 1–4).

The moderate conservative commentator Henry Olsen has noted that Orbán became an icon to many American conservatives because of his "frankly nationalist and traditionalist platform," including his resistance to "refugees from Muslim countries," his "positive endorsement of Christianity," his use of tax policy to "encourage childbearing" in traditionalist families, and his "ethno-nationalism," though Olsen insists that American conservatives instead "must embrace" the reality that America is a "successful multiethnic nation" (Olsen 2023). Yet Orbán's ethnic nationalism is clearly a plus for his many American admirers who raise alarms against America's changing demographics, like Tucker Carlson and Gosar—whose digital director, Wade Searle, has been accused of having sworn "undying allegiance" to Nicholas Fuentes, the white race, and the America First movement (Walker 2023). There can be little doubt that the increasing prominence of nationalist conservative movements on every continent since 2010, and their frequent interactions and mutual cheerleading, are a major source of strength for the American Protect alliance.

Global Racial Equity and Reparations Initiatives

What all the understandable attention to right-wing nationalist leaders obscures, however, is that the transnational alliances among supporters of Black reparations and an array of other racial justice causes are also energized, and they are if anything more broadly and deeply grounded in grassroots support. Like Black Lives Matter, many of the racial equity movements around the globe avoid celebrity leaders. Perhaps partly for that reason, outright advocates of reparations, unlike nationalist conservatives, have not become prominent heads of government, even in most formerly colonial nations. When King Charles III was crowned in 2023, for example, it was primarily leaders of Indigenous peoples within Commonwealth nations, not those nations' leaders, who sent the new monarch a joint letter demanding reparations for British colonialism (Ott 2023). It is also true that previously, the promise—or to some the threat—of the widely heralded World Conference against Racism, Racial Discrimination, Xenophobia and Related Intolerance that the United Nations convened in Durban, South Africa, in 2001, along with Durban Declaration and Programme of Action the conference produced, were squashed by the terrorist attacks on New York City and Washington, DC, on September 11, 2001, just four days after the conference ended. But even during the conference, its proposals met with considerable resistance from the US, Canada, and the European Union (Lantos 2002, 31–32).

The growing and strikingly global focus on racism and reparations for enslavement did not then evaporate, however (Lyons 2002; Achiume and McDougall 2023). Once-rare expressions of contrition for historical injustices have continued to proliferate at many levels of governance and in many places ever since, including, for example, the city of Edinburgh's apology for its role in the enslavement trade and the Dutch prime minister's and the Dutch monarch's apologies for their country's 250-year role in slavery in 2022 and 2023, following on a number of other apologies, as noted in chapter 6 (Brooks 2022; Boztas 2022; Moses 2023). This Repair-favorable trend has shaped and is certain to continue to shape US domestic politics, since links between the demands of civil rights reformers in the United States and progressives globally are long-standing, stretching back to at least the abolitionist movement, through Marcus Garvey's pan-Africanist United Negro Improvement Association, to the anticolonial advocacy of W. E. B. Du Bois and his allies (including Claudia Jones and Paul Robeson) in the 1940s and 1950s, and the conscious emulation of global liberation movements by the Black Panthers in the 1960s and 1970s. Stokely Carmichael and Charles V. Hamilton's demanding and influential book, *Black Power: The Politics of Liberation in America*, explicitly equated the status of colonial peoples and the position of African Americans (Carmichael and Hamilton 1966). Subsequently, as we have seen, American reparations advocates in particular have worked closely with kindred movements in the Caribbean and Central and South America and Africa and have taken inspiration from the movements of Indigenous peoples all over the world.

Since 1993, the UN Human Rights Council has appointed a "Special Rapporteur on contemporary forms of racism," and the Special Rapporteur in 2019, UCLA Law Professor E. Tendayi Achiume, presented to the General Assembly one of the leading examples of contemporary international racial equity and reparations advocacy. Achiume devoted over half of her densely packed report specifically to reparations for colonialism and slavery, tying compensatory schemes to "contemporary structures of racial discrimination, inequality and subordination" (Achiume 2019, 10). To lend her calls credibility, Achiume cited approvingly the success of victims of British oppression of the Mau Mau movement in Kenya in winning compensation, and the continuing claims of the CARICOM's Ten-Point Plan for Reparatory Justice adopted in 2014. She emphasized that "contemporary movements for reparations" center on both "historic racial injustice" and persisting "socioeconomic deprivation for which slavery and colonialism are amongst the root causes" (18). On the basis of such enduring deprivations, Achiume also attacked the "intertemporal principle," the doctrine favored by formerly imperial nations that countries can only be judged by the international laws in effect when they acted, without any retroactive application of new international laws to policies and practices that were not deemed illegal in the times in which they occurred. Against its proponents, she stressed that "when Member States and even international lawyers insist on the application of the intertemporal principle as a bar to pursuing reparation and remediation of racial injustice and inequality, they are, in effect, insisting on the application of the neocolonial law" (19).

Unsurprisingly, however, former imperial powers have continued to dispute Achiume's report on this and many other points. We noted earlier that while Germany has agreed to provide compensation to Namibia for its early twentieth-century genocide of the Ovaherero and Nama peoples, it has done so with retroactive safeguards, citing its payments as products of moral and historical obligations, not requirements of international law (Achiume 2019, 190). Similarly, the British government has resisted the Heirs of Slavery campaign's calls for it to acknowledge and atone for the country's pivotal role in the passage of 3.1 million enslaved people in the Atlantic trade. Members of the Heirs of Slavery group include descendants of Gladstone, the Trevelyans, and others, whose families received compensation when British slavery was abolished in 1833 while enslaved workers did not (Balfour 2023; Fisher 2022; Gentleman 2023; Lashmar and

Smith 2023). Verene A. Shepherd, a historian at the University of the West Indies who has worked with the United Nations Committee on the Elimination of Racial Discrimination, castigates the British state for "simply uttering meaningless statements of regret, remorse and deep sorrow" rather than offering measurable compensation (quoted in Mohdin 2023). Issuing expressions of regret and not formal apologies, much less material compensation, remains the dominant tendency among formerly imperial powers.

The international advocacy group Colonialism Reparations, founded in Italy in 2008, welcomed Achiume's UN report, singling out for praise both the set of recommendations she presented and her rooting of claims to reparations for slavery and colonialism in existing UN agreements and international laws. The report's recommendations included calling for the UN member states to create a generous fund "for the sustained study of paths forward for international action to achieve reparations"; broad educational initiatives, since "a serious barrier to reparations is ignorance" among citizens and leaders about slavery's legacies; and "initiatives by non-State actors," including churches, universities, and financial institutions, of the sort we have identified in the United States (Achiume 2019, 23).

Despite the surge of right-leaning national conservatisms, there is evidence of some trends in these directions. Like the US, European nations are seeing the emergence of a number of groups whose members have great inherited wealth that they seek to use to provide what they term "reparations" for their societies (Bubola 2011). As we have touched on, highly visible reparations movements are also active in the Caribbean and in parts of Africa, seeking to shape the general international political climate and the agendas of a wide range of international economic and political actors and institutions. Consequently, though at present the international movements urging such reparations remain far more remote from governing power than many of their conservative opponents, they provide moral and political support, strategic and policy ideas, and a strong sense of shared endeavor to many members of America's Repair alliance. Many activists believe that in the long run their transnational grassroots movements will prove to have more staying power than today's much-touted nationalist conservative politicians.

The China Factor

The world's future is of course highly unpredictable, since alongside these trends in racial politics, international economic, environmental, and epidemiological catastrophes and unexpected wars may occur, potentially overturning all existing political patterns. Barring any such shattering events, however, it seems a virtual certainty that global politics for many years to come will be heavily shaped by the competition between the United States and China for the status of the world's most sought-after economic and political partner and model. As during much of the Cold War with the Soviet Union, that competition may mean that the United States will support authoritarian regimes in countries like the Philippines and Egypt in return for their allegiance against China. If those are the realpolitik facts of life, many US leaders may show little interest in advancing racial equity policies, at home or abroad, since doing so might suggest sympathy for repressed groups in the countries of their authoritarian allies. The Protect alliance would probably prosper amid such global politics.

Yet China, as an authoritarian one-party, quasi one-person state, may well seem a more attractive partner to many authoritarian leaders than the United States does, since America's troubled democratic system nonetheless still involves regular transfers of power. And precisely because the forces of authoritarian nationalism rather than transnational egalitarian movements appear to be setting the global agenda at present, their visibility may stir countervailing international political forces that could shift the world's political winds in the not-too-distant future. The US might then find it could win more allies by presenting itself as a progressive champion of egalitarian democratic transformations, both domestically and internationally, combating the legacies of European and American imperialism by extending material resources and political power to African Americans and the broader African diaspora and to Indigenous communities, as well as by championing women's rights, LGBTQ+ rights, rights of disabled persons, and environmental justice, and by supporting transnational efforts to combat climate change, international economic inequalities, and related causes. Through such initiatives the US might find that it could rebuild some of the prestige and soft power it possessed in the days of the Marshall Plan and again at the end of the Soviet Union—particularly among nations and movements that might otherwise be inclined to see it simply as a self-seeking white capitalist global hegemon (Dunst 2023). Those foreign and domestic policy stances would obviously assist the Repair alliance.

In sum, transnational networks and other aspects of international politics provide some benefits to each of America's new racial policy alliances, with conservatives taking their inspiration chiefly from kindred traditionalist leaders and progressives primarily from transformative grassroots movements. Though that contrast makes it reasonable to see global political trends as currently most helpful to conservative forces in the United States, it is still true that Sir Hilary Beckles's prediction that the twenty-first century will be the century of reparations is now embraced in many more parts of the world than when he made it.

The impact of international factors on the contestation of America's rival racial orders is, then, unsettled; but it is a near certainty that the international context will play a significant role.

Back to the Domestic

As we turn to the domestic realm, we must also consider two other criticisms of our racial orders framework. Does our focus on clashing policy alliances underestimate and unduly neglect the wide range of regional, state, and local variations in American racial politics? And does our insistence on greater divisions within the American "racial state" mischaracterize what white hegemony theorists perceive as a fundamentally unified, coherent structure of governing power?

Though these criticisms are in some ways at odds with each other, both have validity. It is indisputable that in the next decade as throughout America's past, different racial policy alliances will have the upper hand in different states, cities, smaller towns, and rural regions, and the most salient racial issues will vary in different locales. The racial politics of Alabama and California will continue to be distinct, as will those of Detroit and conservative, predominantly white Ottawa County, Michigan (of which more below).

Indeed, in some respects the diversity in racial politics across America is now greater than in much of the nation's past. State-mandated systems of enslaved labor and, later, de jure racial segregation were regionally concentrated, existing overwhelmingly in the American South, a circumstance that contributed to the Civil War and to the national politics of the civil rights era. Now, not only do cities like Jackson, Mississippi, differ greatly from the more rural-dominated Mississippi state government, but every region has some "purple" states—such as Georgia and North Carolina in the South, Pennsylvania in the Northeast, Michigan and Wisconsin in the Midwest, Nevada and Arizona in the West—whose leaders may shift from members of one racial policy alliance to the other with each election, and which may well elect some state officials from each. These circumstances, among many other factors, make Rep. Marjorie Taylor Greene's call for Red states to "divorce" from Blue states wildly unrealistic: her own state has at this writing two Democratic senators, one a progressive Black man who has been elected twice (Pettypiece 2023).

Yet the very fact that regional divides are less stark than in the antebellum or Jim Crow eras is one of a number of factors, along with a decline of local media, heightened partisan polarization, and more, that have contributed to what Daniel Hopkins has called the "nationalization" of American political behavior (Hopkins 2018). The eruption in many places of controversies over Critical Race Theory and related "cultural" issues is a classic example of this nationalization. We have seen how, aided by conservative media, mobilizing groups, and Republican politicians, after 2020 innumerable local school board and governmental elections across the country have focused on the sorts of disputes that divide the nation's major racial policy alliances. A striking instance came early in 2023, when a MAGA-minded group, "Ottawa Impact," ousted seven "establishment" Republicans from the Ottawa County, Michigan, Board of Commissioners. Among other measures including personnel firings, the new commissioners immediately replaced the county motto of "Where You Belong," which they said derived from the "divisive, Marxist ideology of the race, equity movement," with "Where Freedom Rings," a phrase they said reflected America's "true history as a land of systematic opportunity built on the Constitution, Christianity and capitalism" (quoted in Jaffe and Marley 2023). There can be little doubt that national racial policy debates did far more to motivate this change than any distinctive local concerns.

It is also true that even though the variations in the politics of different places across America are often still extensive, calling into question analyses premised on a unitary American racial state, in the aggregate racial politics have always given the United States contested but predominant patterns that have prevailed across many policy regimes and in many sectors of social life in particular eras. Even when only southern and some midwestern states had Jim Crow segregation laws, the US government's legitimation of those policies made America a country of de jure racial segregation, albeit one in which patterns of segregation varied and were often disputed. Consequently, while the formidable task of mapping the future of racial politics in all their variations across the United States would surely be worthwhile, it is not essential to develop informed reflections on what sorts of racial policies are likely to prevail most widely in America as a whole in the years ahead.

Based on the evidence in the foregoing chapters and on our prior research, we are confident that the predominant pattern across the nation will remain one of contestation between rival racial policy alliances and institutional orders, now organized around the goals of Protect or Repair. Proponents of both positions can reasonably believe that they will be able to build further on the substantial accomplishments each has achieved in recent years. Protect coalitionists especially can claim success in winning federal judicial and state legislative support for newly restrictive voting laws and weaker voting rights protections; legislative and judicial bans on most affirmative action programs and other race-conscious measures in many states and at the national level; bans in many states and local school districts on curriculum seen as favoring Critical Race Theory and LGBTQ+ rights; tougher immigration policies, many enacted under Trump but continued under Biden; new judicial protections for the liberties of traditionalist religious groups; the overturning of *Roe v. Wade* and new restrictions on abortions in strongly conservative states; campaign finance deregulation; and other key concerns of those seeking to resist and reverse transformations in the more traditionalist vision of America they cherish. Moreover, as we have seen, Protect coalition advocates have succeeded in converting many members of the more economically libertarian network of conservative think tanks, policy centers, and advocacy and litigation groups built up in the last quarter of the twentieth century to support for new Protect goals, and they have created many new institutions as well, backed by numerous deep-pocketed donors.

Though the achievements of Repair coalition advocates have been more limited, they are more than substantial enough to sustain optimism of the will, even if often accompanied by pessimism of the intellect (Bacon 2023; Richeson 2020). Chapter 6 documented how for the first time in US history a growing number of cities and states have adopted initiatives explicitly labeled reparations, especially in the areas of housing and public health. Though controversial, police reforms concerned with racial equity have proliferated, especially in the form of new community advisory boards to enable accountability. Despite the efforts to ban Critical Race Theory, many teachers at all levels have given more attention to America's past and present racial injustices than ever before. Innumerable foundations, corporations, churches, and universities are dedicating what promises to be billions of dollars to racial justice causes, many described as reparations. Hundreds if not thousands of efforts to remove statues, monuments, and place names celebrating American champions of white supremacy have succeeded or are still underway, if often against fierce resistance. HR 40 has gained more serious attention in Congress than ever before. Perhaps most significantly, a thick and exceptionally funded infrastructure of NGOs, activists, and donors has been built that now rivals its conservative counterpart and promises to pursue Repair goals persistently far into the future. It is also significant that both policy alliances have linked their racial positions to a wide array of other concerns, with Protect advocates promising to defend traditionalist Americans on many fronts, not just racial issues, and with Repair proponents expressing solidarity with a wide range of disadvantaged groups, not just people of color. The breadth of both coalitions suggests strongly that whichever one will eventually predominate, the clash of today's racial policy alliances is certain to continue.

The Lessons of 2022

Elections will of course shape how extensively each racial policy alliance can become a governing racial institutional order. As we were writing this book, the 2022 midterm elections reinforced the judgment that both Protect and Repair advocates can reasonably hope for future success, continuing the historically dichotomous structure of American racial politics, even as that structure has evolved into a substantively new stage. Despite conservatives' structural advantages, some increases in violent crime, persistent inflation, and the low popularity ratings of President Joe Biden, the 2022 election surprised most political analysts by producing only a modest swing toward Republicans in the House of Representatives, with Democrats unexpectedly gaining a seat in the US Senate. Democrats also retained control of every state legislative chamber they already held, while flipping chambers in key states including Michigan, Pennsylvania, and Minnesota—a feat unmatched in American politics since 1934 (Ewall-Wice 2022). Perhaps most significantly, as we have noted, pro-Trump candidates who denied the legitimacy of Biden's 2020 presidential victory and who sought state-level positions such as secretary of state in order to administer future elections generally ran behind other Republicans in their states, and many lost, especially in closely divided battleground states (Parks 2022).

Yet even though a number of Democratic progressives supportive of reparations won election or reelection in 2022, most Democrats won by promising to defend abortion rights and democratic processes, not racial equity initiatives (Cooper 2022). Across the country Republican candidates for the US House of Representatives won over 3 million more votes than Democrats did, roughly 50.6 percent of all votes cast, exposing a closely divided nation (A. Walter 2022). Prominent proponents of Christian nationalism and white replacement theory, like Representatives Marjorie Taylor Greene and Paul Gosar, easily won reelection in deeply Red congressional districts (Weiner and Zellman 2022). Possibly the biggest winner in either party was Florida Governor Ron DeSantis, one of the nation's most vociferous and ardent champions of a Protect agenda. He had pushed legislation to prevent teaching about Critical Race Theory and sexual diversity and to ban abortions; flown immigrants unannounced to Massachusetts and abandoned them; championed restrictive voting laws; revoked the Disney Corporation's special tax privileges due to its "woke" conduct, and much more (Dixon and Fineout 2022). DeSantis was the first Republican statewide candidate to carry Miami-Dade County in twenty years. Many observers thought he did so by convincing Hispanic voters from a number of Latin American countries, not just Cuba, of his ardent opposition to the kinds of socialist policies they loathed in their homelands, and of his support for their traditionalist religious and social values (Chaffin 2022). Right before the November election, DeSantis ran an ad saying "on the Eight Day, God looked down on his planned paradise, and said 'I need a protector'"; and even as some traditionally religious Americans began to lose their faith that Donald Trump was a divine tribune, some started to turn to DeSantis as their "protector," though whether he could displace his charismatic predecessor remained very much in doubt (Ecarma 2022).

The Possible Futures of America's New Racial Politics

Overall, the 2022 elections delivered no clear verdict beyond confirming that American voters remain more polarized than at any point since the 1870s, giving each side reason to persist in its cause (Abramowitz and McCoy 2019; Dawkins and Hanson 2022). Which side has the better prospects in the years ahead? One way to approach that question is with a thought experiment. What would happen if Americans were given the opportunity to choose definitively between today's rival racial policy alliances—if, for example, they were to vote either in favor of the National Conservatives' Statement of ten principles or NAARC's Ten Point Program?

We think it is overwhelmingly likely that a preponderance of the electorate would favor the NatCons, and so the Protect policy alliance, for the foreseeable future. It is still true that over two-thirds of American registered voters are white; and though many whites support reparations and other major racial equity initiatives, most do not. They are joined in opposition by some non-white traditionalists, especially Hispanics (Gramlich 2020; Reichelmann and Hunt 2021). Although, as we have seen, public opinion data do not always track the scope or efficacy of political organizations and activism, it remains true that those who are advocating for less popular policies face an uphill fight.

And as we have stressed, the Protect alliance holds structural privileges: the Constitution's federal system provides numerous veto points in policy processes, which can be most readily used to obstruct policies benefiting "*vulnerable* (as opposed to powerful) minority groups" (L. Miller 2022, 7, emphasis in the original; cf. L. Miller 2010 and 2019). Because it empowers state legislatures, America's federalism permits most forms of partisan gerrymandering, which both parties have historically engaged in but which is today most often a tool of conservatives in rural-dominated states; and in recent years it has allowed democratic backsliding at the state, county, and city levels in policy regimes such as voting rights, residential zoning and housing laws, and school districts' powers over curriculum, all critical to the Repair agenda (Grumbach 2022, 2023; Rocco 2022; Weir 2005; Weir and King 2021). The nation's future may therefore show considerable continuity with its past in one regard: the conservative racial policy coalition is likely to have more popular support on many issues, and to control more governmental institutions, than its progressive counterpart (Jardina and Piston 2022; Schaffner, MacWilliams, and Nteta 2018; Weiner and Zellman 2022).

However, a number of factors may limit Protect success. It is true that Americans as a whole do not support affirmative action, much less radical reparations. In 2020, voters in the very Blue state of California voted 56 percent to 44 percent not to repeal Proposition 209, the prior referendum that had banned many forms of racial affirmative action in that state (Friedersdorf 2020). Even so, many (probably most) Americans do support at least some other racial equity measures. In a 2023 poll, more than half—once again, 56 percent—strongly or somewhat favored diversity, equity, and inclusion initiatives in higher education, while only 27 percent opposed them (McKown-Dawson 2023). Recent trends may also indicate an increase in the political influence of Americans with more progressive racial views. As residential prices have risen dramatically in many American cities, and as many people have become used to working remotely because of the pandemic, many more college-educated as well as low-wage workers have been moving to suburbs, smaller towns, and even rural regions (Badger, Gebeloff, and Katz 2023). The political consequences of this development are not certain, but because college-educated voters tend to be more liberal on racial issues, especially since the rise of Trump, and because many Democratic voters have long clustered in urban super-majority districts, making many of their votes in legislative races superfluous, it is possible that their diffusion will increase the impact of their support for Democrats, and support for Repair policies, in a greater range of jurisdictions. And though it is not likely to start an urban trend, San Francisco is considering $5 million in reparations for many of its current and former Black residents primarily because they have faced discrimination in the city's housing markets, but also because so many of them have been moving away (Arango 2023).

Perhaps still more significant are recent shifts in Americans' religious adherence. Although as we have seen there are very large numbers of religious groups in the Repair alliance, it remains true that conservative Republicans tend to do better in areas where religious memberships are on the increase, while liberal Democrats fare better in regions that are becoming more secular. In the US as a whole, religious affiliations are in decline, but regional variations are substantial. Democrats and Repair policy supporters can take heart from the fact that most counties in battleground states including Wisconsin, Michigan, and Pennsylvania saw drops in religious adherents between 2010 and 2020, with that pattern expected to continue. Texas and Florida, however, saw growth in their religious memberships, probably to the benefit of the Protect alliance (Burge 2023). Overall, even as Christian nationalists are growing more militant, the perhaps related fact that other Americans are growing more secular may bode well for Repair forces in the years ahead.

While on balance all these factors, taken together, favor conservative positions on racial issues, we do not believe they justify concluding that Protect positions will inevitably become so hegemonic as to be practically synonymous with the nation's racial institutional order, or that Repair advocacy will be almost wholly eclipsed. Not only are there many places in the United States, especially its large cities and a number of states on each coast, in which coalitions of progressive whites and most non-white voters will almost certainly continue to govern. In the nation's heartland, the one-time swing state of Illinois became reliably Democratic in the twenty-first century because its Republican Party too often ran candidates marred by extremism and corruption—thereby serving as a reminder that parties can become so discredited that they lose elections they should be well positioned to win (Pearson 2022). As extremist Republicans gain greater control of state parties in other battleground states like Michigan and Pennsylvania, while key MAGA figures like Ken Paxton, Rudy Giuliani, Steve Bannon, and Trump himself face litigation for corruption, other such examples may arise.

Furthermore, though appeals to racial fears (and sometimes hopes) have often featured in American elections since at least the Lincoln-Douglas debates in 1858, voters are always concerned, and frequently more concerned, about other issues. In every election, the state of the economy matters. National security is sometimes central. As the 2022 midterm elections demonstrated, social issues like abortion rights can play important roles. The fact that elections are rarely decided simply on racial policy issues makes it not only possible but almost certain that progressive candidates will continue to win governing offices in many places, not just the coastal cities. We expect that, given the recent turn of many racial justice advocates toward support for reparations broadly defined, most of those in government who wish to be seen as progressives will strongly contest many elements of a Protect policy agenda, while favoring at least some parts of the Repair agenda. Sometimes they will win.

Much Noise, Little Change?

Consequently, we do not expect that the conflicts between today's racial policy alliances will result in a sweeping victory for either side in the foreseeable future. Though a number of scenarios are conceivable, all plausible paths forward anticipate continuing mixed patterns. In all of them, Protect proponents are expected to govern in some states, cities, towns, and counties; Repair supporters will control others; and many governments, perhaps especially the vast and complex federal government, will have rival alliance members holding office simultaneously.

Indeed, precisely because Americans are deeply divided and politicians may choose to campaign on other issues, it is possible that in the years ahead contestation between supporters of Protect and Repair policies will be waged in legislative hearings, courtrooms, executive agencies, on the internet, and in the streets, without a clear decision between them being put to or provided by American voters. That was the case with the clash between the preceding color-blind and race-conscious racial policy alliances, with the result that neither obtained the kind of clear and consistent popular mandate that might have enabled it to achieve its agenda fully. As we argued in 2011, the nation simply remained a house divided, with limited racial progress (King and Smith 2011). If the battles between the Protect and Repair policy alliances follow a similar course, their most outspoken advocates will garner much media attention, but their clashes will have less impact on now institutionalized racial policies and practices in America, including the extensive patterns of deep racial inequalities. The status quo will, in essence, remain the status quo.

Yet while we cannot rule that scenario out, we do not think it probable. The sharp opposition between Protect and Repair positions across many policy regimes, along with the fervent mobilizations that each has inspired since the end of the Obama years, lead us to consider it more likely that racial issues will play a significant role in national as well as state and local political campaigns. While neither alliance will win across the board, a predominant pattern will probably emerge. That pattern may well arise from one or the other of the racial policy alliances adopting an agenda, adapted to a greater or lesser extent from those we have shown them now to be featuring, that can enable a broadened conservative or progressive coalition to gain governing power in a preponderance of American political institutions. The winners would then establish institutional orders and policy regimes expressive of their commitments on racial issues—and many other issues as well.

To conclude our analysis, we offer six scenarios in which different types of Right and Left coalitions come to power, presented in descending order of what, in light of the evidence of the preceding chapters, we judge to be their probability. We also give our estimates of what are likely to be the sharply varying consequences for the future of America's long-standing racial inequalities, depending on which scenario comes to pass.

1. An Ascendant "Multicultural Protectionist Conservatism"

If we start by assuming that the preponderantly white American electorate would probably vote for the National Conservatives' Statement of Principles over the NAARC Program, but that most whites do not want to see themselves as white supremacists or to abandon all racial equity initiatives, the most likely scenario is one in which a moderate version of national conservatism comes to prevail on racial policies as well as on other issues.

In light of public opinion data and the results of the 2022 elections, in which Republicans narrowly won the national congressional vote despite the unpopularity of many extremist conservative candidates, it is plausible that a moderate national conservative coalition could have substantial electoral success, especially if pitted against proponents of more extreme Repair measures. The NatCons' tenth principle makes clear that, unlike Nicholas Fuentes, most national conservatives wish to be seen as anti-racist, not as white nationalist. That stance has wide appeal to those older conservatives like Linda Chavez, Gail Heriot, and Ward Connerly who have always seen themselves as championing principles of color-blindness; to moderate conservatives like Henry Olsen who see America as a successful multiethnic nation; and to younger conservatives like Reihan Salam and Christopher Rufo who similarly call for a multiethnic or multicultural conservatism—as well as to much of the American electorate.

The racial stances of these older and younger conservatives overlap, but not completely. Rather than insisting on strict adherence to color-blind, individualistic, "meritocratic" policies, today's moderate national conservativism presents itself as (in principle at least) more receptive to *limited* public policies that recognize and accommodate ethnic, racial, and cultural minority identities and concerns. However, such policies would not extend to most forms of affirmative action, or to the robust multiculturalism of the Repair alliance. Ethnic studies programs and student associations would, for example, be welcomed if they celebrated the successes of America's diverse immigration groups, but not if they appeared to convey the anti-American and anti-white messages conservatives associate with Critical Race Theory. Given America's demographic diversity and the power of the Repair coalition, this mildly multicultural yet still protectionist conservatism has better prospects to gain broad political acceptance in the twenty-first century than either a rigid insistence on completely color-blind policies or any open espousal of America as at its core a white nation.

Such multicultural conservativism would be likely to support funding of HBCUs, as the Trump administration came to do, as well as historically Hispanic-serving institutions. It would accept some reforms in criminal justice policies that have resulted in racially disproportionate mass incarceration and police killings of, especially, Black men. It might even endorse some light-touch race-conscious initiatives to support Black entrepreneurship and to expand the pool of applicants for public educational institutions and public employment. Its adherents could similarly accept expanding the diversity of those honored with public statues, memorials, and place names and represented in museums and in public school curricular materials—if, again, the core message is a valorization of America's exceptional inclusiveness, not a condemnation of American systemic racism.

Such a coalition would likely institute some protectionist trade and economic investment policies, consistent with the commitment to put America first that most multicultural conservatives share, that might well benefit many American workers of all races, at least in the short run, and might thus expand this coalition. Some kinds of universalistic social programs, such as Social Security pensions, Medicare, and education funding, promise both to benefit whites directly and to provide them some protection by alleviating the enraging hardships and frustrations many Americans of color experience. Many of the Florida Hispanics who have been crucial in turning their state Red favor bilingualism and a significant measure of multiculturalism, along with many America First economic and social policies (Chaffin 2022). It is therefore possible that moderate multicultural conservatives may win broad support by favoring some protectionist economic policies and modest universalistic redistributive measures, so long as aid programs have work requirements and are minimal enough to not be a slippery slope toward a European-style social welfare state, much less a Latin American-style socialist system. The extent to which a multicultural conservative coalition would support even universalistic redistributive programs is, however, a major question. It is notable that even as Republicans gained control of the House of Representatives in the 2022 election, they signaled goals of reducing federal Social Security and Medicare spending, despite Trump's repeated promises to protect them (Tankersley 2022).

These moderately multicultural protectionist conservatives might also welcome significant, and significantly diverse, immigration to the United States. They are more likely to do so, however, if the nation adopts a point system favoring skilled and prosperous immigrants. Such a system would likely privilege South and East Asian and perhaps eastern European applicants over many of the less affluent would-be migrants from Latin America. Multicultural conservatives would also insist strongly that all immigrants must assimilate to what they take to be core American economic, social, and political values, and must learn English.

Similarly, such conservatives would reject almost all concerted efforts to reconstruct American institutions and practices progressives see as systemically racist. It is not conceivable that they would support any large-scale program of individual cash payments, or any extensive race-targeted initiatives to provide Blacks with guaranteed basic incomes, employment, land, housing, health care, funding for repatriation to Africa, or protection against and compensation for environmental harms. They would also reject the legitimacy of all forms of affirmative action that go beyond efforts simply to expand applicant pools. Even as they affirm what they see as a significant measure of cultural diversity, multicultural conservatives are likely to seek to strengthen the authority of parents and legislatures to ensure that public education and public commemorations do not foster a woke ideology they view as hostile to American traditions and values. They would also oppose efforts to structure city, state, and federal electoral districts explicitly to empower voters of color; they would uphold voting rules imposing barriers to potential voters in the name of combating fraud; and they would resist most efforts to limit police functions and to transfer police funding to other social service agencies. Beyond aid to Black entrepreneurship and education, then, there would be little in the NAARC Ten Point Program that an ascendant multicultural conservatism would support.

What would be the consequences of this moderate multicultural conservative agenda for the nation's enduring patterns of severe racial inequality? In the best case, many of those inequalities would gradually become somewhat less severe, easing some racial conflicts. However, as in the scenario in which racial policies are kept out of electoral politics and decided, if at all, in obscure governmental offices, past experience provides little reason to expect any dramatic transformations in the American status quo if multicultural conservatism, already powerful, becomes still more ascendant. Its policies would after all largely seek to preserve and protect the status quo and would only welcome those outsiders who willingly undergo substantial assimilation to American values and practices as the multicultural conservatives understand them. Consequently, those policies would appease few supporters of transformative Repair measures. Instead, they would perpetuate the nation's historical pattern in which, as one era ends, the issues central to that era's racial debates shift, and some important policies are abandoned—in this case, all strong forms of affirmative action—but most of the nation's long-standing racial inequalities and antagonisms would persist, along with many other controversial inequities.

2. Building a Class/Race Coalition

The widespread existence and harmful effects of economic inequality—not just on Black Americans—makes the next scenario the second most likely.

Again, economic issues always loom large. Moreover, many millions of Americans across the political spectrum have long felt ignored and harmed by the neoliberal policies that both parties predominantly pursued as part of America's Reagan Revolution after 1980. As a result, many progressives now wish for egalitarian economic initiatives to be at least as prominent on their agenda as programs for racial justice. Their position is likely to be significantly strengthened by the Supreme Court's heightened insistence on color-blind policies and the consequent abandonment of most forms of affirmative action, though those developments may also drive some progressives to shift to more radical Repair demands.

But while some on the left favor dropping race-targeted policies entirely, breaking completely with today's Repair agenda, we have noted that many capitalist-centered analysts and advocates still support many forms of affirmative action, even as they decry the Left's turn to "identity politics." At the same time, most Repair agendas already include some universalistic economic initiatives. Consequently, it is not difficult to imagine that many Repair alliance members will prove open to modifying their race-focused agenda somewhat to facilitate their joining with economically focused progressives in advocacy that more prominently features class along with race. Were they to do so, however, it is likely that concerns for a broader array of disadvantaged identity groups would be tacitly assigned secondary importance. Even though modern America exhibits a great and growing variety of identity movements, it remains true that economic and racial issues loom larger than all the rest, so a progressive alliance that chose to feature them above all else might have broad appeal. Most left-leaning Americans know that they have been debating "class v. race" endlessly for generations (Frymer 1999; Frymer and Grumbach 2021; Harris and Rivera-Burgos 2021). As illustrated by the current popularity of the often vaguely defined phrase "racial capitalism," many long to be part of a movement that gives great weight to both.

Consequently, in this scenario, a modified Repair policy alliance would join in a progressive coalition that featured a greater number of universalistic economic and social welfare initiatives in combination with some race-targeted proposals. For example, advocates might urge free higher education for all up through the community college level and heightened aid to HBCUs, while supporting special loans for low-income Black students, if these could be structured to survive constitutional challenges, perhaps by showing that they compensated for past proven discrimination by white institutions and for the advantages that predominantly white legacy students possess in admissions processes. This coalition might also support universal health care that included special initiatives for the distinctive needs of poor communities of color. It might support expanded affordable housing and job programs for all, but again with significant aid targeted to housing, employment, and credit opportunities in more disadvantaged, predominantly Black neighborhoods to address disadvantages arising from segregation (Boustan 2017; Derenoncourt 2022; Wang et al. 2018). Class-and-race proponents could also favor infrastructure programs to provide jobs for many Americans of all backgrounds, while structuring them to include efforts to reduce environmental harms, transit system deficiencies, building disrepair, and other specific needs in Black communities. Advocates might also support heightened funding for social service agencies to assume many functions now being performed by police forces, without urging any "defunding" of police. They could support higher minimum wages, expanded workers' rights, and unions, while also championing private reparations initiatives of many kinds, including the supports for Black entrepreneurship many wealthy private donors favor, but also direct cash payments, tuition and housing assistance, and perhaps forms of community ownership of lands, housing, and commercial enterprises.

Such a progressive coalition would have every incentive to resist voting restrictions and districting systems that limit the political power of African Americans, and to support many forms of Black political organizing. It might also choose to give particular emphasis to race-conscious cultural initiatives, such as public museums, memorials, and place names commemorating Black experiences and historical figures; revised school curricular materials; more inclusive media presentations; and other forms of fuller representation. If its economic agenda tilted toward working-class-oriented universalistic measures, its cultural agenda would be all the more likely to tilt strongly toward enhanced recognition for Black Americans and people of color more generally, within the United States and transnationally.

This "class and race" policy alliance might well disappoint single-minded racial Repair proponents, and also advocates for many other groups, such as disabled persons, LGBTQ+ organizations, and perhaps women's, Indigenous, and immigrant groups, among others, whose concerns would not be so prominently featured. It would also still need to confront the longstanding "profound ignorance of the current reality regarding racial economic inequality" of white Americans, the majority of whom are "deeply committed to the belief that society is currently fair and that Black and White Americans are on equal economic footing" (Onyeador et al. 2021,

764; Taylor 2019). Even so, it is possible that these priorities would permit the establishment of an appealing progressive coalition, especially if efforts were made to structure both universal and targeted measures so that many in the less featured identity categories would still tangibly benefit, along with many less affluent whites. It is also possible, however, that this agenda's race-conscious features would end up doing more simply to promote Black entrepreneurship, Black home and business ownership, and Black representation in existing institutions than to achieve any major systemic transformations, just as in the case of the past generation's neoliberal policies and those likely to be adopted under multicultural conservatism.

Nonetheless, if this class-race alliance proved more politically popular than either a class- or race-based progressive agenda alone, it is conceivable that it might move the US in the direction of becoming a racially inclusive social democratic welfare state, with some significant reductions in racial disparities. The likelihood that such a progressive alliance would face both internal dissension and resolute conservative opposition means, however, that this scenario cannot be deemed the most probable in the years ahead.

3. Triumph for White Extremist Conservatism

The third most likely scenario is one in which the more extreme wing of the modern Protect policy alliance sets the conservative agenda and comes to power in many states and at the national level, with many of its members visibly championing whites against a range of perceived enemies, and many also supporting forms of religious nationalism, often explicitly Christian nationalism. As the National Conservativism Statement of Principles suggests, this strongly conservative alliance would, at a minimum, place a moratorium on virtually all immigration, to be lifted only after adoption of rules that restored some forms of preference for more affluent (and probably predominantly white) immigrants. Conservative lawmakers would seek to restructure American elections in ways that made it more difficult for, especially, non-white Americans to vote, or to elect their preferred representatives if they did vote; and its adherents might also empower state legislatures to override the popular vote in presidential and some other elections in order to stay in power even when, as is likely, they lacked enduring majority support. Unlike moderate multicultural conservatives, this extremist conservative coalition could not truly hope or expect to win support from most Americans. Some of its adherents, like Claremont Institute Research Fellow Glenn Ellmers, have openly contended that "most people living in the United States today—certainly more than half—are not Americans in any meaningful sense of the term," and so must be overridden (Ellmers 2021).

If this brand of conservatism gained power by one means or another, it would probably reduce or end all forms of public assistance explicitly targeted to non-white Americans, as well as programs its members simply perceive as chiefly benefiting minorities, and would be reinforced in these efforts by traditional economic conservatives' opposition to most forms of economic regulation and redistribution. It would be likely to sustain only those governmental programs that might maintain a segregated and unequal structure in American public institutions, such as, perhaps, poorly-funded urban public schools and HBCUs.

For all schools, these conservatives would mandate a patriotic 1776-style curriculum that presents as anti-American governmental efforts to combat systemic injustices in American institutions and to reduce material racial inequalities. They would resist any further changes in American monuments, statutes, and place names, like the etchings on Stone Mountain, Georgia, that would diminish public honoring of past racially conservative—or, indeed, openly white supremacist—American figures. They would support aggressive policing of Black and brown communities, and they would seek to penalize or prohibit any progressive-led government agencies that sought to adopt welcoming policies toward immigrants, or racial justice-oriented employment and education programs, or new restrictions and new forms of accountability to discourage abusive police conduct. At the same time, they would oppose most punishments for vigilante violence like that perpetrated by Kyle Rittenhouse, as well as for those who seek to overthrow elections they regard as having been conducted corruptly. Instead they would probably give such vigilantes medals. Former President Donald Trump provided an example of this extremist Protect stance in his video statement in December 2022, supporting those charged in the January 6 insurrection and their families at a fundraiser hosted by the Patriot Freedom Project. Speaking two days after the conviction of the Oath Keepers' leader, Stewart Rhodes, Trump pugnaciously asserted: "People have been treated unconstitutionally, in my opinion, and very, very unfairly, and we're going to get to the bottom of it" (quoted in Baker 2022).

It is inconceivable that this agenda would contribute to any significant lessening of American racial inequalities, material or symbolic. That would not be its goal. There would still remain some opportunities for particularly gifted and particularly fortunate people of color to flourish in the United States; but many more would experience this route as a retreat from, not progress toward, racial equity. Consequently, this scenario would foster angry resistance on the part of many millions of Americans of all racial backgrounds who believe in trying to achieve greater racial equality, thereby deepening destructive divides and heightening the potential for violence in many if not all venues of American life.

4. Reviving a Working-Class-Centered Progressivism

That very specter, and what many will see as the limited prospects presented by the prior scenarios, could drive Repair-minded Americans in one or the other of two significantly more radical directions. The first of these is symbolized by the recent proliferation of municipal efforts to provide "universal basic incomes," limited though those now are. Many progressive activists like those promoting these initiatives might decide they can achieve more for all Americans, including Black Americans, by pushing a broadly beneficial economic agenda and abandoning race-targeted proposals and "identity politics" completely, except for the politics of economic identities, just as capitalism-focused analysts have urged.

Under this scenario, the Repair goal of reducing racial inequalities would be pursued through, and subsumed under, efforts to achieve robust and inclusive social welfare measures, perhaps including a single-payer national health program, free higher education in public institutions, expansive affordable housing programs, greater access to manageable loans for homeownership and businesses, changes in public policies to favor workers' rights and unions and to regulate, break up, or even nationalize industries that have become oligopolies or monopolies, and job creation programs that could include massive investments in public infrastructure projects in every sector—all funded through higher taxes on the wealthy and, perhaps, protectionist tariff policies. Advocates of this agenda would insist that it would do far more to lift the material conditions of Black Americans and other less advantaged groups in America than any politically feasible form of racial reparations—and far more than multicultural conservative or neoliberal policies would provide.

How far that proved to be true would depend on just how extensive, well-funded, and inclusive these initiatives turned out to be, and whether, if substantial, they also proved to be economically successful. More limited versions of these economically focused measures might only result in a somewhat greater level of African American participation in American capitalism's ownership and benefits (again without major adjustment to systemic racial inequalities), or in the nation's economic system more broadly, with its attendant inequalities of both resources and power. It is not inconceivable, however, that this progressive agenda might move the US much closer to European-style democratic socialism, as Senator Bernie Sanders and others have long urged, while significantly reducing racial disparities.

The more progressives move in this direction, however, the fiercer will be the resistance from proponents of conservative economic policies. History also suggests that many opponents of a strongly Left economic agenda will rely more or less explicitly on accusations that these universal programs would unjustly benefit undeserving people of color. The potential for racial dog whistles or outright racist denunciations to become even more pronounced in American political contests than they are at present is very real.

Meanwhile, current Repair alliance members who support many forms of progressive identity politics might well feel ignored and disrespected by this more purely economic program. Many seek cultural recognition and representation, not simply greater economic resources and opportunities. We have also seen throughout this book that the contemporary Repair alliance, which features such cultural demands, has inspired energetic mass activism to a greater degree than proponents of more traditional Left economic agendas have in recent years. Consequently, though this scenario at its best could achieve significant reductions in racial and economic inequalities and in the stigmatization of many disadvantaged Americans, the obstacles to its success are substantial.

5. Forging a Broad Intersectional Repair Alliance

Rather than homing in on class politics, the alternate radical direction is to seek to build an intersectional progressive coalition with wide appeal by championing as many causes as possible, still including economic concerns along with many others. As we have seen, the platform of the Movement for Black Lives, the most radical Repair agenda we examined, aspires to do just this: to achieve substantial systemic changes by simultaneously advancing the particular causes of Blacks, poor and working-class people, authorized and unauthorized immigrants, Indigenous communities, women, people with diverse sexualities, people with physical and mental disabilities or simply bodies that do not comply with ableist ideals, and more. Through forming numerous intersectional alliances, Black repair advocates aim to gain sufficient political power to enact a sweeping reparations agenda that might include cash payments but also race-targeted systemic reconstructions in the areas of employment; ownership of land, businesses, and homes; education; health and environmental care; and historical and cultural remembrance and recognition. But for such a broad alliance to succeed, progressives would need concurrently to support related initiatives for the other identity groups comprising it as well, not just Blacks. The resulting panoramic array of initiatives could only be funded through systems of massive public taxation and service provision that would substantially transform the nation's economic system.

The pursuit of such an agenda would inevitably arouse not only ferocious conservative opposition, but also conflicts among putative allies. It is true, as Barbara Ransby argues, that Blacks can be found in all categories of oppressed people in America. Still, an agenda that foregrounded Black concerns would undoubtedly stir controversies on the left sooner or later. Disputes might well arise among Indigenous communities, Black Americans, and immigrants as to whose claims to land and control of resources should be honored. More affluent LGBTQ+ groups who could support much of the intersectional alliance's social and cultural agenda might resist its more radical economic measures.

There would also be tensions between those in the intersectional alliance focused on achieving systemic transformations primarily within the United States and those who insist that forming transnational alliances to restructure the global system of unequal nation-states must ultimately take precedence over changes that might only reinforce the international status quo. For many of those advancing intersectional frames, the shift to global politics signaled by the movement against colonial and racist imperial legacies is an unshakable motive and cause.

As a result, while such a broad and radical progressive intersectional alliance might form in the years ahead—because it has indeed already formed to a much greater degree than seemed possible in the opening years of the twenty-first century—it remains exceedingly difficult to envision it gaining predominant political power in the foreseeable future. Were it to do so, the consequences for American patterns of racial inequality, and much else, might well be massive—though here too it is possible that much of the agenda of even an electorally successful intersectional alliance would have to be cut back to be enacted. The results might involve a range of groups obtaining more prominent places and greater shares of resources in American economic, political, and cultural institutions, without otherwise altering those institutions in fundamental ways. Yet under this scenario, the hopes and expectations aroused by the processes of intersectional coalition-building would undoubtedly mean that strong pressures for major changes would persist well into the future, leading to developments of a scope that cannot realistically be foreseen. Precisely because this is potentially the most radically transformative scenario, however, it appears unlikely.

6. Violence Escalation

There is one last scenario which we hope, but cannot assert, is the least likely of all. It is one in which race-related violence in America not only persists but accelerates in the years ahead. The fact that, as we have noted, extremist proponents on the right and the left are not so geographically concentrated as they were in antebellum America makes another all-out civil war between regions improbable. It is also true, however, that today's polarized racial positions are more strongly aligned with opposing political parties than at any time since the 1850s, reinforcing the transition of partisan politics into the dangerously uncompromising, often potentially violent identity politics that recent studies have documented (Kalmoe and Mason 2022). Even if it is not realistic to expect Red and Blue states to "divorce," it is a sign of disturbingly severe divisions when civil rights organizations like the NAACP and the LULAC (League of United Latin American Citizens) issue travel advisories, even if primarily as protests, which warn people of color that it may be dangerous for them to visit Red states like Florida and Missouri (Yan, Alonso, and Gallagher 2023). In this increasingly volatile climate, the possibility cannot be dismissed that the nation will be wracked for years to come by increasing hate-inspired violence and what may approach small- to medium-scale guerrilla warfare in many locales.

A number of factors combine to give rise to this scenario. First, recent years have seen rising numbers of hate crimes that have included vicious killings by embittered individuals, many of them young and emotionally volatile for many reasons, who have embraced extremist theories, including "replacement" fears, and sought to spark race wars (Robertson 2023). There have also been rising numbers of shootings by white homeowners who invoke "stand your ground" laws, sometimes successfully, to defend firing on allegedly trespassing Black Americans as well as racial justice protesters of all colors. So far, the latter have been generally peaceful until attacked; but the more such violence increases, compounding the outrage fueled by the police killings that have often sparked the protests, the greater the likelihood that more on the left will adopt armed tactics in response.

Second, in earlier chapters we have shown that armed groups consciously intent on violent confrontations exist on both the contemporary right and the left, though extremist right-wing groups appear far more numerous and much better organized, and have engaged in more elaborate and deliberate criminal plots, including the January 6 insurrection and the attempted kidnapping of Michigan Governor Gretchen Whitmer.

Third, we have seen that leaders of those extremist Right groups and the Protect alliance more generally, including some state and local officials and, above all, Donald Trump, have repeatedly contended that acts of violence against supporters of the contemporary Left, including officeholders, are justified, and indeed patriotic. Here the asymmetry between the two alliances is especially sharp: unlike in the 1960s, when Nation of Islam's Malcolm X and Black Panther leaders such as Huey Newton and Bobby Seale championed the Second Amendment right to bear arms and sometimes threatened violence, the Repair alliance today has no incendiary figures comparable to Trump, Paul Gosar, or the Oath Keepers' Stewart Rhodes (Bloom and Martin 2013). We have found no evidence that any prominent member of the Repair coalition, including elected politicians, civil rights leaders, NGO activists, and protesters, has deployed violent imagery and calls for violent actions in the manner of many Protect alliance leaders—a major reason why most racial justice protests have been peaceful (Gillion 2012, 2013, 2020; Hinton 2021; Mazumder 2018; Wasow 2020).

That could change.

It is all too easy to imagine these factors combining to create a nation in which violent individual hate crimes continue to escalate and organized group assaults become so frequent that many Americans will feel they are living in war zones. Needless to say, it is impossible to envision any meaningful progress toward easing racial injustices if this scenario should prevail. Instead, the existence of the nation would hang in the balance.

The Context of Mounting Hate Crimes

To grasp the circumstances that make this scenario of violence conceivable, it is important to recognize the corrosive increase in recent years in hate crimes, primarily targeting Black Americans, Asian Americans, and Jewish Americans. It has created an environment ripe both for random killings and for organized group violence. According to FBI data, hate crimes based on race, ethnicity, or ancestry bias spiked sharply in 2020, with 2,871 aimed at African Americans, an increase of 900 over the previous year. Between 2010 and 2020 there were 20,084 instances of anti-Black crimes, and 7,688 anti-Jewish hate crimes (Burch and Vander Ploeg 2022). The upward trend in incidents continued in 2021 (Feuer 2023). That year, fully a third of the nation's HBCUs reported bomb threats, and many Black churches also recorded threats (Burch and Vander Ploeg 2022).

The litany of violent acts that contribute to these hate crime statistics is far too long to report, but it is important to recall a few of the more notable incidents. Some show the impact of the racial theories and conspiratorial accounts circulated by the far Right. As we have noted, after Dylann Roof killed nine of the evening Bible Study participants who had invited him to join them at Charleston's Emanuel African Methodist Episcopal Church in 2015, he explained that his purpose as a white supremacist was to provoke a "race war" (Burnip and Boroff 2020). Seven years later, on May 14, 2022, eighteen-year-old Payton Gendron drove two hundred miles from his hometown of Cronkite, New York, to Buffalo, where he live-streamed his murder of ten African Americans in a Black neighborhood supermarket, again with the intention of mobilizing a race-based conflagration in the United States (Jones 2022a). The three white men who chased and murdered at close range the unarmed Black American Ahmaud Arbery in Georgia in 2021 were revealed at their trial for federal hate crimes to have been circulating in a world of racist language and intent straight out of the nineteenth century (Nakamura 2022). The palpably shaken foreman of the jury, Marcus Ranson, remarked that "'just seeing that it was so much hatred that they had, not only for Ahmaud, but to other people of the Black race ... was a lot to take in'" (quoted in Fausset and Mzezewa 2022). Though police in Allen, Texas, expressed uncertainty about just what thirty-three-year-old Mauricio Garcia hoped to accomplish when he killed eight people and wounded seven, mostly people of color, at the Allen Premium Outlets mall on May 6, 2023, they acknowledged that he was an ardent white supremacist with "neo-Nazi ideation" (Harley 2023). A little over two weeks later, a nineteen-year-old from Chesterfield, Missouri, Sai Varshith Kandula, rammed a truck carrying a Nazi flag into the barriers outside the White House in an attempt to kidnap and possibly kill President Joe Biden (Bushard 2023). The Wolverine Watchmen who previously conspired to kidnap Michigan's Democrat governor, Gretchen Whitmer, represented far more organized violence, but like Roof and Gendron they hoped to provoke massive civil strife (Sidner 2020). On the last Saturday in August 2023, a racially motivated nineteen-year-old who left "racist writings [full] of hatred towards African Americans" murdered three African Americans at a Dollar General store in Jacksonville, Florida (quoted in Betts and Manna 2023). One journalist concluded that "racist attacks" were "now a way of life in the US" (Kaleem 2023).

Other shootings arise not from belief in racial conspiracy theories or hopes of sparking insurrections, but simply from the fear and biases that America's fraught history of racial injustices has instilled in many white Americans, combined with the nation's expansive gun ownership regulations and the "stand your ground" laws authorizing their use that have been adopted in over two dozen states in the last two decades. In 2023, an eighty-four-year-old homeowner in Kansas City shot a sixteen-year-old Black teenager, Ralph Yarl, who was trying to pick up his younger twin siblings and went to the door of the wrong house. Two days later, a sixty-five-year-old homeowner shot a twenty-year-old white woman, Kaylin Gillis, who was in a car that had mistakenly turned into his driveway, as the driver of the car attempted to leave (Sullivan 2023). Though only one of these shootings involved a Black person, they dramatized how the nation's rampant gun use and its new "stand your ground" laws are creating an environment in which race-related violence may well continue to mount throughout the land.

To be sure, the violence is not all on one side. Republican Representative Steve Scalise was shot by a rabid Bernie Sanders supporter who had come prepared with a target list of Republican leaders. The conservative members of the Supreme Court have received death threats that the federal authorities regarded as credible. An Antifa activist killed a right-wing opponent as part of the frequent clashes in Portland (Frum 2022). These brutal incidents only confirm, however, how great the dangers of racially and politically motivated violence now are in America.

The Militia Menace and Protect Alliance Leadership

As we reported in chapter 3, perhaps the most disturbing fact about the armed protectionist groups who form the most extreme wing of the Protect alliance is that they have maintained a steady level of activities and violence even after the many convictions of January 6 insurrectionists won by the Department of Justice. It is in some ways ironic that the Proud Boys' continued activism was aided by their non-hierarchical organizational structure, which has empowered local branches to continue to fan tensions with local acts of protest and violence without much central or national leadership after Enrique Tarrio's conviction, though the subsequent tough twenty-two years in prison sentence may have a sobering effect on activists (Wolfe 2023b; Jackman and Hsu 2023). In this regard, the Proud Boys resemble the decentralized, non-hierarchical structure of many Repair organizations, including the limited and elusive Antifa groups. As a traditional hierarchical group, the Oath Keepers' activities instead receded dramatically after Stewart Rhodes's conviction and sentencing.

But regardless of their modes of organization, right-wing militia leaders have unprecedented access to instruction manuals for violent initiatives and to new media for inciting action (Robertson 2023). Many have regularly amplified the signals sent by Protect alliance politicians that lawless violence against their enemies may well be justified. Those signals have come from some state and local officials and members of Congress, though Donald Trump has been far and away their most important source. Rhodes told his Oath Keeper followers right after the election that the group was "awaiting the president's orders," a strategic ruse to garner "legal cover" before undertaking plans to disrupt the congressional certification of the electoral vote results (quoted in Feuer 2022b). Trump's speeches made them confident that their orders had been issued. A member of the Texas Three Percenters, Guy Wesley Reffitt, also invoked Trump to inspire insurrection, telling his fellow members in an encrypted private chat that "Our President will need us. ALL OF US!! On January 6th. We the People owe him that debt. He sacrificed for us and we must pay that debt" (quoted in Feuer, Schmidt, and Broadwater 2022). Again, hearing Trump, many responded to those admonitions. In the last week of March 2023, a twenty-four-year-old woman, Riley Williams—one of the more than one thousand people charged in connection with the January 6 assault on the Capitol—was sentenced in the US District Court to a three-year jail term. She was a mere twenty-one years old when she rallied other rioters to steal from Speaker Nancy Pelosi's office and urged violent resistance against police officers. Williams's attorney said she had been "fooled and manipulated" by former President Trump and his false claims that Biden's election was fraudulent (Wolfe 2023a). Similarly, David DePape, the forty-two-year-old man who attacked Nancy Pelosi's husband in their home, believed the claims of Trump and his supporters that the Democrats had stolen the election, and that those claims justified his violent response (Vargas and Yang 2022).

Yet as he began his campaign in 2023 to win back the White House in 2024, Trump only ratcheted up his calls for his supporters to break laws in order to achieve power. In December 2022 he posted on his social media site, Truth Social, that a "Massive Fraud" like the 2020 election "allows for the termination of all rules, regulations, and articles, even those found in the Constitution" (Holmes 2023). Trump also chose to hold his first major campaign event in Waco, Texas, where his fiery speech reminded many of the violent battle between federal Bureau of Alcohol, Tobacco, and Firearms officials and the heavily armed right-wing Branch Davidians extremist group in April 1993, which left seventy-five dead. There was little doubt which side the former president of the United States favored: his slogan of "God, Guns and Trump" made no mention of the government (Flores and Leary 2023).

That was perhaps not surprising, since Trump was facing investigation and prosecution by a range of federal, state, and city government prosecutors. The day after Riley Williams's sentencing, Trump made remarks that once again threatened to spark lawless violence, predicting that in the event of his arrest by Manhattan District Attorney Alvin Bragg, America faced "'potential death and destruction'" (quoted in Haberman, Bromwich, and Rashbaum 2023). Trump has also indicated repeatedly that if he regains the presidency, he will extend pardons to most if not all of the January 6 insurrectionists for the federal offenses under which they were convicted (Dodds 2021). Doing so would inevitably encourage more illegal, possibly often violent vigilante actions in ensuing years.

Trump, however, is hardly a lone voice in these regards. Missouri Governor Mike Parson pardoned the wealthy St. Louis couple, Mark and Patricia McCloskey, who had been found guilty of misdemeanors for threatening peaceful BLM protesters with a semiautomatic rifle and handgun (Pereira 2021b). Representative Paul Gosar's infamous video showing himself killing Representative Alexandria Ocasio-Cortez has been matched by numerous political ads showing Republican candidates and officials wielding guns and promising to shoot those who disagree with them. When by the summer of 2023 Trump found himself fighting four criminal indictments, many allied politicians and media figures only ratcheted up their threats of violent reprisals, with Stephen Bannon and Trump-affiliated politicians like Arizona gubernatorial candidate Kari Lake and Washington House candidate Joe Kent contending the nation was effectively already at war (Schmidt et al. 2023). As David Frum, a former speechwriter for President George W. Bush, has written, though extremists on each side engage in lawless destructive acts, only the GOP's leadership "celebrates political violence" (Frum 2022). In towns, counties, cities, and states with such leaders, it is entirely imaginable that in the years ahead violent clashes between partisans of the rival racial policy alliances, and even armed attempts by the Right to seize and hold power, might become frequent.

Conclusion

It is impossible not to be exercised about America's rising violence, so often borne of racial fears and hatreds, and the disdain of Donald Trump and his followers for the rule of law, democratic electoral processes, and many if not most of their fellow citizens. It is discouraging to recognize not only that the visions of today's increasingly mobilized Protect and Repair racial policy alliances are more sharply opposed than those of the preceding color-blind and race-conscious policy coalitions, but that the distrust, and often outright contempt, of each side for the other appear on the increase. This book has compiled extensive evidence in answer to our opening question about what is happening in the politics of race in America today, but we cannot pretend that what we have found is reassuring about the prospects for racial progress now and in the years to come.

We nonetheless believe that the portrait of contemporary American racial politics we have provided can be a basis not for despair but for fresh and constructive thought and action. Though the dangers of severe polarization combined with violent extremism are very real, the emergence of the nation's new racial policy alliances is also a story of how millions of Americans have felt inspired to imagine new political futures and to work actively to bring them into existence. Not all of those so moved are uncompromisingly seeking total victory. Many whom we encountered on each side of the current racial policy divide share the deep anxieties of most

Americans about the dangers the nation faces. A number were seeking in good faith to reformulate their positions in ways that provided for some common ground, without sacrificing their values. Sometimes, staring into the abyss can open eyes, and even minds and hearts.

We think it likely that most Protect alliance supporters genuinely do not wish to embrace the militant white supremacist views of its extremist wing, the disregard for the Constitution that Trump has urged, or the lawless violence he sometimes celebrates. We also think that most Repair proponents sincerely seek, as the N'COBRA website puts it, to help insure that "the nation as a whole will become stronger" through establishing a "just and peaceful society." It is significant that many progressives can accept color-blind policies when such measures can convincingly be shown to improve conditions for all, and that many conservatives, both older and newer, insist that they truly wish to find ways for America to prosper as a multiracial, multicultural nation, albeit one embracing "multicultural conservatism," in Christopher Rufo's phrase. It is notable that even though Virginia Governor Glenn Youngkin got elected by denouncing CRT, in office he has supported reforming Colonial Williamsburg so that it honestly tells the "good and the bad" of its part of the American story. It is equally notable that while Representative Jamaal Bowman strongly endorses reparations, he urges first the creation of a Truth and Reconciliation Commission, to help foster the mutual understandings that might make shared efforts to improve American conditions more feasible. Some progressives are also now acknowledging that many existing diversity, equity, and inclusion initiatives have proven more divisive than transformative. In a surprising (if faint) echo of those on the left who urge coalition-building around widely shared economic interests, some corporate human resource departments are modifying their DEI programs to focus on promoting "diversity and belonging," with a greater emphasis on bridge-building, open conversations, and quests to find ways "we can all rise together" through shared economic success rather than simply by aiding racial minorities—though serious doubts about this direction persist among both conservatives and progressives (Miller 2023).

The point is not that the nation's racial policy divisions are visibly closing. This book shows that they are not. We nonetheless believe that it is on the whole positive that on both the right and particularly on the left, to a greater degree than many have recognized, Americans in recent years have undertaken remarkably energized efforts, at all levels of government and in many social venues, to search for novel ways to address the nation's enduring problems. Most on each side see clearly that neither the conservative nor the liberal stance of the previous era in America's racial history has moved the nation very far forward. Whether they wish to Protect or Repair, most Americans do not wish to see continued increases in destructive violence. At least some on each side are truly committed to finding ways to forge a better future, rather than simply fanning the flames of the nation's long-standing racial fires. There is no guarantee that these constructive efforts will prevail. But if we believe at all in humanity's potential to imagine and to pursue better political directions, as do many Americans who seek to move beyond current oppositions, there is no reason to conclude that these efforts must fail. To the contrary, there is every reason to try to help them succeed.

Acknowledgments

For valuable research assistance during the course of preparing this manuscript we thank Jasper Kauth, Ross Snyder, Tylor-Maria Johnson, Amber Mackey, Nicholas Pangakis, Saanvi Bhatia, Benjamin Rutherford, and Bo Wen Zhu.

For financial support we thank Nuffield College's Mellon Trust Fund and the University of Pennsylvania's Christopher H. Browne Distinguished Chair Research Fund.

During the years of our collaboration studying American racial politics, we have received an immense amount of (critical and positive) intellectual feedback and commentary from many colleagues at professional meetings, seminars, and workshops, and we are grateful for all of it. At a workshop held at the University of Pennsylvania reviewing the penultimate draft of the manuscript we received helpful commentary from workshop panelists Daniel Q. Gillion, Michael Hanchard, Fredrick Harris, Daniel HoSang, Kimberley Johnson, Robert Lieberman, Michelle Margolis, Lisa Miller, and Stephen Skowronek, as well as Amber Mackey, Nora Reikosky, Hadass Silver, Mary Summers, and Heather Swadley.

Many other colleagues gave feedback on drafts, including Touré Reed, Adolph Reed Jr., Lawrie Balfour, Mary Summers, and Joanna Wuest. We received excellent questions and comments from attendees at presentations of our work at Brown University, Campbell University, University of Illinois Chicago, Queen's University Belfast, and the American Political Science Association.

At the University of Chicago Press we have had much appreciated support and guidance from our editor, Sara Doskow, from our copyeditor, Evan Young, and from their colleagues in production. Two readers for the Press provided constructive feedback and comments on a draft of the manuscript.

APPENDIX A

Research Strategies and Methodologies

Chapter 2 elaborates the substance of the revised institutional orders framework we have used to structure our studies. Primarily for the benefit of scholarly readers, this appendix discusses more fully the research methods we have employed to compile evidence for the inquiries the framework poses.

Like most historical institutionalists, we use multiple methodologies in our research, though our work has always rested on close readings of large numbers of primary documents. We believe an extensive base of factual knowledge is the best place to start. While we have experimented with text analysis software systems, we have not found them sufficiently helpful to justify replacing our more traditional methods.

Instead, to gain a preliminary grasp of the terrain we are exploring, we have each, ever since we began studying racial institutional orders in 2003, continually compiled relevant news stories from major media sources such as the *New York Times*, the *Washington Post*, the *Wall Street Journal*, and *The Guardian*, as well as more right- and left-leaning publications, such as the *National Review* and *Jacobin*, and online news and politics websites, such as those of NPR, Fox, the Associated Press, and many others. When these stories have alerted us to popular protests; statements by advocacy groups, candidates, and officeholders; legislative debates; administrative hearings; or judicial cases involving racial policy issues, we have used online sites to review those protests, statements, debates, and hearings, including advocacy and expert testimony and the texts of legislative bills and administrative orders, as well as judicial briefs and decisions.

Through these reviews, we have then compiled lists of advocacy groups, think tanks, commentators, and government agencies active on racial policy issues. We also monitor pertinent academic scholarship in a number of disciplines—chiefly political science, law, history, sociology, political psychology, and political philosophy—for relevant discussions. Those literatures also help us to identify pertinent issues, legislation, and administrative and judicial decisions, as well as advocacy groups, think tanks and governmental agencies, and trends and variations in public opinion on racial topics.

With these studies of political developments and actors on racial policy issues as our starting point, we have then sought to develop more systematic databases for our various specific projects. For example, in our previous book, *Still a House Divided*, we provided partial listings of groups active in racial policy alliances and accounts of their positions by reviewing all the amicus briefs in Supreme Court decisions addressing the racial policies the book examines, accompanied by extensive but less comprehensive examination of testimony in related legislative and administrative hearings, as well as statements by political actors and public opinion data on those policies (King and Smith 2011). For our first article drawn from the research that is the basis of this book, "White Protectionism in America," we examined all of the speeches we could locate that Donald Trump made as a presidential candidate and as president, relying chiefly on the American Presidency Project website based at the University of California-Santa Barbara and the White House's own website of statements and press releases, along with examinations of the websites of all the federal agencies we could identify as active on racial policy issues during the Trump administration. We also reviewed pertinent media coverage of both Trump's speeches and his administration's policies (Smith and King 2020).

As the research for that article persuaded us that America was entering a new stage in its long history of conflicting racial orders, we realized the need to undertake additional forms of research to gain an accurate overview of current developments. We continued, however, to employ all the methods we had used in the past. For example, as indicated in chapter 3, we compiled the list of conservative racial policy groups provided in appendix B by examining organizations that actively sought to be part of advocacy coalitions, such as the State Policy Network and the Conservative Partnership Institute. We identified their allied groups, then looked in turn at other groups associated with those organizations, continuing until we had a reasonably extensive overview of the types of groups forming the emerging Protect policy alliance. We also compiled groups that had filed conservative briefs in federal judicial cases involving racial policy issues, as we did for *Still a House Divided*.

We examined the websites of all these groups as well as pertinent media coverage to see if they advocated any of the positions we identified as Protect policies. These included opposition to Critical Race Theory and the 1619 Project, support for book bans, defenses of symbols and monuments to the Confederacy and other conservative causes, tighter immigration policies, more restrictive voting requirements and changes in electoral rules to reduce the likely power of non-white voters, less stringent enforcement of antidiscrimination laws, more severe policing and punishment for protesters, and opposition to race-targeted aid policies in all areas including education, employment, housing, healthcare, and environmental measures, as well as restrictions on abortion and LGBTQ+ rights and heightened protection for the liberties of traditionalist religious groups and for conservative speech on campuses, in the media, and in other cultural institutions. Research assistants also examined the groups' websites, and online databases like those provided by the IRS, Influence Watch, GuideStar, Charity Navigator, Source Watch, and Cause IQ to obtain information on the groups' founding dates and finances. We preferred to report the founding dates the groups themselves provided, but when those were absent we used the year of the first IRS ruling on their tax status. We also preferred to report their most recent annual expenditures, but lacking that information we have reported most recent annual revenues, endowment, or total assets. In the case of organizations with many diverse expenditure categories, we have sometimes reported the expenditures for their largest programs as an indicator of their financial capacities, while recognizing that racial issues are often not their top priority. As discussed in chapter 3, we then organized the groups in appendix B into categories based on modifications of those used in the analyses of the preceding "Koch network" by Alexander Hertel-Fernandez, Theda Skocpol, and Jason Sclar.

To compile the organizations supportive of Repair measures listed in appendix C, we relied on the signatories to three statements of support for HR 40, as indicated in chapter 6. That list proved so extensive that we decided it would suffice to indicate the breadth and character of the Repair policy alliance, though we noted many other members in the chapters in part 3. Unsurprisingly, many of the signers of the HR 40 endorsements are small groups with limited funding and private businesses whose shares are not publicly traded and whose financial records were unavailable to us. They are nonetheless indicative of the variety of Repair supporters.

Many of the largest funders of racial justice initiatives are not represented on the list, but we have sought to include representatives of all the major categories of supporters, except for individuals. Finding that the categories we used for the conservative groups in appendix B did not capture the greater diversity of organizations in appendix C, we arrived inductively at a more extensive set of classifications to indicate the variety among the groups supporting legislation to create a national reparations commission, whom we judge to be likely to support transformative racial initiatives more generally.

In both appendixes B and C we have indicated when data were not available, and because advocacy groups' finances and very existence can fluctuate rapidly, the information on specific groups does not necessarily describe their circumstances in the years ahead. We are confident, however, that the appendixes convey accurately the categories of groups that form the Protect and Repair policy alliances, their combinations of older and new groups, and the magnitude and range of their financing.

To provide as full an account of today's racial politics as possible, we also embarked on three further types of research.

First, after we had compiled extensive lists of conservative and progressive groups active on racial policy issues, we sent all those for whom we could locate email addresses an online survey seeking to gain their views on racial policy issues today and on whether they perceived racial policy positions as shifting in the ways we hypothesized to be the case. After several rounds of sending out the survey, we concluded that we did not have enough responses, particularly from conservative groups, to report statistically meaningful results. The results we did receive were, however, substantively informative, and they helped us construct the next two methods we employed. We are grateful to Ross Snyder, Amber Mackey, and Nicholas Pangakis for their aid in the construction and administration of this survey, and to Matthew Levendusky, Michele Margolis, Marc Meredith, Daniel Gillion, Daniel Hopkins, and Alexandra Filindra for their advice on survey research.

As reported in chapter 2, we also sought to provide empirical evidence of the existence of what we term "racial policy alliances" by using software to track the frequency of hyperlinks between the websites of conservative and progressive racial policy organizations, thereby undertaking a form of social network analysis (Girvan and Newman 2002). If racial policy groups operate to any nontrivial degree as racial policy alliances, it is reasonable to hypothesize that their websites will have many hyperlinks to other groups

RESEARCH STRATEGIES AND METHODOLOGIES   311

in those alliances, all the more so in the case of groups that are in some way central to their racial policy alliance. It proved unmanageable to compile or to display the hyperlinks among very large numbers of groups, and of course it was not possible to know in advance which groups would prove to be most extensively linked with like-minded racial policy organizations. Consequently, we sought to map the linkages between a relatively small number of groups, chosen to represent both older and newer conservative and liberal groups, as well as more and less prominent ones. We also sought to include a variety of organizational types, particularly advocacy groups, litigation groups, think tanks, religiously and ethnically identified groups, and national, regional, and local organizations. These considerations led us to have slightly more liberal than conservative groups, since our prior research found a greater diversity of types among the groups on the left side of the political spectrum, especially as pertains to ethnically identified organizations. We arrived at the fifty groups listed in table A.1.

Our research assistant, Jasper Kauth, first used the website crawler function of a software system titled "Screaming Frog" to compile lists of all external hyperlinks found on each of the groups' websites (Screamingfrog n.d.; for more on web crawlers, see Vicente 2021). Kauth then wrote code in R with functions he devised using JavaScript to extract from the list of all hyperlinks those links that went to other groups on our list. Finally, Kauth used R packages, especially visNetwork and JavaScript, to create the figures included in chapter 2, showing each group and its links to all the other groups.

As explained in chapter 2, the circles or "nodes" on the figures represent the groups' websites, with larger nodes showing more extensively hyperlinked groups. The lines or "edges" from each node represent their aggregate hyperlinks to each of the other groups, with the thickness of the edges indicating the frequency of the interactions on a logarithmic scale. While the edges show the numbers of hyperlinks between groups, they do not indicate how often those hyperlinks have been clicked by website users. They represent frequent interconnections between the sites, blogs, resources, and other online materials of the groups themselves, evidence pertinent to the hypothesis that the groups are fellow members of racial policy alliances.

We encountered a few unexpected obstacles to this research: some websites — such as those of the Hudson Institute, the Manhattan Institute, and the Texas Public Policy Foundation among conservative groups, and Color of Change, the National Urban League, and the Action Network/

TABLE A.1. **Organizations in Social Network Analyses**

Conservative Groups	Liberal Groups
Alliance Defending Freedom	Alabama New South Coalition
America First Foundation	American Civil Liberties Union
America First Legal	Asian Americans Advancing Justice
American Cornerstone Institute	Black Lives Matter
American Enterprise Institute	Campaign Zero
Californians for Equal Rights	CARICOM Reparations Commission
Center for Equal Opportunity USA	Community Change
Claremont Institute	First Unitarian Society of Denver
Conservative Caucus	Fund for Reparations NOW!
Conservative Headlines	Institute of the Black World 21st Century
Conservative Partnership Institute	Japanese American Citizens League
Eagle Forum	Korematsu Institute
Federation for American Immigration Reform	La Raza Centro Legal
Focus on the Family	Leadership Conference Civil/Human Rights
Heartland Institute	Leadership Conference Women Religious
Heritage Action	Mayors Org. for Reparations and Equity
Judicial Watch	Movement for Black Lives
National Association of Scholars	NAACP
National Conservatism Conference	NAARC
Pacific Legal Foundation	National Association of Black Social Workers
VDARE	National LGBTQ Task Force
Young America's Foundation	N'COBRA
	Nikkei for Civil Rights and Redress
	Partners for Justice
	Racial Justice Rising
	Tsuru for Solidarity
	Vera Institute of Justice
	Workers Center for Racial Justice

Million Hoodies Movement for Justice among progressive groups—block efforts to crawl them via the Screaming Frog software. Some websites, such as those of the American Enterprise Institute and the American Civil Liberties Union, have so many hyperlinks that obtaining a full accounting would require running the software for many days, so they were only partially crawled.

Our results, however, clearly demonstrate that hyperlinks among the groups we are placing within the conservative and progressive racial policy alliances are extensive, while linkages across those alliances are limited. Added to the many other kinds of evidence our research has provided, these mappings of group networking on the internet reinforce the contention that racial policy alliances exist and are actively at work in contemporary American politics.

Finally, and even more productively, we also undertook Zoom and email interviews of contemporary conservative and progressive racial policy advocates and analysts, again to determine both their own views on today's racial policy issues and their perceptions about whether racial politics had changed or were changing, and if they were, whether they were changing in the directions we hypothesized. We again sought to represent a wide range of organizations and perspectives on each side, from leaders of large national organizations to local activist group members, and we included advocacy groups, think tanks, religious and ethnic organizations, and others. We added interviews with some current and former local, state, and national officeholders: Andre Herndon, chief of staff for Los Angeles Mayor Eric Garcetti; US Civil Rights Commissioner Gail Heriot; former Louisiana Governor Bobby Jindal, now leading a center at the America First Policy Institute; and New York Congressman Jamaal Bowman. Two conservatives we contacted chose not to do Zoom interviews but responded to some of our questions via email in ways that were informative. In two cases, once with the conservative religious group Focus on the Family and once with the progressive advocacy group Fund for Reparations NOW!, our interviewee was joined by another member of the person's organization who also participated in the discussion.

Counting the email exchanges, we conducted fifteen interviews with conservatives on racial policy issues and fifteen with liberals, many of whom prefer the designation "progressives." Because of the two interviews with dual participants, there were sixteen interviewees on each side. The conservative interviewees included thirteen men (two of whom participated jointly) and 3 women. Twelve were white, two were African American, and two were Asian American. The liberal interviewees included nine men and seven women (two women participated jointly). Five of these interviewees were white, seven were African American, two were Asian American, one was mixed race (Filipino/African American), and one was Latina. They ranged in age from local activists in their twenties through a veteran activist in his eighties (the longtime opponent of affirmative action Ward Connerly).

Table A.2 lists the organizations with which our interviewees were af-

TABLE A.2. **Organizations Interviewed**

Conservatives	Liberals/Progressives
America First Policy Institute	Campaign Zero
American Civil Rights Institute	Community Change
American Enterprise Institute	First Unitarian Society of Denver
Californians for Equal Rights Foundation	Fund for Reparations NOW!
Claremont Institute	Institute of the Black World 21st Century
Claremont Review of Books	Korematsu Institute
Focus on the Family	Leadership Conference on Civil/Human Rights
Hoover Institute	Mayors Organizing for Reparations and Equity
Hudson Institute	National Japanese American Citizens League
Judicial Watch	N'COBRA
Manhattan Institute	Partners for Justice
National Association of Scholars	Reparation Generation
R Street	Tsuru for Solidarity
Texas Public Policy Foundation	US House of Representatives
US Civil Rights Commission	Vera Institute for Justice

filiated, although one of our Claremont Institute-affiliated interviewees works primarily as a journalist, not as an Institute leader. We have not listed the interviewees by name on the table, as some preferred to remain anonymous. Most of those who waived anonymity are identified at appropriate points in the book's text. The interviewees included both organization leaders and those holding a variety of staff positions.

Apart from the two interviews conducted via email, all interviews were conducted as semi-structured discussions of the interviewee's organization, history, goals, current priorities and activities; the organization's and the interviewee's views as to whether racial policy positions have been shifting, and if so, how; and the organization's and interviewee's perceptions of how others see racial policy history and the contemporary racial policy landscape. We used information from our other interviews and from our review of pertinent primary and secondary sources to explore whether the interviewee's account of his or her own organization, and claims about others, were consistent with depictions provided by others. None of our questions, however, sought to dispute what the interviewee was telling us—only to clarify so that we could record and report their views as accurately as possible.

Overall, the accounts given by interviewees on each side of the current

RESEARCH STRATEGIES AND METHODOLOGIES 315

racial policy divide were remarkably consistent with those of others on their side, both in their characterizations of their own positions and allies and in their characterizations of their opponents' outlooks. Unsurprisingly, those on each side had many more disagreements with how their opponents saw the two sides. Interviewees in each camp firmly believed that racial policy disputes had become more polarized, and in the general directions we describe as Protect or Repair, in recent years; but each side blamed the other for becoming disturbingly more radical and thereby driving the changes. The information provided in the interviews largely reinforced, and often greatly illuminated, the descriptions we were arriving at based on other sources. Consequently, the results of our reading, social network mapping, and interviews, along with the limited results of our survey, all converged in providing extensive evidence that America's long history of conflicting racial orders had entered a new phase.

APPENDIX B

Organizations in the Protect Alliance

TABLE B.1. **A Sampling of Protect Alliance Members**

Organization Type	Founded	Financials
1. Think Tanks		
1. Acton Institute	1990 (o)	$10,887,803 (x)
2. American Enterprise Institute	1938 (o)	$46,953,435 (x)
3. Capital Research Center	1984 (o)	$2,030,597 (x)
4. Center of the American Experiment	1990 (o)	$2,347,617 (x)
5. Center for Security Policy	1988 (o)	$4,167,838 (x)
6. Center for the National Interest	1994 (o)	$3,985,724 (x)
7. Center for Immigration Studies	1985 (o)	$3,416,896 (x)
8. Charlemagne Institute	2018 (o)	$802,178 (r)
9. Claremont Institute	1979 (o)	$5,482,292 (x)
10. Commonwealth Foundation PA	1988 (o)	$2,993,022 (x)
11. Competitive Enterprise Institute	1984 (o)	$7,811,133 (x)
12. Discovery Institute	1990 (o)	$6,865,358 (x)
13. Edmund Burke Foundation	2019 (o)	$930,562 (r)
14. Ethan Allen Institute	1993 (o)	$236,217 (x)
15. Ethics and Public Policy Center	1976 (o)	$3,415,984 (x)
16. Family Research Institute	1972 (o)	$55,508 (r)
17. Gatestone Institute	2008 (o)	$2,337,305 (x)
18. Heartland Institute	1984 (o)	$5,524,414 (x)
19. Hudson Institute	1961 (o)	$18,275,524 (x)
20. Independent Institute	1986 (o)	$3,903,889 (x)
21. Intercollegiate Studies Institute	1953 (o)	$7,276,782 (x)
22. MacIver Institute	2008 (I)	$390,303 (x)
23. Manhattan Institute	1978 (o)	$20,159,557 (x)
24. Mises Institute	1982 (o)	$4,227,370 (x)

(*continued*)

TABLE B.I. (*continued*)

Organization Type	Founded	Financials
25. Pacific Research Institute	1979 (o)	$3,551,430 (x)
26. Pioneer Institute	1988 (o)	$2,124,432 (x)
27. Reason Foundation	1979 (o)	$13,467,708 (x)
28. Steamboat Institute	2008 (o)	$700,546 (x)
2. Policy Advocacy Groups		
1. Advance Arkansas Institute	2009 (o)	$264,384 (x)*
2. AFPI Center for a Healthy America	2021 (o)	N/A
3. AFPI Center for American Freedom	2021 (o)	N/A
4. AFPI Center for American Prosperity	2021 (o)	N/A
5. AFPI Center for American Security	2021 (o)	N/A
6. AFPI Center for American Trade	2021 (o)	N/A
7. AFPI Center for American Value	2021 (o)	N/A
8. AFPI Center for Education Opportunity	2021 (o)	N/A
9. AFPI Center for Election Integrity	2021 (o)	N/A
10. AFPI Center for Energy & Environment	2021 (o)	N/A
11. AFPI Center for Homeland Security and Immigration	2021 (o)	N/A
12. AFPI Center for Law and Justice	2021 (o)	N/A
13. AFPI Center for Opportunity Now	2021 (o)	N/A
14. AFPI Center for 1776	2021 (o)	N/A
15. AFPI Center for the American Child	2021 (o)	N/A
16. AFPI Center for the American Dream	2021 (o)	N/A
17. AFPI Center for the American Worker	2021 (o)	N/A
18. Alabama Policy Institute	1981 (o)	$907,242 (x)
19. Alaska Policy Forum	2009 (o)	$39,486 (x)
20. Alliance for Constructive Ethnic Studies	2021 (o)	≤$50,000 (r)
21. America First Foundation	2017 (o)	$131,606 (x)
22. America First Policy Institute (AFPI)	2021 (o)	$10,830,742 (x)
23. America First Works	2021 (I)	$140,905 (r)
24. American Accountability Foundation	2021 (o)	$551,544 (r)
25. American Civil Rights Institute	1997 (o)	$266,575 (r)
26. American Cornerstone Institute	2021 (o)	$2,963,781 (x)
27. American Greatness Fund	2021 (o)	N/A
28. American Legislative Exchange Council (ALEC)	1973 (o)	$10,237,195 (x)
29. American Moment	2021 (I)	$179,005 (r)
30. American Principles Project	2009 (o)	$2,485,920 (x)
31. Americans for Limited Government	1996 (o)	$300,632 (x)
32. Americans for Tax Reform	1985 (o)	$4,231,786 (x)

Organization Type	Founded	Financials
33. Badger Institute	1987 (o)	$1,008,939 (x)
34. Californians for Equal Rights Foundation	2021 (I)	$167,637 (r)
35. California Policy Center	2010 (I)	$1,803,423 (x)
36. Center for Equal Opportunity	1988 (I)	$511,437 (x)
37. Center for Family and Human Rights	1997 (o)	$1,127,152 (x)
38. Club for Growth	1999 (o)	$12,874,488 (x)
39. Color Us United	2021 (o)	≤$50,000 (r)
40. Concerned Parents of San Diego	N/A	N/A
41. Council for National Policy	1981 (o)	$3,098,641 (x)
42. Council of Conservative Citizens	1985 (I)	$17,365 (x)
43. David Horowitz Freedom Center	1988 (o)	$7,879,872 (x)
44. Eagle Forum	1976 (o)	$4,158,062 (x)
45. Eagle Forum of California	2013 (I)	N/A
46. Educators for Quality and Equality	2012 (o)	N/A
47. Equal Rights for All Foundation	2022 (I)	N/A
48. Fair Education Santa Barbara	2019 (I)	N/A
49. Federation for American Immigration Reform (FAIR)	1979 (I)	$11,246,727 (x)
50. For Kids & Country	2018 (o)	$35,129 (r)
51. Foundation for Government Accountability	2011 (o)	$4,521,285 (r)
52. Freedom Foundation of Minnesota	2007 (o)	$364,627 (x)
53. Freedom Foundation of Washington State	1991 (I)	$4,123,043 (x)
54. FreedomWorks	1984 (o)	$3,273,535 (x)
55. Goldwater Institute	1988 (o)	$4,741,732 (x)
56. Gun Owners of America	1978 (I)	$6,197,962 (x)
57. Heritage Foundation	1973 (o)	$85,427,198 (x)
58. Hoover Institution	1919 (o)	$76,296,000 (r)
59. Independent Women's Forum	1992 (o)	$4,310,866 (x)
60. James G. Martin Center for Academic Renewal	2004 (I)	$654,150 (r)
61. Kansas Policy Institute	1996 (o)	$1,213,485 (x)
62. League of the South	1994 (o)	N/A
63. Mackinac Center for Public Policy	1987	$8,408,449 (x)
64. Maine Policy Institute	2003	$631,379 (x)
65. Mississippi Center for Public Policy	1991 (I)	$766,618 (x)
66. Oklahoma Council of Public Affairs	1993 (o)	$2,486,740 (x)
67. National Association of Scholars	1987 (o)	$1,523,150 (x)
68. National Center for Public Policy Research	1982 (o)	$6,033,559 (x)
69. New Century Foundation	1994 (I)	$439,512 (r)
70. NumbersUSA Action	2002 (I)	$1,063,438 (x)

(*continued*)

TABLE B.1. *(continued)*

Organization Type	Founded	Financials
71. NumbersUSA Education and Research Foundation	1996 (o)	$5,140,817 (r)
72. NumbersUSA Support Organization	2017 (I)	$3,573,622 (e)
73. Platte Institute for Economic Research	2007	$829,246 (x)
74. US Inc./ProEnglish	1982 (I)	$1,328,337 (x)
75. Public Advocate of the United States	1978 (I)	$1,542,072 (r)
76. Secure America Now Foundation	2012 (I)	$54,631 (x)
77. Texas Conservative Coalition Research Institute	1996 (I)	$1,417,959 (x)
78. Texas Public Policy Foundation	1987	$11,303,061 (x)
79. Thomas Jefferson Institute	1985	$246,278 (x)
80. Unhyphenated America	N/A	N/A
81. VDARE	1993 (o)	$681,098 (x)
82. Veterans for Fairness and Merit	2022 (I)	≤$50,000 (r)
83. Virginia Institute for Public Policy	1996 (o)	$144,586 (x)
84. Washington Policy Center	1997	$2,628,708 (x)
3. Constituency Mobilization Groups		
1. Accuracy in Academia	1985 (I)	$120,408 (x)
2. Accuracy in Media	1969 (o)	$843,191 (x)
3. ACT for America	2008 (I)	$202,501 (x)
4. Alliance to Protect Children*	N/A	N/A
5. Allied Educational Foundation	1966 (I)	$393,066 (e)
6. America First Political Action Committee	2017 (o)	N/A
7. America First Political Action Committee (Fuentes)	2020 (o)	N/A
8. America First with Sebastian Gorka	2019 (o)	N/A
9. American Conservative Union Foundation	1983 (o)	$5,470,676 (x)
10. American Freedom Party	2010 (o)	N/A
11. American Greatness Political Action Committee	2021 (o)	N/A
12. American Majority/American Majority Action	2008 (o)	$1,725,296 (x)
13. American Renaissance/New Century Foundation	1990/1994 (o)	$540,638 (x)
14. Americans for Prosperity	2004 (o)	$20,292,795 (x)
15. Americans for Truth about Homosexuality	1996 (o)	$110,000 (r)
16. Better Milpitas	N/A	N/A
17. Center for Renewing America	2021 (o)	$1,100,000 (r)
18. Charles Martel Society 2001 (Occidental Quarterly, Occidental Observer)	2001 (I)	$77,818 (r)
19. Citizens Alliance of Pennsylvania	2017 (I)	$196,199 (e)
20. Citizens for Self-Governance/Convention of States Foundation	2011 (I)	$1,129,391 (e)
21. Civitas Institute	2019 (o)	$1,580,160 (x)
22. Conservative Partnership Institute (CPI)	2017 (o)	$5,958,594 (x)

Organization Type	Founded	Financials
23. Dixie Heritage	N/A	N/A
24. Election Integrity Network/CPI	2018 (o)	N/A
25. Fight Back Now America	2020 (o)	N/A
26. Forge Leadership Network	2015 (o)	$127,962 (x)
27. Forza Nuova USA	N/A	N/A
28. Freedom Caucus	2015 (o)	N/A
29. Future of Freedom Foundation	1989 (I)	$482,401 (x)
30. Heritage Action for America	2010 (o)	$10,340,577 (x)
31. Idaho Freedom Foundation	2009 (I)	$716,579 (x)
32. Informed Parents of California/California Family Council	2004 (I)	$505,337 (x)
33. Jesse Helms Center	1989 (o)	$1,121,065 (x)
34. Job Creators Network	2010 (o)	$5,105,234 (x)
35. John Birch Society	1958 (o)	N/A
36. Leadership Institute	1987 (o)	$18,769,317 (x)
37. Legal Insurrection Foundation	2018 (I)	$286,178 (x)
38. MassResistance	1995 (o)	N/A
39. Media Research Center	1987 (I)	$13,202,105 (x)
40. Moms for Liberty	2021 (o)	$240,033 (x)
41. Nationalist Front	2016 (o)	N/A
42. National Organization for Marriage	2008 (I)	$202,837 (x)
43. National Taxpayers Union	1977 (I)	$4,854,727 (x)
44. National Taxpayers Union Foundation	1978 (I)	$799,561 (x)
45. National Tea Party Inc.	2013 (I)	$2,510,276 (x)
46. National Rifle Association	1871 (o)	$303,387,315 (x)
47. National Right to Life Committee	1974 (I)	$496,464 (x)
48. National Socialist Legion	2018 (o)	N/A
49. Occidental Dissent	2008 (o)	N/A
50. Patriot Front	2017 (o)	N/A
51. Parents Defending Education	2021 (o)	$3,178,345 (r)
52. PragerU (Prager University Foundation)	2010 (I)	$20,514,077 (x)
53. Regnery Publishing/Salem Media Group	1974 (o)	N/A
54. Revere Project/CPI	2018 (o)	N/A
55. Rhode Island Center for Freedom and Prosperity	2011 (o)	$260,429 (x)
56. Rio Grande Foundation	2000 (o)	$248,501 (x)
57. Roughrider Policy Center	2019 (o)	$25,000 (r)
58. Save Our Schools	2003 (I)	$55,000 (x)
59. SFCN Arizona Freedom Caucus/CPI	2018 (o)	≤$50,000 (r)
60. SFCN Georgia Freedom Caucus/CPI	2018 (o)	≤$50,000 (r)

(continued)

TABLE B.1. *(continued)*

Organization Type	Founded	Financials
61. SFCN Illinois Freedom Caucus/CPI	2018 (o)	≤$50,000 (r)
62. SFCN Mississippi Freedom Caucus/CPI	2018 (o)	≤$50,000 (r)
63. SFCN Nevada Freedom Caucus/CPI	2018 (o)	≤$50,000 (r)
64. SFCN S. Carolina Freedom Caucus/CPI	2018 (o)	≤$50,000 (r)
65. SFCN S. Dakota Freedom Caucus/CPI	2018 (o)	≤$50,000 (r)
66. SoCal Patriots	2022 (o)	N/A
67. Speech First	2018 (o)	$1,671,802 (x)
68. State Freedom Caucus Network (SFCN)	2017 (o)	≤$50,000 (r)
69. State Policy Network	1992 (o)	$18,730,675 (x)
70. Susan B. Anthony Pro-Life America	1992 (o)	$15,904,180 (x)
71. Tea Party Patriots Action	2009 (o)	$2,927,908 (x)
72. The Conservative Caucus (a.k.a. Americans for Constitutional Liberty)	1974 (o)	$15,153,036 (x)
73. The Right Stuff.biz	2012 (o)	N/A
74. The Western Journal	2009 (o)	N/A
75. Turning Point USA	2012 (o)	$8,343,094 (x)
76. US English	1987 (I)	$237,180 (x)
77. Vanguard America	2015 (o)	N/A
78. Women for America First	2019 (o)	N/A
79. Young Americans for Liberty	2011 (o)	$9,408,371 (x)
80. Young America's Foundation	1969 (o)	$26,250,582 (x)
4. Litigation and Legal Advocacy Groups		
1. Alliance Defending Freedom	1994 (o)	$59,299,288 (x)
2. America First Legal	2021 (o)	$6,388,442 (r)
3. Atlantic Legal Foundation	1977 (I)	$350,993 (x)
4. Center for Individual Rights	1989 (o)	$1,359,679 (x)
5. Claremont Institute Center for Constitutional Jurisprudence	1999 (o)	$8,071,035 (x)
6. Criminal Justice Legal Foundation	1982 (I)	$676,276 (x)
7. Federalist Society	1982 (o)	$19,604,839 (x)
8. Freedom X	2014 (I)	$112,241 (r)
9. Hamilton Lincoln Law Institute	2019 (I)	$684,797 (x)
10. Individual Rights Foundation	1993 (o)	N/A
11. Judicial Watch	1995 (I)	$49,144,797 (x)
12. The Justice Foundation	1994 (I)	$706,336 (x)
13. Landmark Legal Foundation	1976 (o)	$1,672,353 (x)
14. Liberty Justice Center	2012 (I)	$6,298,778 (r)
15. Mountain States Legal Foundation	1977 (I)	$2,344,402 (x)
16. Pacific Justice Institute	1997 (o)	$3,203,464 (x)

Organization Type	Founded	Financials
17. Pacific Legal Foundation	1973 (o)	$15,441,226 (x)
18. Southeastern Legal Foundation	1976 (o)	$3,057,517 (x)
19. Students for Fair Admissions	2015 (o)	$1,108,390 (x)
20. Wisconsin Institute for Law and Liberty	2011 (I)	$2,518,375 (x)
5. Religious Groups		
1. American Center for Law and Justice	1994 (I)	$23,299,364 (x)
2. American Decency Association	1999 (o)	$328,352 (r)
3. American Family Association	1997 (o)	$19,085,612 (x)
4. California Family Council	2004 (o)	$454,964 (x)
5. Catholic League	1974 (o)	$3,339,191 (x)
6. CatholicVote	2006 (I)	$2,018,302 (x)
7. Center for Christian Virtue	1984 (I)	$789,718 (x)
8. Chalcedon Foundation	1965 (o)	$903,966 (x)
9. Christian Coalition/Christian Coalition of America	1988 (o)	$135,011 (x)
10. Christian Legal Society	1961 (o)	$2,043,611 (x)
11. Concerned Women for America	1979 (o)	$3,964,709 (x)
12. D. James Kennedy Ministries (Coral Ridge)	1994 (I)	$4,925,524 (x)
13. Faith and Freedom Coalition	2009 (I)	$29,681,130 (r)
14. Family Policy Alliance	2005 (I)	$323,095 (x)
15. Family Research Council	1992 (o)	$17,188,410 (x)
16. First Liberty Institute	1973 (o)	$9,964,182 (x)
17. Focus on the Family	1978 (I)	$26,356,776 (x)
18. Foundation for a Christian Civilization/American Society for the Defense of Tradition, Family, and Property	1973 (I)	$13,317,501 (x)
19. Foundation for Moral Law	2005 (I)	$546,789 (x)
20. FRC Action	1993 (o)	$1,918,069 (x)
21. Institute for Faith and Freedom	2005 (o)	$25,434,520 (x)
22. Institute on Religion and Democracy	1985 (I)	$1,384,151 (x)
23. Liberty Counsel	1989 (o)	$5,263,709 (x)
24. Mission: America Coalition	1993 (o)	$117,936 (r)
25. North Carolina Faith and Freedom Coalition	2009 (o)	$298,769 (x)
26. The Family Leader	1997 (I)	$2,778,181 (x)
27. Thomas More Law Center	1999 (o)	$1,370,183 (x)
6. Racial and Ethnic Groups		
1. 80-20 Initiative, DC Chapter	1998 (o)	N/A
2. AMCHA Initiative	2012 (I)	$304,145 (x)

(*continued*)

TABLE B.1. (*continued*)

Organization Type	Founded	Financials
3. American Society of Engineers of Indian Origin	2014 (I)	$5,207 (x)
4. Anhui Association of Texas	2018 (I)	≤$50,000 (r)
5. Asian American Coalition for Education	2000 (I)	$226,910 (x)
6. Asian American Legal Foundation	2013 (I)	≤$50,000 (r)
7. Asian Americans for Political Advancement	2014 (I)	N/A
8. AsianAmericanVoters.org	N/A	N/A
9. Beijing Institute of Technology Alumni Association	2018 (I)	$8,453 (r)
10. BIT Sindri Alumni Association of North India	2013 (I)	$1,063,759 (x)
11. Black Conservative Federation	N/A	N/A
12. Chinese American Association of Orange County	2013 (I)	N/A
13. Chinese American Citizens Alliance NY	2016 (o)	N/A
14. Chinese American Equalization Association	2015 (I)	≤$50,000 (r)
15. Chinese School of Tomorrow	2014 (I)	≤$50,000 (r)
16. Conejo Chinese Cultural Association	1997 (I)	$354,831 (x)
17. Global Organization of People of Indian Origin, Los Angeles Chapter	2016 (I)	$29,984 (r)
18. Great Neck Chinese Association	2002 (I)	$34,305 (r)
19. Hanlin Education Foundation of America	2012 (I)	$52,502 (x)
20. Henan Association of Northern California*	2007 (I)	N/A
21. Houston Chinese Alliance	2014 (I)	≤$50,000 (r)
22. Houston Chinese Civic Center	1995 (o)	$207,444 (x)
23. Houston Jiangsu Association	2005 (I)	N/A
24. Houston Shanghai Association	2012 (I)	N/A
25. Houston Zhiqing Association/US-China Service Center	2001 (I)	$207,444 (x)
26. Howard County (MD) Chinese Parents Group	2016 (I)	$74,501 (x)
27. Huazhong University of Science & Technology Alumni Association of Northern California	1998 (o)	$188,632 (x)
28. International Chinese Transportation Professionals	2021 (I)	≤$50,000 (r)
29. Korean Parents Organization of NJ	N/A	N/A
30. Livingston (NJ) Chinese Association	1973 (o)	$12,331 (x)
31. Livingston Huaxia Chinese School	2007 (I)	$327,386 (x)
32. Long Island Chinese American Association	2014 (I)	$180,500 (x)
33. Long Island School of Chinese	2001 (I)	$264,913 (x)
34. Millburn Short Hills Chinese Association	2015 (I)	$25,031 (r)
35. National Federation of Indian American Associations	1980 (o)	$49,545 (r)
36. Noah Private Foundation	2012 (I)	$19,285 (e)
37. Noble Tree Publishing	2013 (I)	$127,667 (x)

Organization Type	Founded	Financials
38. Northern California Chinese Culture & Athletic Federation	2007 (I)	$56,300 (x)
39. Overseas Chinese Association of Miami	2003 (I)	≤$50,000 (r)
40. Pakistan Policy Institute	N/A	N/A
41. Peking University Alumni Association of So Cal	2003 (I)	$5,811 (x)
42. San Antonio Chinese Alliance	2009 (I)	$99,009 (r)
43. San Diego Asian Americans for Equality	2014 (o)	N/A
44. Shah Latif Cultural Institute of Texas	2014 (I)	≤$50,000 (r)
45. Silicon Valley Chinese Association Foundation	2015 (I)	$52,433 (r)
46. Silicon Valley Women Alliance	2009 (I)	$9,684 (r)
47. Sino Professionals Association	2010 (I)	$55,786 (r)
48. Texas Guangdong Association	2003 (o)	N/A
49. Texas Northeast Chinese Association	2013 (o)	$21,956 (x)
50. Tri-Valley Korean American Parents Association	2014 (o)	$59,076 (x)
51. Tsinghua University Alumni Association of So Cal	2021 (I)	$11,711 (x)
52. United Chinese Association of Utah	2017 (I)	$88,840 (x)
53. United for a Better Community Foundation	2015 (I)	≤$50,000 (r)
54. US Shandong Fellowship Association	1991 (o)	N/A
55. USTC Alumni Association of Greater New York	2015 (I)	$140,510 (x)
7. Armed Protectionists		
1. Anti-Communist Action	2016 (o)	N/A
2. First Amendment Praetorian	2020 (o)	N/A
3. Groypers	2019 (o)	N/A
4. Ku Klux Klan	1946 (o)	N/A
5. Oath Keepers	2009 (o)	N/A
6. Proud Boys	2016 (o)	N/A
7. Three Percenters	2008 (o)	N/A
8. Funding Groups		
1. ActRight Action	2013 (I)	$842,297(x)
2. Lynde & Harry Bradley Foundation	1942 (o)	$61,423,375 (x)
3. Donors Capital Fund	1999 (o)	$5,753,101 (x)
4. Donors Trust, Inc	1999 (o)	$185,809,701 (x)
5. George Edward Durell Foundation	1985 (I)	$32,811,844 (e)
6. George Jenkins Foundation	2003 (I)	$30,240,242 (e)
7. Marble Freedom Trust	2020 (I)	$228,600,000 (x)
8. Mercer Family Foundation	2005 (o)	$24,558,570 (x)

(*continued*)

TABLE B.1. *(continued)*

Organization Type	Founded	Financials
9. National Christian Charitable Foundation	1982 (o)	$1,548,245,914 (x)
10. Pioneer Fund	1937 (o)	$403,102 (x)
11. John William Pope Foundation	1986 (o)	$12,605,782 (x)
12. Edgar and Elsa Prince Foundation	1979 (I)	$4,397,257 (e)
13. Save America PAC	2020 (o)	$121,626,770 (x)
14. Senate Conservatives Fund	2008 (o)	$4,077,803 (x)

Sources of founding dates: (o) = date organization reports, (I) = IRS reporting start.
Financials: (x) = annual expenditures, (r) = revenues, (e)= endowment or total assets.
All data are for most recent year available. N/A = Not Available. * = website closed.
Data compiled from multiple sources including group websites, IRS 990 forms, GuideStar, Charity Navigator, InfluenceWatch, Source Watch, Cause IQ, and others. All references on file with authors.

APPENDIX C

Organizations in the Repair Alliance

TABLE C.1. **A Sampling of Repair Alliance Members/HR 40 Supporters**

Type	Founded	Financials
1.Racial Justice Organizations		
1. Action for Racial Justice	2020 (o)	
2. Advancement Project	1999 (o)	$10,239,352 (r)
3. African American Community Service Agency	1978 (o)	$1,240,214 (r)
4. African American Redress Network	2019 (o)	N/A
5. African Ancestral Society	1992 (I)	≤$50,000 (r)
6. AFRICANS DESERVE REPARATIONS NOW!	@2012 (o)	N/A
7. AmericanAbolitionists.com	2014 (o)	N/A
8. AmericanSlaveryReparations/Center for Jubilee	2014 (o)	N/A
9. Amplify Action	2020 (o)	$1,441 (x)
10. Appeal, Inc.	2022 (o)	≤$50,000 (r)
11. Birmingham Black Economic Alliance	2020 (o)	N/A
12. Black Economic Council of Massachusetts	2016 (o)	$191,423 (x)
13. Black Food Sovereignty Coalition	2018 (o)	$135,596 (x)
14. Black Jewish Justice Alliance	2016 (o)	N/A
15. Black Jewish Justice Alliance, Los Angeles/CLUE	2014 (o)	$890,448 (x)
16. Black Mental Health Task Force	2020 (o)	N/A
17. Black Millennial Political Convention	2018 (I)	N/A
18. Black Millennials 4 Flint	2015 (o)	$819,128 (x)
19. Black Women's Leadership Forum	2005 (o)	N/A
20. #breathewithme Revolution	2020 (o)	≤$50,000 (r)
21. Bridge4Unity	2019 (o)	N/A
22. Brown Grove Preservation Group, Ashland VA	2021 (o)	N/A
23. Brown Grove Preservation Group, Richmond VA	2021 (o)	N/A
24. Clean, Healthy, Educated, Safe & Sustainable Community	2021 (I)	$9,696 (x)

(*continued*)

TABLE C.I. (*continued*)

Type	Founded	Financials
25. Code Switch: Restorative Justice for Girls of Color	2017 (o)	≤$50,000 (r)
26. Collaborising	2017 (I)	$71,337 (x)
27. Color of Change	2005 (o)	$20,468,047 (r)
28. Coming To The Table	2019 (o)	$304,340 (r)
29. Coming To The Table—Virginia Historic Triangle	2019 (o)	N/A
30. Community Healing Network	2009 (o)	$141,813 (x)
31. Democrats Abroad/Reparations Task Force	1964 (o)	N/A
32. End New Jim Crow Action Network Fund	2012 (I)	$251,129 (r)
33. European Network of People of African Descent	2017 (o)	≤$50,000 (r)
34. Exploring Whiteness/Groundworks New Mexico	1996 (I)	$539,834 (x)
35. FirstRepair	2021 (o)	$114,471 (x)
36. Fund for Reparations NOW	2019 (o)	$157,000 (x)
37. Harriet Tubman Center for Freedom and Equity	2019 (o)	N/A
38. HERitage Giving Fund	2017 (o)	N/A
39. I Love Black People	2020 (o)	N/A
40. Institute of the Black World 21st Century	2001 (o)	$200,920 (x)
41. International Black Summit	2015 (o)	≤$50,000 (r)
42. International Black Women's Congress	1986 (o)	$562,996 (x)
43. Irish Americans for Racial Justice	2020 (o)	N/A
44. Just Equity for Health/Sr. Stella Safo	N/A	N/A
45. Justice for Greenwood	2020 (o)	≤$50,000 (r)
46. KC Reparations Coalition	2021 (o)	N/A
47. King Boston/The Boston Foundation	1915 (o)	$175,809,198 (x)
48. Leadership Conference on Civil and Human Rights	1950 (o)	$4,224,383 (r)
49. Liberation Ventures	2022 (o)	$6,000,000 (r)
50. Lost River Racial Justice (SURJ chapter)	2016 (o)	N/A
51. Make It Plain/Harambee Organization Black Unity	2006 (o)	N/A
52. Massachusetts Jews for Reparations	2021 (o)	N/A
53. Movement for Black Lives	2015 (o)	$30,666,918 (r)
54. NAACP	1909 (o)	$29,311,165 (x)
55. NAACP Yonkers Branch	1961 (o)	N/A
56. National Action Network	1991 (o)	$5,821,440 (r)
57. National Af-Am Reparations Commission (NAARC)	2015	N/A
58. National Association for Black Veterans	1983 (o)	$58,959 (x)
59. National Birth Equity Collaborative	2015 (o)	N/A
60. National Black Justice Coalition	2005 (o)	$1,979,393 (r)
61. National Black United Front	1993 (o)	$13,206 (x)
62. National Council of Negro Women/Hudson Valley	1991 (o)	$4,153,228 (x)
63. National Urban League	1911 (o)	$52,244,033 (x)

Type	Founded	Financials
64. N'COBRA	1987 (o)	N/A
65. N'COBRA Atlanta	N/A	N/A
66. N'COBRA Baton Rouge	N/A	N/A
67. N'COBRA Chicago	N/A	N/A
68. N'COBRA Cincinnati	N/A	N/A
69. N'COBRA Dallas	N/A	N/A
70. N'COBRA Detroit	N/A	N/A
71. N'COBRA Evanston	N/A	N/A
72. N'COBRA Indianapolis	N/A	N/A
73. N'COBRA Kansas City	N/A	N/A
74. N'COBRA Miami	N/A	N/A
75. N'COBRA Milwaukee	N/A	N/A
76. N'COBRA New England	N/A	N/A
77. N'COBRA Philadelphia	N/A	N/A
78. New Afrikan Peoples/Malcolm X Grassroots Movement	N/A	N/A
79. Not In Our Town Princeton	1998 (o)	N/A
80. Provisional Government of the Republic of New Africa	1968 (o)	N/A
81. Racial Justice NOW	2020 (I)	$59,362 (r)
82. Racial Justice Rising	2015 (I)	N/A
83. Rare and Black	2020 (I)	N/A
84. RASR (Resolutions Addressing Systemic Racism)	2021 (I)	≤$50,000 (r)
85. Reimagining America Project, Charlotte NC	2020 (o)	N/A
86. Reparation Education Project	2022 (I)	N/A
87. Denver Black Reparations Council/Reparations Circle	2020 (o)	$800,000 (r)
88. Reparations for Amherst, MA	2020 (o)	N/A
89. Reparations4Slavery.com	2019 (o)	N/A
90. Reparations Pledge Community Renewal Society	1937 (I)	$3,700,000 (r)
91. Reparations Project/Quarterman & Keller Fund	2020 (I)	$188,795 (x)
92. Richmond Hill	1987 (o)	$1,039,433 (x)
93. Showing Up for Racial Justice(SURJ)/Social Good Fund	2009 (o)	$3,193,278 (x)
94. SURJ Annapolis and Anne Arundel County	N/A	N/A
95. SURJ Atlanta	N/A	N/A
96. SURJ Biddeford-Saco	N/A	N/A
97. SURJ Blount County	N/A	N/A
98. SURJ Boston	N/A	N/A
99. SURJ Buffalo	N/A	N/A

(*continued*)

TABLE C.1. (*continued*)

Type	Founded	Financials
100. SURJ Central Vermont	N/A	N/A
101. SURJ Clackamas Co., Oregon	N/A	N/A
102. SURJ Corvallis, Oregon	N/A	N/A
103. SURJ Historic Triangle Chapter	N/A	N/A
104. SURJ Indianapolis	N/A	N/A
105. SURJ Kansas City	N/A	N/A
106. SURJ Lakes Area	N/A	N/A
107. SURJ Louisville (SURJ HQ)	2016	$221,073 (x)
108. SURJ Northeast Ohio	N/A	N/A
109. SURJ Northern New Mexico	N/A	N/A
110. SURJ NYC	N/A	N/A
111. SURJ Rochester	N/A	N/A
112. SURJ Sacramento	N/A	N/A
113. SURJ Sacred Heart	N/A	N/A
114. SURJ San Diego	N/A	N/A
115. SURJ San Francisco	N/A	N/A
116. SURJ Santa Barbara	N/A	N/A
117. SURJ Santa Cruz	N/A	N/A
118. SURJ Southeast PA	N/A	N/A
119. SURJ Southern Maine	N/A	N/A
120. SURJ Southwest Washington	N/A	N/A
121. SURJ Springfield-Eugene	N/A	N/A
122. SURJ St. John's Chapter Portland OR	N/A	N/A
123. SURJ Tucson	N/A	N/A
124. SURJ Twin Cities	N/A	N/A
125. SURJ Vashon-Maury	N/A	N/A
126. SURJ Ventura Count	N/A	N/A
127. SURJ Westchester, NY	N/A	N/A
128. SURJ Western Massachusetts	N/A	N/A
129. SURJ Whatcom	N/A	N/A
130. Soul 2 Soul Sisters	2015 (o)	$379,004 (x)
131. Terence Crutcher Foundation	2017 (o)	N/A
132. The Selma Bridge Crossing Jubilee	2012 (o)	N/A
133. Thurgood Marshall Civil Rights Center/ UNIA-African Communities League	1993 (I)	N/A
134. Where Is My Land (S-Corporation)	2020 (o)	N/A
135. White People 4 Black Lives (SURJ)	N/A	N/A
136. Why We Can't Wait Coalition (led by NAARC)	2020 (a)	N/A
137. W. Pa Black Political Assembly*	N/A	N/A

Type	Founded	Financials
2. Social Justice Organizations		
1. Alabama New South Coalition	1986 (o)	N/A
2. Alabama Saving OurSelves*	2018 (o)	N/A
3. Allard Lowenstein International Human Rights Clinic	1981 (o)	N/A
4. All Healers Mental Health Alliance	2005 (o)	N/A
5. Allianza Nacional de Campesinas	2011 (o)	$1,019,458 (x)
6. American Civil Liberties Union	1920 (o)	$144,488,761 (x)
7. American Humanist Association	1980 (o)	$2,211,002 (x)
8. Americans for Democratic Action	1940 (o)	$338,463 (x)
9. Americans for Financial Reform	2018 (o)	$2,872,478 (x)
10. Amnesty International USA	1966 (o)	$51,400,349 (x)
11. Arise for Social Justice	1987 (I)	$399,790 (x)
12. Arizona Coalition for Change	2021 (I)	$878,414 (x)
13. Bayard Rustin Liberation Initiative/FOR-USA	2021 (o)	$366,522 (x)
14. Beloved Community Charlottesville	2022 (o)	N/A
15. Broken Crayons Still Colour Foundation	2021 (I)	≤$50,000 (r)
16. California Alliance for Youth and Community Justice	2014 (o)	N/A
17. Center for Human Rights & Int. Justice, Boston College	2012 (o)	N/A
18. Center for Hunger-Free Communities, Drexel	2004 (o)	N/A
19. Center for Reparatory Justice	2021 (o)	N/A
20. Change the Ref	2018 (o)	$379,672 (x)
21. Children's Defense Fund	1973 (o)	$19,978,433 (x)
22. Children's Defense Fund–California	N/A	N/A
23. Children's Defense Fund–Minnesota	N/A	N/A
24. Collaborating Voices Foundation	2020 (I)	≤$50,000 (r)
25. Community Change	1968 (o)	$22,202,273 (x)
26. Cooperation Jackson for Economic Empowerment	2014 (I)	$1,232,419 (x)
27. Decolonizing Wealth Project/Liberated Capital Fund	2018 (o)	$8,572,314 (r)
28. Demand Progress	2010 (o)	$2,971 (x)
29. Democrats Abroad Global Progressive Caucus	1964 (o)	N/A
30. Detroit Affordable Housing & Homelessness Task Force	2021 (o)	N/A
31. Dreamcatcher Initiative	2021 (I)	$85,415 (x)
32. Evelution INC	2020 (I)	≤$50,000 (r)
33. Fellowship of Reconciliation, Atlanta/FOR-USA	1914 (o)	$605,955 (x)
34. FXB Center for Health and Human Rights, Harvard	1993 (o)	N/A

(*continued*)

TABLE C.1. (*continued*)

Type	Founded	Financials
35. Global Human Rights Clinic, University of Chicago	2020 (o)	N/A
36. Granite State Organizing Project	2002 (o)	$669,432 (x)
37. Haley House	1966 (o)	$2,638,401 (x)
38. Hawaii Institute for Human Rights*	2000 (I)	$4,040 (x)
39. Health and Justice Action Lab, Northeastern Law	N/A	N/A
40. Human Rights Watch	1988 (o)	$70,558,186 (x)
41. Institute for Justice & Democracy in Haiti	2004 (o)	$1,073,914 (x)
42. International Center for Legacies of Trauma	2019 (o)	N/A
43. International Center for Transitional Justice	2001 (o)	$7,585,774 (x)
44. Jacober Kuehner SRI Fund	N/A	N/A
45. Justice & Beyond	2019 (o)	≤$50,000 (r)
46. Justice Strategies	2003 (o)	N/A
47. Marked by COVID	2021 (o)	N/A
48. MK Gandhi Institute for Nonviolence	1991 (o)	$641,529 (x)
49. My Community Too PAC	N/A	N/A
50. National Coalition Against Domestic Violence	1983 (I)	$1,062,107 (x)
51. National Consumers League	1899 (o)	$3,489,257 (x)
52. National Employment Law Project	1969 (o)	$10,193,900 (x)
53. National Health Care for the Homeless Council	1986 (o)	$2,257,555 (x)
54. National Stop the Violence Alliance	N/A	≤$50,000 (r)
55. Network NOVA	2017 (o)	N/A
56. New American Leaders Action Fund	2018 (o)	$274,238 (x)
57. Next Generation Action Network	2014 (o)	$14,401 (x)
58. Nia Foundation	2002 (o)	$4,358,671 (x)
59. Northshore Social Justice Action Group (SURJ)	N/A	N/A
60. Optional Outreach	N/A	N/A
61. Our Revolution	2014 (o)	$3,370,846 (x)
62. Our Voice Our Vote AZ	2022 (I)	$1,812,504 (e)
63. Peace Builders of Orange County (S-Corporation)	2003 (o)	N/A
64. Peace Host.net	1999 (o)	N/A
65. People for the American Way	1981 (o)	$7,513,502 (x)
66. Pillows to Pads	2020 (I)	≤$50,000 (r)
67. Pivot Sac (Sacramento)	2007 (I)	$134,896 (x)
68. Progressive Democrats of America	2004 (o)	$532,693 (x)
69. Radical Health Alliance	2022 (I)	$14,540 (x)
70. Rental Regional Community Foundation	1999 (o)	$1,653,826 (x)
71. RESULTS	1980 (o)	$77,618 (x)
72. Revitalization Strategies LLC	2017 (o)	N/A
73. RiseUp Kingston	2018 (o)	$199,090 (x)

Type	Founded	Financials
74. Rosalyn Cares Foundation	2018 (I)	≤$50,000 (r)
75. San Francisco Black & Jewish Unity Coalition	2016 (o)	N/A
76. Self Grow	N/A	N/A
77. Siyanda Land Collective	N/A	N/A
78. Society for Community Research and Action	1966 (o)	$503,011 (x)
79. South Bay Progressive Alliance	N/A	N/A
80. Southern Poverty Law Center	1971 (o)	$97,403,030 (x)
81. Sowers of Justice Network	2014 (I)	≤$50,000 (r)
82. SSJ-TOSF Social Justice Committee	1945 (o)	N/A
83. Street Meet Company	2005 (o)	$7,000 (x)
84. Sunrise Movement	2017 (o)	$412,722 (x)
85. Treatment Action Group	1992 (o)	$2,764,544 (x)
86. UNESCO Inclusive Policy Lab	2017 (o)	N/A
87. United Parents Against Lead (UPAL)	1996 (o)	$52,652 (x)
88. Universal Human Rights Initiative (UHRI)	2016 (o)	≤$50,000 (r)
89. University Network for Human Rights	2018 (o)	$245,055 (x)
90. URGE: Unite for Reproductive and Gender Equity	1992 (o)	$4,362,765 (x)
91. Vision Walkers	N/A	N/A
92. VOICE Buffalo	1996 (o)	$452,526 (x)
93. WESPAC Foundation	1974 (o)	$319,642 (x)
94. We the Village, Inc.	2020 (I)	$4,560,000 (r)
95. Whm Msw Healing Well, Inc.	2020 (I)	≤$50,000 (r)
96. Woke Vote	2016 (o)	N/A
97. YOUnify	N/A	N/A
3. Criminal Justice Organization		
1. Black and Pink	2005 (o)	$2,192,449 (x)
2. Center for Community Alternatives	1981 (o)	$12,085,975 (x)
3. Criminal Justice Policy Coalition, Boston	2002 (I)	$47,419 (x)
4. Drug Policy Alliance	2000 (o)	$10,883,439 (x)
5. Incarcerated Nation Network	2021 (I)	N/A
6. Justice Roundtable	2002 (o)	N/A
7. Maine Prisoner Advocacy Coalition	2007 (o)	N/A
8. Mass. Against Solitary Confinement/UU Mass Action	2006 (o)	$291,108 (x)
9. Operation Restoration	2016 (o)	$1,659,428 (x)
10. Students for Sensible Drug Policy	1998 (o)	$633,500 (x)
11. The Adolescent Redemptive and Restorative Program	2022 (I)	≤$50,000 (r)
12. The Sentencing Project	1987 (I)	$1,804,673 (x)
13. Vera Institute of Justice	1961 (o)	$156,589,569 (x)

(*continued*)

TABLE C.I. (*continued*)

Type	Founded	Financials
4. Religious Organizations		
1. Adorers of the Blood of Christ	1834 (o)	N/A
2. Adrian Dominican Sisters	1946 (I)	N/A
3. Alliance of Baptists	1967 (o)	N/A
4. All Souls Movement	2022 (o)	N/A
5. American Baptist Churches, USA	1707 (o)	N/A
6. American Friends Service Committee	1917 (o)	N/A
7. American Muslim Voice Foundation	2004 (o)	≤$50,000 (r)
8. AME Zion Church	1821 (o)	N/A
9. Anti-Defamation League	1913 (o)	$76,634,548 (x)
10. Bend the Arc: Jewish Action	1999 (o)	$3,705,357 (x)
11. Bethel AME Church	1816 (o)	N/A
12. Bon Secours Associates	1980 (o)	N/A
13. Boston Workers Circle Center	1892 (o)	$695,004 (x)
14. Braxton Institute	2014 (I)	≤$50,000 (r)
15. Bread for the World	1974 (o)	$5,503,423 (x)
16. The Bridge Community Church Outreach	2013 (o)	N/A
17. Ceremony Heals	N/A	N/A
18. Chicago Benedictines for Peace	N/A	N/A
19. Christian Church (Disciples of Christ)	1832 (o)	N/A
20. Christian Methodist Episcopal Church	1870 (o)	N/A
21. Church of St. Luke and St. Matthew, Brooklyn	1836 (o)	N/A
22. Church World Service	1946 (o)	$73,709,463 (x)
23. Community of Hope AME Church	1816 (o)	N/A
24. Congregation B'nai Israel Tikkun Olam Committee	1924 (o)	N/A
25. Congregation of Our Lady of Charity, US Provinces	1835 (o)	N/A
26. Congregation of St. Joseph—Justice Team	1650 (o)	N/A
27. Council of Jewish Women	1893 (o)	$4,898,518 (x)
28. Creation Justice Ministries	1983 (o)	N/A
29. Disciples Center for Public Witness	2019 (o)	N/A
30. Dominican Sisters Grand Rapids	1877 (o)	≤$50,000 (r)
31. Ebenezer Church, Phoenix AZ	2016 (o)	N/A
32. Ecumenical Peace Institute/Clergy and Laity Concerned	2007 (I)	≤$50,000 (r)
33. Empowerment Temple AME Church	2000 (o)	N/A
34. The Episcopal Church	1789 (o)	N/A
35. Evangelical Lutheran Church in America	1988 (o)	$50,518 (r)
36. Faith Action Network	2011 (o)	$334,084 (x)
37. Faith for Black Lives Action Fund	2022 (I)	N/A

Type	Founded	Financials
38. Faith 4 Justice Asheville	2016 (o)	N/A
39. Faith in Action Bay Area	1972 (o)	$981,973 (x)
40. Faith in Action LA RED	2015 (o)	N/A
41. Faith in Action National Network	1972 (o)	$32,678,024 (x)
42. Faith in Florida	N/A	$2,136,342 (x)
43. Faith in Indiana	2011 (I)	$866,571 (x)
44. Faith in New Jersey	2015 (I)	$338,764 (x)
45. Faith in Public Life	2005 (o)	$3,669,052 (x)
46. First Christian Methodist Episcopal Church	1870 (o)	N/A
47. First Unitarian Society of Denver, Racial Justice Project	2015 (o)	N/A
48. First Unitarian Society of Denver Reparations Group	2020 (o)	$230,000 (r)
49. Franciscan Action Network	2007 (o)	$394,753 (x)
50. Franciscan Sisters of the Sacred Heart	1866 (o)	N/A
51. Friends Committee on National Legislation	1943 (o)	$4,332,577 (x)
52. Grassroots Reparations Campaign/Truth Telling Project	2019 (o)	N/A
53. HealMobile Ministry	N/A	N/A
54. Historic Vernon AME Church	1906 (o)	N/A
55. Holy Spirit Missionary Sisters, USA-JPIC	1889 (o)	N/A
56. ICNA Council for Social Justice (Muslim)	2009 (o)	$121,494 (x)
57. Intercommunity Peace and Justice Center, Seattle	1991 (o)	$506,070 (x)
58. Interfaith Movement for Human Integrity	2015 (o)	$639,154 (x)
59. Lake Street Church	2017 (o)	N/A
60. Leadership Conference of Women Religious	1956 (o)	N/A
61. Leadership Team of the Felician Sisters of NA	1855 (o)	N/A
62. Let My People Vote	2016 (o)	N/A
63. Loretto Community	1986 (o)	$13,453,120 (x)
64. MakeItPlain.com	N/A	N/A
65. Maryknoll Office for Global Concerns	1978 (o)	N/A
66. Meriden Congregational Church, UCC	1779 (o)	N/A
67. Messiah Baptist Church Yonkers NY	1892 (o)	N/A
68. Minnesota Council of Churches	1948 (o)	N/A
69. Missouri Faith Voices	2018 (I)	$327,496 (x)
70. Murph-Emanuel AME Church	1982 (o)	N/A
71. National Advocacy Center Sisters of Good Shepherd	2002 (I)	$8,164 (x)
72. National Council of Churches	1950 (o)	N/A
73. National Religious Campaign Against Torture	2006 (o)	$1,042,927 (x)

(*continued*)

TABLE C.I. (*continued*)

Type	Founded	Financials
74. Network Lobby for Catholic Social Justice	1971 (o)	$1,398,862 (x)
75. New Mexico & El Paso Interfaith Power and Light	2010 (I)	$59,052 (x)
76. North Carolina Council of Churches	1935 (o)	N/A
77. Northminster Presbyterian Church, Evanston IL	1922 (o)	N/A
78. Orange County Congregation Community Organization	1976 (o)	$638,101 (x)
79. Orthodox Church in America	1794 (o)	N/A
80. Outgivers Ministries	2021 (I)	N/A
81. Pax Christi USA	1972 (o)	$405,457 (x)
82. Powerful Community Church	N/A	N/A
83. Presbyterian Church USA Office of Public Witness	1936 (o)	N/A
84. Pure Heart Worship Center	2000 (o)	N/A
85. Reconstructionist Rabbinical Association	1974 (o)	$407,421 (x)
86. Religious of Jesus and Mary, USA-Haiti Province	1877 (o)	N/A
87. RocACTS	1993 (o)	$45,396 (x)
88. Sacred Heart Community Services	1964 (o)	$45,961,299 (x)
89. Samuel DeWitt Proctor Conference	2003 (o)	$1,563,262 (x)
90. San Francisco Friends, Sisters of Mercy	1854 (o)	N/A
91. School Sisters of Notre Dame, Central Pacific Province	1833 (o)	N/A
92. Shtibl Minyan	2010 (I)	N/A
93. Sisters of Bon Secours, USA	1881 (o)	N/A
94. Sisters of Charity Nazareth Congregational Leadership	1812 (o)	N/A
95. Sisters of Charity Nazareth Western Prov. Leadership	1812 (o)	N/A
96. Sisters of Charity of Leavenworth Office of Justice	2012 (o)	N/A
97. Sisters of Charity of New York	1633 (o)	N/A
98. Sisters of Mercy	1827 (o)	N/A
99. Sisters of Mercy of the Americas Justice Team	1843 (o)	N/A
100. Sisters of Notre Dame de Namur	1804 (o)	N/A
101. Sisters of St. Francis of Philadelphia	1855 (o)	N/A
102. Sisters of St. Joseph, Brentwood	1856 (o)	N/A
103. Sisters of St. Joseph of Chestnut Hill, Philadelphia	1847 (o)	N/A
104. Sisters of St. Joseph of Cluny, U.S.A.	1807 (o)	N/A
105. Sisters of St. Joseph of Rochester, NY	1854 (o)	N/A
106. Sisters of the Humility of Mary	1854 (o)	N/A
107. Sisters of the Presentation, Dubuque, Iowa	1874 (o)	N/A
108. Sisters, Servants of the Immaculate Heart of Mary	1845 (o)	N/A
109. Sixth Episcopal Dist. Afr. Methodist Episcopal Church	1865 (o)	N/A

Type	Founded	Financials
110. Society of Helpers, US Province	1856 (o)	N/A
111. Society of the Sacred Heart United States Canada	1800 (o)	N/A
112. South Carolina Christian Action Council	1969 (I)	$77,680 (x)
113. St. Ann & the Holy Trinity Church and Pro Cathedral	1847 (o)	N/A
114. St. James African Methodist Episcopal Church	1842 (o)	N/A
115. St. James African Methodist Episcopal Church, San Jose	1961 (o)	N/A
116. St. Paul's Carroll Street (Episcopal)	1849 (o)	N/A
117. Third Presbyterian Church Rochester NY	1827 (o)	N/A
118. Tikkun Olam and Reparations Committee Amherst	2020 (o)	N/A
119. T-Ruah: The Rabbinic Call for Human Rights	2013 (o)	N/A
120. Union for Reform Judaism	1873 (o)	N/A
121. Unitarian Church in Denver	1871 (o)	N/A
122. Unitarian Universalists for Social Justice	1961 (o)	≤$50,000 (r)
123. United Church of Christ	1957 (o)	$900,000,000 (e)
124. United Methodist Church—Board of Church and Society	1968 (o)	N/A
125. Unity Temple Unitarian Universalist Congregation	1871 (o)	N/A
126. Welcome Home Reparations	2021 (o)	N/A
127. Wesley United Methodist Church	1968 (o)	N/A
5. Hispanic/Latinx and Indigenous Organizations		
1. Centro Legal de La Raza	1969 (o)	$21,743,613 (x)
2. Indigenous Solidarity Network (formerly of SURJ)	2011 (o)	N/A
3. LatinoJustice PRLDEF	1972 (o)	$4,012,171 (x)
4. #WeAllGrow Latina Network	2010 (o)	
6. Asian American Organizations		
1. AAPI Equity Alliance	1976 (o)	N/A
2. API Christians for Social Justice	N/A	N/A
3. API Equality-LA	2008 (o)	N/A
4. API Labor Alliance, AFL-CIO	1992 (o)	$320,159 (x)
5. API Labor Alliance, AFL-CIO, DC	N/A	N/A
6. API Labor Alliance, AFL-CIO, Inland Empire	N/A	N/A
7. API Labor Alliance, AFL-CIO, Maryland	N/A	N/A
8. API Labor Alliance, AFL-CIO, Philadelphia	N/A	N/A
9. API Labor Alliance, AFL-CIO, Sacramento	N/A	N/A
10. API Labor Alliance, AFL-CIO, Seattle	N/A	N/A

(*continued*)

TABLE C.1. (*continued*)

Type	Founded	Financials
11. Asian Americans Advancing Justice (AAJC)	1991 (o)	$4,912,837 (x)
12. Asian & Pacific Islander Health Forum	1991 (I)	$7,750,505 (x)
13. Asian Law Alliance	1977 (o)	$2,641,353 (x)
14. Asian Pacific Partners (APPEAL)	2005 (I)	$920,021 (x)
15. Campaign for Justice: Japanese Latin Americans!	2012 (I)	$56,654 (x)
16. Chinese American Planning Council	1965 (o)	$30,780,992 (x)
17. Densho	1996 (o)	$1,594,184 (x)
18. 18 Million Rising	2012 (o)	N/A
19. Empowering Pacific Islander Communities (EPIC)	2009 (o)	N/A
20. Fred T. Korematsu Institute	2009 (o)	$274,052 (x)
21. Friends of Minidoka	2006 (I)	$179,506 (x)
22. Japanese American Citizens League (JACL)	1929 (o)	$1,701,708 (x)
23. JACL Berkeley	1942 (o)	$27,484 (x)
24. JACL Boise Valley	N/A	N/A
25. JACL Cincinnati	N/A	N/A
26. JACL Dayton	N/A	N/A
27. JACL Florin	N/A	N/A
28. JACL Idaho Falls	N/A	N/A
29. JACL Philadelphia	N/A	N/A
30. JACL Portland	N/A	N/A
31. JACL Puyallup Valley	1964 (I)	≤$50,000 (r)
32. JACL Sacramento	N/A	N/A
33. JACL San Diego	N/A	N/A
34. JACL San Jose	N/A	N/A
35. JACL Seabrook	N/A	N/A
36. JACL Seattle	N/A	N/A
37. JACL Sequoia	N/A	N/A
38. JACL St. Louis	N/A	N/A
39. JACL Twin Cities	N/A	N/A
40. JACL Watsonville-Santa Cruz	N/A	N/A
41. Japanese American Families for Justice	2001 (o)	N/A
42. Japanese American Memorial Pilgrimages	2016 (o)	$241,000 (x)
43. Japanese American Service Committee	1946 (o)	$2,886,096 (x)
44. Japanese Peruvian Oral History Project	1991 (o)	N/A
45. LEAD Filipino	2021 (I)	$24,565 (x)
46. Manzanar Committee	1970 (o)	8,520 (x)
47. Nat'l AP American Families Against Substance Abuse	1988 (o)	$510,432 (x)
48. National Asian Pacific American Bar Association	1988 (o)	$2,331,105 (x)

Type	Founded	Financials
49. National Asian Pacific Women's Forum	1996 (o)	$2,580,495 (x)
50. Nat'l Coalition for AP Amer. Community Development	2001 (I)	$3,383,097 (x)
51. National Council of Asian Pacific Americans	1996 (o)	N/A
52. National Federation of Filipino American Associations	1997 (o)	$254,756 (x)
53. National Japanese American Memorial Foundation	1990 (I)	$92,242 (x)
54. New York Day of Remembrance Committee	N/A	N/A
55. Nihonmachi Outreach Committee	1975 (o)	$3,999,088 (x)
56. Nikkei for Civil Rights & Redress	1980 (o)	$69,325 (x)
57. Nikkei Progressives	2016 (o)	N/A
58. North Carolina Asian Americans Together	2017 (I)	$365,656 (x)
59. OCA—Asian Pacific American Advocates	1973 (o)	N/A
60. OPAWL—Building AAPI Feminist Leadership in Ohio	2016 (o)	$1,202,504 (x)
61. San Jose Nikkei Resisters	2018 (o)	N/A
62. SF Bay Area Day of Remembrance Committee	N/A	N/A
63. South Asian Americans Leading Together (SAALT)	2003 (o)	$625,042 (x)
64. South Bay Youth Changemakers	2020 (o)	N/A
65. Southeast Asia Resource Action Center (SEARAC)	1979 (o)	$1,553,920 (x)
66. Strong Asian Lead	2019 (o)	N/A
67. Tadaima	N/A	N/A
68. Tule Lake Committee	1978 (o)	$33,781 (x)
69. Tsuru for Solidarity	2019 (o)	N/A
70. USC Shinso Ito Center Japanese Religions and Culture	2011 (o)	N/A
7. LGBTQ+ Organizations		
1. Athlete Ally	2011 (o)	$806,944 (x)
2. BreakOUT!	2011 (o)	N/A
3. Center for LGBTQ Economic Advancement & Research	2019 (o)	N/A
4. CenterLink: The Community of LGBTQ Centers	2001 (o)	$1,323,037 (x)
5. Equality North Carolina	1979 (o)	$1,526,738 (r)
6. Family Equality	1985 (o)	$2,186,108 (x)
7. GLSEN	1995 (o)	$7,184,721 (x)
8. LGBT Center of Raleigh	2009 (o)	$533,527 (x)
9. LGBTQ Allyship	2018 (o)	$203,020 (x)
10. Matthew Shepard Foundation	1998 (o)	$1,292,301 (x)

(*continued*)

TABLE C.1. (*continued*)

Type	Founded	Financials
11. National Center for Lesbian Rights	1993 (o)	$4,861,382 (x)
12. National Equality Action Team (NEAT)	2012 (o)	N/A
13. National LGBT Cancer Network	2008 (o)	$626,826 (x)
14. National LGBTQ+ Bar Association	1987 (o)	$238,726 (x)
15. National LGBTQ Task Force Action Fund	1978 (o)	$211,435 (x)
16. National Queer Asian Pacific Islander Alliance	2010 (o)	$775,798 (x)
17. OutNebraska	2011 (o)	$238,239 (x)
18. PFLAG National	1973 (o)	$2,849,515 (x)
19. Success Capital Organization	2015 (o)	N/A
20. TRANScending Barriers	2017 (o)	N/A
21. Whitman-Walker Institute	2018 (o)	$916,911 (x)
8. Immigration Groups		
1. Black Alliance for Just Immigration	2010 (o)	$1,345,423 (x)
2. Center for Gender and Refugee Studies	1999 (o)	N/A
3. Dominican Cultural Association of Yonkers	2016 (o)	$27,143 (r)
4. Don't Look Away Pact	2020 (o)	N/A
5. Immigrant Legal Defense	2019 (o)	$1,757,739 (x)
6. Lights for Liberty	2019 (o)	N/A
7. National Immigration Project	1982 (o)	$1,071,942 (x)
8. National Network for Immigrant and Refugee Rights	2002 (o)	$137,585 (x)
9. National Partnership for New Americans	2012 (o)	$2,562,166 (x)
10. Raleigh Immigration Law Firm	2014 (o)	N/A
11. Services, Immigrant Rights and Education Network	1998 (o)	$1,575,215 (x)
9. Environmental Groups		
1. League of Conservation Voters	1991 (o)	$36,914,836 (x)
10. Disability Groups		
1. Autistic Self Advocacy Network	2011 (o)	$738,688 (x)
2. Brighter View Foundation	2019 (o)	≤$50,000 (r)
3. Center for Disability Rights	1992 (o)	$43,796,112 (x)
4. Disability Rights California	1978 (o)	$33,210,376 (x)
11. Legal Advocacy and Legal Services Groups		
1. American Constitution Society	2001 (o)	$6,524806 (r)
2. Center for Constitutional Rights	1966 (o)	$18,445,910 (r)
3. East Bay Community Law Center	1987 (o)	$10,442,729 (r)

Type	Founded	Financials
4. Justis Connection	2018 (o)	N/A
5. Legal Action Center	1973 (o)	$8,621,714 (r)
6. National Health Law Program	1977 (o)	$11,430,352 (r)
7. National Homelessness Law Center	1989 (o)	$1,094,065 (r)
8. National Lawyers Guild	1936 (o)	$664,891 (r)
9. National Lawyers Guild—International Committee	1937 (o)	N/A
10. Ramirez and Sunnenberg	2018 (o)	N/A
11. Sealing Records	N/A	N/A
12. The Prinz Law Firm PC	2009 (o)	N/A

12. Business Sector

We have not documented the dates and finances of businesses supporting HR 40 as it is not possible to determine whether they have devoted any time or funds to Repair alliance advocacy. For many private businesses not publicly traded, no financial information of any sort was available.

1. ACR Capital LLC
2. Alchemy Space
3. Amorifera Earthwares
4. Arrington & Owens, LLC
5. AshNA WP, LLC
6. AveryEden LLC
7. Batrice & Associates
8. Bethel Business Machines, Inc
9. Big&Chewy LLC
10. Bleeker.co
11. BLK FLWR MRKT
12. BotaniCuisine, LLC
13. Bronze Investments LLC
14. Chi Impact Capital
15. Climestransportation
16. Common Talks Consulting
17. Constructive Communities
18. Dynamic Force Productions LLC
19. Fig nine
20. Freedom Road Consulting
21. Giving Blueprint
22. Groundbreakers
23. Hagans-Jones Consulting LLC
24. HBCUNomics LLC
25. HBCU Pride Nation

(continued)

TABLE C.1. (*continued*)

Type	Founded	Financials
26. HBCU Steam LLC		
27. HBCU Wall Street		
28. Holland & Sherry		
29. Hue of My Brown		
30. Integrative Wellness LLC		
31. Jade Jewel Education Associates		
32. Johnson & Klein, PLLC		
33. Keep the Change LLC		
34. Know Thyself, PC		
35. Lamar Legal PLLC		
36. Let's ReUp Inc.		
37. Life Line Financial Group		
38. McPherson Strategies LLC		
39. Merakai		
40. Mihara Associates		
41. Natalie Molina Niño LLC		
42. Oasis Health and Wellness Center		
43. Pacific Community Ventures		
44. Poo Pourri		
45. Primera Impact		
46. Racial Literacy Groups		
47. Red Horse Financial Group, Inc.		
48. Rhythm of Life Wellness Ministry		
49. Scepter of Righteousness Inc (2019)		
50. ScienceVest		
51. Taranga House Retreat & Spiritual Practice Center		
52. The Chocolate Factory		
53. The Go Trading Company		
54. The Husseini Group LLC		
55. The Jewel Nest		
56. The Josa Group LLC		
57. The Mezzanine Fund		
58. The Taifa Group LLC		
59. Third Avenue Business Improvement District		
60. 3Gen Construction Services		
61. TopKnot Strategies LLC		
62. Ubuntu Village Works LLC		
63. Ujamaa LLC		
66. Umbrelly Welly		

Type	Founded	Financials
65. Ureeka Inc.		
66. World Within Labs		
67. Yard Talk 101		
68. Yoga Center Amherst		
69. Yoga Health		
70. Zehner LLC		
71. 1863 Ventures		
72. 4S Bay Partners LLC		
13. Professional Associations		
1. Black Administrators in Child Welfare	1971 (o)	$22,308 (x)
2. Blacks in Law Enforcement of America*	1965 (o)	N/A
3. National Alliance of Black School Educators	1975 (o)	$1,113,201 (x)
4. National Association of Blacks in Criminal Justice	2014 (o)	≤$50,000 (r)
5. National Association of Black Social Workers	1984 (o)	≤$50,000 (r)
6. National Conference of Black Lawyers	1968 (o)	≤$50,000 (r)
7. The Association of Black Psychologists, Inc.	2016 (o)	≤$50,000 (r)
14. Local and State Governments		
1. Advisory Neighborhood Commission 5E03 (DC)	1976 (o)	N/A
2. Advisory Neighborhood Commission 5E08 (DC)	1976 (o)	N/A
3. City of Durham, NC	1853 (o)	$263,166,339 (r)
4. City of New Bern	1710 (o)	$125,183,571 (r)
5. City of Yonkers, NY	1872 (o)	$1,429,178,934 (r)
6. Connecticut General Assembly	1636 (o)	$21,021,000,000 (r)
15. Civic and Cultural Education Organizations		
1. 1Hood Media	2017 (I)	$569,035 (x)
2. Addy Productions LLC	1990 (o)	N/A
3. Amherst Mindfulness	2016 (o)	N/A
4. Antenna Cloud Farm Music Festival	2017 (o)	N/A
5. Association for Study of Classical African Civilizations	1984 (o)	$44,575 (x)
6. Balanta B'urassa History & Genealogy Society	2019 (o)	N/A
7. Black Music Action Coalition	2021 (I)	N/A
8. Bronx Basketball Association	2016 (o)	N/A
9. Columbia Law School Human Rights Institute	1998 (o)	N/A
10. Cool 2 Be Charity	N/A	N/A
11. Creative Acts	2022 (o)	$1,795 (r)

(*continued*)

TABLE C.1. (*continued*)

Type	Founded	Financials
12. Dance/NYC	2012 (I)	$2,905,391 (x)
13. Discovering U	2020 (I)	≤$50,000 (r)
14. Fit, Fyne and Fabulous LLC	2008 (o)	N/A
15. George Jackson University	2000 (o)	N/A
16. Graduate Assembly of UC-Berkeley	N/A	N/A
17. HenRose Cares Inc.	2020 (o)	≤$50,000 (r)
18. Impact Youth Services	N/A	N/A
20. The Institute for Democratic Education and Culture	1990 (o)	$2,674,011 (x)
19. IU South Bend Civil Rights Heritage Center	2000 (o)	N/A
21. Klassy Gyrlz Empire Social Club	2018 (I)	≤$50,000 (r)
22. Morgan State University	1867 (o)	$41,441,202 (e)
23. National Black Cultural Information Trust, Inc.	2021 (I)	≤$50,000 (r)
24. National Council for Black Studies	1975 (o)	$41,116 (x)
25. New Yorkers for Culture & Arts	2015 (o)	N/A
26. North Forest Bulldog Youth Sports	2011 (I)	≤$50,000 (r)
27. Northampton Parents Center	1986 (o)	$19,588 (x)
28. Occidental College Initiative on Global Political Economy	2012 (o)	N/A
29. One World Exchange	2010 (I)	N/A
30. Progressives Educating New Yorkers	2017 (I)	N/A
31. Project Access to A-Free-Ka	N/A	N/A
32. Project Blueprint (United Way)	2022 (I)	≤$50,000 (r)
33. RaVae Entertainment, Inc.	2014 (o)	N/A
34. Safer Foundation	1972 (o)	$31,860,163 (x)
35. Scene & Heard Podcast	N/A	N/A
36. School of the Art Institute of Chicago	1866 (o)	N/A
37. Shining Stars Leadership Academy	2017 (I)	≤$50,000 (r)
38. SimonSays Entertainment Inc.	2009 (o)	N/A
39. Stetson University College of Law	1900 (o)	N/A
40. Strive Till I Rise	2022 (o)	N/A
41. Think Peace Learning & Support Hub/Hoch Foundation	2021 (I)	$65,833 (x)
42. UMass Amherst	1863 (o)	$5,155,651 (x)
43. University of California Los Angeles	1868 (o)	$5,100,000,000 (e)
44. USC Gould School of Law Human Rights Clinic	2011 (o)	N/A
16. Women's Organizations		
1. Charlottesville National Organization for Women	1979 (I)	N/A
2. College and Community Fellowship	2000 (I)	$2,488,890 (x)

Type	Founded	Financials
3. Georgia National Organization for Women	1979 (I)	N/A
4. Girl Chat 3.0	N/A	N/A
5. Heart to Heart Coalition	2019 (I)	≤$50,000 (r)
6. MomsRising	2007 (I)	$2,929,607 (x)
7. National Council of Jewish Women	1893 (o)	$4,898,518 (x)
8. National Organization for Women (NOW)	1966 (o)	$3,524,343 (x)
9. Positive Women's Network	2013 (o)	$1,209,131 (x)
10. Vote Run Lead	2014 (o)	$1,385,176 (x)
11. WOCStar Fund	2018 (o)	N/A
12. Women's Initiative Supporting Health U. Rochester	N/A	N/A
13. Women's Law Project	1974 (o)	$1,502,704 (x)
14. Woodhull Sexual Freedom Foundation	2003 (o)	$154,277 (x)

Source of founding dates: (o) = date organization reports, (I) = IRS reporting start.
Financials: (x) = annual expenditures, (r) = revenues, (e)= endowment or total assets.
All data are for most recent year available. N/A = Not Available. * = website closed.
Data compiled from multiple sources including group websites, IRS 990 forms, GuideStar, Charity Navigator, InfluenceWatch, Source Watch, Cause IQ, and others. All references on file with authors.

Notes

Chapter One

1. We are indebted to many colleagues for discussions of the strengths and limitations of our framework. For these specific points we wish particularly to acknowledge Cathy J. Cohen, Megan Ming Francis, Daniel Gillion, Michael Hanchard, Ange-Marie Hancock, Fred Harris, Vicky Hattam, Daniel HoSang, Kimberley Johnson, Robert Lieberman, Joseph Lowndes, Michele Margolis, Lisa Miller, Anne Norton, Julie Novkov, Adolph Reed Jr., Ronald Schmidt Sr., Stephen Skowronek, Michael Tesler, Dorian Warren, and Vesla Weaver, with apologies to numerous others who have also made valuable comments on our work.

2. For an important analysis developing the concept of a conservative "coalition for 'profit and protection'" in American cities, see Weir (forthcoming).

3. Because the response rate from conservative advocacy groups we surveyed was low, we do not report any of our survey results here. The answers we did receive were, however, consistent with the arguments we make in this book, and they also led to some valuable interviews that we do report.

Chapter Two

1. That political scientists in general long gave insufficient attention to race as a core topic in their discipline is highlighted by McClain (2021), among others.

2. The *Oxford Handbook of Historical Institutionalism* provides excellent overviews of the origins, theories, methods, and themes of historical institutionalist scholarship, with contributions from "HI" founding figures such as Sven Steinmo, Kathleen Thelen, Peter Hall, and others (Fioretos, Falleti, and Sheingate 2016); see also Steinmo, Thelen, and Longstreth (1992), and the essays in that volume by Hall (1992) and Weir (1992). In conceptualizing ideas within American political development, our work has been most directly influenced by Skocpol (1995),

Lieberman (2002), Orren and Skowronek (2004), and Schmidt (2011); and see the account of ideas and historical institutionalism provided in Blyth, Helgadóttir, and Kring (2016).

3. The term "institutional orders" appears five times in the *Oxford Handbook of Historical Institutionalism* but without any definition or elaboration provided.

4. A conclusion consistent with other recent research on the BLM movement (see for example Tillery 2019; Bonilla and Tillery 2020; Heaney 2022).

5. We are grateful to Michael Hanchard for stressing this point.

6. For a useful overview see Kadushin (2012).

7. We examined a range of particular policies in our previous book, *Still a House Divided: Race and Politics in Obama's America* (King and Smith 2011), in a fashion similar to what we do here, but without using the "policy regimes" terminology.

8. For many other institutional orders, such as those governing gender and disability, we believe these variations are even greater, because those governing orders are extensively structured as compromises among multiple policy alliances, rather than between two major rivals. The institutional orders compromises create have some relative autonomy from any specific policy alliance and often incorporate, with varying levels of efficacy, policies reflecting multiple conflicting conceptions of gender, of the needs and rights of disabled persons, and other positions. But even if the policies shaped by the contestation of rival racial orders fit into a dichotomous frame more neatly than is the case for many other institutional orders, they still produce sets of policy regimes that do not represent consistent victories for either side.

9. We are indebted to Jasper Kauth for his assistance with this research.

10. Our results, however, probably understate the degrees of interconnections, because only publicly accessible websites hosted on the groups' servers were analyzed, and not their social media accounts or private forums. Some sites, like the Hudson Institute and the Manhattan Institute among conservatives and Color of Change and the National Urban League among liberals, bar the software from "crawling" through them and mapping their hyperlinks. Others, like those of the American Enterprise Institute and the ACLU, have such massive numbers of links that the software could provide only a partial mapping in the time available.

11. Murray's book is dedicated to Justice Clarence Thomas's close friend and financial benefactor, the billionaire Harlan Crow.

12. The 2020 edition includes an illuminating Foreword by the renowned historian Robin D. G. Kelley (2000) that, along with Kelley's earlier praise for it, has helped win new audiences for Robinson. Kelley has since stressed that he sees the concept of "racial capitalism" chiefly as strategically useful in revolutionary struggles (Kelley 2023).

13. For critical overviews, see Michael and Singhal (2019) and Levenson and Paret (2022).

14. This first white colonial revolution by the North American rebels was swiftly emulated in Haiti's uprising by the enslaved and its expulsion of the French in

1789, justified through a significantly different version of revolutionary republicanism. Unlike the US, Haiti did not retain enslavement in its founding constitution, prompting a hostile US government to deny it recognition and trade relations until Abraham Lincoln's presidency.

Chapter Three

1. Zoom interview with authors, November 30, 2021, cited with the permission of Professor Swain.
2. See "Smithsonian Removes Infographic about 'Whiteness' After Hawley Demanded Explanation—America First with Sebastian Gorka" (sebgorka.com) and "President Trump Defends Confederate Flag in Exclusive Interview with Chris Wallace—America First with Sebastian Gorka" (sebgorka.com).
3. The organization's website, Women for America First (wfaf.org), became difficult to access via search engines in 2022, even as the organization faced governmental inquiries concerning its role in the January 6, 2021 attack on the Capitol (Paladino 2022).
4. Useful accounts include Phelps-Fein (2009), esp. 158–60; Hacker and Pierson (2010), esp. 117–19; Mayer (2016), esp. 88–92; and MacLean (2018), esp. 125–26.
5. One intriguing detail about these intellectual advocacy efforts comes from the summer camp in 1979 organized by the "law and economics" scholar Henry Manne to convert twenty-two young professors selected from law schools across the country, one of whom was Elizabeth Warren, now a US senator but then a professor at the University of Houston. One participant in the summer camp, John Price, a former dean of the University of Washington Law School, described the event as "sort of pure proselytizing on the part of the dedicated, very conservative law and economics folks" focused on anti-regulatory agendas (Saul 2019).
6. For a profile of Leo, see Toobin (2017).

Chapter Four

1. Authors' interview with Yuval Levin, Senior Fellow, American Enterprise Institute, October 13, 2021; and see Y. Levin (2022).
2. Authors' interview with Chance Layton, Director of Communications, National Association of Scholars, October 13, 2021.
3. Authors' interview with Ward Connerly, President, Californians for Equal Rights, November 9, 2021.
4. Authors' interview with Gail Heriot, US Civil Rights Commission, November 8, 2021.
5. Authors' interview with Christopher Rufo, Senior Fellow, Manhattan Institute, December 3, 2021.

6. In his oral presentation, Trump added, and emphasized, the "only" and the repetition of "America first" to his official written text (compare Trump 2017a to Trump 2017b). Previously the "America First" slogan was most identified with Charles Lindbergh's call in September 1941 for the United States not to oppose Nazi Germany, a lineage Trump may not have known at first and that he has since ignored, despite press coverage highlighting it (Thomas 2016).

7. Authors' interview with Charles Kesler, editor of the *Claremont Review*, on November 18, 2021.

Chapter Six

1. Authors' interview with Dr. Ron Daniels, October 29, 2021. Daniels is the former executive director of the Center for Constitutional Rights and of the National Rainbow Coalition, and he was deputy campaign manager in the Jesse Jackson for President organization in 1988. He played a founding role in creating the National African American Reparations Commission (NAARC 2023a).

2. NAARC 2023a.

3. See Balkan Transitional Justice 2015; Crenzel 2008 (on CONDADEP); US Institute of Peace 1995 (on the South Africa Truth and Reconciliation Commission); Ireland Department of Children, Equality, Disability Integration and Youth 2021; and on Canadian Indigenous children, Shaheen 2021. Canada's Federal Court confirmed a decision made by the Human Rights Tribunal in 2019 to offer C$40,000 to each adult who as a child was involuntarily taken from their home to a residential school for purposes of assimilation between 2006 and 2017. The removal occurred because of deliberate underfunding of schools in their communities, and involved over forty thousand children.

4. Authors' interview with Kamm Howard, co-chair of N'COBRA, October 15, 2021.

5. Kamm Howard interview.

6. Authors' interview with Community Change President Dorian Warren, November 29, 2021.

7. Authors' interview with Steve Brainerd of the First Unitarian Society of Denver Racial Justice Project, October 13, 2021.

8. Authors' interview with DeRay McKesson, Executive Director of Campaign Zero, February 8, 2022.

Chapter Seven

1. Authors' interview with Kamm Howard, National Co-Chair, N'COBRA, October 15, 2021.

2. Authors' interview with Community Change President Dorian Warren, November 29, 2021.

3. For the substantial scholarly literature about reparations as a concept historically and politically and how best to analyze it, see e.g. Boxill 2003; McCarthy 2004; Butt 2009; Cooper 2012; Goodin 2013; Balfour 2014; Page 2019; Franke 2019; Klein and Fouksman 2021; and Page and King 2022.

4. Kamm Howard interview.

5. Authors' interview with Sakira Cook, Senior Director of the Justice Reform Program, Leadership Conference on Civil and Human Rights, April 11, 2021.

Chapter Eight

1. For discussion of how real estate groups and government policies constructed home ownership, in contrast to urban apartment-dwelling, as an American ideal in the second quarter of the twentieth century, see Hayward (2013), esp. 111–50.

2. Authors' interview with Sakira Cook, Director, National Conference on Civil and Human Rights Criminal Justice Program, November 4, 2021.

3. Authors' interview with DeRay McKesson, Executive Director, Campaign Zero, February 8, 2022; Campaign Zero 2023.

4. The historian Annette Gordon-Reed has made Juneteenth the centerpiece of her powerful memoir, *On Juneteenth* (Gordon-Reed 2021).

5. Authors' interview with US Representative Jamaal Bowman, February 15, 2022.

6. E.g., authors' interviews with Erika Weissinger, Reparation Generation National Advisory Board, September 9, 2022; Dorian Warren, President of Community Change, November 29, 2021.

7. Authors' interview with Chance Layton, Director of Communications, National Association of Scholars, October 13, 2021.

References

Abernathy, Gary. 2017. "Why I Support Reparations—and All Conservatives Should." *Washington Post*, April 22. https://www.washingtonpost.com/opinions/2021/04/22/why-i-support-reparations-all-conservatives-should.

Abraham, Roshan. 2022. "Evanston's First 'Reparations' Payments Have Gone Out. Here's How It Was Spent." *Next City*, July 7. https://nextcity.org/urbanist-news/evanstons-first-reparations-have-gone-out-heres-how-it-was-spent.

Abramowitz, Alan, and Jennifer McCoy. 2019. "United States: Racial Resentment, Negative Partisanship and Polarization in Trump's America." *Annals of the American Academy of Political and Social Science* 681: 137–56.

Abramowitz, Alan, and Ruy Teixeira. 2009. "The Decline of the White Working Class and the Rise of a Mass Upper-Middle Class." *Political Science Quarterly* 124 (3/2): 391–422.

Achiume, E. Tendayi. 2019. *Forms of Racism, Racial Discrimination, Xenophobia and Racial Intolerance*. Report to the UN General Assembly, prepared pursuant to General Assembly resolution 73/262, August 21, 2019. UN A/74/321. https://digitallibrary.un.org/record/3827500?ln+en.un.org/record/3827500?ln+en.

Achiume, E. Tendayi, and Gay McDougall. 2023. "Anti-Racism at the United Nations." *American Journal of International Law* 117: 82–87.

ACLED (Armed Conflict Location & Event Data Project). 2021. "A Year of Racial Justice Protests: Key Trends in Demonstrations Supporting the BLM Movement." May 25. https://acleddata.com/2021/05/25/a-year-of-racial-justice-protests-key-trends-in-demonstrations-supporting-the-blm-movement/.

Action St. Louis. 2019. "About Action St. Louis." *Action St. Louis*. https://actionstl.org/mission-vision.

Adams, Liam. 2022. "Civics, Charters, and Classical Ed: What to Know about Hillsdale College's K-12 Efforts in Tennessee." *The Tennessean*, February 2. https://www.tennessean.com/story/news/politics/2022/02/02/hillsdale-college-tennessee-charter-schools-partnership-gov-bill-lee/9303810002/.

ADL (Anti-Defamation League). 2009. "Oath Keepers and Three %ers Part of

Growing Anti-Government Movement." *Backgrounder*, October 26. https://www.adl.org/resources/backgrounder/oath-keepers-and-three-ers-part-growing-anti-government-movement.

ADL (Anti-Defamation League). 2023. "Murder and Extremism in the United States in 2022." February 22. https://www.adl.org/resources/report/murder-and-extremism-united-states-2022.

ADL Center on Extremism. 2018. "White Supremacist Propaganda Nearly Doubles on Campus in 2017–18 Academic Year." June 27. https://www.adl.org/resources/reports/white-supremacist-propaganda-nearly-doubles-on-campus-in-2017-18-academic-year.

ADOS (American Descendants of Slavery) Advocacy Foundation. 2022a. "Reparations Agenda." Last accessed September 4, 2023. https://www.adosfoundation.org/reparations.

ADOS Advocacy Foundation. 2022b. "The Black Agenda." Last accessed September 4, 2023. https://www.adosfoundation.org/black-agenda.

African American Redress Network. 2023a. "About." Last accessed September 4, 2023. https://redressnetwork.org/about/.

African American Redress Network. 2023b. "Redress Map." Last accessed September 4, 2023. https://redressnetwork.org/redress-map/.

Aisch, Gregor, and Alicia Palapiano. 2017. "What Do You Think Is the Most Important Problem Facing the Country Today?" *New York Times*, February 27. https://www.nytimes.com/interactive/2017/02/27/us/politics/most-important-problem-gallup-polling-question/html.

Alba, Richard. 2016. "The Likely Persistence of a White Majority." *American Prospect* 27: 67–71.

Alcorn, Chauncey. 2021. "Homes in Black Neighborhoods Are Undervalued by $46,000 on Average." *CNN Business*, April 20. https://www.cnn.com/2021/04/20/economy/redfin-housing-boom-race-discrimination/index.html.

Aldrich, John H., Bradford H. Bishop, Rebecca S. Hatch, D. Sunshine Hillygus, and David W. Rohde. 2014. "Blame, Responsibility, and the Tea Party in the 2010 Midterm Elections." *Political Behavior* 36 (3): 471–91.

Alexander, Harriet. 2018. "Trump Administration Sides against Harvard in Asian-American Affirmative Action Case." *Daily Telegraph*, August 18. https://www.telegraph.co.uk/news/2018/08/30/trump-administration-sides-against-harvard-asian-american-affirmative/.

Allen, Mike. 2021. "Scoop: Trump Alumni Launch Largest Post-Administration Group." *Axios*, April 13. https://www.axios.com/2021/04/13/trump-policy-institute-brooke-rollins.

Allied Media Projects. 2023. "About." Last accessed September 4, 2023. https://alliedmedia.org/about.

Alter, Alexandra. 2023. "Book Bans Rising Rapidly in the U.S., Free Speech Groups

Find." *New York Times*, April 20. https://www.nytimes.com/2023/04/20/books/book-bans-united-states-free-speech/.

America First Foundation (AFF). 2020–2023a. "About America First." Last accessed September 4, 2023. https://americafirstfoundation.org/about.

America First Foundation (AFF). 2020–2023b. "AFF Through the Years." Last accessed September 4, 2023. https://americafirstfoundation.org/events/.

America First Legal. 2022. "The Mission." https://www.aflegal.org/about.

America First Party. 2022. "Welcome to the Internet Home of the America First Party." https://www.americafirstparty.org/.

America First Policy Institute (AFPI). 2022a. "Our Mission." https://americafirstpolicy.com/about/#team.

America First Policy Institute (AFPI). 2022b. "Jobs *First*." https://americafirstpolicy.com/priorities/category/jobs.

America First Policy Institute (AFPI). 2022c. "Security *First*." https://americafirstpolicy.com/priorities/category/security.

America First Policy Institute (AFPI). 2022d. "Freedom *First*." https://americafirstpolicy.com/priorities/category/freedom.

American Presidency Project. 2022. "2000 Democratic Party Platform." https://www.presidency.ucsb.edu/documents/2000-democratic-party-platform.

Anderson, Meg, and Nick McMillan. 2023. "1,000 People Have Been Charged for the Capitol Riot. Here's Where Their Cases Stand." *NPR*, March 25. https://www.npr.org/2023/03/25/1165022885/1000-defendants-january-6-capitol-riot.

Anderson, Nick. 2023. "How Penn State Abandoned a Big Pledge on Racial Justice." *Washington Post*, January 5. https://www.washingtonpost.com/education/2023/01/05/penn-state-center-for-racial-justice/.

Anderson, Nick, and Moriah Balingit. 2018. "Trump Administration Moves to Rescind Obama-Era Guidance on Race in Admissions." *Washington Post*, July 3. https://www.washingtonpost.com/local/education/trump-administration-moves-to-rescind-obama-era-guidance-on-race-in-admissions/2018/07/03/.

Anderson, Nick, and Lori Rozsa. 2023. "Amid DeSantis Attack, AP African American Studies Course Is Updated." *Washington Post*, February 1. https://www.washingtonpost.com/education/2023/02/01/ap-african-american-studies-curriculum-desantis/.

Anderson, Stuart. 2020. "The Outlook on Immigration in 2020." *Forbes*, January 6. https://www.forbes.com/sites/stuartanderson/2020/01/06/the-outlook-on-immigration-in-2020/?sh=68b155983abdhttps://www.forbes.com/sites/stuartanderson/2020/01/06/the-outlook-on-immigration-in-2020/?sh=68b155983abd.

Andrew, Scottie. 2021. "Jesuits Commit $100 Million to the Descendants of People the Order Once Enslaved." *CNN*, March 16. https://www.cnn.com/2021/03/16/us/georgetown-slavery-descendants-jesuits-100-million-trnd/index.html.

Andrews, Jeff. 2018. "Trump Issues Executive Order on Work Requirements." *Curbed*, April 12. https://www.curbed.com/2018/4/12/17229656/trump-work-requirements-hud-housing-subsidies.

Andrews, Jeff. 2020. "How Ben Carson Tried to Destroy Fair and Affordable Housing." *Curbed*, August 17. https://archive.curbed.com/2020/8/17/21372168/ben-carson-hud-housing-trump.

Aneja, Abhay, and Guo Xu. 2022. "The Costs of Employment Segregation: Evidence from the Federal Government under Woodrow Wilson." *Quarterly Journal of Economics* 137: 911–58.

Anglin, Andrew. 2016. "Trump Retweets Two More White Genocide Accounts Back-to-Back." *Daily Stormer*, January 25. https://dailystormer.name/happening-trump-retweets-two-more-white-genocide-accounts-back-to-back/.

AP News. 2021. "Transcript of Trump's Speech at Rally before US Capital Riot." *AP News*, January 13. https://apnews.com/article/election-2020-joe-biden-donald-trump-capitol-siege-media-e79eb5164613d6718e9f4502eb471f27https://apnews.com/article/election-2020-joe-biden-donald-trump-capitol-siege-media-e79eb5164613d6718e9f4502eb471f27.

AP News. 2022. "Conservative College's '1776 Curriculum' Gets a Foothold in South Dakota." *CBS News Minnesota*, September 12. https://apnews.com/article/education-donald-trump-michigan-south-dakota-sioux-falls.

Arango, Tim. 2023. "Can Reparations Bring Black Residents Back to San Francisco?" *New York Times*, May 16. https://www.nytimes.com/2023/05/16/us/san-francisco-reparations.html.

Armaly, Miles T., David T. Buckley, and Adam M. Enders. 2022. "Christian Nationalism and Political Violence: Victimhood, Racial Identity, Conspiracy and Support for the Capitol Attacks." *Political Behavior* 44: 937–60.

Arpey, Conor. 2017. "The Business Implications of Disparate Impact's Uncertain Future." *BLR Buzz Blog, American University Business Law Review*, April 17. http://www.aublr.org/2017/04/business-implications-disparate-impacts-uncertain-future/.

Asian American Legal Foundation. 2022. "About Us." https://www.asianamericanlegal.com/about-us/.

Atlantic Legal Foundation. 2021. "Effective Education of Our Next Generation(s) of Americans." February 23. https://atlanticlegal.org/news/effective-education-of-our-next-generations-of-americans/.

Atterbury, Andrew. 2023. "Florida's Ban on DEI Becomes Official as DeSantis Enacts College Reforms." *Politico*, May 15. https://www.politico.com/news/2023/05/15/desantis-enacts-floridas-dei-ban.

Autry, Robyn. 2021. "Trump's Commission Tried to Rewrite US History. Biden Had Other Ideas." *NBC News*, January 21. https://www.nbcnews.com/think/opinion/trump-s-1776-commission-tried-rewrite-u-s-history-biden.

Bacon, Perry, Jr. 2023. "Opinion: Today's Civil Rights Movement Is So Different from the '60s." *Washington Post*, March 1. https://www.washingtonpost.com/opinions/2023/03/01/black-lives-matter-sixties-civil-rights-movement/.

Badger, Emily, Robert Gebeloff, and Josh Katz. 2023. "Coastal Cities Priced Out Low-Wage Workers. Now College Graduates Are Leaving, Too." *New York Times*, May 13. https://www.nytimes.com/interactive/2023/05/15/upshot/migrations-college-super-cities.html.

Baker, Peter. 2022. "Trump Embraces Extremism to Fuel His Campaign." *New York Times*, December 2, A15.

Bahney, Anna. 2022. "The Black Homeownership Rate Is Less Now Than It Was a Decade Ago." *CNN Business*, February 25. https://www.cnn.com/2022/02/25/homes/us-black-homeownership-rate/index.html.

Bahr, Sarah. 2021. "Roosevelt Statue to Head West to Presidential Library." *New York Times*, November 20, C3.

Bailey, Phillip M., Chelsey Cox, and Aleszu Bajak. 2021. "How Critical Race Theory Went from Conservative Battle Cry to Mainstream Powder Keg." *USA Today/Yahoo!News*, November 15. https://news.yahoo.com/critical-race-theory-went-conservative-100041316.html.

Baker, Peter. 2017. "President Backs a Plan to Curb Legal Migration." *New York Times*, August 3, A1.

Baldwin, James. 1963. *The Fire Next Time*. New York: Vintage Books.

Balfour, Lawrie. 2014. "Unthinking Racial Realism: A Future for Reparations?" *Du Bois Review* 11: 43–56.

Balfour, Lawrie. 2023. "The Politics of Reparations for Black Americans." *Annual Review of Political Science* 26: 291–304.

Balkan Transitional Justice. 2015. "About the Programme." *BIRN*. https://balkaninsight.com/balkan-transitional-justice-home/balkan-transitional-justice-about/.

Ballotpedia. 2020. "Los Angeles County, California, Measure R, Civilian Police Oversight Commission." March. https://ballotpedia.org/Los_Angeles_County,_California,_Measure_R,_Civilian_Police_Oversight_Commission_and_Jail_Plan_Initiative_(March_2020).

Banks, Adelle M. 2021. "Idaho Church Window Once Depicting Robert E. Lee Now Honors Black Female Bishop." *Religious News Service*, December 22. https://religionnews.com/2021/12/22/idaho-church-window-once-depicting-robert-e-lee-now-honors-black-female-bishop/.

Baptist Joint Committee (BJC) and Freedom from Religion Foundation (FFRF). 2022. "Christian Nationalism and the January 6 2021 Insurrection." *Baptist Joint Committee for Religious Liberty*. https://bjconline.org/wp-content/uploads/2022/02/Christian_Nationalism_and_the_Jan6_Insurrection-2-9-22.pdf.

Barber, C. Ryan. 2023. "Oath Keepers Founder Stewart Rhodes Sentenced to 18

Years for Seditious Conspiracy." *Wall Street Journal*, May 25. https://www.wsj.com/articles/oath-keepers-founder-to-be-sentenced-for-seditious-conspiracy-in-jan-6-attack.

Barr, William P. 2019. "Remarks to the Law School and the de Nicola Center for Ethics and Culture at the University of Notre Dame." United States Department of Justice, October 11. https://www.justice.gov/opa/speech/attorney-general-william-p-barr-delivers-remarks-law-school-and-de-nicola-center-ethics.

Bartels, Larry M. 2020. "Ethnic Antagonism Erodes Republicans' Commitment to Democracy." *PNAS* 117 (37): 22752–59.

Bateman, David. 2023. "The South in American Political Development." *Annual Review of Political Science* 26: 325–45.

Bauer, Greta R., Siobhan M. Churchill, Mayuri Mahendran, Chantel Walwyn, Daniel Lizotte, and Alma Angelica Villa-Rueda. 2021. "Intersectionality in Quantitative Research: A Systematic Review of Its Emergence and Applications of Theory and Methods." *SSM-Population Health* 14. https://doi.org/10.1016/j.ssmph.2021.100798.

Bayer, Casey. 2017. "DeVos Rescinds Guidance Documents for Disabled Students: What Does It Mean?" *Harvard Graduate School of Education*, October 24. https://www.gse.harvard.edu/news/17/10/devos-rescinds-guidance-documents-disabled-students-what-does-it-mean.

BBC News. 2020. "Trump Rejects Calls to Drop Confederate Base Names." June 11. https://www.bbc.com/news/world-us-canada.

BBC News. 2021. "Kyle Rittenhouse: Who Is US Teen Cleared of Protest Killings?" November 19. https://www.bbc.co.uk/news/world-us-canada.

Beam, Adam. 2021. "11 US Mayors Pledge to Pay Reparations for Slavery to Small Groups of Black Residents." *USA Today*, June 19. https://www.usatoday.com/story/news/nation/2021/06/19/reparations-slavery-pledged-11-us-mayors-pilot-program/.

Beaumont, Thomas. 2021. "GOP Ramps Misleading Attacks on Democrats' Policing Policy." *AP News*, June 13. https://apnews.com/article/politics-republicans-democrats-police-defund-crime-murder.

Beckles, Hilary M. 2013. *Britain's Black Debt: Reparations for Caribbean Slavery and Native Genocide*. Kingston, Jamaica: University of the West Indies Press.

Beinart, Peter. 2018. "Trump Shut Programs to Counter Violent Extremism." *The Atlantic*, October 29. https://www.theatlantic.com/ideas/archive/2018/10/trump-shut-countering-violent-extremism-program/.

Bella, Timothy. 2021. "Oregon School Board Bans Pride and Black Lives Matter Symbols in the Classroom." *Washington Post*, September 29. https://www.washingtonpost.com/education/2021/09/29/oregon-newberg-ban-pride-blm/.

Benner, Katie. 2018. "Before Exiting, Sessions Sharply Curbs Agreements That Fight Police Abuse." *New York Times*, November 9, A15.

Benner, Katie. 2020. "Justice Department Establishes Office to Denaturalize Immi-

grants." *New York Times*, February 26. https://www.nytimes.com/2020/02/26/us/politics/denaturalization-immigrants-justice-department.html.
Benner, Katie, and Erica Green. 2021. "Justice Department Seeks to Pare Back Civil Rights Protections for Minorities." *New York Times*, January 5. https://www.nytimes.com/2021/01/05/us/politics/justice-department-disparate-impact.html.
Bennett, Brian. 2018. "How Unlikely Allies Got Prison Reform Done—With an Assist from Kim Kardashian West." *Time*, December 21. https://time.com/5486560/prison-reform-jared-kushner-kim-kardashian-west/.
Benveniste, Alexis, and Kaya Yurieff. 2020. "Meet Rebekah Mercer, the Deep-Pocketed Co-Founder of Parler, a Controversial Conservative Social Network." *CNN*, November 16. https://www.cnn.com/2020/11/15/media/rebekah-mercer-parler/index.html.
Berkowitz, Peter. 2022. "The Intra-Conservative Quarrel Over Universal Principles." *RealClear Politics*, September 9. https://www.realclearpolitics.com/articles/2022/09/09/the_intra-conservative_quarrel_over_universal_principles.
Berman, Mark. 2023. "7 Highlights from Justice Dept.'s Blistering Louisville Police Probe." *Washington Post*, March 8. https://www.washingtonpost.com/national-security/2023/03/08/seven-highlights-justice-departments-blistering-louisville-police-investigation/.
Berry, Kate. 2018. "CFPB's Mulvaney Strips His Fair-Lending Office of Enforcement Powers." *American Banker*, February 1. https://www.americanbanker.com/news/cfpbs-mulvaney-strips-his-fair-lending-office-of-enforcement-powers.
Betts, Anna, and Nichole Manna. 2023. "Grief and Anger Continues to Reverberate from Jacksonville Shootings." *New York Times*, August 28. https://www.nytimes.com/2023/08/28/us/jacksonville-shooting-florida-hbcu.html.
Bickerton, James. 2022. "How Every Known Jan. 6 Participant Fared in US, State Midterm Elections." *Newsweek*, November 11. https://www.newsweek.com/how-every-known-jan-6-participant-fared-us-state-midterm-elections.
Biondi, Martha. 2023. "The Rise of the Reparations Movement." *Radical History Review* 87: 5–18.
Biskupic, Joan. 2021. "Trump's Appointees Are Turning the Supreme Court to the Right with Different Tactics." *CNN News*, July 26. https://www.cnn.com/2021/07/26/politics/trump-kavanaugh-gorsuch-barrett-supreme-court/index.html.
Black Conservative Federation (BCF). n.d. "About." Last accessed September 4, 2023. https://www.bcfaction.com.
Black Freedom Collective. n.d. "Our DNA: Who We Are." https://blackfreedomcollective.org/our-dna/. Last accessed September 4, 2023.
Black Lives Matter. 2020. *Black Lives Matter 2020 Impact Report*. https://blacklivesmatter.com/2020-impact-report/.
BlackPast. 2018. "(1966) The Black Panther Party Ten-Point Program." BlackPast.org, April 5. https://www.blackpast.org/african-american-history/primary-documents-african-american-history/black-panther-party-ten-point-program-1966/.

Blackburn, Piper Hudspeth. 2021. "Despite Racial Reckoning, State Efforts Stall on Reparations." *AP News*, April 25. https://apnews.com/article/race-and-ethnicity-legislature-legislation-coronavirus-pandemic-california.

Blake, Aaron. 2022. "How Badly Election Deniers Cost the GOP in 2022 Elections." *Washington Post*, November 15. https://www.washingtonpost.com/politics/2022/11/14/election-deniers-cost-gop/.

Blazina, Carrie, and Kiana Cox. 2022. "Black and White Americans Are Far Apart in Their Views on Reparations for Slavery." Pew Research Center, November 28. https://www.pewresearch.org/short-reads/2022/11/28/black-and-white-americans-are-far-apart-in-their-views-of-reparations-for-slavery/.

Blight, David W. 2001. *Race and Reunion: The Civil War in American Memory*. Cambridge, MA: The Belknap Press of Harvard University Press.

Blitzer, Ronn. 2021. "Rep. Burgess Owens: 'Unfair and Heartless' for Democrats to Raise Black Americans' Hopes for Reparations." *Fox News*, February 17. https://www.foxnews.com/politics/rep-burgess-owens-democrats-reparations-hearing.

BLM Michigan. 2023. "Black Lives Matter Michigan: Chapters." https://www.blmmichigan.org/.

Blond, Phillip, et al. 2022. "An Open Letter Responding to the Natcon 'Statement of Principles.'" *The European Conservative*, August 29. https://europeanconservative.com/articles/commentary/an-open-letter-to-natcon/.

Bloom, Joshua, and Waldo Martin. 2013. *Black Against Empire: The History and Politics of the Black Panther Party*. Berkeley: University of California Press.

Blyth, Mark, Oddný Helgadóttir, and William Kring. 2016. "Ideas and Historical Institutionalism." In *The Oxford Handbook of Historical Institutionalism*, edited by Orfeo Fioretos, Tulia G. Falleti, and Adam Sheingate, 142–61. New York: Oxford University Press.

Bogel-Burroughs, Nicholas, and J. David Goodman. 2023. "Takeaways from the Impeachment of Texas Attorney General Ken Paxton." *New York Times*, May 28. https://www.nytimes.com/2023/05/28/us/texas-ken-paxton-impeachment-takeaways.html.

Bohannon, Molly. 2023. "Alabama Approves New Map With Only 1 Majority-Black District After Supreme Court Asked for 2." *Forbes*, July 21. https://www.forbes.com/mollybohannon/2023/07/21/alabama-approves-new-house-map-with-only-1-majority-black-district-after-supreme-court-asked-for-2/.

Bonilla, Tabitha, and Alvin B. Tillery Jr. 2020. "Which Identity Frames Boost Support for and Mobilization in the #BlackLivesMatter Movement? An Experimental Test." *American Political Science Review* 114: 947–62.

Bonilla-Silva, Eduardo. 2017. *Racism without Racists: Color-Blind Racism and the Persistence of Racism in America*. New York: Rowman and Littlefield.

Bonilla-Silva, Eduardo. 2023. "*It's Not the Rotten Apples!* Why Family Scholars Should Adopt a Structural Perspective on Racism." *Journal of Family Theory and Review*, May 6. https://doi.org/10.1111/jftr.12503.

Bonta, Rob. n.d. "AB 3121: Task Force to Develop Proposals for Reparations for African Americans." Office of the Attorney General, Department of Justice, State of California. Last accessed September 4, 2023. https://oag.ca.gov/ab3121.

Boorstein, Michelle. 2022. "Va. Episcopal Diocese to Spend $10 Million for Reparations. But How?" *Washington Post*, August 14. https://www.washingtonpost.com/religion/2022/08/14/va-episcopal-diocese-spend-10-million-reparations-how/.

Borealis Philanthropy. 2021. "Borealis Philanthropy Receives Millions from Mackenzie Scott to Support Grassroots Movements." *Borealis News & Updates*, July 15. https://borealisphilanthropy.org/borealis-philanthropy-receives-millions-from-mackenzie-scott-to-support-grassroots-movements/.

Borealis Philanthropy. 2023. "2021 Annual Report." Last accessed September 4, 2023. https://borealisphilanthropy.org/2021-annual-report/.

Bosman, Julie. 2020. "$600 Million for Victims of Lead in Flint Water." *New York Times*, August 20, A23.

Bosman, Julie. 2021. "Chicago Suburb Moves to Shape Reparations for Its Black Residents." *New York Times*, March 23. https://www.nytimes.com/2021/03/22/us/reparations-evanston-illinois-housing.html.

Bosman, Julie, and Mitch Smith. 2017. "Excessive Force Is Rife in Chicago, US Review Find." *New York Times*, January 14, A1.

Bottum, Faith. 2021. "Indecency on Display at the Art Institute of Chicago." *Wall Street Journal*, October 15. https://www.wsj.com/articles/indecency-art-institute-of-chicago-docents-diversity-firing-11634310172.

Boustan, Leah Platt. 2017. *Competition in the Promised Land: Black Migrants in Northern Cities and Labor Markets*. Princeton, NJ: Princeton University Press.

Boxill, Bernard R. 2003. "A Lockean Argument for Black Reparations." *Journal of Ethics* 7 no. 1: 63–91.

Boyer, Dave. 2019. "Far-Right White Nationalists Fracturing Donald Trump's Conservative Base." *Washington Times*, November 28. https://www.washingtontimes.com/news/2019/nov/28/far-right-white-nationalists-fracturing-donald-tru/.

Boztas, Senay. 2022. "Dutch Wrestle with National Apology for 250 Years of Slavery." *The Guardian*, December 4. https://www.theguardian.com/world/2022/dec/04/dutch-wrestle-with-national-apology-for-250-years-of-slavery.

Brennan Center for Justice. 2017. "Voting Laws Roundup 2017." May 10. https://www.brennancenter.org/analysis/voting-laws-roundup-2017.

Brennan Center for Justice. 2021a. "Voting Laws Roundup: May 2021." May 28. https://www.brennancenter.org/our-work/research-reports/voting-laws-roundup-may-2021.

Brennan Center for Justice. 2021b. "Voting Laws Roundup: October 2021." October 4. https://www.brennancenter.org/our-work/research-reports/voting-laws-roundup-october-2021.

Brennan Center for Justice. 2023. "Voting Laws Roundup: February 2023." February 27. https://www.brennancenter.org/our-work/research-reports/voting-laws-roundup-february-2023.

Bridgespan Group. 2022. "2020 Funders, Supporters, and Financials." https://www.bridgespan.org/getmedia/ba8ea40a-7123-4c9f-aa0f-aae17b98544e/Bridgespan-Group-2020-financials.pdf.

Brimelow, Hannah Claire. 2021. "Data Shows Decline in Public Support for BLM." *TIMCAST*, August 10. https://timcast.com/news/data-shows-decline-in-public-support-for-blm/.

Brooklyn Community Foundation. 2016. "About Us." Last accessed September 4, 2023. https://www.brooklyncommunityfoundation.org/about/foundation-overview.

Brooks, Bard. 2020. "Kenosha Police 'Deputized' Militia Ahead of Deadly Shooting, Lawsuit Claims." *Reuters News*, October 18. https://www.reuters.com/world/us/white-nationalists-deputized-by-kenosha-police-led-deadly-shooting-lawsuit-2021-10-16/.

Brooks, David. 2021. "The Terrifying Future of the American Right: What I Saw at the National Conservatism Conference." *The Atlantic*, November 18. https://www.theatlantic.com/ideas/archive/2021/11/scary-future-american-right-national-conservatism-conference/620746/.

Brooks, Libby. 2022. "Edinburgh to Apologise over Its Historical Links to Slavery." *The Guardian*, August 30. https://www.theguardian.com/uk-news/2022/aug/30/edinburgh-to-apologise-over-historical-links-to-slavery.

Brown, Andrew D. 2006. "A Narrative Approach to Collective Identities." *Journal of Management Studies* 43 (4): 731–53.

Brown, Ann. 2021. "Top Reparations Scholar Sandy Darity Continues Attacks on Cities That Call Programs 'Reparations.'" *The Moguldom Nation*, July 23. https://moguldom.com/364895/top-reparations-scholar-dr-sandy-darity-continues-attacks-on-cities-that-call-programs-reparations/.

Brown, Ann. 2022. "After Successful California Reparations Task Force Process, NAASD to Formally Charge the US Government with Genocide." *The Moguldom Nation*, June 15. https://moguldom.com/411937/after-successful-california-reparations-task-force-process-naasd-to-formally-charge-the-us-government-with-genocide/.

Brown, Deneen L. 2020. "Human Rights Watch Calls for Tulsa Race Massacre Reparations a Century after Violence." *Washington Post*, May 29. Reposted at Institute of the Black World 21st Century, May 31. https://ibw21.org/reparations/human-rights-watch-calls-for-tulsa-race-massacre-reparations-a-century-after-violence/.

Brown, Deneen L. 2021a. "Reparations Bill for Tulsa Race Massacre Introduced in Congress." *Washington Post*, May 21. https://washingtonpost.com/history/2021/05/21/tulsa-massacre-reparations-bill/.

Brown, DeNeen L. 2021b. "Tensions Erupt in Tulsa as City Commemorates 1921

Race Massacre." *Washington Post*, May 30. https://www.washingtonpost.com/2021/05/29/tulsa-race-massacre-centennial-reparations-tensions/.

Brown, Jordan D. 2022. "Beach Taken from Black Couple Given Back to Family 100 Years Later: 'We Are Returning Stolen Land.'" *USA Today*, July 21. https://www.yahoo.com/entertainment/beach-taken-black-couple-given-180630758.html.

Brown, Patricia Leigh. 2021. "Telling a Long-Hidden and Painful Truth." *New York Times*, December 19, AR25.

Brown, R. Kari, Ronald E. Brown, and Randall Wyatt. 2023. "Race, Religion, and Black Lives Matter: Assessing the Association between Sermon Content and Racial Justice Attitudes and Behaviors." *Journal for the Scientific Study of Religion*, May 8. https://doi.org/10.1111/jssr.12844.

Brown University. n.d. "Slavery and Justice Report, with Commentary on Context and Impact." Last accessed September 4, 2023. https://slaveryandjusticereport.brown.edu/.

Brownlee, Dana. 2021. "Meet the Founders of 'Where Is My Land' A Movement to Reclaim Stolen Black Land and Wealth." *Forbes*, December 8. https://www.forbes.com/sites/danabrownlee/2021/12/08/meet-the-founders-of-where-is-my-land-a-movement-to-reclaim-stolen-black-land-and-wealth/.

Brownstein, Ronald. 2019. "The Limits of Trump's White Identity Politics." *The Atlantic*, August 15. https://www.theatlantic.com/politics/archive/2019/08/trump-2020.-democrats-racism/.

Brubaker, Rogers. 2017. "Why Populism?" *Theory and Society* 46: 357–85.

Brulliard, Karin. 2021. "Offensive Place Names Dot the American Landscape. Efforts to Change Them Are About to Get a Lot Faster." *Washington Post*, December 17. https://www.washingtonpost.com/nation/2021/12/17/america-offensive-place-names/.

Bubola, Emma. 2022. "She's Inheriting Millions. She Wants Her Wealth Taxed Away." *New York Times*, October 21. https://www.nytimes.com/2022/10/21/world/europe/marlene-engelhorn-wealth-tax.html.

Buchanan, Larry, Quoctrung Bui, and Jugal K. Patel. 2020. "Black Lives Matter May Be the Largest Movement in U.S. History." *New York Times*, July 3. https://www.nytimes.com/interactive/2020/07/03/us/george-floyd-protests-crowd-size.html.

Buhajla, Stephani E. 2022. "Parents Oppose Radical Race and Gender Propaganda, and They Plan to Vote to Prove It." The Foundation for Government Accountability (FGA), October 11. https://thefga.org/blog/parents-oppose-radical-race-and-gender-propaganda.

Bump, Philip. 2017. "Roy Moore: America Was Great in Era of Slavery, Is Now 'Focus of Evil in the World.'" *Washington Post*, December 8. https://www.washingtonpost.com/news/politics/wp/2017/12/08/roy-moore-america-was-great-in-era-of-slavery-is-now-focus-of-evil-in-the-world/.

Bump, Philip. 2020. "An Inescapable Echo between Trump's Campaign Rhetoric and the Deaths of Protesters in Kenosha." *Washington Post*, August 26. https://

www.washingtonpost.com/politics/2020/08/26/inescapable-echo-between-trump-campaign-rhetoric-deaths-protesters-kenosha/.

Bump, Philip. 2022. "Tucker Carlson plays Dumb on 'Replacement Theory'—Then Espouses It." *Washington Post*, May 18. https://www.washingtonpost.com/politics/2022/05/18/tucker-carlson-plays-dumb-replacement-theory-and-then-espouses-it/.

Burch, Audra D. S. 2022. "How a National Movement Toppled Hundreds of Confederate Symbols." *New York Times*, February 28. https://www.nytimes.com/interactive/2022/02/28/us/confederate-statue-removal.html.

Burch, Audra D. S. 2023. "A New Front in Reparations: Seeking the Return of Lost Family Land." *New York Times*, June 14. https://www.nytimes.com/2023/06/08/us/black-americans-family-land-reparations.html.

Burch, Audra D. S., and Luke Vander Ploeg. 2022. "Buffalo Shooting Highlights Rise of Hate Crimes against Black Americans." *New York Times*, May 16. https://www.nytimes.com/2022/05/16/us/hate-crimes-black-african-americans.html.

Burden-Stelly, Charisse. 2020. "Modern U.S. Racial Capitalism: Some Theoretical Insights." *Monthly Review* 72, no. 3 (July–August). https://monthlyreview.org/2020/07/01/modern-u-s-racial-capitalism/.

Burge, Ryan. 2023. "The Religious Landscape Is Undergoing Massive Change. It Could Decide the 2024 Election." *Politico*, May 14. https://www.politico.com/new/magazine/2023/05/15/democrats-religious-secular.

Burnip, Laura, and David Boroff. 2020. "Church Massacre: Who Is Dylann Roof and What Did He Do?" *The U.S. Sun*, December 11. https://www.the-sun.com/news/1955593/dylann-roof-crimes-white-supremacist-south-carolina/.

Bushard, Brian. 2023. "Teen Charged with Threatening to Kill President Biden—After Crashing Truck Carrying Nazi Flag Near White House." *Forbes*, May 23. https://www.forbes.com/sites/brianbushard/2023/05/23/19-year-old-charged-with-threatening-to-kill-president-after-ramming-u-haul-truck-into-dc-gates/.

Butt, Daniel. 2009. *Rectifying International Injustice*. Oxford: Oxford University Press.

Cadava, Geraldo L. 2022. "Latino Voters Are Key to 2024, and They're Not Always Buying What Democrats Are Selling." *New York Times*, January 18. https://www.nytimes.com/2022/01/18/opinion/democratic-party-latino-voters.html.

Caldwell, Christopher. 2020. *The Age of Entitlement: America Since the Sixties*. New York: Simon & Schuster.

California Task Force to Study and Develop Reparation Proposals for African Americans. 2022. "Interim Report." June 1. https://oag.ca.gov/news/press-releases/california-reparations-task-force-releases-interim-report-detailing-harms.

California Task Force to Study and Develop Reparations Proposals for African Americans. 2023. "Final Report." June 29. https://oag.ca.gov/system/files/media/full-ca-reparations.pdf.

Camera, Lauren. 2019. "Trump to HBCU Leaders: No One Has Done More for You

Than Me." *U.S. News*, September 10. https://www.usnews.com/news/education-news/articles/2019-09-10/trump-to-hbcu-leaders-no-one-has-done-more-for-you-than-me.

Cameron, Chris. 2022. "How Army Bases in the South Were Named for Defeated Confederates." *New York Times*, December 2. https://www.nytimes.com/2022/12/02/us/politics/army-base-names-south-confederates.html.

Campaign Zero. n.d. "About." Last accessed September 4, 2023. https://campaignzero.org/about/what-we-do/.

Campaign Zero. 2023. "Mapping Police Violence." July 31. https://mappingpoliceviolence.org/.

Campbell, Adina. 2021. "What Is Black Lives Matter and What Are the Aims?" *BBC News*, June 13. https://www.bbc.com/news/explainers-53337780.

Campbell, Tracy. 2005. *Deliver the Vote: A History of Election Fraud, an American Political Tradition*. New York: Carroll & Graf Publishers.

Campbo-Flores, Arian, and Jennifer Calfas. 2023. "Tulsa Race Massacre: Court Tosses Reparations Case." *Wall Street Journal*, July 9. https://www.wsj.com/articles/tulsa-race-massacre-court-tosses-reparations-case3e39b5e4.

Caputo, Marc. 2022. "The Inside Story of Trump's Explosive Dinner with Ye and Nick Fuentes." *NBC News*, November 29. https://www.nbcnews.com/politics/donald-trump/story-trumps-explosive-dinner-ye-nick-fuentes-rcna59010.

Cargle, Rachel Elizabeth. 2018. "How to Talk to Your Family About Racism on Thanksgiving." *Harper's Bazaar*, November 19. https://www.harpersbazaar.com/culture/politics/a25221603/thanksgiving-dinner-conversation-how-to-talk-to-family-about-politics/.

Caribbean Community Secretariat (CARICOM). 2015. "Reparations for Native Genocide and Slavery." October 13. https://caricom.org/reparations-for-native-genocide-and-slavery/.

Caribbean Community Secretariat. 2023. "Caricom Ten Point Plan for Reparatory Justice." Last accessed September 4, 2023. https://caricom.org/caricom-ten-point-plan-for-reparatory-justice/.

Carmichael, Stokely, and Charles V. Hamilton. 1966. *Black Power: The Politics of Liberation in America*. New York: Vintage Books.

Carpenter, Daniel. 2021. *Democracy by Petition: Popular Politics in Transformation 1790–1870*. Cambridge, MA: Harvard University Press.

Carter Jackson, Kellie. 2019. *Force and Freedom: Black Abolitionists and the Politics of Violence*. Philadelphia: University of Pennsylvania Press.

Carter Jackson, Kellie. 2022. "The Story of Violence in America." *Daedalus* 151 (1): 11–21.

Cawthorne, Cameron. 2022. "Trump Says He Will Pardon Supporters Who Stormed US Capitol on Jan. 6 If He Wins in 2024." *Fox News*, January 30. https://www.foxnews.com/politics/trump-says-he-will-pardon-jan-6-if-he-wins-in-2024.

CBS Chicago. 2021. "Mayor Lori Lightfoot Declares Racism a Public Health Crisis in Chicago: 'It Is Literally Killing Us.'" *CBSNews*, June 17. https://www.cbsnews.com/chicago/news/mayor-lori-lightfoot-systemic-racism-public-health-crisis/.

CBS News Baltimore. 2021. "Baltimore's Memorial Episcopal Church Begins Giving Out $500k in Reparations After Learning Founder Owned Slaves." *CBS Baltimore*, February 19. https://www.cbsnews.com/baltimore/news/baltimores-memorial-episcopal-church-begins-giving-out-500k-in-reparations-after-learning-founder-owned-slaves/.

CBS News Bay Area. 2022. "After California's Groundbreaking Reparations Report, What Next?" June 2. https://www.cbsnews.com/sanfrancisco/news/california-slave-reparations-report-what-next/.

Center for Equal Opportunity. n.d.-a. "Mission Statement Purpose." Last accessed September 4, 2023. https://www.ceousa.org/mission-statement-purpose.

Center for Equal Opportunity. n.d.-b. "Culture & Society." Last accessed September 4, 2023. https://www.ceousa.org/category/culture-and-society/.

Center for International Security and Cooperation. n.d. "Proud Boys Overview." Stanford: Center for International Security and Cooperation. Last accessed September 4, 2023. https://cisac.fsi.stanford.edu/mappingmilitants/profiles/proud-boys.

Center for the Study of the Legacies of British Slavery. 2023. "Home." Department of History, University College London. https://www.ucl.ac.uk/lbs/.

CFER Foundation (Californians for Equal Rights Foundation). 2023. "About." https://cferfoundation.org/about.

Chaffin, Joshua. 2022. "The Surprising Resurgence of Republicans in Miami." *Financial Times*, December 19. https://www.ft.com/content/e962daa7-f3d2-42e9-94ef-8caddd50036d.

Chappell, Bill. 2021. "A Black Nonprofit Got a 6-Figure Payment from Someone Whose Family Enslaved People." *NPR*, June 3. https://www.npr.org/2021/06/03/1002580136/a-black-nonprofit-in-kentucky-got-a-6-figure-reparations-payment-from-a-white-he.

Charland, Maurice. 1987. "Constitutive Rhetoric: The Case of the People Québecois." *Quarterly Journal of Speech* 73 (2): 133–50.

Charlton, Lauretta. 2019. "What Is the Great Replacement?" *New York Times*, August 6. https://www.nytimes.com/2019/08/06/us/politics/grand-replacement-explainer.html.

Chemerinsky, Erwin. 2021. "Why We Need to Reshape the Federal Judiciary." *Free Thought Today* 38 (3), April 3. https://www.freethoughttoday.com/articles/vol-38-no-03-april-2021/erwin-chemerinsky-why-we-need-to-reshape-the-federal-judiciary/.

Chen, Michelle. 2018. "Affirmative Action Is Under Attack." *The Nation*, August 31. https://www.thenation.com/article/affirmative-action-under-attack/.

Chen, Shawna. 2022. "North Carolina Supreme Court: GOP's Redistricting Plans

Unconstitutional." *Axios*, February 5. https://www.axios.com/2022/02/05/north-carolina-redistricting-unconstitutional.

Chenoweth, Erica, Tommy Leung, Nathan Perkins, Jeremy Pressman, and Jay Ulfelder. 2021. "The Trump Years Launched the Biggest Sustained Protest Movement in U.S. History. It's Not Over." *Washington Post*, February 8. https://www.washingtonpost.com/politics/2021/02/08/trump-years-launched-biggest-sustained-protest-movement-us-history-its-not-over/.

Chenoweth, Erica, and Jeremy Pressman. 2021. "This Summer's Black Lives Matter Protesters Were Overwhelmingly Peaceful, Our Research Finds." *Washington Post*, October 16. https://www.washingtonpost.com/politics/2020/10/16/this-summers-black-lives-matter-protesters-were-overwhelming-peaceful-our-research-finds/.

Cherone, Heather. 2022. "Chicago Failed to Enforce Law Requiring City Contractors to Disclose Links to Slavery: Officials." *WTTW News*, June 9. https://news.wttw.com/2022/06/09/chicago-failed-enforce-law-requiring-city-contractors-disclose-links-slavery-officials.

Cho, Sumi, Kimberlé William Crenshaw, and Leslie McCall. 2013. "Toward a Field of Intersectionality Studies: Theory, Applications, and Praxis." *Signs* 38 (4): 785–810.

Christian Legal Society. 2023. "About Us." Last accessed September 4, 2023. https://www.christianlegalsociety.org/who-we-serve/.

Cillizza, Chris. 2021. "How the Ugly, Racist White 'Replacement Theory' Came to Congress." *CNN Politics*, April 15. https://edition.cnn.com/2021/04/15/politics/scott-perry-white-replacement-theory-tucker-carlson-fox-news/index.html.

Church Commissioners for England. 2023. "Church Commissioners' Research into Historic Links to Transatlantic Chattel Slavery." https://www.churchofengland.org/media/29105.

Cineas, Fabiola. 2022. "Could California Become the First State to Provide Reparations?" *Vox.com*, July 3. https://www.vox.com/2022/7/3/23173075/california-reparations-task-force.

City of Alexandria. 2022. "Alexandria Community Policing Review Board." August 19. https://www.alexandriava.gov/public-safety/alexandria-community-policing-review-board.

Coard, Michael. 2021. "It's Time to Stop Asking, and Time to Start Suing, for Reparations." *Pennsylvania Capital-Star*, October 6. https://www.penncapital-star.com/commentary/its-time-to-stop-asking-and-time-to-start-suing-for-reparations-michael-coard/.

Coaston, Jane. 2018. "Self-Described Nazis and White Supremacists Are Running as Republicans Across the Country. The GOP Is Terrified." *Vox.com*, July 9. https://www.vox.com/2018/7/9/17525860/nazis-russell-walker-arthur-jones-republicans-illinois-north-carolina-virginia.

Coates, Ta-Nehisi. 2014. "The Case for Reparations." *The Atlantic*. June. https://www.theatlantic.com/magazine/archive/2014/06/the-case-for-reparations/361631/.

Cobb, Jelani. 2018. "Voter-Suppression Tactics in the Age of Trump." *New Yorker*, October 22. https://www.newyorker.com/magazine/2018/10/29/voter-suppression-tactics-in-the-age-of-trump.

Cohn, D'Vera. 2014. "Millions of Americans Changed Their Racial or Ethnic Identity from One Census to the Next." *Pew Research Center*, May 5. https://www.pewresearch.org/fact-tank/2014/05/05/millions-of-americans-changed-their-racial-or-ethnic-identity-from-one-census-to-the-next/.

Cokely, Kevin. 2020. "Descendants-of-Slavery Movement Undermines the Spirit of Black History Month." *UT News*, February 24. https://news.utexas.edu/2020/02/24/descendants-of-slavery-movement-undermines-the-spirit-of-black-history-month/.

Collins, Patricia Hill. 2021. "Gender, Race and American National Identity: The First Black First Family." In *Why Gender?*, edited by Jude Browne. Cambridge: Cambridge University Press. Online October 15. https://www.cambridge.org/core/books/why-gender/gender-race-and-american-national-identity-the-first-black-first-family/.

Colonialism Reparations. 2019. "Reparations for Colonialism Are Mandatory." November 19. https://www.colonialismreparation.org/en/newsletter-11-19-reparations-for-colonialism-are-mandatory.html.

Community Change. n.d. "Immigrant Rights." Last accessed September 4, 2023. https://communitychange.org/portfolio/immigrant-rights/.

Confessore, Nicholas. 2016. "For Whites Sensing Decline, Donald Trump Unleashes Words of Resistance." *New York Times*, July 14, A1.

Conroy, Meredith, and Perry Bacon Jr. 2020. "White Democrats Are Wary of Big Ideas to Address Racial Inequality." *FiveThirtyEight*, July 14. https://fivethirtyeight.com/features/white-democrats-are-wary-of-big-ideas-to-address-racial-inequality/.

Conservative Partnership Institute. 2023 "We Provide the Support Conservatives Need." Last accessed September 4, 2023. https://www.cpi.org/about/.

Cooper, A. D. 2012. "From Slavery to Genocide: The Fallacy of Debt in Reparations Discourse." *Journal of Black Studies* 43: 107–26.

Cooper, Matthew. 2022. "Why Did Democrats Do So Well in the Midterms?" *Washington Monthly*, November 11. https://washingtonmonthly.com/2022/11/11/why-did-democrats-do-so-well-in-the-midterms/.

Corasaniti, Nick. 2021. "Republicans Target Voter Access in Texas Cities, But Not Rural Areas." *New York Times*, May 30. https://www.nytimes.com/2021/04/24/us/politics/texas-republicans-voting.html.

Corasaniti, Nick, and Alexandra Berzon. 2023. "Under the Radar, Right-Wing Push to Tighten Voting Laws Persists." *New York Times*, May 8. https://www.nytimes.com/2023/05/08/us/politics/voting-laws-restrictions-republicans.html.

Corasaniti, Nick, and Reid Epstein. 2021. "Map by Map, G.O.P. Erasing Black Districts." *New York Times*, December 19, A1.

Cotter, Holland. 2020. "Where 'Horrible Cruelties' Can No Longer Hide." *New York Times*, August 17, A1.

Counter Extremism Project. 2023a. "Far-Left Extremist Groups in the United States." Last accessed September 5, 2023. https://www.counterextremism.com/content/far-left-extremist-groups-united-states.

Counter Extremism Project. 2023b. "Black Bloc." Last accessed September 5, 2023. https://www.counterextremism.com/supremacy/black-bloc.

Covert, Bryce. 2018. "The Not-So-Subtle Racism of Trump Era 'Welfare Reform.'" *New York Times*, May 23. https;//www.nytimes.com/2018/05/23/opinion/trump-welfare-reform-racism.html.

Cox, Oliver Cromwell. 1959. *Caste, Class and Race: A Study in Social Dynamics*. New York: Monthly Review Press. First published 1948 by Doubleday & Co. (New York).

CPAC Hungary. 2023. "Speakers." Last accessed September 5, 2023. https://www.cpachungary.com/en/speakers.

Crampton, Liz. 2021. "States Passed 243 Policing Bills." *Politico*, May 26. https://www.politico.com/news/2021/05/26/states-policing-bills.

Crary, David. 2020. "More US Churches Are Committing to Racism-Linked Reparations." *AP News*, December 13.

Craven, Julia, and Tyler Tynes. 2016. "The Racist Roots of Flint's Water Crisis." *Huffington Post*, March 3. https://www.huffpost.com/entry/racist-roots-of-flints-water-crisis.

Crenzel, Emilio. 2008. "Argentina's National Commission on the Disappearance of Persons: Contributions to Transitional Justice." *International Journal of Transitional Justice* 2 (2): 173–91.

Crimaldi, Laura, Dugan Arnett, and Amanda Milkovitz. 2022. "The White-Nationalist Patriot Front Is Getting Bigger, and More Visible, in New England." *Boston Globe*, July 23. https://www.bostonglobe.com/2022/07/23/metro/far-right-patriot-front-is-getting-bigger-more-visible-new-england.

CTCT (Change Today, Change Tomorrow). 2023. "About CTCT." Last accessed September 5, 2023. https://change-today.org/about-us/.

Cullors, Patrisse. 2020. "Black Lives Matter Began After Trayvon Martin's Death. Ferguson Showed Its Staying Power." *NBC News: Think*, January 1. https://www.nbcnews.com/think/opinion/black-lives-matter-began-after-trayvon-martin-s-death-ferguson.

Curry, Tommy J. 2011. "The Political Economy of Reparations: An Anti-Ethical Consideration of Atonement and Racial Reconciliation under Colonial Moralism." *Race, Gender & Class* 18: 125–46.

Curry, Thomas J. 2021. "Must There Be an Empirical Basis for the Theorization of

Racialized Subjects in Race-Gender Theory?" *Proceedings of the Aristotelian Society* 121, part 1: 21–44.

Daly, Matthew. 2021. "In a First, Congress Overrides Trump Veto of Defense Bill." *AP News*, January 1. https://apnews.com/article/election-2020-donald-trump-defense-policy-bills.

Dawkins, Ryan, and Abigail Hanson. 2022. "'American' Is the Eye of the Beholder: American Identity, Racial Sorting, and Affective Polarization among White Americans." *Political Behavior*, December 4. https://doi.org/10.1007/s11109-022-09834-x.

Darity, William A., Jr. 2016. "How Barack Obama Failed Black Americans." *The Atlantic*, December 22. https://www.theatlantic.com/politics/archive/2016/12/how-barack-obama-failed-black-americans.

Darity, William A., Jr., and A. Kirsten Mullen. 2020. *From Here to Equality: Reparations for Black Americans in the Twenty-First Century*. Chapel Hill: University of North Carolina Press.

Davies, Elizabeth Jordon. 2021. *From Adherents to Activism: The Process of Social Movement Mobilization*. PhD diss., University of Chicago.

Davis, Elliott, Jr. 2020. "US Elections Compare Poorly to Other Democracies." *US News*, October 7. https://www.usnews.com/news/best-countries/articles/2020-10-07/us-elections-compare-poorly-to-other-democracies-research-shows.

Davis, Julie Hirschfeld, and Maggie Haberman. 2017. "Trump Pardons Ex-Sheriff Seen as Migrant Foe." *New York Times*, August 6, A1.

Davis, Michael L., and Kathy J. Hayes. 1990. "Efficiency and Inefficiency in Texas Public Schools." *Texas Public Policy Foundation*, March. https://www.texaspolicy.com/wp-content/uploads/2018/08/1990-03-sf-efficiency.pdf.

Dawson, Michael C. 2016. "Debate: Hidden in Plain Sight: A Note on Legitimation Crises and the Racial Order." *Critical Historical Studies* 3 (1): 143–61.

Dawson, Michael C., and Megan Ming Francis. 2016. "Black Politics and the Neoliberal Racial Order." *Public Culture* 28 (1 [78]): 23–62.

Dazey, Margot. 2021. "Rethinking Respectability Politics." *British Journal of Sociology* 72: 580–93.

DBRC (Denver Black Reparations Council). n.d. "Mission of DBRC." Last accessed September 5, 2023. https://denverblackreparationscouncil.org/mission-of-dbrc/.

DeBonis, Mike. 2021. "Senate Republicans Block Debate on Elections Bill, Dealing Blow to Democrats' Voting Rights Push." *Washington Post*, June 22. https://www.washingtonpost.com/politics/senate-voting-rights-bill/2021/06/22/d63f6a46-d35a-11eb-ae54-515e2f63d37d_story.html.

Delgado, Richard, and Jean Stefancic. 2017. *Critical Race Theory: An Introduction*. Third edition. New York: New York University Press.

DeMuth, Christopher. 2021. "Why America Needs National Conservatism." *Wall*

Street Journal, November 12. https://www.wsj.com/articles/national-conservatism-socialist-progressives-woke-crt-patriotism-social-media-border.

Derenoncourt, Ellora. 2022. "Can You Move to Opportunity? Evidence from the Great Migration." *American Economic Review* 112: 369–408.

Desai, Sahil. 2019. "The First Reparations Attempt at an American College Comes from Its Students." *The Atlantic*, April 18. https://www.theatlantic.com/education/archive/2019/04/why-are-georgetown-students-paying-reparations/587443/.

DeSante, Christopher D., and Candis Watts Smith. 2020. *Racial Stasis: The Millennial Generation and the Stagnation of Racial Attitudes in American Politics*. Chicago: University of Chicago Press.

Desjardins, Lisa. 2017. "How Trump Talks About Race." *PBS News Hour*, August 22. https://www.pbs.org/newshour/politics/every-moment-donald-trumps-long-complicated-history-race.

Devos, Thierry, and Hafsa Mohamed. 2014. "Shades of American Identity: Implicit Relations between Ethnic and National Identities." *Social and Personality Psychology Compass* 8: 739–54.

De Vynck, Gerrit, and Ellen Nakashima. 2021. "Far-Right Groups Move Conversations from Social Media to Chat Apps—And Out of View of Law Enforcement." *Washington Post*, January 18. https://www.washingtonpost.com/technology/2021/01/15/parler-telegram-chat-apps/.

Dias, Elizabeth. 2017. "President Trump Lost a Fight to Allow Churches to Get More Involved in Politics." *Time*, December 15. https://time.com/5067035/president-trump-lost-a-fight-to-allow-churches-to-get-more-involved-in-politics/.

Dias, Elizabeth. 2022. "On the Far Right, Devout Efforts to Get Elected." *New York Times*, July 9, A1.

Diversify Our Narrative. n.d. "About Us." Last accessed September 5, 2023. https://www.diversifyournarrative.com/about-us.

Dixon, Matt, and Gary Fineout. 2022. "DeSantis Wins Big, with an Eye Toward 2024." *Politico*, November 8. https://www.politico.com/news/2022/11/08/florida-governor-2022-ron-desantis-charlie-crist-00065788.

Dodds, Graham G. 2021. *Mass Pardons in America: Rebellion, Presidential Amnesty and Reconciliation*. New York: Columbia University Press.

Donald J. Trump for President. 2020. "The Platinum Plan." https://cdn.donaldjtrump.com/public-files/press_assets/president-trump-platinum-plan-final-version.pdf.

Downey, Caroline. 2022. "President Biden's 2023 Budget Increases Funding for Police." *National Review*, March 28. https://www.nationalreview.com/news/president-bidens-2023-budget-increases-funding-for-police/.

Du Bois, W. E. B. 1920. *Darkwater: Voices from within the Veil*. New York: Harcourt, Brace, and Howe.

Du Bois, W. E. B. 1935. *Black Reconstruction in America*. New York: Harcourt Brace.

Dugan, Andrew. 2015. "Among Republicans, GOP Candidates Better Known Than

Liked." *Gallup: Politics*, July 24. https://news.gallup.com/poll/184337/among-republicans-gop-candidates-better-known-than%20-liked.

Dunbar-Ortiz, Roxanne. 2021. *Not a "Nation of Immigrants": Settler Colonialism, White Supremacy, and a History of Erasure and Exclusion*. Boston: Beacon Press.

Dunst, Charles. 2023. *Defeating the Dictators: How Democracy Can Prevail in the Age of the Strongman*. London: Hodder and Stoughton.

Durr, Barbara. 2021. "Black Home Ownership and the Promise of Reparations." *Blue Ridge Public Radio News*, February 25. https://www.bpr.org/news/2021-02-25/black-home-ownership-and-the-promise-of-reparations.

Dwoskin, Elizabeth. 2022. "Peter Thiel Helped Build Big Tech. Now He Wants to Tear It All Down." *Washington Post*, June 19. https://www.washingtonpost.com/technology/2022/06/19/peter-thiel-facebook-new-right/.

Eagle Forum. 2023. "STOP Racist Critical Race Theory!" Last accessed September 5, 2023. https://eagleforum.org/petitions/stop-racist-critical-race-theory.html.

Ebbs, Stephanie. 2019. "Georgetown University Announces Reparations Fund to Benefit Descendants of Slaves Once Sold by the School." *ABC News*, October 30. https://abcnews.go.com/Politics/georgetown-university-announces-reparations-fund-benefit-descendants-slaves/.

Eberhardt, Jennifer L. 2019. *Biased: Uncovering the Hidden Prejudice That Shapes What We See, Think and Do*. New York: Viking.

Ecarma, Caleb. 2022. "'We Will Get Destroyed': Evangelicals Are Quietly Ditching Donald Trump's 2024 Bid." *Vanity Fair*, December 21. https://www.vanityfair.com/news/2022/12/evangelicals-donald-trump-2024.

Economic Security Project. 2023. "Guaranteed Income: It's More Than a Check, It's the Freedom Everyone Deserves." Last accessed September 5, 2023. https://economicsecurityproject.org/work/guaranteed-income/.

Eder, Steve, and David D. Kirkpatrick. 2021. "D.A.s Reopen Police Killings of Years Past." *New York Times*, December 1, A1.

Edmondson, Catie. 2022. "At the Capitol on Jan. 6, They Hope to Go Back as Members of Congress." *New York Times*, September 3, A13.

Edmondson, Catie, and Luke Broadwater. 2020. "Showdown Brewing over Military Base Names." *New York Times*, November 19, A20.

Edmund Burke Foundation. 2023a. "About." Last accessed September 5, 2023. https://nationalconservatism.org/about/.

Edmund Burke Foundation. 2023b. "National Conservatism: A Statement of Principles." June 15. Last accessed September 5, 2023. https://nationalconservatism.org/national-conservatism-a-statement-of-principles/.

Edwards-Levy, Ariel. 2016. "Nearly Half of Trump Voters Think Whites Face a Lot of Discrimination." *Huffington Post*, November 21. https://www.huffpost.com/entry/discrimination-race-religion.

Einbinder, Nicole. 2019. "The Trump Administration Has Actually Cut Government Resources to Fight White Supremacy and Domestic Terrorism." *Business

Insider, August 6. https://www.businessinsider.com/trump-cut-resources-fight-white-supremacy-domestic-terrorism-2019-8.

Equal Justice Initiative. n.d. "The National Memorial for Peace and Justice." Last accessed September 5, 2023. https://museumandmemorial.eji.org/memorial.

Elam, Stephanie, and Jason Kravarik. 2020. "Black Lives Matter's Surprising Target: Los Angeles County's First Black District Attorney." *CNN*, July 15. https://www.cnn.com/2020/07/10/us/jackie-lacey-la-da-black-lives-matter/index.html.

Elbein, Saul. 2023. "GOP Legislatures Battle for Power with Democratic Cities: Three Flashpoints." *The Hill*, April 7. https://thehill.com/homenews/state-watch/3937969-3-flashpoints-in-the-power-struggle-between-gop-led-state-legislatures-and-democratic-cities/.

Electoral Justice Project. 2023. "Founders & Leaders." Last accessed September 5, 2023. https://electoraljusticeproject.org/.

Ellmers, Glenn. 2021. "'Conservatism' Is No Longer Enough." *The American Mind*, March 24. https://americanmind.org/salvo/why-the-claremont-institute-is-not-conservative-and-you-shouldnt-be-either/.

Empower Mississippi. 2023."Drive Innovation by Trusting Educators." Last accessed September 5, 2023. https://empowerms.org/education/.

Episcopal Diocese of Long Island. 2019. "Diocese of Long Island Designates Funds for Reparations and Relief Efforts." November 20. https://www.dioceseli.org/media/diocesan-news/diocese-of-long-island-designates-funds-for-reparations-and-reli.html.

Episcopal Diocese of Long Island. 2021. "Reparations Committee." https://www.episcopaldioceseli.org/diocese-organizations/reparations/index.html.

Epstein, Reid J., and Patricia Mazzei. 2021. "GOP Bill Targets Protesters." *New York Times*, April 21. https://www.nytimes.com/2021/04/21/us/politics/republican-anti-protest-laws.html.

Estep, Tyler. 2022. "Promised Changes to Confederate Imagery at Stone Mountain Slow Coming." *Atlanta Journal-Constitution*, September 6. https://www.ajc.com/neighborhoods/dekalb/promised-changes-to-confederate-imagery-at-stone-mountain-slow-coming/.

Ewall-Wice, Sarah. 2022. "Democrats Defend Every State Legislative Chamber in Their Control This Year." *CBS News*, November 21. https://www.cbsnews.com/news/2022-midterm-elections-democrats-state-legislatures/.

Fadula, Lola, and Glenn Thrush. 2019. "Democrats Angered by HUD's Hiring of Trump Aide Who Quit After Racist Posts." *New York Times*, July 1. https://www.nytimes.com/2019/07/01/us/politics/trump-aide-racism.html.

Fausset, Richard, and Tariro Mzezewa. 2022. "He Cried, from Seeing 'So Much Hatred.'" *New York Times*, March 3. https://www.nytimes.com/2022/03/01/us/arbery-trial-juror-marcus-ransom.html.

Fausset, Richard, and Michael Wines. 2018. "On Hunt for Illegal Voters, U.S. Subpoenas Election Data in North Carolina." *New York Times*, September 6, A16.

Felton, Emmanuel. 2017. "How the Federal Government Abandoned the *Brown v. Board of Education* Decision." *Hechinger Report*, September 6. http://hechingerreport.org/how-the-federal-government-abandoned-the-brown-v-board-of-education-decision/.

Felton, Emmanuel. 2023a. "What to Know about California's Reparations Proposal for Black Americans." *Washington Post*, May 8. https://www.washingtonpost.com/nation/2023/05/08/california-reparations-black-americans-explained/.

Felton, Emmanuel. 2023b. "Rep. Cori Bush Introduces Resolution on Reparations for Black Americans." *Washington Post*, May 17. https://www.washingtonpost.com/nation/2023/05/17/cori-bush-black-reparations-bill/.

Fergus, Devin. 2018. *Land of the Fee*. New York: Oxford University Press.

Feuer, Alan. 2022a. "Jan. 6 Inquiry Turns Its Focus to New Group." *New York Times*, January 4, A1.

Feuer, Alan. 2022b. "Sedition Trial of Oath Keepers to Get Underway." *New York Times*, September 27. https://www.nytimes.com/2022/09/27/us/jan-6-oath-keepers-trial.html.

Feuer, Alan. 2023. "After Jan. 6 Sedition Convictions, Far-Right Threats Remain." *New York Times*, May 5. https://www.nytimes.com/2023/05/05/us/politics/jan-6-sedition-proud-boys-far-right.html.

Feuer, Alan, and Zach Montague. 2023. "Four Proud Boys Convicted of Sedition in Key Jan. 6 Case." *New York Times*, May 4. https://www.nytimes.com/2023/05/04/us/politics/jan-6-proud-boys-sedition.html.

Feuer, Alan, Michael S. Schmidt, and Luke Broadwater. 2022. "New Focus on How a Trump Tweet Incited Far-Right Groups Ahead of Jan. 6." *New York Times*, March 29. https://www.nytimes.com/2022/03/29/us/politics/trump-tweet-jan-6.html.

Fields, Barbara Jeanne. 1990. "Slavery, Race and Ideology in the United States." *New Left Review* 181 (May/June): 95–118.

Fies, Andy. 2020. "Evanston, Illinois Finds Innovative Solution to Funding Reparations: Marijuana Sales Taxes." *ABC News*, July 19. https://abcnews.go.com/US/evanston-illinois-finds-innovative-solution-funding-reparations-marijuana/.

File, Nate. 2023. "Philly Faith Leaders Meet to Study How Reparations Could Work." *Philadelphia Inquirer*, January 9, B1, B10.

Fioretos, Orfeo, Tulia G. Falleti, and Adam Sheingate, eds. 2016. *The Oxford Handbook of Historical Institutionalism*. New York: Oxford University Press.

Fisher, Anthony L. 2020. "The ADL's Statistics Make It Seem like Ultra-Right Wing Violence in the US Is More Common Than It Actually Is." *BusinessInsider.com*, April 24. https://www.businessinsider.com/adl-extremism-ultraright-wing-violence-statistics-anti-defamation-league-2020-4.

Fisher, Dana R., and Stella M Rouse. 2022. "Intersectionality within the Racial Justice Movement in the Summer of 2020." *PNAS* 119 (30): 1–6.

Fisher, Max. 2022. "Long Road Ahead for Colonial Reparations." *New York Times*, August 27. https://www.nytimes.com/2022/08/27/world/americas/colonial-reparations.html.

Fitzgerald, Sandy. 2021. "Brooke Rollins to Newsmax: Trump's Big Tech Suit Case of 'David Suing Goliath.'" *Newsmax*, July 8. https://www.newsmax.com/politics/brooke-rollins-trump-lawyers-big-tech/2021/07/08/id/1027911.

Flaherty, Colleen. 2021. "Legislating against Critical Race Theory." *Inside Higher Ed*, June 9. https://www.insidehighered.com/news/2021/06/09/legislating-against-critical-race-theory-curricular-implications-some-states.

Flitter, Emily. 2022. "Anatomy of a $30 Billion Pledge to Close the Wealth Gap." *New York Times*, October 21. https://www.nytimes.com/2022/10/21/business/jp-morgan-racial-equity-pledge.html.

Flores, Adolfo, and Alex Leary. 2023. "Thousands Attend Trump Rally in Waco, Texas, as Potential Indictment Looms." *Wall Street Journal*, March 25. https://www.wsj.com/articles/thousands-attend-trump-rally-in-waco-texas-as-potential-indictment-looms-41a3fdf8.

Flowers, Catherine, and Mitchell Bernard. 2021. "Racism That Spews Into Your Sink." *New York Times*, August 26, A23.

Fonger, Ron. 2020. "Genesee County Board of Health Declares Racism a Public Health Crisis." *MLive*, June 4. https://www.mlive.com/news/flint/2020/06/genesee-county-board-of-health-declares-racism-a-public-health-crisis.html.

Fortin, Jacey. 2018. "U.N.C. Chancellor Apologizes for History of Slavery at Chapel Hill." *New York Times*, October 13. https://www.nytimes.com/2018/10/13/us/unc-carolina-apologize-slavery.html.

Fortner, Michael Javen. 2023. "Racial Capitalism and City Politics: Toward a Theoretical Synthesis." *Urban Affairs Review* 39 (2): 630–53.

Fox, Ben. 2020. "Trump Leaves His Mark on Immigration." *APNews*, December 30. https://apnews.com/article/joe-biden-donald-trump-politics-immigration-united-states.

Fox, Ben. 2021. "DOJ Withdraws from Negotiated Settlement with Separated Families, Will Litigate Each Case." *PBS News Hour*, December 16. https://www.pbs.org/newshour/politics/doj-withdraws-from-settlement-negotiations-with-separated-families-will-litigate-each-case.

Francis, Megan Ming. 2014. *Civil Rights and the Making of the Modern American State*. New York: Cambridge University Press.

Francis, Megan Ming. 2019. "The Price of Civil Rights: Black Lives, White Funding, and Movement Capture." *Law and Society Review* 53 (1): 275–309.

Francis, Megan Ming. 2022. "Can Black Lives Matter in U.S. Democracy?" *Annals of the American Academy of Political and Social Science* 699 (1): 186–99.

Francis, Megan Ming, and Leah Wright-Rigueur. 2021. "Black Lives Matter in Historical Perspective." *Annual Review of Law and Social Science* 17: 441–58.

Francis, Theo, and Lauren Weber. 2023. "The Legal Assault on Corporate Diversity Efforts Has Begun." *Wall Street Journal*, August 8. https://www.wsj.com/articles/diversity-equity-dei-companies-blum-2040b173.

Frank, Stephen. 2022. "California's Reparations Plan Would Spend Almost Double the State's Entire Budget on Race-Based Handouts." *California Political Review*, December 4. https://capoliticalreview.com/capoliticalnewsandviews/californias-reparations-plan-would-spend-almost-double-the-states-entire-budget-on-race-based-handouts.

Franke, Katherine. 2019. *Repair: Redeeming the Promise of Abolition*. Chicago: Haymarket Books.

Fraser, Nancy. 2016. "Expropriation and Exploitation in Racialized Capitalism: A Reply to Michael Dawson." *Critical Historical Studies* 3 (1): 163–78.

Freedom Conservatism. 2023. "Freedom Conservatism: A Statement of Principles," July 13. https://www.freedomconservatism.org/p/freedom-conservatism-a-statement.

FreedomWorks. 2022. "Curriculum." https://www.freedomworks.org/issue/curriculum/.

Freking, Kevin. 2021a. "Biden Backs Studying Reparations as Congress Considers Bill." *AP News*, February 17. https://apnews.com/congress-e3c045ece4d0e0eae393a18a09a4a37e.

Freking, Kevin. 2021b. "House Panel Votes to Advance Bill on Slavery Reparations." *AP News*, April 14. https://apnews.com/article/race-and-ethnicity-discrimination-legislation-slavery-john-conyers.

Frenkel, Sheera. 2021. "After Capitol, Proud Boys Quietly Shift Focus to Schools and Town Halls." *New York Times*, December 15, A12.

Friedersdorf, Conor. 2023. "Why California Rejected Racial Preferences, Again." *The Atlantic*, November 10. https://www.theatlantic.com/ideas/archive/2020/11/why-california-rejected-affirmative-action-again/617049/.

Friedland, Roger, and Robert R. Alford. 1991. "Bringing Society Back In: Symbols, Practices, and Institutional Contradictions." In *The New Institutionalism in Organizational Analysis*, edited by Walter W. Powell and Paul J. DiMaggio, 232–67. Chicago: University of Chicago Press.

Friedman, Gillian. 2020. "Here's What Companies Are Promising to Do to Fight Racism." *New York Times*, August 23. https://www.nytimes.com/article/companies-racism-george-floyd-protests.html.

Frum, David. 2022. "Only the GOP Celebrates Political Violence." *The Atlantic*, October 29. https://www.theatlantic.com/ideas/archive/2022/10/pelosi-republicans-partisan-political-violence/671934/.

Frymer, Paul. 1999. *Uneasy Alliances: Race and Party Competition in America*. Princeton, NJ: Princeton University Press.

Frymer, Paul. 2014. "'A Rush and a Push and the Land Is Ours': Territorial

Expansion, Land Policy, and U.S. State Formation." *Perspectives on Politics* 12: 119–44.
Frymer, Paul, and Jacob M. Grumbach. 2021. "Labor Unions and White Racial Politics." *American Journal of Political Science* 65: 225–40.
Funders for Justice. 2012–2021. "Home." Last accessed September 5, 2023. https://fundersforjustice.org/.
Furman Center. 2018. "Policy Minute: HUD Delays Critical Fair Housing Requirement." March 9. http://furmancenter.org/thestoop/entry/policy-minute-hud-delays-critical-fair-housing-requirement.
Furman Center. 2019. "Leading Housing Researchers Challenge Proposed Fair Housing Rule Change." Press release, October 17. https://furmancenter.org/news/press-release/leading-housing-researchers-challenge-proposed-fair-housing-rule-change.
Gabriel, Trip, Maya King, Kurtis Lee, and Shawn Hubler. 2023. "Reparations Are a Financial Quandary. For Democrats, They're a Political One, Too." *New York Times*, May 27. https://www.nytimes.com/2023/05/27/us/politics/reparations-democrats-black-americans.html.
Gaiter, Colette. 2015. "From the Black Panthers to Black Lives Matter." *The Gradient*, December 10. http://walkerart.org/magazine/emory-douglas-black-lives-matter.
Gambino, Lauren. 2020. "Calls for reparations are growing louder. How is the US responding?" *The Guardian*, June 20. https://www.theguardian.com/world/2020/jun/20/joe-biden-reparations-slavery-george-floyd-protests.
Garcia, Jennifer R., and Christopher T. Stout. 2019. "Responding to Racial Resentment: How Racial Resentment Influences Legislative Behavior." *Political Research Quarterly* 73 (4). https://doi.org/10.1177/1065912919857826.
Garcia, Karen, and Jon Healey. 2021. "Biden Administration Wants to Recreate DACA through New Federal Rule." *Los Angeles Times*, November 9. https://www.latimes.com/california/story/2021-11-09/biden-administration-wants-to-re-create-daca-through-new-federal-rule-what-does-that-mean.
García, Uriel J. 2022. "DACA Remains Intact as Appeals Court Sends Case Challenging Its Legality Back to Lower Court in Texas." *Texas Tribune*, Austin, TX, October 5. https://www.texastribune.org/2022/10/05/texas-daca-appeals-court-ruling/.
Garcia-Navarro, Lulu. 2019. "Stephen Miller and 'the Camp of the Saints,' a White Nationalist Reference." *NPR News*, November 19. https://www.npr.org/2019/11/19/780552636/stephen-miller-and-the-camp-of-the-saints-a-white-nationalist-reference.
Gardner, Amy. 2022. "A Majority of GOP Nominees Deny or Question the 2020 Election Results." *Washington Post*, October 12. https://www.washingtonpost.com/nation/2022/10/06/elections-deniers-midterm-elections-2022/.

Gardner, Amy, Todd Hamburger, and Josh Dawsey. 2021. "Trump Works to Place Key Allies in Key Election Posts across the Country." *Washington Post*, November 28. https://www.washingtonpost.com/politics/trump-allies-election-oversight/2021/11/28/.

Garland, David. 2022. "The Current Crisis of American Criminal Justice: A Structural Analysis." *Annual Review of Criminology* 6. https://doi.org/10.1146/annurev-criminol-030722-035139.

Garrett, R. Sam. 2021. "The State of Campaign Finance Policy: Recent Developments and Issues for Congress." *Congressional Research Service*, February 23. https://sgp.fas.org/crs/misc/R41542.pdf.

Garrett-Scott, Shenette. 2021. "What Price Wholeness?" *New York Review of Books*, February 11. https://www.nybooks.com/articles/2021/02/11/what-price-wholeness/.

Garrick, David. 2022. "$500 a Month, No Strings Attached: Guaranteed Income Comes to San Diego with Three Experimental Programs." *San Diego Union-Tribune*, October 2. https://www.sandiegouniontribune.com/news/politics/story/2022-10-02/guaranteed-income-pilot-programs.

Gartland, Michael, and Denis Slattery. 2022. "NYC Mayor Adams Backs Renewed Push for Reparations Bill in Albany." *New York Daily News*, December 8. https://www.nydailynews.com/news/politics/new-york-elections-government/ny-mayor-adams-reparations-albany-legislation.

Gentleman, Amelia. 2023. "Descendants of Slavers to Lobby for Reparations." *The Guardian*, April 24. https://www.magzter.com/stories/newspaper/The-Guardian/DESCENDANTS-OF-SLAVERS-TO-LOBBY-FOR-REPARATIONS.

Gersen, Jeannie Suk. 2023. "The Supreme Court Overturns Fifty Years of Precedent on Affirmative Action." *New Yorker*, June 29. https://www.newyorker.com/news/daily-comment/the-supreme-court-overturns-fifty-years-of-precedent-on-affirmative-action.

Gerstle, Gary. 2022. *The Rise and Fall of the Neoliberal Order*. New York: Oxford University Press.

Gest, Justin. 2016. *The New Minority: White Working Class Politics in an Age of Immigration and Inequality*. New York: Oxford University Press.

Gest, Justin, Tyler Reny, and Jeremy Mayer. 2018. "Roots of the Radical Right: Nostalgic Deprivation in the United States and Britain." *Comparative Political Studies* 51: 1694–1719.

Ghavami, Negin, and Letitia Anne Peplau. 2012. "An Intersectional Analysis of Gender and Ethnic Stereotypes: Testing Three Hypotheses." *Psychology of Women Quarterly* 37 (1): 113–27.

Gilens, Martin. 1999. *Why Americans Hate Welfare: Race, Media, and the Politics of Antipoverty Policy*. Chicago: University of Chicago Press.

Gillion, Daniel Q. 2012. "Protest and Congressional Behavior: Assessing Racial and Ethnic Minority Protests in the District." *Journal of Politics* 74: 950–62.

Gillion, Daniel Q. 2013. *The Political Power of Protest: Minority Activism and Shifts in Public Policy*. New York: Cambridge University Press.

Gillion, Daniel Q. 2016. *Governing with Words: The Political Dialogue on Race, Public Policy and Inequality in America*. New York: Cambridge University Press.

Gillion, Daniel Q. 2020. "The Myth of the Silent Majority." *The Atlantic*, July 30. https://www.theatlantic.com/magazine/archive/2020/09/protest-works/614182/.

Girvan, M., and M. E. J. Newman. 2002. "Community Structure in Social and Biological Networks." *PNAS* 99 (12): 7821–26.

Gittelson, Ben. 2020. "Trump Says No Defunding, Dismantling, or Disbanding of Police." *ABC News*, June 8. https://abcnews.go.com/Politics/trump-defunding-dismantling-disbanding-police/.

Gladstone, Rick, and Satoshi Sugiyama. 2018. "Trump's Travel Ban: How It Works and Who Is Affected." *New York Times*, July 2, A8.

Glover, Julian. 2022. "Noncitizen Voting Rights Gain Traction as Immigrants Vote in SF Unified School Board Recall Election." *ABC7 News*, February 11. https://abc7news.com/noncitizen-voting-san-francisco-recall-election-rights-jose/.

Goble, Danney, compiler. 2022. "Final Report of the Oklahoma Commission to Study the Tulsa Race Riot of 1921." https://tulsareparations.z19.web.core.windows.net/FinalReport.htm.

Goffard, Christopher. 2023. "John Eastman's Bar Trial Resumes, a Week After He Was Indicted with Trump and Others." *Los Angeles Times*, August 22. https://news.yahoo.com/john-eastmans-bar-trial-resumes-100043053.html.

Goldberg, David Theo. 2002. *The Racial State*. New York: Wiley.

Goldberg, Emma. 2020. "How Reparations for Slavery Became a 2020 Campaign Issue." *New York Times*, June 18. https://www.nytimes.com/2020/06/18/us/politics/reparations-slavery.html.

Goldberg, Jonah. 2023. "The Ties That Blind." *The Dispatch*, April 7. https://thedispatch.com/newsletter/gfile/the-ties-that-blind/.

Goldberg, Michelle. 2020. "The Midterm Race That Has It All." *New York Times*, September 24. https://www.nytimes.com/2022/09/24/opinion/house-republican-elections.html.

Goldberg, Michelle. 2023. "Plotting the Hostile Takeover of a Liberal College." *New York Times*, January 10, A19.

Golden, Dan. 2023. "Muzzled by DeSantis, Critical Race Theory Professors Cancel Courses or Modify Their Teaching." *ProPublica*, January 3. https://www.propublica.org/article/desantis-critical-race-theory-florida-college-professors.

Goldman, Adam, Katie Benner, and Alan Feuer. 2021. "Right-Wing Extremists under Rising Scrutiny in Capitol Riot Inquiry." *New York Times*, January 19, A16.

Goldwater Institute. 2023a. "About." https://www.goldwaterinstitute.org/about/.

Goldwater Institute. 2023b. "Issues: Education." https://www.goldwaterinstitute.org/issues/education/.

Golembeski, Dean. 2021. "Washington and Lee Keeps Name, Black Alumni React." *BestColleges*, November 10. https://www.goldwaterinstitute.org/issues/education/.

Golub, Mark. 2018. *Is Racial Equality Unconstitutional?* New York: Oxford University Press.

Gómez, Laura E. 2020. *Inventing Latinos: A New Story of American Racism*. New York: New Press.

Gomez, Melissa. 2021. "L.A. School Board Cuts Its Police Force and Diverts Funds for Black Student Achievement." *Los Angeles Times*, February 16. https://www.latimes.com/california/story/2021-02-16/lausd-diverting-school-police-funds-support-black-students.

Gonyea, Don. 2017. "Majority of White Americans Say They Believe Whites Face Discrimination." *NPR Newscast*, October 24. https://www.npr.org/2017/10/24/559604836/majority-of-white-americans-think-theyre-discriminated-against.

Gonyea, Don. 2020. "After Threatening to Derail It, Trump Signs Covid 19 Relief Package into Law." *NPR*, December 27. https://www.npr.org/2020/12/27/950687654/after-threatening-to-derail-it-trump-signs-covid-19-relief-package-into-law.

Goodin, Robert E. 2013. "Disgorging the Fruits of Historical Wrongdoing." *American Political Science Review* 107: 478–91.

Goodman, Amy. 2019. "Danny Glover & Ta-Nehisi Coates Make the Case for Reparations at Historic Congressional Hearing." *Democracy Now!* July 4. https://www.democracynow.org/2019/7/4/ta_nehisi_coates_danny_glover_make.

Goodman, J. David. 2023. "Texas Republicans Push New Voting Restrictions Aimed at Houston." *New York Times*, May 10. https://www.nytimes.com/2023/05/10/us/texas-election-laws-houston-harris-county.html.

Gordon-Reed, Annette. 2021. *On Juneteenth*. New York: Liveright.

Gorka, Sebastian. 2019. "How to Win the War for America's Soul." *America First: Sebastian Gorka*, October 21. https://www.sebgorka.com/column/how-to-win-the-war-for-americas-soul.

Gorski, Philip S., and Samuel L. Perry. 2022. *The Flag + The Cross: White Christian Nationalism and the Threat to American Democracy*. New York: Oxford University Press.

Gottesman, Isaac. 2016. *The Critical Turn in Education: From Marxist Critique to Poststructuralist Feminism to Critical Theories of Race*. New York: Routledge.

Governor's Office of Tribal Affairs. 2023. "California Truth and Healing Council." https://tribalaffairs.ca.gov/cthc/.

Gramlich, John. 2020. "What the 2020 Electorate Looks like by Party, Race and Ethnicity, Age, Education, and Religion." *Pew Research Center*, October 26. https://www.pewresearch.org/short-reads/2020/10/26/what-the-2020-electorate-looks-like-by-party-race-and-ethnicity-age-education-and-religion/.

Gramlich, John. 2021. "How Trump Compares with Other Recent Presidents in Appointing Federal Judges." *Pew Research Center*, January 13. https://www

.pewresearch.org/short-reads/2021/01/13/how-trump-compares-with-other-recent-presidents-in-appointing-federal-judges/.

Grandoni, Dino. 2023. "National Audubon Society, Pressured to Remove Slave-Owning Nationalist's Name, Keeps It." *Washington Post*, March 15. https://www.washingtonpost.com/climate-environment/2023/03/15/national-audubon-society-name-change/.

Green, Erica L. 2021. "Black Lives Matter, She Wrote, Then 'Everything Just Imploded.'" *New York Times*, October 10. https://www.nytimes.com/2021/10/10/us/politics/maryland-superintendent-racism-black-lives-matter.html.

Green, Erica L., Matt Apuzzo, and Katie Benner. 2018. "Trump Officials Reverse Obama's Policy on Affirmative Action in Schools." *New York Times*, July 4, A1.

Green, Jon, and Sean McElwee. 2018. "The Differential Effects of Economic Conditions and Racial Attitudes in the Election of Donald Trump." *Perspectives on Politics* 17 (2): 358–69.

Greenfield, Nicole. 2022. "Mount Vernon: Where Environmental Injustice Became a Sewage Nightmare." *NRDC: National Resources Defense Council*, June 27. https://www.nrdc.org/stories/mount-vernon-where-environmental-injustice-became-sewage-nightmare.

Greenwood, Max. 2017. "Miller and Bannon Wrote Trump Inaugural Address: Report." *The Hill*, January 21. https://thehill.com/homenews/administration/315464-bannon-miller-wrote-trumps-inauguration-address-report/.

Grumbach, Jacob M. 2022. *Laboratories against Democracy: How National Parties Transformed State Politics*. Princeton, NJ: Princeton University Press.

Grumbach, Jacob M. 2023. "Laboratories of Democratic Backsliding." *American Political Science Review* 117 (3): 1–18.

GRF (Gelman, Rosenberg & Freeman, Auditors). 2021. "Combined Financial Statements: Center for Community Change, Fund for the Center for Community Change." March 12. https://communitychange.org/wp-content/uploads/2021/04/CCC-FCCC-2020-Combined-FS.pdf.

Guarino, Mark. 2021a. "Chicago Links Black Residents' Lower Life Expectancy to Past and Present Racism." *Washington Post*, July 7. https://www.washingtonpost.com/national/chicago-links-black-residents-lower-life-expectancy-to-past-and-present-racism/2021/07/06/.

Guarino, Mark. 2021b. "Evanston, Ill., Leads the Country with First Reparations Program for Black Residents." *Washington Post*, March 22. https://www.washingtonpost.com/national/evanston-illinois-reparations/2021/03/22/.

GuideStar. 2022. "Tides Foundation: Financials." https://www.guidestar.org/profile/51-0198509#financials.

Gutierrez, Gabe. 2018. "Sent by Trump, Soldiers Arrive at Border as Migrant Caravan in Mexico Pushes North." *NBC News*, November 3. https://www.nbcnews.com/news/us-news/sent-trump-soldiers-arrive-border-migrant-caravan-pushes-north-n930751.

Guttentag, Lucas, and Stefano M. Bertozzi. 2020. "Trump Is Using the Pandemic to Flout Immigration Laws." *New York Times*, May 11. https://www.nytimes.com/2020/05/11/opinion/trump-coronavirus-immigration.html.

Guynn, Jessica. 2023. "'Woke Mind Virus'? 'Corporate Wokeness?' Why Red America Declared War on Corporate America." *USA Today*, January 4. https://www.usatoday.com/story/money/2023/01/04/desantis-republicans-woke-big-business-war/.

Guzman, Joseph. 2020. "New Trump Order Seeks to Ban US Service Members, Federal Contractors from Diversity Training." *The Hill*, September 24. https://thehill.com/changing-america/respect/diversity-inclusion/518090-new-trump-order-seeks-to-ban-us-service-members/.

Haberman, Maggie, Jonah E. Bromwich, and William K. Rashbaum 2023. "Trump, Escalating Attacks, Raises Specter of Violence if He Is Charged." *New York Times*, March 24. https://www.nytimes.com/2023/03/24/us/politics/trump-bragg-indictment-protests.html.

Hacker, Jacob S., and Paul Pierson. 2010. *Winner-Take-All Politics: How Washington Made the Rich Richer—and Turned Its Back on the Middle Class*. New York: Simon & Schuster.

Hackett, Ursula, and Desmond King. 2019. "The Reinvention of Education Vouchers as Color-Blind: A Racial Orders Account." *Studies in American Political Development* 33: 234–57.

Hadero, Halaluya. 2021. "Mackenzie Scott Dominates Donations to Racial Equity." *AP News*, September 17. https://apnews.com/article/death-of-george-floyd-health-education-coronavirus-pandemic-race-and-ethnicity.

Hall, Kimberly. 2017. "HUD Suspends Implementation of Key Civil Rights Provision in the Voucher Program." PRRAC: Poverty & Race Research Action Council, August 15. https://www.prrac.org/press-release-august-15-2017-hud-suspends-implementation-of-key-civil-rights-provision-in-the-voucher-program/.

Hall, Peter A. 1992. "The Movement from Keynesianism to Monetarism: Institutional Analysis and British Economic Policy in the 1970s." In *Structuring Politics: Historical Institutionalism in Comparative Analysis*, edited by Sven Steinmo, Kathleen Thelen, and Frank Longstreth, 90–113. New York: Cambridge University Press.

Hall, Stuart. 1999. "From Scarman to Stephen Lawrence." *History Workshop Journal* 48: 187–97.

Hajnal, Zoltan L. 2020. *Dangerously Divided: How Race and Class Shape Winning and Losing in American Politics*. New York: Cambridge University Press.

Hanchard, Michael G. 2018. *The Specter of Race: How Discrimination Haunts Western Democracy*. Princeton, NJ: Princeton University Press.

Hancock, Ange-Marie. 2004. *The Politics of Disgust and the Public Identity of the "Welfare Queen."* New York: New York University Press.

Hancock, Ange-Marie. 2007. "When Multiplication Doesn't Equal Quick Addition:

Examining Intersectionality as a Research Paradigm." *Perspectives on Politics* 5 (1): 63–69.

Hancock, Ange-Marie. 2016. *Intersectionality: An Intellectual History*. New York: Oxford University Press.

Hannah-Jones, Nikole. 2012. "Living Apart: How the Government Betrayed a Landmark Civil Rights Law." *ProPublica*, October 29; updated June 25, 2015. https://www.propublica.org/article/living-apart-how-the-government-betrayed-a-landmark-civil-rights-law.

Hannah-Jones, Nikole. 2017. "The Resegregation of Jefferson County." *New York Times Magazine*, September 6. https://www.nytimes.com/2017/09/06/magazine/the-resegregation-of-jefferson-county.html.

Hannah-Jones, Nikole. 2020. "What Is Owed." *New York Times Magazine*, June 30. https://www.nytimes.com/interactive/2020/06/24/magazine/reparations-slavery.html.

Har, Janie. 2023. "San Francisco Board Open to Reparations with $5M Payouts." *AP News*, March 15. https://apnews.com/article/san-francisco-black-reparations-5-million.

Harley, James. 2023. "Motive in Allen Mall Mass Shooting Is 'Big Question We Don't Know,' Texas DPS Says." *Fort Worth Star-Telegram*, May 7. https://news.yahoo.com/watch-live-texas-dps-fbi-185402420.html.

Harris, Elizabeth A. 2021. "Books on Race Filled Best-Seller Lists Last Year. Publishers Took Notice." *New York Times*, September 15. https://www.nytimes.com/2021/09/15/books/new-books-race-racism-antiracism.html.

Harris, Fredrick C. 2006. "Collective Memory and Collective Action during the Civil Rights Movement." *Social Movement Studies* 5: 19–43.

Harris, Fredrick C. 2013. "Policing the Police." *London Review of Books* 35 (12), June 20. https://www.lrb.co.uk/the-paper/v35/n12/fredrick-harris/policing-the-police.

Harris, Fredrick C. 2014. "Will Ferguson Be a Moment or a Movement?" *Washington Post*, August 22. https://www.washingtonpost.com/opinions/will-ferguson-be-a-moment-or-a-movement/2014/08/22/.

Harris, Fredrick C. 2015. "The Next Civil Rights Movement?" *Dissent* 62 (3): 34–40.

Harris, Fredrick C., and Viviana Rivera-Burgos. 2021. "The Continuing Dilemma of Race and Class in the Study of American Political Behavior." *Annual Review of Political Science* 24: 175–91.

Harris, Leslie, James T. Campbell, and Alfred Brophy, eds. 2019. *Slavery and the University: Histories and Legacies*. Athens: University of Georgia Press.

Harris, Mary. 2022. "A Tiny Christian College in Michigan Is Infiltrating Florida Schools." *Slate*, September 7. https://slate.com/human-interest/2022/09/florida-school-laws-desantis-hillsdale-college-christian-michigan.html.

Hartocollis, Anemona. 2019. "Harvard Won a Key Affirmative Action Battle, but the

War's Not Over." *New York Times*, October 2. https://www.nytimes.com/2019/10/02/us/harvard-admissions-lawsuit.html.

Hartocollis, Anemona. 2023. "Acolyte of the Left Aims to Kill Race-Based College Admission." *New York Times*, March 30, A1.

Hartocollis, Anemona, and Eliza Fawcett. 2023. "Under Pressure, Board Revises AP African American Course." *New York Times*, February 2, A1, A18.

Hasen, Richard L. 2023. "John Roberts Throws a Curveball." *New York Times*, June 8. https://www.nytimes.com/2023/06/08/opinion/milligan-roberts-court-voting-right-act.html.

Hatewatch Staff. 2018. "Stephen Miller: A Driving Force behind the Muslim Ban and Family Separation Policy." *Southern Poverty Law Center*, June 21. https://www.splcenter.org/hatewatch/2018/06/21/stephen-miller-driving-force-behind-muslim-ban-and-family-separation-policy.

Hatzipanagos, Rachel. 2023. "Native Americans Call for Reparations from 'Land-Grab' Universities." *Washington Post*, July 9. https://www.washingtonpost.com/nation/2023/07/09/native-indigenous-reparations-colleges-land/.

Hauser, Christine. 2022. "Judge Allows Part of Lawsuit by Tulsa Massacre Survivors Seeking Reparations." *New York Times*, May 3. https://www.nytimes.com/2022/05/03/us/tulsa-massacre-lawsuit-reparations.html.

Hayes, Christal. 2018. "Here Are 10 Times President Trump's Comments Have Been Called Racist." *USA Today*, August 14. https://www.usatoday.com/story/news/politics/onpolitics/2018/08/14/times-president-trump-comments-called-racist/.

Hayes, Jared. 2021. "Timeline: Black Farmers and the USDA, 1920 to the Present." *Environmental Working Group*, February 1. https://www.ewg.org/research/timeline-black-farmers-and-usda-1920-present.

Hayward, Clarissa. 2013. *How Americans Make Race: Stories, Institutions, Spaces*. New York: Cambridge University Press.

Headley, Tiana. 2021. "Laws Curbing Critical Race Theory May Face Legal Challenges." *Bloomberg Law News*, July 7. https://news.bloomberglaw.com/us-law-week/laws-curbing-critical-race-theory-may-face-legal-challenges.

Heaney, Michael T. 2023. "Who Are Black Lives Matter Activists? Niche Realization in a Multimovement Environment." *Perspectives on Politics* 20: 1–24. https://doi.org/10.1017/S1537592722001281.

Henderson, Kyshia, Samuel Powers, Michele Claibourn, Jazmin L. Brown-Iannuzzi, and Sophie Trawalter. 2021. "Confederate Monuments and the History of Lynching in the American South: An Empirical Examination." *PNAS* 118 (42). https://doi.org/10.1073/pnas.2103519118.

Henry, Charles P. 2007. *Long Overdue: The Politics of Racial Reparations*. New York: New York University Press.

Heriot, Gail L. 2019. "Title VII Disparate Impact Liability Makes Almost Everything Illegal." *New York University Journal of Law & Liberty* 14: 1–170. Revised 2020, 2022. http://dx.doi.org/10.2139/ssrn.3482015.

Heritage Action for America. 2023. "About." Last accessed September 5, 2023. https://heritageaction.com/about.

Hernandez, Javier C. 2021. "Juilliard Gets $50 Million Gift for a Diversity Program." *New York Times*, December 18, C5.

Herndon, Astead W. 2018 "Accusations of Voter Suppression as Some in Georgia Begin to Cast Their Ballots." *New York Times*, October 20, A15.

Herndon, Astead W. 2019a. "For Democrats in 2020, Race-Conscious Policies Could Become a Divide." *New York Times*, February 22, A12.

Herndon, Astead W. 2019b. "'Witch Hunts' and 'Fake News': Trump Grievances Go Local." *New York Times*, March 17, A20.

Herrnstein, Richard J., and Charles Murray. 1994. *The Bell Curve: Intelligence and Class Structure in American Life*. New York: The Free Press.

Hertel-Fernandez, Alexander, Theda Skocpol, and Jason Sclar. 2018. "When Political Mega-Donors Join Forces: How the Koch Network and the Democracy Alliance Influence Organized U.S. Politics on the Right and Left." *Studies in American Political Development* 32: 127–65.

Hinton, Elizabeth. 2021. *America on Fire: The Untold History of Police Violence and Black Rebellion Since the 1960s*. New York: Liveright.

Hochschild, Arlie Russell. 2015. *Strangers in Their Own Land*. New York: New Press.

Hollis-Brusky, Amanda. 2015. *Ideas with Consequences: The Federalist Society and the Conservative Counterrevolution*. New York: Oxford University Press.

Holmes, Jack. 2017. "Trump's Disgusting Retweets Suggest a Larger Problem Is Brewing." *Esquire.com*, November 29. https://www.esquire.com/news-politics/a13974149/trump-retweet-britain-first/.

Holmes, Kristen. 2023. "Trump Calls for the Termination of the Constitution in Truth Social Post." *CNN*, December 4. https://www.cnn.com/2022/12/03/politics/trump-constitution-truth-social/index.html.

Holpuch, Amanda. 2019. "Stephen Miller: The White Supremacist at the Heart of the White House." *The Guardian*, November 24. https://www.theguardian.com/us-news/2019/nov/24/stephen-miller-white-nationalist-trump-immigration-guru.

Honosky, Sarah. 2022. "New Asheville Reparations Project Launches to Do What City, County 'Might Not Be Able to Do.'" *Asheville Citizen Times*, September 13. https://wlos.com/news/local/reparations-program-gets-annual-funding-from-buncombe-county-community-reparations-commission.

Hood, Gregory. 2019. "Western Civilization Is White Civilization." *American Renaissance*, January 21. https://www.amren.com/commentary/2019/01/western-civilization-is-white-civilization/.

Hooijer, Gerda, and Desmond King. 2022. "The Racialized Pandemic: Wave One

Covid19 and the Reproduction of Global North Inequalities." *Perspectives on Politics*, June 20, 507–27.

Hopkins, Daniel J. 2018. *The Increasingly United States: How and Why American Political Behavior Nationalized*. Chicago: University of Chicago Press.

HoSang, Daniel Martinez, and Joseph E. Lowndes. 2019. *Producers, Parasites, Patriots: Race and the New Right-Wing Politics of Precarity*. Minneapolis: University of Minnesota Press.

Howard-Hassmann, Rhoda E. 2004. "Reparations to Africa and the Group of Eminent Persons." *Cahier d'études africaines* 44 (173–74): 81–97.

Howard-Hassmann, Rhoda E. 2019. "Why Japanese-Americans Received Reparations and African Americans Are Still Waiting." *The Conversation*, July 18. https://theconversation.com/why-japanese-americans-received-reparations-and-african-americans-are-still-waiting.

Hughes, Jazmine 2023. "A Year After Buffalo: 'There's No Forgiveness for That. Ever.'" *New York Times*, May 10. https://www.nytimes.com/2023/05/10/magazine/buffalo-shooting-barbara-massey-mapps.html.

Hughey, Matthew W. 2016. "Hegemonic Whiteness: From Structure and Agency to Identity Allegiance." In *The Construction of Whiteness: An Interdisciplinary Analysis of Race Formation and the Meaning of a White Identity*, edited by Stephen Middleton, David R. Roediger, and Donald M. Shaffer, 212–33. Jackson: University Press of Mississippi.

Hunter, Brittany. 2021. "*A Primer on Critical Race Theory*: An Interview with Dr. James Lindsay." Pacific Legal Foundation, September 21. https://pacificlegal.org/a-primer-on-critical-race-theory.

Hurley, Lawrence. 2024. "On Guns, Abortion, and Voting Rights, Trump Leaves Lasting Mark on U.S. Judiciary." *Reuters*, January 15. https://www.reuters.com/article/us-usa-trump-judges-idUSKBN29K162.

Hutchinson, Harold. 2021. "CRT Opponents Win Big in School Board Elections." *Daily Caller*, November 3. https://dailycaller.com/2021/11/03/crt-critical-race-theory-opponents-school-board-elections/.

IAAM (International African American Museum). n.d. "About IAAM." Last accessed September 5, 2023. https://iaamuseum.org/about/.

Iati, Marisa. 2021. "What Is Critical Race Theory, and Why Do Republicans Want to Ban It in Schools?" *Washington Post*, May 29. https://www.washingtonpost.com/education/2021/05/29/critical-race-theory-bans-schools/.

IBW21 (Institute of the Black World 21st Century). n.d. "Our Story." Last accessed September 5, 2023. https://ibw21.org/about/.

Igielnik, Ruth, Scott Keeter, and Hannah Hartig. 2021. "Behind Biden's 2020 Victory: An Examination of the 2020 Electorate." *Pew Research Center*, June 30. https://www.pewresearch.org/politics/2021/06/30/behind-bidens-2020-victory/.

Ignatin, Noel, and Ted Allen. 2011 (1967). "White Blindspot: The Original Essays on Combating White Supremacy and White-Skin Privilege." Reprinted in *Rev-

olutionary Youth and the New Working Class: Lost Writings of SDS, edited by Carl Davidson. Pittsburgh, PA: Changemaker.

ICNL (International Center for Not-for-Profit Law). n.d. "US Protest Law Tracker." Last accessed September 5, 2023. https://www.icnl.org/usprotestlawtracker/.

InfluenceWatch. n.d.-a. "Tides Nexus." Last accessed September 5, 2023. https://www.influencewatch.org/organization/tides-nexus/.

InfluenceWatch. n.d.-b. "Resource Generation." Last accessed September 5, 2023. https://www.influencewatch.org/non-profit/resource-generation/.

InfluenceWatch. n.d.-c. "National Christian Charitable Foundation." Last accessed September 5, 2023. https://www.influencewatch.org/non-profit/national-christian-charitable-foundation/.

Ingham County. 2020. "Ingham County Declares Racism a Public Health Crisis." Health Department, June 11. https://www.scribd.com/document/465245688/Resolution-Ingham-County-declares-racism-public-health-crisis-June-11-2020.

Ingraham, Christopher. 2017. "Here Are the First 10 Members of Trump's Voting Commission." *Washington Post*, July 6. https://www.washingtonpost.com/news/wonk/wp/2017/07/06/here-are-the-first-10-members-of-trumps-voter-fraud-commission/?utm_term=.abadedb44f38.

Ireland Department of Children, Equality, Disability Integration and Youth. 2021. "Final Report of the Commission of Investigation into Mother and Baby Homes." January 12; last updated November 22. https://www.gov.ie/en/publication/d4b3d-final-report-of-the-commission-of-investigation-into-mother-and-baby-homes/.

Italiano, Laura. 2023. "The Proud Boys Seditious Conspiracy Trial Is Underway. But the New Leadership Has Moved On from the 2020 Election to LGBQT Issues." *Business Insider*, February 14. https://www.businessinsider.com/proud-boys-2022-break-records-anti-lgbtq-protests-extremism-watchdog-2023-1.

Itkowitz, Colby. 2019. "1 in Every 4 Circuit Court Judges Is Now a Trump Appointee." *Washington Post*, December 21. https://www.washingtonpost.com/politics/one-in-every-four-circuit-court-judges-is-now-a-trump-appointee/2019/12/21/.

Jabali, Malaika. 2019. "Plantation Weddings Are Wrong. Why Is It So Hard for White Americans to Admit That?" *The Guardian*, December 11. https://www.theguardian.com/commentisfree/2019/dec/11/plantation-weddings-are-wrong-why-is-it-so-hard-for-white-americans-to-admit-that.

Jackson, Tom, and Spencer S. Hsu. 2023. "Ex-Proud Boys Leader Enrique Tarrio Sentenced to 22 Years for Jan. 6." *Washington Post*, September 5. https://www.washingtonpost.com/dc-md-va/2023/09/05/proud-boys-sentencing-enrique-tarrio-jan-6-seditious-conspiracy/.

Jacobs, Lawrence R. 2022. *Democracy Under Fire: Donald Trump and the Breaking of American History*. New York: Oxford University Press.

Jaffe, Greg, and Patrick Marley. 2023. "In a Thriving Michigan County, a Community Goes to War with Itself." *Washington Post*, April 22. https://www.washingtonpost.com/politics/2023/04/22/ottawa-county-commission/.

Jaffe, Logan. 2020. "The Nation's First Reparations Package to Survivors of Torture Included a Public Memorial. Survivors Are Still Waiting." *ProPublica*, July 23. https://www.propublica.org/article/the-nations-first-reparations-package-to-survivors-of-police-torture-included-a-public-memorial-survivors-are-still-waiting.

Jamerson, Joshua. 2019. "Reparations for Slavery, Shelved for Decades, Are on the Table for the 2020 Election." *Wall Street Journal*, April 12. https://www.wsj.com/articles/reparations-for-slavery-shelved-for-decades-is-on-the-table-for-2020-election-11554989520.

Jan, Tracy, Jena McGregor, and Meghan Hoyer. 2021. "Corporate America's $50 Billion Promise." *Washington Post*, August 24. https://www.washingtonpost.com/business/interactive/2021/george-floyd-corporate-america-racial-justice/.

Janzer, Cinnamon. 2021. "What Role Can Cities Play in Reparations? Some Aim to Find Out." *Next City*, February 10. https://nextcity.org/urbanist-news/what-role-can-cities-play-in-reparations-some-aim-to-find-out.

Jardina, Ashley J. 2019. *White Identity Politics*. New York: Cambridge University Press.

Jardina, Ashley, and Spencer Piston. 2022. "The Effects of Dehumanizing Attitudes about Black People on Whites' Voting Decisions." *British Journal of Political Science* 52: 1076–98.

Jardina, Ashley, and Michael Traugott. 2019. "The Genesis of the Birther Rumor." *Politics* 4: 60–80.

Jaschik, Scott. 2018. "Kavanaugh Evades Questions on Affirmative Action in Higher Education." *InsideHigherEd*, November 14. https://www.insidehighered.com/quicktakes/2018/09/14/kavanaugh-evades-questions-affirmative-action.

Jasko, Katarzyna, Gary LaFree, James Piazza, and Michael H. Becker. 2022. "A Comparison of Political Violence by Left-Wing, Right-Wing, and Islamist Extremist Groups in the United States and the World." *PNAS*, July 18. https://doi.org/10.1073/pnas.2122593119.

Jay, Erin. 2023. "Relocation, Preservation of the Williamsburg Bray School Celebrated." *W&M News*, February 14.

Jervis, Rick, and Jessica Guynn. 2023. "When the Officers Are Black: Tyre Nichols' Death Raises Tough Questions about Death in Policing." *USA Today*, January 30. https://www.usatoday.com/story/news/nation/2023/01/28/tyre-nichols-death-black-police-officers/11136520002/.

Jilani, Zaid. 2017. "New Report Looks at How Obama's Housing Policies Destroyed Black Wealth." *The Intercept*, December 8. https://theintercept.com/2017/12/08/barack-obama-housing-policy-racial-inequality/.

Johnson, Kimberley S. 2010. *Reforming Jim Crow*. New York: Oxford University Press.

Johnson, Kimberley S. 2016. "The Color Line and the State: Race and American Political Development." in *The Oxford Handbook of American Political Devel-

opment, edited by Richard M. Valelly, Suzanne Mettler, and Robert C. Lieberman, 593–624. New York: Oxford University Press.

Johnson, Jenna. 2018. "With Trump in the White House, Candidates Who Sound Like Him Hit the Campaign Trail." *Washington Post*, July 16. https://www.washingtonpost.com/politics/with-trump-in-the-white-house-candidates-who-sound-like-him-hit-the-campaign-trail/2018/07/15/2ff71b5a-86c5-11e8-8553-a3ce89036c78_story.html?utm_term=.ffc2c685f2d9/.

Johnson, Richard. 2020. *The End of the Second Reconstruction: Obama, Trump and the Crisis of Civil Rights*. London: Polity.

Johnson, Richard, and Lisa L. Miller. 2023. "The Conservative Policy Bias in Senate Malapportionment." *PS: Political Science and Politics* 56 (1): 10–17.

Jones, Dustin. 2022a. "What Is the 'Great Replacement' and How Is It Tied to the Buffalo Shooting Suspect?" *NPR*, May 16. https://www.nprillinois.org/2022-05-15/what-is-the-great-replacement-and-how-is-it-tied-to-the-buffalo-shooting-suspect.

Jones, Dustin. 2022b. "Republican Leaders Denounce Trump's Dinner with White Nationalist Nick Fuentes." *NPR: Politics*, November 29. https://www.npr.org/2022/11/29/1139742844/republicans-denounce-trump-dinner-white-supremacist-nick-fuentes.

Jones, Ellen E. 2020. "Opal Tometi, Co-Founder of Black Lives Matter: 'I Do This Because We Deserve to Live.'" *The Guardian*, September 24. https://www.theguardian.com/society/2020/sep/24/opal-tometi-co-founder-of-black-lives-matter-i-do-this-because-we-deserve-to-live.

Jones, Zoe Christen. 2021. "Black Lives Matter Foundation Raised $90 Million in 2020." *CBS News*, February 24. https://www.cbsnews.com/news/black-lives-matter-raises-90-million-2020/.

Jopson, Barney. 2018. "Rebekah Mercer, the Mega-Donor Who Bankrolled Trump's Campaign." *Financial Times*, January 12. https://www.ft.com/content/9d896ac0-f6fa-11e7-88f7-5465a6ce1a00.

Jordan, Miriam. 2020. "They Lost Their Jobs, Now They May Have to Leave the US." *New York Times*, May 5. https://www.nytimes.com/2020/05/12/us/foreign-workers-visas-immigrants.html.

Joyce, Kathryn. 2022. "Did Christian Nationalism Lose in the Midterms? Sort of— But It's Not Going Away." *Salon*, November 10. https://www.salon.com/2022/11/10/did-christian-nationalism-lose-in-the-midterms-sort-of--but-its-not-going-away/.

Kadushin, Charles. 2012. *Understanding Social Networks: Theories, Concepts, and Findings*. New York: Oxford University Press.

Kaleem, Jaweed. 2023. "Racist Attacks Now a Way of Life in the U.S." *Los Angeles Times*, September 1. https://www.latimes.com/world-nation/story/2023-08-31/jacksonville-shooting-racism-white-supremacy-gun-attacks.

Kalmoe, Nathan P., and Liliana Mason. 2022. *Radical American Partisanship: Map-*

ping Violent Hostility, Its Cause and Consequences for Democracy. Chicago: University of Chicago Press.

Kang, Jay Caspian. 2022. "The Anti-CRT Movement and a Vision for a New Right Wing." *New York Times*, February 10. https://www.nytimes.com/2022/02/10/opinion/anti-crt-politics.html.

Karni, Annie, Maggie Haberman, and Sydney Ember. 2021. "Trump Plays on Racist Fears of Terrorized Suburbs to Court White Voters." *New York Times*, July 29, 2020, updated January 20, 2021. https://www.nytimes.com/2020/07/29/us/politics/trump-suburbs-housing-white-voters.html.

Kasakove, Sophie. 2022. "In Tennessee, 'Maus' Fight Is Part of Bigger Battle." *New York Times*, March 5, A19.

Kashyap, Monika Batra. 2019. "Unsettling Immigration Laws: Settler Colonialism and the U.S. Immigration Legal System." *Fordham Urban Law Journal* 46: 548–79.

Kato, Daniel. 2016. *Liberalizing Lynching: Building a New Racialized State*. New York: Oxford University Press.

Kaufman, Ellie. 2022. "West Point Is Displaying a Ku Klux Klan Plaque at Entrance to Science Building, Congressional Naming Commission Finds." *CNN Politics*, August 31. https://www.cnn.com/2022/08/31/politics/west-point-kkk-plaque/index.html.

Kaur, Harmeet. 2019. "A New Jersey Religious College Will Set Aside Nearly $28 Million for Slavery Reparations." *CNN*, October 26. https://www.cnn.com/2019/10/26/us/princeton-seminary-slavery-reparations-trnd/.

Kaylor, Brian, and Beau Underwood. 2022. "Christian Nationalism as the Keystone." *Word&Way*, May 12. https://publicwitness.wordandway.org/p/christian-nationalism-as-the-keystone.

KCRG News Staff. 2021. "Iowa City Community Police Review Board Formally Recommends Policy Changes." *KCRG.com*, July 20. https://www.kcrg.com/2021/07/20/iowa-city-community-police-review-board-formally-recommends-policy-changes/.

Keegan, Harrison. 2020. "Springfield NAACP Leaders Call on Police to End Neck Restraints, Reform Review Board." *Springfield News-Leader*, July 27. https://www.news-leader.com/story/news/crime/2020/07/27/springfield-police-department-naacp-leaders-call-reform-change/5471206002/.

Kelley, Robin D. G. 2000. "Foreword." In *Black Marxism: The Making of the Black Radical Tradition*. Chapel Hill: University of North Carolina Press.

Kelley, Robin D. G. 2022. *Freedom Dreams: The Black Radical Imagination*. Boston: Beacon Press.

Kelley, Robin D. G. 2023. "Racial Capitalism: An Unfinished History." *Ethnic and Racial Studies*, June. https://doi.org/10.1080/01419870.2023.2219301.

Kesler, Charles R. 2021. *Crisis of the Two Constitutions: The Rise, Decline, and Recovery of American Greatness*. New York: Encounter Books.

Kim, Eunji. 2023. "Entertaining Beliefs in Economic Mobility." *American Journal of Political Science* 67 (1): 39–54.

Kim, Seung Min. 2021. "Juneteenth Holiday Marking the End of Slavery Becomes Law after Decades of Inaction." *Washington Post*, June 17. https://www.washingtonpost.com/politics/juneteenth-holiday-marking-the-end-of-slavery-becomes-law-after-decades-of-inaction/2021/06/17/.

Kinder, Donald R., and Lynn M. Sanders. 1994. *Divided by Color*. Chicago: University of Chicago Press.

King, Desmond. 1995. *Separate and Unequal: African Americans and the US Federal Government*. New York: Oxford University Press.

King, Desmond. 2000. *Making Americans: Immigration, Race, and the Origins of the Diverse Democracy*. Cambridge, MA: Harvard University Press.

King, Desmond. 2007. *Separate and Unequal: African Americans and the US Federal Government*. Rev. ed. Oxford: Oxford University Press.

King, Desmond. 2014. "America's Civil Rights State: Amelioration, Stagnation or Failure?" In *Developments in American Politics 7*, edited by Gillian Peele, Christopher J. Bailey, Bruce E. Cain, and B. Guy Peters, 263–83. London: Palgrave.

King, Desmond. 2017. "Forceful Federalism against Racial Inequality." *Government and Opposition* 52: 356–82.

King, Desmond, and Robert C. Lieberman. 2017. "The Civil Rights State: How the American State Develops Itself." In *The Many Hands of the State: Theorizing Political Authority and Social Control*, edited by Kimberly J. Morgan and Ann Shola Orloff, 178–202. New York: Cambridge University Press.

King, Desmond S., and Rogers M. Smith. 2005. "Racial Orders in American Political Development." *American Political Science Review* 99 (1): 75–92.

King, Desmond S., and Rogers M. Smith. 2011. *Still a House Divided: Race and Politics in Obama's America*. Princeton, NJ: Princeton University Press.

King, Desmond S., and Rogers M. Smith. 2014. "'Without Regard to Race': Critical Ideational Development in Modern American Politics." *Journal of Politics* 76 (4): 958–71.

King, Desmond S., and Rogers M. Smith. 2016. "The Last Stand? Shelby County v. Holder, White Political Power, and America's Racial Policy Alliances." *Du Bois Review* 13: 25–44.

King, Hope. 2021. "Online Reparations Revolution." *Axios*, June 25. https://www.axios.com/2021/06/25/reparations-online-twitter-venmo-cashapp.

King, Maya. 2020. "Black Lives Matter Goes Big on Policy Agenda." *Politico*, August 28. https://www.politico.com/news/2020/08/28/black-lives-matter-breathe-act-403905.

Klaas, Brian. 2017. "Gerrymandering Is the Biggest Obstacle to Genuine Democracy in the United States. So Why Is No One Protesting?" *Washington Post*, February 10. https://www.washingtonpost.com/news/democracy-post/wp/2017/

02/10/gerrymandering-is-the-biggest-obstacle-to-genuine-democracy-in-the-united-states-so-why-is-no-one-protesting/.

Klarman, Michael J. 2016. *The Framers' Coup: The Making of the U.S. Constitution.* New York: Oxford University Press.

Klein, E., and E. Fouksman. 2021. "Reparations as a Rightful Share: From Universalism to Redress in Distributive Justice." *Development and Change* 53 (1): 31–57.

Kleinfeld, Rachel. 2021. "The Rise of Political Violence in the United States." *Journal of Democracy* 32: 160–76.

Klinkner, Philip A., with Rogers M. Smith. 1999. *The Unsteady March: The Rise and Decline of Racial Equality in America.* Chicago: University of Chicago Press.

Koch, Makenzie. 2023. "Kansas City Mayor Appoints 13 to Reparations Commission." *Fox4 News*, May 1. https://fox4kc.com/news/kansas-city-mayor-appoints-13-to-reparations-commission/.

Kopan, Tal. 2016. "Donald Trump Retweets 'White Genocide' Twitter User." *CNN Politics*, January 22. https://www.cnn.com/2016/01/22/politics/donald-trump-retweet-white-genocide/index.html.

Kotch, Alex. 2019. "America's Biggest Charities Are Funneling Millions to Hate Groups from Anonymous Donors." *Sludge*, February 19. https://www.readsludge.com/2019/02/19/americas-biggest-charities-are-funneling-millions-to-hate-groups-from-anonymous-donors/.

Kranish, Michael. 2022. "They Rallied in D.C. on Jan. 6. Now They'll Join Congress." *Washington Post*, November 15. https://www.washingtonpost.com/politics/2022/11/15/derrick-van-orden-congress/.

Kraus, Michael. 2022. "Deep Racial Inequality Persists in the U.S.—But Many Americans Don't Want to Believe It." *Los Angeles Times*, February 28. https://www.latimes.com/opinion/story/2022-02-28/american-perception-racial-inequality.

Krinsky, Miriam Aroni. 2021. "How (Some) Prosecutors Changed the Face of Justice in 2021." *The Crime Report*, Center on Media Crime and Justice at John Jay College, December 7. https://fairandjustprosecution.org/.

Kroll, Andy, Andrea Bernstein, and Nick Surgey. 2023. "Inside the 'Private and Confidential' Conservative Group That Promises to 'Crush Liberal Dominance.'" *ProPublica*, March 9. https://www.propublica.org/article/leonard-leo-teneo-videos-documents.

Kromash, Wendi. 2022. "First United Methodist Sets Example for Reparations with Major Gift." *Evanston Roundtable*, March 1. https://evanstonroundtable.com/2022/03/01/first-united-methodist-sets-example-for-reparations-with-major-gift/.

Kutner, Brad, Martin Macias Jr., and Nicholas Iovino. 2020. "Demand for Citizen Police Review Boards Spreads Across US." *Courthouse News Service*, July 18. https://www.courthousenews.com/demand-for-citizen-police-review-boards-spreads-across-us/.

La Raja, Raymond J. 2012. "Why Super PACs? How the American Party System Outgrew the Campaign Finance System." *The Forum* 10 (4): 91–104.

Ladson-Billings, Gloria. 2021. *Critical Race Theory in Education: A Scholar's Journey*. New York: Teachers College Press.

Laila, Cristina. 2021. "'Black Power!—New Black Panther Party Stages Armed 'March for Reparations' in Tulsa, Oklahoma." *The Gateway Pundit*, May 29. https://www.thegatewaypundit.com/2021/05/black-power-new-black-panther-party-stages-armed-march-reparations-tulsa-oklahoma-video/.

Lakhani, Nina, and Jonathan Watts. 2020. "Environmental Justice Means Racial Justice, Say Activists." *The Guardian*, June 18. https://www.theguardian.com/environment/2020/jun/18/environmental-justice-means-racial-justice-say-activists.

Lantos, Tom. 2002. "The Durban Debacle: An Insider's View of the UN World Conference Against Racism." *The Fletcher Forum of World Affairs* 26 (1): 31–52.

LaPonsie, Maryalene. 2022. "What Is Universal Basic Income?" Shah Family Foundation, March 1. https://www.shahfoundation.org/press/universal-basic-income.

Lashmar, Paul, and Jonathan Smith. 2023. "'My Forefather Did Something Horribly Wrong': British Slave Owners' Family to Apologise and Pay Reparations." *The Guardian*, February 4. https://www.theguardian.com/world/2023/feb/04/british-slave-owners-family-apologise-reparations-trevelyans.

Late, Michele. 2022. "Racism Declarations Pass New Milestone." *Public Health Newswire*, July 25. http://www.publichealthnewswire.org/?p=racism-public-health.

Laughland, Oliver. 2022. "Glenn Youngkin Attempts to Ban Critical Race Theory on Day One as Virginia Governor." *The Guardian*, January 16. https://www.theguardian.com/us-news/2022/jan/16/virginia-governor-glenn-youngkin-sworn-into-office-critical-race-theory.

Laurel, Raymond. 2017. "Trump Administration Eliminates Funding for Group Countering White Nationalism." *ThinkProgress*, June 23. https://thinkprogress.org/white-nationalism-group-funding-f1d35fb5604e/.

Lawrence, Charles R. III. 2020. "Book Review: Implicit Bias in the Age of Trump." *Harvard Law Review* 133: 2304–57.

Leadership Conference on Civil and Human Rights. 2023. "Trump Administration Civil and Human Rights Rollbacks." Last accessed September 4, 2023. https://civilrights.org/trump-rollbacks/.

LeBlanc, Paul. 2020. "Trump Condemns 'All White Supremacists' after Refusing to Do So at Presidential Debate." *CNN Politics*, October 1. https://www.cnn.com/2020/10/01/politics/trump-proud-boys-white-supremacists/index.html.

LeBlanc, Paul. 2021. "Trump Endorses Gosar One Day after He Was Censured for Violent Video Targeting AOC and Biden." *CNN Politics*, November 18. https://edition.cnn.com/2021/11/18/politics/trump-gosar-endorsement/index.html.

Lee, Kurtis. 2022. "California Contemplates Billions in Reparations." *New York Times*, December 2, A1.

Lee, Kurtis. 2023. "California Panel Calls for Billions in Reparations for Black Residents." *New York Times*, May 6. https://www.nytimes.com/2023/05/06/business/economy/california-reparations.html.

Leong, Nancy. 2013. "Racial Capitalism." *Harvard Law Review* 126 (8): 2151–2226.

Lepore, Jill. 2022. "Why the School Wars Still Rage." *New Yorker*, March 14. https://www.newyorker.com/magazine/2022/03/21/why-the-school-wars-still-rage.

Levenson, Zachary, and Marcel Paret. 2022. "The Three Dialectics of Racial Capitalism: From South Africa to the U.S. and Back Again." *Du Bois Review: Social Science Research on Race*, 1–19. https://doi.org/10.1017/S1742058X22000212.

Levin, Sam T. 2022. "Black Lives Matter Grassroots Chapters Sue Global Foundation over Funds." *The Guardian*, September 2. https://www.theguardian.com/world/2022/sep/02/black-lives-matter-grassroots-lawsuit-global-foundation.

Levin, Yuval. 2022. "Democrats Lost the Midterms, Too." *New York Times*, November 19, A11.

Levine, Mike. 2016. "What Jeff Sessions Has Said About Race and Civil Rights." *ABCNews*, November 18. https://abcnews.go.com/Politics/jeff-sessions-race-civil-rights/story?id=43633501.

Levine, Sam. 2021. "Supreme Court Deals Blow to Voting Rights by Upholding Arizona Restrictions." *The Guardian*, July 1. https://www.theguardian.com/us-news/2021/jul/01/us-voting-rights-supreme-court-arizona.

Levinson, Jonathan. 2023. "Despite Setbacks, Far-Right Extremists Are Winning Positions in Mainstream Northwest Politics." Oregon Public Broadcasting, March 28. https://www.opb.org/article/2023/03/28/far-right-extremists-government-oregon-washington-idaho/.

Lewis, Kaitlin. 2022. "Photos of Marjorie Taylor Greene with Nick Fuentes Resurface. 'This You?'" *Newsweek*, November 29. https://www.newsweek.com/photos-marjorie-taylor-greene-nick-fuentes-resurface-this-you.

Lieberman, Robert C. 2002. "Ideas, Institutions, and Political Order: Explaining Political Change." *American Political Science Review* 96 (4): 697–712.

Lieberman, Robert C. 2023. "Can Social Movements Save American Democracy?" *Political Research Quarterly* 138: 77–86.

Lillis, Mike and Scott Wong. 2019. "Reparations Bill Wins New Momentum in Congress." *The Hill*, April 4. https://thehill.com/homenews/house/437286-reparations-bill-wins-new-momentum-in-house/.

Liptak, Adam. 2019. "Supreme Court Leaves Census Question on Citizenship in Doubt," *New York Times*, June 27. https://www.nytimes.com/2019/06/27/us/politics/census-citizenship-question-supreme-court.html.

Liptak, Adam. 2021. "Supreme Court Upholds Arizona Voting Rights Restrictions." *New York Times*, July 1. https://www.nytimes.com/2021/07/01/us/politics/supreme-court-arizona-voting-restrictions.html.

Liptak, Adam. 2022. "Justices Restore Vote Map Said to Dilute Rights." *New York Times*, February 8, A1.

Liptak, Adam. 2023. "Court Rules State Control of U.S. Voting Has Limits." *New York Times*, June 28, A1.

Liptak, Kevin, and Kristen Holmes. 2020. "Trump Calls Black Lives Matter a 'Symbol of Hate' as He Digs In on Race." *CNN*, July 1. https://www.cnn.com/2020/07/01/politics/donald-trump-black-lives-matter-confederate-race/index.html.

Lopez, German. 2019. "Donald Trump's Long History of Racism, from the 1970s to 2019." *Vox*, February 14. https://www.vox.com/2016/7/25/12270880/donald-trump-racist-racism-history.

Lopez Bunyasi, Tehama. 2019. "The Role of Whiteness in the 2016 Presidential Primaries." *Perspectives on Politics* 17: 679–98.

Lowell, Hugo. 2022a. "Steve Bannon Given Four Months in Prison for Contempt of Congress." *The Guardian*, October 21. https://www.theguardian.com/us-news/2022/oct/21/steve-bannon-sentenced-prison-contempt-congress.

Lowell, Hugo. 2022b. "Donald Trump 'Shied Away from Criticizing Nick Fuentes.'" *The Guardian*, November 28. https://www.theguardian.com/us-news/2022/nov/28/donald-trump-shied-away-from-criticising-nick-fuentes.

Lowery, Wesley. 2018. "Police Are Still Killing Black People. Why Isn't It News Anymore?" *Washington Post*, March 16. https://www.washingtonpost.com/outlook/police-are-still-killing-black-people-why-isnt-it-news-anymore/2018/03/12/.

Lyons, Michelle E. 2002. "World Conference against Racism: New Avenues for Slavery Reparations?" *Vanderbilt Journal of Transnational Law* 35 (4): 1235–68.

Mac, Ryan, and Brianna Sacks. 2020. "'The Black Lives Matter Foundation' Raised Millions. It's Not Affiliated with the Black Lives Matter Movement." *BuzzFeed News*, June 15. https://www.buzzfeednews.com/article/ryanmac/black-lives-matter-foundation-unrelated-blm-donations.

MacFarquhar, Neil. 2020. "When a Vigilante's Call to Action Is Only a Facebook Post Away." *New York Times*, October 17, A1.

MacLean, Nancy. 2018. *Democracy in Chains: The Deep Roots of the Radical Right's Stealth Plan for America*. New York: Penguin Books.

MacPherson, Sir William of Cluny. 1999. "The Stephen Lawrence Inquiry." *Home Department*, February. https://www.gov.uk/government/publications/the-stephen-lawrence-inquiry.

Maher, Kris. 2022. "Cities Struggle with Columbus Statues as Holiday Approaches." *Wall Street Journal*, October 9. https://www.wsj.com/articles/cities-struggle-with-columbus-statues-as-holiday-approaches-11665281361.

Manfredi, Lucas. 2021. "BLM Shared Detailed Look at Finances: Report." *Fox Business*, February 23. https://www.foxbusiness.com/politics/blm-reveals-detailed-look-at-finances-report.

Manjoo, Farhad. 2022. "Biden Has Helped the Quiet Revolution of Giving People

Money." *New York Times*, September 23. https://www.nytimes.com/2022/09/23/opinion/columnists/child-tax-credit-basic-income.html.

Mann, Ted. 2017. "White House Won't Require Firms to Report Pay by Gender, Race." *Wall Street Journal*, August 29. https://www.wsj.com/articles/white-house-wont-require-firms-to-report-pay-by-gender-race-1504047656.

Marans, Daniel. 2018. "GOP State Lawmakers Pal Around with White Supremacists. Party Group Backs Them Anyway." *HuffPost*, October 22. https://www.huffpost.com/entry/republican-state-lawmakers-white-nationalists-rslc-silent_n_5bcd82e4e4b0a8f17eee0a1d.

Marcelo, Philip. 2022. "Rhode Island Reparations Report Suggests Programs, Not Cash." *WPRI.com12*, August 23. https://www.wpri.com/news/local-news/providence/rhode-island-reparations-report-suggests-programs-not-cash.

Margalit, Yotam. 2012. "Lost in Globalization: International Economic Integration and the Sources of Populist Discontent." *International Studies Quarterly* 56 (3): 484–500.

Mark, Julian, and Eli Tan. 2023. "Affirmative Action Ruling Puts Target on Corporate Diversity Programs." *Washington Post*, June 29. https://www.washingtonpost.com/business/2023/06/29/affirmative-action-business-diversity/.

Marley, Patrick, and Robert Barnes. 2023. "N.C. Supreme Court Reverses Redistricting Ruling in a Win for Republicans." *Washington Post*, April 28. https://www.washingtonpost.com/politics/2023/04/28/north-carolina-courts-redistricting-voter-id/.

Martin, Lisa. 2020. "Modern Day Militias Rise in Virginia." *Crozet Gazette*, October 2. https://www.crozetgazette.com/2020/10/02/modern-day-militias-rise-in-virginia/.

Mason, Lilliana. 2018. *Uncivil Agreement: How Politics Became Our Identity*. Chicago: University of Chicago Press.

Masuoka, Natalie. 2017. *Multiracial Identity and Racial Politics in the United States*. New York: Oxford University Press.

Mayer, Carla. 2022. "7th Anniversary of the Reparations Ordinance." *Chicago Torture Justice Center*, May 6. https://www.chicagotorturejustice.org/newsandevents/7th-anniversary-of-the-reparations-ordinance.

Mayer, Jane. 2016. *Dark Money: The Hidden History of the Billionaires Behind the Rise of the Radical Right*. New York: Anchor Books.

Mayors for a Guaranteed Income. 2023. "About MGI." Last accessed September 4, 2023. https://www.mayorsforagi.org/about.

Mays, Jeffery C. 2022. "Court Rejects Law Giving Non-Citizens Vote in N.Y.C." *New York Times*, June 28, A19.

Mays, Jeffery C., and Annie Correal. 2021. "City Council's Vote Gives Non-Citizens Legal Right to Vote in Local Elections." *New York Times*, December 10, A20.

Mays, Jeffery C., and Zachary Small. 2021. "Jefferson Knocked Off Pedestal in New York Council Chamber." *New York Times*, October 19, A1.

Mazumder, Soumyajit. 2018. "The Persistent Effect of the U.S. Civil Rights Movement on Political Attitudes." *American Journal of Political Science* 62: 922–35.

Mazzei, Patricia. 2019. "Ex-Felons in Florida Have the Right to Vote, But It's Not That Simple." *New York Times*, May 4, A11.

McCarthy, Bill. 2022. "Tucker Carlson Feigned Ignorance about 'Great Replacement' Theory, Despite Talking about It Often." *Politifact*, May 19. https://www.politifact.com/article/2022/may/19/tucker-carlson-feigned-ignorance-over-great-replac/.

McCarthy, Lauren. 2023. "Court Ruling Revives Reparations Claim Filed by Tulsa Massacre Survivors." *New York Times*, August 16. https://www.nytimes.com/2023/08/16/tulsa-race-massacre-lawsuit-appeal.html.

McCarthy, Thomas. 2004. "Coming to Terms With Our past, Part II: On the Morality and Politics of Reparations for Slavery." *Political Theory* 32: 750–72.

McCaskill, Nolan D. 2020. "Trump's Policies for Black Americans." *Politico*, November 1. https://www.politico.com/news/2020/11/01/trump-black-americans-policies-433744.

McClain, Paula D. 2021. "Crises, Race, Acknowledgement: The Centrality of Race, Ethnicity, and Politics to the Future of Political Science." *Perspectives on Politics* 19: 7–18.

McDaniel, Polly. 2021. "Asheville City Council Hears Next Steps in Reparations Process." News, The City of Asheville, October 12. https://www.ashevillenc.gov/news/asheville-city-council-hears-next-steps-in-reparations-process/.

McDermott, Jennifer. 2021. "Brown Expands Slavery Report, But No Plans for Reparations." *AP News*, November 14. https://apnews.com/article/brown-university-slavery-education.

McFadden, Syreeta. 2020. "Black Lives Matter Just Entered Its Next Phase." *The Atlantic*, September 3. https://www.theatlantic.com/culture/archive/2020/09/black-lives-matter-just-entered-its-next-phase/615952/.

McGee, Jamie. 2021. "In a Tennessee City, a Confederate Statue Stays, but Gets Company." *New York Times*, October 25, A12.

McGirt, Ellen. 2020. "The Ford Foundation Announces $180 Million in New Racial Justice Grants, Supported by Proceeds from Social Bonds." *Fortune*, October 9. https://fortune.com/2020/10/09/ford-foundation-racial-justice-grants-social-bonds/.

McGraw, Meredith. 2022. "Trump's Criminal Justice Reform Bill Becomes Persona Non Grata among GOPers." *Politico*, May 1. https://www.politico.com/news/2022/05/01/trump-republicans-first-step-act.

McKown-Dawson, Eli. 2023. "How Do Americans Feel about Regulation of Public Universities?" *YouGov*, March 15. https://today.yougov.com/topics/politics/articles-reports/2023/03/15/how-americans-feel-regulation-public-universities.

McWhirter, Cameron. 2022. "Debate on Police in Jackson, Miss. Adds Tension to City Divided by Water Crisis." *Wall Street Journal*, October 30. https://www.wsj

.com/articles/debate-on-police-in-jackson-miss-adds-tension-to-city-divided-by-water-crisis.

McWhorter, John. 2023. "Reparations Should Be an End, Not a Beginning." *New York Times*, June 22. https://www.nytimes.com/2023/06/22/opinion/reparations-race-housing.html.

Mead, Lawrence M. 2019. *Burdens of Freedom: Cultural Difference and American Power*. New York: Encounter Books.

Mead, Lawrence M. 2021. "Poverty and Culture." *Academic Questions* 34 (1): 100–110.

Meckler, Laura, and Devlin Barrett. 2019. "Trump Administration Considers Rollback of Anti-Discrimination Rules." *Washington Post*, January 3. https://www.washingtonpost.com/local/education/trump-administration-considers-rollback-of-anti-discrimination-rules/2019/01/02/.

Mendelberg, Tali. 2001. *The Race Card*. Princeton, NJ: Princeton University Press.

Mendez, Dara D., Jewel Scott, Linda Adodoadji, Christina Toval, Monica McNeil, and Mahima Sindu. 2021. "Racism as a Public Health Crisis: Assessment and Review of Municipal Declarations and Resolutions Across the United States." *Frontiers in Public Health*, August 11. https://www.frontiersin.org/articles/10.3389/fpubh.2021.686807/full.

Mercer, Ilana. 2021. "Conservatives Won't Say It: The Problem Is 'Systemic Anti-Whiteness.'" *COCC: Conservative Headlines*, May 8. http://www.cofcc.us/.

Mervosh, Sarah. 2023. "DeSantis Faces Swell of Criticism Over Florida's New Standards for Black History." *New York Times*, July 21. https://www.nytimes.com/2023/07/21/us/desantis-florida-black-history-standards.html.

Mettler, Suzanne, and Robert C. Lieberman. 2020. *Four Threats: The Recurring Crises of American Democracy*. New York: St. Martin's Press.

Michael, Mark. 2020. "Diocese of Texas to Fund $13 Million in Slavery Reparations." *The Living Church*, February 17. https://www.edotracialjustice.org/news/diocese-of-texas-to-fund-13-million-in-slavery-reparations.

Michael, Ralph, and Maya Singhal. 2019. "Racial Capitalism." *Theory and Society* 48: 851–81.

Michelson, Melissa. 2002. "The Black Reparations Movement: Public Opinion and Congressional Policy Making." *Journal of Black Studies* 32 (5): 574–77.

Migdon, Brooke. 2022. "What Is DeSantis's 'Stop WOKE Act?'" *The Hill*, August 19. https://thehill.com/changing-america/respect/diversity-inclusion/3608241-what-is-desantiss-stop-woke-act/.

Millard, Egan. 2019. "Diocese of New York Establishes Reparations Fund, Adopts Anti-Slavery Resolutions from 1860." *ENS: Episcopal News Service*, November 12. https://www.episcopalnewsservice.org/2019/11/12/diocese-of-new-york-establishes-reparations-fund-adopts-anti-slavery-resolutions-from-1860/.

Miller, Hayley. 2020. "William Barr: BLM 'Not Interested in Black Lives.'" *NPR*,

September 18. https://www.huffingtonpost.co.uk/entry/william-barr-black-lives-matter.

Miller, Joe. 2023. "Law Firms Become Latest Battleground in US Diversity Fight." *Financial Times*, September 3. https://www.ft.com/content/a4dd5adf-d6e8-452d-8ec6-5e7fdacc7a4a.

Miller, Jennifer. 2023. "Why Some Companies Are Saying 'Diversity and Belonging' Instead of 'Diversity and Inclusion.'" *New York Times*, May 13. https://www.nytimes.com/2023/05/13/business/diversity-equity-inclusion-belonging.html.

Miller, Kim. 2022. "Announcement of New City of Asheville Reparations Commission Members." News, The City of Asheville, March 8. https://www.ashevillenc.gov/news/announcement-of-new-city-of-asheville-reparations-commission-members/.

Miller, Lisa L. 2010. "The Invisible Black Victim: How American Federalism Perpetuates Racial Inequality in Criminal Justice." *Law & Society Review* 44: 805–43.

Miller, Lisa L. 2015. "What's Violence Got to Do with It? Inequality, Punishment, and State Failure in US Politics." *Punishment and Society* 17: 184–210.

Miller, Lisa L. 2019. "Amending Constitutional Myths." *Drake University Law Review* 67: 947–75.

Miller, Lisa L. 2022. "Up from Federalism." *Boston Review*, July 18. https://www.bostonreview.net/articles/up-from-federalism/.

Miller, Paul D. 2022. *The Religion of American Greatness: What's Wrong with Christian Nationalism*. Downers Grove, IL: InterVarsity Press.

Miller-Idriss, Cynthia. 2022. "America's Most Urgent Threat Now Comes from Within." *New York Times*, January 6, A23.

Minnite, Lorraine C. 2010. *The Myth of Voter Fraud*. Ithaca, NY: Cornell University Press.

Mirahmadi, Hedieh. 2021. "The Assault on 'White America.'" *Christian Post*, April 8. https://www.christianpost.com/news/the-assault-on-white-america.html.

Miranda, Carolina. 2021. "LA's Memorial for 1871 Chinese Massacre Will Mark a Shift in How We Honor History." *Los Angeles Times*, October 22. https://www.latimes.com/entertainment-arts/story/2021-10-22/how-a-planned-monument-marking-the-chinese-massacre-of-1871-begins-to-fill-historical-gaps.

Miroff, Nick. 2018. "Family Ties Drive U.S. Immigration. Why Trump Wants to Break the 'Chains.'" *Washington Post*, January 2. https://www.washingtonpost.com/world/national-security/how-chain-migration-became-a-target-in-trumps-immigration-agenda/2018/01/02/dd30e034-efdb-11e7-90ed-77167c6861f2_story.html?utm_term=.cc0823472c94.

Mishan, Ligaya. 2020. "The Long and Tortured History of Cancel Culture." *New York Times*, December 3. https://www.nytimes.com/2020/12/03/t-magazine/cancel-culture-history.html.

Mitchell, Damon. 2022. "The Fallout over Hillsdale College, Charter Schools, and Tennessee School Districts, Explained." *WPLN News*, July 24. https://wpln.org/

post/the-fallout-over-hillsdale-college-charter-schools-and-tennessee-school-districts-explained/.

Mitchell, Ellen. 2022. "Renaming Army Bases Named after Confederate Leaders to Cost $21M." *The Hill*, August 10. https://thehill.com/policy/3596192-renaming-army-bases-named-after-confederate-leaders-to-cost-21m/.

Mogannam, Laura. n.d. "Honoring the Oppressed: Sisters Began Reparations with Descendants of Enslaved People." Last accessed September 4, 2023. *Society of the Sacred Heart United States-Canada*. https://rscj.org/sisters-begin-reparations.

Mohdin, Aamna. 2023. "UK Government and Royals Called On to Investigate Slavery Links after *Guardian* Apology." *The Guardian*, March 29. https://www.theguardian.com/news/2023/mar/29/uk-government-royals-called-on-investigate-slavery-links-after-guardian-apology.

MORE (Mayors Organized for Reparations and Equity). 2021. "MORE Mission." Last accessed September 4, 2023. https://moremayors.org/mission.

Moreau, Julie. 2018. "Transgender Workers Not Protected by Civil Rights Law, DOJ Tells Supreme Court." *NBC News*, October 25. https://www.nbcnews.com/feature/nbc-out/transgender-workers-not-protected-civil-rights-law-doj-tells-supreme-n924491.

Morgan, Jennifer L. 2021. *Reckoning with Slavery: Gender, Kinship, and Capitalism in the Early Black Atlantic*. Durham, NC: Duke University Press.

Morris, Kevin, and Myrna Perez. 2018. "Purges: A Growing Threat to the Right to Vote." *Brennan Center for Justice*, July 18. https://www.brennancenter.org/our-work/research-reports/purges-growing-threat-right-vote.

Morris, Sarah. 2018. "All I Want This Holiday Season Is for FCC's Terrible Lifeline Proposal to Go Away." *Slate*, December 27. https://slate.com/technology/2018/12/fcc-lifeline-reform-proposal.html.

Morrison, Aaron. 2021. "AP Exclusive: Black Lives Matters Opens Up about Its Finances." *AP News*, February 23. https://apnews.com/article/black-lives-matter-90-million-finances.

Morton, Neal. 2023. "Some Districts That Removed Police From Schools Brought Them Back." *Teen Vogue*, October 19. https://www.teenvogue.com/story/districts-removed-police-schools-bringing-back.

Moscufo, Michela. 2021. "Crowdfunding Campaigns Start Their Own Form of Reparations in Lieu of a Federal Push." *NBC News*, August 13. https://www.nbcnews.com/news/nbcblk/crowdfunding-campaigns-start-form-reparations-lieu-federal-push.

Moscufo, Michela. 2022. "Harvard Sets Up $100 Million Endowment Fund for Slavery Reparations." *Reuters*, April 26. https://www.reuters.com/world/us/harvard-sets-up-100-million-endowment-fund-slavery-reparations-2022-04-26/.

Moses, Claire. 2023. "King Apologizes for Netherlands' Role in the Slave Trade." *New York Times*, July 3, A10.

Movement for Black Lives (M4BL). 2023. "Vision for Black Lives." Last accessed September 4, 2023. https://m4bl.org/policy-platforms/.

Movement for Black Lives (M4BL). n.d. "The BREATHE Act." Electoral Justice Project of the Movement for Black Lives. Last accessed September 4, 2023. https://breatheact.org/wp-content/uploads/2020/07/The-BREATHE-Act-PDF_FINAL3-1.pdf.

Mullen, Kirsten A., and William A. Darity Jr. 2021. "Evanston, Ill., Approved 'Reparations.' Except It Isn't Reparations." *Washington Post*, March 28. https://www.washingtonpost.com/opinions/2021/03/28/evanston-ill-approved-reparations-housing-program-except-it-isnt-reparations/.

Mullins, Dexter. 2013. "14 Caribbean Nations Sue European Countries for Slavery Reparations." *Al Jazeera America*, September 27. http://america.aljazeera.com/articles/2013/9/27/14-caribbean-nationssueeuropeancountriesforreparationsoverslaver.html.

Muravchik, Stephanie, and Jon A. Shields. 2022. "Liz Cheney and the Twilight of the Old Republican Elite." *New York Times*, August 16. https://www.nytimes.com/2022/08/16/opinion/liz-cheney-wyoming.html.

Murray, Charles. 2020. *Human Diversity: The Biology of Gender, Race, and Class*. New York: Twelve.

Mutz, Diana C. 2018. "Status Threat, Not Economic Hardship, Explains the 2016 Presidential Vote." *PNAS* 115 (19): E4330–E4339.

Mylonas, Harris, and Maya Tudor. 2023. *Varieties of Nationalism: Communities, Narratives, Identities*. New York: Cambridge University Press.

NAARC (National African American Reparations Commission). 2023a. "About NAARC." Last accessed September 4, 2023. https://reparationscomm.org/about-naarc/.

NAARC. 2023b. "Ten-Point Reparations Plan." Last accessed September 4, 2023. https://reparationscomm.org/reparations-plan/.

NAASD (National Assembly of American Slavery Descendants). n.d. "Be the Change." Last accessed September 4, 2023. https://www.naasdla.org/.

Nakamura, David. 2022. "Arbery Hate-Crimes Trial Highlights Everyday Racism—and Casual Gun Culture." *Washington Post*, February 20. https://www.washingtonpost.com/national-security/2022/02/20/arbery-guns-trial-mcmichaels/.

Napoletano, E. 2022. "An Unexpected Outcome of the Covid 19 Pandemic: A Slew of Universal Income Programs." *Forbes Advisor*, May 12. https://www.forbes.com/advisor/personal-finance/universal-basic-income-programs/.

Natanson, Hannah. 2020. "High School Students Are Demanding Schools Teach More Black History, Including Black Authors." *Washington Post*, August 17. https://www.washingtonpost.com/local/education/high-schoolers-across-the-country-are-banding-together-to-demand-their-schools-teach-more-black-history-and-read-more-black-authors/2020/08/15/.

Natanson, Hannah. 2022. "Parent-Activists, Seeking Control over Education, Are Taking over School Boards." *Washington Post*, January 19. https://www.washingtonpost.com/education/2022/01/19/parents-school-boards-recall-takeover/.

National Conservatism. n.d. "A Conference in London, UK." Last accessed September 5, 2023. https://nationalconservatism.org/natcon-uk-2023/.

National Immigration Law Center. 2019. "Status of Current DACA Litigation." February 7. https://www.nilc.org/issues/daca/status-current-daca-litigation/.

N'COBRA (National Coalition of Blacks for Reparations in America). 2004. "How Will the United States and Its Residents Benefit?" May. Last accessed September 4, 2023. https://ncobra.org/default.

Nefzi, Samiar. 2022. "Reparations Program Gets Annual Funding from Buncombe County." *ABC13News*, July 19. https://wlos.com/news/local/reparations-program-gets-annual-funding-from-buncombe-county-community-reparations-commission.

New York Times Staff. 2021. "How George Floyd Died, and What Happened Next." *New York Times*, November 1. https://www.nytimes.com/article/george-floyd.html.

Nguyen, Tina. 2019. "Nobody Wants to Start a Populist Revolution with Steve Bannon." *Vanity Fair*, March 15. https://www.vanityfair.com/news/2019/03/steve-bannon-populist-movement-europe.

Norton, Michael I., and Samuel R. Sommers. 2011. "Whites See Racism as a Zero-Sum Game That They Are Now Losing." *Perspectives on Psychological Science* 6 (3): 215–18.

NYC Antifa. n.d. "About Us." Last accessed September 5, 2023. https://nycantifa.wordpress.com/about-us/.

O'Brien, Rebecca Davis. 2023. "Group Tied to Influential Conservative Activist Spent $183 Million in a Year." *New York Times*, May 12. https://www.nytimes.com/2023/05/12/us/politics/leonard-leo-marble-freedom-trust.html.

Office of Special Education and Rehabilitative Services. 2018. "Regulation Postponed Two Years to Insure Effective Implementation." *IDEA*, July 3. https://sites.ed.gov/idea/regulation-postponed-two-years-to-ensure-effective-implementation/.

Olsen, Henry. 2023. "U.S. Conservatives Have Found an Alarming Model for Their Movement." *Washington Post*, May 15. https://www.washingtonpost.com/opinions/2023/05/15/viktor-orban-republican-party-conservativism/.

Oltermann, Philip. 2021. "Germany Agrees to Pay Namibia €1.1bn over Historical Herero-Nama Genocide." *The Guardian*, May 28. https://www.theguardian.com/world/2021/may/28/germany-agrees-to-pay-namibia-11bn-over-historical-herero-nama-genocide.

Omi, Michael, and Howard Winant. 1986. *Racial Formation in the United States: From the 1960s to the 1980s*. New York: Routledge.

Omi, Michael, and Howard Winant. 1994. *Racial Formation in the United States: From the 1960s to the 1990s*. New York: Routledge.

Omi, Michael, and Howard Winant. 2014. *Racial Formation in the United States*. 3rd ed. New York: Routledge.

On the Issues. 2016. "Donald Trump on Social Security." http://www.ontheissues.org/2016/Donald_Trump_Social_Security.htm.

Onyeador, Ivuoma, Natalie M. Daumeyer, Julian M. Rucker, Ajua Duker, Michael W. Krause, and Jennifer A. Richeson. 2021. "Disrupting Beliefs in Racial Progress: Reminders of Persistent Racism Alter Perceptions of Past, But Not Current, Racial Economic Equality." *Personality and Social Psychology Bulletin* 47 (5): 753–65.

Orren, Karen, and Stephen Skowronek. 2004. *The Search for American Political Development*. New York: Cambridge University Press.

Osnos, Evan. 2015. "The Fearful and the Frustrated: Donald Trump's Nationalist Coalition Takes Shape—For Now." *New Yorker*, August 31. https://www.newyorker.com/magazine/2015/08/31/the-fearful-and-the-frustrated.

Ott, Haley. 2023. "King Charles Urged to Acknowledge Britain's 'Legacy of Genocide and Colonization' on Coronation Day." *CBS News*, May 4. https://www.cbsnews.com/news/king-charles-coronation-letter-commonwealth-reparations-genocide-colonization/.

Oxenden, McKenna, and Jessica Jaglois. 2023. "An 11-Year-Old Boy Called 911. Police Then Shot Him." *New York Times*, May 27. https://www.nytimes.com/2023/05/27/us/mississippi-11-year-old-boy-police-shooting.html.

Page, Jennifer M. 2019. "Reparations for Police Killings." *Perspectives on Politics* 17 (4): 958–72.

Page, Jennifer, and Desmond King. 2022. "Truth and Reparation for Mass Incarceration in the United States." *Du Bois Review* 19 (2): 209–32.

Paladino, Jason. 2022. "Meet the Kremers, Leaders of MAGA Group Women for America First in the Crosshairs of a Jan. 6 Grand Jury." *The Messenger*, September 15. https://themessenger.com/grid/meet-the-kremers-leaders-of-maga-group-women-for-america-first-in-the-crosshairs-of-a-jan-6-grand-jury.

Paletta, Damien, Mike DeBonis, and John Wagner. 2019. "Trump Declares National Emergency on Southern Border in Bid to Build Wall." *Washington Post*, February 15. https://www.washingtonpost.com/politics/trumps-border-emergency-the-president-plans-a-10-am-announcement-in-the-rose-garden/2019/02/15/f0310e62-3110-11e9-86ab-5d02109aeb01_story.html?utm_term=.c469303871c1.

Palmer, Chris, Tommy Rowan, and Jeremy Roebuck. 2021. "Organized Anarchists? Homegrown Rabble-Rousers? Philly Police Say They Aren't Sure What Motivated Vandals." *Philadelphia Inquirer*, January 5. https://www.inquirer.com/news/vandalism-graffiti-arrests-philadelphia-new-years-eve-antifa-20210105.html#loaded.

Palmer, Ewan. 2023. "Steve Bannon's Connection to Brazil Insurrection by Bolsonaro Supporters." *Newsweek*, January 9. https://www.newsweek.com/steve-bannon-brazil-bolsonaro-supporters-insurrection-1772183.

Pandolfo, Chris. 2023. "Arkansas Gov. Sarah Huckabee Sanders Bans Critical Race Theory in Schools." *Fox News*, January 11. https://www.foxnews.com/politics/arkansas-gov-sarah-huckabee-sanders-bans-critical-race-theory-schools.

Papaycik, Matt. 2022. "New Law Allows Florida Parents to Contest School Library Books, Reading Lists." *WPTV*, March 25. https://www.wptv.com/news/education/new-law-allows-florida-parents-to-contest-school-library-books-reading-lists.

Parker, Ashley, Amy Gardner, and Josh Dawsey. 2022. "How Republicans Became the Party of Trump's Election Lie after Jan. 6." *Washington Post*, January 5. https://www.washingtonpost.com/politics/republicans-jan-6-election-lie/2022/01/05/.

Parker, Christopher Sebastian. 2022. "Many White People Feel the Need to Take Drastic Measures to Maintain White Supremacy." *The Guardian*, November 6. https://www.theguardian.com/us-news/2022/nov/06/how-close-is-the-us-to-civil-war-barbara-f-walter-stephen-march-christopher-parker.

Parker, Christopher S., and Matt A. Barreto. 2013. *Change They Can't Believe In: The Tea Party and Reactionary Politics in America*. Princeton, NJ: Princeton University Press.

Parkinson, Robert G. 2021. "You Can't Tell the Story of 1776 Without Talking about Race and Slavery." *Time*, July 4. https://time.com/6077468/united-states-1776-racism-slavery/.

Parks, Miles. 2022. "Election Deniers Performed Especially Poorly in Races to Oversee Voting in Key States." *NPR News*, November 19. https://www.npr.org/2022/11/19/1137129319/secretary-of-state-election-denialism-underperformed.

Pavilonis, Valerie. 2022. "Fact Check: Thousands of Black Lives Matter Protesters Were Arrested in 2020." *USA Today*, February 22. https://www.usatoday.com/story/news/factcheck/2022/02/22/fact-check-thousands-black-lives-matter-protesters-arrested-2020/6816074001/.

Paxson, Christina H. n.d. "Foreword." In *Brown's Slavery & Justice Report*, Brown University. Last accessed August 31, 2023. https://slaveryandjusticereport.brown.edu/essays/foreword-paxson/.

Pearson, Rick. 2022. "The Future of the Illinois GOP—and How Far Right It May Go—Lie with This Month's Primary." *Chicago Tribune*, June 19. https://www.chicagotribune.com/politics/elections/ct-what-is-an-illinois-republican.

Peiser, Jaclyn. 2020. "Barr Slams BLM." *Washington Post*, August 10. https://www.washingtonpost.com/nation/2020/08/10/barr-fox-antifa-blm/.

People's Advocacy Institute. n.d. "Home." Last accessed September 5, 2023. https://peoplesadvocacyinstitute.com.

Pereira, Ivan. 2021a. "Asheville City Council Approves Reparations Plans as Providence Explores Idea." ABC News, July 16. https://abcnews.go.com/US/city-council-asheville-north-carolina-unanimously-approves-reparation/.

Pereira, Ivan. 2021b. "Governor Pardons St. Louis Couple Who Pointed Guns at Black Lives Matter Protesters." *ABC News*, August 3. https://abcnews.go.com/US/governor-pardons-st-louis-couple-pointed-guns-black/.

Perez, Andrew, Andy Kroll, and Justin Elliott. 2022. "How a Secretive Billionaire Handed His Fortune to the Architect of the Right-Wing Takeover of the Courts." *ProPublica*, August 22. https://www.propublica.org/article/dark-money-leonard-leo-barre-seid.

Perez, Juan, Jr. 2023. "Why GOP Culture Warriors Lost Big in School Board Races This Month." *Politico*, April 17. https://www.politico.com/news/2023/04/17/gop-school-board-races-midwest-00092232.

Pérez-Bustillo, Camillo. 2022. "Migrants Have Rights to Truth Commission and Reparations for Abuses at the Border." *TruthOut*, February 7. https://www.politico.com/news/2023/04/17/gop-school-board-races-midwest.

Perreault, Daniel. 2022. "Iowa City Truth and Reconciliation Chair Under Fire for 'Racist and Offensive Comments' on a Podcast." *KWWL.com*, August 23. https://www.kwwl.com/news/top-stories/iowa-city-truth-and-reconciliation-commission-chair-under-fire-for-racist-and-offensive-comments-on/.

Perry, Andre M., and Rashawn Ray. 2021. "Evanston's Grants to Homeowners Aren't Enough. But They Are Reparations." *Washington Post*, April 1. https://www.washingtonpost.com/outlook/evanston-housing-reparations/2021/04/01/.

Perry, Samuel L., and Cyrus Schleifer. 2022. "My Country, White or Wrong: Christian Nationalism, Race, and Blind Patriotism." *Ethnic and Racial Studies* 46 (7): 1249–68.

Perry, Samuel L., and Andrew L. Whitehead. 2019. "Christian America in Black and White: Racial Identity, Religious-National Group Boundaries, and Explanations for Racial Inequality." *Sociology of Religion: A Quarterly Review* 80 (3): 277–98.

Perry, Samuel L., and Andrew Whitehead. 2022. "Why White Christian Nationalism Isn't Going Away." *Time*, November 13. https://time.com/6233438/white-christian-nationalism-isnt-going-away/.

Peterson, Dana M., and Catherine L. Mann. 2020. "Closing the Racial Inequality Gaps: The Economic Cost of Black Equality in the U.S." *Citi GPS: Global Perspectives and Solutions*, September. https://icg.citi.com/icghome/what-we-think/citigps/insights/closing-the-racial-inequality-gaps-20200922.

Petrizzo, Zachary. 2020. "White Nationalist Groypers Are Taking Trump's Retweet as Endorsement." *Daily Dot*, May 17. https://www.dailydot.com/debug/trump-nicholas-fuentes-groypers-retweet/.

Pettus, Emily Wagster. 2020. "Mississippi Approves Flag with Magnolia, 'In God We Trust.'" *PBS*, November 4. https://www.pbs.org/newshour/politics/mississippi-approves-flag-with-magnolia-in-god-we-trust.

Pettypiece, Shannon. 2023. "Marjorie Taylor Greene Calls for a 'National Divorce' between Liberal and Conservative States." *NBC News*, February 20. https://www

.nbcnews.com/politics/congress/marjorie-taylor-greene-calls-national-divorce-liberal-conservative-sta-rcna71464.

Pew Research Center. 2021. "Wide Racial, Ethnic and Partisan Gaps in Support for Black Lives Matter." September 24. https://www.pewresearch.org/short-reads/2021/09/27/support-for-black-lives-matter-declined-after-george-floyd-protests-but-has-remained-unchanged-since/.

Phelps-Fein, Kim. 2009. *Invisible Hands: The Making of the Conservative Movement from the New Deal to Reagan*. New York: Norton.

Phillips, Nancy, and Craig R. McCoy. 2017. "Antifa, Black-Clad and Often Violent, Is Strong in Philly." *Philadelphia Inquirer*, August 29. https://www.inquirer.com/philly/news/pennsylvania/philadelphia/antifa-black-clad-and-often-violent-is-strong-in-philly-20170829.html.

Philly Antifa. n.d. "About." Last accessed August 31, 2023. https://phillyantifa.org/about/.

Pitts, Jonathan M. 2020. "Maryland Episcopal Diocese Commits $1 Million Towards Reparations for Slavery, Racial Injustice." *Baltimore Sun*, September 15. https://www.baltimoresun.com/maryland/bs-md-episcopal-reparations.

Pogrebin, Robin. 2021. "Museum Ousts Volunteers in Diversity Push. Uproar Ensues." *New York Times*, October 22, A10.

Poor People's Campaign. n.d. "About." Poor People's Campaign: A National Call for Moral Revival. Last accessed August 31, 2023. https://www.poorpeoplescampaign.org/about/.

Powell, Catherine, and Camille Gear Rich. 2020. "The 'Welfare Queen' Goes to the Polls: Race-Based Fractures in Gender Politics and Opportunities for Intersectional Coalitions." *Georgetown Law Journal* 108 (19th Amendment Special Edition): 105–65.

Powell, Michael. 2020. "'Supremacy?' Divide Grows Over a Phrase." *New York Times*, October 18, A1.

Powers, Kelly, and Sammy Gibbons. 2022. "Are US Churches Setting the Tone for Reparations? How a Movement Is Growing." *USA Today Network*, June 16. https://news.yahoo.com/u-churches-setting-tone-reparations-085510880.html.

President's Advisory 1776 Commission. 2021. *The 1776 Report*. January. https://trumpwhitehouse.archives.gov/wp-content/uploads/2021/01/The-Presidents-Advisory-1776-Commission-Final-Report.pdf.

Pressley, Ayanna. 2021. "Pressley, Warren, Lee Reintroduce Bold Legislation to Confront Structural Racism as a Public Health Crisis." February 1. https://pressley.house.gov/2021/02/01/pressley-warren-lee-reintroduce-bold-legislation-confront-structural-racism/.

Pressman, Jeremy, Erica Chenoweth, Tommy Leung, L. Nathan Perkins, and Jay Ulfelder. 2022. "Protests under Trump, 2017–2021." *Mobilization* 27 (1): 13–26.

Pride, Nicole. 2019. "Princeton Theological Seminary Announces Plan to Repent for Ties to Slavery." *Gather: Princeton Theological Seminary Magazine*, October

18. https://gather.ptsem.edu/princeton-theological-seminary-announces-plan-to-repent-for-ties-to-slavery/.

Program on Extremism and NCITE (National Counterterrorism, Innovation Technology and Education Center). 2021. "Anarchist/Left Wing Violent Extremism in America: Trends in Radicalization, Recruitment, and Mobilization." Program on Extremism, George Washington University, November. https://extremism.gwu.edu/sites/g/files/zaxdzs5746/files/Anarchist%20-%20Left-Wing%20Violent%20Extremism%20in%20America.pdf.

PRRI. 2018. "Partisan Polarization Dominates Trump Era: Findings from the 2018 American Values Survey." October 19. https://www.prri.org/research/partisan-polarization-dominates-trump-era-findings-from-the-2018-american-values-survey/.

Public Arts Foundation. 2021. "Kerry James Marshall, Elizabeth Alexander to Reimagine Confederate Windows." Press release, Washington National Cathedral, September 23. https://cathedral.org/about/news-media/kerry-james-marshall-elizabeth-alexander-to-reimagine-confederate-windows/.

Public Interest Legal Foundation. 2018a. "PILF Commends DOJ Vote Monitoring Plan." November 5. https://publicinterestlegal.org/blog/pilf-commends-doj-vote-monitoring-plan/.

Public Interest Legal Foundation. 2018b. "PILF to SCOTUS: Census Needs Citizenship Question." November 13. https://publicinterestlegal.org/blog/pilf-to-scotus-2020-census-needs-citizenship-question/.

Puget Sound John Brown Gun Club. n.d. "Home." Last accessed August 31, 2023. https://psjbgc.org/.

Pulitzer Center. n.d. "Our Mission and Model." Last accessed August 31, 2023. https://pulitzercenter.org/about/our-mission-and-model.

Queen Anne's County Public Schools. n.d. "Board of Education." Last accessed August 31, 2023. https://www.qacps.org/board-of-education/.

Rankin, Sarah, and Denise Lavoie. 2021. "Gen. Lee Statue Comes Down in Former Confederate Capital." *AP News*, September 9. https://apnews.com/article/robert-e-lee-statue-virginia-removed.

Ransby, Barbara. 2018. *Making All Black Lives Matter: Reimagining Freedom in the Twenty-First Century*. Oakland: University of California Press.

Rappeport, Alan. 2022. "Congress Rewrites Aid Program Black Farmers Pinned Hopes On." *New York Times*, August 13, B3.

Rahal, Sarah. 2022. "Who Should Be Able to Receive Detroit Reparations?" *Detroit News*, March 4. https://www.governing.com/now/who-should-be-eligible-to-receive-detroit-reparations.

Ray, Rashawn. 2022. "Black Lives Matter at 10 Years: 8 Ways the Movement Has Been Highly Effective." *Brookings*, October 12. https://www.brookings.edu/articles/black-lives-matter-at-10-years-what-impact-has-it-had-on-policing/.

Ray, Rashawn, and Alexandra Gibbons. 2021. "Why Are States Banning Critical

Race Theory?" *Brookings*, November. https://www.brookings.edu/articles/why-are-states-banning-critical-race-theory/.

Ray, Rashawn, and Keon L. Gilbert. 2020. "Has Trump Failed Black Americans?" *Brookings*, October 15.

Raymond, Laurel. 2017. "Trump Administration Eliminates Funding for Group Countering White Nationalism." *ThinkProgress*, June 23. https://thinkprogress.org/white-nationalism-group-funding-f1d35b5604e/.

Redell, Jordan. 2020. "Reparations Task Force to Hold First Meeting." Press release, City of Burlington (VT), November 11. https://www.burlingtonvt.gov/Press/reparations-task-force-to-hold-first-meeting.

Redneck Revolt. n.d.-a. "About." Last accessed August 31, 2023. https://www.redneckrevolt.org/about.

Redneck Revolt. n.d.-b. "Ways to Support." Last accessed August 31, 2023. https://www.redneckrevolt.org/support.

Reed, Adolph, Jr. 2022. *The South: Jim Crow and Its Afterlives*. New York: Verso.

Reed, Touré F. 2020. *Toward Freedom: The Case Against Race Reductionism*. New York: Verso.

Reichelmann, Ashley V., and Matthew O. Hunt. 2021. "How We Repair It: White Americans' Attitudes toward Reparations." *Brookings*, December 8. https://www.brookings.edu/articles/how-we-repair-it-white-americans-attitudes-toward-reparations/.

Reilly, Katie. 2022. "Republicans Are Increasingly Targeting 'Divisive Concepts' at Colleges and Universities." *Time*, March 29. https://time.com/6162489/divisive-concepts-colleges/.

Reilly, Ryan J. 2019. "5 years After Ferguson, the Justice Department Has All but Ended Federal Police Reform." *Huffington Post*, August 9 https://www.huffpost.com/entry/ferguson-justice-department-police-reform-trump-pattern-or-practice_n_5d4b18b3e4b0066eb70bad87.

Rein, Lisa. 2018. "Don't Condemn White Nationalists, Veterans Affairs' Diversity Chief Was Told after Charlottesville, E-Mails Show." *Washington Post*, December 5. https://www.washingtonpost.com/politics/dont-condemn-white-nationalists-veterans-affairs-diversity-chief-was-told-after-charlottesville-emails-show/2018/12/05/.

Reinhard, Beth, Jacqueline Alemany, and Josh Dawsey. 2021. "Low-Profile Heiress Who 'Played a Strong Role' in Financing Jan. 6 Rally Is Thrust into Spotlight." *Washington Post*, December 8. https://www.washingtonpost.com/investigations/publix-heiress-capitol-insurrection-fancelli/2021/12/08/.

Reinhard, Beth, and Josh Dawsey. 2022. "How a Trump-Allied Group Fighting 'Anti-White Bigotry' Beat Biden in Court." *Washington Post*, December 12. https://www.washingtonpost.com/politics/2022/12/12/stephen-miller-america-first-legal-biden-race-policies/.

Reinhard, Beth, and Josh Dawsey. 2023. "Gov. Ron DeSantis used secretive panel to

flip state Supreme Court." *New York Times*, June 20. ttps://www.washingtonpost.com/politics/2023/06/20/gov-ron-desantis-used-secretive-panel-flip-state-supreme-court/.
Reitman, Janet. 2018. "U.S. Law Enforcement Failed to See the Threat of White Nationalism. Now They Don't Know How to Stop It." *New York Times Magazine*, November 11, 38.
Reparations Circle Denver. 2023. "About." Last accessed September 5, 2023. https://reparationsdenver.com/about/.
Reparation Generation. n.d. "Racial Healing + Repair + Renewal." Last accessed September 5, 2023. https://reparationgeneration.org/.
Reparations: Requests and Offerings. n.d. "About." Last accessed September 5, 2023. https://www.facebook.com/groups/reparations.me/.
Reparations Roundtable 2023. "About Us." Patreon profile. https://www.patreon.com/ReparationsRoundtable/about.
Resnick, Brian. 2017. "White Fear of Demographic Change Is a Powerful Psychological Force." *Vox*, January 28. https://www.vox.com/science-and-health/2017/1/26/14340542/white-fear-trump-psychology-minority-majority.
Resource Generation. n.d. "History." Last accessed August 31, 2023. https://resourcegeneration.org/who-we-are/history/.
Reuters. 2021. "US Republicans Bring Defense Bill into Social Spending Debate." *Yahoo Finance*, November 2. https://finance.yahoo.com/news/u-republican-senators-bring-defense-182851610.html.
Richeson, Jennifer A. 2020. "Americans Are Determined to Believe in Black Progress." *The Atlantic*, September. https://www.theatlantic.com/magazine/archive/2020/09/the-mythology-of-racial-progress/614173/.
Rickford, Randall. 2015. "Black Lives Matter: Toward a Modern Practice of Mass Struggle." *New Labor Forum* 25, no.1 (December). https://doi.org/10.1177/1095796015620I.
Rising Majority. n.d. "About Us." Last accessed August 31, 2023. https://therisingmajority.com/about-us/.
Ritchie, Andrea, and Marbre Stahly-Butts, eds. 2019. *M4BL: Reparations Now Toolkit*. https://m4bl.org/wp-content/uploads/2020/05/Reparations-Now-Toolkit-FINAL.pdf.
Roberts, Frank Leon. 2018. "How Black Lives Matter Changed the Ways Americans Fought for Freedom." *ACLU*, July 13. https://www.aclu.org/news/racial-justice/how-black-lives-matter-changed-way-americans-fight.
Robertson, Campbell. 2023. "The Synagogue Attack Stands Alone, But Experts Say Violent Rhetoric Is Spreading." *New York Times*, August 4. https://www.nytimes.com/2023/08/04/us/pittsburgh-synagogue-shooting-antisemitism-bowers.
Robinson, Cedric J. 2020. *Black Marxism: The Making of the Black Radical Tradition*. 3rd ed. Chapel Hill: University of North Carolina Press.
Robinson, Martin. 2022. "Boris Slams Canadian Anti-Colonial Protestors Who

Raged 'Tear This B**** Down' as They Toppled Statues of the Queen and Queen Victoria and Threw One of Captain Cook in a Harbor amid Anger over the Deaths of Nearly 1,000 Indigenous Children Found in Mass Graves." *DailyMail.com*, July 2, 2021, updated April 27, 2022. https://www.dailymail.co.uk/news/article-9749001/Angry-protestors-topple-deface-statues-Queen-great-great-grandmother-Victoria.html.

Robinson, Randall. 2000. *The Debt: What America Owes to Blacks*. New York: Dutton.

Rocco, Philip. 2022. "Laboratories of What? American Federalism and the Politics of Democratic Subversion." In *Democratic Resilience: Can the United States Withstand Rising Polarization?*, edited by Robert C. Lieberman, Suzanne Mettler, and Kenneth M. Roberts, 297–319. New York: Cambridge University Press.

Roesler, Shannon. 2021. "Racial Segregation and Environmental Injustice." *Environmental Law Reporter* 51 (September): 10773–84.

Rogers, Katie, and Jason DeParle. 2019. "The White Nationalist Websites Cited by Stephen Miller." *New York Times*, November 18. https://www.nytimes.com/2019/11/18/us/politics/stephen-miller-white-nationalism.html.

Rogers, Taylor Nicole. 2021. "Black American Workers Need Widespread Economic Reform." *Financial Times*, May 24. https://www.ft.com/content/377a163d-fdbf-4f11-bb4a-e26465f8c2aa.

Rojas, Rick. 2020. "Alliance Brings the Flag Down in Mississippi." *New York Times*, July 11, A1.

Romo, Vanessa. 2020. "NASCAR Bans Confederate Flag." *NPR*, June 10. https://www.npr.org/sections/live-updates-protests-for-racial-justice/2020/06/10/874393049/nascar-bans-confederate-flag.

Rose City Antifa. n.d. "Home." Last accessed August 31, 2023. https://rosecityantifa.org/.

Ross, Megan, Brooks Hepp, and Kianna Gardner. 2018. "White Extremist Groups Are Growing—and Changing." *Center for Public Integrity*, September 5. https://publicintegrity.org/federal-politics/white-extremist-groups-are-growing-and-changing/.

Rossing, Emily. 2022. "Pursuing Reparations." *The Clarion*, Bethel University, St. Paul, MN, April 19. https://bethelclarion.com/38065/news/pursuing-reparations/.

Roston, Aram. 2021. "Proud Boys Leader Enrique Tarrio Was an FBI Informant." *The Guardian*, January 27. https://www.theguardian.com/us-news/2021/jan/27/proud-boys-leader-enrique-tarrio-fbi-informant.

Roth, Zachary. 2023. "Noncitizens Allowed to Vote in Some Local Elections, Spurring Backlash from GOP." *Georgia Recorder*, March 14. https://georgiarecorder.com/2023/03/14/noncitizens-allowed-to-vote-in-some-local-elections-spurring-backlash-from-gop/.

Rucker, Julian M., and Jennifer A. Richeson. 2021. "Toward an Understanding of Structural Racism: Implications for Criminal Justice." *Science* 374: 286–90.

Rucker, Karah, and Stacey Chamberlain. 2023. "San Francisco NAACP Opposing $5 Million Reparations Plan." *SAN: Straight Arrow News*, March 16. https://san.com/cc/san-francisco-naacp-opposing-5-million-reparations-plan/.

Rucker, Philip. 2018. "Trump Says Chicago Police Should Use 'Stop and Frisk' Tactics to Curb Shootings." *Washington Post*, October 8. https://www.washingtonpost.com/politics/trump-says-chicago-police-should-use-stop-and-frisk-tactics-to-curb-shootings/2018/10/08/a4afaaa0-cb0f-11e8-a3e6-44daa3d35ede_story.html?utm_term=.2a583df23974.

Ruiz, Rebecca R., Robert Gebeloff, Steve Eder, and Ben Protess. 2020. "A Conservative Agenda Unleashed on the Federal Courts." *New York Times*, March 14. https://www.nytimes.com/2020/03/14/us/trump-appeals-court-judges.html.

Russell, Jim. 2022. "Amherst Town Council Paves Way for $2 Million Reparations Bank." *Mass Live*, June 28. https://www.masslive.com/news/2022/06/amherst-town-council-paves-way-for-2-million-reparations-bank.html.

Sacchetti, Maria. 2017. "Immigration Judges Say Proposed Quotas from Justice Dept. Threaten Independence." *Washington Post*, October 12. https://www.washingtonpost.com/local/immigration/immigration-judges-say-proposed-quotas-from-justice-dept-threaten-independence/2017/10/12/.

Sacchetti, Maria, Felicia Sonmez, and Nick Miroff. 2019. "Trump Tightens Asylum Rules, Will Make Immigrants Pay Fees to Seek Humanitarian Refuge." *Washington Post*, April 30. https://www.washingtonpost.com/politics/trump-issues-memo-calling-for-changes-to-handling-of-asylum-cases/2019/04/29/.

Salozar, Carolyn. 2019. "Kavanaugh Slams 'Pure Discrimination' against Churches as Court Declines to Hear Religious Liberty Case." *Fox News*, March 4. https://www.foxnews.com/politics/kavanaugh-slams-pure-discrimination-against-churches-as-court-declines-to-hear-religious-liberty-case.

Sampson, Robert J., and Alix Winter. 2016. "The Racial Ecology of Lead Poisoning: Toxic Inequality in Chicago Neighborhoods, 1995–2013." *Du Bois Review* 13: 261–83.

Sanders, Ron. 2018. "Inactive Registered Voters No Longer Purged in Kentucky." *SurfKY News Group*, November 14. https://www.surfky.com/index.php/ohio/179-news/kentucky/130688-inactive-registered-voters-no-longer-purged-in-kentucky.

Sanger, David E., Michael D. Shear, and Eric Schmitt. 2021. "Trump's Pentagon Chief Squashed Idea to Send 250,000 Troops to the Border." *New York Times*, October 19. https://www.nytimes.com/2021/10/19/us/politics/trump-border.html.

Sankin, Aaron, and Will Carless. 2018. "President Trump Is Pushing White Nationalist Ideas into the Mainstream." *Washington Post*, August 24. https://www.washingtonpost.com/outlook/2018/08/24/president-trump-is-pushing-white-nationalist-ideas-into-mainstream/.

Saul, Stephanie. 2019. "Warren's Awakening to a World of Desperation." *New York Times*, August 26, A1.

Saul, Stephanie. 2023. "At U.Va, an Alumnus Attacked Diversity Programs. Now He Is on the Board." *New York Times*, April 23. https://www.nytimes.com/2023/04/23/us/uva-diversity-board-bert-ellis.html.

Savage, Charlie. 2017. "Justice Dept. to Take On Affirmative Action in College Admissions." *New York Times*, August 2, A1.

Savage, Niara. 2020. "UCLA Professor Suggests America Should Provide Reparations to Latinos." *Atlanta Black Star*, November 19. https://atlantablackstar.com/2020/11/19/ucla-professor-suggests-america-should-provide-reparations-to-latinos/.

Schaffner, Brian F., Matthew MacWilliams, and Tatishe Nteta. 2018. "Understanding White Polarization in the 2016 Vote for President: The Sobering Role of Racism and Sexism." *Political Science Quarterly* 133 (1): 9–34.

Schenker, Laura, David Sylvan, Jean-Louis Arcand, and Ravi Bhavnani. 2023. "Segregation and 'Out of Placeness': The Direct Effect of Neighborhood Racial Composition on Police Stops." *Political Research Quarterly*. https://doi.org/10.1177/10659129231171516.

Schlinkmann, Mark. 2022. "St. Louis Mayor Signs Bill Allowing Voluntary Reparations Donations as 'First Step.'" *St. Louis Post-Dispatch*, April 2. https://www.stltoday.com/news/local/govt-and-politics/st-louis-mayor-signs-bill-allowing-voluntary-reparations-donations-as-first-step/.

Schmail, Emily. 2023. "Stripping Confederate Ties, the U.S. Navy Renames Two Vessels." *New York Times*, March 11. https://www.nytimes.com/2023/03/11/us/navy-ship-confederate-robert-smalls.html.

Schmidt, Michael A., Alan Feuer, Maggie Haberman and Adam Goldman. 2023. "Trump Supporters' Violent Rhetoric In His Defense Disturbs Experts." *New York Times*, June 14. https://www.nytimes.com/2023/06/10/us/politics/trump-supporter-violent-rhetoric.html.

Schmidt, Ronald Sr. 2020. *Interpreting Racial Politics in the United States*. New York: Routledge.

Schmidt, Samantha. 2019. "'Victory For Equal Pay': Judge Rules Trump Administration Must Require Companies to Report Pay by Gender, Race." *Washington Post*, March 5. https://www.washingtonpost.com/dc-md-va/2019/03/05/victory-equal-pay-judge-rules-trump-administration-must-require-companies-report-pay-by-gender-race/?utm_term=.6eefb8fd8010.

Schmidt, Vivien A. 2011. "Reconciling Ideas and Institutions through Discursive Institutionalism." In *Ideas and Politics in Social Science Research*, edited by Daniel Béland and Robert Henry Cox, 47–64. New York: Oxford University Press.

Schneider, Gregory S. 2023. "White Contractors Wouldn't Remove Confederate Statues. So a Black Man Did It." *Washington Post*, January 2. https://www.washingtonpost.com/dc-md-va/2023/01/02/devon-henry-confederate-statues-richmond/.

Schnurer, Eric. 2017. "The Rise of Zero-Sum Politics." *U.S. News*, September 14.

https://www.usnews.com/opinion/thomas-jefferson-street/articles/2017-09-14/donald-trump-and-the-rise-of-zero-sum-politics.

Schroeder, Robert. 2016. "Trump Has Gotten Nearly $3 Billion in 'Free' Advertising." *MarketWatch*, May 6. https://www.marketwatch.com/story/trump-has-gotten-nearly-3-billion-in-free-advertising-2016-05-06.

Schuessler, Jennifer. 2020. "Initiative Will Reimagine Monuments." *New York Times*, October 5, C2.

Schwartz, Brian. 2021. "Trump-Allied Dark Money Group Joins Forces with a Think Tank Run by Ex-President's Former Aides." *CNBC*, November 22. https://www.cnbc.com/2021/11/22/trump-alumni-think-tank-joins-forces-with-america-first-works-dark-money-group.html.

Schwartz, Matthew S. 2020. "Trump Tells Agencies to End Trainings on 'White Privilege' and 'Critical Race Theory.'" *NPR News*, September 5. https://www.npr.org/2020/09/05/910053496/trump-tells-agencies-to-end-trainings-on-white-privilege-and-critical-race-theor.

Schwartz, Sarah. 2023. "Map: Where Critical Race Theory Is Under Attack." *Education Week*, March 23. https://www.edweek.org/policy-politics/map-where-critical-race-theory-is-under-attack/2021/06.

Scott, Eugene. 2018. "Trump Said It Is 'Racist' to Ask Him about His Nationalism. Here's Why It's Necessary." *Washington Post*, November 8. https://www.washingtonpost.com/politics/2018/11/08/trump-said-it-is-racist-ask-him-about-his-nationalism-heres-why-its-necessary/?utm_term=.3b7b570f57c1.

Scott, Mackenzie. 2021. "Seeding by Ceding." *Medium*, June 15. https://mackenzie-scott.medium.com/seeding-by-ceding-ea6de642bf.

Screamingfrog. n.d. "Screaming Frog SEO Spider." Last accessed August 31, 2023. https://www.screamingfrog.co.uk/seo-spider/.

Seisdedos, Iker. 2023. "A US City Took Down Its Racist Statues. Where Do They Go Next?" *The Guardian*, February 28. https://www.theguardian.com/us-news/2023/feb/27/the-statue-graveyard-where-torn-down-confederate-monuments-lie.

Serwer, Adam. 2017. "Jeff Sessions' Unqualified Praise for a 1924 Immigration Law." *The Atlantic*, January 10. https://www.theatlantic.com/politics/archive/2017/01/jeff-sessions-1924-immigration/512591/.

Sessions, Jefferson. 2018. "Remarks at the Department of Justice's Religious Liberty Summit." *United States Department of Justice*, July 30. https://www.justice.gov/opa/speech/attorney-general-sessions-delivers-remarks-department-justice-s-religious-liberty-summit.

Settles, Gabrielle. 2021. "How Many Newly Elected Officials and Congressional Candidates Were 'Involved' in the Capitol Riot?" *PolitiFact*, December 3. https://www.politifact.com/article/2021/dec/03/how-many-newly-elected-officials-and-congressional/.

Shah, Areeba. 2023. "Watchdog Accuses Right-Wing Supreme Court Takeover Architect of Funneling $73 Million in Non-Profit Funds." *Salon*, April 8. https://

www.salon.com/2023/04/08/watchdog-accuses-right-wing-takeover-architect-of-funneling-73m-in-non-profit-funds/.

Shaheen, Kareem. 2021. "Canada Faces Reckoning on Abuse of Indigenous Children after Court Ruling." *Financial Times*, October 5. https://www.ft.com/content/20faa21c-fff2-42c2-8aca-f321e0d5809d.

Sharkey, Patrick. 2022. "The Crime Spike Is No Mystery." *The Atlantic*, November 23. https://www.theatlantic.com/ideas/archive/2022/11/crime-wave-gun-violence-chicago-causes/672216/.

Sharkey, Patrick, Keeanga-Yamahtta Taylor, and Yaryna Serkez. 2020. "The Gaps between White and Black America, in Charts." *New York Times*, June 19. https://www.nytimes.com/interactive/2020/06/19/opinion/politics/opportunity-gaps-race-inequality.html.

Sheasley, Chelsea. 2022. "One Country, Two Histories: What Does It Mean to Be an American?" *Christian Science Monitor*, June 14. https://www.csmonitor.com/USA/Education/2022/0614/One-country-two-histories-What-does-it-mean-to-be-an-American.

Shepard, Paul. 2000. "Group to Seek Slavery Reparations." *Washington Post*, November 5. https://www.washingtonpost.com/archive/politics/2000/11/05/group-to-seek-slavery-reparations/.

Sherman, Mark, Kevin Freking, and Matthew Daly. 2020. "Trump's Impact on Courts Likely to Last beyond His Term." *AP News*, December 21. https://apnews.com/article/joe-biden-donald-trump-mitch-mcconnell-elections-judiciary.

Sides, John, Michael Tesler, and Lynn Vavreck. 2017. "The 2016 Election: How Trump Lost and Won." *Journal of Democracy* 28 (2): 34–44.

Sides, John, Michael Tesler, and Lynn Vavreck. 2018. *Identity Crisis: The 2016 Election and the Battle for the Meaning of America*. Princeton, NJ: Princeton University Press.

Sidner, Sara. 2020. "Sheriff Spoke in Defense of Accused Domestic Terrorists." *CNN*, October 14. https://edition.cnn.com/2020/10/14/us/michigan-sheriff-militias/index.html.

Silver, Hadass. 2022. "Inventing 'White Privilege': Pseudo-progressivism in American Political Discourse." *American Political Thought* 11 (4): 437–66.

Silverstein, Jake. 2021. "The 1619 Project and the Long Battle over U.S. History." *New York Times Magazine*, November 9, updated November 12. https://www.nytimes.com/2021/11/09/magazine/1619-project-us-history.html.

Simien, Evelyn M. 2007. "Doing Intersectionality Research: From Conceptual Issues to Practical Examples." *Politics and Gender* 3 (2): 264–71.

Simmons, Ruth J. 2004. "Facing Up to Our Ties to Slavery." *Boston Globe*, April 28. http://archive.boston.com/news/globe/editorial_opinion/oped/articles/2004/04/28/facing_up_to_our_ties_to_slavery/.

Simpson, April. 2022. "Reparations for Racist Laws? Idea Gaining Traction at State,

Local Level." *Center for Public Integrity*, July 1. https://publicintegrity.org/inside-publici/newsletters/watchdog-newsletter/reparations-gain-traction-local-levels/.

Skewl. n.d. "Reparations Initiative." Instagram profile. Last accessed September 5, 2023. https://www.instagram.com/p/CHVholSL7v5/?img_index=1.

Skocpol, Theda. 1995. "Why I Am an Historical Institutionalist." *Polity* 28 (1): 103–6.

Skocpol, Theda, and Caroline Tervo, eds. 2020. *Upending American Politics*. Cambridge, MA: Harvard University Press.

Smart, Sara. 2021. "A Statue of Thomas Jefferson Is Removed from New York City Hall after 187 Years." *CNN*, November 24. /www.cnn.com/2021/11/24/us/thomas-jefferson-statue-removed/index.html.

Smedley, Audrey, and Brian D. Smedley. 2012. *Race in North America: Origin and Evolution of a World-View*. 4th ed. Boulder, CO: Westview Press.

Smith, Alexandra. 2021. "Why Critical Race Theory Is Essential to an Honest Education in America." *Human Rights Pulse*, September 2. https://www.humanrightspulse.com/mastercontentblog/why-critical-race-theory-is-essential-to-an-honest-education-in-america.

Smith, David. 2017. "Q&A: What Are Trump and the White House's Links to the Far Right?" *The Guardian*, August 14. https://www.theguardian.com/us-news/2017/aug/14/donald-trump-steve-bannon-breitbart-news-alt-right-charlottesville.

Smith, David. 2020. "Donald Trump Announces Surge of Police Officers in Democratic Cities." *The Guardian*, July 23. https://www.theguardian.com/us-news/2020/jul/22/donald-trump-federal-officers-police-surge-chicago.

Smith, David. 2022. "Biden's Message Drowned Out by Beat of the Republican Culture-War Drum." *The Guardian*, April 24. https://www.theguardian.com/us-news/2022/apr/24/joe-bidens-message-drowned-out-by-beat-of-the-republican-culture-war-drum.

Smith, Mitch, and Tim Arango. 2021. "Minneapolis Voters Hold Future of Police Dept. in Their Hands." *New York Times*, October 29, A1.

Smith, Mitch, Ernesto Londoño, and Glenn Thrush. 2023. "Here Are the Most Significant Findings Against the Minneapolis Police." *New York Times*, June 16. https://www.nytimes.com/2023/06/16/us/police-doj-report-highlights-minneapolis.html.

Smith, Paige, and Louis C. LaBrecque. 2021. "Biden to Seek Pay Data to Help End Gender, Racial Disparities." *Bloomberg News*, January 4. https://news.bloomberglaw.com/daily-labor-report/biden-to-seek-pay-data-to-help-end-gender-racial-disparities.

Smith, Rogers M. 1997. *Civic Ideals*. New Haven, CT: Yale University Press.

Smith, Rogers M. 2015. *Political Peoplehood*. Chicago: University of Chicago Press.

Smith, Rogers M., and Desmond King. 2020. "White Protectionism in America." *Perspectives on Politics* 19 (2): 1–19.

Smith, Rogers M., and Desmond King. 2021. "Racial Reparations against White

Protectionism: America's New Racial Politics." *Journal of Race, Ethnicity and Politics* 6: 82–96.

Solidaire. 2022a. "Solidaire Network Form 990." https://solidairenetwork.org/wp-content/uploads/2022/09/SOLIDAIRE-FY21-990-Public-Disclosure-Copy-3.pdf.

Solidaire. n.d. "Who We Are." Last accessed August 31, 2023. https://solidairenetwork.org/who-we-are/.

Solomon, Adina. 2021. "A Look at the First Official Act of Reparations in Georgia." *Facing South*, June 9. https://www.facingsouth.org/2021/06/look-first-official-act-reparations-georgia.

Somvichian-Clausen, Austa. 2021. "Biden Rescinds Trump's 1776 Commission." *The Hill*, January 21. https://thehill.com/changing-america/enrichment/education/535323-biden-rescinds-trumps-1776-commission-a-report/.

Sonnenberg, Rhonda. 2022. "Under Attack: Virginia Military Institute's Culture Is Forced to Change—But How Much?" *Southern Poverty Law Center*, June 17. https://www.splcenter.org/news/2022/06/17/under-attack-virginia-military-institutes-culture-forced-change-how-much.

Sotomayor, Marianna. 2021. "House Panel Approves Bill to Create a Commission on Slavery Reparations." *Washington Post*, April 14. https://www.washingtonpost.com/politics/reparations-slavery-commission/2021/04/14/.

Soul 2 Soul Sisters. n.d. "Our Story." Last accessed August 31, 2023. https://soul2soulsisters.org/our-story/.

South Carolina Policy Council. 2021. "Bills to Watch in 2022." December 14. https://www.scpolicycouncil.org/bills_to_watch_in_2022.

Southern Poverty Law Center. n.d. "White Nationalist." Last accessed August 31, 2023. https://www.splcenter.org/fighting-hate/extremist-files/ideology/white-nationalist.

Spence, Lester K. 2015. *Knocking the Hustle: Against the Neoliberal Turn in Black Politics*. New York: Punctum Books.

Spielman, Fran. 2022. "City Council Urged to Create Guaranteed Annual Income Program for Black Men." *Chicago Sun-Times*, June 9. https://chicago.suntimes.com/city-hall/2022/6/9/23161878/chicago-reparations-evanston-african-americans-black-men-city-council-subcommittee-guaranteed-income.

Sprunt, Barbara. 2021. "The Brewing Political Battle over Critical Race Theory." *NPR*, June 29. https://www.npr.org/2021/06/02/1001055828/the-brewing-political-battle-over-critical-race-theory.

State Freedom Caucus Network. n.d. "Find Your Local Representative." Last accessed August 31, 2023. https://statefreedomcaucus.org/.

State Policy Network. n.d. "History." Last accessed August 31, 2023. https://spn.org/history/.

Steakin, Will. 2021. "How the Far-Right Group behind AFPAC Is Using Twitter to

Grow Its Movement." *ABC News*, March 12. https://abcnews.go.com/US/group-afpac-twitter-grow-movement/story?id=76418773.

Stein, Letitia. 2018. "Politics Clouds Felon Voting Rights Restoration in Florida." *Reuters*, December 15. www.reuters.com/article/us-usa-florida-felons/politics-cloud-felon-voting-rights-restoration-in-florida-idUSKBN1OE0C2.

Stein, Perry. 2021. "Wisconsin Congressman Introduces Bill to Ban Critical Race Theory in D.C. Schools." *Washington Post*, June 18. https://www.washingtonpost.com/local/education/dc-schools-critical-race-theory/2021/06/18/8d7afbd0-d04f-11eb-a7f1-52b8870bef7c_story.html.

Steinmo, Sven, Kathleen Thelen, and Frank Longstreth, eds. 1992. *Structuring Politics: Historical Institutionalism in Comparative Analysis*. New York: Cambridge University Press.

Steinmetz, Katy. 2019. "'The Most Hated Person on Campus': Why Some College Republicans Are Channeling Trump." *Time*. Last accessed August 31, 2023. http://time.com/the-most-hated-person-on-campus-why-some-college-republicans-are-channeling-donald-trump/.

Stephens-Dougan, LaFleur. 2021. "The Persistence of Racial Cues and Appeals in American Politics." *Annual Review of Political Science* 24: 301–20.

Stewart, Katherine. 2020. *The Power Worshippers: Inside the Dangerous Rise of Religious Nationalism*. New York: Bloomsbury Publishing.

Stofan, Jake. 2021. "Fight over Felon Voting Rights Head Back to Federal Court." *News4jax*, July 22. https://www.news4jax.com/news/florida/2021/07/22/fight-over-felon-voting-rights-heads-back-to-federal-court/.

Strauss, Valerie, Danielle Douglas-Gabriel, and Moriah Balingit. 2018. "DeVos Seeks Cuts from Education Department to Support School Choice." *Washington Post*, February 13. www.washingtonpost.com/news/education/wp/2018/02/12/devos-seeks-massive-cuts-from-education-department-to-support-school-choice/?utm_term=.fb52fe56d13f.

Streep, Abe. 2023. "How Montana Took a Hard Right toward Christian Nationalism." *New York Times Magazine*, January 11. https://www.nytimes.com/2023/01/11/magazine/montana-republicans-christian-nationalism.html.

Students Deserve. n.d. "Black Lives Matter Partnership." Last accessed August 31, 2023. https://www.schoolslastudentsdeserve.com/black-lives-matter-partnership.html.

Sugrue, Thomas J. 2016. "Jeff Sessions' Other Civil Rights Problem." *New York Times*, November 21. https://www.nytimes.com/2016/11/21/opinion/jeff-sessions-other-civil-rights-problem.html.

Sullivan, Becky. 2023. "2 Shootings at Mistaken Addresses Renew the Focus on Controversial Self-Defense Laws." *NPR*, April 18. https://www.npr.org/2023/04/18/1170648617/how-stand-your-ground-laws-have-proliferated-in-the-last-decade.

Summers, Madison. 2019. "Cruz Addresses the 'Overheated' Rhetoric between

POTUS and the Freshmen Democrat 'Squad.'" *IJR*, August 1. https://ijr.com/cruz-addresses-overheated-rhetoric-potus-freshmen-dems/.

Swan, Jonathan, Alan Feuer, Luke Broadwater, and Maggie Haberman. 2023. "How Mark Meadows Pursued a High-Wire Legal Strategy in Trump Inquiries." *New York Times*, August 22. https://www.nytimes.com/2023/08/22/us/politics/mark-meadows-trump-legal-strategy.html.

Swan, Sarah, and Donnalie Jamnah. 2021. "Teaching the 1619 Project: Insights for Educators and Librarians." 1619education.org, December 22. https://1619education.org/stories/teaching-1619-project-insights-educators-and-librarians.

Swarns, Rachel L. 2022. "Catholic Order Struggles to Raise $100 Million to Atone for Slave Labor." *New York Times*, August 16. https://www.nytimes.com/2022/08/16/us/jesuits-reparations.html.

Sylvester, Sherry, and Carol Swain. 2021. "Critical Race Theory Bans Protect Our History and Students." *Washington Examiner*, November 10. https://www.washingtonexaminer.com/restoring-america/patriotism-unity/critical-race-theory-bans-protect-our-history-and-students.

Tackett, Michael and Michael Wines. 2018. "Trump Shutters His Commission on Voter Fraud." *New York Times*, January 4, A1.

Tankersley, Jim. 2022. "G.O.P. Signals Plan to Shrink Social Security." *New York Times*, November 3, A1.

Tankersley, Jim. 2023. "Black Americans Are Much More Likely to Face Tax Audits, Study Finds." *New York Times*, February 1, A18.

Tavernise, Sabrina. 2021. "New Chapter in Richmond as Lee Statue Comes Down." *New York Times*, September 9, A9.

Taylor, Keeanga-Yamahtta. 2016. *From #BlackLivesMatter to Black Liberation*. Chicago: Haymarket Books.

Taylor, Keeanga-Yamahtta. 2019. *Race for Profit: How Banks and the Real Estate Industry Undermined Black Homeownership*. Chapel Hill: University of North Carolina Press.

Taylor, Keeanga-Yamahtta. 2023. "The Meaning of African American Studies." *New Yorker*, February 3. https://www.newyorker.com/culture/q-and-a/the-meaning-of-african-american-studies.

TCCRI (Texas Conservative Coalition Research Institute). n.d. "About TCCRI." Last accessed August 31, 2023. https://www.txccri.org/about.

TeaParty.org. 2021. "JUST IN: Marjorie Taylor Greene Introduces Bill to Award Congressional Gold Medal to Kyle Rittenhouse." November 23. https://www.teaparty.org/just-in-marjorie-taylor-greene-introduces-bill-to-award-congressional-gold-medal-to-kyle-rittenhouse-472224.

Teles, Steven M. 2008. *The Rise of the Conservative Legal Movement: The Battle for Control of the Law*. Princeton, NJ: Princeton University Press.

Tesler, Michael. 2012. "The Spillover of Racialization into Health Care: How President Obama Polarized Public Opinion by Race and Racial Attitudes." *American Journal of Political Science* 56 (3): 690–704.

Tesler, Michael. 2013. "The Return of Old Fashioned Racism to White Americans' Partisan Preferences in the Early Obama Era." *Journal of Politics* 75 (1): 110–23.

Tesler, Michael. 2016a. *Post-Racial or Most-Racial? Race and Politics in the Obama Era*. Chicago: University of Chicago Press.

Tesler, Michael. 2016b. "Views about Race Mattered More in Electing Trump Than in Electing Obama." *Washington Post/Monkey Cage*, November 22. https://www.washingtonpost.com/news/monkey-cage/wp/2016/11/22/peoples-views-about-race-mattered-more-in-electing-trump-than-in-electing-obama/.

Tesler, Michael. 2016c. "Trump Is the First Modern Republican to Win the Nomination on Racial Prejudice." *Washington Post/Monkey Cage*, August 1. https://www.washingtonpost.com/news/monkey-cage/wp/2016/08/01/trump-is-the-first-republican-in-modern-times-to-win-the-partys-nomination-on-anti-minority-sentiments/.

Tesler, Michael. 2017. "Trump Voters Think African Americans Are Much Less Deserving Than 'Average Americans.'" *Huffington Post*, December 20. https://www.huffpost.com/entry/trump-voters-think-africa_b_13732500.

Thomas, Louisa. 2016. "America First, for Charles Lindbergh and Donald Trump." *New Yorker*, July 24. https://www.newyorker.com/news/news-desk/america-first-for-charles-lindbergh-and-donald-trump.

Thompson, Andrew. 2018. "The Measure of Hate on 4Chan." *Rolling Stone*, May 10. https://www.rollingstone.com/politics/politics-news/the-measure-of-hate-on-4chan-627922/.

Thompson, Erin L. 2022. "Confederate Heritage Groups Are Keeping the Lost Cause on Life Support." *Washington Post*, January 23. https://www.washingtonpost.com/opinions/2022/01/23/confederate-heritage-groups-are-keeping-lost-cause-life-support/.

Thomson-DeVeaux, Amelia, and Laura Bronner. 2022. "The Supreme Court's Partisan Divide Hasn't Been This Sharp in Generations." *FiveThirtyEight.com*, July 5. https://fivethirtyeight.com/features/the-supreme-courts-partisan-divide-hasnt-been-this-sharp-in-generations/.

Thornton, Patricia H., William Ocasio, and Michael Lounsbury. 2012. *The Institutional Logics Perspective: A New Approach to Culture, Structure and Process*. New York: Oxford University Press.

Thurston, Chloe N. 2018. *At the Boundaries of Homeownership*. New York: Cambridge University Press.

Tides. n.d. "Our Approach." Last accessed August 31, 2023. https://www.tides.org/approach/.

Tillery, Alvin B., Jr. 2019. "What Kind of Movement Is Black Lives Matter? The View from Twitter." *Journal of Race, Ethnicity and Politics* 4: 297–323.

Toobin, Jeffrey. 2017. "The Conservative Pipeline to the Supreme Court." *New Yorker*, April 17. https://www.newyorker.com/magazine/2017/04/17/the-conservative-pipeline-to-the-supreme-court.

Torbati, Yeganeh. 2018. "Trump Administration Bars Haitians from U.S. Visas for Low-Skilled Work." *Reuters*, January 17. www.reuters.com/article/us-usa-immigration-haiti/trump-administration-bars-haitians-from-u-s-visas-for-low-skilled-work-idUSKBN1F702O?feedType=RSS&feedName=politicsNews.

Totenberg. Nina. 2023. "Supreme Court Unexpectedly Upholds Provision Prohibiting Racial Gerrymandering." NPR, June 8. https://www.npr.org/2023/06/08/1181002182/supreme-court-voting-rights.

Trump, Donald J. 2015. "Remarks Announcing Candidacy for President in New York City." June 16. *The American Presidency Project*. https://www.presidency.ucsb.edu/documents/remarks-announcing-candidacy-for-president-new-york-city.

Trump, Donald J. 2016a. "Remarks on Foreign Policy." April 27. *The American Presidency Project*. https://www.presidency.ucsb.edu/documents/remarks-foreign-policy.

Trump, Donald J. 2016b. "Remarks in Virginia Beach, Virginia." July 11. *The American Presidency Project*. https://www.presidency.ucsb.edu/documents/remarks-virginia-beach-virginia-0.

Trump, Donald J. 2016c. "Address Accepting the Presidential Nomination at the Republican National Convention in Cleveland, Ohio." July 21. *The American Presidency Project*. https://www.presidency.ucsb.edu/documents/address-accepting-the-presidential-nomination-the-republican-national-convention-cleveland.

Trump, Donald J. 2016d. "Remarks at Youngstown State University in Youngstown, Ohio." August 15. *The American Presidency Project*. https://www.presidency.ucsb.edu/documents/remarks-youngstown-state-university-youngstown-ohio.

Trump, Donald J. 2016e. "Remarks at the Washington County Park Fair in West Bend, Wisconsin." August 16. *The American Presidency Project*. https://www.presidency.ucsb.edu/documents/remarks-the-washington-county-fair-park-west-bend-wisconsin.

Trump, Donald J. 2016f. "Remarks at the Summit Sports and Ice Complex in Dimondale, Michigan." August 19. *The American Presidency Project*. https://www.presidency.ucsb.edu/documents/remarks-the-summit-sports-and-ice-complex-dimondale-michigan.

Trump, Donald J. 2016g. "Remarks at Great Faith International Ministries in Detroit, Michigan." September 3. *The American Presidency Project*. https://www.presidency.ucsb.edu/documents/remarks-great-faith-international-ministries-detroit-michigan.

Trump, Donald J. 2016h. "Remarks at the Cleveland Arts and Sciences Academy in Cleveland, Ohio." September 8. *The American Presidency Project*. https://www.presidency.ucsb.edu/documents/remarks-the-cleveland-arts-and-social-sciences-academy-cleveland-ohio.

Trump, Donald J. 2016i. "Remarks to the 11th Annual Values Voter Summit in Washington, D.C. Omni Shoreham Hotel." September 9. *The American Presidency Project.* https://www.presidency.ucsb.edu/documents/remarks-the-11th-annual-values-voter-summit-washington-dc-omni-shoreham-hotel-washington.

Trump, Donald J. 2016j. "Remarks at a Rally at Sun Center Studios in Chester Township, Pennsylvania." September 22. *The American Presidency Project.* https://www.presidency.ucsb.edu/documents/remarks-rally-sun-center-studios-chester-township-pennsylvania.

Trump, Donald J. 2016k. "Remarks at the South Florida Fair Expo Center in West Palm Beach, Florida." October 13. *The American Presidency Project.* https://www.presidency.ucsb.edu/documents/remarks-the-south-florida-fair-expo-center-west-palm-beach-florida.

Trump, Donald J. 2017a. "The Inaugural Address." January 20. https://www.whitehouse.gov/briefings-statements/the-inaugural-address/.

Trump, Donald J. 2017b. "Donald Trump's Inauguration Speech—Full Speech." https://www.youtube.com/watch?v=FFH7QMZ5N1k.

Trump, Donald J. 2018. "Congresswoman Maxine Waters." June 25. https://twitter.com/realdonaldtrump/status/1011295779422695424?lang=en.

Trump, Donald J. 2019. "Remarks by President Trump at 2019 Second Step Presidential Justice Forum." October 25. https://www.whitehouse.gov/briefings-statements/remarks-president-trump-2019-second-step-presidential-justice-forum-columbia-sc/.

Trump, Donald J. 2020a. "July 4th Speech at Mount Rushmore." https://singjupost.com/full-transcript-president-trumps-july-4-2020-speech-at-mount-rushmore/.

Trump, Donald J. 2020b. "Executive Order on Establishing the President's 1776 Advisory Commission." November 2. https://trumpwhitehouse.archives.gov/presidential-actions/executive-order-establishing-presidents-advisory-1776-commission/.

Tucson Reparations. 2022. "Intro." Facebook post, February 6, 2022. https://www.facebook.com/tucsonreparations/.

Turner, Jack. 2018. "Douglass and Political Judgment: The Post-Reconstruction Years." In *A Political Companion to Frederick Douglass*, edited by Neil Roberts, 203–35. Lexington: University Press of Kentucky.

Uhuru Solidarity. n.d. "Reparations Legacy Project." Last accessed August 30, 2023. https://www.uhurusolidarity.org/reparationslegacy.

Ujifusa, Andrew. 2018. "Betsy DeVos Revokes Obama Discipline Guidance Designed to Protect Students of Color." *Education Week: Politics K-12*, December 21. http://blogs.edweek.org/edweek/campaign-k-12/2018/12/betsy_devos_revokes_obama_discipline_guidance_students_of_color_protect.html.

Underwood, Lauren. 2021. "Underwood, Adams, Booker Unveil the Black Maternal Health Omnibus Act to Address America's Maternal Health Crisis." February 8. https://underwood.house.gov/media/press-releases/underwood-adams-booker-unveil-black-maternal-health-momnibus-act-address.

Union Presbyterian Seminary. 2020. "Union Presbyterian Seminary Creates $1M Endowment in Support of Reparations for Enslaved African Americans." December 2. https://www.upsem.edu/newsroom/union-seminary-creates-1m-endowment-in-support-of-reparations-for-enslaved-african-americans/.

United Nations. 2005. "Basic Principles and Guidelines on the Right to a Remedy and Reparation for Victims of Gross Violations of International Human Rights Law and Serious Violations of International Humanitarian Law." *United Nations Human Rights: Office of the High Commissioner*. December 15. https://www.ohchr.org/en/instruments-mechanisms/instruments/basic-principles-and-guidelines-right-remedy-and-reparation.

US Department of Justice. 2023. "Attorney General Merrick B. Garland Delivers a Statement Following the Jury Verdict in the Proud Boys Trial." May 4. https://www.justice.gov/opa/speech/attorney-general-merrick-b-garland-delivers-statement-following-jury-verdict-proud-boys.

US Department of Justice Civil Rights Division. 2015. "Investigation of the Ferguson Police Department." March 4. https://www.justice.gov/sites/default/files/opa/press-releases/attachments/2015/03/04/ferguson_police_department_report.pdf.

US Department of Justice Civil Rights Division and U.S. Attorney's Office Western District of Kentucky Civil Division. 2023. "Investigation of the Louisville Metro Police Department and Louisville Metro Government." March 8. https://www.justice.gov/d9/press-releases/attachments/2023/03/08/2023.3.8_lmpd_findings_report_0.pdf.

US Department of Justice Office of Public Affairs. 2016. "Justice Department and City of Ferguson, Missouri Resolve Lawsuit with Agreement to Reform Ferguson Police Department." March 17. https://www.justice.gov/opa/pr/justice-department-and-city-ferguson-missouri-resolve-lawsuit-agreement-reform-ferguson.

United States Institute of Peace. 1995. "Truth Commission: South Africa." December 1. https://www.usip.org/publications/1995/12/truth-commission-south-africa.

Vadum, Matthew. 2019. "Ben Carson Seeks Fairer, More Efficient Disparate Impact Rules." *Washington Times*, October 30. https://www.theepochtimes.com/ben-carson-seeks-fairer-more-efficient-disparate-impact-rule_3132184.html.

Valentino, Nicholas A., Fabian G. Neuner, and L. Matthew Vandenbroek. 2018. "The Changing Norms of Racial Political Rhetoric and the End of Racial Priming." *Journal of Politics* 80 (3): 751–68.

Vargas, Ramon Antonio, and Maya Yang. 2022. "What We Know So Far about the Man Who Attacked Nancy Pelosi's Husband." *The Guardian*, October 28. https://www.theguardian.com/us-news/2022/oct/28/paul-pelosi-nancy-pelosi-attack-david-depape.

Vasilogambros, Matt. 2021. "Noncitizens Are Slowly Gaining Voting Rights." *PEW:*

Stateline, July 1. https://stateline.org/2021/07/01/noncitizens-are-slowly-gaining-voting-rights/.

Vicente, Vann. 2021. "What Is a Web Crawler, and How Does It Work?" How-To Geek, July 9. https://www.howtogeek.com/731787/what-is-a-web-crawler-and-how-does-it-work/.

Vickery, Amanda, Kyra Trent, and Cinthia Salinas. 2019. "'The Future Is Intersectional': Using the Arts to Reinsert Black Women Into the Civil Rights Narrative." *Multicultural Perspectives* 21 (4): 224–32.

Victor, Daniel. 2020. "'Gone With the Wind' Is Pulled." *New York Times*, June 11, C3.

Viswanatha, Aruna. 2017. "Trump Administration Lifts Obama's Ban on Military Surplus Gear Going to Police." *Wall Street Journal*, August 28. www.wsj.com/articles/trump-administration-allows-police-agencies-to-get-surplus-military-gear-in-reversal-of-obama-rule-1503934284.

Vogel, Kenneth P., and Shane Goldmacher. 2022a. "Denouncing Dark Money, Then Deploying It in 2022." *New York Times*, January 22, A1.

Vogel, Kenneth P., and Shane Goldmacher. 2022b. "Complex $1.6 Billion Donation Enriches Conservative War Chest." *New York Times*, August 23, A1.

Waldmeir, Patti. 2020. "Black Lives Matter Co-Founder Tometi: 'We Have Taken the Baton.'" *Financial Times*, August 14. https://www.ft.com/content/71efd9a2-c1bb-47b6-b4c5-7795b1a66cac.

Walker, Hunter. 2023. "EXCLUSIVE: Capitol Hill Staffer Is a Prominent Follower of Neo-Nazi Nick Fuentes." *TPM*, May 14. https://talkingpointsmemo.com/muckraker/paul-gosar-nick-fuentes-staffer-wade-searle.

Wallace-Wells, Benjamin. 2021. "How a Conservative Activist Invented the Conflict over Critical Race Theory." *New Yorker*, June 18. https://www.newyorker.com/news/annals-of-inquiry/how-a-conservative-activist-invented-the-conflict-over-critical-race-theory.

Walmart. 2021. "The Walmart.org Center for Racial Equity Awards Over $14 Million in First Round of Grants." February 1. https://philanthropynewsdigest.org/news/walmart-awards-14-million-through-center-for-racial-equity.

Walter, Amy. 2022. "2022 National House Vote Tracker." *The Cook Report*. Last accessed September 13, 2023. https://www.cookpolitical.com/charts/house-charts/national-house-vote-tracker/2022.

Walter, Barbara F. 2022. *How Civil Wars Start: And How to Stop Them*. New York: Crown.

Walters, Dan. 2023. "California's Budget Deficit May Be Even Larger Than Predicted." *Cal Matters*, February 23. https://calmatters.org/commentary/2023/02/budget-deficit-may-be-larger/.

Wang, Hansi Lo. 2023. "Alabama's congressional map is struck down again for diluting Black voters' power." *NPR*, September 5. https://www.npr.org/2023/09/05/1193749552/alabama-congressional-map.

Wang, Qi, Nolan Edward Phillips, Mario L. Small, and Robert J. Sampson. 2018.

"Urban Mobility and Neighborhood Isolation in America's 50 Largest Cities." *PNAS* 115: 7735–40.

Washington Policy Center. 2021. "Governor Inslee: Don't Impose Divisive and Harmful Critical Race Theory on Our Schools." April 18. https://www.washingtonpolicy.org/publications/detail/governor-inslee-dont-impose-divisive-and-harmful-critical-race-theory-on-our-schools-2.

Washtenaw Health Plan Staff. 2020. "Racial Justice and Health Equity." https://www.washtenaw.org/3182/Racial-Justice-and-Health-Equity.

Wasow, Omar. 2020. "Agenda Seeding: How 1960s Black Protests Moved Elites, Public Opinion and Voting." *American Political Science Review* 114: 638–59.

Weaver, Timothy. 2017. "Urban Crisis: The Genealogy of a Concept." *Urban Studies* 54 (9): 2039–55.

Weber, Travis. 2019. "Justices Alito, Thomas, Gorsuch, and Kavanaugh: We See Religious Freedom Problems with Coach Kennedy Case." *Family Research Council*, January 22. https://www.frcblog.com/2019/01/justices-alito-thomas-gorsuch-and-kavanaugh-we-see-religious-freedom-problems-coach-kennedy-case/.

Weiner, Amanda, and Ariel Zellman. 2022. "Mobilizing the White: White Nationalism and Congressional Politics in the American South." *American Politics Research* 50: 707–22.

Weir, Margaret. 1992. "Ideas and the Politics of Bounded Innovation." In *Structuring Politics: Historical Institutionalism in Comparative Analysis*, edited by Sven Steinmo, Kathleen Thelen, and Frank Longstreth, 188–216. New York: Cambridge University Press.

Weir, Margaret. 2005. "States, Race and the Decline of New Deal Liberalism." *Studies in American Political Development* 19: 157–72.

Weir, Margaret. Unpublished manuscript. "The New Metropolis: Political Power and Spatial Inequality in Twenty-First Century America." Microsoft Word document, accessed 2022.

Weir, Margaret, and Desmond King. 2021. "Redistribution and the Politics of Spatial Inequality in America." In *Who Gets What? The New Politics of Insecurity*, edited by Frances McCall Rosenbluth and Margaret Weir, 188–210. New York: Cambridge University Press.

Weisman, Jonathan. 2022. "Jewish Allies Call Trump's Dinner with Antisemites a Breaking Point." *New York Times*, November 28. https://www.nytimes.com/2022/11/28/us/politics/trump-kanye-west-nick-fuentes-antisemitism.html.

Weisman, Jonathan and Trip Gabriel. 2023. "Talk of Racism Proves Thorny for G.O.P. Candidates of Color." *New York Times*, June 1. https://www.nytimes.com/2023/06/01/us/politics/republicans-race-scott-haley.html.

Weissert, Will, and Calvin Woodward. 2020. "Trump Wholly Distorts Biden on Immigration." *AP News*, July 16. https://apnews.com/article/5c0bfde98f11556abc4339dd18c6f5af.

Wellemeyer, James. 2020. "Want to Know Where All Those Corporate Donations for #BLM Are Going? Here's the List." *NBC News*, June 5. https://www.nbcnews.com/business/consumer/want-know-where-all-those-corporate-donations-blm-are-going-n1225371.

Wells, Nicole. 2022. "A New 'Squad' Is Headed to Washington." *Newsmax*, November 10. https://www.newsmax.com/newsfront/squad-progressives-congress/2022/11/10/id/1095848/.

Wessler, Seth Freed. 2018. "Denaturalized." *New York Times Magazine*, December 23, 36.

Wheeler, Russell. 2020. "How Close Is Trump to His Goal of Record-Setting Judicial Appointments?" *Brookings Review*, May 5. https://www.brookings.edu/articles/how-close-is-president-trump-to-his-goal-of-record-setting-judicial-appointments/.

Wheeler, Russell. 2021. "Trump's Last-Minute Judicial Appointments: Impact on Norms and on Biden's Appointments Opportunities." *Brookings Review*, January 22. https://www.brookings.edu/articles/trumps-last-minute-judicial-appointments-impact-on-norms-and-on-bidens-appointment-opportunities/.

White, Angela. 2017. "Tax Reform Act of 1969." *Learning to Give*. Last accessed August 30, 2023. https://www.learningtogive.org/resources/tax-reform-act-1969.

White, Ed. 2022a. "Court Orders Charges Dismissed against Ex-Governor, 8 Others over Flint Water." *PBS News Hour*, June 28. https://www.pbs.org/newshour/politics/michigan-supreme-court-orders-charges-dismissed-against-ex-governor-8-others-over-flint-water.

White, Ed. 2022b. "Ex-Michigan Governor Rick Snyder Wins Appeal over Flint Water Testimony." *Click On Detroit*, November 9. https://www.usnews.com/news/best-states/michigan/articles/2022-11-09/ex-michigan-governor-wins-appeal-over-flint-water-testimony.

Why We Can't Wait Coalition. 2022a. "Immediately Pass H.R. 40." February 5. http://americanhumanist.org/wp-content/uploads/2022/02/H.R.-40-Letter-To-Congress.pdf.

Why We Can't Wait Coalition. 2022b. "Statement on Failure to Establish H.R. 40/S. 40 Commission." *Human Rights Watch*, August 23. https://www.hrw.org/news/2020/07/31/why-we-cant-wait-coalition-statement-urges-us-congress-pass-hr-40-reparations-bill.

Wiessner, Daniel. 2023. "Ex-Trump administration officials target corporate diversity efforts." *Reuters*, August 18. https://www.reuters.com/sustainability/ex-trump-administration-officials-target-corporate-diversity-efforts-2023-08-18/.

Wilder, Craig Steve. 2013. *Ebony and Ivy: Race, Slavery and the Troubled History of America's Universities*. New York: Bloomsbury.

Wilderson, Frank B. III. 2020. *Afropessimism*. New York: Liveright.

Williams, Jordan. 2021. "Biden Reverses Trump Ban on Diversity Training." *The Hill*, January 20. https://thehill.com/homenews/administration/535135-biden-reverses-trump-executive-order-on-diversity-training/.

Williamson, Vanessa, and Isabella Gelfand. 2019. "Trump and racism: What Do the Data Say?" *Brookings*, August 14. https://www.brookings.edu/articles/trump-and-racism-what-do-the-data-say/.

Wiltz, Teresa. 2019. "These States Are Considering Reparations in Apology for Slavery." *HuffPost*, October 4. https://www.huffpost.com/entry/reparations-slavery-african-americans_b_5d963d5de4b0bae8dd6189d4.

Wines, Michael. 2018. "U.S. Shifts Stance on Voting Rights, Embracing Limits." *New York Times*, August 13, A1.

Wines, Michael. 2020a. "Federal Court Rejects Trump's Effort to Exclude Undocumented from Census." *New York Times*, September 10. https://www.nytimes.com/2020/09/10/us/census-undocumented-trump.html.

Wines, Michael. 2020b. "Here Are the Threats Terrorizing Election Workers." *New York Times*, December 3. https://www.nytimes.com/2020/12/03/us/election-officials-threats-trump.html.

Wines, Michael. 2021a. "After Record Turnout, Republicans Are Trying to Make It Harder to Vote." *New York Times*, January 30. https://www.nytimes.com/2021/01/30/us/republicans-voting-georgia-arizona.html.

Wines, Michael. 2021b. "In Statehouses, Stolen-Election Myth Fuels a G.O.P. Drive to Rewrite Rules." *New York Times*, February 27. https://www.nytimes.com/2021/02/27/us/republican-voter-suppression.html.

Wines, Michael. 2021c. "After a Nightmare Year, Election Officials Are Quitting." *New York Times*, July 2. https://www.nytimes.com/2021/07/02/us/politics/2020-election-voting-officials.html.

Wines, Michael, and Richard Fausset. 2020. "With Census Count Finishing Early, Fears of a Skewed Tally." *New York Times*, August 4. https://www.nytimes.com/2020/08/04/us/2020-census-ending-early.html.

Witness at the Border. 2022. "Open Letter to President Biden, Vice President Harris, Attorney General Garland, and Secretary Mayorkas." January 17. Google Doc. https://static1.squarespace.com/static/5e221cacff87ba2d2833cf54/t/61e6e2b99a48c041b08ab6f2/1642521273617/WITNESS+FAMILY+SEPARATION+CASES+LETTER+%281%29.pdf.

Wolfe, Jan. 2023a. "Jan. 6 Rioter Gets Three-Year Sentence for Storming Nancy Pelosi's Office." *Wall Street Journal*, March 23. https://www.wsj.com/articles/jan-6-rioter-gets-three-year-sentence-for-storming-nancy-pelosis-office-28a22a9e.

Wolfe, Jan. 2023b. "Proud Boys Step Up Activity after Jan. 6 Attacks, Despite Criminal Convictions." *Wall Street Journal*, May 6. https://www.wsj.com/articles/proud-boys-step-up-activity-after-jan-6-attack-despite-criminal-convictions-9f2e05fa.

Woodly, Deva. 2019. "Black Feminist Visions and the Politics of Healing in the Movement for Black Lives." In *Women Mobilizing Memory*, edited by Ayse Gul Altmay, Maria Jose Contreras, Marianne Hirsch, Jean Howard, Banu Karaca, and Alisa Solomon, 279–310. New York: Columbia University Press.

Woodly, Deva R. 2021. *Reckoning: Black Lives Matter and the Democratic Necessity of Social Movements*. New York: Oxford University Press.
World Population Review. 2022. "States That Have Banned Critical Race Theory 2022." Last updated April 2023. https://worldpopulationreview.com/state-rankings/critical-race-theory-ban-states/.
Wright, Colleen. 2021. "St. Petersburg City Council Approves 'Reparations' to Address Structural Racism." *Tampa Bay Times*, December 10. https://www.tampabay.com/news/st-petersburg/2021/12/10/st-petersburg-city-council-accepts-structural-racism-study-to-right-wrongs/.
Wright, Peter. 2022. "'Are There Racists in Yugoslavia?' Debating Racism and Anti-Blackness in Socialist Yugoslavia." *Slavic Review* 81 (2): 418–41.
Wright, Robert. 2023. "Church of England Sets Aside £100mn to Address 'Shameful Past' of Slave Trade." *Financial Times*, January 10. https://www.ft.com/content/6cd0dd01-dfbc-4758-8efb-267d2978edf5.
Wright, Will. 2021. "Seminary Starts Paying Reparations for Labor in Slavery and Jim Crow." *New York Times*, May 31, A14. https://www.nytimes.com/2021/05/31/us/reparations-virginia-theological-seminary.html.
Yan, Holly, Melissa Alonso, and Dianne Gallagher. 2023. "'Beware, Your Life Is Not Valued': NAACP Travel Advisory Warns Florida Is 'Openly Hostile toward African Americans.'" *CNN US*, May 22. https://edition.cnn.com/2023/05/21/us/naacp-florida-travel-advisory/index.html.
Yancy, Nina M. 2022. *How the Color Line Bends: The Geography of White Prejudice in Modern America*. New York: Oxford University Press.
Yankowski, Peter. 2020. "CT Police Accountability Law Takes Effect Today. Here Are 5 Things to Know." *CTPost*, October 1. https://www.ctpost.com/local/article/CT-police-accountability-law-takes-effect-today-15611136.php.
Zerofsky, Elizabeth. 2022. "How the Claremont Institute Became a Nerve Center of the American Right." *New York Times*, August 3, updated September 9. https://www.nytimes.com/2022/08/03/magazine/claremont-institute-conservative.html.

Index

Page numbers followed by an *f* or *t* refer to figures or tables, respectively.

Abbott, Greg, 147
Abernathy, Gary, 166
abolitionism, 19–20, 223, 259
Abrams, Stacey, 242
Abuja Proclamation, 159
Achiume, E. Tendayi, 273, 274
Action Network/Million Hoodies Movement for Justice, 311–12
Action St. Louis, 242
Adams, Eric, 29
Adarand Constructors v. Peña, 6–7
affirmative action, 3, 4, 129t, 153, 215; ADOS's view of, 169; conservative opposition to, 12, 43–48, 70, 72, 75, 94, 101, 132, 134, 278, 285, 287; corporate support of, 172, 174; Hispanics and, 83, 173; progressive views of, 31, 56; public opinion on, 281; and Supreme Court, 6, 12, 27, 102, 288
AFL-CIO, 172
African American Cultural Heritage Fund, 175
African American Museum of History and Culture, 234
African American Redress Network, 179
African Americans: and affirmative action, 3; billionaires, 263; churches, 181–83; community, 166, 167; conservative, 313; DeSantis's ban of course on, 26; disenfranchisement of, 232; education, 154, 226; elected officials, 146; emancipation, 155; evictions of, 189; in Flint, MI, 238; and hate crimes, 229, 297–98; history, 26, 136; housing and employment opportunities, 29; housing for, funded by cannabis tax, 184; integration, 101, 202; Juneteenth, 166; leaders, 177; liberal, 313; life expectancy of, 237; low unemployment rates, 140; and lynchings, 234; massacres of, 188; mischaracterizations of, 6; in Mount Vernon, NY, 237; and "multicultural conservativism," 118; Obama, conservatives' accusations of favoritism of, 14; participation in capitalism, 293; police violence against, 99, 139, 161, 163, 204; and progressives, 275, 289; protests of police killings by football players, 115; and racist monuments, 230–32; repair measures for, 22; slavery, 198–99; violence against, 139; voting, 140, 143, 145, 240. *See also* reparations
African People's Socialist Party, 177
Afropessimism, 58, 262, 264
AirBnB, 191
Alexandria Community Policing Review Board, 224
Alford, Robert R., 37, 40
Allen, Leah C., 146
Allen, Ted, 200
Alliance for Free Citizens, 26
Allied Media Projects, 190
Amazon, 175, 191
America First, 78, 122
America First Foundation, 47f, 81
America First Legal, 25, 77–78, 246
America First Party, 109
America First Policy Institute (AFPI), 25, 47f, 49f, 75–76, 108; and America First Foundation, 81; and color-blind policies, 77

430　INDEX

America First Political Action Committee, 77
America First Political Action Conference (AFPAC), 79, 81, 270
America First Works, 77
American Baptist Churches USA, 171
American Civil Liberties Union (ACLU), 46, 47f, 48f, 139, 174, 312t, 348n10
American Descendants of Slavery (ADOS), 169–70, 173, 210–12, 214, 215, 217, 219, 239, 265
American Enterprise Institute, 46, 47f, 91, 99, 105, 312, 348n10
American Freedom Party, 113
American Legislative Exchange Council (ALEC), 91
American Library Association, 138
American Populist Union (now America Virtue), 117
Americans for Prosperity, 91
Amherst (MA) Town Council, 185
Andrew W. Mellon Foundation, 191
Anglin, Andrew, 113
Anti-Defamation League (ADL), 195
Antifa, 195–96, 298, 299
anti-LGBTQ+ groups, 93
Apple, 163, 191
Arabella Advisors, 96
Arbery, Ahmaud, 297
Armed Conflict Location and Event Data Project, 91
Arnn, Larry, 227
Arpaio, Joe, 81, 115, 129t
Art Institute of Chicago, 178
Asheville (NC) City Council, 185, 222
Asian American Legal Foundation, 82
Asian Pacific American Labor Alliance, 172
Atlantic Legal Foundation, 74
Away (luggage brand), 191

Baker, Ella, 204
Baldwin, James, 6, 269
Bank of America, 163, 190
Bannon, Steve, 94, 113, 126, 283, 301
Baptist Joint Committee for Religious Liberty (BJC), 85
Barbara C. Harris Scholars Program for Truth and Reparations, 183
Barber, William J., II, 182
Barr, William, 126, 133

Barrett, Amy Coney, 133
Beckles, Hilary, 153, 159, 165, 276
Bell, Derrick, 106
Bendapudi, Neeli, 181
Benning, John Lewis, 232
Bertino, Jeremy, 89
Bethel Business Machines, 172
Bezos, Jeff, 175
Biden, Joe: administration, 245–46; appointments of, exceeding Trump's pace, 127; from centrist to "New New Left," 105; HR 40, endorsement of, 28; immigration policies from Trump years, 278; Interagency Task Force on the Reunification of Families, 239; Juneteenth National Independence Day Act, 233; low popularity ratings, 279; migrant families, accountability for separation and detention of, 240; Naming Commission, 233; plot to kidnap and possibly kill, 298; police funding, increase of, 223; and pro-Trump election deniers, 279, 300; racial sensitivity training bans, rescinding of, 134; refusal to create reparations commission via executive order, 168, 242; reparations, support for study of, 166; 1776 Commission, termination of, 135; violent crime, increase in funding to combat, 140
Bittker, Boris, 155
Black American Descendants of Chattel Slavery (BADOCS), 212
Black Bloc, 196–97
Black Conservative Federation (BCF), 84
Black Feminist Project, 194
Black Freedom Collective, 176
Black-Led Movement Fund, 193
Black Liberation Pooled Fund, 194
Black Lives Matter (BLM), 43f, 47f, 48f; activists, 160, 208, 224–25, 232; conservatives' views of, 107; Foundation, 30; growth of, 15, 204, 224; leadership, 174; movement, 7, 28, 107, 161–64, 165, 205, 207; and racial justice, 192; support for, 197; threats against BLM protestors, 300
Black Lives Matter Global Network, 15, 164
Black Lives Matter Grassroots, 224
Black Manifesto, 202
BlackOUT Collective, 194
Black Panthers, 98; Black Bloc activists'

INDEX

invocations of, 197; Declaration of Independence, invocations of, 201, 256; global liberation movements, 272; mentorship of by Audley Moore, 200; Party demands, 28; Ten-Point Program, 200–201, 204, 257
Black Women Build, 183
Black Women's Leadership Forum, 170
Blake, Jacob, 90
Blankenstein, Eric, 126
BLM Political Action Committee, 164
Blum, Edward, 132
Boebert, Lauren, 86
Bolsonaro, Eduardo, 270
Bolsonaro, Jair, 126, 270, 271
Booker, Cory, 131, 140, 165
Borealis Philanthropy, 175, 193
Bostock v. Clayton County, 133
Bowman, Jamaal, 30, 166, 189; proposed Truth and Reconciliation Commission, 243, 302
Bragg, Alvin, 300
Braithwaite, Peter, 184–85
Bray School, 235
BREATHE Act, 223
Brennan Center for Justice, 145
Bridgespan Group, 30, 193
Brimelow, Peter, 46
Brnovich v. Democratic National Committee, 142–43
Brog, David, 78
Brooklyn Community Foundation, 194
Brooks, David, 79, 100
Brown, Michael, 15, 107, 190
Brown University, 180
Bruce, Charles and Willa, 189
Bryant, Phil, 76
Buchanan, Pat, 109
Burge, John, 186
Bush, Cori, 30, 189, 243
Bush, George H. W., 102
Bush, George W., 13, 301
Bush, Jeb, 121
Butterfield, G. K., 146
Byrd, Jessica, 242

Caldwell, Christopher, 75, 89, 101–2, 104, 107
California African American Freedman Affairs Agency, 29, 187, 213

California Indian Heritage Center, 189
Californians for Equal Rights Foundation, 47f, 49f, 82
California State Assembly, 29, 189
California Task Force to Study and Develop Reparation Proposals, 29, 187, 199, 213, 214
Cameron, Daniel, 63
Campaign for Accountability, 95
Campaign Zero, 191, 205, 221, 224
Camus, Renaud, 80
capitalism: African American participation in, 293; "Black capitalism," 246; constraints of, 268; crony capitalism, 119; as inherently racially exploitative system, 53; M4BL's proposals to transform, 209; neoconservatives' mission to spread, 266; overthrowing of, 56, 194; racial, 52–53, 199, 200, 207, 208, 244; racial inequalities and, 53–54; racialization of labor, disentanglement from, 54; racialized, 60
"capitalism-focused" perspective, 50, 55–57, 257–60
Caribbean Community and Common Market (CARICOM), 47f, 158–59, 165, 216, 273
Carlson, Tucker, 25, 80, 259, 271
Carmichael, Stokely (Kwame Ture), 98, 204, 272
Carson, Ben, 126, 140–41, 261
Cash App, 176
Castro, Julian, 242
Cato Institute, 91
Cause IQ, 309
Center for Community Change, 175
Center for Equal Opportunity, 69, 72–73
Center for Immigration Studies, 120
Center for Racial Equity, 191
Change Today, Change Tomorrow (CTCT), 176
Charity Navigator, 81, 309
Charles III (king), 272
Chauvin, Derek, 163
Chavez, Linda, 72, 75, 285
Cheney, Liz, 147
Chicago City Council, Subcommittee on Reparations, 156, 186
China, as influence on US policies, 274–75
Chinese American Planning Council, 172
Chocolate Factory, 172

Chowdhury, Shaniyat, 243
Christian Legal Society, 82
Christian nationalism, 85, 87, 96, 120, 280, 290
Christians United for Israel, 78
Church of England, 160
CitiBank, 166, 219
Citizens United v. Federal Elections Commission, 94
Civil Rights Act (1964), 102, 129t
Civil Rights Act (1991), 102
Claremont Institute, 47f, 49f, 101, 105, 117, 120, 121, 290–91, 314; Center for Constitutional Jurisprudence, 105
Claremont Review, 105
Clinton, Hillary, 242
Coates, Ta-Nehisi, 107, 158, 165, 167, 204
Coleman, Stephanie, 156
Colonialism Reparations, 274
color-blind policies: in American politics, 3; America's failure to commit to, 98; and conservatives, 5, 18–19, 62, 75, 77, 120, 285; late twentieth-century, 18; and liberals, 20, 23; policy disputes, 42; and progressives, 302; vs. race-targeted policies, 7; and Supreme Court, 288
Color of Change, 170, 191, 234, 311, 348n10
Columbia Institute for the Study of Human Rights, 179
Columbia School of International Affairs, 179
Committee for Reparations for Descendants of US Slaves, 155
Common Talks Consulting, 172
Communities Transforming Police Fund, 193
Community Change, 21, 47f, 48f, 171, 175, 205, 239, 245
Community Police Review Board, 224–25
Community Reparations Commission (Asheville, NC), 28, 185
Concord Fund (formerly Judicial Crisis Network), 95
Congressional Black Caucus (CBC), 146, 165, 189, 233
Connecticut General Assembly, 224
Connerly, Ward, 75, 101–2, 104, 285, 313
Conservative Headlines, 46, 47f, 49f
Conservative Partnership Institute (CPI), 47f, 49, 77–78, 81, 118, 120, 308
Conservative Political Action Conference (CPAC), 78–79, 97, 270

conservative racial policy positions, 20
Conyers, Ian, 222
Conyers, John, 27, 155, 157, 165, 218, 222
Cook, Sakira, 223
Coors Brewing family, 91
Copeland-Hanzas, Sarah, 188
Cornell, Yvette, 169, 212
Council of Conservative Citizens, 84
COVID-19 pandemic, 16, 237, 244; and constraints on financial environment, 181; disparate impacts of, 237; and environmental racism, 236; impact on foreign workers, 138–39; pandemic funds, 185; and regulation of Big Tech companies, 76; and Republican National Convention, 90; schools' response to, 137; Trump's response to, 116
Cox, Oliver Cromwell, 55
Crenshaw, Kimberlé, 106
Crews, Trahern, 3–4, 160–61
Critical Race Theory (CRT): as anti-white messages, conservatives' view of, 285; attacks on, 73–74, 110, 233, 309; bans and restrictions of, 26, 69–70, 95, 134, 136, 278, 280; conservative response to, 136, 137; as dangerous, conservatives' view of, 77, 100; development of, 106; Eagle Forum against, 72; in education, 16; and fear of students' indoctrination, 228; in higher education, 228; and identity politics, 73, 77; and intersectionality, 103; Left's championing of, 102; and nationalization, 277; and "New New Left," 104; racial progressives' view of, 202; Rollins on, 76; and Rufo, 103, 106, 200; and social justice movements, 193; as takeover of public education, conservatives' view of, 226; teaching of, 71; versions of, 72
Croney, Nannie Grace, 176–77
Crow, Harlan, 348n11
Cruz, Ted, 115
Cullors, Patrice, 15, 162, 205
Cumbo, Laura, 240
Curry, Tommy J., 58–59

Daley, Richard J., 144
Daniels, Ron, 156, 157, 158, 185, 350n1 (chap. 6)
Darity, William, Jr., 30, 31; and calculating the costs of reparations, 161, 214, 215;

criticism of Evanston's reparations initiative, 184; on Douglass, 200; *From Here to Equality*, 166, 214; on racial inequality, 199; on reparations, definition and forms of, 178, 215, 217, 219
"dark money," 93, 96
Davis, Angela, 98, 103
Davis, Jefferson, 231
Davis, Tawana, 184
Dawson, Michael, 59
Debt, The (R. Robinson), 13, 154, 166
Delgado, Richard, 228
DeMint, Jim, 120
Democrats: accusations against, 25; agenda, 28; Black voters' loyalty to, 14; border wall, opposition to, 138; centrists' rejection of "big government," 12; college-educated voters' support for, 282; and "dark money," 95; election cheating, Republicans' belief of, 69, 144, 300; and gerrymandering, 146; and local contests, 137; National Voter Registration Act, 12, 144; neoliberal, 94; and "New New Left," 105; and police funding, increases in, 140; and race-conscious measures, 13, 154; and religion, 282; reparations, opposition to, 31, 157; results of 2022 election, 279–80; supporting Republicans due to race, 6; and voting access, increases in, 145, 147
DeMuth, Christopher, 99
Denver Black Reparations Council, 177, 183
DePape, David, 300
DeSantis, Ron, 95; Claremont Institute's influence on, 105; Critical Race Theory, opposition to, 26; diversity training restrictions, 108; educational restrictions, 26–27, 137–38; and Leonard Leo, 95; Protect agenda, 280
Descendants Truth & Reconciliation Foundation, 29
DeVos, Betsy, 141
DeVos family, 91
DiAngelo, Robin, 107
DiMaggio, Paul J., 38
#DiversifyOurNarrative, 227
diversity, equity, and inclusion (DEI): advocates, 103, 219; concerns, 174; consultants, 154; corporate departments, 255; industry, 17, 98, 102, 104, 154, 172, 198, 202;

initiatives and programs, 108, 181, 202, 257, 302; officials, 102; policies, 174
Donors Trust, 93, 95
Douglass, Frederick, 61, 200, 202, 256
Du Bois, W. E. B., 153, 159, 200, 258, 272
Duke, David, 75, 113
Dunbar-Ortiz, Roxanne, 58
Duval, Dawn Riley, 184

Eagle Forum, 47f, 49f, 72
Eastman, John, 105
Economic Security Project, 245
Edmund Burke Foundation, 78, 118, 120
Edwards, Ana, 230
Electoral Justice Project, 242
Ellis, Bert, 181
Ellmers, Glenn, 291
Emanuel African Methodist Episcopal Church, 229, 297
Emerging LGBTQ Leaders of Color Fund, 193
Empower Mississippi, 7
Episcopal dioceses, 182–83
Equal Justice Initiative, 191, 234
Erdoğan, Recep, 271
Evanston (IL) City Council, 184
Evanston Community Foundation, 183
Evanston Reparations Community Fund, 222
Ex-Slave Mutual Relief and Bounty and Pension Association, 200

Facebook, 76, 78, 162, 164, 176, 177, 191, 245
Fair and Just Prosecution, 225
Fair Immigration Reform Movement, 239
Faith and Freedom Coalition, 85
Family Research Council, 85
Fancelli, Julie, 78
federalism and fragmented power, 21, 281
Federalist Society, 93, 95
Fidelity Charitable, 92, 93
1st Amendment Praetorian, 88
FirstRepair, 170, 222
First Step Act, 131t, 139–40
First Unitarian Society, 47f, 48f, 171, 183, 184, 350f
First United Methodist Church of Evanston, 183
Fisher, Anthony L., 195
Fletcher, Viola, 188

Floyd, George, 15, 16, 24, 90, 139, 140, 149, 157, 181, 187, 190
Ford Foundation, 92, 191, 192, 193
Forman, James, 155, 202
Fortner, Michael Javen, 53
Foster, Natalie, 245
Foundation for Government Accountability, 73
Francis, Megan Ming, 35
Fraser, Nancy, 59
Frederick, Lew, 188
Freedom Conservatism, 121, 122
Freedom from Religion Foundation (FFRF), 85
FreedomWorks, 74
Freeskewl, 176
Friedland, Roger, 37, 40
Frum, David, 301
Fuentes, Nicholas: America First Foundation, 79–81; America First Political Action Conference, 270; far-right counter-protester following, 90; white-governed Christian America, 112, 117–18, 259
Fullilove v. Klutznick, 5–6
Funders for Justice, 193
Fund for Reparations NOW! (FFRN), 30, 47f, 48f, 170, 313

Gandhi Institute for Nonviolence, 171
Garcetti, Eric, 187, 261, 313
Garcia, Mauricio, 298
Garvey, Marcus, 272
Garza, Alicia, 15, 162
Garza, Jose, 225
Gates Foundation, 193
Gendron, Payton, 26, 297, 298
George Jenkins Foundation, 78
Georgetown University, 29, 178–80
gerrymandering, 146
Gianforte, Greg, 86
Gibbons, Isabel, 180
Gillis, Kaylin, 298
Gilroy, Paul, 159
Giuliani, Rudy, 283
Glass-Steagall Act, 209
Global Human Rights Clinic, 171
Glossier, 191
Glover, Danny, 167
Goldberg, Jonah, 118, 121
Goldwater Institute, 71–72, 73

Gómez, Laura, 173
Goodrich, Pierre, 92
Google, 76, 190
Gordon, John Brown, 232
Gordon-Reed, Annette, 351n4 (chap. 8)
Gore, Al, 154
Gorka, Sebastian, 78
Gorsuch, Neil, 133
Gosar, Paul, 81, 270–71, 280, 296, 300
Gottesman, Isaac, 103, 228
Great Recession, 17, 107
Great Society, 91, 104, 105
Greene, Marjorie Taylor, 74, 81, 86, 277, 280
Guggenheim Museum, 178
GuideStar, 81, 309

Haaland, Deb, 231
Hall, Peter A., 347n2 (chap. 2)
Hall, Stuart, 36, 60
Hamilton, Charles V., 272
Hanchard, Michael, 348n5
Hancock, Ange-Marie, 64
Hancock, Michael, 187
Hannah-Jones, Nikole, 158, 166, 226
Harris, Fredrick, 35, 162, 164
Harris, Kamala, 242
Harvard University, 2, 9, 81, 129t, 132, 179
Hawley, Josh, 79
Hazony, Yoram, 78–79, 120, 270
HBO Max, 234
hegemonic white nation-states, 21
Height, Dorothy, 204
Heirs of Slavery, 273
Henry, Devon, 230
Heriot, Gail, 101, 102, 104, 285, 313
Heritage Action for America, 47f, 49f, 82
Heritage Foundation, 91, 105, 120
Herndon, Andre, 313
Herrnstein, Richard, 6, 51
Hertel-Fernandez, Alexander, 82, 309
Herzl Institute, 79
Hewlett Foundation, 192
Hey, John Pittman, 109
Heyer, Heather, 88, 229
Hillsdale College, 120, 121, 137, 227
Hispanic National Bar Association, 173
historical institutionalism, 34
Historically Black Colleges and Universities (HBCUs): aid and donations to, 170, 175, 288; bomb threats, 297; creation of after

the Civil War, 179; funding of, 129t, 182, 190, 211, 285; HR 40, endorsement of, 178; leaders, 132
Hoover Institution, 120
Hopkins, Daniel, 277
House, Callie, 155, 200
Housing and Urban Development (HUD), 131t, 140–41, 261
Howard, Kamm, 165–66, 203, 214
Howard University Thurgood Marshall Civil Rights Center, 179
HR 40, 27–28, 154–55, 157, 165–81, 189, 202, 210, 218, 239–42, 279, 309
Hudson Institute, 99, 120, 311, 348n10
Hughes, Chris, 245
Human Rights Tribunal, 350n3

ICNA Council for Social Justice, 171
Ignatiev (Ignatien), Noel, 103, 200
I Love Black People, 170
Immigration and Customs Enforcement (ICE), 107, 223
Indigenous Solidarity Network, 173
Inflation Reduction Act (2022), 246
InfluenceWatch, 193, 309
Institute of the Black World 21st Century, 30, 46–47, 47f, 48f, 156
institutional orders, 34, 37, 38, 40, 348n3, 348n8; color-blind and race-conscious, 12; framework, 33, 50, 54; and ideational contexts, 36; and policy alliances, 34, 35, 37, 41–44; Protect and Repair, 31; racial, 7, 8, 9, 11, 23–24, 34, 35, 37, 38, 44–45, 54–55, 56; research agenda, 39–40
institutional racism, 36, 60, 62, 99, 102, 103
integration, 6, 16, 19–20, 62, 70–72, 75, 101–3, 116, 131–32, 141, 202, 215
Intercollegiate Studies Institute, 120
Internal Revenue Service (IRS), 31, 81, 309
International African American Museum, 234
International Center for Non-Profit Law, 149
International Convention on the Elimination of All Racial Discrimination, 158
intersectional perspective, 50, 54, 63–64
intersectional systems of inequality, 50

Jackson, Andrew, 116
Jackson, Jesse, 156, 204, 205
Jackson, Stonewall, 180, 231, 234
Janisha R. Gabriel Movement Protection Fund, 194
January 6 insurrection, 88, 105, 126, 195
Japanese American Citizens League, 47f, 48f, 240
Jefferson, Thomas, 51, 180, 230
Jesuit Conference of Canada and the United States, 29, 179
Jindal, Bobby, 76, 313
John Brown Gun Clubs, 196
Johnson, Andrew, 155
Johnson, Derrick, 233
Johnson, Hank, 189
Johnson, Lyndon, 102
Johnson, William, 113
Johnson Amendment, 111, 133
Jones, Claudia, 272
Jones, Melanie C., 180
Jones, Tishaura O., 186
JPMorgan Chase, 190
Juilliard School, 178
Juneteenth, 166–67, 233

Kaepernick, Colin, 163
Kagan, Elena, 143
Kahlenberg, Richard, 56
Kandula, Sai Varshith, 298
Kane, Andrea, 3–4
Kardashian, Kim, 139
Kashyap, Monika Batra, 58
Katie Geneva Cannon Center for Womanist Leadership, 180
Kavanaugh, Brett, 133
Kelley, Robin G. D., 348n12
Kellogg Foundation, 191, 192
Kelly, Leontine T. C., 234
Kendi, Ibram X., 107
Kennedy, Robert F., 175, 239
Kent, Joe, 117, 301
Kesler, Charles, 101, 104–5, 117–18, 255
Khan-Cullors, Patrisse, 205
King, Desmond, 5–7
King, Martin Luther, Jr., 76–77, 135, 181–82, 202, 204, 205, 256
Kirk, Charlie, 90, 120
Klein, Morton, 81
Klingenstein, Thomas, 105
Knights Party, 113
Knot Worldwide, 234

Kobach, Kris, 142
Koch brothers, 25, 74, 82, 91, 139, 309
Kremer, Amy, 78
Kresge Foundation, 191
Krinsky, Miriam, 225
Kudlow, Larry, 76
Ku Klux Klan (KKK), 113, 231, 232

Lacey, Jackie, Jr., 225–26
LA County Museum, 178
Ladson-Billings, Gloria, 228
Lake, Kari, 301
La Raza Centro Legal, 47f, 240
Lawrence, Stephen, 36
Leadership Conference on Civil and Human Rights, 27, 47f, 48f, 170
League of Revolutionary Black Workers, 155, 202
League of United Latin American Citizens (LULAC), 173, 295
Lee, Barbara, 238
Lee, Opal, 233
Lee, Robert E., 229, 231, 234
Lee, Sheila Jackson, 27, 165, 167
Legacy Museum and National Memorial for Peace and Justice, 234
Leo, Leonard, 95
Leong, Nancy, 53
Levenson, Zachary, 53
Levin, Yuval, 99, 107
LGBTQ+ groups, 98, 174, 192, 289, 294
LGBTQ+ people and identities, 35, 65, 100, 138, 265, 267; rights, 83, 91, 120, 170, 275, 278, 309
liberal racial policy positions, 20–21
Lieberman, Robert C., 348n2
Lindbergh, Charles, 350n6 (chap. 5)
Lorde, Audre, 98
Los Angeles Reparations Commission, 187
Los Angeles Times, 178
Lounsbury, Michael, 38–39
Lumumba, Rukia, 242

MacArthur Foundation, 192
Make America Great Again (MAGA) movement, 87, 203; key figures, 283; National Conservativism Conference, 270; "Ottawa Impact," 277; Republicans, 260
Manhattan Institute, 69, 104, 118, 120, 311, 348n10

Manheimer, Esther, 261
Manne, Henry, 349n5 (chap. 3)
Marble Freedom Trust, 95
Marcus, Kenneth, 132
Markham, Ian S., 180
Martin, Trayvon, 15, 107, 158, 190
Marx, Karl, 253
Mastriano, Doug, 86
Mayor's Commission on Faith-Based and Interfaith Affairs (Philadelphia, PA), 185
Mayors for a Guaranteed Income, 244–45
Mayors Organized for Reparations and Equity (MORE), 47f, 48f, 187, 261
McAuliffe, Terry, 69
McCarthy, Kevin, 80
McClellan, Jennifer, 230
McCloskey, Mark and Patricia, 300
McConnell, Mitch, 127
McKesson, DeRay, 191, 205, 224
McMahon, Linda, 76
McVeigh, Timothy, 195
McWhorter, John, 19
Mead, Lawrence, 51
Meadows, Mark, 77, 120, 270
Meloni, Giorgia, 271
Memorial Episcopal Church of Baltimore, 183
Mercer, Rebekah, 94–95
Mercer, Robert, 94–95
Mercer Family Foundation, 95
Meriden Congregational Church, 171
Metropolitan Museum of Art (New York), 178
Mexican American Legal Defense and Education Fund, 173
Miller, Stephen, 5, 25, 77, 113, 126–27, 139, 246
Minnesota Alliance for Volunteer Advancement, 178
Minnesota Council of Churches, 183
Mitchell, John J., 230
Modi, Narendra, 271
Moore, Antonio, 169
Moore, Audley, 155, 156, 200
Moore, Kamilah, 187
Moore, Roy, 115
Moore v. Harper, 147
Morgan, Jennifer L., 53
Morial, Mark, 31, 191
Mother and Baby Homes Commission, 160

Movement for Black Lives (M4BL), 15, 47f, 48f, 169, 175, 204, 208, 265, 268, 273; decentralized structure, 164; M4BL Toolkit, 200, 202–3, 207–10, 213, 217. *See also* Vision for Black Lives

Mullen, Kirsten: and calculating the costs of reparations, 161, 214, 215; criticism of Evanston's reparations initiative, 184; on Douglass, 200; *From Here to Equality*, 166, 214; on racial inequality, 199; on reparations, definition and forms of, 178, 215, 217, 219

"multicultural conservatism," 20, 118, 125, 285, 287, 290, 302

"multicultural neoliberalism," 57

Murray, Charles, 6, 7, 51, 348n11

Murray, Pauli, 204

Murry, Aderrien, 36

Museum of Fine Arts (Boston), 178

Museum of Fine Arts (Houston), 178

Musk, Elon, 27

Mutz, Diana, 112

Nadler, Jerrold, 167

NASCAR, 234

National African American Reparations Commission (NAARC), 47f, 48f, 170, 201; and Black Panthers' Ten-Point Program, 201; creation of, 204; HR 40, endorsement of, 168, 170; and Institute of the Black World 21st Century (IBW21), 46; and Repair policy agenda, 48; reparations initiatives, 30, 165, 216–19, 280, 284, 287; *Why We Can't Wait* Coalition, 168

National Assembly of American Slavery Descendants (NAASD), 169–70, 210, 212, 214, 215, 217, 219

National Association for the Advancement of Colored People (NAACP), 47f, 48f, 125, 146, 157, 168, 174, 186, 190, 191, 192, 295

National Association of Scholars, 46, 47f, 49f

National Christian Charitable Foundation, 84

National Coalition against Domestic Violence, 171

National Coalition of Blacks for Reparations in America (N'COBRA), 47f, 48f; creation of, 202; HR 40, endorsement of, 157, 170; reparations initiatives, 30, 160, 218; website, 302

National Coalition of Latino Clergy and Christian Leaders, 173

National Commission on the Disappearance of Persons (CONDADEP), 160

National Conservatism, 118, 119, 121, 122, 124, 280, 285

National Conservatism Conference, 41, 47f, 49f, 78, 79, 99, 108, 118

National Conservatism Statement of Principles, 121, 122, 124, 280, 284–85, 290

National Consumers League, 171

National Council of Churches, 171

National Council of La Raza, 173

National Defense Authorization Act, 135, 142, 231

National Ex-Slave Mutual Relief, Bounty, and Pension Association (MRBP), 155

National Network for Immigrant and Refugee Rights, 240

National Urban League, 31, 170, 311, 348n10

National Voter Registration Act, 12, 144

New Black Panthers, 234

New College of Florida, 26, 137

New Left of the 1960s, 98, 103, 104, 228

"New New Left," 104–5, 106, 198

Newsom, Gavin, 189

Newton, Huey, 103, 204, 296

New York City Council, 230

Next Generation Action Network, 171–72

Nichols, Tyre, 31, 36

Nike, 191

Norquist, Grover, 121

Northam, Ralph, 229, 231

NYC Antifa, 195–96

Oath Keepers, 13–14, 87–89, 103, 291, 296, 299

Obama, Barack: Black voters' loyalty to, 14; and color-blind policy alliance, 63; conservative reaction and opposition to, 13–14, 87, 103; DACA creation, court ruling on, 138; judicial appointments, vs. Trump's, 127; presidency, 15, 103, 157, 165, 198, 263, 284; racial integration in housing efforts, ended by Trump's HUD, 116, 141; racial politics, 9, 63; and Reagan Revolution, 92; on reparations, 242; school diversity, Trump's rescinding of, 132, 141

Ocasio, William, 38–39

Ocasio-Cortez, Alexandria, 81, 300
Ogletree, Charles, 13, 154, 155
Olin, John M., 91
Olin Foundation, 92
Olsen, Henry, 271, 285
Omi, Michael, 59
Orbán, Viktor, 270, 271
Oregon Reparations Task Force, 188
O'Rourke, Beto, 242
Orren, Karen, 348n2
Ottawa County (MI) Board of Commissioners, 277
Owens, Burgess, 167, 261

Pacific Legal Foundation, 47f, 49f, 74, 91–92
Packard Foundation, 192
Paret, Marcel, 53
Parson, Mike, 300
Patriot Front, 88
Paxton, Kenneth, 89, 283
PayPal, 30, 176, 190
Peace Builders of Orange County, 172
Pelosi, Nancy, 300
PEN America, 138
Pence, Mike, 116
Pennsylvania State University, 181
People for the American Way, 171
People's Advocacy Institute, 242
PepsiCo, 163
Perkins, Tony, 85
Perry, Rick, 76
Perry, Scott, 80
Philadelphia Antifa, 195–96
Pigford v. USDA, 245
Pinterest, 234
policy alliances, 8, 11–12, 15, 17, 20, 22–24; distinction from institutional orders, 34–37, 43f
policy regimes, 42–44
Pompeo, Mike, 115
Poor People's Campaign, 182
Powell, Lewis, 91, 96, 108, 270
Powell, Walter W., 38
Prairie View A&M University, 175
Prendergraft, Rachel, 113
Pressley, Ayanna, 223, 238
Price, John, 349n5 (chap. 3)
Princeton Theological Seminary, 179
propertied white Christian men, 64–65
Proud Boys, 88–89, 90, 91, 197, 299

Providence Municipal Reparations Commission, 185
public health crisis declarations, 236–37
Puget Sound John Brown Gun Club, 196
Pulitzer Center, 226–27
Putin, Vladimir, 271

racial capitalism, 52–54, 199–200, 207–8, 244, 257–58, 288
racial equity initiatives: absence of in Democratic platforms, 279; in Blue states, 261; cities' and states', 169; discrimination against Black Americans, 213; repairing systemic racism, 21, 27; white support for, 281
Racial Equity in Journalism Fund, 193
Racial Equity in Philanthropy Fund, 193
Racial Equity to Accelerate Change (REACH) Fund, 193
Racial Justice Project, 183–84
Racial Literacy Groups, 172
racial policies: alliances, 17, 35, 43f, 45, 47; American, 260, 277; battles over, 261; coalition-building, 10; color-blind vs. race-conscious, 43; conservative, 7, 96, 128, 284; and electoral politics, 287; historical, 256; institutionalized, 284; making of, 41; and Obama's critics, 103; progressive, 121; in *Still a House Divided* (King and Smith), 308; survey respondents on, 81; Trump's, 114; and young people, 13
racial politics: academic and activist understandings of, 3, 33, 57, 66, 249, 264; aggregate, 277; analysis of, 40, 54, 55, 268, 313; and Black Lives Matter, 35, 162, 164; and capitalism, 256; clashing policy alliances, 276; color-blind policies, 3; complexity of American, 61; contemporary, 256; "deep structure" of, 7; different theoretical approaches to, 17, 33, 50, 52; diversity in, 10, 268, 276; and elites' policy formulation, 44; framework for studying, 7, 9, 11; future of, 277, 280–83; Hispanics and, 84; historical institutionalist framework of, 34–50, 253; historically dichotomous structure of, 279; institutionalist analysis, 33, 36, 37; intersectional politics, 65, 264; Obama's effect on, 9; polarized, 4; Protect or Repair dichotomy, 31; racial

INDEX 439

orders framework, 17, 52; reparations at the margins of, 27–28; rival claims about, 55; transformative racially egalitarian orders, 61; transnational, 60, 269; trends in, 274; and white settler-colonial identity, 59
Radical Reconstruction, 20, 41, 155, 200
Radical Republicans, 41, 200
Randle, Lessie Benningfield, 188
Ransby, Barbara, 204, 205, 207, 294
Ranson, Marcus, 297
Reagan, Ronald, 6, 12, 75, 84, 105, 270
Reagan coalition, 84
Reagan era, 6, 16–17, 57, 71–75, 122
Reagan Revolution, 92, 144, 154, 288
Redneck Revolt, 196
Reed, Adolph, Jr., 55
Reed, Kayla, 242
Reed, Ralph, 85
Reed, Touré, 56
Reffitt, Guy Wesley, 299
Religious Liberty Task Force, 133
Reparation Generation, 177, 222, 351f
reparations: activism, 192; advocates, 158, 166, 203, 205, 212, 271–73, 283, 294; and affirmative action, 281; African, 159, 274; agricultural, 245–46; American Descendants of Slavery (ADOS), 169; and Asian Americans, 174; Caribbean, 158–59, 274; changing meanings of, 19–20, 28, 243–44; commission, 242, 261, 310; congressmembers and, 189, 302; Darity and Mullen on, 214–15; Democrats and, 31; to detained migrant families, 240; economic benefits of, 166; federal, 213; in Germany, 160; and Hispanics, 83, 173; history of, 155; in housing and employment opportunities, 222; and immigrants, 239; international, 198; justification for, 22, 176, 274; legitimacy of, 172; Audley Moore and, 200; in municipalities, 184–87, 221; National Assembly of American Slavery Descendants (NAASD) "R.E.P.A.I.R." agenda, 169–70; and Native Americans, 173; in New York and California, 29; nonprofits, 177, 194; opposition to, 157, 167, 259; in other countries, 108; private, 30, 175, 176, 222; progressive legislation, 30; proposals, 216, 267; racial, 292; and religious groups, 182–84; Repair alliance proponents, 162, 165, 168, 206, 210, 242; in San Francisco, 282; smaller initiatives, 178; state legislatures and, 187–89; support for, 14, 168, 243, 276; "torts model" of, 246–48; and universities, 178–81; US, 160–61, 166, 167, 170; white support for, 263, 281. *See also* Movement for Black Lives (M4BL); racial equity initiatives; Vision for Black Lives
Reparations Assessment Group, 154
Reparations Circle Denver, 183
Reparations Legacy Project, 177
Reparations: Requests and Offerings, 177
Reparations Roundtable (RR), 176
Reparations Stakeholder Authorities, 183, 222
Reparations Task Force (Burlington, VT), 185
Reparations Task Force (Detroit), 186
Reparations Working Group, US Green Party, 161
Republicans: candidates, 3, 25, 69, 128; and Christian nationalism, 86; diversity training, opposition to, 134; "divisive concepts," bans and restrictions on, 26; on election integrity and noncitizen voting, 144, 241; "establishment," 79; extremists in control of state parties, 283; federal judgeships under, 94, 127; and Fuentes, 80, 117; and guns, 301; militantly conservative, 14; National History Standards, 70; organizations, 89; politicians, 102, 109, 277; presidents, 5; and prison reform, 140; race-conscious measures, opposition to, 13; redrawing of state electoral maps, 145–46; and religion, 282; and removal of Confederate names, 116; reparations, opposition to, 167; Republican National Convention, 90; Republican Party, 91, 96, 117, 282; spending, vs. Democrats, 95; state legislatures, 12, 144, 260; and Supreme Court, 85–86, 146–47; 2020 congressional election, 285; 2020 election denial, 147–48; 2022 congressional election, 223, 243, 279, 286; Trump and older economic policies, 125; university autonomy, reductions of, 137; violence against, 298; voting reforms, 147; voting restrictions, 145, 148

Republic of New Afrika, 200
Resource Generation, 193
Rhodes, Stewart, 88, 291, 296, 299
Rising Majority, 208
Rittenhouse, Kyle, 74, 90, 150, 291
Roberts, Frank Leon, 221
Roberts, Kevin, 270
Robertson Foundation, 193
Robeson, Paul, 272
Robinson, Cedric, 52–53, 55
Robinson, Randall, 13, 30, 154, 155, 166, 215
Rockefeller Foundation, 92, 191, 192
Roe, Tom, 73
Roe v. Wade, 85, 278
Rollins, Brooke, 76, 77
Romanoff, Andrew, 166, 243
Roof, Dylann, 229, 297, 298
Roosevelt, Franklin Delano, 104
Roosevelt, Theodore, 230
Rose City Antifa, 196
Rosendale, Matthew, 233
Rosewood Scholarship, 188
Ross, Wilbur, 143
Rove, Karl, 121
Rubio, Marco, 108
Rufo, Christopher: on Critical Race Theory, 103, 106, 107, 136, 200, 255; diversity training, attacks on, 134; on future of public education, 69; as militant conservative leader, 101; "multicultural conservatism," 118, 285, 302; New College, 137; rejection of white nationalism, 120
Rule of Law Trust, 95
Rustin, Bayard, 204
Rutte, Mark, 159
Ryan, Taylor, 177

Sabato, Ernesto, 160
Salam, Reihan, 104, 118, 285
Sanders, Bernie, 207, 242, 293, 298
Sanders, Sarah Huckabee, 136
San Francisco Board of Supervisors, 186
Santos, George, 89
Sawyers, Hewitt, 232
Scaife, Richard Mellon, 91
Scalise, Steve, 298
Schlafly, Phyllis, 72
Schmidt, Ronald, Sr., 348n2
Schwab Charitable, 93

Sclar, Jason, 82, 309
Scott, Mackenzie, 30, 175, 193
Scott, Rick, 97
Scott, Tim, 63
Seale, Bobby, 204, 296
Searle, Wade, 271
Seid, Barre, 95
Sessions, Jefferson, 125–26, 132, 133, 139
settler colonialism, 58
1776 Commission, 134, 135, 136, 137, 227
1776 Project Political Action Committee, 137
Shapiro, Ben, 81
Shelby County v. Holder, 12, 144, 147
Shepherd, Verene A., 274
Showing Up for Racial Justice (SURJ), 30, 170, 173, 224
Simmons, Robin Rue, 184, 222
Sims, Kirstie, 191
Sisters of Bon Secours, 171
1619 Project (*New York Times*), 74, 134, 158, 204, 226–27, 309
1619 Project Education Network, 227
Skocpol, Theda, 82, 309, 347n2 (chap. 2)
Skowronek, Stephen, 348n2
Slave Era Disclosure Act, 156
Smith, Richard, 3–4, 255
Smith, Rogers, 5–7
Snyder, Rick, 238
Society of the Sacred Heart, 182
Sojourner Truth Organization, 103
Solidaire Network, 193–94
Soros, George, 95
Soul 2 Soul Sisters, 184
Source Watch, 309
South Carolina Policy Council, 73
Southern Christian Leadership Conference, 27, 125
Southern Poverty Law Center, 93, 172, 243
Spalding, Matthew, 137
Spencer, Richard, 113
State Policy Network (SPN), 73–74, 81, 82, 121, 154, 308
Stefancic, Jean, 228
Steinberg, Darrell, 261
Steinmo, Sven, 347n2 (chap. 2)
Stevens, Thaddeus, 200
Stevenson, Bryan, 191, 234
Stewart, Katherine, 85

INDEX 441

Still a House Divided (King and Smith), 7, 9, 308, 309, 348n7
Stone Mountain Park, GA, 231, 291
St. Petersburg (FL) City Council, 186
Student Non-Violent Coordinating Committee, 202
Students Deserve, 226
Students for a Democratic Society (SDS), 98, 103, 200
Students for Fair Admissions v. Harvard, 81
Sumner, Charles, 200
Supreme Court: and affirmative action, 7, 12, 27, 132, 288; amicus briefs in decisions addressing racial policies, 308; Christian traditionalists and, 85; and citizenship question on census, 143; color-blind policies, 288; and congressional districting plan, 145; death threats to conservative justices, 298; decisions, 5, 6, 12, 41, 81, 85, 94, 127, 129–31t, 133, 135, 142–43, 144, 147, 153, 298, 308; dismissal of Tulsa Massacre lawsuit, 247; liberal decisions of, 102; opposition to Reconstruction legislation, 41; on protections to transgender persons, 133; Republican appointments, 5; Trump appointments, 127. *See also individual Supreme Court cases*
Sutton, Everett Taylor, 183
Swain, Carol, 77, 120

Tarrio, Enrique, 88
Task Force for the Study and Development of Reparation Proposals, 213
Tax Reform Act (1969), 92
Taylor, Breonna, 15, 16, 190
Taylor, Jared, 113
Teaching Racial and Universal Equality (TRUE) Act, 26
Tea Party, 14, 35, 44, 74, 78
Teneo Network, 95
Texas Conservative Coalition Research Institute, 82
Texas Public Policy Foundation, 70, 72, 76, 77, 120, 311
Texas Public Policy Institute, 73
Thelen, Kathleen, 347n2 (chap. 2)
Theoharis, Liz, 182
Thiel, Peter, 78, 120

Thomas, Clarence, 105, 348n11
Thornton, Patricia, 38–39
Three Percenters, 14, 87–88, 103, 299
Tides Foundation, 192, 193
Tlaib, Rashida, 223
Tometi, Opal, 15, 162
Transnational Justice program, 160
Trump, Donald: administration, 16, 25, 76, 77, 115, 118, 122, 227, 239, 285, 308; and affirmative action, 132; America First philosophy, 114, 350n6 (chap. 5); appointments, 125–28; and Christian nationalists, 85–86; Claremont Institute, 105–6; Constitution, disregard for, 302; corruption litigation, 283; COVID-19 response, 116; criminal indictments, 301; and Critical Race Theory, 110; culture war, 134–38; defense of Confederate flag and Confederate names, 78, 232–33; discrimination against whites, 27, 111, 116–17, 132–34, 219; and education, 106, 141; Electoral College, 263; and Fuentes, 79, 80; and Gosar, 81; housing policy, 140–41; immigration policy, 138–39, 278; inauguration, 113–14, 115, 124, 197; January 6 insurrection, 78, 85, 291, 299, 300; Make America Great Again, 16, 44, 109; and Mercers, 94–95; policies, 15, 124–25, 128–32; on policing, 139–40; presidency, 105; and Protect alliance, 24–25, 43, 84, 87, 109, 110–13, 116, 117, 118–19, 122, 129–31t, 148–50; and Proud Boys, 90; racial inequalities due to liberal policies, 110, 255; racial policies, 35, 114; religious leaders and, 86, 280; Repair alliance's lack of comparable figure, 207, 296; rise of, 4, 7, 15–16, 203, 282; on Social Security and Medicare, 286; and social welfare, 141–42; speeches and tweets, 111, 112, 115, 299, 308; stolen election claim, 116, 300; supporters, 80, 81, 88, 245; Supreme Court appointments, 85–86; and Tea Party, 74; on violence against Left, 296; and voting rights and election systems, 142–48; and white nationalism, 112; years in office, 11, 14, 15, 95, 106; and Youngkin, 69
Truth and Reconciliation Commission (Argentina), 160

Truth and Reconciliation Commission (Iowa City), 186
Tucson Reparations, 177
Tulsa Massacre, 188–89, 235, 247
Ture, Kwame. *See* Carmichael, Stokely (Kwame Ture)
Turner, Jack, 61
Turning Point USA, 90, 120
Tutu, Desmond, 160
Twitter, 15, 27, 76, 95, 111, 176
2020 election deniers, 128, 148
Tzedek, 222

Uber, 191
UCL Centre for the Study of the Legacies of British Slavery, 159
Uhuru Solidarity Movement, 177
UNESCO Inclusive Policy Lab, 172
Union Presbyterian Seminary, 180
United Church of Christ, 174
United Nations, "Basic Principles and Guidelines on the Right to a Remedy and Reparation for Victims of Gross Violations of International Human Rights Law and Serious Violations of International Humanitarian Law," 218
United Nations Working Group of Experts on People of African Descent, 202
United Nations World Conference against Racism, Racial Discrimination, Xenophobia and Related Intolerance, 159, 272
Unite the Right rally, 80, 87, 115, 195, 229
Universal Basic Income (UBI), 244–45, 248, 292
University Network for Human Rights, 172
University of Georgia, 186
University of North Carolina, 132, 180
University of Virginia, 180–81
Urban League, 21, 31, 170, 190–91
US Colored Troops, 232
USC Shinso Ito Center for Japanese Religions and Culture, 170

Vance, J. D., 79, 270
Van Ellis, Hughes, 188
Vanguard Charitable, 92, 93
Van Oden, Derrick, 89
VDare, 46, 47f, 49f

Venmo, 30, 176
Virginia Defenders for Freedom, Justice and Equality, 230
Virginia Military Institute, 231
Virginia Theological Seminary, 179–80
Vision for Black Lives: focus on intersectionality, 205; platform, 15, 28, 207; Repair alliance, 215–16; six headings, 208–10
Voting Rights Act, 144
Vrdolyak, Edward, 6

Walker, Herschel, 167
Wall, Caroline, 247
Walmart Corporation, 191
Warby Parker, 191
WarnerMedia, 191
Warren, Dorian, 245
Warren, Elizabeth, 238, 242, 349n5 (chap. 3)
Washington, Booker T., 20
Washington, Harold, 6
Washington (State) Policy Center, 73
Washington and Lee University, 181
Weir, Margaret, 347n2 (chap. 1)
"welfare queens," 64, 70
Westley, Robert, 154
Where Is My Land, 189
white hegemony analysts, 63
"white hegemony" perspective, 50, 54, 57–60, 62
white supremacy, 7, 13, 20, 55, 60, 70, 75, 90, 115, 176–78, 196, 199, 208, 219, 255, 278; and Christianity, 87, 112
Whitmer, Gretchen, 150, 195, 296, 298
Will, George, 121
Willem-Alexander (king of the Netherlands), 159
Williams, Riley, 299
Williams, Roger, 121
Williamson, Marianne, 242
Wilson, Woodrow, 104, 200
Winant, Howard, 59
Wins, Cedric, 231
"woke" corporations, 57
Wolverine Watchmen, 150, 298
Women for America First, 78, 349n3 (chap. 3)
Wyss, Hansjorg, 95–96

X, Malcolm, 197, 296
Xi Jinping, 271

Yarl, Ralph, 298
Ye (formerly Kanye West), 80, 139
Youngkin, Glenn: appointment of Ellis to UVA Board of Trustees, 181; and Colonial Williamsburg, support for reforming, 302; and Critical Race Theory, opposition to, 26, 69, 137, 234–35

Zimmerman, George, 15, 203
Zionist Organization of America, 81
Zuckerberg, Mark, 147, 191

Chicago Studies in American Politics

A series edited by Susan Herbst, Lawrence R. Jacobs, Adam J. Berinsky, and Frances Lee; Benjamin I. Page, editor emeritus

Also in the series:

WHY PARTIES MATTER: POLITICAL COMPETITION AND DEMOCRACY IN THE AMERICAN SOUTH by John H. Aldrich and John D. Griffin

NEITHER LIBERAL NOR CONSERVATIVE: IDEOLOGICAL INNOCENCE IN THE AMERICAN PUBLIC by Donald R. Kinder and Nathan P. Kalmoe

STRATEGIC PARTY GOVERNMENT: WHY WINNING TRUMPS IDEOLOGY by Gregory Koger and Matthew J. Lebo

POST-RACIAL OR MOST-RACIAL? RACE AND POLITICS IN THE OBAMA ERA by Michael Tesler

THE POLITICS OF RESENTMENT: RURAL CONSCIOUSNESS IN WISCONSIN AND THE RISE OF SCOTT WALKER by Katherine J. Cramer

LEGISLATING IN THE DARK: INFORMATION AND POWER IN THE HOUSE OF REPRESENTATIVES by James M. Curry

WHY WASHINGTON WON'T WORK: POLARIZATION, POLITICAL TRUST, AND THE GOVERNING CRISIS by Marc J. Hetherington and Thomas J. Rudolph

WHO GOVERNS? PRESIDENTS, PUBLIC OPINION, AND MANIPULATION by James N. Druckman and Lawrence R. Jacobs

TRAPPED IN AMERICA'S SAFETY NET: ONE FAMILY'S STRUGGLE by Andrea Louise Campbell

ARRESTING CITIZENSHIP: THE DEMOCRATIC CONSEQUENCES OF AMERICAN CRIME CONTROL by Amy E. Lerman and Vesla M. Weaver

HOW THE STATES SHAPED THE NATION: AMERICAN ELECTORAL INSTITUTIONS AND VOTER TURNOUT, 1920–2000 by Melanie Jean Springer

WHITE-COLLAR GOVERNMENT: THE HIDDEN ROLE OF CLASS IN ECONOMIC POLICY MAKING by Nicholas Carnes

HOW PARTISAN MEDIA POLARIZE AMERICA by Matthew Levendusky

CHANGING MINDS OR CHANGING CHANNELS? PARTISAN NEWS IN AN AGE OF CHOICE by Kevin Arceneaux and Martin Johnson

THE POLITICS OF BELONGING: RACE, PUBLIC OPINION, AND IMMIGRATION by Natalie Masuoka and Jane Junn

TRADING DEMOCRACY FOR JUSTICE: CRIMINAL CONVICTIONS AND THE DECLINE OF NEIGHBORHOOD POLITICAL PARTICIPATION by Traci Burch

POLITICAL TONE: HOW LEADERS TALK AND WHY by Roderick P. Hart, Jay P. Childers, and Colene J. Lind

LEARNING WHILE GOVERNING: EXPERTISE AND ACCOUNTABILITY IN THE EXECUTIVE BRANCH by Sean Gailmard and John W. Patty

THE SOCIAL CITIZEN: PEER NETWORKS AND POLITICAL BEHAVIOR by Betsy Sinclair

FOLLOW THE LEADER? HOW VOTERS RESPOND TO POLITICIANS' POLICIES AND PERFORMANCE by Gabriel S. Lenz

THE TIMELINE OF PRESIDENTIAL ELECTIONS: HOW CAMPAIGNS DO (AND DO NOT) MATTER by Robert S. Erikson and Christopher Wlezien

ELECTING JUDGES: THE SURPRISING EFFECTS OF CAMPAIGNING ON JUDICIAL LEGITIMACY by James L. Gibson

DISCIPLINING THE POOR: NEOLIBERAL PATERNALISM AND THE PERSISTENT POWER

OF RACE *by Joe Soss, Richard C. Fording, and Sanford F. Schram*

THE SUBMERGED STATE: HOW INVISIBLE GOVERNMENT POLICIES UNDERMINE AMERICAN DEMOCRACY *by Suzanne Mettler*

SELLING FEAR: COUNTERTERRORISM, THE MEDIA, AND PUBLIC OPINION *by Brigitte L. Nacos, Yaeli Bloch-Elkon, and Robert Y. Shapiro*

WHY PARTIES? A SECOND LOOK *by John H. Aldrich*

OBAMA'S RACE: THE 2008 ELECTION AND THE DREAM OF A POST-RACIAL AMERICA *by Michael Tesler and David O. Sears*

NEWS THAT MATTERS: TELEVISION AND AMERICAN OPINION, UPDATED EDITION *by Shanto Iyengar and Donald R. Kinder*

FILIBUSTERING: A POLITICAL HISTORY OF OBSTRUCTION IN THE HOUSE AND SENATE *by Gregory Koger*

US AGAINST THEM: ETHNOCENTRIC FOUNDATIONS OF AMERICAN OPINION *by Donald R. Kinder and Cindy D. Kam*

THE PARTISAN SORT: HOW LIBERALS BECAME DEMOCRATS AND CONSERVATIVES BECAME REPUBLICANS *by Matthew Levendusky*

DEMOCRACY AT RISK: HOW TERRORIST THREATS AFFECT THE PUBLIC *by Jennifer L. Merolla and Elizabeth J. Zechmeister*

IN TIME OF WAR: UNDERSTANDING AMERICAN PUBLIC OPINION FROM WORLD WAR II TO IRAQ *by Adam J. Berinsky*

AGENDAS AND INSTABILITY IN AMERICAN POLITICS, SECOND EDITION *by Frank R. Baumgartner and Bryan D. Jones*

THE PARTY DECIDES: PRESIDENTIAL NOMINATIONS BEFORE AND AFTER REFORM *by Marty Cohen, David Karol, Hans Noel, and John Zaller*

THE PRIVATE ABUSE OF THE PUBLIC INTEREST: MARKET MYTHS AND POLICY MUDDLES *by Lawrence D. Brown and Lawrence R. Jacobs*

SAME SEX, DIFFERENT POLITICS: SUCCESS AND FAILURE IN THE STRUGGLES OVER GAY RIGHTS *by Gary Mucciaroni*